Springer Proceedings in Business and Economics

More information about this series at http://www.springer.com/series/11960

Nicos Sykianakis • Persefoni Polychronidou •
Anastasios Karasavvoglou
Editors

Economic and Financial Challenges for Eastern Europe

Proceedings of the 9th International
Conference on the Economies of the
Balkan and Eastern European Countries
in the Changing World (EBEEC)
in Athens, Greece, 2017

 Springer

Editors
Nicos Sykianakis
Piraeus University of Applied Sciences
Egaleo, Greece

Persefoni Polychronidou
International Hellenic University
Serres, Greece

Anastasios Karasavvoglou
International Hellenic University
Kavala, Greece

ISSN 2198-7246   ISSN 2198-7254   (electronic)
Springer Proceedings in Business and Economics
ISBN 978-3-030-12168-6   ISBN 978-3-030-12169-3   (eBook)
https://doi.org/10.1007/978-3-030-12169-3

This Springer imprint is published by the registered company Springer Nature Switzerland AG.
The registered company address is: Gewerbestrasse 11, 6330 Cham, Switzerland

Preface

This volume includes papers presented at the 9th international conference "The Economies of the Balkan and the Eastern European Countries in the Changing World"—EBEEC 2017. It was organized jointly by the TEI of Eastern Macedonia and Thrace, Department of Accounting and Finance (Greece); the Piraeus University of Applied Sciences, Department of Accounting and Finance (Greece); and the University of Piraeus, Department of International and European Studies. It took place in Athens, Greece, on April 28–30, 2017. The conference's general aim to present scientific papers and researches of theoretical and empirical character about the economies and business in this region brought together more than 140 papers prepared by more than 300 authors from 30 countries from the region and all over the world.

The proceedings of the conference are of great interest since the papers are the scientific results of researches regarding current issues in international economies, European integration, economic growth, economic crises, macroeconomics, finance, banking, stock market, accounting, education, tourism, labor market, energy, innovation, management, and marketing in the wider area of Eastern Europe.

Our aim is to highlight that there are new and genuine knowledge and ideas of scientists in economics and in several specific fields like business, finance, European economies, macroeconomics, tourism, labor market, management, and marketing. The region of the Balkans and Eastern Europe is, after all, a region that has played an important role in the European and world history and has affected processes and changes in the economies of all European countries.

Egaleo, Greece   Nicos Sykianakis
Serres, Greece   Persefoni Polychronidou
Kavala, Greece   Anastasios Karasavvoglou

Contents

Financial Crisis and Brain Drain: An Investigation of the Emigration Intentions of Greek Scientists

George Theodossiou, Ioannis Rigas, Eleni Thanou, and Apostolos Goulas

Abstract

Purpose This study intends to identify and assess the emigration intentions of Greek scientists due to the continuing economic crisis in Greece from 2009 onward.

Methodology/Approach The subject of this paper is investigated with the help of factor analysis applied to a data set collected from a nationwide sample of 342 young people aged 18–45 years. The questionnaire consists of two categories (scales) of questions which refer to (a) the reasons that compel young people to emigrate (A scale) and (b) the reasons for not considering emigration (B scale). The factor analysis identified five factors in the scale A and three in the scale B, which explain the 78.53% and 78.64% of the total variance in the respective data sets. The same results were reached both with the method of hierarchical analysis in clusters for grouping the subjects of the two scales and with the method of residuals for each subject.

Results The analysis and processing of the data showed that young people who want to emigrate are well aware of the reasons which have led them to this important decision, while those who do not consider to emigrate are not so clear about the reasons that lead them to the rejection of emigration as an option for a better future.

Practical Implications The research findings indicate that young unemployed scientists believe that core EU countries offer an excellent environment for

G. Theodossiou (✉)
Department of Business Administration, School of Business and Economics, TEI of Thessaly, Larissa, TK, Greece
e-mail: geortheo@teilar.gr

I. Rigas
Department of Finance, Morgan Stanley, London, UK

E. Thanou
Graduate Program on Banking, Hellenic Open University, Patras, Greece

A. Goulas
Department of Planning and Regional Development, School of Engineering, University of Thessaly, Volos, Greece

© Springer Nature Switzerland AG 2019
N. Sykianakis et al. (eds.), *Economic and Financial Challenges for Eastern Europe*,
Springer Proceedings in Business and Economics,
https://doi.org/10.1007/978-3-030-12169-3_1

professional advancement plus other professional and social benefits compared to those available or not available in Greece during the crisis.

Originality/value This is an original research which contributes to the international literature on the investigation of the emigration intentions and motives of young scientists.

Keywords Brain drain · Migration intention · Greek scientists · Financial crisis · Austerity · Crisis impact · Government spending · Universities

1　Introduction

Greece has been in the grip of a persisting and severe economic crisis since 2009. The crisis has stripped more than a quarter of the country's GDP since its inception and has left many unemployed. Unemployment is particularly high among the young, peaking at 48% in 2013 (see Table 1). This study aims to investigate and assess the attitude and intentions toward emigration of young Greek scientists as a result of the prolonged economic crisis in the country.

The term *brain drain* is used to describe both the movement of people and the socioeconomic costs associated with emigration. The first instance where this phenomenon has been noted and studied was in Nazi Germany, where the nature of the regime of the Third Reich and its attack on Jews and intellectuals resulted in a massive emigration of scientists, mostly to the USA. The phenomenon continued after the end of World War II, where aspiring scientists from many of the ruined European countries emigrated to the USA.

The phenomenon, however, took massive dimensions in the era of globalization, since 1991. The creation of basic educational institutions in the former colonies, the breakdown of the scientific and academic powerhouse of the former Soviet Union,

Table 1 Greece: Unemployment rate for total population and for persons aged 15–29 years[a], 2007–2015

Year	Total	Persons aged 15–29
2007	8.4	17.3
2008	7.8	16.2
2009	9.6	18.8
2010	12.7	24.4
2011	17.9	34.8
2012	24.4	43.7
2013	27.5	48.7
2014	26.5	45.0
2015	24.9	41.3

Source: Population and Labour Market Statistics Division ELSTAT (http://www.statistics.gr/el/statistics/pop)
[a]Data refer to the annual average

and the nature of the economic globalization all contributed to the global dimensions of the emigration of skilled and educated people.

The term brain drain was coined by the British institute Royal Society, to describe the emigration of scientists and mechanics to North America from postwar Europe (Cervantes and Guellec 2002). During the following decades, brain drain was characterized as a "North-South," developing-developed country issue (Carrington and Detragiache 1999). The same term was used later to describe the influx of Indian scientists and mechanics to the UK.

There are two main factors that contribute to the generation and evolution of this phenomenon: on the one hand, the living conditions in the country of origin of the young scientist and on the other his or her own choices (Balmer et al. 2009). The brain drain or human capital flight refers to the emigration of people with a high level of education and skills. The main reason for the emigration of these individuals is the pursuit of new economic opportunities, recognition, better rewards, and improved living conditions (Anastasiu 2014). Another factor that encourages this phenomenon is that the labor market for graduate workers is more flexible and flowing than that for workers with lower schooling levels (Cardoso and Ferreira 2009). Shirley L. Chang (1992) tried to explain the brain drain of graduates from Taiwan to the USA using a pull-and-push approach. That is, they examine both the "pull" factors in the USA for the scholar-immigrants' decisions to immigrate and the "push" factors in Taiwan for their decisions not to return.

According to Alexander Haupt and Eckhard Janeba (2009), "The debate over the merits of skilled migration and the increasing degree of competition for educated workers features two opposing views. On the one hand, the emigration of human capital gives rise to many concerns. The threat of brain drain puts pressure on governments to adjust their economic policy to the benefit of skilled workers, for example, by lowering the effective tax burden for high-income earners. The ensuing erosion of tax revenues, restricts government redistribution toward those who are less educated and less mobile, which in turn increases inequality. In addition, it constrains a government's ability to publicly fund accumulation of human capital."

Various studies provide statistics that indicate the magnitude of the various forms of migration globally. The number of individuals migrating from the South to the North increased from 14 million in 1960 to 60 million in 2000 (Ozden et al. 2011). At the same time, the percentage of migrants with tertiary education increased dramatically. According to the Ratha et al. (2010), during the last 50 years (1960–2010), international migration increased from 75 million to 215,8 million people. This phenomenon is attributed to various local wars, especially in Africa and Asia, the absolute poverty, the poor living conditions and minimum level of social benefits, the political instability in many countries, and the growing gap in incomes (Lawan Ngoma Abubakar and Wana Ismail Normaz 2013).

In Turkey, the emigration of scientists was growing steadily from 1960 up to 2000, when Turkey introduced measures to discourage the emigration of scientists, which, along with economic growth, succeeded to curb the brain drain phenomenon. In Latin American countries, with proximity to the target country for most scientists, the USA, the phenomenon also reached large dimensions. During the 1990s,

Argentina lost 19,1% of its scientists, Chile 15,6%, and Peru 10% (Sevris 2014). The numbers are even more striking if we focus on poorer counties such as Haiti, Guyana, and Grenada: 80% of university graduates with nationalities from these countries live in the USA (Özden 2006).

More recently, the financial crisis of 2008, which caused high unemployment in many developed European countries such as France, Spain, Italy, and Greece, also gave rise to waves of brain drain-type migration (Migration and Remittances Factbook 2011). A study was conducted in France by the Centre d'Etudes et de Recherches sur les Qualifications (Céreq) and was published on September 24, 2015, indicated that higher studies no longer ensure entry into the labor market. The study shows that the unemployment level 3 years after obtaining a degree was 13% and resulted from the financial crisis of 2007 (Benoit 2015).

Regarding intra-European migration, Katrin Nussmayr (2014) notes that from 2003 to 2013, 276,124 EU citizens have applied to go to another member state to work on a permanent basis with their profession. The countries experiencing the most brain drain have been Poland (33,207 professionals), Germany (29,670), Romania (26,496), Greece (22,260), and the UK (21,519). At the same time, the UK has been the country with the most brain gain as well: 76,956 professionals moved there after obtaining their qualification in another EU country, followed by Germany (38,343), Belgium (22,835), Cyprus (22,834), and Austria (19,625). The most mobile professions within the EU since 2003 are:

1. Secondary school teacher 54,040
2. Doctor of medicine 47,998
3. Nurse 39,773
4. Physiotherapist 12,529
5. Dental practitioner 8907

The German Federal Statistical Office reports that inflow of Spanish migrants to Germany increased by 37.1% in 2012 compared to 2011; the respective rates for Portugal and Greece were 41.1% and 53.0% (Vena Nedeljkovic 2014).

2   Brain Drain and Growth: A Literature Review

Most modern theories agree that the three main factors that contribute to economic growth are capital, human capital, and technology. Human capital is defined as the set of knowledge, capacities, and skills that can be obtained by humans through studies and professional experience. It can be quantified by taking the present value of all the relevant earnings during the professional lifetime. The investment in education does not result in the acceleration of economic growth rates, unless it is combined with the minimization of the emigration of talented and skilled individuals, the growth of invested capital, and the continuous update of technology. The high-quality work force contributes to innovation, technology, productivity, and rational capital distribution, so that it can promote the growth process of a country. This is justified, because knowledge dispersion only occurs via humans.

Therefore, governments should safeguard and enrich the human capital factor and facilitate its development; otherwise these people will move on to countries that will ensure suitable work and living conditions for them.

Modern theories of endogenous growth have considerably renewed the analysis of the relations between education, migration, and growth. Since education has been pointed out as a major determinant of long-term growth (Lucas 1988), common wisdom suggests that the migration of people endowed with a high level of human capital—the so-called brain drain—is detrimental for the country of emigration. The brain drain can indeed be seen as a negative externality on the population left in the source country (Bhagwati and Hamada 1974), due, for example, to imperfect substitution between skilled and unskilled labor (Piketty 1997).

The negative impact of the brain drain has also been stressed in the new growth literature (Miyagiwa 1991; Haque and Kim 1995; Galor and Tsiddon 1997). Most studies underline the positive impact of migrations on human capital formation but, when turning to the issue of the brain drain, conclude that there is a detrimental growth effect.[1] A United Nations study showed that only from the emigration of computer specialists, India is losing 2 billion dollars per year. The emigration of Indians for educational or professional reasons leads to the loss of $10 billion per year (United Nations 2006).

A series of theoretical papers over the past 15 years, summarized in Docquier and Rapoport (2011), have shown that it is possible that high-skilled emigration can lead to a rise in human capital levels in the home country. The rationale is roughly the following: in a poor economy with an inadequate growth potential, the return to human capital is likely to be low and hence would lead to limited incentive to acquire education, which is the engine of growth. However, the world at large does value education, and hence, allowing migration to take place from this economy would increase the returns to the educated fraction of its population. The models of brain drain, i.e., when labor is heterogeneous and when only the most skilled residents emigrate (Mountford 1997; Docquier and Rapoport 1997), differ from models with homogenous labor (Stark et al. 1998; Vidal 1998) and from models with imperfect information and return migrations.

One common characteristic of recent economic crises (during the last 30 years) in countries including Argentina, Uruguay, Turkey, Greece, Cyprus, Poland, Estonia, etc. is the emigration of university graduates and the impoverization of the middle class.

---

[1]For example, Haque and Kim (1995) find that a brain drain reduces the growth rate of the effective human capital that remains in the economy and hence generates a permanent reduction of per capita growth in the home country. See also Miyagiwa (1991), who finds that contrary to the presumption that brain drain hurts the unskilled individuals left in a source country, it is actually those professionals possessing intermediate-level abilities who are hurt by brain drain.

3   Brain Drain and Greece

In Greece, the fiscal adjustment imposed by the two memoranda had as a result the increase in unemployment from 9% in 2008 to 24,9% in 2015 and the loss of 25% of the country's GDP over that period. Disposable incomes fell by over 30% on average, and the reduction was most severe among high-wage earners and skilled employees. During that period according to a recent Bank of Greece study, 223,000 young people emigrated to developed countries. "I think what we are seeing in Greece is a lost generation," said Kevin Featherstone, a professor at the London School of Economics who is an expert on modern Greek society (Steven Zeitchik 2015).

Labrianidis and Vogiatzis (2013a, b) studied a sample of 2700 young scientists who left Greece. Among them were 54% PhD holders and 37% with postgraduate degrees, and 42% of them left the country right after obtaining their basic university degree, aged between 24 and 29 years old. The main reason cited for their decision to leave was to seek better career opportunities.

The negative effects of this brain drain are:

- Demographic—increase in the proportion of older people and reduction of birth rates
- Reduced contributions to pension funds, depletion of reserves, and subsequent increase in public expenditure which contributes to public deficits
- Deterioration in the average quality of the work force
- Increase in the tax revenue of the receiving country with simultaneous decrease in the tax revenues of the country of origin

According to data from receiving countries and Greek studies, the human capital reduction between 2008 and the present is between 350.000 (Endeavor estimate) and 427.000 (Bank of Greece estimate). According to calculations of the Endeavor study (http://endeavor.org.gr), the emigrants contribute every year €12,9 billion to the GDP of the receiving countries, mostly to Germany and Britain, and €9,1 billion in tax revenues. From 2008 to date, Greek brain drain members have contributed cumulatively more than €50 billion to the GDPs of their new "home countries." It is interesting to note, further, that the Greek government has spent approximately €8 billion for their education (http://endeavor.org.gr/).

4   Methodology and Data

We have collected a countrywide sample of 342 people aged 18–45 facing employment problems, who are either employed in the private sector with temporary or open-ended contracts or are unemployed. The methodology applied is the following:

(a) Questionnaire. We used a structured questionnaire of 28 questions that consists of four parts. First are demographic questions, second, questions referring to employment search issues, third, questions relating to the reasons for a possible migration, and, fourth, questions addressed to those not considering emigration. As a result, our responses are grouped into two sets, one that includes the responses in parts 1,2, and 4 of 90 people considering to emigrate and a second one consisting of the responses to parts 1,2, and 3 of 252 individuals who are not considering emigration at this moment. Apart from the first set of demographic questions, each group contains a number of factors, nine for group A (variables 14–23) and six for group B (variables 23–28).

The questions of both groups were structured around a five-point scale, 1 = totally disagree, 2 = disagree, 3 = neither agree nor disagree, 4 = agree, and 5 = totally agree. Principal component analysis was applied to the factors of both groups in order to identify appropriate subgroups.

(b) Data collection. The questionnaire was initially tested during January 2016 in the 13 prefectures of the country, where its functionality and ease of use were established and minor revisions not altering its structure were applied. Between February 2016 and April 2016, we collected 342 questionnaires through telephone interviews and local visits. The phone numbers and addresses of the participants were obtained randomly from the lists of OAED (Organization for the Employment of the Work Force) from young people registered as unemployed during the last 2 years. There was an effort to communicate with many more people, but only 342 responded positively and filled the questionnaire. According to Lawley and Maxwell (1971), the maximum likelihood method in factor analysis requires a sample that exceeds the number of factors under measurement by at least 51. In our case, given the nine factors for group A and six for group B, the sample sizes satisfy this condition.

(c) Reliability analysis. The statistical analysis was conducted with the Statistical Package for Social Sciences (SPSS 15.0). We first performed the reliability analysis to both factor groups, A (variables 14–22) and B (variables 23–28). The internal cohesion of the three sets of responses was estimated using the Cronbach index and was found acceptable.

(d) Factor analysis—analysis in clusters. We then applied factor analysis to the answers of groups A and B using the principal component analysis method, aiming to group the variables in factor subgroups, in order to use them in further analysis. The factor analysis was conducted in four steps: (a) We created correlation tables among all subjects and investigated the suitability of using the factor model. (b) We determined the number of factors that are sufficient to describe the data, and we evaluated the good fit of the chosen model. (c) For the final factor solution, we used axis rotation so that the factor interpretation could be optimized. (d) We calculated the grades for each factor.

The determination of the number of factors for each group (A and B) was performed based on the graphic analysis of the eigenvalues. Following that, we applied the hierarchical cluster analysis (average linkage between groups method) for the grouping of the variables in groups A and B and used the hierarchical cluster analysis dendrogram. Lastly, we compared the clusters that were formed for each group separately.

(e) Variance analysis. We used the ANOVA statistical method in order to perform tests for the statistical significance of the difference of the means in the responses among the various independent variables (age, sex, family status, degree, family income, and employment status).

(f) Correlation coefficients and descriptive statistics. The Pearson's index r was used to measure correlation among variables.

5   Results and Interpretation

5.1   *Reliability Analysis: Factor and Cluster Analysis*

The internal cohesion of the response to the questionnaires was measured using the index alpha of Cronbach. For group A, "Reasons for which young people want to emigrate," the value was found to be a-$Cr_A = 0,629$, and for group B, "Reasons for not considering to emigrate," the value was a-$Cr_A = 0,683$. According to most researchers, the reliability of a questionnaire is high if a-$Cr_A > 0,60$ which is satisfied by both our subsamples.

The KMO indexes for groups A and B, respectively, were 0,618 and 0,719, and Bartlett's sphericity index was found to be 152,69 and 488,983 ($p < 0,001$), respectively, which implies that factor analysis is an appropriate statistical method for both data sets.

Next we proceeded to a preliminary factor extraction using principal component analysis. For every group and every question, we calculated the communalities, that is, the percentage of the variance that can be explained by the common factors. When communalities are close to zero, this means that the common factors cannot explain an important part of its variance, and this means that this question measures something unique. This is the case only for question 23 in group A which had a value of 0,482 (all other values were higher).

Factor analysis identified five factors for group A and three for group B that explain 78,53% and 78,64% of the total variance, respectively.

For the group "Reasons for which young people want to emigrate", these factors are:

A1: Potential for professional growth and specialization.
A2: Negative working environment in Greece.
A3: Limited social benefits in Greece.
A4: Better opportunities abroad for my profession.
A5: The improvement of economic conditions is a motivation to return.

The factors for group B "Reasons for not considering to emigrate" that support the theoretical dimensions of the subject are the following:

B1: Strong bonds with the country and faith in its potential
B2: Independent with a strong desire to offer to the country
B3: Lack of courage

In order to support and confirm the above findings, we also performed the hierarchical cluster analysis (average linkage between groups method) for the grouping of the variables in groups A and B. The hierarchical cluster analysis dendrograms identified precisely the same clusters of questions as the factor analysis above for both groups.

5.2 Descriptive Statistics

Some highlights are the following: The distribution of men and women in the various age groups is balanced, with the exception of the age group 36–45 in group A, where there are 38% men and 62% women. Regarding education levels, in group A 63% of the respondents who belong in the age group 26–35 and 62% in the age group 36–45 are holding university degrees, 100% of the people with PhD belong to the 6–35 age group, and women with basic degrees are 10% more than men, while among the postgraduate and PhD holders, there are as many women as men.

Tables 2 and 3 show, respectively, the average, median, and variance for the five factors of group A and the three factors of group B identified by the factor analysis.

5.3 ANOVA Results

The ANOVA statistical method was used in order to tests for possible statistically significant differences of the means in the responses among the various independent variables (age, sex, family status, degree, family income, and employment status).

Table 2 The average, median and variance for the 5 factors of Group A

A/A	Subgroup	Average	Standard error	Std deviation	Median
A1	Potential for professional growth and specialization	4,30	0,060	0,565	4,50
A2	Negative working environment in Greece	4,27	0,064	0,605	4,50
A3	Limited social benefits in Greece	4,43	0,057	0,542	4,50
A4	Better opportunities abroad for my profession	4,34	0,063	0,594	4,50
A5	Improvement of economy is a motivation to return	3,73	0,115	1,089	4.00

Table 3 The average, median and variance for the 3 factors of Group B

A/A	Subgroup	Average	Standard error	Std deviation	Median
B1	Strong bonds with the country and faith in its potential	3,50	0,039	0,618	3,50
B2	Independent with a strong desire to offer to the country	3,62	0,042	0,666	4,00
B3	Lack of courage	2,67	0,058	0,923	3,00

3A. ANOVA results for group A (with an intention to emigrate). There were no statistically significant differences at the 5% level among the sample subgroup's responses for all the categorical variables. We only found some differences at the 10% level.

3B. Among the group that is not considering to emigrate, the ANOVA analysis revealed several statistically significant differences at the 5% level. More specifically, factor B2 "Independent with a strong desire to offer to the country" with independent variable "age," factor B1 "Strong bond with the country and faith in its potential," and factor B3 "Lack of courage" with independent variable "family status" as well as with the independent variables "degree" and "annual family income."

5.4 Correlation Coefficients

4A. For the investigation of the correlation among the variables, we calculated the Pearson coefficient r. For group A we identified the following strong positive correlations (at the $p = 0,01$ level) among the factors: A1 with A3 ($r = 0,287$), A1 and A4 ($r = 0,289$), and A2 and A3 ($r = 0,287$). At the level $p = 0,05$, there is strong correlation between A1 and A2 ($r = 0,262$), A2 and A4 ($r = 0,248$), and A3 and A4 ($r = 0,254$).

4B. The calculation of the Pearson coefficient for all the pairs of variables showed strong correlation ($p = 0,01$) among variables B1 and B2 ($r = 0,404$).

6 Conclusions

The present paper investigated two issues in the context of the brain drain literature: (a) the reasons for which young people want to emigrate and (b) the reasons behind the decision to stay.

The reliability analysis for both sets of responses to the relevant questions showed a strong internal cohesion (a-Cr > 0,60) so that factor analysis methods could be successfully applied. The table of the correlation coefficients among the factors for each group revealed that there are zero correlation coefficients with values below 0,2, which ensures that the definitions and meaning of the factors with high loadings are real.

The factor analysis identified five factors for group A and three for group B, which explain, respectively, 78,53% and 78,64% of the total variance. These results were confirmed also with the method of hierarchical analysis in clusters and the residuals method.

The ANOVA analysis in group A showed that the differences in the means of the five independent categorical variables were not significantly different at the 5% level. On the contrary, we identified statistically significant differences at the 5%

level among some of the variables for group B. These were the following: B2 "Independent with a strong desire to offer to the country" with independent variable "age," B1 "Strong bond with the country and faith in its potential," and B3 "Lack of courage," with independent variable "family status" as well as with independent variables "degree" and "annual family income."

Regarding the five factors explaining the decision to emigrate (group A), the people who consider leaving agree almost totally in all five factors. Among those not considering emigration (group B), they have a tendency to "almost agree" ($\mu_{B1} = 3,50$) in factor B1 "Strong bond with the country and faith in its potential" and B2 "Independent with a strong desire to offer to the country" ($\mu_{B2} = 3,62$) but neither agree nor disagree with factor B3 "Lack of courage" ($\mu_{B3} = 2,67$).

From the above, we conclude that those wishing to leave have a good understanding and strong feelings regarding the reasons that lead them to this decision. On the contrary, those who identify themselves as not wishing to leave have less clear views for the reasons for which they reject the option to emigrate.

From the analysis of innovation chains, we know that an economy needs an upstream innovation system in order to be able to initiate entrepreneurial activities on a broader basis with innovative and productive firms. It means that Greece needs a developed innovation system that consist of high-quality schools and universities, as well as professional education systems and excellent research with the public sector (Herrmann and Kritikos 2013). The importance of the contribution of human capital and especially of the skilled human capital to economic growth has been stressed by many researches in the international literature; therefore its departure in large numbers constitutes a blow to the country's efforts to recover.

Once the phenomenon of brain drain has manifested itself, there are two possible responses that the country of origin can adopt. The first is to try to attract them back (return option), while the second is to accept that this human capital will stay abroad in the long term and try to take advantage of it (diaspora option).

The policy of any government should focus in facilitating the contacts and cooperation of these people with their homeland from the country where they live and also to create a framework allowing them to work on a temporary basis in Greece. Thus, they will be able to transfer some ideas and know-how through their cooperation with universities and research centers but also private organizations or even through the creation of their own enterprises. Specific policy measures include but are not limited to:

- Encouragement of the employment of skilled personnel through a point system.
- Incentives to the research and development units of private companies and creation of new/better funding of existing research centers.
- Start-up companies or research proposals with the participation of Greeks living and working abroad should be subsidized or prioritized.
- Legislation should be introduced to allow the possibility of dual appointments in universities in Greece and abroad.

These ideas could create the necessary "bridges" to allow for the possibility that the people who left may return at some point in the future, contributing to the Greek economy and society in general.

References

Anastasiu, A. (2014). *The brain drain phenomenon within the European Union*. http://one-europe. info/brain-drain-eu

Balmer, B., Godwin, M., & Gregory, J. E. (2009). The Royal Society and the 'brain drain': Natural scientists meet social science. *Notes and Records of the Royal Society, 63*(4), 339–353. https:// doi.org/10.1098/rsnr.2008.0053.

Benoit, F. (2015, September 24). «*Sur le marché de l'emploie, le diplôme protégé un peu moins qu'avant*». LE MONDE. http://www.lemonde.fr/education/article/2015/09/24/sur-le-marche-l-emploi-le-diplome-protege-un-peu-moins-qu-avant_4769240_1473685.htm

Bhagwati, J., & Hamada, K. (1974). The brain drain, international integration of markets for professionals and unemployment: A theoretical analysis. *Journal of Development Economics, 1*(1), 19–42.

Cardoso, A. R., & Ferreira, P. (2009). The dynamics of job creation and destruction for university graduates: Why a rising unemployment rate can be misleading. *Applied Economics, Taylor & Francis (Routledge), 41*(19), 2513–2521.

Carrington, W., & Detragiache, E. (1999). International migration and the "brain drain". *The Journal of Social, Political and Economic Studies 24*, 163–171. In Comparative analysis of brain drain, brain circulation and brain retain: a case study of Indian Institutes of Technology by Varma, R., & Kapur, D. (2013). *Journal of Comparative Policy Analysis, 15*(4), 315–330.

Cervantes, M., & Guellec, D. (2002, January). The brain drain: Old myths, new realities. *OECD Observer* No. 230. http://www.oecdobserver.org/news/archivestory.php/aid/673/The_brain_drain:_Old_myths,_new_realities.html

Chang, S. L. (1992, Spring). Causes of brain drain and solutions: The Taiwan experience. *Studies in Comparative International Development, 27*(1), 27–43. http://www.ncbi.nlm.nih.gov/pubmed/?term=Chang%20SL%5BAuthor%5D&cauthor=true&cauthor_uid=12285391

Docquier, F., & Rapoport, H. (1997). *La fuite des cerveaux, une chance pour les pays en developpement?* Meeting of the French economic association, Paris, September in Human Capital Flight: Stratification, Globalization and the Challenges to Tertiary Education in Africa* By B.J. Ndulu

Docquier, F., & Rapoport, H. (2011). *Globalization, brain drain and development IZA*. Discussion Paper No. 5590.

Galor, O., & Tsiddon, D. (1997). The distribution of human capital and economic growth. *Journal of Economic Growth, 2*(1), 93–124.

Haque, N. U., & Kim, S.-J. (1995). Human capital flight: Impact of migration on income and growth. *IMF Staff Papers, 42*(3), 577–607.

Haupt, A., & Janeba, E. (2009). Education, redistribution and the threat of brain drain. *International Tax and Public Finance, 16*, 1–24.

Herrmann, B., & Kritikos, A. S. (2013). Growing out of the crisis: Hidden assets to Greece's transition to an innovation economy. *IZA Journal of European Labor Studies, 2*, 14. https://doi.org/10.1186/2193-9012-2-14.

Labrianidis, L., & Vogiatzis, N. (2013a). The mutually reinforcing relation between international migration of highly educated labour force and economic crisis: The case of Greece. *Southeast European and Black Sea Studies, 13*(4), 525–551. http://www.tandfonline.com/doi/pdf/10.1080/14683857.2013.859814.

Labrianidis, L., & Vogiatzis, N. (2013b). Highly skilled migration: What differentiates the 'brains' who are drained from those who return in the case of Greece? *Population, Space and Place, 19* (5), 472–486. http://onlinelibrary.wiley.com/enhanced/doi/10.1002/psp.1726.

Lawan Ngoma, A., & Wana Ismail, N. (2013). The determinants of brain drain in developing countries. *International Journal of Social Economics, 40*(8), 744–754. https://doi.org/10.1108/IJSE-05-2013-0109.

Lawley, D. N., & Maxwell, A. E. (1971). *Factor analysis as a statistical method* (2nd ed.). London: Butterworths.

Lucas, R. E. (1988). On the mechanics of economic development. *Journal of Monetary Economics, 22*(3), 3–42.

Miyagiwa, K. (1991). Scale economies in education and the brain drain problem. *International Economic Review, 32*(3), 743–759.

Mountford, A. (1997). Can a brain drain be good for growth in the source economy? *Journal of Development Economics, 53*(2), 287–303.

Nedeljkovic, V. (2014). *Brain drain in the European Union: Facts and figures*. Bridging Europe Rethink Education working paper No 4.

Nussmayr, K. (2014). *Where do the European brains move?* European Forum Alpbach. http://www.alpbach.org/alpbuzz/2014/08/26/where-the-european-brains-move/

Özden, Ç. (2006). *«Brain drain in latin America»*. UN/POP/EGM-MIG/2005/10.

Ozden, C., Parsons, C. R., Schiff, M., & Walmsley, T. L. (2011). *Where on earth is everybody ? The evolution of global bilateral migration 1960–2000*. Policy Research Working Paper Series 5709, The World Bank.

Piketty, T. (1997). Immigration et justice sociale. *Revue Economique, 48*(5), 1291–1309. http://www.persee.fr/doc/reco_0035-2764_1997_num_48_5_409941.

Ratha, D., Mohapatra, S., & Silwal, A. (2010). *Migration and remittances factbook 2011*. Washington, DC: World Bank Group. http://documents.worldbank.org/curated/en/630421468163744010/Migration-andremittances-factbook-2011

Sevris Constandis. (2014). *Brain drain to Germany*, Journal ARDIN V.93, (in Greek) http://ardin-rixi.gr/archives/14227

Stark, O., Helmenstein, C., & Prskawetz, A. (1998). Human capital formation, human capital depletion, and migration: A blessing or a curse? *Economics Letters, 60*(3), 363–367.

United Nations. (2006, July 12). *Migrants human rights, cost of "brain drain", protecting remittances among issues raised as general assembly holds civil society hearings on migration*, GA/10482. http://www.un.org/press/en/2006/ga10482.doc.htm

Vidal, J.-P. (1998). The effect of emigration on human capital formation. *Journal of Population Economics, 11*(4), 589–600. http://link.springer.com/article/10.1007/s001480050086#page-1.

Zeitchik, S. (2015). With jobless rate above 50%, disillusioned Greek youths becoming a 'lost generation'. *Los Angeles Times*. http://www.latimes.com/world/europe/la-fg-greece-youth-economic-woes-20150602-story.html

Complexity in a Bertrand Duopoly Game with Heterogeneous Players and Differentiated Goods

Georges Sarafopoulos and Kosmas Papadopoulos

Abstract In this paper we investigate the dynamics of a nonlinear discrete-time Bertrand duopoly game with differentiated goods. The players have heterogeneous expectations and the game is modeled with a system of two difference equations. Existence and stability of equilibria of this system are studied. We show that the model gives more complex chaotic and unpredictable trajectories as a consequence of change in the parameter of horizontal product differentiation. If this parameter is varied, the stability of Nash equilibrium is lost through period doubling bifurcations. The chaotic features are justified numerically via computing Lyapunov numbers and sensitive dependence on initial conditions.

Keywords Bertrand duopoly game · Discrete dynamical system · Heterogeneous expectations · Stability · Chaotic behavior

1 Introduction

An oligopoly is a market structure between monopoly and perfect competition, where there are only a few number of firms in the market producing homogeneous products. The dynamic of an oligopoly game is more complex because firms must consider not only the behaviors of the consumers but also the reactions of the competitors, i.e., they form expectations concerning how their rivals will act. Cournot in 1838 has introduced the first formal theory of oligopoly. In 1883 another French mathematician Joseph Louis Francois Bertrand modified Cournot game suggesting that firms actually choose prices rather than quantities. Originally Cournot and Bertrand models were based on the premise that all players follow naïve expectations, so that in every step, each player (firm) assumes the last values

G. Sarafopoulos (✉) · K. Papadopoulos
Department of Economics, Democritus University of Thrace, Komotini, Greece
e-mail: gsarafop@econ.duth.gr

© Springer Nature Switzerland AG 2019   15
N. Sykianakis et al. (eds.), *Economic and Financial Challenges for Eastern Europe*,
Springer Proceedings in Business and Economics,
https://doi.org/10.1007/978-3-030-12169-3_2

that were taken by the competitors without estimation of their future reactions. However, in real market conditions, such an assumption is very unlikely since not all players share naïve beliefs. Therefore, different approaches to firm behavior were proposed. Some authors considered duopolies with homogeneous expectations and found a variety of complex dynamics in their games, such as appearance of strange attractors (Agiza 1999; Agiza et al. 2002; Agliari et al. 2005, 2006; Bischi and Kopel 2001; Kopel 1996; Puu 1998, 2005; Sarafopoulos 2015a, b; Zhang et al. 2009). Also models with heterogeneous agents were studied (Agiza and Elsadany 2003, 2004; Agiza et al. 2002; Den Haan 2001; Hommes 2006; Fanti and Gori 2012; Gao 2009; Tramontana 2010; Zhang et al. 2007; Wu et al. 2010).

In the real market, producers do not know the entire demand function, though it is possible that they have a perfect knowledge of technology, represented by the cost function. Hence, it is more likely that firms employ some local estimate of the demand. This issue has been previously analyzed by (Baumol and Quandt 1964; Singh and Vives 1984; Puu 1991, 1995; Westerhoff 2006; Naimzada and Ricchiuti 2008; Askar 2013, 2014). Bounded rational players (firms) update their strategies based on discrete time periods and by using a local estimate of the marginal profit. With such local adjustment mechanism, the players are not requested to have a complete knowledge of the demand and the cost functions (Agiza and Elsadany 2004; Naimzada and Sbragia 2006; Zhang et al. 2007; Askar 2014).

In this paper we study the dynamics of a Bertrand-type duopoly with differentiated goods where each firm behaves with heterogeneous expectation strategies. We show that the model gives more complex chaotic and unpredictable trajectories as a consequence of change in the parameter of horizontal product differentiation. The paper is organized as follows: In Sect. 2, the dynamics of the duopoly game with heterogeneous expectations, linear demand, and a quadratic cost function including emission costs is analyzed. The existence and local stability of the equilibrium points are also analyzed. In Sect. 3 numerical simulations are used to show complex dynamics via computing Lyapunov numbers and sensitive dependence on initial conditions.

2 The Game

2.1 The Construction of the Game

In this study we consider heterogeneous players, and more specifically, we consider that the Firm 1 chooses the price of its product in a rational way, following an adjustment mechanism (bounded rational player), while the Firm 2 decides with naïve way by selecting a price that maximizes its output (naïve player). We consider a simple Bertrand-type duopoly market where firms (players) produce differentiated goods and offer them at discrete-time periods on a common market. Price decisions are taken at discrete time periods $t = 0, 1, 2,\ldots$. At each period t, every firm must form an expectation of the rival's strategy in the next time period in order to determine the corresponding profit-maximizing prices for period $t + 1$. We suppose that q_1, q_2 are the production quantities of each firm. Also, we consider that the preferences of consumers represented by the equation:

$$U(q_1, q_2) = a(q_1 + q_2) - \frac{1}{2}\left(q_1^2 + q_2^2 + 2dq_1q_2\right) \tag{1}$$

where α is a positive parameter ($\alpha > 0$), which expresses the market size, and $d \in (-1, 1)$ is the parameter that reveals the differentiation degree of products. For example, if $d = 0$ then both products are independent, and each firm participates in a monopoly. But, if $d = 1$ then one product is a substitute for the other, since the products are homogeneous. It is understood that for positive values of the parameter d the larger the value, the less diversification we have in both products. On the other hand, negative values of the parameter d are described that the two products are complementary, and when $d = -1$ then we have the phenomenon of full competition between the two companies. The inverse demand functions (as functions of quantities) coming from the maximizing of (1) are given by the following equations:

$$p_1(q_1, q_2) = a - q_1 - dq_2 \text{ and } p_2(q_1, q_2) = a - q_2 - dq_1 \tag{2}$$

The direct demand functions (as functions of prices):

$$q_1(p_1, p_2) = \frac{a(1 - d) - p_1 + dp_2}{1 - d^2} \text{ and } q_2(p_1, p_2) = \frac{a(1 - d) - p_2 + dp_1}{1 - d^2} \tag{3}$$

We suppose that the cost functions are linear:

$$C_i(q_i) = cq_i, \tag{4}$$

$i = 1, 2$ and $c > 0$ is the same marginal cost.

With these assumptions the profits of the firms are given by:

$$P_1(p_1, p_2) = \frac{(p_1 - c)[a(1 - d) - p_1 + dp_2]}{1 - d^2} \text{ and}$$

$$P_2(p_1, p_2) = \frac{(p_2 - c)[a(1 - d) - p_2 + dp_1]}{1 - d^2} \tag{5}$$

Then the marginal profits at the point of the strategy space are given by:

$$\frac{dP_1}{dp_1} = \frac{1}{1 - d^2}[a(1 - d) + c - 2p_1 + dp_2] \text{ and}$$

$$\frac{dP_2}{dp_2} = \frac{1}{1 - d^2}[a(1 - d) + c - 2p_2 + dp_1] \tag{6}$$

We suppose that first firm decides to increase its level of adaptation if it has a positive marginal profit or decreases its level if the marginal profit is negative (bounded rational player). If $k > 0$ the dynamical equation of the first player is:

$$\frac{p_1(t+1) - p_1(t)}{p_1(t)} = k\frac{dP_1}{dp_1} \tag{7}$$

k is the speed of adjustment of player 1; it is a positive parameter which gives the extent price variation of the firm following a given profit signal. Moreover it captures the fact that relative variations of the price are proportional to the marginal profit. The second firm decides with naïve way by selecting a price that maximizes its profits (naïve player):

$$\frac{dP_2}{dp_2} = 0 \Rightarrow p_2(t+1) = \frac{a(1-d) + c + dp_1(t)}{2} \tag{8}$$

The dynamical system of the players is described by:

$$\begin{cases} p_1(t+1) = p_1(t) + k \cdot p_1(t)\dfrac{dP_1}{dp_1} \\ p_2(t+1) = \dfrac{a(1-d) + c + dp_1(t)}{2} \end{cases} \tag{9}$$

We will focus on the dynamics of this system to the parameter d.

2.2   Dynamical Analysis

2.2.1   The Equilibriums of the Game

The equilibriums of the dynamical system (9) are the nonnegative solutions of the algebraic system:

$$\begin{cases} k \cdot p_1^* \dfrac{1}{1-d^2}[a(1-d) + c - 2p_1^* + dp_2^*] = 0 \\ p_2^* = \dfrac{a(1-d) + c + dp_1^*}{2} \end{cases} \tag{10}$$

which obtained by setting $p_1(t+1) = p_1(t) = p_1^*$ and $p_2(t+1) = p_2^*$ in Eq. (9).

- If $p_1^* = 0$, then $p_2^* = \dfrac{a(1-d) + c}{2}$ and we have the boundary equilibrium:

$$E_0 = \left(0, \frac{a(1-d) + c}{2}\right) \tag{11}$$

- If $\dfrac{dP_1}{dp_1} = \dfrac{dP_2}{dp_2} = 0$, then we form the system:

$$\begin{cases} p_1^* = \dfrac{a(1-d) + c + dp_2^*}{2} \\ p_2^* = \dfrac{a(1-d) + c + dp_1^*}{2} \end{cases} \qquad (12)$$

The solutions are $p_1^* = p_2^* = \dfrac{a(1-d) + c}{2-d}$, giving the Nash equilibrium:

$$E_* = \left(\dfrac{a(1-d) + c}{2-d}, \dfrac{a(1-d) + c}{2-d} \right) \qquad (13)$$

2.2.2   Stability of Equilibriums

The study of the local stability of the equilibrium is based on the localization on the complex plane of the eigenvalues of the Jacobian matrix of the dimensional map Eq. (9). In order to study the local stability of equilibrium points of the model (9), we consider the Jacobian matrix $J(p_1, p_2)$ along the variable strategy (p_1, p_2) (Gandolfo 1997; Medio and Gallo 1995; Medio and Lines 2001, 2005; Sedaghat 2003):

$$J(p_1, p_2) = \begin{bmatrix} f_{p_1} & f_{p_2} \\ g_{p_1} & g_{p_2} \end{bmatrix} \qquad (14)$$

where

$$\begin{aligned} f(p_1, p_2) &= p_1 + k \cdot p_1 \dfrac{dP_1}{dp_1} = p_1 + k \cdot p_1 \dfrac{1}{1-d^2}[a(1-d) + c - 2p_1 + dp_2] \\ g(p_1, p_2) &= \dfrac{a(1-d) + c + dp_1}{2} \end{aligned} \qquad (15)$$

The Jacobian matrix is:

$$J(p_1, p_2) = \begin{bmatrix} 1 + \dfrac{k}{1-d^2}[a(1-d) + c - 4p_1 + dp_2] & \dfrac{kdp_1}{1-d^2} \\ \dfrac{d}{2} & 0 \end{bmatrix} \qquad (16)$$

At the equilibrium E_0:

$$J(E_0) = \begin{bmatrix} 1 + \dfrac{k}{1-d^2} \cdot \dfrac{(2+d)[a(1-d)+c]}{2} & 0 \\[3mm] \dfrac{d}{2} & 0 \end{bmatrix} \tag{17}$$

with

$$Tr = 1 + \frac{k}{1-d^2} \cdot \frac{(2+d)[a(1-d)+c]}{2} \text{ and } Det = 0.$$

The characteristic equation of $J(E_0)$ is:

$$l^2 - Tr \cdot l + Det = 0 \tag{18}$$

with solutions

$$l_1 = 0 \text{ and } l_2 = Tr = 1 + \frac{k}{1-d^2} \cdot \frac{(2+d)[a(1-d)+c]}{2} \tag{19}$$

Since $l_2 > 1$, the equilibrium E_0 is unstable.

At the Nash equilibrium point E_*, the Jacobian matrix is:

$$J(E_*) = \begin{bmatrix} 1 + \dfrac{k}{1-d^2}[a(1-d)+c-(4-d)p^*] & \dfrac{kdp^*}{1-d^2} \\[3mm] \dfrac{d}{2} & 0 \end{bmatrix} \tag{20}$$

with

$$Tr = 1 - \frac{2kp^*}{1-d^2} \text{ and } Det = -\frac{kd^2p^*}{2(1-d^2)}.$$

The Nash equilibrium is asymptotically stable if the following conditions are hold (Elaydi 2005; Gandolfo 1997):

$$\begin{aligned} &i) \quad 1 - Det > 0 \\ &ii) \quad 1 - Tr + Det > 0 \\ &iii) \quad 1 + Tr + Det > 0 \end{aligned} \tag{21}$$

Since

$$1 - Det = 1 + \frac{kd^2p^*}{2(1-d^2)} > 0 \tag{22}$$

and

$$1 - Tr + Det = \frac{kp^*(4 - d^2)}{2(1 - d^2)} > 0 \tag{23}$$

the conditions (i) and (ii) are always satisfied.

The third condition becomes

$$1 + Tr + Det > 0 \Leftrightarrow kp^*(4 + d^2) - 4(1 - d^2) < 0 \tag{24}$$

with

$$p^* = \frac{a(1 - d) + c}{2 - d}$$

then

$$\begin{aligned} &k[a(1 - d) + c](4 + d^2) - 4(2 - d)(1 - d^2) < 0 \Leftrightarrow \\ &-(4 + ak) \cdot d^3 + (ak + ck + 8) \cdot d^2 + 4(1 - ak) \cdot d + 4k(a + c) - 8 < 0 \end{aligned} \tag{25}$$

It follows that:

Proposition *The Nash equilibrium* $E_*\left(p_1^*, p_2^*\right)$ *of the dynamical system Eq. (9) is locally asymptotically stable if:*

$$-(4 + ak) \cdot d^3 + (ak + ck + 8) \cdot d^2 + 4(1 - ak) \cdot d + 4k(a + c) - 8 < 0$$

2.2.3 Numerical Simulations

To provide some numerical evidence for the chaotic behavior of the system Eq. (9), as a consequence of change in the parameter d of the product differentiation degree, we present various numerical results here to show the chaoticity, including its bifurcation diagrams, strange attractor, Lyapunov numbers, and sensitive dependence on initial conditions (Kulenonic and Merino 2002). In order to study the local stability properties of the equilibrium points, it is convenient to take the parameter values as follows $a = 5$, $c = 1$, $k = 0.3$, so the Eq. (25) becomes $-5.5 \cdot d^3 + 8.8 \cdot d^2 - 2d - 0.8 < 0$ and its graph is the Fig. 1, in which we can see that it becomes negative for values of parameter d from about -0.2 to 0.6. This means that when d is between these values the Nash equilibrium of the system Eq. (9) is stable.

Numerical experiments are computed to show the bifurcation diagram with respect to d, strange attractor of the system Eq. (9) in the phase plane (p_1, p_2), and Lyapunov numbers. Figure 2 shows the bifurcation diagrams with respect to the parameter d against variable p_1 (left) and p_2 (right). Also in Fig. 3, we plot the

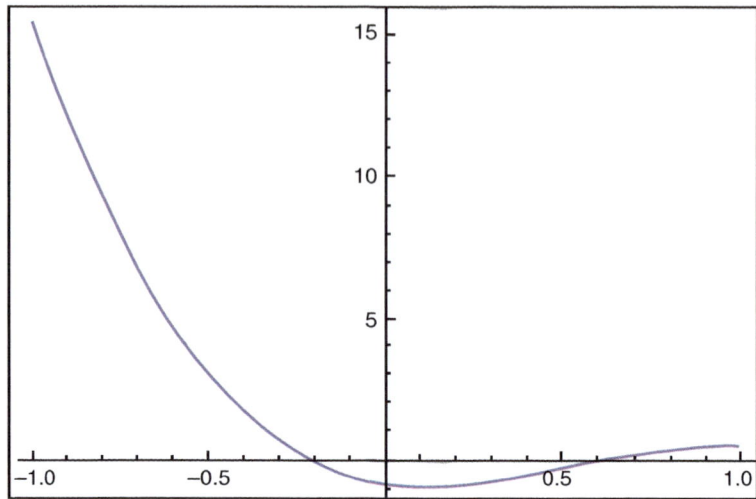

Fig. 1 Graph of the function: $f(d) = -5.5 \cdot d^3 + 8.8 \cdot d^2 - 2d - 0.8$, with $d \in [-1, 1]$

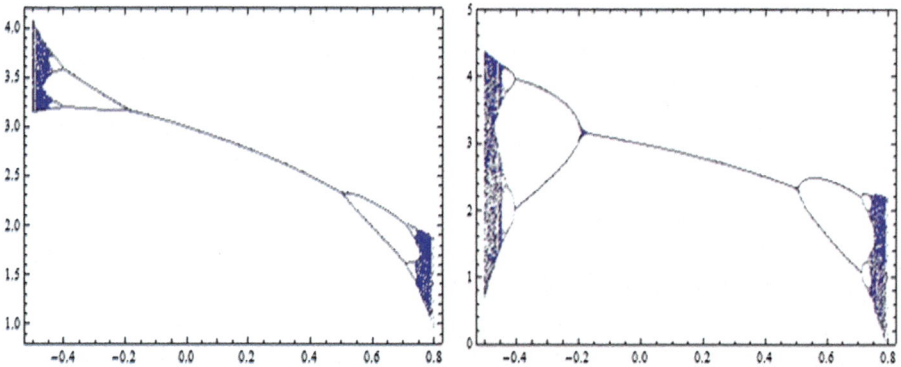

Fig. 2 Bifurcation diagrams with respect to the parameter d against variable p_1 (left) and p_2 (right), with 400 iterations of the map Eq. (9) for $a = 5$, $c = 1$, $k = 0.3$

last two bifurcation diagrams in one to show the common stability space for parameter d. In these figures the Nash equilibrium E^* is locally asymptotically stable for $-0.2 < d < 0.6$. For $d > 0.6$ and $d < -0.2$, the Nash equilibrium E^* becomes unstable, and one observes complex dynamics behavior such as cycles of higher order and chaos. Figure 4 shows the Lyapunov numbers' diagram of the same orbit for $a = 5$, $c = 1$, $k = 0.3$, $d = 0.75$. If the Lyapunov number is greater of 1, one has evidence for chaos. Figure 5 shows the graphs of the orbit of the point $(0.1, 0.1)$ (strange attractors) for $a = 5$, $c = 1$, $k = 0.3$, $d = -0.49$ (left), $a = 5$, $c = 1$, $k = 0.3$, $d = -0.5$ (middle), and $a = 5$, $c = 1$, $k = 0.3$, $d = 0.75$ (right). From these results when all parameters are fixed and only d is varied, the structure of the game becomes

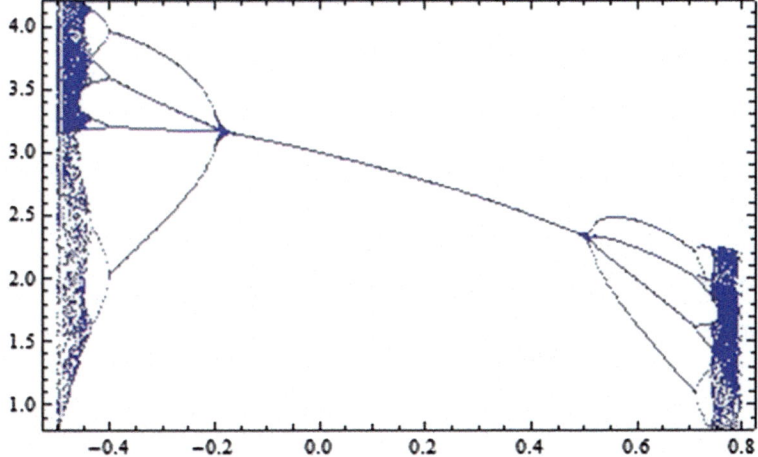

Fig. 3 Two bifurcation diagrams of Fig. 2 are plotted in one

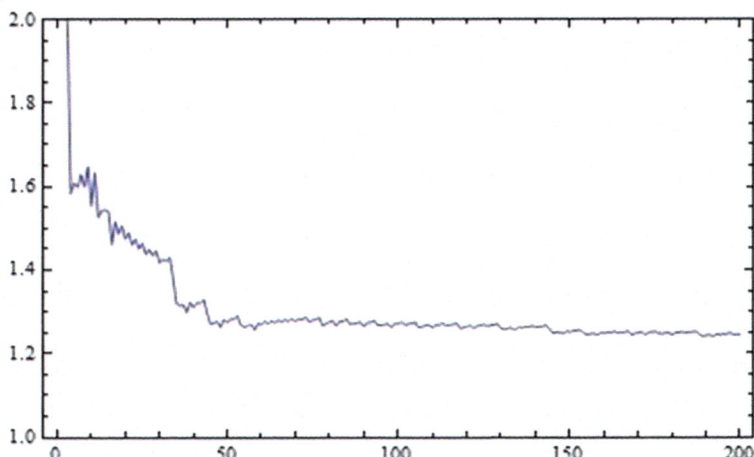

Fig. 4 Lyapunov numbers of the orbit of the point A(0.1,0.1) versus the number of iterations for $a = 5, c = 1, k = 0.3, d = 0.75$

complicated through period doubling bifurcations; more complex bounded attractors are created which are aperiodic cycles of higher order or chaotic attractors.

To demonstrate the sensitivity to initial conditions of the system Eq. (9), we compute two orbits with initial points (0.1,0.1) and (0.101,0.1), respectively. Figure 6 shows sensitive dependence on initial conditions for x-coordinate of the two orbits, for the system Eq. (9), plotted against the time with the parameter values $a = 5$, $c = 1, k = 0.3, d = 0.75$. At the beginning the time series are indistinguishable; but after a number of iterations, the difference between them builds up rapidly, which is clearly shown in Fig. 7. From Figs. 6 and 7, we show that the time series of the

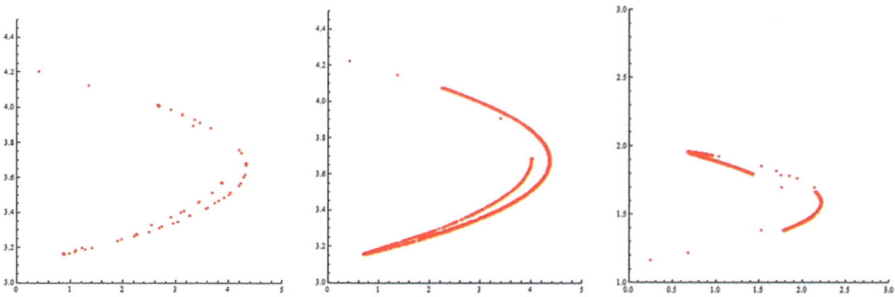

Fig. 5 Phase portrait (strange attractors). The orbit of (0.1,0.1) with 2000 iterations of the map Eq. (9) for $a = 5$, $c = 1$, $k = 0.3$, $d = -0.49$ (left), for $a = 5$, $c = 1$, $k = 0.3$, $d = -0.5$ (middle), and for $a = 5$, $c = 1$, $k = 0.3$, $d = 0.75$ (right)

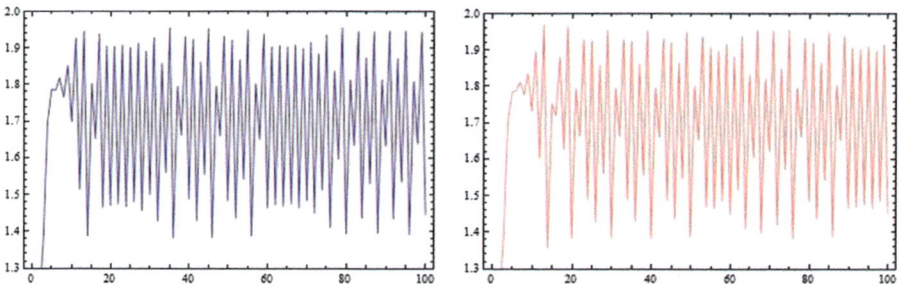

Fig. 6 Sensitive dependence on initial conditions for x-coordinate plotted against the time: the two orbits, the orbit of (0.1,0.1) (left) and the orbit of (0.101,0.1) (right), for the system Eq. (9), with the parameter values $a = 5$, $c = 1$, $k = 0.3$, $d = 0.75$

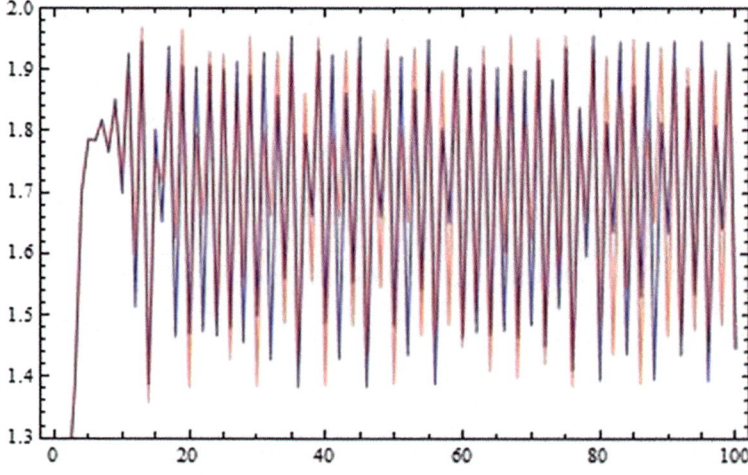

Fig. 7 Two graphs of Fig. 6 are plotted in one

system Eq. (9) is sensitive dependent on initial conditions, i.e., complex dynamics behavior occur in this model.

3 Conclusion

In this study, we analyzed through a discrete dynamical system based on the marginal profits of the players, the dynamics of a nonlinear discrete-time Bertrand-type duopoly game, where the players have heterogeneous expectations. The stability of equilibria, bifurcation, and chaotic behavior is investigated. We proved that a parameter (product differentiation degree) may change the stability of Nash equilibrium and cause a structure to behave chaotically, through period doubling bifurcation. The chaotic features are justified numerically via computing Lyapunov numbers and sensitive dependence on initial conditions.

References

Agiza, H. N. (1999). On the analysis of stability, bifurcation, chaos and chaos control of Kopel map. *Chaos, Solitons & Fractals, 10*, 1909–1916.

Agiza, H. N., & Elsadany, A. A. (2003). Nonlinear dynamics in the Cournot duopoly game with heterogeneous players. *Physica A, 320*, 512–524.

Agiza, H. N., & Elsadany, A. A. (2004). Chaotic dynamics in nonlinear duopoly game with heterogeneous players. *Applied Mathematics and Computation, 149*, 843–860.

Agiza, H. N., Hegazi, A. S., & Elsadany, A. A. (2002). Complex dynamics and synchronization of duopoly game with bounded rationality. *Mathematics and Computers in Simulation, 58*, 133–146.

Agliari, A., Gardini, L., & Puu, T. (2005). Some global bifurcations related to the appearance of closed invariant curves. *Mathematics and Computers in Simulation, 68*(3), 201–219.

Agliari, A., Gardini, L., & Puu, T. (2006). Global bifurcations in duopoly when the Cournot point is destabilized via a subcritical Neimark bifurcation. *International Game Theory Review, 8*(1), 1–20.

Askar, S. S. (2013). On complex dynamics of monopoly market. *Economic Modelling, 31*, 586–589.

Askar, S. S. (2014). Complex dynamic properties of Cournot duopoly games with convex and log-concave demand function. *Operations Research Letters, 42*, 85–90.

Baumol, W. J., & Quandt, R. E. (1964). Rules of thumb and optimally imperfect decisions. *American Economic Review, 54*(2), 23–46.

Bischi, G. I., & Kopel, M. (2001). Equilibrium selection in a nonlinear duopoly game with adaptive expectations. *Journal of Economic Behavior and Organization, 46*, 73–100.

Den Haan, W. J. (2001). The importance of the number of different agents in a heterogeneous asset-pricing model. *Journal of Economic Dynamics and Control, 25*, 721–746.

Elaydi, S. (2005). *An introduction to difference equations* (3rd ed.). New York: Springer.

Fanti, L., & Gori, L. (2012). The dynamics of a differentiated duopoly with quantity competition. *Economic Modelling, 29*(2), 421–427.

Gandolfo, G. (1997). *Economic dynamics*. Berlin: Springer.

Gao, Y. (2009). Complex dynamics in a two dimensional noninvertible map. *Chaos, Solitons Fractals, 39*, 1798–1810.

Hommes, C. H. (2006). *Heterogeneous agent models in economics and finance*. In L. Tesfatsion & K. L. Judd (Eds.), *Handbook of computational economics, agent-based computational economics* (Vol. 2, pp. 1109–1186). Amsterdam: Elsevier Science BV.

Kopel, M. (1996). Simple and complex adjustment dynamics in Cournot duopoly models. *Chaos, Solitons Fractals, 12*, 2031–2048.

Kulenonic, M., & Merino, O. (2002). *Discrete dynamical systems and difference equations with mathematica*. Boca Raton: Chapman & Hall/CRC.

Medio, A., & Gallo, G. (1995). *Chaotic dynamics: Theory and applications to economics*. Cambridge, MA: Cambridge University Press.

Medio A, Lines M. (2001).*Nonlinear dynamics. A primer*. Cambridge, MA: Cambridge University Press.

Medio, A., & Lines, M. (2005). Introductory notes on the dynamics of linear and linearized systems. In M. Lines (Ed.), *Nonlinear dynamical systems in economics* (CISM) (pp. 1–26). New York: Springer.

Naimzada, A. K., & Ricchiuti, G. (2008). Complex dynamics in a monopoly with a rule of thumb. *Applied Mathematics and Computation, 203*, 921–925.

Naimzada, A., & Sbragia, L. (2006). Oligopoly games with nonlinear demand and cost functions: Two boundedly rational adjustment processes. *Chaos, Solitons Fractals, 29*, 707–722.

Puu, T. (1991). Chaos in duopoly pricing. *Chaos, Solitons Fractals, 1*, 573–581.

Puu, T. (1995). The chaotic monopolist. *Chaos, Solitons & Fractals, 5*(1), 35–44.

Puu, T. (1998). The chaotic duopolists revisited. *Journal of Economic Behavior and Organization, 37*, 385–394.

Puu, T. (2005). Complex oligopoly dynamics. In M. Lines (Ed.), *Nonlinear dynamical systems in economics* (CISM) (pp. 165–186). New York: Springer.

Sarafopoulos, G. (2015a). On the dynamics of a duopoly game with differentiated goods. *Procedia Economics and Finance, 19*, 146–153.

Sarafopoulos, G. (2015b). Complexity in a duopoly game with homogeneous players, convex, log linear demand and quadratic cost functions. *Procedia Economics and Finance, 33*, 358–366.

Sedaghat, H. (2003). *Nonlinear difference equations: Theory with applications to social science models*. London: Kluwer Academic Publishers (now Springer).

Singh, N., & Vives, X. (1984). Price and quantity competition in a differentiated duopoly. *The RAND Journal of Economics, 15*, 546–554.

Tramontana, F. (2010). Heterogeneous duopoly with isoelastic demand function. *Economic Modelling, 27*, 350–357.

Westerhoff, F. (2006). *Nonlinear expectation formation, endogenous business cycles and stylized facts. Studies in Nonlinear Dynamics and Econometrics, 10*(4), Article 4.

Wu, W., Chen, Z., & Ip, W. H. (2010). Complex nonlinear dynamics and controlling chaos in a Cournot duopoly economic model. *Nonlinear Analysis: Real World Applications, 11*, 4363–4377.

Zhang, J., Da, Q., & Wang, Y. (2007). Analysis of nonlinear duopoly game with heterogeneous players. *Economic Modelling, 24*, 138–148.

Zhang, J., Da, Q., & Wang, Y. (2009). The dynamics of Bertrand model with bounded rationality. *Chaos, Solitons and Fractals, 39*, 2048–2055.

A Performance Measurement System for Staff of the Logistics Section: A Case Study for an Oil & Gas Company

Filippos Gegitsidis and Pavlos Delias

Abstract Companies recognize the central role performance measurement plays in their success and are therefore becoming increasingly enthusiastic about their performance measurement efforts. Performance measurement indicators not only support the daily operation of the organization, but they are valuable in formulating any emerging problems as well. Logistics encompasses a complex set of activities that require an equally complex collection of metrics to adequately measure performance. However, many performance measurement systems have neither kept up with the changing role and scope of logistics nor have they been systematically examined or evaluated. Performance measurement systems should be evaluated at both the individual metric and system-wide levels in order to maintain relevance and effectiveness. This study aims to present the empirical findings and lessons learned from a field research on the development of the performance measurement system (PMS) for the logistics department of an Oil & Gas company. The implementation focuses on the procedure rather than on the structure of PMS offering a conceptual procedural framework with information and insights on how to design, implement, use, and assess a PMS, addressing an important gap identified in the literature. This research focuses on the evaluation of staff of the supply chain. Specifically, we propose a set of recommended criteria that can be applied to evaluate staff of the relevant department and demonstrate the use of these criteria through the evaluation of drivers' performance. The primary motivation for evaluating performance at that level is that measurement systems guide management decisions. A well-crafted system of metrics will lead toward better decision-making by managers. The entire research effort lasted almost 6 months, involving multiple interactions between a researcher from academia and a practitioner from the company. Ultimately, the main

F. Gegitsidis (✉)
Department of Petroleum & Natural Gas Technology, Eastern Macedonia and Thrace Institute of Technology, Kavala, Greece

P. Delias
Department of Accounting and Finance, Eastern Macedonia and Thrace Institute of Technology, Kavala, Greece
e-mail: pdelias@teiemt.gr

© Springer Nature Switzerland AG 2019
N. Sykianakis et al. (eds.), *Economic and Financial Challenges for Eastern Europe*,
Springer Proceedings in Business and Economics,
https://doi.org/10.1007/978-3-030-12169-3_3

27

findings are as follows: (1) how we can evaluate a drive; (2) the indicators and their parameters that contribute in revealing our assumptions about "good" and "bad" driver; (3) developing a prototype PMS; and (4) the use and review of the new PMS has led to improvements in people's behavior, development of organizational capabilities, and improved performance results.

Keywords Performance measurement · Decision support system · Staff of logistics · Multicriteria analysis

1   Introduction

The petroleum industry includes roughly the global processes of exploration, extraction, refining, transporting (often by oil tankers and pipelines), and marketing petroleum products. The largest volume products of the industry are fuel oil and gasoline (petrol). The industry is usually divided into three major streams: upstream, midstream, and downstream. The upstream oil sector is also commonly known as the exploration and production (E&P) sector. The upstream sector includes searching for potential underground or underwater crude oil and natural gas fields, drilling exploratory wells, and subsequently drilling and operating the wells that recover and bring the crude oil and/or raw natural gas to the surface. The downstream sector commonly refers to the refining of petroleum crude oil and the processing and purifying of raw natural gas, as well as the marketing and distribution of products derived from crude oil and natural gas (PSAC 2017).

In this work, we focus on the part of the transportation of the final product via road tankers to retail sellers. Petroleum is transported by rail cars, trucks, tanker vessels, and through pipelines. Which method is used to move this oil depends on the amount that is being moved and where it is being moved to. The biggest problems with moving this oil are pollution and the chance that the oil can spill. Petroleum oil is very hard to clean up and is very toxic to living animals.

These road tankers (trucks) are used in situations where it would be illogical to use railcars, pipelines, and tanker ships. Places like gas stations or some infrastructures, which are not able to be accessed by marine vessels, and do not demand the volume that is delivered by pipelines or trains, would get their fuel from tanker trucks. This allows a rational and cost-effective way to deliver the fuel to the consumers.

Undoubtedly, transportation of petroleum products is very important for the industries in economic-fiscal terms, because the customer pays for the products and the industries want to carry forward appropriately. To this end, the logistics section is responsible for the transportation and correspondingly requires qualified staff. At this point, a significant issue emerges, because a detailed monitoring of the whole process, and consequently the evaluation of the involved staff, is required.

This can be resolved with a performance measurement system (Folan and Browne 2005; Platts and Gregory 1990; Platts 1994).

Performance measurement enables organizations to collect data that help identify potential improvements to their business models. By acting on the knowledge provided by this data, an organization can ultimately increase its financial performance. As Neely and Al Najjar explain (2006), a "business model is just a model. It is based on a series of assumptions that might not be valid." Performance measurement can help turn assumptions into well-understood facts and show the way to improvements that lead to more effective business models.

According to this context, the following research question has emerged: How should a company successfully manage the evolution of its PMS, considering the entire PMS life cycle from design through implementation and use/review? The research focuses on the procedure and structure of PMS offering a conceptual procedural framework that provides information and insights on how to design, implement, use, and assess a PMS (Folan and Browne 2005; Platts 1994; Platts and Gregory 1990).

The Petroleum Company that was studied has been facing increased complexity of its operations, resulting in the growth of its logistics department's importance. Thus, performance measurement of the logistics activities has become critical to the company. Therefore, this study presents the main lessons learned in a real-life setting and contributes to filling the identified gap in the PMS literature. It aims to examine the procedures and techniques that are relevant for the development of a PMS. In particular the research objectives are as follows: (1) identify the relevant factors for drivers, (2) combine multiple factors in an aggregated score, and (3) develop a system to support the pertinent decisions.

The next section briefly reviews the relevant theoretical aspects, while the methodological approach is presented in Sect. 3. The analytical results of our application are illustrated and discussed in Sect. 4, and our efforts to wrap up and present our thoughts for future work and limitations of this study conclude the paper.

2   Theoretical Background

In today's competitive business world, enterprises must continually improve the quality of their products and services to stay ahead of the competition. Despite dramatic changes in the business environment, performance measurement systems have been affected only marginally: both top management and lower management assess enterprise performance mainly through financial measures and nonfinancial aspects such as customer satisfaction or job satisfaction having a modest role (Akhtar and Mittal 2015; Elg and Kollberg 2012).

Over the last decade, the role of logistics in business has increased in both scope and strategic importance. Logistics encompasses a complex set of activities which require a collection of metrics to adequately measure performance. Initiatives, such as supply chain integration, quick response, and just-in-time inventory management, have revolutionized not only the way companies manage their logistics activities but also how they run their entire business (Hoek 2001; Bichou and Gray 2004).

Performance measurement systems (PMSs) have become a relevant issue for scholars and practitioners since the end of the 1980s. Despite the great volume of research on PMSs, research gaps still exist, offering many opportunities for future research (Bititci et al. 2012; Taylor and Taylor 2013). The balanced scorecard is the largest or most visible achievement of the performance measurement revolution foreseen by Eccles (1991) and Neely (1999) during the 1990s.

A performance indicator or key performance indicator (KPI) is a type of performance measurement. KPIs evaluate the success of an organization or of a particular activity (such as projects, programs, products, and other initiatives) in which it engages. Often success is simply the repeated, periodic achievement of some levels of operational goal (e.g., zero defects, 10/10 customer satisfaction, etc.), and sometimes success is defined in terms of making progress toward strategic goals. Accordingly, choosing the right KPIs relies upon a good understanding of what is important to the organization. "What is important" often depends on the department measuring the performance—e.g., the KPIs useful to finance will differ from the KPIs assigned to sales. Since there is a need to understand well what is important, various techniques to assess the present state of the business, and its key activities, are associated with the selection of performance indicators. These assessments often lead to the identification of potential improvements, so performance indicators are routinely associated with "performance improvement" initiatives.

Unfortunately, many performance measurement systems have neither kept up with the changing role and scope of logistics nor have they been systematically examined or evaluated (Caplice and Sheffi 1995). Performance measurement systems should be evaluated at both the individual metric and system-wide levels in order to maintain relevance and effectiveness (Delias and Matsatsinis 2009). This research addresses the evaluation of staff of the logistics performance measurement systems. Specifically, establish useful criteria which can be applied to evaluate logistics performance measurement systems and demonstrate the use of these criteria through the evaluation of drivers' performance measurement systems. The primary motivation for evaluating performance measurement at the system level is that measurement systems guide management decisions. A well-crafted system of metrics will lead toward better decision-making by managers. A measurement system, therefore, should be more than a disparate assortment of individual metrics; it must be cohesive, comprehensive, and complementary.

As Gunasekaran et al. (2004) mentioned in his work, supply chain management (SCM) has been a major component of competitive strategy to enhance organizational productivity and profitability. The literature on SCM that deals with strategies and technologies for effectively managing a supply chain is quite vast. In recent years, organizational performance measurement and metrics have received much attention from researchers and practitioners. The role of these measures and metrics in the success of an organization cannot be overstated because they affect strategic, tactical, and operational planning and control. Performance measurement and metrics have an important role to play in setting objectives, evaluating performance, and determining future courses of actions. Performance measurement and metrics pertaining to SCM have not received adequate attention from researchers or practitioners. We developed a framework to promote a better understanding of the importance of SCM performance measurement and metrics. Using the current literature and the results of an empirical study of selected British companies, we developed the framework presented herein, in hopes that it would stimulate more interest in this important area.

3   Methodology

3.1   About the Company

The target Oil & Gas company (which we shall keep anonymous throughout this paper, referring to it as "The Company") is committed to being a leader in the petroleum refining business, thus providing the region that it serves with a reliable and affordable supply of energy. Through its evolution the company is now considered as one of the major contributors to the domestic economy and a key market player in the region. The company is listed in the Athens Exchange and is a constituent of the ATHEX COMPOSITE INDEX, FTSE/ATHEX LARGE CAP INDEX, as well as of additional various sectorial indices.

3.2   Decision Support Systems with Multiple Criteria

In decision-making involving multiple criteria, the basic problem stated by analysts and decision-makers concerns the way that the final decision should be made. In many cases, however, this problem is posed in the opposite way: assuming that the decision is given, how is it possible to find the rational basis for the decision being made? Or equivalently, how is it possible to assess the decision-maker's preference model leading to exactly the same decision as the actual one or at least the most "similar" decision? The philosophy of preference disaggregation in multicriteria analysis is to assess/infer preference models from given preferential structures and to address decision-aiding activities through operational models within the aforementioned framework.

UTA methods (Siskos et al. 2005) refer to the philosophy of assessing a set of value or utility functions, assuming the axiomatic basis of MAUT (Dyer 2005) and adopting the preference disaggregation principle. UTA methodology uses linear programming techniques in order to optimally infer additive value/utility functions, so that these functions are as consistent as possible with the global decision-maker's preferences (inference principle).

In the traditional aggregation paradigm, the criteria aggregation model is known a priori, while the global preference is unknown. On the contrary, the philosophy of

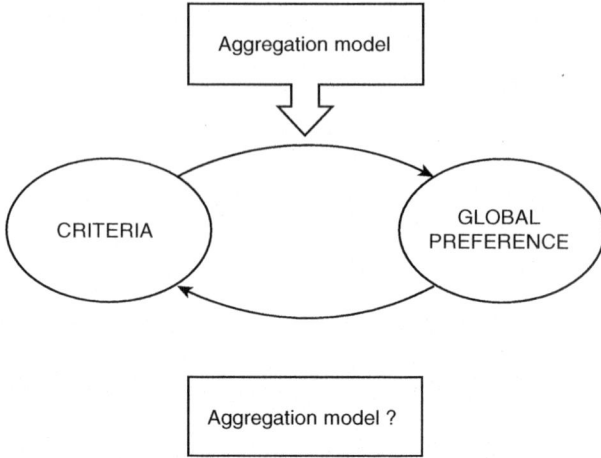

Fig. 1 The aggregation and disaggregation paradigms in MCDA adapted from (Siskos et al. 2005)

disaggregation involves the inference of preference models from given global preferences (Fig. 1).

The disaggregation-aggregation approach (Jacquet-Lagrèze and Siskos 2001; Siskos and Yannacopoulos 1985; Siskos et al. 1993) aims at analyzing the behavior and the cognitive style of the decision-maker (DM). Special iterative interactive procedures are used, where the components of the problem and the DM's global judgment policy are analyzed and then they are aggregated into a value system (Matsatsinis and Delias 2003). The goal of this approach is to aid the DM to improve his/her knowledge about the decision situation and his/her way of preferring that entails a consistent decision to be achieved.

3.3 The UTASTAR Algorithm

The UTASTAR method proposed by Siskos and Yannacopoulos (1985) is an improved version of the original UTA model. In the original version of UTA, for each packed action $\alpha \in AR$, a single error $\sigma(\alpha)$ is introduced to be minimized. This error function is not sufficient to minimize completely the dispersion of points all around the monotone curve of Fig. 2. The problem is posed by points situated on the right of the curve, from which it would be suitable to subtract an amount of value/utility and not increase the values/utilities of the others.

In this study, Talos project (Christodoulakis 2015) was used to find the significance weights for the KPIs through the UTASTAR method. Talos project runs UTASTAR algorithm and it was developed by University of Piraeus through Thales Development Program. This decision support system is designated to help the decision-maker in situations where he wishes to rank several actions (alternatives, proposals, strategies, projects, etc.) defined on several criteria. The performance of

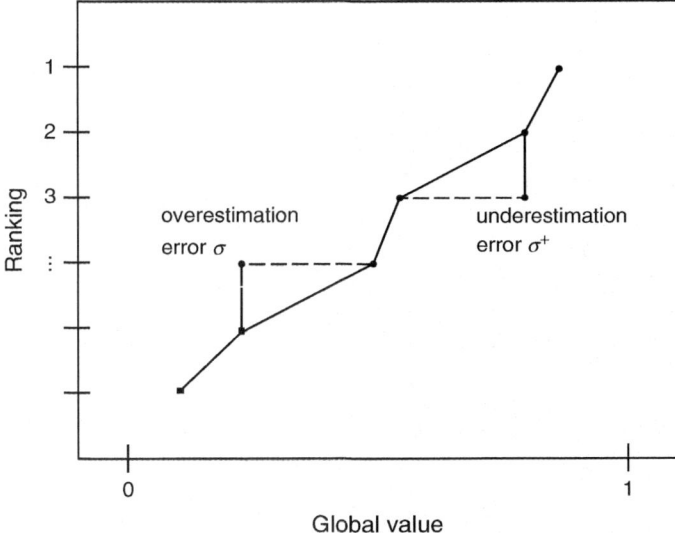

Fig. 2 Ordinal regression curve (ranking versus global value) (Siskos et al. 2005)

these actions on any criterion can be known with a certain level of uncertainty in the sense that they are characterized by a probability distribution on the variation interval of the criterion. In general terms, the DSS provides a ranking of all the actions which are assessed with a "utility" function build to represent the decision-maker's system of preferences (Christodoulakis 2015).

3.4 Data Gathering

The company provided available data (SAP files) for this research aiming in a perfect evaluation of its drivers. However, there were so many information from a very large scale of parameters; therefore, domain expertise was necessary to bring in the pertinent knowledge. For this purpose, we conducted a series of in-depth interviews with the contract and own fleet manager at the company facilities. The interviews were unstructured, and they were conducted during a guided tour at the company's facilities. Their goal was to clarify the importance of the factors that reflect a driver's performance with respect to the organizational goals. As long as for the data format, it is important to note that all the quantitive information, i.e., the files with the data of driver's performance, was provided by the company in MS EXCEL ® files. The original data were preprocessed to result in aggregated formats of information about drivers.

3.5 Validity in Research

Qualitative research methodology is considered to be suitable when the researcher or the investigator either investigates new field of study or intends to ascertain and theorize prominent issues (Corbin and Strauss 2008; Creswell 2007). There are many qualitative methods that are developed to have an in-depth and extensive understanding of the issues by means of their textual interpretation, and the most common type is interviewing.

Quantitative research is the conduct of investigations primarily using numerical methods, whereas qualitative research tends to use exploratory approaches and produce textual data rather than numbers or measurements. Quantitative or statistical methods have been used in research since the early nineteenth century, and Florence Nightingale was one of the pioneers.

Validity describes the extent to which a measure accurately represents the concept it claims to measure (Punch 1998). There are two broad measures of validity—external and internal. External validity addresses the ability to apply with confidence the findings of the study to other people and other situations and ensures that the "conditions under which the study is carried out are representative of the situations and time to which the results are to apply." Internal validity addresses the reasons for the outcomes of the study and helps to reduce other, often unanticipated, reasons for these outcomes.

Validity is assessed in terms of how well the research tools measure the phenomena under investigation (Punch 1998). A potential difficulty in achieving validity in qualitative research is researcher bias, arising out of selective collection and recording of data, or from interpretation based on personal perspectives (Johnson 1997). In the case of interviews, a common method of data collection in qualitative research, the validity of the interview data needs to be considered. While the interviewer should assume that self-reporting is accurate and therefore valid (Burns and Grove 2005), distortions can arise through the process of analysis and interpretation.

In this research we use triangulation for the validity, because the benefits of this method include "increasing confidence in research data, creating innovative ways of understanding a phenomenon, revealing unique findings, challenging or integrating theories, and providing a clearer understanding of the problem" (Thurmond 2001). These benefits largely result from the diversity and quantity of data that can be used for analysis. At this point it is important to refer that all data and results are verified by the executives and managers of company.

3.6 Developing the Algorithm for the PMS

After the collection and the preprocess of company's data, the next step is finding out the KPIs and their parameters for the evaluation of drivers. For a sound PMS, we chose to model the PMS through an algorithm based on MS EXCEL VBA

	QUANTITY	TOTAL WORKING HOURS	TOTAL DAYS OFF	Trips/hr	Drops/hr	euro/m^3	OVERTIME/HR
KALOCHORI	4320,665	597,54					
30161	995,782	107,31	7	0,298	0,522	3,96	0,031
30162	121,141	24,27	7	0,165	0,206	29,93	0,000
30177	604,02	93,94	7	0,202	0,468	6,66	0,000
30192	505,031	69,11	7	0,246	0,492	7,54	0,190
30274	1032,899	156,85	8	0,210	0,383	2,83	0,133
30281	1061,792	146,06	8	0,233	0,418	2,53	0,069
KORINTHOS	1309,015	253,71					
30181	757,043	146,47	8	0,164	0,314	5,03	0,071
30329	551,972	107,24	8	0,205	0,476	4,90	0,329
PERAMA	14576,081	3502,1					
30051	845,113	185,86	7	0,145	0,360	6,03	0,225
30143	1064,017	196,92	8	0,183	0,472	3,95	0,309
30153	870,467	210,28	7	0,143	0,333	5,33	0,315
30157	765,352	182,1	8	0,143	0,351	6,84	0,253
30158	812,082	173,32	7	0,150	0,438	5,03	0,215
30160	658,478	163,11	8	0,129	0,405	7,44	0,264
30163	457,364	90,04	7	0,144	0,455	9,94	0,289
30164	63,409	11,55	8	0,173	0,433	66,53	0,307
30165	607,011	159,41	8	0,138	0,339	7,01	0,197
30166	389,954	109,86	8	0,118	0,309	9,81	0,199
30167	661,883	164,66	8	0,134	0,225	6,02	0,174
30169	772,569	197,18	7	0,208	0,558	5,25	0,270
30182	334,278	103,48	8	0,174	0,454	13,23	0,150
30189	748,368	188,86	8	0,143	0,339	5,82	0,280
30190	510,353	112,24	8	0,160	0,330	8,60	0,216
30194	689,882	166,61	8	0,132	0,444	6,84	0,232
30195	601,431	145,96	7	0,226	0,555	7,40	0,287
30217	832,724	188,28	8	0,159	0,372	4,90	0,320
30219	746,673	168	8	0,143	0,363	5,05	0,238

Fig. 3 Data of parameters for operational indicator

MACROS and import the right data. First of all, it is necessary to create a table with information that help us afterward to give the scores for the operational KPIs like trips/hour, drops/hour, cost/quantity, and overtime/hour (Fig. 3), which are the parameters.

After this step, we need the algorithm to import all these data and calculate the final results for operation KPIs, i.e., the points that every driver of the company collects, based only on the operational parameters. For this reason we applied a novel formula for calculating the operational points. There is an average for every parameter, and every driver has a deviation from this average, so the formula for the drivers, who are above the average, is $P = 10+(\%\text{deviation} \times 100)$ and from the other hand for below is $P = 10 + (\%\text{deviation} \times 10)$. The final results after running the algorithm are presented in the next section.

The second step is about the health, safety, security, and environment (HSSE) KPIs. In this KPI there are eight parameters: MVIs, PIs, road traffic offenses, LSR violations, crossovers, leakage, shortages, and wrong fuel delivery process. For every occurrence the user of program should input the right data in program in the worksheet "HSSE Input" with the proper measurement of parameter. More

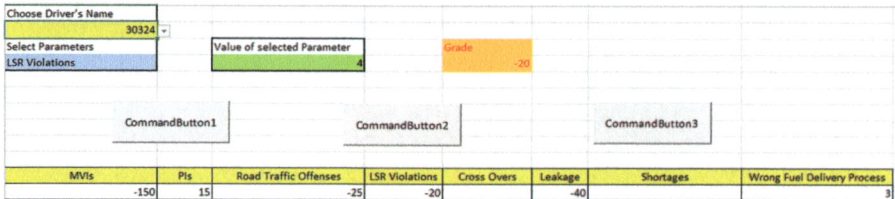

Fig. 4 Input form for health, safety, and secure parameters

specifically we have in this sheet (Fig. 4) three different sections for completing. These are the "Choose Driver's Name."

Driver's code for every available driver of the company, the "Select Parameters" to choose what happened, and the "Value of selected Parameter" to put the proper measurement based on the measurement type of selected parameter. After the completion of gaps, one may run the code by clicking the "Command Button1," and as a result, the algorithm delivers the score of the driver for the selected parameter, while in another sheet, a database for every new entry is developed simultaneously. This acts as a logging and monitoring procedure. A similar procedure runs for the total score of drivers about the HSSE KPIs, as shown in Fig. 5.

The other KPI is called behavioral KPIs, with several parameters. There are six parameters for the evaluation of the driver's behavior. More specifically: customer complaints, itinerary refusal, late arrival, delayed incident report, checklist fail, and participation in seminars. The logic that was followed for the input is the same with HSSE input sheet, i.e., starting with the proper selection of driver and of the parameter that occurred, and subsequently, the right value depends on the measurement unit of the selected parameter.

The fourth KPI is the rate from team, which is an assessment of drivers from five different heads of departments in the company, namely, the chief, the shipping manager, the router-man, the security manager, and the infrastructure manager. Each one should put a mark ranging from the worst performance (zero—0) to the excellent performance (ten—10) for every driver. Since each manager is characterized by a weight (based on the department to which she belongs), a marginal score is calculated. The next KPI is about the defensive driving ranking (DDR) in which an affiliate examination center examines and provides a score for each driver based on the evaluation of some tests. These tests concern 13 categories, which are presented in Table 1. To achieve an excellent score at each module, a driver has to collect 46.15 points, so consequently the overall maximum score for DDR is almost 600.

Because all the other KPIs are ranged in 0–100, to get the DDR score for our algorithm, we divide the score of the examination center by 6.

So, until now we have described five different KPIs for the evaluation of drivers. To this set, we may add one extra, which reflects the past score of the evaluation system to account for seasonal variations in drivers' performance. Of course, this is valid only after the first round of results.

Name	Parameter	Date	Grade		Driver's Name ▾	Total Score
30051	Wrong Fuel De	16/9/2016	-20,00			
30051	PIs	17/9/2016	15,00		Driver's Name ▾	Total Score
30144	Shortages	16/9/2016	3,00		30051	-5
30158	Road Traffic Of	16/9/2016	-25,00		30144	3
30160	Road Traffic Of	16/9/2016	-20,00		30158	-25
30161	MVIs	16/9/2016	-50,00		30160	-20
30161	MVIs	16/9/2016	-150,00		30161	-200
30162	PIs	16/9/2016	3750,00		30162	3600
30162	MVIs	17/9/2016	-150,00		30166	-50
30166	Road Traffic Of	16/9/2016	-25,00		30177	-175
30166	Road Traffic Of	16/9/2016	-25,00		30181	-50
30177	Road Traffic Of	16/9/2016	-25,00		30192	-25
30177	MVIs	17/9/2016	-150,00		30194	-50
30181	MVIs	16/9/2016	-50,00		30273	-25
30192	LSR Violations	16/9/2016	-25,00		30274	-110
30194	Leakage	16/9/2016	-25,00		30276	3
30194	Leakage	16/9/2016	-25,00		30281	3
30273	Road Traffic Of	16/9/2016	-25,00		30282	-250
30274	Cross Overs	16/9/2016	5,00		30283	-25
30274	Leakage	16/9/2016	-25,00		30329	20
30274	MVIs	17/9/2016	-50,00		(κενό)	
30274	Leakage	18/9/2016	-40,00		30219	-25
30281	Shortages	16/9/2016	3,00		30324	-20
30282	Cross Overs	16/9/2016	-250,00		Genaral Total (HSSE)	2574
30283	Leakage	16/9/2016	-25,00			
30329	PIs	16/9/2016	60,00			
30329	Leakage	18/9/2016	-40.00			

Fig. 5 Sample of HSSE incidents and HSSE KPI score for drivers

Table 1 Categories of defensive driving ranking

1. Observation	2. Use of warning signal	3. Position on the street	4. Behavior
5. Ability prediction	6. Communication with other	7. Distances	8. Ability to maneuver
9. Use of mirrors	10. Collection of information	11. Use of vehicle controls	12. Concentration

4 Results and Discussion

This section presents the application of the algorithm described in the previous section. These results will enable the drawing of conclusions about the impact of the KPIs and their parameters and ultimately about what makes a "good" driver for the company. To demonstrate our application, let's select one driver and let's follow all the results of the program and the final score for this driver.

	m₃	Working Hours	Day-off	m₃/h	Working Days	Overall costs	€/overtime hr	Overtime hrs	Trips	Drops	Trips/hr	Drops/hr	euro/m³	overtime/hr
KALOCHORI	4320,665	597,54		7,23	71									
30161	995,782	107,31	7	9,28	13	3.940	23,0		3,31	32	56	0,298	0,522	3,96	3,1%
30162	121,141	24,27	7	4,99	5	3.625	22,6		0	4	5	0,165	0,206	29,93	0,0%
30177	604,02	93,94	7	6,43	12	4.022	23,2		0	19	44	0,202	0,468	6,66	0,0%
30192	505,031	69,11	7	7,31	7	3.808	24,4		13,11	17	34	0,246	0,492	7,54	19,0%
30274	1032,899	156,85	8	6,59	17	2.924	23,0		20,85	33	60	0,210	0,383	2,83	13,3%

Fig. 6 Parameters of operational KPI for the evaluation

		% ABOVE / BELOW OF AVERAGE m³					% ABOVE / BELOW OF AVERAGE m³/hr				overtime/hr
		KALOCHORI	KORINTHOS	PERAMA	CHANIA		KALOCHORI	KORINTHOS	PERAMA	CHANIA	
	AVERAGE	720,11	654,51	633,74	335,04	AVERAGE	6,98	5,16	4,20	2,81	
KALOCHORI	4320,67					AVERAGE	7,23				
30161	995,782	38,3%					9,28	33,0%			3,1%
30162	121,141	-83,2%					4,99	-28,5%			0,0%
30177	604,02	-16,1%					6,43	-7,8%			0,0%
30192	505,031	-29,9%					7,31	4,7%			19,0%
30274	1032,9	42,4%					6,59	5,6%			13,3%

Fig. 7 Performance in operational KPI

4.1 An Instantiation for a Specific Driver

First of all, to better demonstrate the functionality of the program, let us make the assumption that this driver has some *malus* from penalties .The PMS tool described previously demands as the very first step to select a driver. Let us assume the driver with the code (Driver's Name) 30161 and whose region is Kalochori. Another important assumption is that every driver lies in the same category of traffic volumes.

Then, we have to trace back all the operational parameters like the transferred quantity for the period of evaluation. For example, let us consider an evaluation period of the third quarter of 2016. In particular, the illustrations refer to July 2016. Considering the PMS algorithm, we take account only of the parameters about the total transferred quantity, the quantity per hour, and the coefficient of overtime hour per working hour. As Fig. 6 shows, there are plenty additional fields available; however, their value in reflecting the performance of a driver is low, as justified by the company's expert.

So, first of all we calculate the average per region for the total transferred quantity (m^3), the quantity per hour (m^3/h), as well as the deviation of every driver within the same region (Fig. 7). For every driver who is above the average, the mark is calculated as follows: Points = 10 + (%deviation of average × 100) and on the other hand if a driver is below the average, there is another formula: Points = 10 − I %deviation of average × 10I. For the overtime coefficient, drivers are rewarded for small percentage of overtime per hour, so the formula is Points = 100 − (% overtime per hour × 100).

In practice, the selected driver delivered 995.782 m^3, while the average (across all drivers) transferred quantity for Kalochori was 720.11 m^3. So, our driver was 38.3% above the average that means that he transfers more than other colleagues. In terms of points, he gathers Points = 10 + (38.3% × 100) = 10 + 38.3 = 48.3. In the same way, we calculate the second parameter about quantity per hour (m^3/h), and our driver was 33% up from the average; thus his Points = 10 + 33 = 43 (Fig. 8).

	OPERATIONAL KPIs SCORE			
	m^3	m^3/hr	overtime/hr	TOTAL SCORE
KALOCHORI				
30161	48,3	43,0	96,9	57,9
30162	1,7	7,2	100,0	27,4
30177	8,4	9,2	100,0	30,7
30192	7,0	14,7	81,0	27,7
30274	53,4	9,4	86,7	44,7

Fig. 8 Parameter and total score in operational KPI

	Chief	Shipping Manager	Router-man	Security Manager	Infrastructure Manager	Rate from Team
KALOCHORI						
30161	8	6,5	7	7	6	7,08
30162	5	4,5	4,2	5	1	4,28
30177	10	9	9,7	10	10	9,68

Fig. 9 Rate from team input form (Driver's Name: 30161)

Continuing with operational KPIs score, the driver was very consistent, without delaying, and as a result, he achieves a low percentage in overtime per hour (just 3.1%). This means that he will have a very small decrease from the perfect score for this parameter which is a hundred (100) points. Points = 100−3.1 = 96.9. Until this step, we have calculated the score for the parameters in the operational dimension, but every parameter has a different weight in the final score of the operational dimension. More specifically, the significance weights are 38% for the transferred quantity (m^3), 38% for quantity per hour (m^3/h), and 24% for the overtime per hour ratio. Therefore, the final score can be calculated as a weighted sum: $0.38 \times 48.3 + 0.38 \times 43 + 0.24 \times 96.9 = 57.9$ (Fig. 8).

At this step of our PMS, we consider different managers of the company from different departments who evaluate the driver based on their performance. The subjectivity of the managers in their evaluation is an inherent element of the PMS, so the system does not impose any normative actions on their marks. For instance, the selected driver gathered 7.08 from the RFT KPI because he got an 8 from the chief, a 6.5 from the shipping manager, a 7 from the router-man, a 7 from the security manager, and a 6 from the infrastructure manager. Assuming the managers' weights of 30%, 25%, 25%, 10%, and 10%, respectively, the weighted sum, which delivers the RFT KPI, equals 7.08 for this particular driver (Fig. 9). However, scores of this KPI is on a different scale from the other KPIs. Nevertheless, a normalization is trivial by multiplying the result of RFT KPI by ten (10).

For the defensive driving ranking indicator, the company provided us with a scorecard for every driver. The scorecard was designed and rated by an examination center in which the drivers were tested in 13 different categories about defensive driving. Our driver was rated with 481.68 points, but in the proposed PMS, we

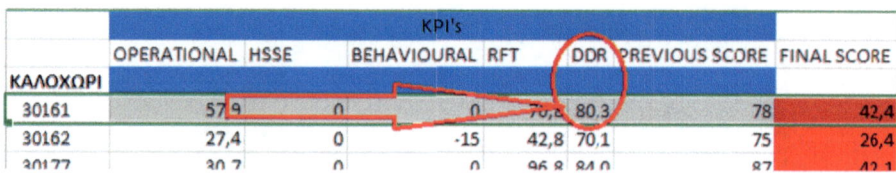

Fig. 10 DDR score (normalized) in the final evaluation sheet

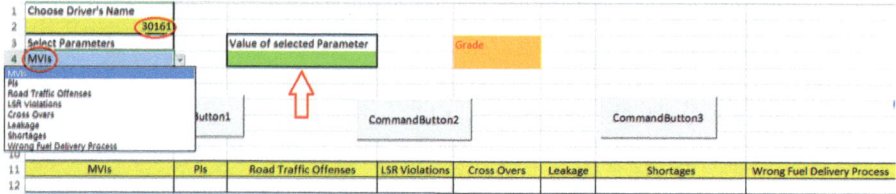

Fig. 11 HSSE input form

NAME	PARAMETER	DATE	GRADE
30324	Pls	21/10/2016	30,00
30324	Pls	23/10/2016	30,00
30276	Pls	23/10/2016	30,00
30324	Pls	23/10/2016	30,00
30324	LSR Violations	23/10/2016	-10,00
30161	MVls	23/10/2016	-100,00
30161	Pls	23/10/2016	30,00

Ετικέτες γραμμής ▾	Total Grade
30161	-70
30276	30
(κενό)	
30324	80
Γενικό Άθροισμα	40

Fig. 12 HSSE incidents database

normalize the points of the driver by dividing the original score by 6 because we want the same scale in all indicators (a scale from 0 to 100). The normalization of course is automatically calculated, so the user has just to enter the original score and does not have to worry about the scales. For example, our driver has $481.68/6 = 80.3$ as shown below (Fig. 10) in the sheet of the final evaluation with all indicators.

About health, safety and security, and behavioral indicators, as described in the previous section, we assume that the scores are ready for use, so the user selects the driver, and right after she enters the corresponding value to the respective parameter. In this paragraph, we shall present the recommendations of the proper values for every selected parameter. Through VBA macros the program accepts some specific values, and by clicking the command button, it gives us the score in HSSE and behavioral KPIs for every driver. So starting from the input sheet (Fig. 11), we select our driver, and then we should select the parameter and the value.

Also, we can see (Fig. 12) another sheet after the running of the code that contains a database similar to what was mentioned before with the date, the parameter, the score for every parameter in the left part of table (red rectangular), and in the right part of table the total score for every driver, for our driver is "−70 points," about

	KPI's						
	OPERATIONAL	HSSE	BEHAVIOURAL	RFT	DDR	PREVIOUS SCORE	FINAL SCORE
KALOCHORI							
>30161	57,9	-70	0	70,8	80,3	78	24,9
30162	27,4	0	-15	42,8	70,1	75	26,4
30177	30,7	0	0	96,8	84,0	87	42,1

Fig. 13 Final evaluation sheet, connection of the score for the HSSE from the database

	KPI's					
	OPERATIONAL	HSSE	BEHAVIOURAL	RFT	DDR	PREVIOUS SCORE
KALOCHORI						
30161	57,9	30	9	70,8	80,3	50
30162	27,4	0	0	42,8	70,1	40
30177	30,7	0	0	96,8	84,0	38
30192	27,7	0	0	46,3	88,3	45

Fig. 14 Evaluation sheet (final step of the program)

HSSE KPIs. This value is transferred immediately through a connection in the final evaluation sheet (Fig. 13).

The same procedure is followed for the behavioral KPIs.

4.2 Final Evaluation Sheet

This is the last step of the application, since this sheet is connected with all indicators which are presented previously. Every cell in this sheet is automatically filled by formulas using the scores from the other sheets. In Fig. 14 we present the final sheet with some sample drivers and all KPIs.

To calculate the final score, every KPI contributes with a different weight to the score. These weights are assessed via the UTASTAR method as described in the previous section and we will analyze in the next subsection.

4.3 Decision Support System Results

To calculate the weights for the KPIs, the Talos tool was used. Talos is using UTASTAR to disaggregate the decision model of the managers. The results for the KPIs weights were 35.47% for the rate from team, 17.97% for the operational, 17.53% for the defensive driving ranking, 16.79% for the HSSE, and 12.24% for the behavioral KPIs, as illustrated in Fig. 15. Talos provide us with the utility functions, and with the help of linear interpolation method, we calculate the utility values for every indicator.

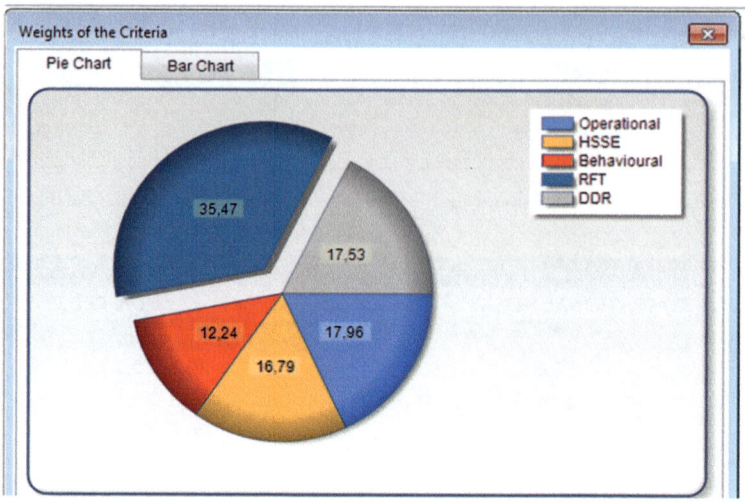

Fig. 15 Weights of the criteria (pie chart)

	KPI's							
	OPERATIONAL	HSSE	BEHAVIOURAL	RFT	DDR	PREVIOUS SCORE	FINAL SCORE
KALOCHORI							
30161	57,9	30	9	70,8	80,3	50	54,6
30162	27,4	0	0	42,8	70,1	40	33,9
30177	30.7	0	0	96.8	84.0	38	51.2

Fig. 16 Evaluation sheet with score of KPIs

4.4 Driver Evaluation Based on Utilities Value and Weights

Toward the completion of evaluation, we have two final sheets. The first contains the score of every KPI and the weights for the final mark, and the other sheet contains the evaluations based on utility values of KPIs. First of all let's assume that we want to evaluate our drivers only with weights of KPIs, so it is obvious that we have to multiply the score from every KPI with the proper weight factor and come up with a score. The final mark is arising from 80% of the score of weighted KPIs and 20% of the previous score, as discussed in previous section. Figure 16 presents the final score for Driver "30161" which is calculated as:

$$\text{Final} = 80\% \times (17.97\% \times \text{Oper} + 16.79\% \times \text{HSSE} + 12.24\% \times \text{Behav} + 35.47\% \times \text{RFT} + 17.53 \times \text{DDR}) + 20\% \times \text{Previous Score}$$

The other way to evaluate the drivers is by using the utilities functions for every KPI based on the score of KPI. So in Fig. 17, we have for our selected driver the utilities value for every KPI.

	UTILITIES OF KPI's				
	OPERATIONAL	HSSE	BEHAVIOURAL	RFT	DDR
KALOCHORI					
30161	0,18	0,047	0,04428	0,1336	0,168
30162	0,168	0	0	0	0,168
30177	0,18	0	0	0,356	0,176

Fig. 17 Utilities values of KPIs

UTILITIES OF KPI's					
OPERATIONAL	HSSE	BEHAVIOURAL	RFT	DDR	FINAL
99,9	27,965	35,99964	37,408	95,424	57,05015
93,24	0	0	0	95,424	33,48306
99,9	0	0	99,68	99,968	70,83292
93 24	0	0	4 655	99 968	35 93075

Fig. 18 Normalized utilities values and final utility score

For better understanding, we changed the scale of utilities, for example, for operational the scale is 0–0.18, and we made it 0–100, so we have to multiply every utility value of operational with 555.55 (because 100/0.18 = 555.55). The same procedure was followed for the other KPIs, and we have to multiply with a factor which stems from the maximum utility value divided by 100, and finally we come up with the results illustrated in Fig. 18. After the calculation, we multiply every KPI utility value with the corresponding weight, and the final score for our Driver "30161" is almost 57. It is obvious that for this calculation, we ignored the previous score. We can see that sum of the utilities is greater than final score. This is a clear indication that the utilities reflect better the situations in which the ratings are not linearly improved, but there is a different "preference" shape.

5   Conclusion

In modern globalized markets, fierce competition is forcing companies to seek new ways of effective service customer. In recent years, companies are increasingly aware that the efficiency of their operations depends largely on cooperation and coordination with their suppliers, as well as with the customers. This role of the coordinators is played by logistics and its staff. Optimizing the performance of a company majorly involves the optimization of logistics processes that constitute it. Proper charting of the performance of logistics procedures and all the parties can enable great potentials and prevent many situations. The references to measurement indicators help both daily operations of the system as well as the easy fix of the problems resulting from it. A performance measurement tableau should be easily accessible and readable from all over company, could be improved regarding their enrichment with new data, and often is a powerful element in the company's hands regarding control of the internal environment.

Internal environment is the staff of logistics, and it is important and crucial for the company, the evaluation of this staff with unbiased and objective criteria. These criteria are the indicators, and the evaluation of these and finally through the developed PMS is the best possible illustration of the chain to have a reliable and constantly improved supply chain based on the proper evaluation.

In this work we tried to show the importance of logistics processes and performance indicators through a development of a PMS prototype with the purpose of evaluation of drivers of logistic section of an Oil & Gas company. To conclude this, it is important to note that the utility functions and utility values are the proper manner than the conservative method with collecting points for every indicator.

References

Akhtar, M., & Mittal, R. K. (2015). Implementation issues and their impact on strategic performance management system effectiveness – an empirical study of Indian oil industry. *Measuring Business Excellence, 19*(2), 71–82.

Bichou, K., & Gray, R. (2004). A logistics and supply chain management approach to port performance measurement. *Maritime Policy & Management, 31*(1), 47–67.

Bititci, U., Garengo, P., Dörfler, V., & Nudurupati, S. (2012). Performance measurement: Challenges for tomorrow. *International Journal Manager Review, 14*(3), 305–327.

Burns, N., & Grove, S. (2005). *The practice of nursing research: Conduct, critique, and utilization* (5th ed.). Philadelphia, PA: WB Saunders.

Caplice, C., & Sheffi, Y. (1995). A review and evaluation of logistics performance measurement systems. *The International Journal of Logistics Management, 6*(2), 61–74.

Christodoulakis, N. (2015). *Analytical methods and multicriteria decision support systems under uncertainty: The Talos system.* Piraeus: University of Piraeus (UNIPI).

Corbin, J., & Strauss, A. (2008). *Basics of qualitative research: Techniques and procedures for developing grounded theory* (3rd ed.). Thousand Oaks, CA: Sage.

Creswell, J. (2007). *Qualitative inquiry and research design: Choosing among five approaches: International student edition.* Thousand Oaks, CA: Sage.

Delias, P., & Matsatsinis, N. (2009). A genetic approach for strategic resource allocation planning. *Computational Management Science, 6*(3), 269–280.

Dyer, J. (2005). MAUT—multiattribute utility theory. In *Multiple criteria decision analysis: State of the art surveys* (pp. 265–292). New York: Springer.

Eccles, R. (1991, January–February). The performance measurement manifesto. *Harvard Business, 131–137,* 69.

Elg, M., & Kollberg, B. (2012). Conditions for reporting performance measurement. *Journal of Total Quality Management & Business Excellence, 23*(1), 63–77.

Folan, P., & Browne, J. (2005). A review of performance measurement: Towards performance management. *Computers & Industrial Engineering, 56*(7), 663–680.

Gunasekaran, A., Patel, C., & Gaughey, R. E. M. (2004). A framework for supply chain performance measurement. *International Journal of Production Economics, 87*(3), 333–347.

Hoek, R. I. v. (2001). The contribution of performance measurement to the expansion of third party logistics alliances in the supply chain. *International Journal of Operations & Production Management, 21*(1/2), 15–29.

Jacquet-Lagrèze, E., & Siskos, Y. (2001). Preference disaggregation: 20 years of MCDA experience. *European Journal of Operational Research, 130*(2), 233–245.

Johnson, R. (1997). Examining the validity structure of qualitative research. *Education, 118*(2), 282–292.

Matsatsinis, N., & Delias, P. (2003). AgentAllocator: An agent-based multi-criteria decision support system for task allocation. In *Holonic and multi-agent systems for manufacturing* (pp. 1082–1083). Berlin: Springer.

Neely, A. (1999). The performance measurement revolution: Why now and what next? *International Journal of Operations & Production Management, 19*(2), 205–228.

Neely, A., & Al Najjar, M. (2006). Management learning not management control: The true role of performance measurement. *California Management Review, 48*(3), 101–114.

Platts, K. W. (1994). Characteristics of methodologies for manufacturing strategy formulation. *Computer Integrated Manufacturing Systems, 7*(2), 93–99.

Platts, K. W., & Gregory, M. J. (1990). Manufacturing audit in the process of strategy formulation. *International Journal of Production and Operations Management, 10*(9), 5–26.

PSAC. (2017). *Industry overview*. Calgary: Petroleum Service Association of Canada.

Punch, K. (1998). *Introduction to social research*. London: Sage.

Siskos, Y., & Yannacopoulos, D. (1985). UTASTAR: An ordinal regression method for building additive value functions. *Investigação Operacional, 5*(1), 39–53.

Siskos, J., Spyridakos, A., & Yannacopoulos, D. (1993). MINORA: A multicriteria decision aiding system for discrete alternatives. *Journal of Information Science and Technology, 2*(2), 136–149.

Siskos, Y., Grigoroudis, E., & Matsatsinis, N. F. (2005). UTA methods. In *Multiple criteria decision analysis: State of the art surveys* (pp. 297–334). New York: Springer.

Taylor, A., & Taylor, M. (2013). Antecedents of effective performance measurement system implementation: An empirical study of UK manufacturing firms. *International Journal of Production Research, 51*(18), 5485–5498.

Thurmond, V. (2001). The point of triangulation. *Journal of Nursing Scholarship, 33*(3), 254–256.

Banks' Income Smoothing in the Basel Period: Evidence from European Union

Konstantinos Vasilakopoulos, Christos Tzovas, and Apostolos A. Ballas

Abstract This paper investigates whether European banks smooth income and regulatory capital ratios through loan loss provisions in the Basel period. Using a sample of 1064 bank-year observations from 26 European Union countries, we find that banks use loan loss provisions in order to smooth income after the adoption of IFRS and the Basel regulatory framework. However, our results do not support the regulatory capital management hypothesis. In addition, we find that the risk level and direct market discipline affect bank managers' accounting discretion. On the other hand, we do not find evidence to support the hypothesis that the legal environment plays a substantial role in banks' accounting policy decisions.

Keywords Banks · Provisions · IFRS · Regulation · Capital

1 Introduction

The introduction of the Basel Accords I and II in 1988 and 2005, respectively, has changed the regulatory framework within which the banks operate. Empirical findings have provided substantial evidence that banks had smoothed income in the period prior to the introduction of the Basel agreement (Ma 1988; Greenawalt and Sinkey 1988; Collins et al. 1995; Laeven and Majnoni 2003; Kanagaretnam et al. 2004; Fonseca and González 2008). Beatty and Liao (2014) suggest that research could focus in examining the accounting policy decisions of banks under the new regulatory regime. In particular, they suggest that it can be investigated whether banks smooth income in order to avoid violating various regulatory

This research is financed by the Research Centre of Athens University of Economics and Business, in the framework of the project entitled "Original Scientific Publications."

K. Vasilakopoulos (✉) · C. Tzovas · A. A. Ballas
Athens University of Economics and Business, Athens, Greece
e-mail: kvasilakopoulos@aueb.gr; ctzovas@aueb.gr; aballas@aueb.gr

© Springer Nature Switzerland AG 2019
N. Sykianakis et al. (eds.), *Economic and Financial Challenges for Eastern Europe*,
Springer Proceedings in Business and Economics,
https://doi.org/10.1007/978-3-030-12169-3_4

constraints. In addition, they propose that it can be examined whether bank managers use accounting discretion opportunistically in order to further their own personal goals.

This paper attempts to address these issues within a European Union (EU hereinafter) context, by investigating the accounting policy decisions of EU banks in the Basel period. In particular, we examine whether EU bank managers smooth income and regulatory capital through loan loss provisions after the adoption of Basel regulatory framework. The elimination of loan loss provisions from the calculation of Tier I capital, after the adoption of Basel regulatory framework, creates incentives for a simultaneous management of income and regulatory capital (Kim and Kross 1998). Undercapitalized banks may understate provisions in order to increase income and offset a possible decline of earnings and regulatory capital. The adoption of the Basel II framework introduced a risk-adjusted capital ratio and a series of mandatory disclosures in order to enhance bank transparency and limit excessive risk taking. Thus, the stricter regulatory capital requirements of the new framework may prompt bank managers to engage in earnings management practices in order to reduce regulatory capital volatility.

In line with previous research, we examine loan loss provisions (LLPs hereinafter) as a smoothing accounting choice. Banks have substantial latitude in determining the amount of provisions (Scholes et al. 1990; Beaver and Engel 1996; Fonseca and González 2008),[1] while banks' high leverage makes them quite vulnerable to volatility in asset values. Thus, banks need adequate provisions to cover possible loan losses that may hamper bank capital.

European Union comprises an appropriate environment for investigating the income smoothing hypothesis, since all member countries have adopted IFRS and the Basel regulatory capital framework. Thus, even if we use cross-country data, the uniformity of accounting and regulatory figures enhances the comparability of our results. In order to test our hypotheses, we use a sample of 133 systemic banks from 26 countries of the European Union for the period of 2006–2013. We further control if bank managers take into account any regulatory capital regulations. We also investigate whether market discipline and legal environment comprise possible determinants for bank managers' accounting decisions. Furthermore, we compare if there is any difference between high- and low-risk banks as far as income smoothing is concerned.

In contrast with previous research, which provided evidence that the adoption of IFRS limits the EU bank managers' discretion to smooth income through loan loss provisions (Gebhardt and Novotny-Farkas 2011), our results provide evidence that the managers of European Union banks smooth income through loan loss provisions. On the other hand, banks do not appear to manage regulatory capital, while legal

---

[1]In May 2006, the Public Company Accounting Oversight Board (PCAOB) issued a report on large firms accounting deficiencies. The American Institute of Certified Public Accountants (AICPA 2006) found that banks' loan loss allowance ranks number one among the various deficiencies found by inspectors.

environment does not affect managers' accounting decisions. We found that market discipline and bank risk level affect managers discretion for manipulating LLPs.

Despite that EU has attempted to constrain bank managers' discretion through the adoption of Basel agreement and IFRS, bank managers continue to exert their discretion on accounting numbers. This study, by investigating the income smoothing practices of EU banks, ultimately examines the quality of financial statements prepared by EU banks. The findings of this study suggest that accounting standard setters and regulators have to work further in order to improve accounting quality in the banking industry.

The rest of this paper is organized as follows. Section 2 discusses the hypotheses regarding income and regulatory capital management and possible determinants as well. Section 3 describes our sample and the methodology. Section 4 reports the empirical results of univariate and multivariate analyses. Section 5 presents our conclusions.

2 Hypotheses

EU banks recognize provisions for loan losses according to the guidelines of IAS 39. The Standard adopts an incurred loan loss model, which implies that loan losses should only be recognized when there is objective evidence that a "loss event" has already occurred at the balance sheet date. When there is evidence of impairment, the amount of the loss is measured as the difference between loans' carrying amount and the present value of estimated future cash flows. A bank has to assess whether impairment exists for loans that are individually significant or for a group of smaller loans with similar credit risk characteristics. In contrast with forward looking provision models, IAS 39 adopts an incurred loan loss model which prohibits banks from recognizing impairment losses that are expected to occur in future periods. Yet, they should only recognize impairment when there is objective evidence about the deterioration of the counterparty's credit quality. The standard does not provide specific guidelines about the existence of the objective evidence but only refers an indicative and not restrictive list of loss events.

Within this context, managers have considerable discretion to determine whether there is objective evidence for a loss event. Managers may have incentives to overstate provisions when income is high. Subsequently, managers may reverse the overstated provisions or understate the current year's provisions in order to offset the negative effect of different factors on earnings.

The interest of investors, analysts, creditors, and tax authorities for accounting numbers may comprise a strong incentive for managers to smooth income. In the case of banks, capital regulation may encourage bank managers to smooth income (Moyer 1990; Bishop 1996). Banks that do not comply with the minimum requirements of capital standards may attract the interest and the subsequent intervention of bank supervisors. The adoption of the Basel regulatory framework caused the elimination of loan loss provisions from Tier I capital and created incentives for a simultaneous management of earnings and regulatory capital (Kim and Kross 1998). Although prior research has found that the incentives for income and capital management may be discrete (Collins et al. 1995; Beatty et al. 1995), we follow Kim and Kross (1998) and examine the simultaneous management of regulatory capital and income.

Furthermore, prior literature argues that income smoothing in the form of managing loan loss provisions (LLPs) varies from country to country depending on variables such as investor protection, disclosure, regulation, supervision, financial structure, and financial development (Leuz et al. 2003; Fonseca and González 2008). Within this context we examine if market discipline, legal enforcement, and bank risk level may influence bank managers' decision among EU countries.

2.1   Income Smoothing Hypothesis

Prior literature assumes that managers face strong incentives to smooth income through accounting adjustments. Managers are concerned about the level of reported income because shareholders, regulators, depositors, and other stakeholders are interested in banks' income and cash flows. Under an effective contracting perspective, the interests of managers and shareholders may be aligned. Thus, income smoothing may lead to the maximization of shareholders' wealth (Lambert 1984). Agency problems comprise another factor that may encourage managers to smooth income. Healy (1985) provided evidence that managers systematically manage earnings in order to maximize their compensation, while Kanagaretnam et al. (2003) found that managers adjust income due to job security concerns. In addition, Beatty et al. (1995) argued that high competition and increased interest from analysts and investors may lead managers to outperform earnings of other banks.

In the case of banks, incentives for income smoothing tend to be stronger due to the existence of bank capital regulation (Scholes et al. 1990; Beatty et al. 1995). Banks should maintain a minimum level of capital in order to cover unexpected loss due to credit risk. When a bank does not comply with capital requirements, it may attract regulatory intervention, which in turn may cause the dismissal of the current management, the reduction of dividend payments, the disallowance of merger activity, etc.

In the Pre-Basel period, loan loss provisions comprised a component of primary regulatory capital. Thus, banks with low profits had incentives to increase loan loss provisions in order to offset a primary capital decline[2] and avoid this way regulatory intervention at the expense of accounting earnings. Moyer (1990) argued that if regulators base their assessments on accounting measures, bank managers are

---

[2]The increase of loan loss provisions by 1 euro would lead to an equal decline of earnings and capital by $1 \times$ (1-tax rate). Also, capital will increase by 1 euro since loan loss provisions would be added back to capital.

expected to manage regulatory capital with accounting adjustments in order to reduce intervention costs. Similarly, Bishop (1996) argued that banks would use accounting accruals for managing regulatory capital but only if the costs of violating the minimum capital standards are high. Moreover, she stated that the probability of a possible regulatory intervention is related to factors beyond a violation of the capital standards, including bank size, liquidity, growth, intangibles or off-balance sheet instruments, and previous intervention.

Moyer (1990) and Beatty et al. (1995) investigated the regulatory capital hypothesis and provided evidence that loan loss provisions were positively associated with capital ratio. These results implied that banks with inadequate regulatory capital increased provisions in order to offset the negative effect of a profit decline on capital. In contrast, the results of Collins et al. (1995) and Bishop (1996) did not support the capital management hypothesis through loan loss provisions.

The adoption of the Basel regulatory framework eliminated loan loss provisions from the calculation of Tier I capital ratio. Within this context, an increase of provisions will lead to a primary capital decline. Thus, bank managers could simultaneously manage both earnings and regulatory capital. Kim and Kross (1998) and Ahmed et al. (1999) investigated the effect of the regulatory regime switch on bank managers' incentives for capital management with loan loss provisions. Both studies' findings showed that banks recognized lower provisions for loan losses after the adoption of the new regime.

The recent financial crisis and the introduction of the Basel II regulatory framework may further affect bank managers' incentives for income smoothing and regulatory capital management. During the financial crisis, banks faced capital pressure due to the high loan losses and the credit quality deterioration of their counterparties. Furthermore, although the Basel II framework did not alter the computation for regulatory capital ratios, it imposed further restrictions for risk weighted-based assets by introducing the standardized and the IRB approach (Hamadi et al. 2016). Within this context, managers of under-capitalized banks are encouraged to understate loan loss provisions in order to avoid regulatory costs. However, the shortfall of adequate provisions may cause greater capital pressures during an economic downturn, when banks have to recognize large losses due to credit risk (Gebhardt and Novotny-Farkas 2011). Therefore, we formulate the following hypothesis:

H1 There is a positive association between loan loss provisions and earnings (before taxes and loan loss provisions) during the period of 2006–2013.

2.2   Market Discipline

The banking literature distinguishes two different types of market discipline: direct and indirect. Indirect market discipline is imposed via regulatory intervention, which is triggered by a market signal such as price movements of bank securities (Rochet

2005; Hovikimian and Kane 2000; Kane 2004; Flannery and Thakor 2006). In contrast, direct market discipline refers to the influence that market participants themselves exert on a bank's risk-taking behavior. Depositors may discipline excessive risk taking by demanding higher deposit interest rates or by withdrawing their deposits. Further, in the case of listed banks, investors may impose direct market discipline through stock price (Demirgüç-Kunt and Huizinga 2004).

The third pillar of Basel Accord II posits a central role for market discipline and determines a set of disclosures that may enhance transparency and make market discipline more efficient. The lack of transparency increases informational asymmetry and its negative connotations. Thus, depositors' uncertainty about the true value of a bank's assets may cause liquidity problems and a subsequent bank run which may hamper the whole financial system (Santos 2001).

Although bank runs are generally considered costly, they can prevent opportunistic behavior by bank managers (Calomiris and Kahn 1991). Within this context, bank managers may be encouraged to signal their private information about the true value of a bank's assets and alter stakeholders' risk perceptions. Beaver et al. (1989) and Wahlen (1994) found that there was a positive association between the market value of banks and an increase of loan loss provisions. These results imply that managers try to convey their private information about banks' ability to absorb credit losses and about favorable future cash flows. Also, the findings of Kanagaretnam et al. (2004) support the hypothesis that the incentives for signaling and income smoothing may be distinct and hierarchical depending on a bank's performance. In conclusion, direct market discipline may comprise a monitoring tool that prevents from management's opportunistic behavior. Thus, bank managers may take into account the perception of depositors for the bank's risk before they engage in discretionary accounting adjustments. Therefore, we formulate the following hypothesis:

H2 The propensity to signal through loan loss provisions is higher for banks with a decline of deposits than for banks with an increase of deposits.

2.3 Legal Environment

The legal protection of outside investors is often asserted to be a key determinant for financial market development, regulation, and ownership structures (Shleifer and Vishny 1997; La Porta et al. 2000). La Porta et al. (1998) argue that all outsiders who are willing to protect their benefits by limiting insiders' private control benefits design contracts that rely on a country's legal system. Within this context, accounting rules may reflect the influence of a country's legal and institutional framework. Leuz et al. (2003) state that "countries with strong outsider legal protection are expected to enact and enforce accounting and securities laws that limit the manipulation of accounting information reported to outsiders" (p. 8). Furthermore, Ball et al. (2000) argued that the demand for timely incorporation of economic income in accounting income is lower under the code-law "stakeholder" model of corporate governance than under the common-law "shareholder model."

Prior literature investigated the association of the legal environment with income smoothing practices. Ball et al. (2000) provided evidence that showed that common-law accounting income does indeed exhibit significantly greater timeliness than code-law accounting income but that this is due to greater sensitivity to economic losses (income conservatism). The findings of Leuz et al. (2003) also supported that strong legal enforcement and high extent of investor protection reduce earnings management. On the other hand, Shen and Chih (2005) report a negative relation between the rights of minority shareholders and earnings management but do not find a negative influence for the quality of legal enforcement. Yet, Fonseca and González (2008) concluded that higher investor protection reduces incentives for income smoothing through loan loss provisions.

Within this context, bank managers' accounting decisions may be affected by the legal environment of each country. Despite the fact that EU has adopted uniform accounting and regulatory standards, different legal environments among member countries may affect bank managers' income smoothing behavior. Therefore, our fourth hypothesis is:

H3 There is difference in the association between loan loss provisions and earnings between code-law and common-law countries.

2.4 Risk Taking

Excessive risk taking from banks may affect economic growth and financial fragility (Calomiris and Mason 1997; Keeley 1990). Excessive risk taking may lead to bank runs and contagion. Within this context, banks operate in a strictly regulated environment, where regulators act on behalf of taxpayers and monitor banks. Except for regulation, agency theory suggests that ownership structure influences corporate risk taking (Jensen and Meckling 1976; John et al. 2005). Demsetz et al. (1997) argue that the owner/manager agency problem may offset the moral hazard problem. Managers, who stand to lose invested wealth, firm-specific human capital or the benefits associated with control of the firm, may adopt a risk-averse strategy rather than a value maximizing one. The absence of effective shareholder discipline encourages managers to choose safer assets or choose to operate with higher capital than shareholders would desire.

Risk-based regulation influences diversified owners' risk-taking incentives in a different manner than those of debt holders and non-shareholder managers. For instance, capital regulations aim to reduce the risk-taking incentives of owners by forcing owners to place more of their personal wealth at risk in the bank (Kim and Santomero 1994). However, these restrictions may encourage owners to select a riskier investment portfolio in order to compensate for the loss of utility encouraging management to take over excessive risk.

Previous research has not attempted to investigate a direct association between income smoothing policies and risk level. Laeven and Levine (2009) argued that the ownership structure of a bank influences managers' risk-taking decisions and their findings provide evidence that risk taking varies positively with the comparative power of shareholders within the corporate governance structure of each bank. Nichols et al. (2009) also notified that risk-taking decisions may differ between privately held and publicly held banks. Yet, Bushman and Williams (2012) found that accounting discretion varies with changes in risk. Furthermore, Hamadi et al. (2016) argued that bank managers' accounting discretion depends on the selected model of measuring credit risk. Their findings provided evidence that banks' income smoothing behavior differs between IRB and standardized banks.

In order to provide further evidence for the association between risk and accounting quality, we argue that the decision for smoothing income depends on risk-taking activities of bank managers. Banks that take on excessive risk may increase provisions in order to signal the economic strength of a bank in order to avoid regulatory intervention or market discipline. On the other hand, under risk-based capital framework, an increase of provisions will indirectly (through income decrease) lead to a decline of regulatory capital, thus creating a need for capital replenishment from shareholders' or cut lending. Therefore we formulate the following hypothesis:

H4 There is a difference in the association of loan loss provisions with earnings between high-risk and low-risk banks.

3   Sample Selection and Model

Our sample consists of 1064 annual observations from 26 countries of the EU for the period from 2006 to 2013. We exclude Croatia because it joined the EU in 2014 and Luxembourg due to lack of data. Furthermore, we exclude 2005 because it contains accounting adjustments due to the first time adoption of IFRS. The European Union adopted IFRS from the 1/1/2005. Consequently, all banks report their financial statements under a uniform accounting framework. Further, the European Union has adopted both Basel Accords (I and II); thus a uniform regulatory environment also exists. Within this context we include every bank with available data, which publishes its financial statements under IFRS.

Beatty and Liao (2014) made a review of the empirical models that are used by different studies for capturing income smoothing. Based on their analysis, we use the following model in order to examine income smoothing (H1) through loan loss provisions.

$$\begin{aligned}
\mathbf{LLPt} = {} & b0 + b(1) \times \Delta NPLt + b(2) \times \Delta NPLt - 1 + b(3) \times SIZEt - 1 \\
& + b(4) \times \Delta LOANt + b(5) \times \Delta GDPt + b(6) \times \Delta UNEMPt + b(7) \\
& \times ALWt - 1 + b(8) \times EBTPt
\end{aligned} \tag{1}$$

where

LLP	Loan loss provision scaled by lagged total loans
ALW	Loan loss allowance divided by total loans
LOAN	Total loans divided by total assets
NPL	Nonperforming assets divided by lagged total loans
ΔGDP	Change in GDP
ΔLOAN	Change in total loans divided by lagged total loans
ΔNPL	Change in nonperforming assets divided by lagged total loans
ΔUNEMP	Change in unemployment rates
EBPT	Earnings before taxes and provisions scaled by lagged total loans
SIZE	The natural log of total assets

Loan loss provisions in year *t* reflect managers' expectations of loan losses based on information about loans that became delinquent during the previous year (ΔNPLt $-$ 1) or the current year (ΔNPLt). Nonperforming loans are expected to be positively correlated with loan loss provisions. A high amount of past-due loans is associated with current year's write-offs and subsequently with previous year's loan loss provisions. We control for bank size because banks of different sizes may be subject to different level of regulatory scrutiny or monitoring. Although the "political costs" hypothesis of Watts and Zimmerman (1986) implies a positive sign, we have no clear prediction for the sign of size. Moyer (1990) investigated the political costs hypothesis and did not find any evidence. Alternatively, the "too big to fail"[3] hypothesis implies a nonsignificant coefficient. Furthermore, we control for loan growth (ΔLOAN) because loan loss provisions may be higher when the bank extends credit to more clients with lower credit. Thus, we expect that loan growth is positively related with loan loss provisions. We also include variable ALWt $-$ 1 to control for past year's loan loss allowances. The rationale of controlling for past allowance is that if banks recognize sufficiently high provision in the past, then the current provision may be lower. Within this context, we expect a negative sign as far as the relation between ALWt $-$ 1 and LLPt is concerned. We also include ΔGDPt[4] and ΔUNEMPt in order to control for macroeconomic trends in the overall economy. During economic booms, GDP growth is positive, and unemployment decreases. Subsequently, we expect a positive sign for GDP, since banks are

---

[3]This hypothesis was suggested by Bishop (1996) and suggests that regulators are reluctant to intervene in operations of large banks.

[4]Laeven and Majnoni (2003) argued that income smoothing through loan loss provisions is suggested by regulators in order to offset pro-cyclical effect of banks' capital. Within this context, they argue that when loan loss provisions are negatively associated with GDP growth, bank managers show an imprudent loan loss provisioning behavior.

expected to increase loans. On the other hand, we expect a negative sign for unemployment, because it is used as proxy for individuals' credit quality.

The variable EBPTt equals earnings before loan loss provisions and taxes at the end of the year t and is used as a proxy for income smoothing (H1), since if a manager is interested in smoothing or managing earnings, then this independent variable will be positively associated with loan loss provisions.

In order to control for regulatory capital considerations, we use the variable TIERIt to proxy for capital management. TIERIt equals the published Tier I capital at the end of the year t. According to Basel Accord, Tier I consists of shareholders' equity and disclosed reserves. Within this context, an increase of provisions will lead to a decrease of Tier I capital engendering capital pressure for a bank. Thus, bank managers may be willing to simultaneously smooth earnings and primary capital in a good year in order to avoid capital pressures in bad years. Subsequently, we expect a positive relation between TIERIt and LLPs.

Our second hypothesis examines the direct influence of market discipline by depositors. If depositors perceive that a bank manager invests in risky assets, they will probably withdraw deposits from this bank. Within this context, banks with a decline of their deposits may be willing to send a signal for their financial strength by increasing provisions. On the other hand, if the level of deposits remains stable, managers may be prompted to retain the current level of risk or smooth income opportunistically. In order to test this hypothesis, we estimate our base model for two separate subsamples. The first cluster consists of banks that face a decline of deposits at the end of the year t, while the other cluster includes banks with an increase of deposits. If the estimated coefficients of the variable EBPTt are statistically different, then bank managers' income smoothing behavior is affected by direct market discipline.

Our third hypothesis investigates the effect of legal origins on bank managers' accounting estimates. It is asserted that common-law and code-law countries adopt different approaches as far as legal enforcement, investor and creditor rights, and accounting rules are concerned. In order to test our fourth hypothesis, we use the classification of legal origins from La Porta et al. (2007).[5] We divide our pooled sample into smaller clusters according to the legal origins of each country: English, French, German, and Scandinavian. This analysis will provide evidence if income smoothing behavior differs across the EU.

Finally, in order to test the fourth hypothesis, we classify banks into clusters of high and low risk. The difference in the coefficient of earnings will provide evidence for differences in the incentives of managers to smooth earnings. Since bank risk of our sample is unobservable, we classify banks as risky by using z-score. Following Laeven and Levine (2009), we compute z-score as the return on assets plus the

---

[5]Common-law countries have the strongest protection of outside investors, both shareholders and creditors, whereas French civil law countries have the weakest protection. German civil law and Scandinavian countries fall in between, although comparatively speaking they have stronger protection of creditors, especially secured creditors.

Table 1 Descriptive statistics

	LLPt	ΔNPAt	ΔNPAt	ΔGDPt	ΔUNEMPt	EBTPt
Mean	0.009	0.012	0.071	0.007	0.086	0.017
Median	0.005	0.004	0.039	0.011	0.078	0.013
Maximum	0.141	0.834	1.918	0.110	0.275	0.401
Minimum	−0.012	−0.387	−0.619	−0.177	0.031	−0.127
Std. Dev.	0.013	0.047	0.195	0.034	0.040	0.024
N	1.064	1.064	1.064	1.064	1.064	1.064

capital-asset ratio divided by the standard deviation of asset returns. Thus, z indicates the number of standard deviations that a bank's ROA has to drop below its expected value before equity is depleted. A higher z-score indicates that the bank is more stable. Banks with a z-score that is higher than the sample median are classified as low risk and high risk otherwise. If the estimated coefficients of the variable EBPTt are statistically different between clusters, then bank managers' income smoothing behavior is affected by the level of risk.

4 Results

The descriptive statistics for the pooled sample for the period 2006–2013 are presented in Table 1. The results indicate that the banks of our sample appear on average for the selected period, since the mean of earnings before provision and taxes is 0.017. Furthermore, they operate in an area with a positive annual growth of GDP (0.007). However, the cluster analysis of Table 2 indicates a negative impact of the financial crisis in Greece, Ireland, Italy, Spain, and Portugal, since the median of GDP growth is negative. Further, the average Tier I capital of the pooled sample is 11.4%, a finding that indicates that the banks of our sample comply with the capital regulation of the Basel Accord (banks should present a minimum Tier I capital of 4%).

The Spearman rank correlations (Table 3) show that there is a positive association between loan loss provisions and nonperforming loans of the current and previous period. Furthermore, there is a positive association with past year's loan loss allowance. This finding implies that over(under)stated provisions of past years have an impact on the current year's provisions. Finally, the correlation analysis provides evidence that there is a positive relation between loan loss provisions and earnings, which means that bank managers smooth income through loan loss provisions. Despite the fact that this income smoothing behavior may be prudent under a regulatory perspective, the negative association between provisions and both loan and GDP growth implies a pro-cyclical effect of provisions on capital.[6]

---

[6]Laeven and Majnoni (2003) argue that loan loss provisioning behavior is susceptible to have pro-cyclical effect on banks' capital if loan loss provisions are negatively related to loan growth or GDP growth.

Table 2 Summary statistics per country

Country	Mean LLPt	Mean EBPTt	Mean TierIt	Mean ΔLOANt	Mean ΔGDPt	Obs.
Austria	0.008	0.010	0.148	0.029	0.016	72
Belgium	0.003	0.006	0.122	−0.030	0.014	24
Bulgaria	0.012	0.040	0.126	0.252	0.013	16
Cyprus	0.017	0.017	0.101	0.072	0.008	16
Czech Republic	0.006	0.038	0.119	0.072	0.021	24
Denmark	0.007	0.014	0.132	0.013	0.007	40
Estonia	0.005	0.018	0.150	0.042	0.039	24
Finland	0.000	0.013	0.136	0.084	0.015	16
France	0.003	0.012	0.104	0.103	0.009	80
Germany	0.003	0.007	0.110	0.026	0.022	128
Greece	0.020	0.011	0.098	0.120	−0.035	40
Hungary	0.027	0.029	0.106	0.064	0.010	24
Ireland	0.018	0.003	0.139	−0.028	−0.000	40
Italy	0.006	0.011	0.085	0.098	−0.004	144
Latvia	0.037	0.132	0.162	0.197	0.046	8
Lithuania	0.009	0.017	0.119	0.106	0.035	16
Malta	0.003	0.028	0.196	0.229	0.027	8
Netherlands	0.007	0.012	0.116	0.049	0.012	40
Poland	0.007	0.042	0.138	0.175	0.042	32
Portugal	0.009	0.023	0.093	0.029	−0.006	40
Romania	0.023	0.044	0.119	0.196	0.029	8
Slovakia	0.006	0.033	0.120	0.082	0.037	24
Slovenia	0.026	0.021	0.117	0.091	0.010	48
Spain	0.010	0.020	0.096	0.081	−0.000	48
Sweden	0.001	0.011	0.113	0.078	0.022	48
United Kingdom	0.008	0.019	0.123	0.081	0.014	56
All	0.009	0.017	0.114	0.071	0.011	1064

The empirical results for our first hypothesis of income smoothing are provided on Table 4. Our findings show that there is a positive and significant association between loan loss provisions and earnings before provisions and taxes. These results are in line with the previous findings of Ma (1988), Greenawalt and Sinkey (1988), Laeven and Majnoni (2003), Fonseca and González (2008), and Hamadi et al. (2016). This positive association provides evidence that European bank managers smooth income through loan loss provision during the period of 2006–2013. Further, consistent with the univariate results and our expectations, loan loss provisions are positively and significantly associated with nonperforming loans. In contrast with our expectations, we find a positive relation with loan loss allowances in the previous year. Beatty and Liao (2014) suggest that if past allowance reflects the overall credit quality of the bank's clients, lagged allowance and provision may be positively

Table 3 Correlation matrix

Variable	LLPt	ΔNPLt	ΔNPLt−1	SIZEt−1	ΔLOANt	ΔGDPt	ΔUNEMPt	ALWt−1	EBTPt
LLPt									
ΔNPLt	0.488								
ΔNPLt−1	0.453	0.262							
SIZEt−1	0.052	−0.115	0.015						
ΔLOANt	−0.151	0.074	−0.108	−0.232					
ΔGDPt	−0.410	−0.306	−0.251	−0.235	0.386				
ΔUNEMPt	0.254	0.176	0.252	−0.010	−0.216	−0.233			
ALWt−1	0.575	0.190	0.416	0.173	−0.279	−0.281	0.322		
EBTPt	0.247	0.112	0.034	−0.155	0.418	0.224	−0.005	0.059	

Table 4 Income smoothing hypothesis. $LLP_t = b0 + b(1) \times \Delta NPL_t + b(2) \times \Delta NPL_{t-1} + b(3) \times SIZE_{t-1} + b(4) \times \Delta LOAN_t + b(5) \times \Delta GDP_t + b(6) \times \Delta UNEMP_t + b(7) \times ALW_{t-1} + b(8) \times EBTP_t + b(9) \times TIER_{It}$

| | Income smoothing hypothesis |
Independent variable	Coefficients (t-stat)
INTERCEPT	0.006
	(4.88) ***
ΔNPL_t	0.052
	(3.30) ***
ΔNPL_{t-1}	0.029
	(2.55) **
SIZE $t-1$	−0.000
	(−4.55) ***
$\Delta LOAN_t$	−0.001
	(−0.58)
ΔGDP_t	−0.112
	(−7.43) ***
$\Delta UNEMP_t$	0.003
	(0.26)
ALW $t-1$	0.274
	(8.29) ***
EBTP t	0.055
	(2.26) **
TIER$_{It}$	−0.011
	(−1.84)
R-squared	0.48
N	1.064

***, **, and * represent 1%, 5%, and 10% significance (two-tailed or one- tailed, as appropriate), respectively

Variable definition: *LLP* Loan loss provision scaled by lagged total loans, *ALW* Loan loss allowance divided by total loans, *LOAN* Total loans divided by total assets, *NPL* Nonperforming assets divided by lagged total loans, *ΔGDP* Change in GDP, *ΔLOAN* Change in total loans divided by lagged total loans, *ΔNPL* Change in nonperforming assets divided by lagged total loans, *ΔUNEMP* Change in unemployment rates, *EBPT* Earnings before taxes and provisions scaled by lagged total loans, *SIZE* The natural log of total assets, *TIERI* Reported Tier I capital at the end of the year

correlated. Finally, in line with univariate results, we find a negative association with ΔGDP and ΔLOAN. This result implies that bank managers do not take into account economic cycles when they recognize loan loss provisions.

We also include the variable Tier I in order to proxy for regulatory capital management (Table 4). The inclusion of the new variable in our model does not differentiate the R-squared of our model since it remains 48%. Also, our findings still show a positive and significant association of loan loss provisions and earnings. In contrast with our expectations, the multivariate analysis shows that there is a negative but not significant association between loan loss provisions and regulatory capital. These results are in line with Perez et al. (2008) who investigated whether Spanish banks use loan loss provisions to manage capital ratios during the period of 1986–2002. They examined if the capital ratio at the start of the year had an impact on current year's loan loss provisions, but they did not find any evidence to support the capital management hypothesis. On the other hand, our results are not consistent with Kim and Kross (1998) and Ahmed et al. (1999) who showed that banks decrease loan loss provisions in order to manipulate capital ratios after the adoption of the Basel capital framework. These findings are consistent with results of the univariate analysis, which show that the average Tier I capital (11.7%) of the sample is far away from the minimum level of 4%. This finding may be explained by the study of Berger et al. (2008), who provided evidence that banks target a specific capital ratio that typically exceeds the regulatory capital requirements.[7] Furthermore, this finding may imply that banks manage earnings for other purposes rather than regulatory capital management.

Our second hypothesis aims to investigate if managers' incentives for smoothing are affected by depositors' behavior. In order to examine this hypothesis, we investigate if there is a difference in association between income and LLP for banks that face a decline of deposits versus those with a deposit increase. In Table 5, multivariate results show that there is a positive and significant association between loan loss provisions and earnings for the banks with an increase of deposits. In contrast, there is a negative but not significant association for banks with a decline of the deposit level. The previous findings imply that bank managers may exert their discretion when they perceive that depositors' trust is high. Within this context, they may smooth income opportunistically or for purposes other than signaling a bank's financial wealth.

In order to examine our third hypothesis, we classify our sample into four groups, based on their legal origin. The multivariate analysis results (Table 6) show that there is a positive association between loan loss provisions and earnings for banks that operate in countries with German, French, and English legal origin. By contrast, the results show a negative association for banks of Scandinavian law. However, the former associations are not statistically significant.

Our fourth hypothesis posits that the level of risk affects bank managers' discretion. The results of the multivariate analysis are presented in Table 7.[8] The findings show that there is a positive and significant association between LLPs and earnings for the low-risk group. On the other hand, although the relation between LLPs and earnings is also positive for the high-risk group, it is not significant. These findings show that capital restriction may deter income smoothing for banks which have taken up excessive risk. An increase of provisions will lead to negative impact on Tier I capital, creating a need for capital replenishment. In contrast, low-risk banks

---

[7]They provide the example of Citigroup who disclosed in their SEC filings a target Tier 1 capital ratio of 7.5% which is substantially above the 6% required to be considered "well capitalized".

[8]We perform the same tests by excluding the observations from the 33rd to the 66th percentile, and we find the same results.

Table 5 Income smoothing and market discipline. $LLPt = b0 + b(1) \times \Delta NPLt + b(2) \times \Delta NPLt{-}1 + b(3) \times SIZEt{-}1 + b(4) \times \Delta LOANt + b(5) \times \Delta GDPt + b(6) \times \Delta UNEMPt + b(7) \times ALW\ t{-}1 + b(8) \times EBTPt$

Independent variable	Deposit decrease Coefficients (t-stat)	Deposit increase Coefficients (t-stat)
INTERCEPT	0.008	0.002
	(3.01) ***	(2.29) **
ΔNPLt	0.065	0.055
	(2.20) **	(2.90) ***
ΔNPLt−1	0.063	0.029
	(2.13) **	(2.52) **
SIZE t−1	−0.000	−0.000
	(−3.52) ***	(−2.380) **
ΔLOANt	−0.000	0.000
	(−0.04)	(0.42)
ΔGDPt	−0.096	−0.107
	(−4.25) ***	(−5.92) ***
ΔUNEMPt	−0.021	0.024
	(−0.94)	(2.62) ***
ALW t−1	0.441	0.126
	(9.68) ***	(7.34) ***
EBTP t	−0.019	0.092
	(−0.307)	(3.64) ***
R-squared	0.61	0.49
N	294	770

***, **, and * represent 1%, 5%, and 10% significance (two-tailed or one- tailed, as appropriate), respectively
Variable definition: *LLP* Loan loss provision scaled by lagged total loans, *ALW* Loan loss allowance divided by total loans, *LOAN* Total loans divided by total assets, *NPL* Nonperforming assets divided by lagged total loans, *ΔGDP* Change in GDP, *ΔLOAN* Change in total loans divided by lagged total loans, *ΔNPL* Change in nonperforming assets divided by lagged total loans, *ΔUNEMP* Change in unemployment rates *EBPT* Earnings before taxes and provisions scaled by lagged total loans, *SIZE* The natural log of total assets

may adopt more easily an income smoothing behavior, since they do not face the same risk-based regulatory restrictions.

5 Conclusions

Prior literature has investigated the incentives of bank managers to smooth income through loan loss provisions. Further, the recent financial crisis led to a debate about the effect of the incurred loan loss model on bank capital pro-cyclicality. Beatty and

Table 6 Legal origin and income smoothing. LLPt = b0 + b(1) × ΔNPLt + b(2) × ΔNPLt−1 + b(3) × SIZEt−1 + b(4) × ΔLOANt + b(5) × ΔGDPt + b(6) × ΔUNEMPt + b(7) × ALW t−1 + b(8) × EBTPt

	German	French	Scandinavian	English
Independent variable	Coefficients (t-stat)	Coefficients (t-stat)	Coefficients (t-stat)	Coefficients (t-stat)
INTERCEPT	0.007	0.003	−0.000	0.002
	(2.95) ***	(2.44) **	(−0.02)	(0.77)
ΔNPLt	0.038	0.085	0.174	0.272
	(2.39) **	(4.26) ***	(1.12)	(4.20) ***
ΔNPLt−1	0.025	0.027	0.087	0.036
	(1.78)	(1.83)	(1.28)	(0.71)
SIZE t−1	−0.000	−0.000	0.000	−0.000
	(−4.03) *	(−2.10) **	(0.31)	(−0.33)
ΔLOANt	0.003	−0.003	0.003	−0.002
	(0.89)	(−1.77)	(0.86)	(−0.57)
ΔGDPt	−0.142	−0.100	−0.024	−0.039
	(−5.96) ***	(−5.65) ***	(−2.82)***	(−1.00)
ΔUNEMPt	0.013	0.025	0.011	0.013
	(0.54)	(2.61) ***	(0.48)	(0.37)
ALW t−1	0.365	0.101	0.063	0.240
	(6.98)***	(4.88) ***	(0.70)	(2.63)**
EBTP t	0.050	0.044	−0.031	0.044
	(1.77)	(0.99)	(−0.72)	(0.37)
R-squared	0.56	0.48	0.44	0.72
N	368	536	64	96

***, **, and * represent 1%, 5%, and 10% significance (two-tailed or one- tailed, as appropriate), respectively

Variable definition: *LLP* Loan loss provision scaled by lagged total loans, *ALW* Loan loss allowance divided by total loans, *LOAN* Total loans divided by total assets, *NPL* Nonperforming assets divided by lagged total loans, *ΔGDP* Change in GDP, *ΔLOAN* Change in total loans divided by lagged total loans, *ΔNPL* Change in nonperforming assets divided by lagged total loans, *ΔUNEMP* Change in unemployment rates, *EBPT* Earnings before taxes and provisions scaled by lagged total loans, *SIZE* The natural log of total assets

Liao (2014) pointed out that there is little evidence for earnings and regulatory capital management in the post-Basel Period.

This study attempted to investigate if European bank managers smooth income through loan loss provisions. Our findings show that during 2006–2013, there is a positive association between loan loss provisions and bank earnings, a finding that is indicative of income smoothing behavior. On the other hand, we do not find evidence that concerns for regulatory capital management have any impact on bank managers' income smoothing decisions.

Our findings also suggest that the level of risk and direct market discipline have an impact on managers' decisions about income smoothing. In contrast, we do not

Table 7 Risk level and income smoothing.
$$LLPt = b0 + b(1) \times \Delta NPLt + b(2) \times \Delta NPLt-1 + b(3) \times SIZEt-1 + b(4) \times \Delta LOANt + b(5) \times \Delta GDPt + b(6) \times \Delta UNEMPt + b(7) \times ALW\ t-1 + b(8) \times EBTPt$$

Independent variable	Low-risk coefficients (t-stat)	High-risk coefficients (t-stat)
INTERCEPT	−0.000	0.008
	(−0.69)	(4.14) ***
ΔNPLt	0.047	0.052
	(4.23) ***	(3.07) **
ΔNPLt−1	0.003	0.029
	(0.20)	(2.35) **
SIZE t−1	0.000	−0.000
	(0.95)	(−4.04) **
ΔLOANt	−0.002	−0.000
	(−2.08) **	(−0.14)
ΔGDPt	−0.061	−0.146
	(−7.83) ***	(−6.25) ***
ΔUNEMPt	0.007	0.002
	(0.74)	(0.13)
ALW t−1	0.137	0.282
	(8.01) ***	(6.64) ***
EBTP t	0.216	0.035
	(10.40) ***	(1.19)
R-squared	0.58	0.454
N	536	528

***, **, and * represent 1%, 5%, and 10% significance (two-tailed or one- tailed, as appropriate), respectively
Variable definition: *LLP* Loan loss provision scaled by lagged total loans, *ALW* Loan loss allowance divided by total loans, *LOAN* Total loans divided by total assets, *NPL* Nonperforming assets divided by lagged total loans, *ΔGDP* Change in GDP, *ΔLOAN* Change in total loans divided by lagged total loans, *ΔNPL* Change in nonperforming assets divided by lagged total loans, *ΔUNEMP* Change in unemployment rates, *EBPT* Earnings before taxes and provisions scaled by lagged total loans, *SIZE* The natural log of total assets

find supportive evidence that the legal environment influences the exertion of accounting discretion.

Despite the fact that the European Union has attempted to implement uniform accounting and regulatory frameworks, the opacity of banks still allows the exertion of accounting discretion. European Union institutions, accounting standard setters, and regulators should work in order to ensure that financial reporting does not have negative implications on bank transparency and that monitoring mechanisms limit any opportunistic accounting discretion that may hamper financial stability.

References

Ahmed, A., Takeda, C., & Thomas, S. (1999). Bank loan loss provisions: A reexamination of capital management, earnings management and signaling effects. *Journal of Accounting and Economics, 28*, 1–25.

AICPA. (2006). Large firm PCAOB inspection deficiency analysis.

Ball, R., Kothari, S. P., & Robin, A. (2000). The effect of international institutional factors on properties of accounting earnings. *Journal of accounting and economics, 29*(1), 1–51.

Beatty, A., Chamberlain, S. L., & Magliolo, J. (1995). Managing financial reports of commercial banks: The influence of taxes, regulatory capital, and earnings. *Journal of Accounting Research, 33*, 231–261.

Beatty, A., & Liao, S. (2014). Financial accounting in the banking industry: A review of the empirical literature. *Journal of Accounting and Economics, 58*(2), 339–383.

Beaver, W., Eger, C., Ryan, S., & Wolfson, M. (1989). Financial reporting, supplemental disclosures, and bank share prices. *Journal of Accounting Research, 27*, 157–178.

Beaver, W. H., & Engel, E. E. (1996). Discretionary behavior with respect to allowances for loan losses and the behavior of security prices. *Journal of Accounting and Economics, 22*(1), 177–206.

Berger, A. N., et al. (2008). How do large banking organizations manage their capital ratios? *Journal of Financial Services Research, 34*(2–3), 123–149.

Bishop, M. L. (1996, June). *Managing bank regulation through accruals*. Working paper, New York University, New York.

Bushman, R. M., & Williams, C. D. (2012). Accounting discretion, loan loss provisioning, and discipline of banks' risk-taking. *Journal of Accounting and Economics, 54*(1), 1–18.

Calomiris, C., & Kahn, C. (1991). The role of demandable debt in structuring optimal banking arrangements. *American Economic Review, 81*, 497–513.

Calomiris, C., & Mason, J. (1997). Contagion and bank failures during the great depression: The Chicago banking panic of June 1932. *American Economic Review, 87*, 863–884.

Collins, J. H., Shackleford, D. A., & Wahlen, J. M. (1995). Bank differences in the coordination of regulatory capital, earnings and taxes. *Journal of Accounting Research, 33*, 263–291.

Demirgüç-Kunt, A., & Huizinga, H. (2004). Market discipline and deposit insurance. *Journal of Monetary Economics, 51*(2), 375–399.

Demsetz, R. S., Saidenberg, M. R., & Strahan, P. E. (1997). *Agency problems and risk taking at banks*. FRB of New York Staff Report 29.

Flannery, M., & Thakor, A. (2006). Accounting, transparency and bank stability. *Journal of Financial Intermediation, 15*, 281–284.

Fonseca, A. R., & González, F. (2008). Cross-country determinants of bank income smoothing by managing loan-loss provisions. *Journal of Banking & Finance, 32*(2), 217–228.

Gebhardt, G., & Novotny-Farkas, Z. (2011). Mandatory IFRS adoption and accounting quality of European banks. *Journal of Business Finance & Accounting, 38*(3–4), 289–333.

Greenawalt, M. B., & Sinkey, J. F., Jr. (1988). Bank loan-loss provisions and the income-smoothing hypothesis: An empirical analysis, 1976–1984. *Journal of Financial Services Research, 1*(4), 301–318.

Hamadi, M., et al. (2016). Does Basel II affect the market valuation of discretionary loan loss provisions? *Journal of Banking & Finance, 70*, 177–192.

Healy, P. M. (1985). The effect of bonus schemes on accounting decisions. *Journal of accounting and economics, 7*(1), 85–107.

Hovikimian, A., & Kane, E. (2000). Effectiveness of capital regulation at U.S. commercial banks, 1985 to 1994. *Journal of Finance, 55*(1), 451–469.

Jensen, M. C., & Meckling, W. H. (1976). Theory of the firm: Managerial behavior, agency costs, and ownership structure. *Journal of Financial Economics, 3*, 305–360.

John, K., Litov, L. P., & Yeung, B. Y. (2005). *Corporate governance and managerial risk taking: Theory and evidence*. Available at SSRN 687206.

Kanagaretnam, K., Lobo, G. J., & Dong-Hoon, Y. (2004). Joint tests of signaling and income smoothing through bank loan loss provisions. *Contemporary Accounting Research, 21*(4), 843–884.

Kanagaretnam, K., Lobo, G. J., & Mathieu, R. (2003). Managerial incentives for income smoothing through bank loan loss provisions. *Review of Quantitative Finance and Accounting, 20*(1), 63–80.

Kane, E. (2004). Financial regulation and bank safety nets: An international comparison. Working Paper, Boston College.

Keeley, M. (1990). Deposit insurance, risk, and market power in banking. *American Economic Review, 80*, 1183–1200.

Kim, M.-S., & Kross, W. (1998). The impact of the 1989 change in bank capital standards on loan loss provisions and loan write-offs. *Journal of Accounting and Economics, 25*, 69–99.

Kim, D., & Santomero, A. (1994). Risk in banking and capital regulation. *Journal of Finance, 43*, 1219–1233.

La Porta, R., Lopez-de-Silanes, F., & Schleifer, A. (2007). *The economic consequences of legal origins. No. w13608.* Cambridge, MA: National Bureau of Economic Research.

La Porta, R., Lopez-de-Silanes, F., Schleifer, A., & Vishny, R. (1998). Law and finance. *Journal of Political Economy, 106*, 1113–1155.

La Porta, R., Lopez-de-Silanes, F., Schleifer, A., & Vishny, R. (2000). Investor protection and corporate governance. *Journal of Financial Economics, 58*, 3–27.

Laeven, L., & Levine, R. (2009). Bank governance, regulation and risk taking. *Journal of Financial Economics, 93*(2), 259–275.

Laeven, L., & Majnoni, G. (2003). Loan loss provisioning and economic slowdowns: Too much, too late? *Journal of Financial Intermediation, 12*(2), 178–197.

Lambert, R. A. (1984). Income smoothing as rational equilibrium behavior. *Accounting Review, 59* (4), 604–618.

Leuz, C., Nanda, D., & Wysocki, P. D. (2003). Earnings management and investor protection: An international comparison. *Journal of financial economics, 69*(3), 505–527.

Ma, C. K. (1988). Loan loss reserves and income smoothing: The experience in the US banking industry. *Journal of Business Finance & Accounting, 15*(4), 487–497.

Moyer, S. E. (1990). Capital adequacy ratio regulations and accounting choices in commercial banks. *Journal of Accounting and Economics, 13*, 123–154.

Nichols, D. C., Wahlen, J. M., & Wieland, M. M. (2009). Publicly traded versus privately held: Implications for conditional conservatism in bank accounting. *Review of Accounting Studies, 14* (1), 88–122.

Perez, D., Salas-Fumás, V., & Saurina, J. (2008). Earnings and capital management in alternative loan loss provision regulatory regimes. *European Accounting Review, 17*(3), 423–445.

Rochet, J. C. (2005, October). Prudential policy. *Monetary and Economic Studies* (Special Edition). pp 93–119.

Santos, J. A. C. (2001). Bank capital regulation in contemporary banking theory: A review of the literature. *Financial Markets, Institutions & Instruments, 10*(2), 41–84.

Scholes, M. S., Wilson, G. P., & Wolfson, M. A. (1990). Tax planning, regulatory capital planning, and financial reporting strategy for commercial banks. *Review of financial Studies, 3*(4), 625–650.

Shen, C.-H., & Chih, H.-L. (2005). Investor protection, prospect theory, and earnings management: An international comparison of the banking industry. *Journal of Banking & Finance, 29*(10), 2675–2697.

Shleifer, A., & Vishny, R. (1997). A survey of corporate governance. *Journal of Finance, 52*, 737–783.

Wahlen, J. (1994). The nature of information in commercial bank loan loss disclosures. *The Accounting Review, 69*, 455–478.

Watts, R. L., & Zimmerman, J. L. (1986). *Positive accounting theory.* Englewood Cliffs, NJ: Prentice-Hall.

Evaluating Perception, Expectation of Consumers, and Service Quality Gap in Greek Banking in a Period of Financial Crisis and Capital Controls

Zafeiria E. Papadaki and Sofia D. Anastsasiadou

Abstract The principal objective of this paper is to investigate the interrelationships of major constructs related to customer satisfaction regarding bank services. The aim of the paper is to assess the quality of Greek banking services in a period of financial crisis and capital controls. The paper examines the relationship or gap between the perceived and expected levels of service quality as such relate to its dimensions, namely, tangibility, reliability, assurance, responsiveness, empathy, and accessibility. The survey aims to reveal the causes promoting the satisfaction of Greek bank customers as well as those hindering it. The instrument employed to measure customer satisfaction relating to service quality is SEVQUAL. The research findings draw our attention to the significant effects of tangibility, reliability, assurance, responsiveness, empathy, and accessibility on service quality in banks. In addition, it highlights customers' negative attitudes and obstacles or positive behaviors toward bank services. Moreover, the research findings point out the necessity of understanding the current situation as it relates to the economic crisis and accepts the real need for changes to initiatives in order to find appropriate solutions which will satisfy customer needs and consolidate their commitment to their bank. The study was referring to Greek banks customers' satisfaction from bank services during capital control. Future research could supply new empirical results in relation to the current situation still in a period of capital controls. The paper contributes to describe a total new situation, capital control for more than a year regarding Greek bank services to their customers.

Keywords Bank customer · Service quality · Capital controls

Z. E. Papadaki
Democritus University of Thrace, Xanthi, Greece

S. D. Anastsasiadou (✉)
University of Western Macedonia, Kozani, Greece
e-mail: sanastasiadou@uowm.gr

© Springer Nature Switzerland AG 2019
N. Sykianakis et al. (eds.), *Economic and Financial Challenges for Eastern Europe*,
Springer Proceedings in Business and Economics,
https://doi.org/10.1007/978-3-030-12169-3_5

1   Theoretical Framework

Greek economy remains in the grip of recession, and the private sector and business world still face enormous financial difficulties and have accumulated high debts, while the hiring of new personnel is frozen for the public sector, even for health services. The financial crisis became even more adverse for Greece with the unprecedented enactment of capital controls for the first time almost 2 years ago. Banks did not open to the public on Monday June 29, 2015, and remained closed until Monday July 6, 2015. Upon the enhancement, most banking services to the public are suspended or severely limited, and people could not transact with the banks, pensioners could not withdraw their pensions, merchants could not pay their suppliers, and withdrawals were for a period of time limited to 60 Euros per day. The media Greek and international media documented the disheartening and discouraging endless queues of Greek people waiting in front of ATMs to withdraw the 60 Euros, the only money with which to live as well as settle their bills, on a day-by-day basis. ATMs used to run out of bills, and the queue would shift to a different machine, as people run around trying to find a machine that had bills and became increasingly frustrated, even furious. Bank customers became dissatisfied and questioned both the quality and the reliability of bank services. Thus their loyalty to the banking system as a whole came to be questioned.

Wisniewski (2001) claims that the concept of service quality is not well defined since there are difficulties in defining and measuring it, on account of the lack of overall consensus on both the definition and appropriate measurement. Parasuraman et al. (1988) defined perceived quality as "global judgment or attitude to the superiority of the service." Zeithaml et al. (1996) claim that perceived service quality can be described as customers' outlook of a service that leads to their satisfaction and their future buying intentions. Eshghi et al. (2008) argue that service quality has been defined as the overall appraisal of a service by customers. In addition, Culiberg and Rojsck (2010) suggest that service quality regarding the banking sector and more specifically a bank's superiority should be correlated with customers' preferences.

According to Musaba et al. (2014), customers judge quality as low if performance does not meet their expectations and deem quality to be high if performance exceeds their expectations. Deming (1994) and Gale (1994) observe that expected service quality is the level of quality customer demand and expect from service providers.

Service quality can be evaluated in terms of the gaps between customers' expectations and perceptions (Hoffman and Bateson 2006), while Parasuraman et al. (1985) suggest that customers' appraisal of service quality taken as a whole depends on the gaps between the expected and the perceived service. They have identified five distinct gaps between customers' expectations and perceptions. These five gaps are illustrated in Fig. 1:

(a) Gap 1: The knowledge gap, which refers to the difference between what customers expect of a service and what management perceives that customers expect (Musaba et al. 2014). Mohammand and Moghadam (2016) argued that management might have a wrong perception of customers' actual perception. In

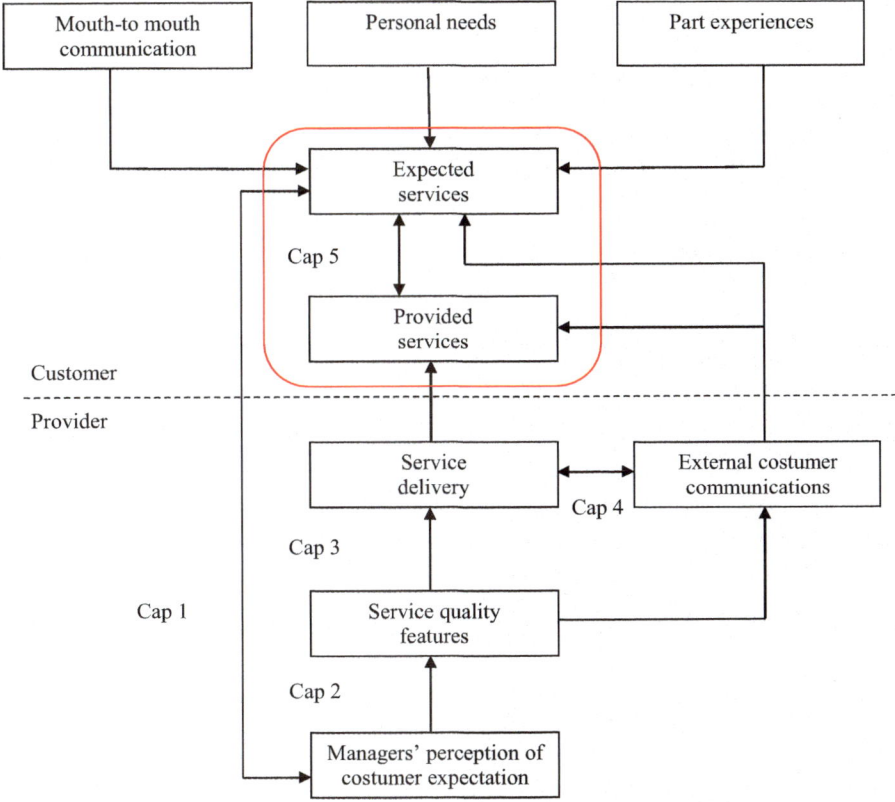

Fig. 1 GAP model (Source: https://www.ncbi.nlm.nih.gov/pmc/articles/PMC4963340/figure/Fig1/)

addition, they pointed out that this gap has its roots in the lack of focus on customers or the market (Mohammand and Moghadam 2016).

(b) Gap 2: The standard gap, which refers to the difference between what management perceives that customers expect and the quality and specifications set for service delivery (Musaba et al. 2014). Mohammand and Moghadam (2016) argued that the organization might not be able to translate customers' expectations into service specifications/features. This gap relates with aspects of service design (Mohammand and Moghadam 2016).

(c) Gap 3: The delivery gap, referring to the difference between the quality specifications set for a service delivery and the actual quality of service delivery. Mohammand and Moghadam (2016) argued that, with respect to services rendered, banking organizations do not offer high-quality services. They argued that the organization might be faced with, among others, personnel and communication problems, the unpredictability of frontline personnel and shortcomings relating to processes.

(d) Gap 4: The communications gap refers to the difference between the actual quality of service delivered and the quality of service described in the firm's external communications, such as brochures and mass media advertising (Musaba et al. 2014). Mohammand and Moghadam (2016) argued that customers' expectation might be strongly influenced by the external relations of the organization. This gap relates to unrealistic expectations shaped by the promotion of positive perceptions that the organization is not capable of sustaining (Mohammand and Moghadam 2016).

(e) Gap 5: The service gap which summarizes all the other gaps and describes the difference between customers' expectations and their perceptions of the service they receive (Musaba et al. 2014). Perceived quality of the service relates to difference between expectation and perception. A negative difference between customer's perceptions and expectations shows a level of service quality below customers' expectations (Mohammand and Moghadam 2016).

Gap 5 between the expected and the perceived service is considered to be the most significant one (Katler and Armostrong 2000; Musaba et al. 2014).

2 Aim of the Study

The main aim of this paper is to investigate the interrelationships of major constructs related to customer satisfaction regarding bank services. The aim of the paper is to assess the service quality offered by the Greek banking system, in a period of financial crisis and capital controls, by evaluating gaps between customers' expectations and perceptions as they relate to SERVQUAL dimensions with respect to customers' loyalty. Thus this study will focus on Gap 5 between expected and perceived service.

3 The Instrument

The instrument employed to measure the satisfaction of Greek bank customers with respect to quality is SEVQUAL (Parasuraman et al. 1988, 1990). According to Gronroos (1982), SEVQUAL has been the predominant method used to measure consumers' perceptions relating to service quality.

This tool consists of 25 items referring to 6 different attitude sub-scales, as follows:

(a) Tangibility—respondents' positive or negative attitudes toward organization facilities and equipment, environment and brochures about services (Tan1, Tan 2, Tan3, Tan 4, Tan5), (e.g., Tan1: Bank has up-to-date and well-maintained facilities and equipment). According to Parasuraman et al. (1985), tangibility strongly relates to the appearance of physical facilities, equipment, personnel, prospectuses, and brochures. Ananth et al. (2011) claim that the tangibility of the private bank sector is strongly associated with modern looking equipment, physical facilities, and personnel dressing code.

(b) Reliability—respondents' positive or negative attitudes toward services, timing, consistency of charges, staff professionalism, and competence (items: Rel1, Rel2, Rel3, Rel4, Rel5, Rel6) (e.g., Rel1: Services should be provided at appointed times). According to Parasuraman et al. (1985, 1988), reliability strongly relates to the way customers are handled and service-related problems, and this factor is of a great importance in conventional service. Yang and Fang (2004) claim that the reliability factor is the most important factor for banking services.

(c) Responsiveness—respondents' positive or negative attitudes toward concerning prompt services and staff responsiveness (four items: Res1, Res2, Res3, Res4) (Res1: e.g., Customers should be given prompt services). According to Parasuraman et al. (1985, 1988), responsiveness is strongly related to the timeliness of services.

(d) Assurance—respondents' positive or negative attitudes toward staff friendliness and courteousness, behavior, and knowledge (four items: Ass1, Ass2, Ass3, and Ass4) (e.g., Ass1: Friendly and courteous personnel). According to Parasuraman et al. (1985, 1988), assurance strongly relates to personnel knowledge and courtesy. Moreover, assurance is also closely associated with personnel professionalism to inspire trust and confidence. Additionally, according to Sadek et al. (2010), assurance of the British bank sector relates, among others, to personnel politeness and friendliness, to knowledgeable personnel and to the provision of financial advice.

(e) Empathy—respondents' positive or negative attitudes toward service availability, customers' feedback, staff interest, and empathy (four items: Emp1, Emp2, Emp3, and Emp4) (e.g., Emp1: Obtain feedback from customers). Parasuraman et al. (1985, 1988) named empathy as the compassionate and individual attention the organization offers to its customers. Ananth et al. (2011) claim that the empathy of private bank sector is strongly related to both customers and personal attention, to understanding customers' needs and their best interests and to convenient working hours.

(f) Accessibility—respondents' positive or negative attitudes toward parking facilities and availability and organization position (three items: Acc1, Acc2, and Acc3) (e.g., Acc1: There are adequate parking facilities).

Each item of the instrument used a 7-point Likert scale that ranged from 1-Strongly Disagree to 7-Strongly Agree. The value of the Cronbach's α-coefficient for this instrument in the sample of this study was 0.904.

4　Data Analysis

Respondents' Demographic Profile　In total, a sample of 138 respondents from 4 different banks participated in the survey. Details of the respondents' demographic profile are presented in Table 1.

Table 1 Demographic characteristics

Demographic characteristics		Frequency	%
Gender	Men	66	47.8
	Women	72	52.2
Age	1. 20–30	12	8.7
	2. 31–40	20	14.5
	3. 41–50	14	10.1
	4. 51–60	39	28.3
	5. 61–80	53	38.4
Occupation	1. Private sector employee	7	5.1
	2. Government employee	13	9.4
	3. Self-employed	22	15.9
	4. Retire	70	50.7
	5. Unemployed	26	18.8
Years of experience	1. 0–10	23	16.7
	2. 11–20	31	22.5
	3. 21–30	22	15.9
	4. 31–40	42	30.4
	5. Above 40	20	14.5
Education	1. Elementary education	17	12.3
	2. High school	30	21.7
	3. Lyceum	35	25.4
	4. Vocational training school IEK	4	2.9
	5. Technical institute graduated (TEI)	18	13.0
	6. University graduated (AEI)	34	24.6
Other studies	1. Second degree	15	10.9
	2. Master's degree	6	4.3
	3. PhD	2	1.4
Bank	1. National bank	46	33.3
	2. Piraeus bank	38	27.5
	3. Eurobank bank	23	16.7
	4. Alpha bank	31	22.5

Table 2 Cronbach's Alpha of all the items

Dimensions	Perception	Expectation
Tangibility	0.911	0.927
Reliability	0.941	0.913
Responsiveness	0.628	0.703
Assurance	0.825	0.792
Empathy	0.671	0.745
Accessibility	0.658	0.756

5 Reliability Test

Before proceeding with the analysis, a reliability test was carried out to ensure that the data collected is reliable. The coefficient Cronbach's α is calculated to measure the reliability of the six dimensions, i.e., tangibility, reliability, responsiveness, etc. (Table 2).

6 Analysis of Mean Scores and Service Quality Gap of Perception and Expectation of Bank Customers

Mean and standard deviation of perception and expectations and the Service Gap of Bank's Customers on Tangibility:

Table 3 Mean scores and service quality of perceptions and expectations and service gap on tangibility

Tangibility	Mean (Std. deviation) perception	Mean (Std. deviation) expectation	Gap
Tab1: Bank has up-to-date and well-maintained facilities and equipment	3.805 (0.7843)	3.968 (0.8463)	−0.163
Tab2: The physical facilities are visually appealing	3.383 (1,2239)	3.572 (1.5562)	−0.189
Tab3: Personnel is neat and professional in appearance	2.906 (1.1801)	3.232 (1.4812)	−0.326
Tab4: Materials associated with the service such as brochures, pamphlets, or statements are visually appealing	2.914 (1.4088)	3.674 (1.1971)	−0.760
Tab5: Services are provided at appointed time	3.172 (1.3228)	3.536 (1.2966)	−0.464

From the results presented in Table 3, it can be observed that the mean expectation scores are greater than the mean perception scores in relation to all five attributes, fact that it can certify that customers are dissatisfied. However, in terms of magnitudes of the gap scores, it was found the gap scores ranged from -0.760 to -0.163. Attribute Tab1 referring to whether the bank has up-to-date and well-maintained facilities and equipment has the highest mean both in terms of expectation and perception and the lowest in the dimension of tangibility, where attribute Tab3 refers to whether personnel is neat and professional in appearance both in terms of expectation and perception. It should also be noted that attribute 4, which refers to whether materials associated with the service such as brochures, pamphlets, or statements are visually appealing, has the highest negative sign.

Mean and standard deviation of perception and expectations and the Service Gap of Bank's Customers on Reliability:

Table 4 Mean scores and service quality of perceptions and expectations and service gap on reliability

Reliability	Mean (Std. deviation) perception	Mean (Std. deviation) expectation	Gap
Rel6: Bank' services are reliable and carried out right the first time	3.195 (1.4745)	3.609 (1.3586)	-0.414
Rel7: When a customer has a problem, the bank shows genuine interest in solving it	3.281 (1.1901)	3.587 (1.2365)	-0.306
Rel8: Director and staff are both professional and competent	2.883 (1.1475)	3.435 (1.3178)	-0.552
Rel9: Bank provides services once promised to do	2.828 (1.2804)	3.471 (1.3996)	-0.643
Rel10: Bank maintains accurate records for clients	2.992 (1.2391)	3.125 (1.3711)	-0.133

From the results presented in Table 4, it can be easily observed that the mean expectation scores are greater than the mean perception scores in relation to all four attributes. The results show that customers are not satisfied as far as reliability is concerned. However, in terms of magnitudes of the gap scores, these ranged from -0.643 to -0.133. It must be said at this point that attributes Rel9 and Rel0 have the highest negative signs and state that customers are dissatisfied with both the provision services that they promised by the bank and managers' and staffs' professionalism and competence.

Attribute Rel6 refers to whether the bank's services are reliable and carried out right the first time has the highest mean in terms of expectation. Attribute Rel10 referring to whether the bank maintains accurate records for clients has the lowest mean in terms of expectation.

Attribute Rel7 refers to whether when a customer has a problem, the bank shows genuine interest in solving it and has the highest mean in terms of perception, while Rel9 which refers to whether the bank provides services once promised to do has the lowest mean in terms of perception.

Mean and standard deviation of perception and expectations and Service Gap of Bank's Customers on Responsiveness:

Table 5 Mean scores and service quality of perceptions and expectations and service gap on responsiveness

Responsiveness	Mean (Std. deviation) perception	Mean (Std. deviation) expectation	Gap
Res11: Customers should be given prompt services	2.867 (1.0068)	3.696 (1.1437)	-0.729
Res12: Personnel is responsive	3.430 (0.9195)	3.754 (1.1765)	-0.324
Res13: Bank personnel/staff is always willing to help customers	3.359 (0.8487)	3.775 (0.7643)	-0.416
Res14: Bank personnel/staff is never too busy to respond to customers' requests	3.625 (0.9961)	4.283 (0.7922)	-0.658

From the results presented in Table 5, it can be effortlessly observed that the mean expectation scores are greater than the mean perception scores in relation to all four attributes, fact that it can again confirm customers' dissatisfaction. Nevertheless in terms of the magnitudes of the gap scores, it was found that gap scores ranged from −0.729 to −0.324. It ought to be mentioned that attributes 11 and 14 have the highest negative sign and signify customer dissatisfaction in relation to the offer of prompt services and to the responsiveness vis-a-vis their requests.

It should be noted that the highest mean in terms of expectations involves attributes Res14 and Res13 which shows that the customers feel that these two are the attributes that matter the most to them.

The highest mean in terms of expectation is observed in attribute Res14, which relates to the bank's personnel never being too busy to respond to customers' requests. Attribute Res13 relates to the willingness of the bank's staff to always help customers and has the second highest mean score in terms of expectation. Attribute Res14 also has the highest mean score in terms of perception. Nevertheless, attribute Res14 which refers to whether customers should be given prompt services scored the lowest mean in terms of perception.

Mean and standard deviation of perception and expectations and Service Gap of Bank's Customers on Assurance:

Table 6 Mean scores and service quality of perceptions and expectations and service gap on assurance

Assurance	Mean (Std. deviation) perception	Mean (Std. deviation) expectation	Gap
Ass15: Director and staff are friendly and courteous	3.664 (1.0293)	4.370 (0.6402)	−0.706
Ass16: Personnel (director and stuff) has the knowledge to answer customers' questions	3.469 (1.0344)	4.268 (0.8243)	−0.798
Ass17: Customers are treated with dignity and respect	3.898 (0.9868)	4,428 (0.6823)	−0.530
Ass18: The behavior of personnel instills confidante in customers	3.883 (0.9771)	4.623 (0.7270)	−0.740

From the results presented in Table 6, it is manifest that the mean expectation scores are greater than the mean perception scores in relation to all four attributes on assurance, fact that once again confirms customers' dissatisfaction. Even so, in terms of magnitudes of the gap scores, it was found that the gap scores ranged from −0.798 to −0.530.

It should be pointed out that attributes Ass16, Ass18, and Ass15 have the highest negative sign and thus were revealing customers' disappointment and dissatisfaction. Assurance attributes had the highest mean expectation scores and the highest mean perception scores in relation to all four attributes and to other dimensions (tangibility, reliability, responsiveness, empathy, and accessibility). It can be noted that the highest negative sign of the gap, −0.798, is connected with Ass16, namely, whether personnel (manager and staff) have the knowledge to answer customers' questions. Equally high was the negative gap, −0.740, of attribute Ass18 indicating that the behavior of personnel instills no confidante in customers.

In line was also attribute Ass15 which manifested a large gap, −0.706, showing that the customers were not satisfied with the behavior of personnel. They argued that the staff and manager were not friendly and courteous. It should be observed that the highest mean in terms of expectation involves attributes Ass18 and Ass17, which shows that the customers feel that these two attributes are of a major importance to them. Attributes Ass18 and Ass17 show that customers demanded from personnel to instill confidante in them and to be treated with dignity and respect. It can be noted that the highest mean in terms of perception involves attributes Ass17 and Ass18, 3.898 and 3.883, respectively.

Attribute Ass16 refers to whether personnel has adequate knowledge to answer customers' questions and has the lowest mean in terms of both perception and expectation.

Overall, respondents expressed their greatest dissatisfaction with respect to the inadequacy of the manager and staff to answer their question, which regarded to the new and unprecedented for Greece state of capital controls. This resulted to the manager's overall conduct not to inspire the confidence of customers. Additionally, the manager's and staff's conduct was deemed by customers not to be friendly, since there was tension and discontent among the customers who could not withdraw their monies from the bank and had to wait for a long time to be served.

Mean and standard deviation of perception and expectations and Service Gap of Bank's Customers on Empathy:

Table 7 Mean scores and service quality of perceptions and expectations and service gap on empathy

Empathy	Mean (Std. deviation) perception	Mean (Std. deviation) expectation	Gap
Emp19: Director and staff obtain feedback from customers	3.867 (1.0300)	4.297 (1.0138)	−0.420
Emp20: Opening hours of the bank must be suitable, and there is 24-hour online service available	3.578 (1.0840)	4.232 (0.9688)	−0.654

(continued)

Table 7 (continued)

Empathy	Mean (Std. deviation) perception	Mean (Std. deviation) expectation	Gap
Emp21: Director and staff have customers' best interest at heart	3.156 (1.4166)	4.449 (0.8377)	−0.293
Emp22: Director and staff understand the specific needs of customers	2.820 (1.4818)	3.181 (1.9603)	−0.361

From the results presented in Table 7, it can be observed without doubt that the mean expectation scores are greater than the mean perception scores with respect to all four attributes on empathy, fact that further verifies customer dissatisfaction.

It is ought to be mentioned that attribute Emp20 has the highest negative sign and signifies the discord by customers for the unavailability of the electronic services round-the-clock, as ATMs were short in notes. Customers stated that the opening and closing hours are extremely important for them. Attribute Emp21 refers to whether it was thought that the manager and staff had the customers' best interests at heart, and it had the highest mean score in terms of expectation. Attribute Emp22 regards whether the manager and staff understood the specific needs of customers and scored the lowest mean in terms of expectation. Attribute Emp19, which refers to whether the personnel and the manager obtained feedback from customers had the highest mean score in terms of perception. Finally, attribute Emp22 which regards whether the manager and staff were capable of understanding their specific needs had the lowest mean score in terms of perception.

Mean and the standard deviation of perceptions and expectations and the Service Gap of Bank Customers on Accessibility:

Table 8 Mean scores and service quality of perceptions and expectations and service gap on accessibility

Accessibility	Mean (Std. deviation) perception	Mean (Std. deviation) expectation	Gap
Acc23: There was enough parking space	3.547 (1.2158)	3.826 (1.5231)	−0.279
Acc24: Bank position is easily accessible	3.242 (1.3847)	4.652 (0.8932)	−0.410
Acc25: Bank services provided are of affordable charges	3.031 (1.2098)	3.312 (1.1888)	−0.281

From the results presented in Table 8, it can be observed that the mean expectation scores are greater than the mean perception scores in relation to all three attributes on accessibility, fact that verifies the customers' dissatisfaction.

It must be observed at that attribute Acc24 has the highest negative sign, -0.410, which stands for customers' dissatisfaction with respect to the accessibility of their location.

Attribute Emp25 which relates to whether the services provided by the bank were at an affordable charge exhibited the lowest mean score in terms both of perception and expectation. The highest mean score was observed in attribute Emp25, whether there were enough parking spaces.

7 Conclusion

In conclusion, one could claim that the customers of the four banks, National Bank of Greece, Piraeus Bank, Eurobank, and Alpha Bank, are not satisfied by the quality of the services rendered by these particular banks. Above all, customers are dissatisfied with respect to the assurance attributes meaning that customers are disappointed with staff friendliness and courteousness, behavior and knowledge, as well as the level of service. It is worth observing that there was a negative gap for all 25 attributes.

References

Ananth, A., Ramesh, R., & Prabaharan, B. (2011). Service quality GAP analysis in private sector banks. A customer perspective. *International Indexed Journal, II*(1), 245–252.

Culiberg, B., & Rojsck, I. (2010). Identifying service quality dimensions as antecedents to customer satisfaction in retain banking. *Economic and Business Review, 12*(3), 151–166.

Deming, W. E. (1994). *The new economics for industry. Government education*. Cambridge, MA: MIT Press.

Eshghi, A., Roy, S., & Ganguli, S. (2008). Service quality and customer satisfaction: An empirical investigation in Indian mobile telecommunications services. *Marketing Management Journal, 18*(2), 119–144.

Gale, B. T. (1994). *Managing customer value: Creating quality and services that customers can see*. New York: Free Press.

Gronroos, C. (1982). *Strategic management and marketing in the service sector*. Helsingfors: Swedish School of Economics and Business Administration.

Hoffman, K. D., & Bateson, J. E. G. (2006). *Services marketing: Concepts, strategies, and cases* (3rd ed.). Ohio: Thomson South-Western.

Katler, P., & Armostrong, G. (2000). *Marketing principles*. Tehran: Adabestan Publication.

Mohammand, G., & Moghadam, N. S. (2016). The reviews of gap between customers expectations and perceptions of electronic service quality Saderat bank in Zahedan. *International Business Management, 10*(10), 2017–2022.

Musaba, C. N., Musaba, E. C., & Hoabeb, S. I. R. (2014). Employee perceptions of service quality in the Namibian hotel industry: A SERVQUAL approach. *International journal of Asian Social Science, 4*(4), 533–543.

Parasuraman, A., Zeithaml, V. A., & Berry, L. L. (1985). A conceptual model of service quality and its implications for future research. *Journal of Marketing, 49*(4), 41–50.

Parasuraman, A., Zeithaml, V. A., & Berry, L. L. (1988). SERVQUUAL: A multi-item scale for measuring consumer perceptions of service quality. *Journal of Retailing, 64*(1), 12–40.

Parasuraman, A., Berry, L. L., & Zeithaml, V. A. (1990). *An empirical examination of relationships in an extended service quality model.* Cambridge, MA: Marketing Science Institute.

Sadek, D., Zainal, N., Taher, M., & Yahya, A. (2010). Service quality perceptions between cooperative and Islamic banks of Britain. *American Journal of Economics and Business Administration, 2*(1), 1–5.

Wisniewski, M. (2001). Using SERVQUAL to assess customer satisfaction with public sector services. *Managing Service Quality, 11*(6), 380–388.

Yang, Z., & Fang, X. (2004). Online service quality dimensions and their relationships with satisfaction: A content analysis of customer reviews of securities brokerage services. *International Journal of Service Industry Management., 15*(3), 302–326.

Zeithaml, V. A., Berry, L. L., & Parasuraman, A. (1996). The behavioral consequences of service quality. *Journal of Marketing, 60*, 31–46.

The Role of Tertiary Education in Regional Development in Greece

Th. Stefanos Papailias

Abstract The purpose of this paper is to evaluate the economic as well as the social contribution of tertiary education in the region of Greece.

Since 1980 in Greece, tertiary education is growing rapidly, and a huge amount of universities and faculties have been established all over the country, especially in the regional areas.

In the following article, regional inflow–outflow tables are compiled that illustrate the connection between education and other domains of economy. They also illustrate the contribution of tertiary education in gross production value for the period 1995–2010.

Furthermore, it presents an extended research using questionnaires in regard to the economic impact of tertiary education in the regional areas.

Therefore, a comparison of the research findings (micro approach) with the results of the inflow–outflow tables (macro approach) is made in order to indicate the positive multiplier effects of tertiary education in regional areas.

The innovation–contribution of this study is that there will be an estimation of the benefits of tertiary education in regional areas, using macro approach, through inflow–outflow tables, an approach Greek bibliography lacks in this day and age. Lastly, these tables will be compared with the results of the above research.

Keywords Tertiary education · Regional development · Inflow–outflow tables · Gross production value · Benefits

T. S. Papailias (✉)
Hellenic Quality Assurance and Accreditation Agency (HQA), Athens, Greece

© Springer Nature Switzerland AG 2019

81

N. Sykianakis et al. (eds.), *Economic and Financial Challenges for Eastern Europe*,
Springer Proceedings in Business and Economics,
https://doi.org/10.1007/978-3-030-12169-3_6

1 Introduction

After 1950 throughout the countries, there has been an increasing trend for further education as this is considered to be an important factor for economic development.[1] Especially in 1960 the idea of investing in human capital was introduced as an essential term in economics.[2]

The subject of this paper is to analyze further the role of tertiary education in regional development in Greece. Tertiary education includes universities and technological educational institutes also known as University of Applied Sciences (TEI). Hence, the expenses of relocated students (micro approach) are illustrated and subsequently the benefits that stem from tertiary education in regional areas, especially their gross domestic product (macro approach). In the end, it contrasts the results of the micro approach with those of the macro.

As far as Greece is concerned, there has been a boost in educational development, mainly at tertiary education. This trend has increased since the Second World War and especially after 1960. The continuous establishment of new universities and TEI afterward (in the 1970s) resulted in the establishment of numerous schools and faculties. Regional institutes of tertiary education are established in every regional town, mostly after 1980. Funding from the European Union was of great assistance for the establishment of buildings and hiring staff.

Regional areas ended up with many universities and TEI abruptly. In the aftermath, the following happened, although in 1950 and 1960, people used to relocate from rural areas to urban in order to study, after 1980 students tended to relocate from central cities to regional ones. The cost burdened the middle and lower levels of society, since the privileged upper classes were stable in their preferences studying abroad (France, the UK, the USA, etc.). The total number of Greek students (relative to the population size) became the largest in the world, and Greece came close to the USA, Canada, and Sweden since the early 1990s for people aged 18–30 attending postsecondary education. However, due to the fact that the access to tertiary education in Greece was limited, as it required for a student to sit an exam in order to enter a university, those from privileged upper classes of society preferred studying abroad to sitting an exam. As a consequence, student migration to the East and West was and remained the world's largest per citizen until 2010 (year of economic recession in Greece).[3]

The methodology followed is:

1. A questionnaire filled in by people who studied away from their hometown (relocated students). These results were compared with similar findings in studies

---

[1]Schultz (1960), Becker (1964), Barro (1997), Bartik (2004), Bloom et al. (2005)
[2]Schultz (1960, 1961, 1964), Becker (1962, 1964), Yotopoulos and Nugent (1976)
[3]OECD (2011)

conducted a decade ago.[4] In this way, it reflected a more complete picture of students' expenditure.

2. A questionnaire for the benefits in economic, social, and cultural development, filled in by elected (in municipalities and prefectures), so as the previous conclusions can be verified.

3. Along with the research findings, an attempt was made to estimate to a macro level the benefits of tertiary education in regional areas. Regional input–output tables were compiled for this purpose. Approach was formed concerning years 1995, 1998, 2000, 2007, and 2010.

The contribution of the study appeared to be of utmost importance, as it examines the benefits resulting from tertiary education's operation. This was accomplished through the micro approach, which was based on questionnaires, but also through macro approach, which was based on the estimation of regional inflow–outflow tables, e.g., estimation of national and economic data. These estimations remained totally absent from Greek bibliography[5] for many years. As yet, in Greece, researches remained at a general stage, without further analysis. Some (such as Psaharopoulos and Kazamias 1985; Papakostantinou 2000, 2003) tried to evaluate the benefits of education considering the theory of human capital. Since 2000 some researches seem to only focus on regional development (Gikas et al. 2006).

The results of the study, concerning years 1995–2010, demonstrate the crucial role of tertiary education in the development of many regional areas and particularly of those that were less developed. It is clear that the benefits of tertiary education are not only economic but also extended throughout society. Therefore, in areas such as Western Macedonia and Epirus, the contribution of higher education in the creation of gross production value was essential. In other regions where tourism is prevalent (South Aegean) or tourism and agricultural production (Crete), the contribution of higher education was less substantial. It would be even feasible for region areas to be revived, if universities and TEI continued their operation.[6]

---

[4]Gikas et al. (2006), Tsounis (2006), Western Macedonia University of Applied Sciences, Department of Florina (2005), Technological Educational Institute of Epirus, Department of Igoumenitsa (2004), Technological Educational Institute of Epirus, Department of Preveza (2004), Technological Educational Institute of Peloponnese, Department of Local Government (2004).

[5]For the years 1995, 1998, and 2000, tables were estimated only referring to the regions of the Peloponnese, Epirus, the Ionian Islands, and Western Greece (the signatory participated as researcher and using this methodology assessed the regional tables throughout the country in the coming years).

[6]Arbo and Benneworth (2007)

Table 1 Students in the region of Western Macedonia (5-year average)

		1975/ 1979	1980/ 1984	1985/ 1989	1990/ 1994	1995/ 1999	2000/ 2004	2005/ 2009	2010/ 2014
University of Western Macedonia	Students	0	0	0	490	980	2980	3170	4120
	Active	0	0	0	392	784	2384	2536	3296
	Relocated	**0**	**0**	**0**	**294**	**588**	**1788**	**1902**	**2472**
University of Applied Sciences of Western Macedonia	Students	407	910	2190	2487	3652	7417	7365	7380
	Active	326	728	1752	1990	2922	5934	5892	5904
	Relocated	**244**	**546**	**1314**	**1492**	**2191**	**4450**	**4419**	**4428**
Total number of students in regional areas	Students	407	910	2190	2977	4632	10,397	10,535	11,500
	Active	326	728	1752	2382	3706	8318	8428	9200
	Relocated	**244**	**546**	**1314**	**1786**	**2779**	**6238**	**6321**	**6900**

Source: research data

2 The Results of Micro Approach (Questionnaire)

Through the use of questionnaires students' expenses were defined, while the findings were compared with those of earlier surveys.[7] For a common family in the period 2005–2014, the monthly expenses were estimated between 700 and 850 €, exceeding the average wage of an unskilled worker. Due to the high informal economy (non-declared incomes), parents were able to cover the educational expenses (e.g., providing financial aid to their children for 5 or more years of their education). The maintenance of strong family bonds in Greece has made the enrollment in universities or TEI for the lower levels of society possible.

Tables 1, 2, 3, and 4 indicate the average number of students per 5 years at Western Macedonia's, Epirus', Western Greece's, and Crete's[8] regions for the period 1975 till 2014.

The following assumption was illustrated:

From the estimations that have been done,[9] in the region of Western Greece and Epirus, it seems that from the total number of students, just 80% of them are active. While 75% of the active students were relocated (who are studying away from their hometowns), an assumption that is considered to be somehow conservative. It is

---

[7]Gikas et al. (2006), Tsounis (2006), Western Macedonia University of Applied Sciences, Department of Florina (2005), etc.

[8]The Region of South Aegean is not included, since universities are relatively recent and the number of departments low.

[9]Gikas et al. (2006), Tsounis (2006), Western Macedonia University of Applied Sciences, Department of Florina (2005), etc.

Table 2 Students in the region of Epirus (5-year average)

		1975/ 1979	1980/ 1984	1985/ 1989	1990/ 1994	1995/ 1999	2000/ 2004	2005/ 2009	2010/ 2014
University of Ioannina	Students	2939	4080	5541	5817	5065	7548	7491	7760
	Active	2351	3264	4433	4654	4052	6038	5993	6208
	Relocated	**1763**	**2448**	**3325**	**3490**	**3039**	**4529**	**4495**	**4656**
Technological Educational Institute of Epirus	Students	0	57	1222	429	2065	5767	5713	5920
	Active	0	46	978	343	1652	4614	4570	4736
	Relocated	**0**	**34**	**733**	**257**	**1239**	**3460**	**3428**	**3552**
Total number of students in regional areas	Students	2939	4137	6763	6246	7130	13,315	13,204	13,680
	Active	2351	3310	5411	4997	5704	10,652	10,563	10,944
	Relocated	**1763**	**2482**	**4057**	**3747**	**4278**	**7989**	**7922**	**8208**

Source: research data

obvious that the percentage of inactive students differs slightly depending on universities and regions. A general average of 20% was estimated as acceptable.

Thus, the tables for each educational institute include three rows; the first one includes the average of total students per 5 years. The second row shows the average of active students, and the third shows the estimated average of relocated students.

Western Macedonia includes the prefectures of Florina, Kastoria, Kozani, and Grevena. According to Table 1, university students of this region in 2014 exceeded 4000. Active students reached 3.3 thousand and relocated students approached approximately 2.5 thousand.

In 1975/1979, at the University of Applied Sciences of Western Macedonia, which is one of the oldest universities, there were 407 students of whom 326 students were active and approximately 245 were relocated. In 2010/2014 the estimated number of relocated students was 4.4 thousand. Consequently, the total number of students of tertiary education in this region was 407 in 1975/1979, 4.6 thousand in 1995/1999, and 11.5 thousand in 2010/2014. The total number of relocated students was 244, 2.8 thousand, and 6.9 thousand, respectively.

Based on the results of questionnaires and also on previous similar studies,[10] the average annual expenses for each relocated student amounted to 5.2 thousand euro in 1995, while in 2014 they amounted to approximately 7.2 thousand euro (Table 5).

These expenses although they refer to an annual basis, they were estimated according to the cost of accommodation for 9.5 months. According to micro approaching, it issued that 2–2.5 months per year, relocated students returned to their families (so the expenditure for that period was either just the accommodation expenses or after agreement with the landlords there were no expenses at all).

Hence, as for Western Macedonia, the total expenses of relocated students amounted to 14.5 million in 1995 and 50 million in 2014 (Table 6).

---

[10]Gikas et al. (2006), Tsounis (2006), Western Macedonia University of Applied Sciences, Department of Florina (2005), etc.

Table 3 Students in the region of Western Greece (5-year average)

		1975/1979	1980/1984	1985/1989	1990/1994	1995/1999	2000/2004	2005/2009	2010/2014
University of Patras	Students	3874	5138	7442	8975	7806	10,859	10,805	10,940
	Active	3099	4110	5954	7180	6245	8687	8644	8752
	Relocated	**2324**	**3083**	**4465**	**5385**	**4684**	**6515**	**6483**	**6564**
Technological Educational Institute of Patras	Students	1275	2292	4358	3593	4526	8143	8077	8210
	Active	1020	1834	3486	2874	3621	6514	6462	6568
	Relocated	**765**	**1375**	**2615**	**2156**	**2716**	**4886**	**4846**	**4926**
Technological Educational Institute of Messolonghi	Students	69	370	1501	429	1920	3568	3538	3740
	Active	55	296	1201	343	1536	2854	2830	2992
	Relocated	**41**	**222**	**901**	**257**	**1152**	**2141**	**2123**	**2244**
Total number of students in regional areas	Students	5218	7800	13,301	12,997	14,252	22,570	22,420	22,890
	Active	4174	6240	10,641	10,398	11,402	18,056	17,936	18,312
	Relocated	**3131**	**4680**	**7981**	**7798**	**8551**	**13,542**	**13,452**	**13,734**

Source: research data

Table 4 Students in the region of Crete (5-year average)

		1975/1979	1980/1984	1985/1989	1990/1994	1995/1999	2000/2004	2005/2009	2010/2014
University of Crete	Students	355	1497	3281	4242	4144	6016	5988	6210
	Active	284	1198	2625	3394	3315	4813	4790	4968
	Relocated	213	898	1969	2545	2486	3610	3593	3726
Technical University of Crete	Students	0	25	368	623	722	1170	1163	1550
	Active	0	20	294	498	578	936	930	1240
	Relocated	0	15	221	374	433	702	698	930
Technological Educational Institute of Crete	Students	1258	2204	5222	4161	4570	7671	7638	7690
	Active	1006	1763	4178	3329	3656	6137	6110	6152
	Relocated	755	1322	3133	2497	2742	4603	4583	4614
Total number of students in regional areas	Students	1613	3726	8871	9026	9436	14,857	14,789	15,450
	Active	1290	2981	7097	7221	7549	11,886	11,831	12,360
	Relocated	968	2236	5323	5416	5662	8914	8873	9270

Source: research data

Table 5 Average annual expenses per student (euro)

1995	1998	2000	2007	2010	2014
5230	5490	5770	6640	6980	7250

Table 6 Students' expenses (thousand euro)

1995	1998	2000	2007	2010	2014
14,534	15,257	35,993	41,971	48,162	50,025

Advances in Epirus' region appeared more positive than those of Western Macedonia. The University of Ioannina operates in the city of Ioannina, whereas the Technological Educational Institute operates in four prefectures: Thesprotia, Preveza, Arta, and Ioannina. According to Table 2, students in Epirus' region in 1975/1979 were around 3000 while in 2010/2014 around 14,000. Namely, in 1975/1979 students of the University of Ioannina amounted at 3000, active students at 2.4 thousand, and relocated students at 1.8 thousand. In 2010/2014 the total number of students reached 7.8 thousand, active students reached 6.2 thousand, and relocated reached 4.6 thousand.

At the TEI of Epirus, the total number of students was estimated at 1.2 thousand in 1985/1989, whereas in 2010/2014 it was estimated at 6000 reaching approximately the total number of students in the University of Ioannina. In 2010/2014, active students were more than 4.7 thousand, while relocated students outnumbered 3.6 thousand. It is remarkable that those 8000 relocated students, attending lessons at the University of Ioannina and also at the TEI of Epirus, in 2010/2014 were considered a significant financial support for the region.

The annual expenses of relocated students studying in Epirus in 1995 amounted at 22.5 million euros whereas in 2014 at 60 million euros (Table 7).

Table 3 describes the advances in Western Greece. The University of Patras, although it used to get the majority of students, has recently lost its dynamics. In 1975/1979 the average of students was around 3.9 thousand, whereas in 2010/2014 it was 10.9 thousand. Active students increased from 3 thousand to 8.7 thousand, respectively. Relocated students in 1975/1979 were estimated at 2.3 thousand while in 2010/2014 at 6.6 thousand.

The TEI of Patras and the TEI of Messolonghi are also operating in Western Greece. The TEI of Patras received from 1.3 thousand (1975/1979) to 8.2 thousand (2010/2014) students. The average number of active students amounted at one thousand for the first 5 years, while it came to about 6.5 thousand in 2010/2014. The number of relocated students of the TEI of Patras was estimated at 765 in 1975/1979, while in 2010/2014 it approached approximately 5000. Fewer advances occurred in the TEI of Messolonghi; relocated students reached 2.2 thousand in 2010/2014, from only 41 students who were studying there, in the beginning of the period. The total expenses of relocated students studying at Western Greece totaled from 45 million euros in 1995 to 100 million euros in 2014 (Table 8).

Table 7 Students' expenses (thousand euro)

1995	1998	2000	2007	2010	2014
22,374	23,486	46,097	52,602	57,292	59,508

Table 8 Students' expenses (thousand euro)

1995	1998	2000	2007	2010	2014
44,722	46,945	78,137	89,321	95,863	99,572

Table 9 Students' expenses (thousand euro)

1995	1998	2000	2007	2010	2014
29,612	31,084	51,434	58,917	64,705	67,208

Last but not the least, Table 4 shows the total number of students in Crete. Crete has one university, a technical university and a TEI. Thus, in 1975/1979 the total number of students of the university was 355 (284 were active students of whom the relocated were 213), whereas in 2010/2014 the total number reached 6.2 thousand (active students were 5000 of whom 3.7 were relocated).

At the technical university, there was a little increase in the number of students. In 2010/2014 the total number of students was 1.5 thousand (1.2 thousand were active of whom 930 were relocated), whereas in 1985/1989 there were 368 (294 active of whom 221 were relocated).

The TEI of Crete is the most populated institution of this region. In 1975/1979 the total number of students was 1.260 (1000 active, 755 relocated), whereas in 2010/ 2014 it was 7.7 thousand (6.1 thousand active, 4.6 relocated).

In conclusion, the total number of students in Crete reached 1.6 thousand in 1975/ 1979, while in 2010/2014 it reached 15.5 thousand. Regarding the expenses of relocated students, in 1995 they were estimated at 30 million euros, whereas in 2014 they exceeded 67 million euros (Table 9).

Table 10 illustrates the total expenses of relocated students (7.1.1 up to 7.1.4) as well as of educational and administrative staff (most of whom were relocated).[11] Additional expenses have also been illustrated regarding the educational institutes' operation. For instance, in Epirus and also in Florina, the Department of Plant and Animal Production was in operation. The expendables of laboratories and any other educational expenses have also been illustrated. While in 1995 the expenses of relocated students reached 14.5 million euros in the region of Western Macedonia, in 2014 it was estimated at 50 million. The total expenses were estimated though, at 16.4 million and 57.4 million euros, respectively.

In Epirus, the total number of expenses for the same years reached 25 million and 67.9 million euros, respectively.

---

[11]Gikas et al. (2006), Western Macedonia University of Applied Sciences, Department of Florina (2005), etc.

Table 10 Total expenses (students, educational administrative staff, etc.) in euros

Regions	Expenses	1995	1998	2000	2007	2010	2014
Western Macedonia	Students	14,534,170.00	15,256,710.00	35,993,260.00	41,971,440.00	48,162,000.00	50,025,000.00
	Educational administrative, etc.	1,816,902.00	1,983,515.04	4,859,245.89	6,043,887.36	6,983,490.00	7,353,675.00
	Total	**16,351,072.00**	**17,240,225.04**	**40,852,505.89**	**48,015,327.36**	**55,145,490.00**	**57,378,675.00**
Epirus	Students	22,373,940.00	23,486,220.00	46,096,530.00	52,602,080.00	57,291,840.00	59,508,000.00
	Educational administrative, etc.	2,707,246.74	2,912,291.28	6,038,645.43	7,320,480.48	8,078,149.44	8,331,120.00
	Total	**25,081,186.74**	**26,398,511.28**	**52,135,175.43**	**59,922,560.48**	**65,369,989.44**	**67,839,120.00**
Western Greece	Students	44,721,730.00	46,944,990.00	78,137,340.00	89,321,280.00	95,863,320.00	99,571,500.00
	Educational administrative, etc.	5,008,950.91	5,586,584.47	9,610,892.82	11,969,051.52	12,300,239.76	14,681,250.00
	Total	**49,730,680.91**	**52,531,574.47**	**87,748,232.82**	**101,290,331.52**	**108,163,559.76**	**114,252,750.00**
Crete	Students	29,612,260.00	31,084,380.00	51,433,780.00	58,916,720.00	64,704,600.00	67,207,500.00
	Educational administrative, etc.	3,109,067.64	3,729,862.08	6,943,716.09	7,777,357.63	8,476,302.60	9,005,805.00
	Total	**32,721,327.64**	**34,814,242.08**	**58,377,496.09**	**66,694,077.63**	**73,180,902.60**	**76,213,305.00**

Source: research data

In Western Greece, the cost amounted to 50 million euros in 1995, whereas in 2014 it exceeded 114 million euros.

Lastly, in Crete, the total amount of the expenses from 32.7 million in 1995 exceeded 76.2 million in 2014.

Summarizing from the above, we conclude that there has been a significant relocation of financial resources to the aforesaid regions and especially in cities where the tertiary institutes were operating.

3 Macro Approach Results (Inflow–Outflow Tables)

The second subject of this study was the contribution of higher education in gross production value. The estimation of regional inflow–outflow tables for 1995, 1998, 2000, 2007, and 2010 shows the amount of gross production value in regional areas. Table 11 demonstrates the important increase that appeared. While in Epirus in 1995 tertiary education contributed 127 million euros to regional product, in 2010 it reached 395 million under conservative assumptions (e.g., since 2005 the Hellenic Statistical Authority did not estimate the educational product alone, but the estimation was done including also the public administration product and health product so the educational product was seemed lower).[12]

In 1995 at Crete, the contribution of the university's, the technical university's, and the TEI's operation was 64 million euros to gross production value whereas in 2010 was 521 million. Apart from the field of tourism and agricultural, such a positive economic development has only appeared in few fields.

Comparing the results of Table 10 (micro approach) with those of Table 11 (macro approach), we can assume that the expenses of relocated students along with the expenses for infrastructure bring about positive numerous results. At the beginning these results were not so numerous as the number of students was to increase later on. With the passing of time, positive results increased. Thus, although in 1995 the contribution of relocated students at Epirus was 25 million euros and in 2010 was 65 million euros (Table 10), according to Table 11 gross production value totaled 127 and 395 million euros, respectively.

In Western Greece, in 1995 and 2010, the relocated students' expenses (including expenses of educational staff) were estimated at 50 million and 108 million, respectively. Gross production value was estimated at 98 million and 420 million, respectively. Those are the positive multiple results from tertiary education about the aforesaid regions.

Tables 10 and 11, which were noted previously, illustrate the households' expenses as well as the benefits for the regional areas. Practically, cities benefit more from this economic situation. Therefore, the city of Preveza (or Heraklion of

---

[12]Livas (1994), Skountzos and Livas (2000), Skountzos (2004), Skountzos and Stroblos (2007)

Table 11 Gross production value of tertiary education 1995–2010 (million euros)

Years\regions	1995	1998	2000	2007	2010
Western Macedonia	26	73	82	132	184
Epirus	127	170	181	242	395
Western Greece	98	140	195	298	420
South Aegean	0	45	55	130	173
Crete	64	173	212	307	521

Source: research data

Crete or the city of Florina) benefits predominantly from profits derived from relocated students. The same is true for the rest of the regional areas.

4 Conclusion

The results of the study pointed out the following:

Firstly, tertiary education plays an important role in regional development. Remote areas, such as Epirus and Western Macedonia, would have less gross domestic product, if institutes of tertiary education hadn't been established, as it is concluded not only from inflow–outflow tables but also from the micro approach. Unfortunately there wasn't enough regional policy in order for tertiary educational institutes to give rise to social, cultural, and economic development. The education industry only had a connection with the construction industry, food industry, and real estate industry, whereas a connection with other industries came to be limited.

Secondly, under these circumstances, we come to the conclusion that a way to enhance regional development is just the reinforcement of educational departments through better educational policies.

Since 1990, mainly with the EU's contribution, there has been an increase in employing university professors. Till now, the only step that has been made by the state is building constructions for education. Therefore, parents were bearing students' costs as the idea of scholarships or student loans still remains unknown in Greece.

Thirdly, due to the foundation of tertiary educational institutes in every regional town, there has been a significant relocation of financial resources from urban areas to rural. At the same time, similar changes occurred in regional areas; new buildings were constructed, and entertainment facilities, clothing stores, and restaurants emerged, changing the city planning of the regional areas abruptly. As a result, regional areas became areas with vacancies, helping local people find a job, who would otherwise migrate to urban areas in order to be employed. Agricultural and industrial production has expanded as the demand increased.

However, since 2009 the economic crisis in Greece has as a result in the inability of families to provide financial aid to relocated students. At such crisis, the state is unable to employ more professors and also incapable to fund tertiary educational institutes. Due to Greek legislation, tertiary educational institutes are not able to set their own policy, with their financial resources deriving mainly from the state, in contrast to what is happening in countries such as the USA, the UK, Scandinavia, etc.

The proposed solutions are:

Firstly, the exclusion of education from the memorandum (therefore the increase of the tertiary education funding).

Secondly, faculties should receive financial support coming from resources of prefectures and also financial support coming from nonpublic sector. The connection between industry production and education production is another proposed solution that is likely to increase the universities–TEI's revenues.

Thirdly, with the universities' participation in conducting surveys concerning companies, there would be definitely more revenues to tertiary educational institutes. This tripartite participation of the state, prefecture, and of private sector could prevent regional tertiary educational institutes from collapse, until the country would elude from bankruptcy.

References

Arbo, P., & Benneworth, P. (2007). *Understanding the regional contribution of higher education institutions. A literature review*. OECD, Institutional Management in Higher Education Programme.

Barro, J. (1997). *Determinants of economic growth: A cross-section empirical study*. Cambridge, MA: MIT Press.

Bartik, T. J. (2004). *Increasing the economic development benefits of higher education in Michigan*. W.E. Upjohn Institute for Employment Research, No. 04–106.

Becker, G. S. (1962). Investment in human capital: A theoretical analysis. *Journal of Political Economy, 70*(5, Part 2), 9–49.

Becker, G. S. (1964). *Human capital*. Princeton, NJ: Princeton University Press.

Bloom, D., Canning, D., & Chan, K. (2005). *Higher education and economic development in Africa*. Research commissioned by the World Bank. Cambridge: Harvard University.

Gikas, G., Bitxava, A., & Diakomixalis, M. (2006). Estimation of economic impact at the local economy from the Operation of Technological Educational Institute of Epirus. In *Conference Proceedings 3rd International Research of Technological Educational Institute of Epirus, Education and Economic Development* (pp. 103–113). Preveza.

Livas, P. (1994). *Analysis inflow-outflow*. Athens: Stamoulis.

OECD. (2011). *Education at a glance*. Paris: OECD.

Papakostantinou, G. (2000). *The cost of education: Since the withdrawal of the state in "competitive" infiltration family*. Athens: National Centre for Social Research.

Papakostantinou, G. (2003). *Supply and demand of higher education*. Athens: Metexmio.

Psaharopoulos, G., & Kazamias, A. (1985). *Education and development in Greece: Social and economic study of higher education*. Athens: National Centre for Social Research.

Schultz, T. (1960). Capital formation by education. *Journal of Political Economy, 68*, 571–583.

Schultz, T. (1961). Education and economic growth. In N. B. Henry (Ed.), *Social forces influencing American education*. Chicago, IL: University of Chicago Press.

Schultz, T. (1964). *The economic value of education*. New York: Columbia University Press.

Skountzos, Th. (2004). *Regional economic analysis and policy* (Vol. B). Athens: Stamoulis.

Skountzos, T., & Livas, P. (2000). *National economic accounts*. Athens: Stamoulis.

Skountzos, T., & Stroblos, N. (2007). *Relations branch of the Greek economy in national and regional level*. Athens: Athens Academy.

Technological Educational Institute of Epirus, Department of Igoumenitsa. (2004). *Reforming course of study*.

Technological Educational Institute of Epirus, Department of Preveza. (2004). *Reforming course of study*.

Technological Educational Institute of Peloponnese, Department of Local Government. (2004). Reforming course of study.

Tsounis, N. (2006). Universities and Regional Development: The case of TEI of Western Macedonia. In *Conference Proceedings of 3rd International Research of Technological Educational Institute of Epirus, Education and Economic Development* (pp. 65–80). Preveza.

Western Macedonia University of Applied Sciences, Department of Florina. (2005). *Reforming course of study*.

Yotopoulos, P., & Nugent, J. (1976). Economics of development, empirical investigations (Vol. 59, No. 2, pp. 406–408). Oxford: Oxford University Press.

The Importance of Trade with the Balkan Countries for Turkey

Turker Susmus and S. Ozgur Baslangic

Abstract In our present age, international business is growing very fast since buyers and sellers can easily connect each other without hardly any limit. However, despite the ease and speed of communication, geographical realities are still an important factor in evaluating trade opportunities. Thus, to transport and deliver commodities as cheaply and quickly as possible to their destination is as important as it is to make online deals at the touch of a button. Naturally, the fastest and cheapest logistics operations can be conducted at shorter distances, so trade with neighbours is still of great importance.

For the purposes of international trade, Balkan countries are strategically located both in terms of their European neighbourhood and also in the wider global context. Moreover, a shared history and culture is an important factor encouraging a strengthened cooperation amongst these countries themselves as well as the neighbouring countries like Turkey. Turkey's trade relations with these countries have gained an increased significance in recent years as it has started to enjoy a positive balance in its trade with the region.

In this study, import and export values between Turkey and Balkan countries are carefully presented in detail, and the advantages and benefits of trade with these countries for Turkish economy are considered.

Keywords Import · Export · International business

T. Susmus (✉)
Department of Business Administration, Ege University, Izmir, Turkey
e-mail: turker.susmus@ege.edu.tr

S. O. Baslangic
International Business and Logistics Expert, Izmir, Turkey

© Springer Nature Switzerland AG 2019
N. Sykianakis et al. (eds.), *Economic and Financial Challenges for Eastern Europe*,
Springer Proceedings in Business and Economics,
https://doi.org/10.1007/978-3-030-12169-3_7

95

1   Introduction

Mutual opportunities presented by an ever-expanding foreign trade enabled by globalisation are of great importance for all countries in the world. The importance of relocating goods and services can be specified as follows (Susmus and Baslangic 2015: 321):

- Opportunities provided by technology
- Different environmental and health conditions
- High demand for manufactured goods
- Inequality of resource distribution

Both developed and developing countries are making great efforts to increase their exports. Countries try to make more exports to increase their scarce foreign exchange resources, and this is amongst the first priorities of foreign economic policy. It can be said that the situation is similar in Turkey as well, and the most reliable way of obtaining foreign exchange is through export (Takim and Ersungur 2010: 289). Turkey has adopted an open market economy model and export-oriented growth strategy since the early 1980s. The economic measures taken created a model that aimed to integrate the national economy with the world economy and to provide national growth through foreign trade and industrialisation strategy which can compete in international markets easily. Even though there have been and still are conjuncture-based troubles from time to time, Turkey's exports and imports have continued to increase every year (Doğanlar et al. 2004: 83).

Today, with the increasing use of information and communication technologies, countries' growth and trade with each other is increasing every day (Kalayci 2013: 145). In Turkey, these developments have been adapted rapidly, and, as a result, Turkey has managed to increase its foreign trade, especially with its neighbouring countries. Today, Turkey has an annual export volume of nearly $150 billion and import volume of nearly $200 billion. The annual foreign trade volume of around $350 billion in Turkey shows the result of past economic steps (TUIK 2017).

However, the difference of approximately $50 billion between imports and exports represents a significant foreign trade deficit. In this study, general exports and general imports of Turkey are examined. In addition, commercial transactions with Balkan countries were examined and compared with general trade.

2   Turkey's International Business

Foreign trade volume of Turkey is rapidly increasing each year. This increase can be seen more clearly when the volume of foreign trade is examined from the date of the major economic decisions taken in the early 1980s to present day. Compared to 35 years ago, Turkey boosts a 25 times more foreign trade volume at present. In particular, the rise seen after 2007 is very important, and it attracts considerable attention. However, the rise in the volume of foreign trade was accompanied by a simultaneous increase in foreign trade deficit. In the last decade, an average foreign trade deficit of $75 billion has been formed (TUIK 2017).

The last 35 years of foreign trade of Turkey can easily be seen in Table 1. Since the imports and exports have increased continuously, the foreign trade deficit has not steadily come down for the last 35 years (TUIK 2017).

According to Table 2, Turkey makes half of its annual exports to the top ten countries specified. These are Germany, the UK, Iraq, Italy, the USA, France, UAE, Spain, Iran and the Netherlands. Turkey's exports to these countries have a very important share in its overall exports. Table 2 presents a general overview of the last 10 years of exports to these countries (TUIK 2017).

On the other hand, the top ten countries with the largest share in Turkey's imports are specified in Table 3. According to the table, more than half of Turkey's general imports are made from these countries. The top ten countries with the largest share in Turkey's imports are China, Germany, Russia, the USA, Italy, France, South Korea, India, Spain and the UK. Table 3 has a general overview of the last 10 years of imports from these countries (TUIK 2017) (Fig. 1).

If we compare Tables 2 and 3, countries such as Germany, the UK, Italy, Spain, the USA and France seem to have a very important place in the foreign trade volume of Turkey. On the other hand, it is clearly seen that the European Union countries have a very important place in terms of export as foreign exchange earning activity (TUIK 2017) (Fig. 2).

Table 4 shows the situation of exports and imports made in 2016 according to the international standard industry classification. It can be seen that, the vast majority of exports and imports are in the manufacturing industry. Agriculture and Forestry and Mining and Quarrying sectors are also the other sectors that influence the foreign trade volume of Turkey. The figures for the year 2016 reflect Turkey's foreign trade structure in the past years (TUIK 2017).

3 The Importance of Trade with the Balkan Countries for Turkey

The Balkans constitutes a geographical peninsula in the eastern and southeastern parts of the European continent. In this region, there are 12 countries with a common historical and political background. At present these countries are Albania, Bosnia and Herzegovina, Bulgaria, Croatia, FYRM, Greece, Kosovo, Montenegro, Romania, Serbia, Slovenia and Turkey. Some of these countries are entirely located geographically within the Balkans region, while others are partly located within it (SETAV 2017).

The Balkans is of great importance both for Turkey and the European Union. It is very important for Turkey, because the Balkan societies and the Turkish people have

Table 1 Foreign trade by years, 1982–2016

Years	Exports value	Imports value	Balance of foreign trade value	Volume of foreign trade value	Proportion of imports covered by exports %
1982	5,745,973	8,842,665	−3,096,692	14,588,639	65.0
1983	5,727,834	9,235,002	−3,507,168	14,962,836	62.0
1984	7,133,604	10,757,032	−3,623,429	17,890,636	66.3
1985	7,958,010	11,343,376	−3,385,367	19,301,386	70.2
1986	7,456,726	11,104,771	−3,648,046	18,561,497	67.1
1987	10,190,049	14,157,807	−3,967,757	24,347,856	72.0
1988	11,662,024	14,335,398	−2,673,374	25,997,422	81.4
1989	11,624,692	15,792,143	−4,167,451	27,416,835	73.6
1990	12,959,288	22,302,126	−9,342,838	35,261,413	58.1
1991	13,593,462	21,047,014	−7,453,552	34,640,476	64.6
1992	14,714,629	22,871,055	−8,156,426	37,585,684	64.3
1993	15,345,067	29,428,370	−14,083,303	44,773,436	52.1
1994	18,105,872	23,270,019	−5,164,147	41,375,891	77.8
1995	21,637,041	35,709,011	−14,071,970	57,346,052	60.6
1996	23,224,465	43,626,642	−20,402,178	66,851,107	53.2
1997	26,261,072	48,558,721	−22,297,649	74,819,792	54.1
1998	26,973,952	45,921,392	−18,947,440	72,895,344	58.7
1999	26,587,225	40,671,272	−14,084,047	67,258,497	65.4
2000	27,774,906	54,502,821	−26,727,914	82,277,727	51.0
2001	31,334,216	41,399,083	−10,064,867	72,733,299	75.7
2002	36,059,089	51,553,797	−15,494,708	87,612,886	69.9
2003	47,252,836	69,339,692	−22,086,856	116,592,528	68.1
2004	63,167,153	97,539,766	−34,372,613	160,706,919	64.8
2005	73,476,408	116,774,151	−43,297,743	190,250,559	62.9
2006	85,534,676	139,576,174	−54,041,498	225,110,850	61.3
2007	107,271,750	170,062,715	−62,790,965	277,334,464	63.1
2008	132,027,196	201,963,574	−69,936,378	333,990,770	65.4
2009	102,142,613	140,928,421	−38,785,809	243,071,034	72.5
2010	113,883,219	185,544,332	−71,661,113	299,427,551	61.4
2011	134,906,869	240,841,676	−105,934,807	375,748,545	56.0
2012	152,461,737	236,545,141	−84,083,404	389,006,877	64.5
2013	151,802,637	251,661,250	−99,858,613	403,463,887	60.3
2014	157,610,158	242,177,117	−84,566,959	399,787,275	65.1
2015	143,838,871	207,234,359	−63,395,487	351,073,230	69.4
2016	142,545,946	198,616,139	−56,070,193	341,162,085	71.8

TUIK, http://www.tuik.gov.tr/ (Accessed date 15.03.2017)

a shared culture and a history of coexistence since the Ottoman era. However, this region is also important for Europe because most of the Balkan countries are members of the European Union (Aytüre and Berki 2015: 197).

Table 2 Exports by country and year (top ten country in exports) (Value: US$1000)

Rank	Country	2016	2015	2014	2013	2012	2011	2010	2009	2008	2007
1	Germany	14,000,020	13,417,033	15,147,423	13,702,577	13,124,375	13,950,825	11,479,066	9,793,006	12,951,755	11,993,232
2	United Kingdom	11,686,650	10,556,393	9,903,172	8,785,124	8,693,599	8,151,430	7,235,861	5,937,997	8,158,669	8,626,776
3	Iraq	7,637,880	8,549,967	10,887,826	11,948,905	10,822,144	8,310,130	6,036,362	5,123,406	3,916,685	2,844,767
4	Italy	7,581,176	6,887,399	7,141,071	6,718,355	6,373,080	7,851,480	6,505,277	5,888,958	7,818,988	7,480,060
5	USA	6,623,447	6,395,842	6,341,841	5,640,247	5,604,230	4,584,029	3,762,919	3,240,597	4,299,941	4,170,688
6	France	6,022,938	5,845,032	6,464,243	6,376,704	6,198,536	6,805,821	6,054,499	6,211,415	6,617,511	5,974,462
7	UAE	5,407,149	4,681,255	4,655,710	4,965,630	8,174,607	3,706,654	3,332,885	2,896,572	7,975,400	3,240,940
8	Spain	4,989,045	4,742,270	4,749,584	4,334,196	3,717,345	3,917,559	3,536,205	2,818,470	4,047,267	4,579,995
9	Iran	4,966,510	3,663,760	3,886,190	4,192,511	9,921,602	3,589,635	3,044,177	2,024,546	2,029,760	1,441,190
10	Netherlands	3,589,630	3,154,867	3,458,689	3,538,043	3,244,429	3,243,080	2,461,371	2,127,297	3,143,835	3,018,878
	Top 10 total	72,504,446	67,893,818	72,635,750	70,202,291	75,873,947	64,110,642	53,448,623	46,062,265	60,959,812	53,370,990
	Grand total	142,545,946	143,838,871	157,610,158	151,802,637	152,461,737	134,906,869	113,883,219	102,142,613	132,027,196	107,271,750

TUIK, http://www.tuik.gov.tr/ (Accessed date 15.03.2017)

Table 3 Imports by country and year (top ten country in imports) (Value: US$1000)

Rank	Country	2016	2015	2014	2013	2012	2011	2010	2009	2008	2007
1	China	25,440,726	24,873,457	24,918,224	24,685,885	24,295,242	21,693,336	17,180,806	12,676,573	15,658,210	13,234,092
2	Germany	21,474,093	21,351,884	22,369,476	24,182,422	21,400,614	22,985,567	17,549,112	14,096,963	18,687,197	17,539,955
3	Russia	15,162,363	20,401,757	25,288,597	25,064,214	26,625,286	23,952,914	21,600,641	19,450,086	31,364,477	23,508,494
4	USA	10,867,787	11,141,462	12,727,562	12,596,170	14,130,546	16,034,121	12,318,745	8,575,737	11,975,929	8,166,068
5	Italy	10,219,003	10,639,042	12,055,972	12,884,864	13,344,468	13,449,861	10,139,888	7,591,645	10,682,037	9,751,280
6	France	7,364,722	7,597,687	8,122,571	8,079,840	8,589,896	9,229,558	8,176,600	7,091,795	9,022,015	7,849,709
7	South Korea	6,384,163	7,057,439	7,548,319	6,088,318	5,660,093	6,298,483	4,764,057	3,118,214	4,091,711	4,369,903
8	India	5,757,172	5,613,515	6,898,577	6,367,791	5,843,638	6,498,651	3,409,938	1,902,607	2,457,908	2,299,732
9	Span	5,679,305	5,588,524	6,075,843	6,417,719	6,023,625	6,196,452	4,840,062	3,776,917	4,548,182	4,342,994
10	United Kingdom	5,320,631	5,541,277	5,932,227	6,281,414	5,629,455	5,840,380	4,680,611	3,473,433	5,258,923	5,477,102
	Top 10 Total	113,669,965	119,806,043	131,937,368	132,648,637	128,542,862	132,179,321	104,660,460	81,756,971	113,746,590	96,539,329
	Grand Total	198,616,139	207,234,359	242,177,117	251,661,250	236,545,141	240,841,676	185,544,332	140,928,421	201,963,574	170,062,715

TUIK, http://www.tuik.gov.tr/ (Accessed date 15.03.2017)

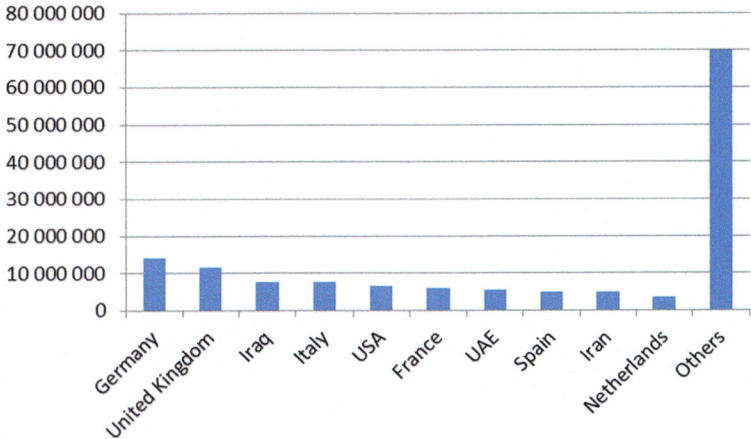

Fig. 1 Exports of Turkey–2016. TUIK, http://www.tuik.gov.tr/ (Accessed date 15.03.2017)

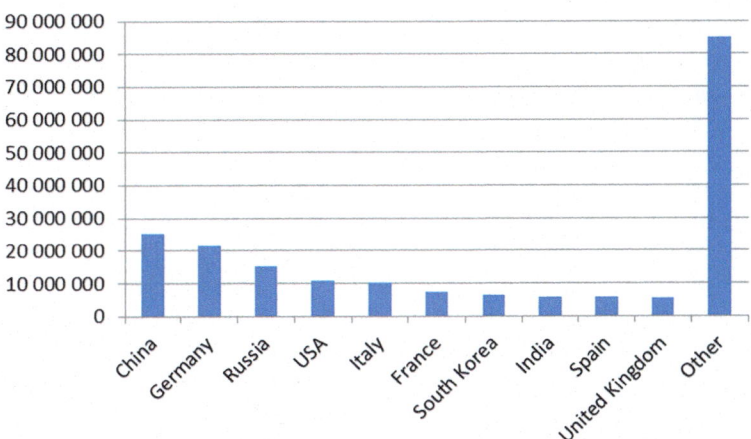

Fig. 2 Imports of Turkey-2016. TUIK, http://www.tuik.gov.tr/ (Accessed date 15.03.2017)

The Balkan countries have suffered from various political troubles and ethnic tensions in the recent past after the disintegration of Yugoslavia, but today the region has been stabilised and the present political boundaries are formed. In the present political configuration, Turkey holds a privileged position with respect to its bilateral relations with some of the countries of the region. Indeed, there are very strong links between the people living in Turkey and the Balkan countries. Relatives of Turkish origin live as a minority in the Balkan countries, and on the other hand some Balkan citizens live in Turkey (MFA 2017).

In addition, Turkey believes that Balkan countries can make the greatest contribution to the future of the wider region. For this reason, Turkey puts an emphasis on the development of unique cooperation mechanisms in the Balkans. In this context,

Table 4 Exports and imports 2016 by ISIC (Value: US$1000)

Classification	Exports 2016	Imports 2016
Agriculture and forestry	5,397,482	7,041,734
Fishing	413,953	55,956
Mining and quarrying	2,676,845	19,009,172
Manufacturing	133,611,857	167,240,660
Electricity, gas and water supply	13,590	213,614
Wholesale and retail trade	423,714	5,010,752
Real estate, renting and business activities	794	1856
Other community, social and personal service activities	7711	42,395
Total	142,545,946	198,616,139

TUIK, http://www.tuik.gov.tr/ (Accessed date 15.03.2017)

the Southeast European Cooperation Process (SEECP) is of great importance in terms of Turkey and the other regional countries. The number of participating countries in which Turkey is a founding member, together with Slovenia, reaches 12 and covers all countries in the region (MFA 2017).

As in with most of the world, foreign trade policy constitutes an important part of general economic policy for Balkan countries, too. These two policies must be in a perfect harmony. The politics of the countries that have an important place in the world global economy are also influential in other countries due to these reasons. In this case, we can easily say that the economic policies of the European Union are very important for the countries in the region (Seyidoğlu 2015: 142).

Details of the last 5 years of exports made from Turkey to Balkan countries are presented in Table 5. Exports to Balkan countries represent an average of 6% of Turkey's overall exports. This is an important export volume for Turkey, and it is equivalent to approximately 9 billion dollars annually. The countries which receive the highest exports volume from Turkey are Greece, Romania, Bulgaria and Slovenia. On the other hand, Turkey has a very low export capacity in its trade with Montenegro, Kosovo, Croatia, Albania, FYRM and Bosnia and Herzegovina when compared to other countries.

Table 6 gives details of the imports of Turkey from the Balkan countries. According to this, Turkey's imports from the Balkan countries are about 4% of its total imports. The Balkan countries, which have an import volume of approximately 8–9 billion USD, are in a position to be considered as important for Turkish trade. The Balkan countries that Turkey imports the most are Greece, Bulgaria and Romania. On the other hand, import volumes from Kosovo, FYRM, Albania, Montenegro and Croatia are in quite low levels.

Table 7 presents a comparative comparison of Turkey's general foreign trade with its foreign trade with Balkan countries. According to the table, the foreign trade volume with Balkan countries is close to 20 billion dollars. The general foreign trade volume of Turkey is around 360 billion dollars. When the general trade volume is compared with the Balkan trade volume, the latter may not be very impressive. However, the exports to Balkan countries are higher than the imports, according to

Table 5 Exports to Balkan countries (Value: US$1000)

Country	2016	2015	2014	2013	2012
Albania	304,610	287,374	318,541	266,544	255,950
Bosnia and Hezegovnia	308,963	292,570	322,022	274,086	251,523
Bulgaria	2,383,741	1,675,928	2,040,157	1,971,247	1,684,989
Crotia	278,251	251,652	287,401	201,597	200,575
FYRM	378,038	324,613	347,965	293,976	274,497
Greece	1,427,228	1,400,566	1,536,658	1,437,443	1,401,401
Kosovo	260,728	240,676	275,645	278,998	254,784
Montenegro	51,807	38,297	35,040	29,140	29,131
Romania	2,671,406	2,815,506	3,008,011	2,616,313	2,495,427
Serbia	581,776	492,472	506,419	440,650	380,869
Slovenia	928,151	810,405	742,817	666,164	548,314
Exports to Balkans	9,574,699	8,630,060	9,420,675	8,476,158	7,777,461
Total Exports	142,545,946	143,838,871	157,610,158	151,802,637	152,461,737
Balkan ratio in total exports (%)	7	6	6	6	5

TUIK, http://www.tuik.gov.tr/ (Accessed date 15.03.2017)

Table 6 Imports from Balkan countries (Value: US$1000)

Country	2016	2015	2014	2013	2012
Albania	20,602	49,578	96,281	82,390	98,989
Bosnia and Hezegovnia	288,291	250,089	171,424	124,330	111,649
Bulgaria	2,141,160	2,254,180	2,846,185	2,760,303	2,753,650
Crotia	133,517	135,757	136,889	193,262	209,766
FYRM	82,581	80,929	79,194	81,518	103,224
Greece	1,187,058	1,860,935	4,043,839	4,206,020	3,539,869
Kosovo	8507	7864	12,783	9951	9093
Montenegro	23,364	8001	7373	11,515	17,936
Romania	2,195,671	2,598,908	3,363,233	3,592,568	3,236,425
Serbia	288,237	238,299	273,901	251,957	205,538
Slovenia	296,053	343,784	301,868	304,256	311,875
Imports From Balkans	6,665,040	7,828,323	11,332,972	11,618,070	10,598,013
Total Imports	198,616,139	207,234,359	242,177,117	251,661,250	236,545,141
Balkan ratio in total imports (%)	3	4	5	5	4

TUIK, http://www.tuik.gov.tr/ (Accessed date 15.03.2017)

that Turkey is covering the imports with exports and also giving foreign trade surplus in recent years. Obviously this situation is very important and meaningful for Turkey. Especially the surplus data for 2015 and 2016 are very important for Turkey.

Table 7 Imports and exports comparison of Turkey (Value: US$1000)

Years	General					Balkans				
	Exports	Imports	Balance of foreign trade	Proportion of imports covered by exports(%)	Foreign trade volume	Exports	Imports	Balance of foreign trade	Proportion of imports covered by exports (%)	Foreign trade volume
2016	142,545,946	198,616,139	−56,070,193	72	341,162,085	9,574,699	6,665,040	2,909,658	144	16,239,739
2015	143,838,871	207,234,359	−63,395,487	69	351,073,230	8,630,060	7,828,323	801,737	110	16,458,382
2014	157,610,158	242,177,117	−84,566,959	65	399,787,275	9,420,675	11,332,972	−1,912,297	83	20,753,647
2013	151,802,637	251,661,250	−99,858,613	60	403,463,887	8,476,158	11,618,070	−3,141,912	73	20,094,227
2012	152,461,737	236,545,141	−84,083,404	64	389,006,877	7,777,461	10,598,013	−2,820,552	73	18,375,475

TUIK, http://www.tuik.gov.tr/ (Accessed date 15.03.2017)

Table 8 Foreign trade volume of Turkey with Balkan countries (Value: US$1000)

Country	2016	2015	2014	2013	2012
Albania	325,212	336,952	414,822	348,934	354,939
Bosnia and Hezegovnia	597,254	542,659	493,446	398,416	363,172
Bulgaria	4,524,901	3,930,108	4,886,341	4,731,550	4,438,639
Crotia	411,769	387,409	424,291	394,859	410,341
FYRM	460,619	405,542	427,159	375,494	377,721
Greece	2,614,286	3,261,502	5,580,497	5,643,463	4,941,270
Kosovo	269,234	248,540	288,428	288,949	263,877
Montenegro	75,170	46,299	42,413	40,656	47,067
Romania	4,867,077	5,414,415	6,371,244	6,208,880	5,731,852
Serbia	870,013	730,771	780,320	692,607	586,407
Slovenia	1,224,204	1,154,189	1,044,684	970,420	860,190
Total	16,239,739	16,458,382	20,753,647	20,094,227	18,375,475

TUIK, http://www.tuik.gov.tr/ (Accessed date 15.03.2017)

Table 9 Balance of foreign trade with Balkan countries (Value: US$1000)

Country	2016	2015	2014	2013	2012
Albania	284,008	237,796	222,260	184,154	156,961
Bosnia and Hezegovnia	20,673	42,481	150,598	149,756	139,875
Bulgaria	242,581	−578,252	−806,028	−789,056	−1,068,661
Crotia	144,734	115,894	150,512	8335	−9190
FYRM	295,457	243,684	268,770	212,458	171,273
Greece	240,171	−460,369	−2,507,181	−2,768,577	−2,138,468
Kosovo	252,221	232,812	262,862	269,048	245,691
Montenegro	28,443	30,296	27,667	17,625	11,196
Romania	475,735	216,598	−355,222	−976,255	−740,998
Serbia	293,539	254,173	232,518	188,693	175,332
Slovenia	632,097	466,622	440,949	361,908	236,439
Total	2,909,658	801,737	−1,912,297	−3,141,912	−2,820,552

TUIK, http://www.tuik.gov.tr/ (Accessed date 15.03.2017)

Table 8 gives us details of foreign trade volumes of Balkan countries. According to the table, Turkey has the highest level of commercial relations in the region with Romania, Bulgaria, Greece and Slovenia. The trade volume of these four countries is higher than the trade volume of the remaining countries. Despite the decrease in trade volumes in the last 2 years, this decline is in parallel with the general foreign trade of Turkey.

The balance of foreign trade with Balkan countries is shown in Table 9. According to this table, in the years 2015 and 2016, Turkey exports more than it imports, thus having a surplus in its foreign trade with the Balkan countries. It is very important in terms of sustainability that this trade surplus is achieved not only by countries with very high commercial volume but by almost all countries.

4   Conclusion

Turkey has been suffering from a serious trade deficit it its foreign trade for a long time now. In this context, Turkey's positive foreign trade balance with Balkan countries is an example that needs to be well understood and if possible replicated in its foreign trade relations with all countries. Nonetheless, it must also be noted that although trade with Balkan countries is favourable to Turkey, the volume of trade has not yet reached the desired levels.

Turkey's mutual trade with Greece, Romania, Bulgaria and Slovenia is maturing owing to high levels of trade. Moreover, the historical and cultural ties with these countries can be utilised in the development of this trade. The fact that these four countries are members of the European Union places a special emphasis on trade structure and development of the trade with these countries.

Countries such as Kosovo, Albania, Montenegro, FYRM, and Bosnia and Herzegovina, where Turkey has had a very strong cultural and political presence in the past, have very low levels of presence in Turkey's foreign trade. Since these countries are not yet European Union members and they are still recovering after Yugoslavia's disintegration, Turkey should support them, both politically and commercially. A strong commercial relationship with these countries today will become much more effective and stronger in the future when they become members of the European Union.

As a result, the strategies that Balkan countries adopt for developing commercial ties with each other will be very beneficial for both these countries themselves and Turkey also. In addition, common institutions to assist their cooperation will be very useful for almost every country. At this point, all professional and civil society structures, especially the economy ministries of these countries, should facilitate their operations. In terms of contributing to this study, the following topics can be examined by future researchers:

- Examining the trade volumes of the Balkan countries
- Detailed analysis of product groups in the Balkan countries' trade with each other
- Logistics advantages of Balkan countries trading
- Payment methods for Balkan countries' trade with each other

References

Aytüre, S., & Berki, Ö. (2015). Avrupa Birliği, Türkiye ve Balkan Ülkeleri Ticaret İlişkileri. *İstanbul Ticaret Üniversitesi Sosyal Bilimler Dergisi, 14*(28), 197–212.
Doğanlar, M., Bal, H., & Özmen, M. (2004). Uluslararası Ticaret ve Türkiye'nin İhracat Fonksiyonu. *Manas Üniversitesi Sosyal Bilimler Dergisi, 4*(7), 83–109.
Kalayci, E. (2013). Dijital Bölünme, Dijital Yoksulluk ve Uluslararası Ticaret; Atatürk Üniversitesi İktisadi ve. *İdari Bilimler Fakültesi Dergisi, 27*(3), 145–162.
MFA. Accesed March 28, 2017., from http://www.mfa.gov.tr/balkanlar_ile-iliskiler.tr.mfa
SETAV. Accesed March 28, 2017., from https://setav.org/assets/uploads/2017/02/72Rapor.pdf

Seyidoğlu, H. (2015). *Uluslararası İktisat* (1. Basım). İstanbul: Gizem Yayınları.

Susmus, T., & Baslangic, S. O. (2015). The new payment term BPO and its effects on Turkish International Business. *Procedia Economics and Finance, 33*, 321–330.

Takim, A., & Ersungur, M. Ş. (2010). Dahilde İşleme Rejimi: İthalat ve İhracat Üzerindeki Etkisi. *Atatürk Üniversitesi İktisadi ve İdari Bilimler Fakültesi Dergisi, 24*(2), 289–305.

TUIK. Accessed March 15, 2017., from http://www.tuik.gov.tr/

Barriers in the Calculation of Residual Income in Slovak Companies

Ivana Podhorska and Tomas Kliestik

Abstract The question of the value of company and the value of company's goodwill is an actual topic not only in Slovakia but also abroad. The often interest of scientific researchers is a difference between the market value of company and the book value of company. Because this difference is often a situation, which is created in real economic conditions. In general, scientific literature states the idea that difference between the market value of company and the book value of company represents relevant valuation for company's goodwill. It means that company's goodwill is the source of the market value of company creation. This paper deals with the issue of relevant valuation of company's goodwill. This paper uses, as basic concept, the idea of residual income for valuation of the value of company and the value of company's goodwill. According to the theory of residual income, residual income represents the value of income which company creates over the level of its cost of equity. Required income from the side of company's owners represents basic normal income which the company had to create. Any income which the company creates over the level of its cost of equity represents residual income. Based on these facts, residual income is defined as a difference between net income and the equity charge. The concept of residual income uses, for example, Feltham-Ohlson model, which determines the value of company as the sum of the book value of company's equity and the present value of its future residual income. Application of information from company's financial statements represents the advantage of this model. The main aim of this paper is to calculate the value of company's residual income (calculation consists of earnings after taxes, book value of equity, and the cost of equity). On these outputs, this paper determines other statistically significant variables, which could have impact on the value of company's residual income. The secondary aim of this paper is to discover the statistically significant variables, which could be considered as the sources of company's goodwill. This paper works with the data set of Slovak companies. The data set consists of 11,483 financial statements

I. Podhorska (✉) · T. Kliestik
Faculty of Operation and Economics of Transport and Communications, Department of Economics, University of Zilina, Zilina, Slovak Republic
e-mail: ivana.podhorska@fpedas.uniza.sk; tomas.kliestik@fpedas.uniza.sk

© Springer Nature Switzerland AG 2019
N. Sykianakis et al. (eds.), *Economic and Financial Challenges for Eastern Europe*,
Springer Proceedings in Business and Economics,
https://doi.org/10.1007/978-3-030-12169-3_8

of Slovak companies. For calculation of earnings after taxes and the book value of equity, this paper uses information from financial statements of this data set of companies. For calculation of cost of equity, this paper uses the capital asset pricing model, according to the recommendation of Feltham-Ohlson model. Calculation of secondary variables, which could have impact on the company's goodwill, is primary based on the information from financial statements of the data set of Slovak companies. This paper uses, as a relevant statistical method for determination of statistically significant variables, the multiple linear regression.

Keywords Residual income · Feltham-Ohlson model · Equity · Goodwill · Multiple linear regression

1 Introduction

Economic concept of residual income has a long history. First, in 1920s General Motors applied this concept in the process of evaluating the business segments. Later, residual income has received renewed attention as an economic profit or abnormal earnings. Based on the idea of residual income, were created residual income valuation models. These models try to define the value of company as the sum of the book value of company's equity and the present value of future residual income of company. Feltham-Ohlson model also provides this calculation concept of the value of company. It is residual income that creates the difference between the market value of company and the book value of company, given that residual income represents the basic concept for calculation of the company's goodwill. Due to the review of scientific literature, we can state that it is company's goodwill, which creates the difference between the market value of company and the book value of company. Subsequently, the value of residual income is equal to the company's goodwill. This view is shared by the Kliestik et al. (2015) and Vochozka (2010).

Basic idea of residual income says that income which company creates over the level of required income from the owners of company represents residual income. However, the question is what represents the required income from the company's owners. According to this idea, residual income represents the difference between net income of company and its equity charge. Equity charge represents the product of the cost of equity and the book value of equity. Given that, required income from the company's owners is equal to the cost of equity. The calculation of the cost of equity has some special barriers. The company's income statement contains a charge for the cost of debt capital as an interest expense. However, company's income statement does not contain the information about the cost of equity. Based on these facts, we had to use relevant economic method for the calculation of the cost of equity (Spuchlakova and Michalikova-Frajtova 2016).

In this paper, we use these patterns of calculation and basic assumptions and procedures of calculation. This paper contains the data set of 11,483 Slovak companies. In this paper, we provide the calculation of residual income in this data set of companies. In addition, we try to determine statistically significant variables, which could have impact on the residual income creation and represent the sources of company's goodwill creation. We apply the multiple linear regression for the determination of statistically significant source of company's goodwill creation.

2 Theoretical Framework

This chapter, provides theoretical framework. We describe basic theoretical aspects of residual income and its calculation. In addition, chapter describes theoretical background of variables, which could represent the sources of company' goodwill, because, as we mentioned above, the main aim of this paper is to calculate the value of company's residual income (calculation consists of earnings after taxes, book value of equity, and the cost of equity). The secondary aim of this paper is to discover the statistically significant variables, which could be considered as the sources of company's goodwill. The research in the area of relevant variables is performed based on the scientific literature.

2.1 Theoretical Aspects of Residual Income

Residual income represents income which company creates over the level of its cost of equity. Cost of equity represents required income from the side of company's owners. According to this fact, residual income represents the difference between the net income and equity charge. Equity charge is the product of the cost of equity and the book value of equity. If the company creates income, which is equal to the required income from the side of company's owner, it means cost of equity; this company creates only normal income. However, if the company creates income, which is higher than the required income from the side of company's owner, it means cost of equity in this company creates residual income. In both theory and practice exist the difference between the market value of company and the book value of company. In accordance with Kimbro and Xu (2016). This difference represents residual income. In addition, we can find view that the difference between the market value of company and the book value of company is caused by company's goodwill. Based on these literature conclusions, we can state that the determination and calculation of residual income could represent value for company's goodwill.

As we mentioned in introduction, calculation of the book value of company according to the theory of residual income has one big advantage. This approach combines the book value of equity and present value of future residual income. It means that this approach arises from the accounting data. In this paper we work with the data set of 11,483 financial statements of Slovak companies, and thanks to the concept of this model, we are able to calculate the value of residual income in these companies. Linking between accounting data and earnings in the valuation model represents very interesting possibility of the company's valuation. This concept is actual in the theory of corporate finance. The genesis of accounting-based model can be traced back to works of Preinreich (1936), Edwards and Bell (1961), and Peasnell (1982) but reappeared if that is a correct word in this sense in the work of Ohlson (1999) and Feltham and Ohlson (1995). Collins et al. (1997) show that value-relevancy of earnings and book value has not declined, and while the incremental value-relevance of "bottom line" earnings has declined, it has been replaced by increasing value-relevance of book value. Liu and Ohlson (1999) conclude that residual income valuation (RIV) model rests solely on the expected evolution of accounting data without ad hoc dividend policies and in this respect succeed in articulating how market value depends on anticipated accounting data realizations in addition to current realizations.

2.2 Theoretical Aspects of Potentially Significant Variables

This paper contains assumption that the value of residual income is equal to the value of company's goodwill. Residual income represents relevant method for the determination of company's goodwill. Basic variables, which influence residual income, are net income, book value of equity, and cost of equity. In the context of these circumstances, we decided to find other statistically significant variables, which could be considered, as the sources of company's goodwill creation. We performed a robust analysis of domestic and foreign scientific literature dealing with issues of the value of company or the value of company's goodwill. We present some of them—Jakubec et al. (2011), Marik et al. (2011), Zelenka (2006), Ballaster et al. (2003), Kariuki et al. (2013), Cheng (2005), Jansky (2011), and Bartosova and Kral (2016).

We focused on the literature review, and we tried to choose relevant variables, which could be the sources of company's goodwill. We chose variables from the financial analysis of company. In addition, we tried to choose variables, which capture the cost of marketing and some categories of company's profit. We also find variables, which capture investments into the property, plant and equipment in company, or variables, which capture the value of intellectual property of company. In the process of finding of relevant sources of company's goodwill, we discovered other barriers in calculation. *The barrier* is the problem with the calculation of these variables. In scientific literature, we can find many variables, which could have impact on the company's goodwill, but we are able to calculate only few of them. Some relevant variables we are able to obtain from the financial statements of company, but some of them we have to derive from other values from financial statements of company.

3 Methodology

In this chapter, we provide methods and methodology which were used in the process of residual income calculation and determination of statistically significant sources of company's goodwill. In this chapter, we describe methodology of residual income calculation. In second part of this chapter, we describe methodology of potentially significant sources of company's goodwill calculation. Our methods of calculation of all variables correspond with the theory of scientific literature.

3.1 Methodology of Residual Income Calculation

Based on the literature of theoretical aspects, we provide Eq. (1) of residual income calculation. Residual income represents the difference between net income and the equity charge:

$$I_{res} = NI - equity\ charge \tag{1}$$

where

I_{res}	residual income
NI	net income
equity charge	The product of the book value of equity and the cost of equity

Determinants of equity charge represents the key calculation of residual income, because equity charge is the product of the cost of equity and book value of equity. This fact is captured in Eq. (2):

$$equity\ charge = r_e \times BV_E \tag{2}$$

where

r_e	cost of equity
BV_E	book value of equity

In the formulation of these equations and relationships, we discovered the first barriers in calculation. *The first barrier* is the question of net income calculation. In literature, we can find the different views on this problem. In literature exists approach, where net income is equal to the earnings after taxes (EAT). In addition, in scientific literature exists approach, where net income is equal to the net operating profit after taxes (NOPAT). Focus is on the distribution of operating and financial activities of the company. In addition, we can find studies, where net income is equal to earnings without specific explanation. Finally, we decided to use the concept of earnings after taxes (EAT) for residual income calculation. *The second barrier* is linked with the question of the relevant method for the determination of the cost of

Table 1 Methodology of potentially significant variables calculation

Variable	Mark	Calculation
Cash ratio	CR	(Cash + cash equivalents)/current liabilities
Debt-equity ratio	DER	Equity/total liabilities
Turnover ratio from short-term payables	TUR	(Short-term payables from business/costs) × 365
Return on equity	ROE	Earnings after taxes/equity
Net income	NI	Earnings after taxes from previous year
Retained earnings from previous years	RE	Retained earnings from previous year from balance sheet
Valuable rights	VR	Valuable rights from balance sheet
Research and development costs	R&D	Research and development costs from balance sheet
Marketing costs	MC	½ (15% × service costs from income statement)
Investments into the property, plant, and equipment	INV	Annual change from balance sheet
Age of company	AC	Time since the company's establishment to 2015
Company market share	CS	Sales from operating activities/sales from operating activities in industry

equity. In Slovak literature, we can find several approaches to the calculation of cost of equity. Typical methods are methods INFA and build-up model. However, concept of capital asset pricing model (CAPM) represents universal method for the calculation of the cost of equity. Feltham-Ohlson model also recommends using capital asset pricing model for the determination the cost of equity. We can also find this opinion in the Slovak scientific literature (Svabova and Kral 2016; Corejova and Al Kassiri 2016).

3.2   Methodology of Potentially Significant Variable Calculation

As we mentioned in the chapter of theoretical framework, according to the robust analysis of domestic and foreign scientific literature dealing with issues of the value of company or the value of company's goodwill, we chose several potential sources of company's goodwill. We defined 12 variables. Chosen variables and their calculation methodology are captured in Table 1.

We derived 15% for the marketing costs based on the discussion with accountants. The time during which these costs have effect on the company income is limited. We decided to determine this time for 2 years according to the scientific literature (Jansky 2011).

4   Results

In this chapter we focused on outputs of our calculation of residual income and potentially significant sources of company's goodwill in data set of 11,483 Slovak companies in 2015.

4.1   Calculation of Residual Income

As we mentioned in the chapter of theoretical framework, we calculated residual income as the difference between the earnings after taxes and the equity charge. We calculated equity charge as the product of the book value of equity and the cost of equity. The value of earnings after taxes we obtained from the income statements of companies in 2015. The book value of companies we obtained from the balance sheets of companies in 2015. For the calculation of the cost of equity, we decided to use capital asset pricing model according to the Feltham-Ohlson model.

We calculated the cost of equity according to Eq. (3):

$$r_e = r_f + r_p \times \beta + r_s \tag{3}$$

where

r_e cost of equity
r_f risk-free rate
r_p market risk premium
β beta coefficient
r_s specific risk premium for company size

We determined risk-free rate (r_f) as annual average of 10-year government bonds according to the data of The National Bank of Slovakia. Market risk premium (r_p) was calculated according to the information from Damodaran's website by A. Damodaran—professor of finance at the Stern School of Business at New York University. Information from Damodaran's website we also used in the process of β coefficient determination. This coefficient explains the risk premium for riskiness of industry; on the website in the section Data/Discount Rate Estimation, Damodaran provides the values for "Levered and Unlevered Betas by Industry." The last variable was specific risk premium for company size (r_s); we decided to determine the value of this risk premium according to the information from the company Morningstar/Ibbotson. Its determination of this risk premium is based on the information about market capitalization of companies in the US market. Because in Slovak Republic we do not have this information, we decided to inspire additional fee, which is determined by Morningstar/Ibbotson, but we replaced intervals of market capitalization. Instead of market capitalization, we used the value of the assets according to data set of companies (Kliestikova and Misankova 2016).

Table 2 shows results of residual income calculation. Table provides the values of earnings after taxes (EAT), book value of equity (BV_E), equity charge (ECH), and residual income (I_{res}) in euros and the values of risk-free rate (r_f), market risk premium (r_p), beta coefficient (β), specific risk premium for company size (r_s), and cost of equity (r_e) in decimal numbers.

The same value of r_s (-0.0036) and β (0.45) in all rows is caused by filter, which we created when we worked with this big data (it is random situation).

In the process of residual income calculation, we discovered other *barriers* in the calculation:

The first barrier = five companies from data set of companies do not have SK NACE. We were not able to determine beta coefficient in these companies. We decided to exclude these companies from the data set of companies.

The second barrier = for the determination of cost of equity, we used method CAPM. But this method is not exact in Slovak conditions; we had a problem with the negative value of cost of equity in 1405 companies from database (because r_s was negative). We decided to exclude these companies from the data set of companies.

The third barrier = we had another problem in our calculation of residual income. The problem was with companies, which had the negative value of equity. In Slovak Republic, by course of law no. 7/2005 Z.z. Bankruptcy and Restructuring, "company in bankrupt" is the company which has the negative value of equity. Given that companies with the negative value of equity (1068 companies) much misrepresented our calculation, we decided to exclude these companies from next calculation.

After exclusion of these barriers, our data set consists of 9005 Slovak companies.

4.2 Calculation of Potentially Significant Variables

Based on the information and circumstances which we described in the theoretical framework and methodology, we tried to calculate the value of potentially significant variables in data set of 11,483 companies from Slovak Republic in 2015. Table 3 shows results of potentially significant variables.

In the process of potentially significant variables calculation, we discovered other *barriers* in the calculation:

The first barrier = we were not able to calculate the value of cash ratio in some companies (because they lacked the necessary values). Alternatively, we discovered companies, which had negative value of cash ratio. We had to exclude these companies from next calculation. This problem was associated with 172 companies.

The second barrier = we were not able to calculate the value of debt-equity ratio in some companies (because they lacked the necessary values). On the other hand,

Table 2 Illustration of residual income calculation in data set of 11,483 Slovak companies in 2015

EAT	r_f	r_p	β	r_s	r_e	BV_E	ECH	I_{res}
22,914	0.00885	0.0659	0.45	−0.0036	0.06794	1,991,662	135,304	−112,390
144,291	0.00885	0.0659	0.45	−0.0036	0.11873	1,018,130	120,879	23,412
200,820	0.00885	0.0659	0.45	−0.0036	0.05942	2,198,467	130,628	70,191
30,582	0.00885	0.0659	0.45	−0.0036	0.74466	141,952	105,706	−75,123
−437,575	0.00885	0.0659	0.45	−0.0036	0.03782	3,977,060	150,424	−587,999
107,981	0.00885	0.0659	0.45	−0.0036	0.12499	893,687	111,698	−3718
−14,215	0.00885	0.0659	0.45	−0.0036	0.05176	2,416,471	125,073	−139,288
639,049	0.00885	0.0659	0.45	−0.0036	0.03578	3,953,627	141,465	497,585
−77,587	0.00885	0.0659	0.45	−0.0036	0.13221	748,252	98,926	−176,513
−219,342	0.00885	0.0659	0.45	−0.0036	0.09526	1,073,401	102,254	−321,596

Table 3 Illustration of potentially significant sources of company's goodwill in data set of 11,483 Slovak companies in 2015

CR	DER	TUR	ROE	NI	RE	VR	R&D	MC	INV	AC	CS
0.638	0.522	9.471	0.801	5385	0	0	0	135	854	10	0.000001543
0.700	3.555	10.257	0.578	5022	0	0	0	1569	11,567	11	0.000002433
0.460	0.734	7.634	0.527	4026	0	0	0	2410	2389	11	0.000002681
0.317	1.368	0.000	0.216	2247	0	0	0	10	0	7	0.000002692
0.212	0.228	12.464	0.851	2656	0	0	0	718	3141	22	0.000004798
0.232	0.191	54.657	0.297	3448	0	0	0	1227	12,502	7	0.000006163
0.521	0.203	1.872	0.633	11,965	0	0	0	8317	8381	10	0.000009878
0.503	0.411	39.670	0.769	3857	0	0	0	1675	4663	7	0.000010220
0.372	0.098	10.194	0.729	3804	0	0	0	1517	11,500	12	0.000011764
0.684	0.705	46.269	1.173	54,733	0	0	0	1918	38,314	8	0.000013117

we discovered companies, which had negative value of debt-equity ratio. We had to exclude these companies from next calculation. This problem was associated with one company.

The third barrier = we were not able to calculate the value of turnover ratio from short-term payables in some companies (because they lacked the necessary values). Alternatively, we discovered companies, which had negative value of this ratio. We had to exclude these companies from next calculation. This problem was associated with 250 companies.

The fourth barrier = we discovered companies which had negative value of its marketing costs. We had to exclude these companies from next calculation. This problem was associated with six companies.

The fifth barrier = we were not able to calculate the value of market share in some companies, or some companies had negative value of their market share. We decided to exclude these companies from next calculation. This problem was associated with five companies.

The sixth barrier = we discovered companies which had negative value of retained earnings from previous years, and we decided to exclude these companies from next calculation. This problem was associated with 44 companies.

After exclusion of these barriers, our data set consists of 8532 Slovak companies.

4.3 Statistical Testing of Significance of Potential Sources of Company's Goodwill

In this paper, we defined two basic aims. The first aim was to calculate residual income. The secondary aim of this paper is to discover the statistically significant variables, which could be considered as the sources of company's goodwill. As a statistical method for determination of the significant sources of company's goodwill, we used multiple linear regression. Because we tried to determine sources of company's goodwill, we had to exclude companies, which did not create residual income. In our data set of 8532 Slovak companies, 4469 companies did not create residual income. After exclusion of companies with negative residual income, our data set consists of 4063 Slovak companies. This amount of companies enters into the multiple linear regression.

For multiple linear regression, we used statistical program XLSTAT section modelling data/linear regression. We had to verify the hypothesis about the significance of the correlation coefficient. As the test of significance for the individual parameters, we used partial t-test. We formulated two-tailed hypotheses:

H_0 $\beta_i = 0$ there is not significant relationship between variables.

H_1 $\beta_0 \neq 0$ there is significant relationship between variables.

Table 4 Output of multiple linear regression in data set of 4469 Slovak companies in 2015

Model variables	β coefficient	Standard error	$|t|$	$t_{\alpha,n-2}^{crit}$	p-value	Upper limit (95%)	Lower limit (95%)
Intercept	−11,321	3006.65	−4243	1965	<0.0001	−18,664.7	−6848.2
ROE	41,530	6261.94	7271	1965	<0.0001	33,225.7	57,835.9
NI	1.14	0.05	21,768	1965	<0.0001	1.0	1.2
RE	0.08	0.03	3486	1965	0.001	0.0	0.1
VR	9.61	2.73	4618	1965	<0.0001	7.2	18.0
MC	0.19	0.08	3774	1965	0.000	0.1	0.4
INV	10.34	6.35	2100	1965	0.036	0.9	25.8

Test statistic has following form:

$$t = \frac{b_1}{s_{b1}} \tag{4}$$

where s_{b1} is the standard error of regression coefficient b_1:

$$s_{b1} = \frac{s_{res}}{\sqrt{\sum_{i=1}^{n} x_i^2 - \frac{1}{n} \times \left(\sum_{i=1}^{n} x_i \right)^2}} \tag{5}$$

We rejected hypothesis H_0 on the significance level α; if the value of t test statistic is higher than the critical value of t statistic $t_{\alpha,n-2}$, it means the critical value of student t-distribution with n − 2 degree of freedom on the significance level $\alpha = 0.05$ (Kliestik and Majerova 2015).

We defined following decision rules:

1. $|t| \geq t_{\alpha,n-2}^{crit}$, we reject hypothesis H_0, and we accept hypothesis H_1; there is significant relationship between variables.
2. $p - \text{value} \leq \alpha$, we reject hypothesis H_0, and we accept hypothesis H_1; there is significant relationship between variables.

Output of multiple linear regression is shown in Table 4.

Based on the results of multiple linear regression in Table 4, we can state that we were able to discover statistically significant sources of company's goodwill. Significant relationship exists between residual income and variables return on equity, net income, retained earnings from previous years, valuable rights, and marketing costs and investments into the property, plant, and equipment.

5 Discussion

The first aim of this paper was to calculate residual income. The secondary aim of this paper was to discover the statistically significant variables, which could be considered as the sources of company's goodwill. We achieved first aim of this paper in the chapter results where we managed to calculate residual income. In the process of residual income calculation, we worked with an assumption that residual income represents the difference between net income and equity charge. Equity charge represents the product of the cost of equity and the book value of equity. In addition, according to the scientific literature, we determined that the value between the market value of company and the book value of company is caused by residual income. Subsequently, we proposed that this difference could be caused by company's goodwill. For this reason, we defined the value of company's goodwill as the amount, which is equal to company's residual income. Elementary variables, which have impact on the value of company's goodwill, are earnings after taxes, cost of equity, and book value of equity (we calculated residual income from these variables). However, we tried to find other variables, which could have impact on the company's goodwill, according to the robust analysis of domestic and foreign scientific literature. Based on these assumptions, we tried to achieve the second aim of this paper—to discover the statistically significant variables, which could be considered as sources of company's goodwill. For discovery of statistically significant relationship between variables, we used multiple linear regression. Multiple linear regression showed that from the 14 potential sources of company's goodwill, statistically significant sources of company's goodwill are return on equity, net income, retained earnings from previous years, valuable rights, and marketing costs and investments into the property, plant, and equipment.

6 Conclusion

In this paper, we calculated the value of residual income in the Slovak companies. We worked with the data set of 11,483 companies. Because in the process of its calculation we discovered several problems, we decided to exclude these barriers and adjust our sample. Finally, we calculated residual income in the data set of 9005 Slovak companies. Thanks to this calculation, we obtained the first aim of this paper. Subsequently, based on the multiple linear regression, we decided to discover statistically significant variables, which could have impact on the residual income. It means we tried to determine sources of company's goodwill. Based on the literature review, we chose 12 potentially significant variables, which could have impact on the company's goodwill. Subsequently, we calculated these variables in the data set of companies. In the process of their calculation, we also discovered several barriers. We decided to exclude these barriers. After these adjustments, our data set consisted of 8532 Slovak companies. Because we tried to determine sources of company's goodwill, we also decided to exclude companies, which did not create residual income. After this adjustment our data set consisted of 4063 Slovak companies. Thanks to the multiple linear regression, we discovered six statistically significant variables which could be considered for sources of company's goodwill, and we achieved the second aim of this paper.

Acknowledgment This research was financially supported by the Slovak Research and Development Agency—Grant No. APVV-14-0841: Comprehensive Prediction Model of the Financial Health of Slovak Companies.

References

Ballaster, M., Garcia-ayuso, M., & Livnat, J. (2003). The economic value of the R&D intangible asset. *European Accounting Review, 12*(4), 605–633.

Bartosova, V., & Kral, P. (2016). Methodological framework of financial analysis results objectification in Slovak Republic. In *The European Proceedings of Social & Behavioural Sciences EpSBS* (pp. 2357–1330). Selangor.

Cheng, Q. (2005). What determines residual income? *The Accounting Review, 80*, 85–112.

Collins, D. W., Maydew, E., & Weiss, I. (1997). Changes in the value-relevance of earnings and book values over the past forty year. *Journal of Accounting and Economics, 24*, 36–68.

Corejova, T., & Al Kassiri, M. (2016). Knowledge triangle, innovation performance and global value chain. In *16th International Scientific Conference on Globalization and its Socio-Economic Consequences 2016* (pp. 329–336). Rajecke Teplice.

Edwards, E. O., & Bell, P. W. (1961). *The theory and measurement of business income*. Berkeley, CA: University of California Press.

Feltham, G., & Ohlson, J. A. (1995). Valuation and clean surplus accounting for operating and financial activities. *Contemporary Accounting Research, 11*(2), 689–731.

Jakubec, M., Kardoš, P., & Kubica, M. (2011). *Riadenie hodnoty podniku – zbierka príkladov*. Bratislava: Iura Edition, spol. s r.o., Slovak Republic.

Jansky, M. (2011). *The Feltham-Ohlson model: Goodwill and price volatility* (Working Paper). Charles University in Prague, Czech Republic.

Kariuki, B. W., et al. (2013). Testing the residual income valuation model in a Nascent stock exchange: The case of Nairobi securities exchange. *International Journal of Business and Social Science, 4*, 69–77.

Kimbro, M. B., & Xu, D. (2016). The accounting treatment of goodwill, idiosyncratic risk, and market pricing. *Journal of Accounting Auditing and Finance, 31*, 365–387.

Kliestik, T., & Majerova, J. (2015). Selected issues of selection of significant variables in the prediction models. In *Financial Management of Firms and Financial Institutions: 10th International Scientific Conference* (pp. 537–543). Ostrava, Proceedings.

Kliestik, T., Majerova, J., & Lyakin, A. N. (2015). Metamorphoses and semantics of corporate failures as a basal assumption of a well-founded prediction of a corporate financial health. In *Economics and Social Science: 3rd International Conference on Economics and Social Science* (pp. 150–154). Paris.

Kliestikova, J., & Misankova, M. (2016). European insolvency law harmonisation in terms of global challenges. In *Proceedings of International Scientific Conference Globalization and Its Socio-Economic Consequences 2016* (pp. 914–921). Rajecke Teplice, Slovakia.

Liu, J., & Ohlson, A. J. (1999). *The Feltham-Ohlson (1995) model: Empirical implications* (Working Paper). Arizona State University and University of California at Los Angeles.

Marik, M., Čada, K., Dušek, D., Maříková, P., Rýdlová, B., & Rajdl, J. (2011). *Metody oceňování podniku*. Praha: Ekopress, s.r.o.

Ohlson, J. (1999). Discussion of an analysis of historical and future-oriented information in accounting-based security valuation models. *Contemporary Accounting Research, 16*(2), 381.

Peasnell, K. (1982). Some formal connections between economic values and yields and accounting numbers. *Journal of Business Finance & Accounting, 9*(3), 361–381.

Preinreich, G. (1936). The fair value and yield of common stock. *The Accounting Review*, 130–140.

Spuchlakova, E., & Michalikova-Frajtova, K. (2016). Investment certificates as an instrument of structured products. *Ekonomicko manažerské spektrum, 10*(2), 13–25.

Svabova, L., & Kral, P. (2016). Selection of predictors in bankruptcy prediction models for Slovak companies. In *10th International Scientific Conference International Days of Statistics and Economics* (pp. 1759–1768). Prague.

Vochozka, M. (2010). Development of methods for comprehensive evaluation of business performance. *Politicka ekonomie, 58*(5), 675–688.

Zelenka, V. (2006). *Goodwill principy vykazování v podniku*. Praha: Ekopress, s.r.o.

Social Choice and Multicriterion Decision-Making: Decision Modeling Career of Students in Secondary Education Using Multicriteria Analysis

Ioannis Dimitrakopoulos and Kostas Karamanis

Abstract The aim of this paper is to offer an applicable evaluation framework relating to the right choice of one's profession via his/her studies. The first part of the paper consists of the basic principles of multicriteria decision-making. To begin with, the paper initially focuses on the MACBETH method. This helps to provide a perspective for procedural types of decisions in which various qualitative and quantitative aspects are incorporated. In the second part of the paper, the abovementioned multicriteria method is applied to a "real-world" case concerning a specific case of a student, Eva. For this specific study, it is concluded that the factors of greatest importance that lead to choosing the university Eva finally chose were four: the cost of undergraduate studies, the reputation-status of the university, its logistics and infrastructure, and its interconnections with other universities and other academic institutions.

Keywords Social science · Personnel management · IT management · Multicriteria decision-making · MACBETH method · Career

1 Introduction

According to the theories of occupational decision-making and development, it is maintained that the optimal decisions are based upon sound stances-behaviors leading to the right choice of career which in turn offer stability and satisfaction in one's life (Hilton 1962; Gelatt 1962; Tiedeman and O'Hara 1963; Katz 1963; Vroom 1964; Kaldor and Zytowsky 1969; Harren 1979; Gati 1986). Deciding on what career to follow is twofold consisting of the mechanism of choice and the outcome of this mechanism, that is, the decision or choice. One of the most popular approaches

I. Dimitrakopoulos · K. Karamanis (✉)
Technological Educational Institute of Epirus, Preveza, Greece
e-mail: kkaraman@teiep.gr

© Springer Nature Switzerland AG 2019
N. Sykianakis et al. (eds.), *Economic and Financial Challenges for Eastern Europe*,
Springer Proceedings in Business and Economics,
https://doi.org/10.1007/978-3-030-12169-3_9

to studying educational intention is the theory of planned behavior. The underlying assumption of the theory is that behavior is under volitional control, namely, personal attraction to the behavior, subjective norms, and perceived behavioral control explain much of the variance in intention and, in turn, explain a significant amount of behavioral variance (Sahinidis et al. 2014).

Therefore the right choices lead to the rational decision-making when it comes to facing the complexities of life and career matters. Many studies concluded that the factors influencing one in decision-making are grouped as follows (Yip and Côté 2013; Zeelenberg et al. 2008, 1998; Goldstein and Hogarth 1997; Rosenhead 1996):

- *Individual factors.* It is about biological and hereditary factors; acquired, personal factors, ones related to personality, motivation, self-awareness, and self-esteem; as well as factors related to one's beliefs, stance in life, and values or one's personal needs.
- *Background or otherwise nonpersonal factors.* In this case we refer to one's family, school, community, and the circumstances and context one is living that affect the person dramatically in taking decisions.
- *Factors relevant to the decision.* These are external factors that are directly interrelated to the decision itself such as the quality and the quantity of information, the level of risk taking, time anxiety, the possibility of revising one's decision, the possible consequences of the decision, etc.

The three ways according to Harren (1979) in which people usually take a decision are (Leong et al. 1987; Phillips et al. 1985):

- *The rational mode.* People take responsibility of their actions based on their rationale since their actions are conscious and they seek for information relevant to the decision-making; therefore they act responsibly.
- *The intuitive mode.* It focuses on intuition rather than reasoning or rationale. The decisions are spontaneous and require little time and not much information or planning.
- *The reliant mode.* When the decision-making relies on the opinions, wishes, and expectations of others, the reliant mode is used so as to deny any personal responsibility involved because the others are to blame for whatever the consequences of that choice are.

According to Tiedeman and O'Hara (1963), a balanced decision should involve elements of the three modes of decision-making. When a decision is sound and balanced, it takes into account information from internal to external sources. The effectiveness of a decision depends on how well one knows himself /herself and his/her surroundings, environment. As we can notice, the decision-makers generally are influenced by many factors, such as self-interest, personality, and peer pressure (Mousiolis et al. 2015; Fernandez-Huerga 2008; Rocha and Ghoshal 2006; Enns and McFarlin 2003). In the same direction, Li and Davies (2001) deal with some key issues in using and developing information systems for strategic marketing decisions, and they concluded that hybrid intelligent support systems, coupled with such techniques as group decision support and knowledge management, will have a part to play in support of strategic marketing decisions, with the decision-makers as a core and in control. Nikolopoulos (2003) finds out that subjectivity plays a very important role in managerial decision-making. Subjectivity differs in quantity and quality according to the characteristics of the company and the decision-maker and to the kind of decision to be taken. La Scalia et al. (2016) found out that fuzzy technique for order performance by similarity to ideal solution can be a useful decision-making tool combined with the automatable methodology for data acquisition.

There have been significant changes in the global economy during the last 30 years. Since the early 1980s, a series of changes in the economy, social structure, and way of life of peoples took place. It is without doubt, common knowledge, that the decision concerning what kind of studies and career one chooses is one of the most important and determining decisions taken in one's life (Karamanis and Hyz 2016). Due to their age, students differ to one another in terms of readiness to take a sound decision concerning their future career (Super et al. 1996; Crites and Savickas 1995). The occupational development of people is not in line with their mental, physical, social, or emotional development. Therefore, experts on this field should be able to define the readiness of their students who are on the verge of taking a decision concerning their studies and career and further on choosing among the available educational and occupational prospects.

The aim of this paper is the development of such methods and the support of such techniques that will help students take optimal decisions taking advantage of the information available. The resolution of multifaceted real problems with the use of criteria renders the use of suitable "equipment" for decision-making imperative such as multicriteria decision-making. The basic principles of multicriteria decision-making are presented here, and great emphasis is given on the MACBETH method. Based on this joint method, it presents an empirical application for sustainable road planning in choice of one's career by our students.

2 Multicriteria Decision Analysis as a Decision Support System in a Complex Decision-Making Process

2.1 General

During the last decades, we have seen an increasing and widespread use of multicriteria analysis. The multicriteria methods are a complex and multidimensional process, which looks into all the criteria involved in the analytical process of defining the object of decision, construction of the model of preference, and support of that decision combining decisions under circumstances of certainty and uncertainty (David 2009; Siskos et al. 2005; Figueira and Roy 2002; Belton and Stewart 2002; Lahdelma and Hokkanen 2002; Bouyssou et al. 2000; Hokkanen and Salminen 1997; Roy and Bouyssou 1993; Roy 1985). These methods serve to make a complex multidimensional choice problem more transparent. They are usually called multiple criteria methods, and they pay particular attention to major constituents of choice problems, including (Nijkamp et al. 2002):

- The identification of relevant choice options
- The definition of appropriate evaluation criteria (emanating from conflicting objectives)
- Assessment of the numerical value of each evaluation criterion for each choice option
- The collection of measurable prior information about each of the relevant decision criteria (e.g., by means of weights or interactive computer methods)
- The identification of the relevant decision level or of the proper institutional decision procedure (in case of a multi-actor choice situation)
- The specification of a suitable measurement scale for the available information (e.g., ratio, ordinal, or fuzzy information)

The multicriteria analysis is deployed in order to support the decision-making with emphasis on the following (Anwar et al. 2014; Montibeller and Franco 2011; Franco and Rouwette 2011; Franco and Montibeller 2010):

- Both the concept of decision and the process of taking it
- The basic characteristics of the decision as well as its long-term consequences
- The discontinuity characterizing the creation and negotiation of decisions

Thus, the multicriteria methodology for the support of the decision should encompass the following gradual stages (Richard 1981):

(a) Preliminary diagnosis
(b) Choice of fields and criteria
(c) Implementation of this reasoning
(d) Plan selection for execution
(e) Convergence of feedback cycles

The problem of classification during the multicriteria decision analysis (MCDA) is tackled by placing the data of all the alternative actions into categories. The classification is achieved by examining the value of the attributes of these alternatives via predetermined rules. There are three basic categories according to the research approaches of the classification problem in the international bibliography (Manski 1980, 2004; Mcfadden 1981):

- Statistics and econometrics
- Nonparametric
- Direct and indirect

Nowadays there is plurality in terms of methods of multicriteria analysis. The most widely used techniques of such analysis require judgment and reason and differentiate in the way they combine the data with the result. Because of the bulk of complex information, the aim of these techniques is to confront the difficulties the decision-makers face in handling this information with consistency and reason. The applied techniques of multicriteria analysis can be used to define the most attractive choice, to classify the criteria, to numerate a limited number of choices, and to separate acceptable from unacceptable reasoning (Hwang and Yoon 1981).

The application of mathematics in the applied techniques in every multicriteria decision problem focuses on the quantification of preferences and is mainly expressed through the concept of dual relationship. So the adoption of different mathematical models of dual relationships leads to different methodologies. In our days the methods of multicriteria analysis have evolved greatly due to the progress of the main three theoretical classes and other methods which are (Siskos and Spyridakos 1999):

(a) The method based on functional models (theory of usefulness)
(b) Methods based on relational models (outranking relations) among the alternative actions
(c) Interactive methods

We will focus our attention on the MACBETH method that will be concisely discussed in Sect. 2.2.

2.2   The MACBETH Method

The MACBETH method of taking decisions (measuring attractiveness by a categorical-based evaluation technique) was first presented in 1994 (Bana e Costa and Vansnick 1994) and constitutes a development and substantial improvement of the analytic hierarchy process (AHP) of Thomas Saaty. It has been successfully implemented in a wide range of decision problems. Specifically, the decision maker is called upon making comparisons every pair of criteria (pairwise comparisons) and the final model the criteria synthesis is a balanced average of marginal rates/index of attractiveness. The outcome of the attractiveness criteria should envelope the concept of consistent unit concessions (trade-off).

The goal of this method is the creation of quantitative models for the evaluation of the attractiveness of alternative solutions that belong to a finite group A. This is mathematically achieved by the solution of linear programs for the creation of value functions based on a process of question and answers between the analyst and the decision-maker.

We can detect domination relationships among the actions which are expressed in a seven-degree scale. Basically, the scale requires the decision-maker to verbally express the differences concerning attractiveness between two actions (criteria and/or alternatives). To this effect the process of quantification is achieved (Table 1).

The process of questioning and answering is carried out in two stages. First the analyst classifies the data of the decision of the whole in the first phase A in descending order according to the decision-maker's preferences. Then in phase two, the charts which compare the actions in pairs are filled out according to the

Table 1 Scale of difference attractiveness MACBETH

Preference rate (C_k)	Difference of attractiveness	Scale of intensity (k)
C_0	Indifference	0
C_1	Little	1
C_2	Mild	2
C_3	Medium	3
C_4	Strong	4
C_5	Very strong	5
C_6	Extreme utmost	6

decision-maker's preferences in line with the seven-degree scale which is suggested by this method.

We have to take into consideration the following conditions of consistency so that the differences of attractiveness can be expressed (Bana e Costa and Vansnick 1994, 1999):

$$\forall a, b, c \in A \text{ with } aPb \text{ and } bPc \text{ and } \forall k, k' \in \{1, 2, 3, 4, 5, 6\}$$

$$if \ (a, b) \in C_k \ and \ (b, c) \in C_k$$

$$then \ (a, c \in C_k) \ with \ k'' \geq max\{k, k''\}$$

where a, b, and c are the alternatives of the analysis and k, k', and k'' are the rates of the MACBETH scale.

In effect, the preferences among alternatives are defined by the above conditions as follows (de Lima and Damiani 2009): "if alternative a is strongly preferred to alternative b and alternative b is medially preferred to alternative c then the difference of attractiveness between alternative a and b can't be smaller than that between alternatives a−b and b−c."

Consequently, MACBETH method presupposes qualitative judgment/reasoning exclusively, concerning the differences in attractiveness so that the decision-maker can quantify the relevant value of the alternative actions. We are talking about an interactive approach that helps the decision-maker to estimate and evaluate the whole attractiveness aspect (global attractivity) of different actions bearing in mind multiple criteria. The estimation and evaluation of the value (of attractiveness) of the alternatives in question are accomplished through a procedure of posing questions to the person who is going to take a decision—questions dealing with the expression of qualitative bilateral (non-numeric) comparisons of alternatives in a qualitative seven-degree scale as mentioned above.

There has been a tremendous development in the supportive computer software in realizing MACBETH in the recent years (Bana e Costa and Vansnick 1999). The latest development of the computer software (Bana e Costa et al. 2005) allows the modeling of problems and applications of multicriteria analysis and via the use of computer that supports the direct creation of results such as the model of added value that expresses the preferences of the person who decides as well as sensitivity and robustness analysis.

The MACBETH computer software of multicriteria analysis is a very useful tool as it allows:

- Creation of value trees
- Development of descriptive criteria
- Grading of the choices concerning the criteria
- Creation of value functions
- Estimation of the importance of the criteria
- Sensitivity analysis
- Robustness analysis in terms of the relevant and real value of the alternatives

The computer software is available on https://www.m-macbeth.com.

3 A Case Study on Eva's Case

3.1 The Problem

Eva is an 18-year-old high school student living in Preveza. Both her parents are civil servants; she has got a brother, and her parent's financial situation is good. Eva wishes to become an architect, and her parents encourage her to do so. Her performance at school is quite good, and it is as follows:

- Mathematics: 14
- Physics: 15
- Chemistry: 16
- Ancient Greek: 14
- Modern Greek: 12
- Foreign languages: excellent knowledge of French, very good knowledge of English, and good knowledge of Italian

After discussion with the responsible vocational guidance school consultant and her parents, taking into account her strong wish to realize her dream as well, she decides not to sit the Greek general exams and to attend a university abroad instead. Her choice was based on the following data:

1. Her school performance does not allow her to have an entry in relevant of her preferred university in Greece.
2. Her parent's financial status gives the green light to her studying abroad.
3. Her good command of foreign languages allows her to study abroad as well.

Eva's dilemma is which university she should attend abroad.

3.2   Application of the MACBETH Computer Software

The MACBETH approach will be applied as it was discussed in detail previously so that a decision will be taken considering the problem in question which is the optimal choice of studies abroad for Eva. Then the data of this application, the analysis, and the resolution are presented, and the final decision is to be taken.

Initially the decision-maker has to set the criteria upon which the attractiveness of the student's decision will be evaluated. These attractiveness criteria upon which Eva's decision was evaluated are the following four (4) which are illustrated in the tree of values we created in M-MACBETH:

1. k_1—cost of studies abroad
2. k_2—reputation of the university
3. k_3—logistic infrastructure
4. k_4—interconnections with other universities and institutions

Defining the criteria allows subsequently that the nodes, the value tree of criteria and the three alternative options the student has, are registered: University U-F, University U-E, and University U-I as in:

$$U - F = \{University\ in\ France\}$$
$$U - E = \{University\ in\ England\}$$
$$U - I = \{University\ in\ Italy\}$$

In Fig. 1 you can see the nodes, the value tree of criteria and the relevant options/ choices.

The properties of the nodes of the value tree are defined as:

- *Criterion k_1—cost of undergraduate studies*: It involves tuition fees and relevant costs such as that of accommodation, transportation, and eating. This criterion is described quantitatively ranging from 10,000 € (the most attractive option) to 30,000 € (the least attractive option) per year (Fig. 2).
- *Criterion k_2—the reputation (status) of the university*: It refers to the international recognition of the university, the quality of its syllabus, the professional standing of its professors, the multiannual tradition of the establishment, and the possibility of realizing postgraduate studies or a doctoral degree (Fig. 3).
- *Criterion k_3—logistics infrastructure*: It denotes the availability and accessibility of logistics infrastructure such as technological or computing infrastructure (computer labs, databases) reference works, a library (Fig. 4).
- *Criterion k_4—interconnections with other universities and scientific institutions*: This refers to how flexible the university is in terms of interconnecting and cooperating with other national and international educational institutions and universities as well as scientific institutions (Fig. 5).

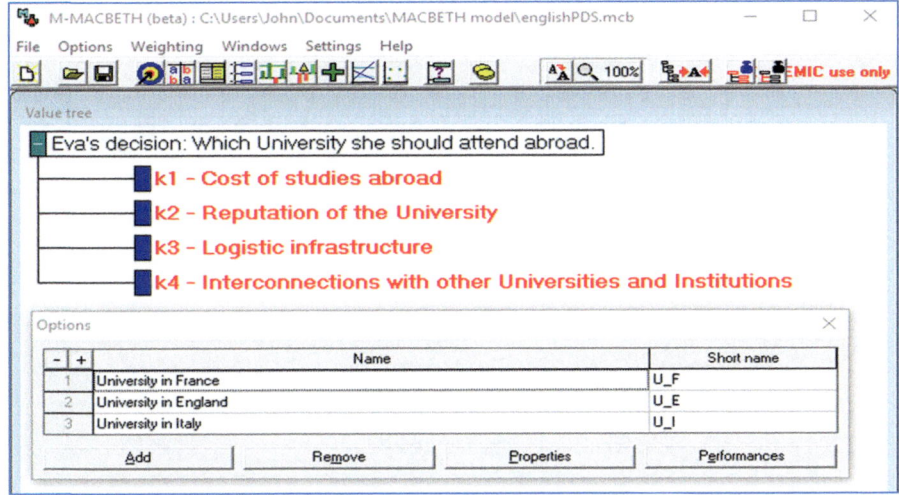

Fig. 1 Nodes, the value tree of criteria and the relevant options/choices

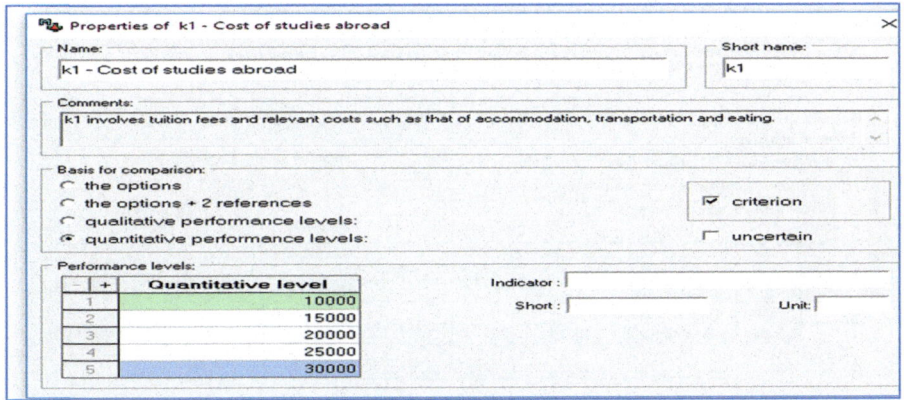

Fig. 2 Properties of k_1—cost of undergraduate studies

The evaluation of criteria k_2, k_3, and k_4 is described in a qualitative manner. Thus, the person who is to take a decision gives to each option one and only one description for each criterion.

Then the Fig. 6 of performances is registered. For example, the option U-F (University in France) was linked by the analyst as follows: 22,000 € costs, REPU-TATION 1—R1 (long tradition in architectural studies, a great number of prestigious professors, many possible mentors, the international status of the university very good), LOG. INFRASTRUCTURE 1—INF1 (very well-equipped laboratories, availability of technological or computing infrastructure, databases, library), and

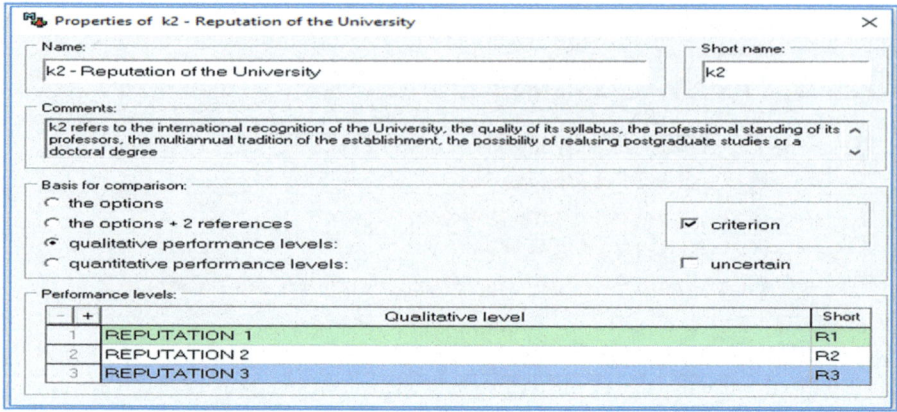

Fig. 3 Properties of k_2—the reputation of the university

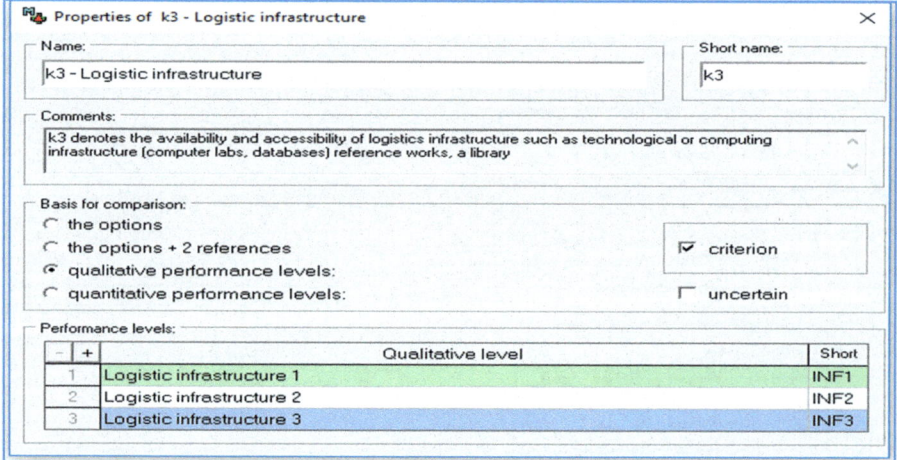

Fig. 4 Properties of k_3—logistics infrastructure

INTERCONNECTIONS 3 (lectures during the morning; the courses are carried out in French; alternative language, English).

The difference in attractiveness for the criterion related to the cost of undergraduate studies (judgment) is defined as such: the most attractive and the least attractive levels are compared to the next level of attractiveness, the less attractive level. Then the most attractive level is compared to all the other levels, and afterward the most attractive is compared to the second most attractive level, and then the second is compared to the third, and so on and so forth. The verbal scale is formed separately for each criterion depending on the range and the gap/difference of ratings (5000 €). In case the ratings are exactly the same, there is no comparison carried out between

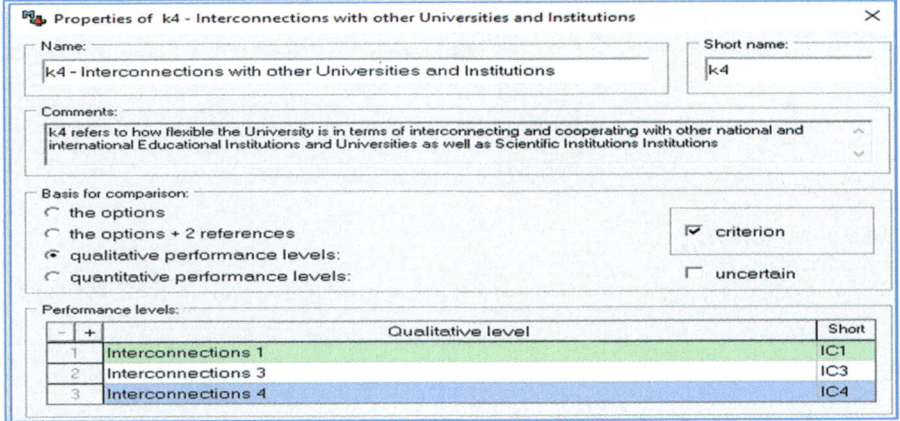

Fig. 5 Properties of k_4—interconnections of the university

Options	k1	k2	k3	k4
U_F	22000	R1	INF1	IC3
U_E	12000	R2	INF2	IC1
U_I	26000	R3	INF3	IC4

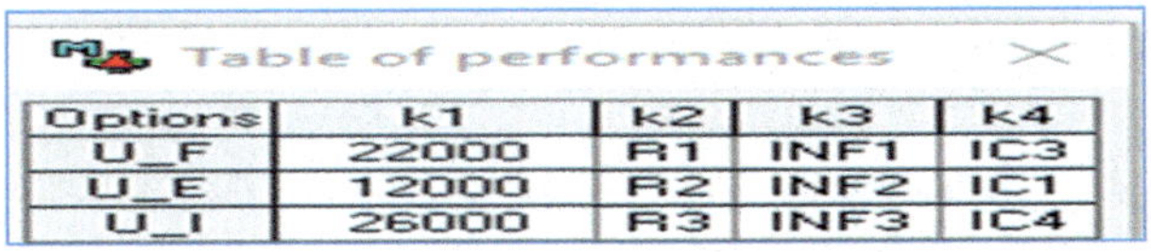

Fig. 6 Table of performances

k1 - Cost of studies abroad

	10000	15000	20000	25000	30000	Current scale
10000	no	moderate	strg-vstr	extreme	vstrg-extr	100.00
15000		no	moderate	strg-vstr	extreme	76.92
20000			no	strong	v. strong	53.85
25000				no	moderate	23.08
30000					no	0.00

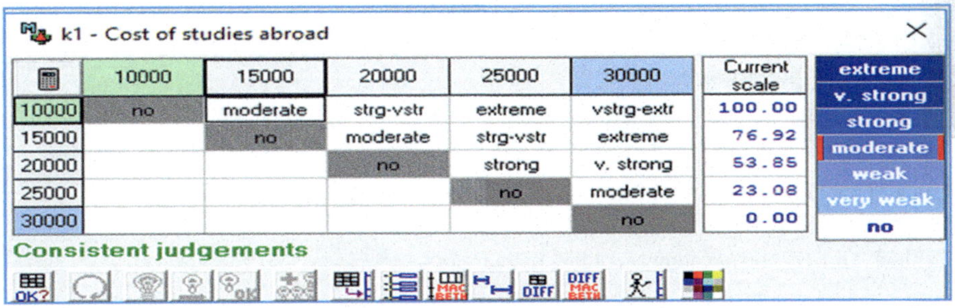

Fig. 7 Differences of attractiveness k_1—cost of undergraduate studies

them because there's no issue of difference in attractiveness. Figure 7 depicts the differences of attractiveness for criterion k_1—cost of undergraduate studies.

Based on the patterns of decisions for the differences of attractiveness in criteria, the MACBETH computer software forms a pericardial scale that can be evaluated in linear representation. Figure 8 represents the pericardial linear scale for criterion k_1.

The decision-maker was asked to classify the criteria from the most important to the least important (Table 2) and to fill in the twofold criteria comparisons (Fig. 9) as these are expressed in the MACBETH evaluation scale in order to estimate the

Fig. 8 Pericardial scale for criterion k_1

k1 - Cost of studies abroad	Current scale	MACBETH anchored	MACBETH basic
10000	100.00	100.00	13.00
15000	76.92	76.92	10.00
20000	53.85	53.85	7.00
25000	23.08	23.08	3.00
30000	0.00	0.00	0.00

Table 2 MACBETH evaluation scale

C_0	No difference
C_1	Very weak difference
C_2	Weak difference
C_3	Moderate difference
C_4	Strong difference
C_5	Very strong difference
C_6	Extreme difference

Weighting (Eva's decision: Which University she should attend abroad.)						Current scale	
	[k1]	[k2]	[k3]	[k4]	[all lower]		extreme
[k1]	no	moderate	moderate	strong	v. strong	43.48	v. strong
[k2]		no	moderate	moderate	moderate	30.43	strong
[k3]			no	weak	moderate	17.39	moderate
[k4]				no	weak	8.70	weak
[all lower]					no	0.00	very weak
							no

Consistent judgements

Fig. 9 Twofold comparisons of the criteria in the MACBETH evaluation scale

Table 3 Criteria classification according to their importance

1	k_1	Cost of studies abroad
2	k_2	Reputation of the university
3	k_3	Logistic infrastructure
4	k_4	Interconnections with other universities and institutions

importance of the four criteria (Table 3). The result of this is the importance of the criteria (Fig. 10).

In order to specify and define the importance of the criteria, twofold comparisons are carried out and are expressed in the MACBETH evaluation scale. Initially the decision-maker is asked to evaluate his option which is neutral to each and every one of the criteria and respond by qualitative judgments in questions like: "in the overall

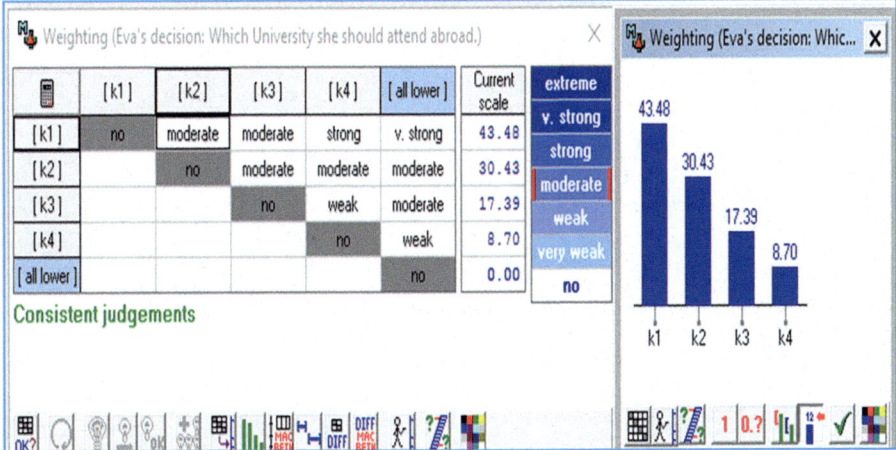

Fig. 10 Chart of attractiveness and scale of importance

Table 4 Importance of criteria

	Criterion	Weighting factor
k_1	Cost of studies abroad	43.48
k_2	Reputation of the university	30.43
k_3	Logistic infrastructure	17.39
k_4	Interconnections with other universities and institutions	8.70

differences of attractiveness of each criterion, how much should a situation which is neutral be placed further on, in order to be classified as attractive?" Then the analyst is called upon to compare the most attractive situation with the next following most attractive situation, by answering the question of how much more attractive a situation is from neutral to better from one criterion to another. The comparisons of attractiveness among the criteria as well as the results of their importance are very well portrayed in the software (Fig. 10).

3.3   Final Results and References

Based on all the above, we've come up with a chart of all the sub-ratings of each criterion (Table 4).

Figure 11 gives us the final results of the candidates' choices as these were derived by M-MACBETH. In the table of scores, we see the total scoring/rating each prospective university gathered keeping in mind the sub-ratings in each criterion. We note that the University in France (U-F) gets the highest score (69.61), the University in England comes second (U-E) with a small difference in scoring (68.66), and last is the University in Italy (U-I) with a very low score (8.03).

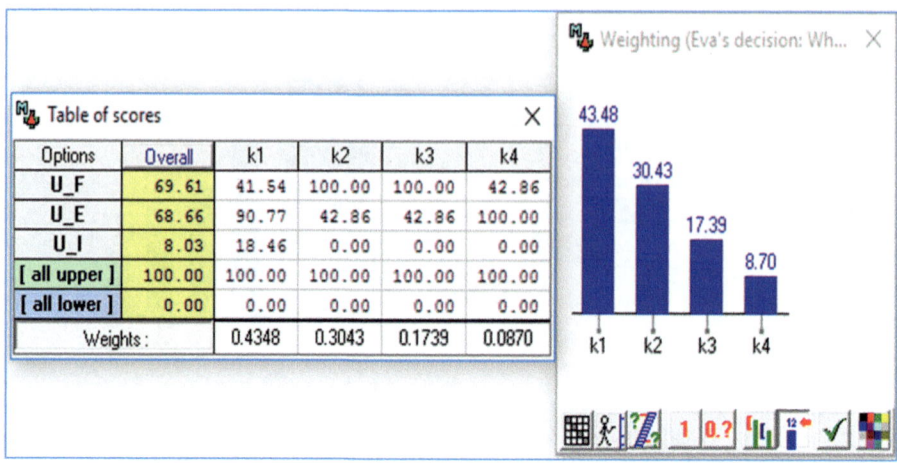

Fig. 11 Final table of scores and performance (weighting) of the best university

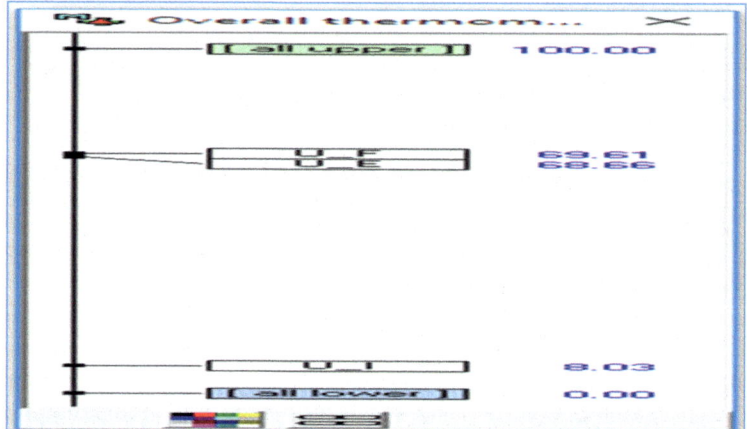

Fig. 12 Overall thermometer

The above results are also depicted in the overall thermometer where we see that the universities U-F and U-E dramatically differ from university U-I (Fig. 12).

The concept of sub-importance each candidate gives to a specific criterion is depicted in the bar graph of performance relating to the prospective options (U-F, U-E, U-I). Taking into consideration the bar graphs and the university profiles, we notice that U-F has achieved the highest relatively score in two criteria, k_2—university reputation—and k_3, logistics infrastructure, and falls short with almost the same scoring in criteria k_1 and k_4. Although U-A has achieved the highest score in one criterion k_4—interconnections with other universities and academic institutions—and reached excellence in k_1, cost of undergraduate studies, it still falls short

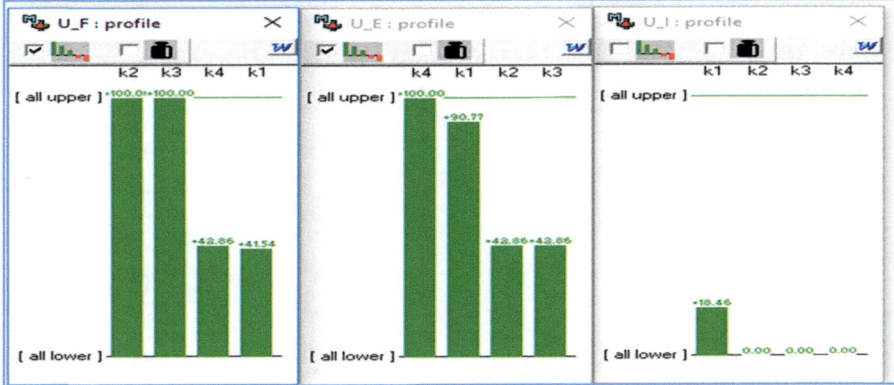

Fig. 13 Profile U-F, U-E, and U-I classified per criterion

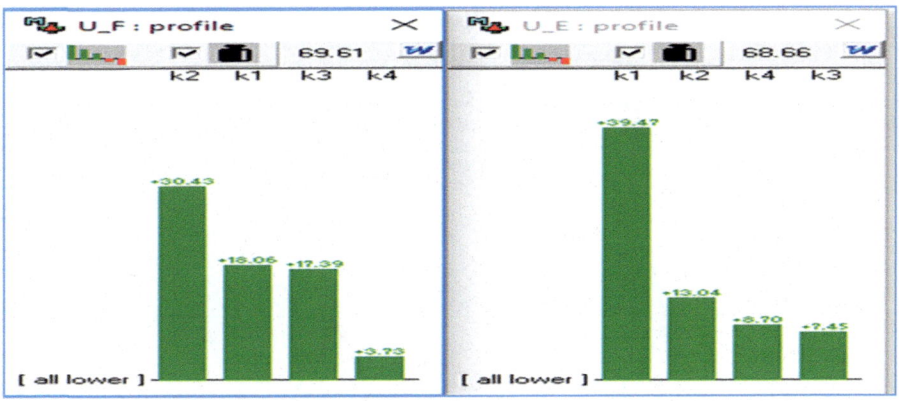

Fig. 14 Bar graph of U-F, U-E, and U-I along with weights

significantly in criteria k_2 and k_3 (42.86). Finally, U-I has zero scoring in k_2, k_3, and k_4 and very low scoring in k_1 (18.46) (Fig. 13).

In the bar graph (Fig. 14), each bar of choice correlates to weight-result of the criterion and the university scoring U-F and U-E. Therefore, the profile relating to weights represents the individual importance the scorings/ratings of each criterion hold in relation to the overall scoring of the criterion, and this is depicted in the upper part of the bar graph, which in our case is 69.61 and 68.66 respectively.

Additionally, on evaluating the results, the computer software enables us to compare the first and second candidate universities U-F and U-E. The positive differences depicted in green color in the first bar graph denote the criteria (k_2, k_3) for which the first university beats per choice the second. Orange color is used to specify the criteria (k_1, k_4) in the bar graph with which U-E is better than U-F (Fig. 15).

Fig. 15 Bar graph of differences of U-F and U-E

Fig. 16 Bar graph of differences of U-F and U-E with weights

The bar graph (Fig. 16) with the weighted bars that enables us to analyze the range in which the differences counterbalance or not in favor of the first choice that is U-F or the second choice U-E. The total is shown automatically on the top right part of the bar graph and is 0.95.

The software enables us to observe the outcome of the model in graphic representations in the form of XY map. These graphic representations help us compare the scores of choices in two criteria or group criteria. At the same time, the effective border for each case we examined is depicted by the red line with all the efficient solutions. Some indicative combinations are presented in Figs. 17, 18, and 19.

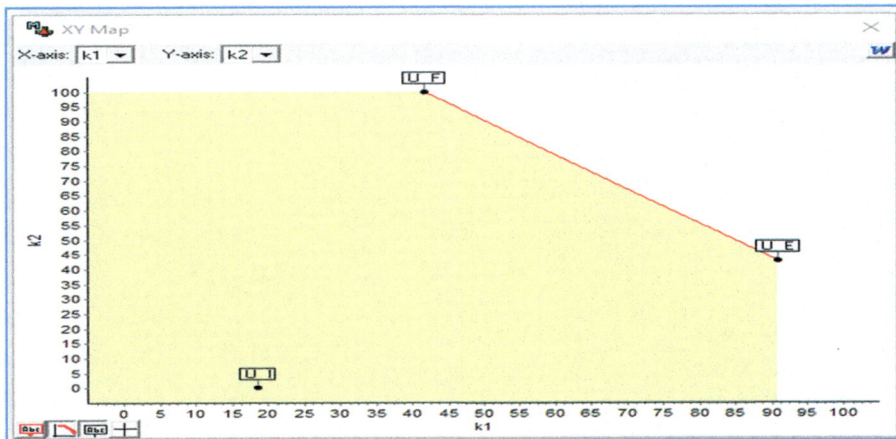

Fig. 17 Graphic depiction of the cost criterion k_1 in relation to the reputation criterion k_2

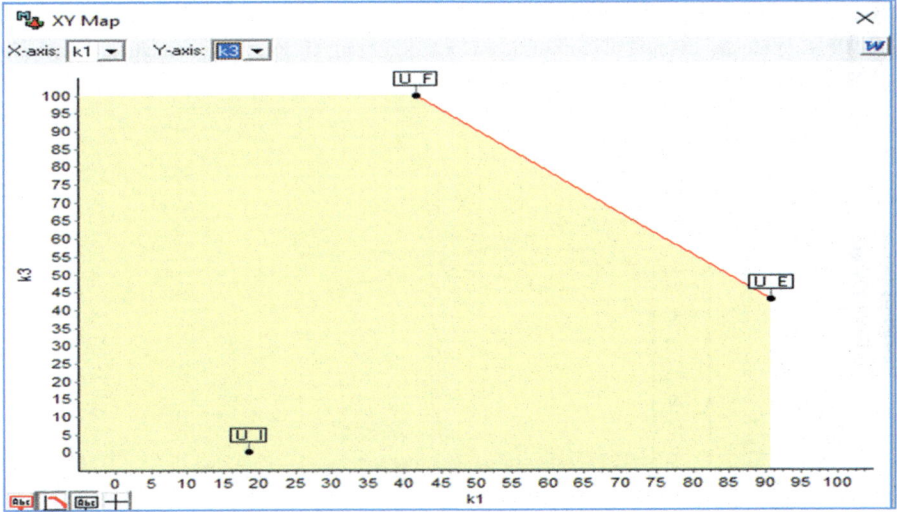

Fig. 18 Graphic depiction of the infrastructure criterion k_3 in relation to the cost criterion k_1

3.4 Sensitivity Analysis

This kind of analysis allows us to detect how the rate of each criterion changes when the total value of the options changes. Its application to one criterion gives us the visual perception of the range, the width, in which the model's suggestion would change as a result of the changes occurring at the expense of the criterion.

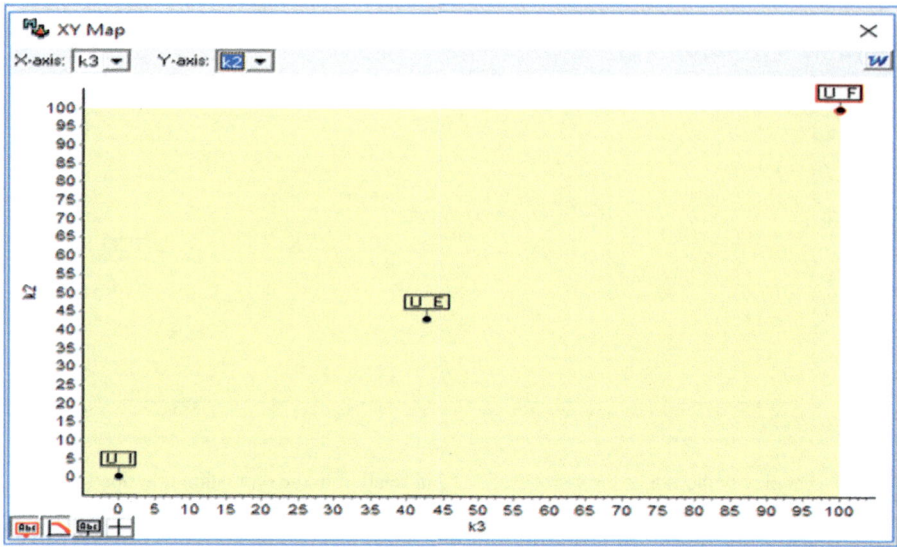

Fig. 19 Graphic depiction of the infrastructure criterion k_3 in relation to the reputation criterion k_2

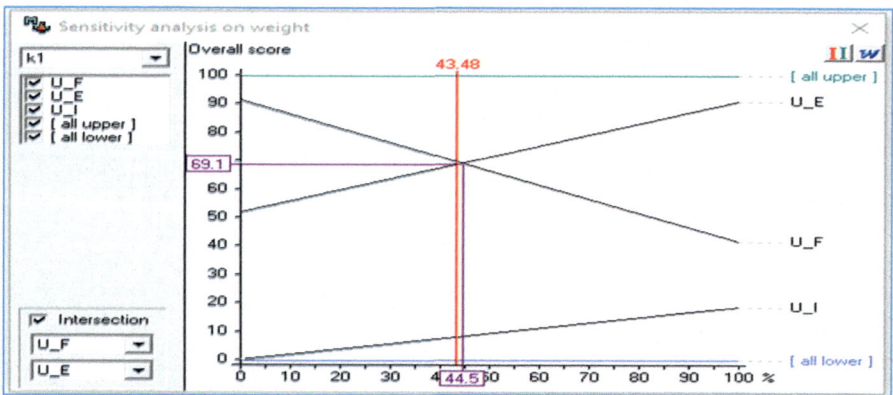

Fig. 20 Sensitivity analysis concerning the cost criterion

The line of each choice in the graph shows the differential in the total scores of the choices, when the weight of the criterion ranges from 0 to 100%. The vertical red line represents the current weight of the criterion (Figs. 20, 21, 22, and 23).

The detection of weight which causes change in the classification of total attractiveness with the use of sensitivity analysis of U-F and U-E in the criterion of cost of undergraduate studies can be analyzed in the following way.

The overall scores are crossed on the point 44.5 and 69.1. This indicates that the lesser the weight is given on k_1 than 44.5, the better scoring U-F will get. However, if the weight given on the cost increases over 44.5, then the U-F will receive better total

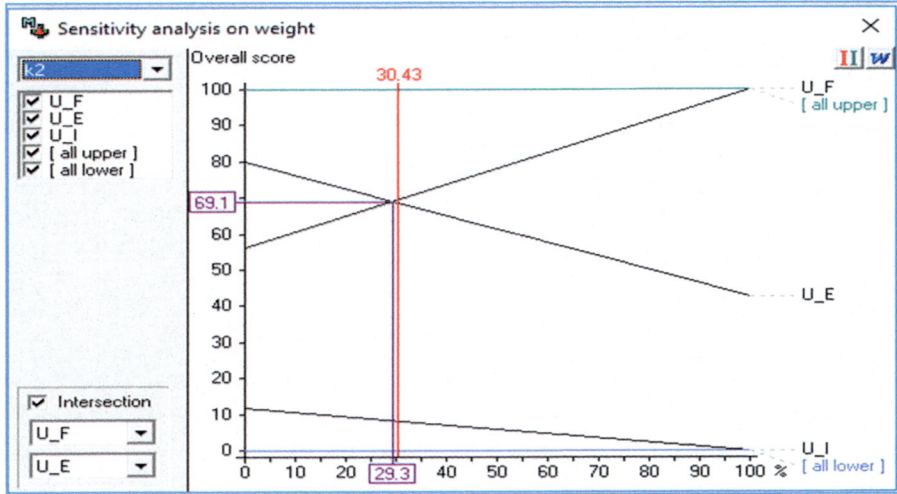

Fig. 21 Sensitivity analysis of the reputation criterion

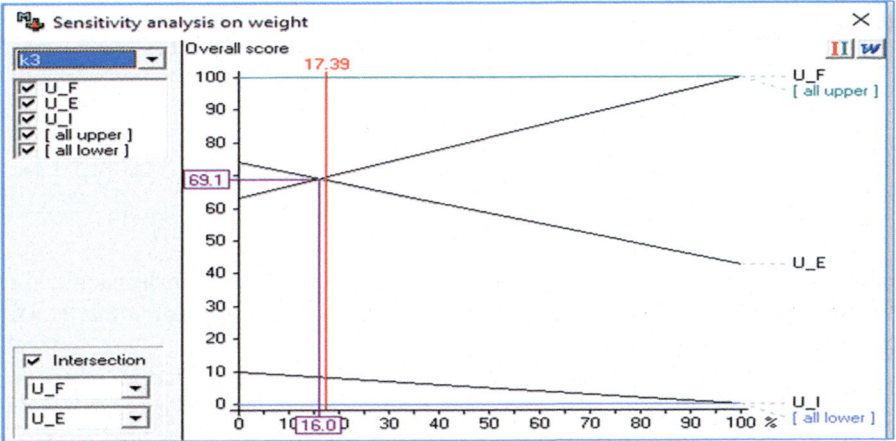

Fig. 22 Sensitivity analysis of the logistics-infrastructure criterion

scoring. If the lines of two options are not crossed, the one option is always more attractive than the other, whatever weight might be given to them. We can make relative comparisons with other criteria, respectively.

3.5 Robustness Analysis

When taking decisions, it would be useful to define the range of making deductions of the quantity of the information due to different degrees of inaccuracy or

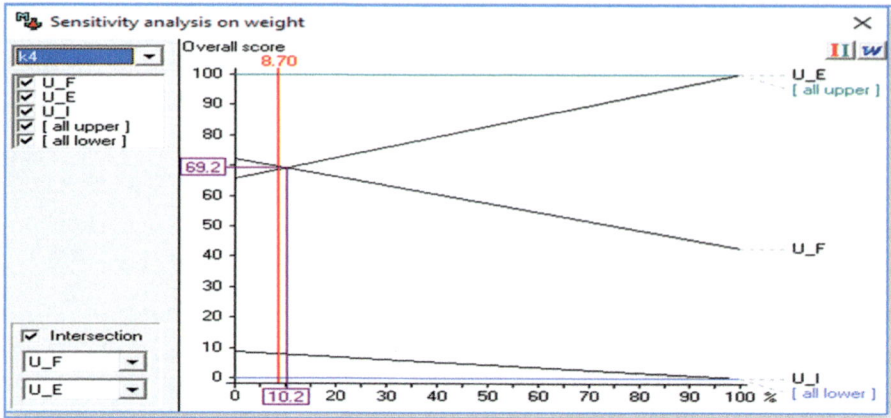

Fig. 23 Sensitivity analysis of the logistics-infrastructure criterion

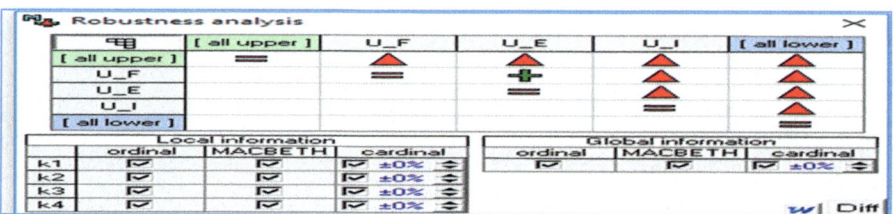

Fig. 24 Robustness analysis (ordinal and MACBETH global-ordinal and MACBETH local information)

uncertainty. This is due to the fact that when making deductions, the decision-taking process often leads to uncertain, inaccurate, or incomplete information that is why the robustness analysis is recommended.

In this kind of analysis, the triangle symbolizes dominance, that is, when one option dominates over the other and when the former is as attractive as the latter in terms of the criteria but the former is more attractive than the other in at least one criterion.

The symbol of the cross (✛) symbolizes dominance, that is, when one option dominates over the other and when the former is as attractive as the latter in terms of the criteria but the former is more attractive than the other in at least one criterion. The M-MACBETH software organizes the incoming model information into three types (Fig. 24):

• Ordinal
• MACBETH and
• Cardinal

and two areas:

- (Local) and
- Global information

The ordinal information refers only to the classification excluding whatever information is characterized by differences of attractiveness. MACBETH information consists of conceptual judgments that are introduced to the model, and it does not disassociate possible numerical scales which are compatible with these judgments. On the contrary, the cardinal information denotes the precise, accurate numerical scale evaluated by the analyst. The local information is all the information specifically for only one criterion, whereas the global refers to the weights of the model.

The robustness analysis along with the ordinal, the MACBETH, the cardinal, the global, and local information confirms the additive dominance of U-F in relation to the rest.

4   Conclusions

The present article attempted to develop the methods and support the techniques that will help students take the optimal decision taking advantage of the information available along with the use of multicriteria analysis of decisions. The development of skills in decision-taking is one of the most difficult problems concerning students that have to be tackled in this stage of their life.

The student who has all this information can assess and evaluate all the possible outcomes of his/her options and can process the importance of various options so as to choose the best solution. One crucial decision students of secondary education are asked to take is what kind of educational and occupational studies they will follow and what career to choose. Choosing to further one's education by attending a university abroad for undergraduate studies is a complex process since multidimensional decisions have to be taken in that respect.

We examined a specific case of a student, Eva, who chooses the University of France via the application of MACBETH software. For this specific study, the factors of greatest importance that lead to choosing the university Eva finally chose were four: the cost of undergraduate studies, the reputation-status of the university, its logistics and infrastructure, and its interconnections with other universities and other academic institutions. MACBETH software is a clever and relatively practical tool for making decisions simple or complex in the field of multicriteria analysis. It is worth mentioning also that this software is a very useful tool, enabling the decision-maker in registering, evaluating, and analyzing the options based on choice-criteria depending on each case every time. The education received by undergraduate studies is a long-lasting process which requires great commitment on the part of the prospective candidates in universities so that this (education) is substantial and effective for their future career and is therefore defined by many factors.

There is an abundance of software in the field of multicriteria analysis, which are used as useful tools in decision-making. We have to take into account though that the way we take decisions does not follow the same pattern and the person who decides has always the last word since there are suitable and unsuitable methods in relation to the problem, the data, and the people involved. The analyst should register, analyze, and evaluate each possible consequence for each possible outcome and each choice criterion for alternative solutions and actions relating to the problem.

References

Anwar, A., Bwisa, H., Otieno, R., & Karanja, K. (2014). Strategic decision making: Process, models, and theories. *Business Management and Strategy, 5*(1), 78–104. https://doi.org/10.5296/bms.v5i1.5267.

Bana e Costa, C. A., & Vansnick, J. C. (1994). MACBETH: An interactive path towards the construction of cardinal value functions. *International Transactions in Operations Research, 1*(4), 488–500. https://doi.org/10.1111/j.1475-3995.1994.00325.x.

Bana e Costa, C. A., & Vansnick, J. C. (1999). The MACBETH approach: Basic ideas, software, and an application. In N. Meskens & M. Roubens (Eds.), *Advances in decision analysis* (pp. 135–152). Dordrecht: Springer. https://doi.org/10.1007/978-94-017-0647-6_9.

Bana e Costa, C. A., De Corte, J. M., & Vansnick, J. C. (2005). On the mathematical foundations of MACBETH. In J. Figueira, S. Greco, & M. Ehrgott (Eds.), *Multiple criteria decision analysis: The state of the art surveys* (pp. 409–442). New York: Springer. https://doi.org/10.1007/0-387-23081-5_10.

Belton, V., & Stewart, T. (2002). *Multiple criteria decision analysis: An integrated approach.* Dordrecht: Kluwer Academic. https://doi.org/10.1007/978-1-4615-1495-4.

Bouyssou, D., Marchant, T., Pirlot, M., Perny, P., Tsoukiàs, A., & Vincke, P. (2000). *Evaluation and decision model. A critical perspective.* Dordrecht: Kluwer Academic. https://doi.org/10.1007/978-1-4615-1593-7.

Crites, J., & Savickas, M. (1995). Career maturity inventory. California: McGraw-Hill.

David, F. R. (2009). *Strategic management: Concepts and cases.* Upper Saddle River, NJ: Prentice Hall.

De Lima, A., & Damiani, J. H. (2009). *Proposed method for modeling research and development (R&D) project prioritization criteria.* PICMENT 2009 Proceedings, August 2–6, Portland, OR.

Enns, H., & McFarlin, D. (2003). When executives influence peers: Does function matter? *Human Resource Management, 42*(2), 125–142. https://doi.org/10.1002/hrm.10072.

Fernandez-Huerga, E. (2008). The economic behavior of human beings: The institutional/post-Keynesian model. *Journal of Economics Issues, 42*(3), 709–726. https://doi.org/10.1080/00213624.2008.11507175.

Figueira, J., & Roy, B. (2002). Determining the weights of criteria in the ELECTRE type methods with a revised Simos procedure. *European Journal of Operational Research, 139*, 317–326. https://doi.org/10.1016/S0377-2217(01)00370-8.

Franco, L. A., & Montibeller, G. (2010). Facilitated modelling in operational research. *European Journal of Operational Research, 205*(3), 489–500. https://doi.org/10.1016/j.ejor.2009.09.030.

Franco, L. A., & Rouwette, E. A. J. A. (2011). Decision development in facilitated modelling workshops. *European Journal of Operational Research, 212*(1), 164–178. https://doi.org/10. 1016/j.ejor.2011.01.039.

Gati, I. (1986). Making career decisions: A sequential elimination approach. *Journal of Counseling Psychology, 33*, 408–417. https://doi.org/10.1037/0022-0167.33.4.408.

Gelatt, H. (1962). Decision making: A conceptual frame of reference for counseling. *Journal of Counseling Psychology, 9*, 240–245. https://doi.org/10.1037/h0046720.

Goldstein, W. M., & Hogarth, R. M. (1997). Judgment and decision research: Some historical context. In W. M. Goldstein & R. M. Hogarth (Eds.), *Research on judgment and decision making: Currents, connections, and controversies* (pp. 3–65). Cambridge: Cambridge University Press.

Harren, V. (1979). A model for career decision making for college students. *Journal of Vocational Behavior, 14*, 119–133. https://doi.org/10.1016/0001-8791(79)90065-4.

Hilton, T. (1962). Career decision making. *Journal of Counseling Psychology, 9*(4), 291–298. https://doi.org/10.1037/h0048309.

Hokkanen, J., & Salminen, P. (1997). Choosing a solid waste management system using multicriteria decision analysis. *European Journal of Operational Research, 98*(1), 19–36. https://doi.org/10.1016/0377-2217(95)00325-8.

Hwang, C. L., & Yoon, K. (1981). *Methods for multiple attribute decision making* (pp. 58–191). Berlin: Springer. https://doi.org/10.1007/978-3-642-48318-9.

Kaldor, D., & Zytowsky, D. (1969). A maximizing model of occupational decision making. *Personnel and Guidance Journal, 47*, 781–788. https://doi.org/10.1002/j.2164-4918.1969. tb03006.x.

Karamanis, K., & Hyz, A. (2016). How flexible working influence unemployment? Evidence from Greek labour market. In P. E. Petrakis (Ed.), *A new growth model for the Greek economy: Requirements for long-term sustainability* (pp. 235–249). Basingstoke: Palgrave/Macmillan.

Katz, M. (1963). *Decisions and values. A rationale for secondary school guidance.* New York: College Entrance Examination Board.

La Scalia, G., Marra, F. P., Rühl, J., Sciortino, R., & Caruso, T. (2016). A fuzzy multi-criteria decision-making methodology to optimise olive agro-engineering processes based on geo-spatial technologies. *International Journal of Management and Decision Making, 15*(1), 1–15.

Lahdelma, P. S., & Hokkanen, J. (2002). Locating a waste treatment facility by using stochastic multicriteria acceptability analysis with ordinal criteria. *European Journal of Operational Research, 142*, 345–356. https://doi.org/10.1016/S0377-2217(01)00303-4.

Leong, S., Leong, F., & Hoffman, M. (1987). Counseling expectations of rational, intuitive, and dependent decision makers. *Journal of Counseling Psychology, 34*(3), 260–265. https://doi.org/10.1037/0022-0167.34.3.261.

Li, S., & Davies, B. J. (2001). Key issues in using information systems for strategic marketing decisions. *International Journal of Management and Decision Making, 2*(1), 16–34. https://doi.org/10.1504/IJMDM.2001.001219.

Manski, C. F. (1980). An empirical analysis of household choice among motor vehicles. *Transportation Research Part A: General, 14*(1–2), 349–366. https://doi.org/10.1016/0191-2607(80) 90054-0.

Manski, C. F. (2004). Measuring expectations. *Econometrica, 72*(5), 1329–1376. https://doi.org/10. 1111/j.1468-0262.2004.00537.x.

Mcfadden, D. (1981). Econometric models for probabilistic choice among products. *The Journal of Business, 53*(3), S13–S29.

Montibeller, G., & Franco, L. A. (2011). Raising the bar: Strategic multi-criteria decision analysis. *Journal of the Operational Research Society, 62*(5), 855–867. https://doi.org/10.1057/jors. 2009.178.

Mousiolis, D., Zaridis, A., Karamanis, K., & Rontogianni, A. (2015). Corporate social responsibility in SMEs and MNEs. The different strategic decision making. *Procedia-Social and Behavioral Sciences, 175*, 579–583. https://doi.org/10.1016/j.sbspro.2015.01.1240.

Nijkamp, P., Torrieri, F., & Vreeker, R. (2002). A decision support system for assessing alternative projects for the design of a new road network: Methodology and application of a case study. *International Journal of Management and Decision Making, 3*(2), 114–138. https://doi.org/10.1504/IJMDM.2002.002468.

Nikolopoulos, A. (2003). Assessing subjective influences on managerial decisions. *International Journal of Management and Decision Making, 3*(3/4), 337–352. https://doi.org/10.1504/IJMDM.2002.002482.

Phillips, T. L., Peppers, R. A., & DeMichele, D. W. (1985). Stratigraphic and interregional changes in Pennsylvania coal-swamp vegetation: Environmental influences. *International Journal of Goal Geology, 5*, 43–109. https://doi.org/10.1016/0166-5162(85)90010-2.

Richard, J. L. (1981). Aid to the strategic decision in SMES. In E. Jacquet-Lagrèze & J. Siskos (Eds.), *Method of multicriteria decision* (pp. 119–142). Paris: Men and Techniques.

Rocha, H., & Ghoshal, S. (2006). Beyond self-interest revisited. *Journal of Management Studies, 43*(3), 585–619. https://doi.org/10.1111/j.1467-6486.2006.00603.x.

Rosenhead, J. (1996). What's the problem? An introduction to structuring to methods. *Interfaces, 26*(6), 117–131. https://doi.org/10.1287/inte.26.6.117.

Roy, B. (1985). *Multicriteria methodology: To aid in the decision.* Paris: Economica.

Roy, B., & Bouyssou, D. (1993). *Multicriteria support to the decision: Methods and case.* Paris: Economica.

Sahinidis, A., Vassiliou, E., & Hyz, A. (2014). Factors affecting entrepreneurs' intention to start a new venture: An empirical study. *International Journal on Strategic Innovative Marketing, 1*, 148–162.

Siskos, Y., & Spyridakos, A. (1999). Intelligent multicriteria decision support: Overview and perspectives. *European Journal of Operational Research, 113*, 236–246. https://doi.org/10.1016/S0377-2217(98)00213-6.

Siskos, Y., Grigoroudis, E., & Matsatsinis, N. F. (2005). UTA methods, in multiple criteria decision analysis: State of the art surveys. In J. Figuera, S. Greco, & M. Ehrgott (Eds.), *International series in operations research management science* (pp. 297–343). New York: Springer.

Super, D., Savickas, M., & Super, C. (1996). The life-span, life-space approach to careers. In D. Brown, L. Brooks, & Associates (Eds.), *Career choice & development* (3rd ed., pp. 121–178). San Francisco: Jossey Bass.

Tiedeman, D., & O'Hara, R. (1963). *Career development, choice and adjustment.* New York: College Entrance Examination Board.

Vroom, V. (1964). *Work and motivation.* New York: Wiley.

Yip, J. A., & Côté, S. (2013). The emotionally intelligent decision maker: Emotion—understanding ability reduces the effect of incidental anxiety on risk taking. *Psychological Science, 24*, 48–55. https://doi.org/10.1177/0956797612450031.

Zeelenberg, M., Van Dijk, W. W., Van der Pligt, J., Manstead, A. S. R., Van Empelen, P., & Reinderman, D. (1998). Emotional reactions to the outcomes of decisions: The role of counterfactual thought in the experience of regret and disappointment. *Organizational Behavior and Human Decision Processes, 75*, 117–141. https://doi.org/10.1006/obhd.1998.2784.

Zeelenberg, M., Nelissen, R. M. A., Breugelmans, S. M., & Pieters, R. (2008). On emotion specificity in decision making: Why feeling is for doing. *Judgment and Decision Making, 3*, 18–27.

Greek Banks Abroad: A Historic Examination

Simeon Karafolas

Abstract Greek banks have a long history of presence abroad; it dates from the beginning of the twentieth century due mainly to the presence of the National Bank of Greece in London related to Greek merchant navy and the Greek shipowners. The important movement of Greek banks abroad began at the decade of the 1960s; it is related mainly to the Greek immigration. Greek banks followed Greek immigrants to the host countries. From the decade of the 1990s, the presence abroad has changed. Greek banks are settled in the Balkan countries because they followed Greek companies to these countries and because they focused to take a part of the local banking market. Banking systems in these countries were created from the beginning presenting big opportunities for the foreign banks. The current economic and financial crisis in Greece had as consequence the reduction of the banking network abroad. The banking presence abroad has not been homogenous neither by the banks implemented abroad nor by the host countries. The form of presence was influenced by the host country's legislation, the parent bank's policy, and bank's economic potential.

Keywords Internationalization · Banks · Greece

1 Introduction

Greek banking internationalization presents an interesting historic evolution on a theoretical and practical matter. It is very much related to the evolution of the Greek economy and society, and in many issues it presents innovative theoretical aspects that differentiate it to other country cases. Banking presence abroad followed

S. Karafolas (✉)
Department of Accounting and Finance, Western Macedonia University of Applied Sciences, Kozani, Greece

© Springer Nature Switzerland AG 2019   149
N. Sykianakis et al. (eds.), *Economic and Financial Challenges for Eastern Europe*,
Springer Proceedings in Business and Economics,
https://doi.org/10.1007/978-3-030-12169-3_10

different reasons during the period from the decade of the 1960s to date by distinguishing three main periods.

The important movement of Greek banks abroad began at the decade of the 1960s; it is influenced by the opening of the Greek economy to the world economy, but mainly it is related to the immigration of Greeks. Greek banks followed Greek immigrants to several continents, in Europe, North America, Oceania, and Africa. From the decade of the 1990s, the presence abroad has changed. Greek banks are settled in the Balkan countries because they followed Greek companies to these countries and because they focused to take a part of the local banking market. Banking systems in these countries were created from the beginning presenting big opportunities for the foreign banks. The current economic and financial crisis in Greece had as consequence the reduction of the banking network abroad. The banking presence abroad has not been homogenous neither by the banks implemented abroad nor by the host countries. The form of presence was influenced by the host country's legislation, the parent bank's policy, and bank's economic potential. Referring to the degree of internationalization (see Slager 2005), the Greek banking presence abroad does not have the same degree as multinational banks (MNB).

The paper will examine three distinct periods of the Greek banking internationalization. These periods are characterized by specific reasons of development and shrinkage. After the introduction a first section examines the forms of presence abroad and the reasons the literature describes for the banking presence abroad. The rest of the study will distinguish the three periods of the internationalization of Greek banks: the first period till the decade of the 1980s with the immigration as the main reason for this movement; the second period where Greek banks follow their clients to the host countries and they try to take part at these new banking markets, mainly in Balkan and East Europe countries; the third period is this of the crisis; during this period the network abroad is reduced partly because Greek banks have to cover capitalization needs by selling affiliates abroad. Conclusions follow the above sections.

2 Forms and Reasons of Banking Internationalization

2.1 Forms of Banking Presence Abroad

Banking internationalization can be either indirect through corresponding banks in host countries or autonomous presence as this paper is interested to do. The autonomous banking presence abroad can be of the following three forms: affiliate, branch, and representative office (Karafolas 2006, 2012):

Affiliate bank is a banking institution, under the law of the host country, in which the parent bank has the majority or the whole of the stock capital. The affiliate may be the result of a new institution or the acquisition of a bank already existing. The affiliate publishes its own balance sheet and income statement.

Branch is directly related to the parent company. It depends on the home country law and the parent bank is entirely responsible for its activities. Branch's activities are registered directly to parent's bank balance sheet and income statement.

Representative office is a bureau created from the parent bank in order to give information on the banking system and economic and political situation of the host and home countries to bank's clients. Contrary to the affiliate and the branch, the representative office cannot provide banking services.

2.2   Reasons of Banking Presence Abroad

According to literature, banking internationalization is based to several reasons. Banks follow productive investments to the host country. In that case banks follow multinational companies in the host countries. Several authors concluded on this relation (Hultman and McGee 1989; Gross and Goldberg 1991; Nigh et al. 1986; Goldberg and Johnson 1990; Yamori 1998). This explanation is called also defensive policy (Williams 2002; Qian and Delios 2008). In some cases, especially in less developed markets such as in former socialist nations, multinational firms can use home banks or a third nation multinational bank (Berger et al. 2003). The defensive expansion may increase multinational size but has little impact upon multinational bank profits according to Williams (2002).

The population movement can be also a reason for the banking expansion abroad since banks follow the immigrant population (Karafolas 1992, 1998).

The growth of trade between the country of origin of banks and the host country has been considered as a principal reason for the banking presence in the host country by several authors such as Goldberg and Saunders (1980), Gross and Goldberg (1991), Bagghi-Sen (1995), and Bassouamina (1999).

Some studies found a positive relation between the exchange rate and the expansion of banks abroad (Goldberg and Saunders 1980; Hultman and McGee 1989).

The local banking market may be a significant reason to attract foreign banks according to its size and opportunities it offers. On this positive relation are concluded numerous studies such as Hultman and McGee (1989), Gross and Goldberg (1991), Bagghi-Sen (1995), Yamori (1998), and Claessens et al. (2001).

The opportunity of the local markets appears very crucial in the former socialist countries, mainly East European countries. The change of economic and social regime destroyed the previous ancient banking system and showed the need of the new banking system. The new system needs the contribution of well-established banks having a strong capital basis and appropriate technology. Balkan countries presented an excellent opportunity for these banks (Karafolas 2006, 2012).

Other studies focused on specific issues as, for example, Qian and Delios; on the case of Japanese banks abroad, note that this expansion permits to *exploit* the intangible assets as managerial and production skills, marketing abilities, and consumer goodwill (Qian and Delios 2008). Buch et al. (2011) notice that through internationalization foreign assets abroad increase the position of the bank at the home market but also increase risks. Focarelli and Franco Pozzolo (2005) notice that lower regulatory restrictions in host countries encourage the creation of subsidiaries by multinational banks.

3 Evolution of Greek Banking Presence Abroad

The decade of the 1960s marks the autonomous internationalization of Greek banks. From the decade of the 1970s, Greek banks began to have a significant banking network abroad. Three main periods are distinguished according to the development of the network, the reasons, and the geographic implementation abroad:

- The first period till the end of the 1980s
- The second period that began the decade of the 1990s
- The third period is placed the period of Greek economic crisis

3.1 Immigration as the Main Reason of Greek Banks Abroad

Contrary to multinational banks of developed countries that followed clients to host countries because of productive investments or international trade, Greek banks followed Greek economic immigrants to host countries. Neither investments nor international trade can explain the Greek banking presence abroad.

Table 1 presents the implementation of Greek banks by host country and form of presence in several years the time period 1960–1986, just before the change of the political and economic regime of East European countries. In some countries we have several forms of presence; in others only the form of affiliate or the representative office. The decade of the 1960s' banking networks were hosted in the United States of America (USA) and South Africa with two affiliates of the National Bank of Greece, the Atlantic Bank of New York (ABNY) and the South Africa Bank of Athens (SABA). Banking networks are hosted in the United Kingdom (UK) and Cyprus under the form of branch and in West Germany and France under the form of representative office. It is quite interesting to notice that the National Mortgage Bank of Greece (NMBG) had in Germany a banking network under this form. In the decade of the 1970s, the network grew up considerably regarding the number of offices, branches, and the new host countries. Three new affiliates were created in France, the UK (NBG's affiliates), and Germany (Emporiki Bank's affiliate). Canada, the Netherlands, Egypt, and Australia were the new host countries of Greek banking network, mainly of the National Bank of Greece. In the decade of the 1980s, the network was extended to three new host countries, Belgium and

Table 1 Greek banking network abroad, by host country and form of presence

	Branches						Representation office						Number of affiliates					
	1960	1965	1970	1975	1980	1986	1960	1965	1970	1975	1980	1986	1960	1965	1970	1975	1980	1986
West Germany				1	1	7		2	3	6	9	9	1	1	1	1	1	1
United States of America				1	2	3			2		1	3		1	1	1	1	1
United Kingdom	1	1	2	3	3	3						1			1			
South Africa													1	1	1	1	1	1
Cyprus	3	3	9	8	11	18												
France								1	1	1	1	1			1		1	1
Canada									2	2								1
Holland				1	1	1					1	1						
Sweden											2	2						
Egypt					1	1				1								
Australia										1	2	2						
Bahrain											1	1						
Belgium												1						
Total	4	4	11	14	19	33	0	3	8	11	17	21	2	2	4	3	4	5

Source: Karafolas (1988)

Table 2 Greek immigrant population, by host countries

	1960	1970	1980
USA	378,586	1,260,515	3,000,000
Canada		125,000	n.a.[a]
Australia	140,089	n.a.	300,000[b]
West Germany	179,000	265,000	297,500
United Kingdom		120,000	n.a.
:of which Greco Cypriots		110,000	150,000
Belgium	26,191	26,647	10,700
Sweden		8000	7400
The Netherlands			4500
France			4500
Egypt	27,500	n.a.	8000
South Africa		33,000	50,000

Source: Karafolas (1988)
[a]Not available
[b]Estimation

Sweden, with NMBG representative offices, and Bahrain because of Greek companies that undertook construction projects in this country.

During this period the following banks had an autonomous banking presence abroad: NBG, Emporiki Bank, NMBG, Agriculture Bank of Greece, Ergasias Bank and Crete Bank, and Macedonia and Thrace Bank. According to the network, we can distinguish them in three categories. NBG by its network approached more than any other Greek bank the character of a multinational bank. NMBG had an important network of offices not authorized to offer banking services. NMBG used these offices to attract immigrants' deposits. If we consider immigrants' deposits, this network may be important for the bank, according to Slager's criteria of degree of internationalization (Slager 2005). The third group includes all other banks; their banking network is limited by the number of host countries and the network.

Main reason for the banking presence is the immigrant population in these countries. As it appears on Table 2, immigrant population is very important in most of these countries. Serve this population in the host countries and collect the saving of immigrants are main reasons for their presence (Karafolas 1988). To this reason we may add the need of presence in London to serve Greek shipowners and Bahrain to serve Greek construction companies.

3.2 The Expansion to New Market of East European Countries

In the second period, autonomous internationalization of Greek banks approaches the characteristics of multinational banks. Since the decade of the 1990s, Greek banks followed the Greek companies who invested mainly to Balkan countries and developed important trade relations. Since this decade Greece is a major investor in Balkan countries (Tsantilas 2009). In the period 1996–2008, Greek investments in South Europe, mainly in Balkan countries, exceeded 16 billion euros (Kathimerini 2010). The extension of Greek banks to ex-socialist countries in particular to Balkan differentiates the strategy they followed the previous period. Tables 3 and 4 give the presence of Greek banks under the form of affiliate and branch, respectively.

During the examined period, the National Bank of Greece had seven affiliates in Balkan countries, including Turkey and Cyprus, on a total of 11 affiliates. These affiliates were created during the decades of the 1990s and the 2000s (Table 3). The same bank opened branches in seven countries; under the exception of the United Kingdom and Egypt, all other branches were opened in Balkan countries during the decades of the 1990s and the 2000s. It is quite characteristic of the policy followed that on 2006 this bank sold its affiliates in New York and Canada in order to buy the affiliate Finansbank in Turkey. The strategy of the bank was to discontinue business in mature markets with limited growth prospects and focus to more dynamic markets of South Eastern Europe (National Bank of Greece 2007, 2006; Karafolas 2006). Emporiki Bank had six affiliates, on a total of seven affiliates, in Balkan and Black Sea countries, all of them created in the decades of the 1990s and the 2000s (Table 3). Piraeus Bank has affiliates in six Balkan and East Europe countries, all of them created in the decades of the 1990s and the 2000s, and only two affiliates in other countries (Table 3). On a total of three branches, one was opened in Bulgaria and two others were opened in Germany and the United Kingdom (Table 4). Alpha Bank has five affiliates in Balkan countries and one other in the United Kingdom. All affiliates were created in the decades of the 1990s and the 2000s. In this period, the bank opened also branches in three Balkan countries (Table 4). Eurobank has affiliates in five Balkan and East Europe countries on a total of six countries (Table 3). The bank opened branches in two other countries, the United Kingdom and Poland (Table 4). Egnatia Bank created an affiliate in Romania in the same period, and Agrotiki Bank had a branch in Germany. It appears that Greek banks based their policy on the extension to Balkan and East Europe countries trying to take advantage of new banking markets and following Greek companies installed to these countries.

3.3   The Reduction of the Network Abroad

The third period is during the economic crisis 2009–2016, and it is very much influenced by the consequences of the economic restrictions imposed to the Greek economy. During this period a strong reduction of the Greek presence abroad took place. It is the consequence mainly of the necessity for the Greek banks to cover the capital needs resulting from financial losses Greek banks had in this period. These losses were the consequence of the recession of the economy that created enormous nonpaid loans and the haircut imposed to the Greek bonds on 2012 (Bank of Greece 2014). Greek banks had to sell some of their affiliates mainly those in Balkan and

Table 3 Greek banks abroad, by host country, 2015

Bank	Country	Affiliate bank	Opening–close[a]	Branches
National Bank of Greece	FYROM	Stopanska Banka	2000	47
	Romania	Banca Romaneasca	2003	45
	Bulgaria	United Bulgarian Bank	2000	117
	Canada	National Bank of Greece (Canada)	1969–2006	10
	Cyprus	National Bank of Greece (Cyprus)	1993	19
	South Africa	The South African Bank of Athens	1954	10
	USA[a]	Atlantic Bank of New York	1953–2006	19
	Turkey	Finansbank	2006–2016	642
	Malta	NBG Bank Malta	2009	1
	Serbia	Vojvodoska Banka NoviSad and NBG Beograd	2006	244
	Albania	NBG Albania	2012	27
Emporiki Bank	Albania	Emporiki Bank (Albania)	1999–2012	3
	Bulgaria	Emporiki Bank (Bulgaria)	1994–2012	7
	Romania	Emporiki Bank (Romania)	1996–2012	7
	Germany	Emporiki Bank (Germany)	1972–2006	4
	Cyprus	Emporiki Bank (Cyprus)	2001–2012	12
	Armenia	Commercial Bank of Greece	2000–2005	1
	Georgia	International Commercial Bank	2000–2005	1
Piraeus Bank	Albania	Tirana Bank	1996	33
	Romania	Piraeus Bank (Romania)	1995	30
	Bulgaria	Piraeus (Bulgaria)	2005	49
	Serbia	Piraeus Atlas Bank	2005	11
	USA	Marathon National Bank of NY	1999–2012	11
	Egypt	Piraeus Bank Egypt	2005–2015	25
	Ukraine	International Commerce Bank	2007	86
	Cyprus	Piraeus Bank Cyprus	2008	14
Alpha Bank	Romania	Alpha Bank Romania	1995	130
	FYROM	Alpha Bank, Skopje	2000	7
	Serbia	Jubanka	2005	86
	Great Britain	Alpha Bank London	1995	2
	Cyprus	Alpha Bank	1998	26
	Albania	Alpha Bank Albania	1998	40
EFG Eurobank	Bulgaria	Eurobank Bulgaria	1998	143
	Romania	Banc Post	2000	151
	Serbia	Eurobank, Beograd	2002	27
	Serbia	Nacionalna Stedionica-Banka	2005	70
	Luxembourg	Private Bank (Luxembourg)	1997	1
	Cyprus	Eurobank Cyprus	2008	8
	Ukraine	Universal Bank	2008–2016	48

(continued)

Table 3 (continued)

Bank	Country	Affiliate bank	Opening–close[a]	Branches
Egnatia Bank	Romania	Egnatia Bank (Romania)	1998–2010	3

Source: Hellenic Bank Association (2016)
[a]Close when the year appears
Notes: In January 2016 the affiliate of the NBG in Turkey, Finansbank, was sold to the Qatar National Bank (Papadogiannis 2016)
In 2015, acquisition of the operations of Alpha Bank's Bulgarian Branch by Eurobank's subsidiary in Bulgaria, Eurobank Bulgaria AD ("Postbank")

ex-socialist countries in order to cover capital needs. Reduction of affiliates is also the result of acquisition and merging of Greek banks (Karafolas 2016). The acquisition of Emporiki Bank from Alpha Bank and the Agrotiki Bank by the Piraeus Bank resulted in the absorption or the sale of their network abroad. By the end of 2012, the network of Emporiki Bank in Balkan countries was sold or absorbed; earlier the network in Germany, Armenia, and Georgia was sold (Table 3). On 2016 and 2017 three main banks were obliged to sale part of their networks. The National Bank of Greece, the main international Greek bank, had to abandon a serious part of its network abroad. The most important loss was the sale of the affiliate Finansbank in Turkey on 2016 (Papadogiannis 2016). On 2017 NBG agreed to sale the affiliates in Bulgaria and Cyprus (Papadogiannis 2017). Piraeus Bank sold on 2012 and 2015 two of its affiliates in New York and Egypt. On 2016 Piraeus Bank sold its affiliate in Cyprus (Naftemporiki 2016). On 2016 Eurobank sold its affiliate in Ukraine. On 2016 Alpha bank sold its affiliate in Bulgaria to Eurobank (Eurobank 2016). Greek banks reduced progressively their presence abroad through the branch form (Table 4). Of the most serious sales considering the number of branches was this of Eurobank in Poland and this of Alpha Bank in Bulgaria.

4   Conclusion

Greek banks have a long history of presence abroad; it dates from the beginning of the twentieth century due mainly to the presence of the National Bank of Greece in London related to Greek merchant navy and the Greek shipowners. The important movement of Greek banks abroad began at the decade of the 1960s; it is related mainly to the Greek immigration. Greek banks followed Greek immigrants to the host countries. From the decade of the 1990s, the presence abroad has changed. Greek banks are settled in the Balkan countries and other ex-socialist countries because they followed Greek companies to these countries and because they focused to take a part of the local banking market. Banking systems in these countries were created from the beginning presenting big opportunities for the foreign banks. The current economic and financial crisis in Greece had as consequence the reduction of

Table 4 Network of branches abroad of Greek banks, end 2015

Bank	Country	Opening year	Number of branches
National Bank of Greece	Albania	1996–2012	6
	Serbia	2001–2006	25
	Egypt	1979	1
	Cyprus	2004	1
	Great Britain	1960	2
Piraeus Bank	Bulgaria	1993–2005	16
	Great Britain	2000	1
	Germany	2000–2003	1
Alpha Bank	Albania	1998	9
	Bulgaria	1995–2016	82
	Serbia	2002–2005	3
	Great Britain	1990	1
Eurobank	Great Britain	1990–2015	1
	Poland	2005–2011	190
Emporiki Bank	Great Britain	2012	1
	Cyprus	2004	
Agrotiki Bank	Germany	1986–2012	1

Source: Idem Table 3
Notes: Two branches of the National Bank of Greece opened one in Bulgaria in 1993 and one in Romania in 1996 have been absorbed by BNG's affiliates. On 2006, NBG's branches in Serbia were absorbed by NBG's affiliate in Serbia. On 2012 NBG's branches in Albania have been absorbed by NBG's affiliate in Albania. On 2005 Piraeus Bank's branch in Bulgaria was absorbed by the bank's affiliate. On 2016, Alpha Bank sold its branches in Bulgaria to the Eurobank's affiliate in Bulgaria Post Bank (Eurobank Bulgaria) (Kathimerini 2016)
On 2012 the branch of Agrotiki Bank was transferred to Piraeus Bank
On 2016 Piraeus bank sold the affiliate in Cyprus to Lebanese investors (Naftemporiki 2016)

the banking network abroad since Greek banks had to face capital needs. The reduction of the network resulted also from the acquisitions policy followed by Greek banks during the crisis period. The banking presence abroad has not been homogenous neither by the banks implemented abroad nor by the host countries. The form of presence was influenced by the host country's legislation, the parent bank's policy, and bank's economic potential.

References

Bagghi-Sen, S. (1995). FDI in US producer services: A temporal analysis of foreign direct investment in the finance, insurance and real estate sectors. *Regional Studies, 29*, 159–170.
Bank of Greece. (2014). *The chronicle of the great crisis.* Athens: Center of Cultural Research and Documentation. Bank of Greece.
Bassouamina, J. M. (1999). Les déterminants de la présence bancaire étrangère en France. *Revue d'Economie Financière, 55*, 99–111.

Berger, A., Dai, Q., Ongena, S., & Smith, D. (2003). To what extent will the banking industry be globalized? A study of bank nationality and reach in 20 European nations. *Journal of Banking and Finance, 27*, 383–415.

Buch, C., Tahmee Koch, C., & Koetter, M. (2011). *Do banks benefit from internationalization? Revisiting the market power-risk nexus.* Received April 3, 2017, from https://www.aeaweb.org/conference/2012/retrieve.php

Claessens, S., Demirguc-Kunt, A., & Huizinga, H. (2001). How does foreign entry affect domestic banking markets? *Journal of Banking and Finance, 25*, 891–911.

Eurobank. (2016). *History of Eurobank.* Received April 20, 2017, from https://www.eurobank.gr/online/HOME/generic.aspx?id=1294&lang=en&mid=

Focarelli, D., & Pozzolo, F. (2005). Where do banks expand abroad? An empirical analysis. *The Journal of Business, 78*(6), 2435–2464.

Goldberg, L. G., & Johnson, D. (1990). The determinants of US banking activity abroad. *Journal of International Money and Finance, 9*, 123–137.

Goldberg, L. G., & Saunders, A. (1980). The causes of US bank expansion overseas: The case of Great Britain. *Journal of Money, Credit and Banking, 12*(3), 630–643.

Gross, R., & Goldberg, L. G. (1991). Foreign bank activity in the United States: An analysis by country of origin. *Journal of Banking and Finance, 15*, 1093–1112.

Hellenic Bank Association. (2016). *Greek banks abroad.* Received January 15, 2017, from http://www.hba.gr/Statistics/List?type=AbroadGreekBanksNetwork

Hultman, C. W., & McGee, L. R. (1989). Factors affecting the foreign banking presence in the US. *Journal of Banking and Finance, 13*, 383–396.

Karafolas, S. (1988). Les banques grecques à étranger, Cahier Monnaie et Financement, Décembre, pp. 121–149.

Karafolas, S. (1992). *Le rôle de l'immigration dans internationalisation des banques (quatre cas: Espagne, Grèce, Italie, Portugal).* Université Lumière – Lyon 2, Lyon.

Karafolas, S. (1998). The migrant remittances in Greece and Portugal: An examination of the distribution by country of provenance and the role of the banking presence. *International Migration, 36*(3), 357–381.

Karafolas, S. (2006). *Activities of Greek banks in Balkan countries: A comparative balance sheet and income analysis between affiliate banks in Balkan countries.* European Regional Science Association Annual Conference, Enlargement, Southern Europe and Mediterranean University of Thessaly, August 30 – September 3, Volos

Karafolas, S. (2012). *The role of the banking affiliates at the Balkan countries for the Greek banks.* Management of International Business and Economics Systems, TEI of Larisa, Larisa, May 25–27. Received March 5, 2017, from mibes.teilar.gr/proceedings/2012/oral/

Karafolas, S. (2016). *Courses on banking environment.* Master of Banking and Finance, Western Macedonia University of Applied Sciences. Received 5 March 2017, from http://eclass.teiwm.gr/modules/document/?course=MBF102 (in Greek).

Kathimerini. (2010). *11,88 billion euros Greek investments in Balkan countries.* Received March 7, 2017, from http://www.kathimerini.gr/383400/article/oikonomia/epixeirhseis/sta-1188-dis-oi-ellhnikes-ependyseis-sta-valkania (in Greek).

Kathimerini. (2016). *Deal completed between Alpha Bank – Eurobank in Bulgaria.* Received March 5, 2017, from http://www.kathimerini.gr/851542/article/oikonomia/epixeirhseis/oloklhrw8hke-to-ntil-alpha-bank%2D%2D-eurobank%2D%2Dsth-voylgaria (in Greek).

Naftemporiki. (2016). *Piraeus Bank: Deal for the sold of the affiliate in Cyprus.* Received April 3, 2017, from http://www.naftemporiki.gr/finance/story/1125855/trapeza-peiraios-sumfoniagia-tin-polisi-tis-thugatrikis-tis-stin-kupro (in Greek).

National Bank of Greece. (2006). *Annual report 2005.* National Bank of Greece, Athens.

National Bank of Greece. (2007). *Annual report 2006.* National Bank of Greece, Athens.

Nigh, D., Cho, K. R., & Krighnan, S. (1986). The role of location-related factors in U.S. banking involvement abroad: An empirical examination. *Journal of International Business Studies Fall*, 59–72.

Papadogiannis, I. (2016, June 16). The sold of 99.81% of Finansbank to QNB was completed. *Kathimerini*. Received April 4, 2017, from http://www.kathimerini.gr/863909/article/ oikonomia/epixeirhseis/oloklhrw8hke-h-pwlhsh-toy-9981-ths-finansbank-sthn-qn (in Greek).

Papadogiannis, I. (2017, January 4). Within 2017 the withdrawal of NBG from Cyprus. *Kathimerini*. Received April 4, 2017, from http://www.kathimerini.gr/890327/article/ oikonomia/epixeirhseis/entos-2017-h-apoxwrhsh-ete-apo-kypro (in Greek).

Qian, L., & Delios, A. (2008). Internationalization and experience: Japanese Bank's international expansion, 1980–1998. *Journal of International Business Studies, 39*(2), 231–248.

Slager, A. (2005). *Internationalization of banks: Strategic patterns and performance*. SUERF Studies 2005/4.

Tsantilas, F. (2009). *Greek investments in Balkan countries*. Diploma thesis for the Master on Business Administration, University of Macedonia, Thessaloniki (in Greek).

Williams, B. (2002). The defensive expansion approach to multinational banking: Evidence to date. *Financial Markets Institutions & Instruments, 11*(2), 127–203.

Yamori, N. (1998). A note on the location choice of multinational banks: The case of Japanese financial institutions. *Journal of Banking and Finance, 22*, 109–120.

Corporate Financial Modeling Using Quantitative Methods

Panagiotis M. Spanos, Christos L. Galanos, and Konstantinos J. Liapis

Abstract The purpose of this research is the application of quantitative methods in corporate financial modeling under uncertainty conditions. Most firms forecast their capital requirements by constructing pro forma financial statements. Pro forma financial statements are the base for using the additional funds needed (AFN) methodology to estimate capital requirements in a deterministic perspective. The question is if AFN methodology can also be employed in volatile financial data conditions, in order to enhance policy-making. By using Monte Carlo simulation and mathematical programming, it was found that the AFN formula is an appropriate methodology to calculate the capital requirements under uncertainty and thus apply any optimization techniques. The expected financial elements usually depend on various factors, so a quantitative range is more useful in financial planning. The importance of this research is that capital requirements forecasting can be used as an envelope of scenarios that can support financial planning and decision-making. Moreover, financial modeling becomes a useful tool in the restructuring planning processes for estimating base, adverse, and best business scenarios.

Keywords AFN · Financial modeling · Capital requirements · Monte Carlo simulation · Optimization

1 Introduction

The query in this research is to find a suitable way to construct a corporate business plan by ensuring the application of pro forma accounting techniques and including the management approach. The classic or deterministic view of financial planning follows individual steps, which drive the decision-making of each administration.

P. M. Spanos (✉) · C. L. Galanos · K. J. Liapis
Faculty of Sciences of Economy and Public Administration, Department of Economic and Regional Development, Panteion University of Social and Political Sciences, Athens, Greece
e-mail: pspanos@panteion.gr

© Springer Nature Switzerland AG 2019   161
N. Sykianakis et al. (eds.), *Economic and Financial Challenges for Eastern Europe*,
Springer Proceedings in Business and Economics,
https://doi.org/10.1007/978-3-030-12169-3_11

Briefly, after analyzing the company's existing financial position, if current yield exceeds or at least is equal to the objectives set by the budgeting processes, then these objectives can be better redefined. On the other hand, if the current yield is below the budget objectives, it is necessary to look for alternative decisions. At this point, individual decision-making models with available data and relevant tests are carried out. The input of these tests sometimes is predetermined, but, in most cases, the key variables of these tests ought to be in volatility. The purpose of this paper is the implementation of the stochastic processes in financial planning and especially on the basis of the AFN model. Budgeting framework is presented as well as the steps of the AFN model, which is an analytical implementation of the AFN formula, demonstrated in a typical corporate example. The AFN formula requires a growing revenue, while the other determinants, such as the retention ratio, remain stable. By constructing pro forma financial statements, the AFN formula is applied as an *AFN technique* in corporate modeling which requires more determinants to be considered, such as cost of capital or free cash flows. This is necessary to set corporate targets, and thus financial modeling becomes a useful tool in the restructuring planning process for estimating base, adverse, and best business scenarios. In order to estimate the range of the previously mentioned scenarios, the Monte Carlo simulation is applied on our model, assuming that the financial data follows the PERT distribution. The PERT probability distribution function gets its name as it uses the same assumption, regarding the mean/norm in program evaluation and review technique (PERT) networks used in project planning. The results show that capital requirements forecasting create an envelope of scenarios to support financial planning and decision-making. Finally, by mathematical programming the optimization technique is used in applying policy-making. Basically, this procedure enforces decision-making in short term periods where econometric models are more difficult to be implemented.

2 The Budgeting Framework

The operation of any company requires continuous capital reinforcement, which is necessary for developing its strategy. This requires planning of action to achieve the purpose (e.g., adding value to shareholders) which the company has established by implementing specific goals (objectives). These objectives should be qualitative, quantitative, or both. The programming of operations can be divided into the operational (1–12 months), the tactical (1–5 years), or the strategic level (over 5 years). Therefore, the management of resources in the operational level occurs in the framework of regular and strategic planning. Quantification of programming expressed in financial figures constitutes (a) the budget when we refer to the operating level (short-term period) and (b) the financial plan when referring to tactical-strategic level (long-term period). In other words, the financial plan of short-term period is the business budget (Sizer 1988). The financial plan is consisted in three levels: (a) the provision of sales growth, (b) the preparation and modeling of

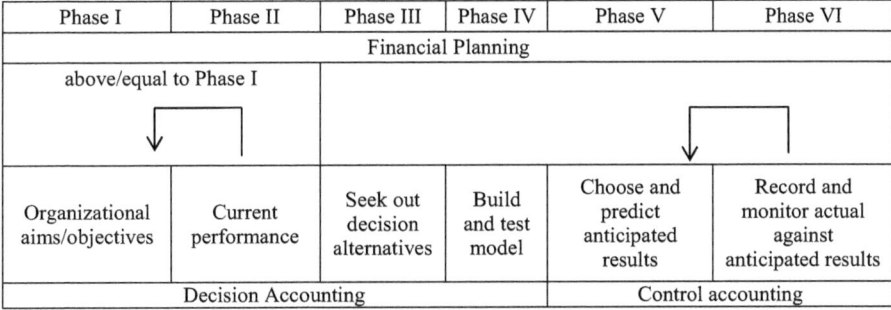

Phase I	Phase II	Phase III	Phase IV	Phase V	Phase VI
Financial Planning					
above/equal to Phase I					
Organizational aims/objectives	Current performance	Seek out decision alternatives	Build and test model	Choose and predict anticipated results	Record and monitor actual against anticipated results
Decision Accounting				Control accounting	

Fig. 1 Phases of financial planning. Source: Wright (1996)

financial statements for budgeting procedure, and (c) the identification of the additional funds needed (AFN). One of the most important steps which are included in the process of financial planning is the forecasting of a company's revenues. For example, revenues can be estimated based on long-term agreements, the trends in the market, the supply conditions, and/or the demand and the share in the market.

The preparation of the financial program requires the process of financial planning. Financial planning includes viewing the projection of financial statements (balance sheet, income statement, and cash flow statement) in which the effects are presented in profitability and financial ratios. According to Wright (1996) financial planning includes six phases (Fig. 1). Loopbacks could be found between Phase II and Phase I in the field of decision accounting and between Phase VI and Phase V in the control accounting field. This specific approach which is analyzed in this paper focuses on the link between control accounting and decision accounting in the financial planning. We place emphasis on the point between Phase V and Phase IV via a stochastic approach, with the implementation of mathematical programming techniques. Therefore, a pre-controlled procedure emerges to create a prediction envelope of anticipated results by testing the models.

3 Budgeting, Key Variables, and Basic Steps

Most firms forecast their capital requirements by constructing pro forma income statements and balance sheets as described in previous chapters. However, if the ratios are expected to remain constant, then formula (1) can be used to forecast financial requirements (Brigham and Daves 2007). This equation under appropriate modification is adjusted in financial statements (Winkler 1994).

$$\text{AFN} = \frac{\text{A}^*}{\text{S0}} \Delta S - \frac{\text{L}^*}{\text{S0}} \Delta S - \text{MS1}(\text{RR}) \tag{1}$$

- AFN: Additional funds needed
- A*: Assets that are tied directly to sales, hence they must increase if sales are to increase. Note that A designates total assets and A* designates those assets that must increase if sales are to increase.
- S0: Sales during the last year.
- A*/S0: Percentage of required assets to sales, which also show the required dollar increase in assets per $1 increase in sales.
- L*: Liabilities that increase spontaneously. L* is normally much less than the total liabilities (L). Spontaneous liabilities include accounts payable and accruals, but not bank loans and bonds.
- L*/S0: Liabilities that increase spontaneously as a percentage of sales, or spontaneously generated financing per $1 increase in sales.
- M: M = NI/S0
- RR: Retention ratio, which is the percentage of net income that is retained or RR = 1 − D/NI

After assessing either the revenues or the sales growth rates, pro forma or projected financial statements are prepared, and the percentage of the revenue growth method is implemented. With this method, most of the data found in the financial statements are expressed as a percentage of sales. The processing of budgeting and modeling statements is performed in Microsoft Excel. It should be noted that the circular repetitive movements require settings as such (Options-Formulas-Enable Iterative Calculations) in Microsoft Excel. Firstly, we define the model input (Table 1), all constant for the forecasting period except for those that represent cash reserves. Following this, we present the forecasted balance sheet (Table 2), the forecasted income statement (Table 3), and the model output in the forecasted period (Table 4) which include key financial data and ratios to be controlled.

Table 1 Model input

Model input	Historical period (t) (%)	Forecasted period (t + 1) (%)
Target of sales		10.00
Depreciation expense % ratio of Net assets	10	10
Tax rate	26	26
Dividends per share growth rate		10
Costs of goods sold as percentage of sales	87.21	87.21
Accounts receivable as percentage of sales	12.50	12.50
Inventory as percentage of sales	20.50	20.50
Interest rate loans	10.19	10.19
Cash target (amount)		14
Accounts payable as percentage of sales	2.00	2.00
Accruals as percentage of sales	4.67	4.67
Net plant and equipment as percentage of sales	33.33	33.33

Source: Own calculations, based on volatility assumptions

Table 2 Forecasted balance sheet

Balance sheet	Historical period (t)	Forecasted period (t + 1)
Assets		
1. Cash	10	14
2. Accounts receivable	375	413
3. Inventories	615	677
4. Total current assets	1000	1103
5. Net plant and equipment	1000	1100
6. Total assets	2000	2203
Liabilities and equity		
7. Accounts payable	60	66
8. Accruals	140	154
9. Notes payable	110	198
10. Total current liabilities	310	418
11. Long-term bonds	754	754
12. Total liabilities	1064	1172
13. Preferred stock	40	40
14. Common stock	130	130
15. Retained earnings	766	861
16. Total common equity	936	1031
17. Total liabilities and equity	2000	2203
18. Required assets		2203
19. Specified sources of financing		2115
20. Additional funds needed (AFN)		88

Source: Own calculations, based on volatility assumptions

The equations from (2) to (7) are the set of mathematical relationships which form the basis for calculating the amount of accounts in the budgeting period (t + 1). Each component of the financial statements should be expressed in the programming period, as:

Cash and cash equivalents (cash and cash equivalents) (C): They are cash, deposits, or expired coupons. These assets are immediately liquidated, and for them to be estimated in the planning, we take as a compliance case a minimum cash reserve (in the example presented in this research paper, we assume $14).

Accounts receivable, trade (receivable) (AR): These are mainly amounts, deriving from sales which have indeed been invoiced but not yet received. It is calculated on the basis of total income (R) according to the relative Eq. (2):

$$AR (t + 1) = \{AR (t)/R (t)\} * R (t + 1) \qquad (2)$$

Inventories (I): It includes mostly finished or semifinished products. These are calculated according to formula (3) :

Table 3 Forecasted income statement

Income statement	Historical period (t)	Forecasted period (t + 1)
1. Sales	3000.00	3300.00
2. Costs except for depreciation	2616.20	2877.93
3. Depreciation expense	100.00	109.99
4. Total operating costs	2716.20	2987.92
5. EBIT	283.80	312.08
6. Less interest	88.00	92.50
7. Earnings before taxes (EBT)	195.80	219.58
8. Taxes (26%)	50.91	57.09
9. NI before preferred dividends	144.89	162.49
10. Preferred dividends	4.00	4.00
11. NI available to common	140.89	158.49
12. Shares of common equity (number)	50	50
13. Dividends per share	1.15	1.27
14. Dividends to common	57.50	63.25
15. Additions to retained earnings	83.39	95.24

Source: Own calculations, based on volatility assumptions

Table 4 Model output

Output	Historical period (t)	Forecasted period (t + 1)
Net operating profit after taxes (NOPAT)	210	231
Net operating working capital (NOWC)	800	883
Total operating capital (TOC)	1800	1983
Free cash flows (FCF)		48.16
AFN		88
Ratios	t	t + 1
Current ratio	3.23	2.64
Inventory turnover	4.88	4.88
Days sales outstanding	45.63	45.63
Total assets turnover	1.50	1.50
Debt ratio	48.00%	47.99%
Profit margin	4.70%	4.80%
Return on assets	7.04%	7.19%
Return on equity	15.05%	15.37%
(NOPAT/total operating capital)	11.67%	11.65%

Source: Own calculations, based on volatility assumptions

$$I\,(t+1) = \{I\,(t)/R\,(t)\} * R\,(t+1) \tag{3}$$

Property and equipment, net (property and equipment, net amounts) (PR),

$$PR\,(t+1) = \{PR\,(t)/R\,(t)\} * R\,(t+1) \tag{4}$$

Accounts payable, trade, and others (accounts payable, credit suppliers)

$$APAY\,(t+1) = \{APAY\,(t)/R\,(t)\} * R\,(t+1) \tag{5}$$

Accrued liabilities (AL),

$$AL\,(t+1) = \{AL\,(t)/R\,(t)\} * R\,(t+1) \tag{6}$$

The account retained earnings (REAR) include profits which are not divided to shareholders and are calculated from the subtraction of previous year retained earnings minus dividends of the same year DIV plus the profits (NIAC—net income available to common). That is:

$$REAR\,(t+1) = REAR\,(t) - DIV\,(t) + NI\,(t+1) \tag{7}$$

Finally, the account which is the reconciliation of the assets and liabilities of the programming period (t + 1) is notes payable (NP) as presented in Eq. (9). In order to support the new volume of revenues in the year t + 1, the method of the percentage of revenues requires the assets to be adapted to new business requirements. The new assets should result from an additional capital support. In other words, additional requested funds (ADDITIONAL FUND NEEDED/AFN (t + 1)) will be the amount of liabilities which will support the new volume of revenues. It is calculated using Eq. (8):

$$
\begin{aligned}
AFN = {}& TA(t+1) - APAY(t+1) - AL(t+1) - NP(t) - LTB(t+1) \\
& - PS(t+1) - CS(t+1) - REAR(t+1)
\end{aligned}
\tag{8}
$$

Balance Sheet Balancing Account (Notes Payable (NP)), NP (t + 1)
$$= NP(t) + AFN \tag{9}$$

The balance sheet accounts are stock variables, in contrast to the accounts of the income statement, which are flow variables.

The income statement presents the operating results of the company. Additionally, based on various sales growth estimation techniques (g), we assume that the rate is 10%. The total revenues will be increased depending on the budgeted growth rate or according to formula (10):

$$R\,(t+1) = R\,(t) * (1+g) \tag{10}$$

Interest costs (IC) are calculated using the estimated interest rate (i) and the average borrowed amount over a 2-year time span. Therefore,

$$i\,(t+1) = i\,(t) = IC\,(t)/\{NP(t) + LTB(t)\} \tag{11}$$

The average lending (average debt) (ADE) is:

$$ADE = \{NP\,(t) + LTB\,(t+1) + AFN/2\} \tag{12}$$

For the year t + 1, the calculation of interest costs results from the relationship:

$$IC\,(t+1) = i\,(t+1) * ADE \tag{13}$$

After constructing the projected financial statements, key financial data are calculated threw Eqs. (14)–(17). Therefore,
Net operating profit after taxes (NOPAT):

$$NOPAT = EBIT * (1 - \text{Tax rate}) \tag{14}$$

Net operating working capital (NOWC):

$$NOWC = C + AR + I - APAY - AL \tag{15}$$

Total operating capital (TOC):

$$TOC = NOWC + \text{Net plant and equipment} \tag{16}$$

Free cash flows (t + 1) (FCF), O'Byrne (1999) are calculated in Eq. (17):

$$FCF(t+1) = NOPAT(t+1) - (TOC(t+1) - TOC(t) \text{ or } \Delta\text{capital}) \tag{17}$$

4 Budgeting Under Uncertainty

4.1 Monte Carlo Simulation

Approximately 50 years ago, Hertz (1964) proposed a method which applied the Monte Carlo simulation technique to business decisions under uncertainty due to the gambling aspect of the process. Since then, this method has been popularized by the rapid development in information technology. Nowadays, many practical and theoretical problems involving risk and uncertainty in the area of economics and management are solved using approaches which follow the same principles originating from his work. According to Bennett and Ormerod (1984), the Monte Carlo technique or *stochastic* simulation approach, due to the presence of random processes, typically generates the estimates by randomly calculating a feasible value for each variable, from a statistical probability distribution function, which represents the range and pattern of possible outcomes. To ensure that the chosen values are representative of the pattern of possible outcomes, a quite large number of repetitive deterministic calculations, known as iterations, are made.

Lorance and Wendling (1999), as cited in Loizou and French (2012), list the various steps of carrying out a Monte Carlo simulation: the first step is to define the capital resources by developing the deterministic model of the estimate. The second step is to identify the uncertainty in the estimate by specifying the possible values of the variables in the estimate with probability ranges (distributions). The third step is to analyze the estimate with simulation—the model is run (iterated) repeatedly to determine the range and probabilities of all possible outcomes of the model. Prior to running the simulation, the model produces a single-point value (result) for the estimate. This value is known as the deterministic result and generally is referred to as the base estimate before adding contingency. There are a number of software tool environments in which Monte Carlo simulations can be run with add-ins to spread sheets being the most popular (such as *Crystal Ball, @Risk and ModelRisk* commercial software packages). The risk analysis and simulation package which is used in this research is Microsoft® Office Excel® add-in @RISK® by Palisade Corporation® (@RISK).

4.2 PERT Probability Distribution Function

The PERT probability distribution function (Vose 1996) acquired its name as it utilizes the same assumptions, regarding the mean/norm in PERT (program evaluation and review technique) networks used in project planning procedures. Technically, it is a version of the beta distribution and is widely employed in risk analysis for modeling expert opinion of a variable's uncertainty. It is based on the assumption that the mean $(\mu) = (minimum + 4 * most\ likely + maximum)/6$; therefore, the mean for the PERT distribution is four times more sensitive to the *most likely* value than to the *minimum* and *maximum* values. It requires the same three parameters as the triangular distribution (*minimum-a, most likely-b, maximum-c*) without suffering to the same extent the potential systematic bias problems of the triangular distribution, that is, in producing too great a value for the mean of the risk analysis results where the maximum for the distribution is very large. The standard deviation of the PERT distribution is also less sensitive to the estimate of the extremes and systematically lower than the triangular distribution, particularly where the distribution is highly skewed. As for the triangular distribution, the PERT distribution is *bounded* on both sides, hence, may not be adequate for some modeling purposes when it is desired to capture tail or extreme events. The equation of the PERT distribution is related to the beta distribution as presented in Eq. (18):

$$\text{PERT}(a, b, c) = \text{Beta}(\alpha_1, \alpha_2)^*(c-a) + a \tag{18}$$

where:

$$a1 = [(\mu-a)^*(2b-a-c)]/[(b-\mu)^*(c-a)] \tag{19}$$

$$a2 = [a1^*(c-\mu)]/(\mu-a) \tag{20}$$

and the mean is:

$$\mu = (a + 4 * b + c)/6. \tag{21}$$

The variance of the PERT distribution derives from the equation:

$$\sigma^2 = \frac{(\mu - a) * (c - \mu)}{7} \tag{22}$$

The probability density function of the PERT distribution is:

$$f(x) = \frac{(x - a)^{\alpha_1 - 1} * (c - x)^{\alpha_2 - 1}}{\text{Beta}\,(\alpha_1, \alpha_2) * (c - a)^{\alpha_1 + \alpha_2 - 1}} \tag{23}$$

5 Estimations-Results

5.1 The Model Without Uncertainty (Deterministic Approach)

The employed methodology mentioned in this research without uncertainty in the corporate financial model is presented in chapter "A Performance Measurement System for Staff of the Logistics Section: A Case Study for an Oil and Gas Company." In order to apply three different scenarios, we suppose that the target of sales growth is 10%. The results are demonstrated in Table 5 for the change of taxation, in Table 6 for dividend policy changing, and, finally, in Table 7 for the change of the cost of debt.

a. First Scenario: The taxation environment changes, assuming the tax rate increases from 26 to 30%:

Table 5 Model output 2

Model output	Historical period (t)	Forecasted period (t + 1)
NOPAT	199	219
Net operating working capital	800	883
Total operating capital	1800	1983
Free cash flows (FCF)		35.53
AFN		97
Current ratio	3.23	2.58
Inventory turnover	4.88	4.88
Days sales outstanding	45.63	45.63
Total assets turnover	1.50	1.50
Debt ratio	48.00%	48.45%
Profit margin	4.44%	4.53%
Return on assets	6.65%	6.78%
Return on equity	14.22%	14.62%
(NOPAT/total operating capital)	11.04%	11.02%

Source: Own calculations, based on volatility assumptions

b. Second Scenario: Dividend policy changes, so dividends per share growth rate decreases from 10 to 5%:

Table 6 Model output 3

Model output	Historical period (t)	Forecasted period (t + 1)
NOPAT	210	231
Net operating working capital	800	883
Total operating capital	1800	1983
Free cash flows (FCF)		48.01
AFN		85
Current ratio	3.23	2.66
Inventory turnover	4.88	4.88
Days sales outstanding	45.63	45.63
Total assets turnover	1.50	1.50
Debt ratio	48.00%	47.84%
Profit margin	4.70%	4.81%
Return on assets	7.04%	7.20%
Return on equity	15.05%	15.34%
(NOPAT/total operating capital)	11.67%	11.65%

Source: Own calculations, based on volatility assumptions

c. Third Scenario: Cost of debt increases from 10.19 to 12%:

Table 7 Model output 4

Model output	Historical period (t)	Forecasted period (t + 1)
NOPAT	210	231
Net operating working capital	800	883
Total operating capital	1800	1983
Free cash flows (FCF)		48.01
AFN		100
Current ratio	3.23	2.56
Inventory turnover	4.88	4.88
Days sales outstanding	45.63	45.63
Total assets turnover	1.50	1.50
Debt ratio	48.00%	48.63%
Profit margin	4.70%	4.42%
Return on assets	7.04%	6.62%
Return on equity	15.05%	14.32%
(NOPAT/total operating capital)	11.67%	11.65%

Source: Own calculations, based on volatility assumptions

5.2 The Model Under Uncertainty

The implemented methodology mentioned on our budget model has been constructed in this paper (previous Chap. 3, *Budgeting, Key Variables, and Basic Steps*). The expected revenue growth usually depends on various factors, so the revenue growth range is more useful in financial planning. Thus, we suppose that the revenue growth variable is fitted in PERT distribution as shown in Fig. 2:

According to Fig. 2, for the forecasted sales target, there is a volatility range between 5% and 15% approximately. For the company, sales growth of 5% could be associated with an adverse business scenario, while a value of 10% with a base one, and finally a value of 15% could be the best. With a given variance and statistical measures, we apply the Monte Carlo simulation (Minimum: 0.0511, Maximum: 0.1479, Mean: 0.1000, Std Dev: 0.0189, Values:10,000) resulting in the estimations for a group of dependent variables of our model in Figs. 3, 4, 5, 6, and 7.

The estimations in Table 8 compose the main range of our planning, when there is a volatility of sales target. For each key ratio, we take the smallest and largest value, thus constructing an interval of values for each key variable, while anticipating the fluctuating figures.

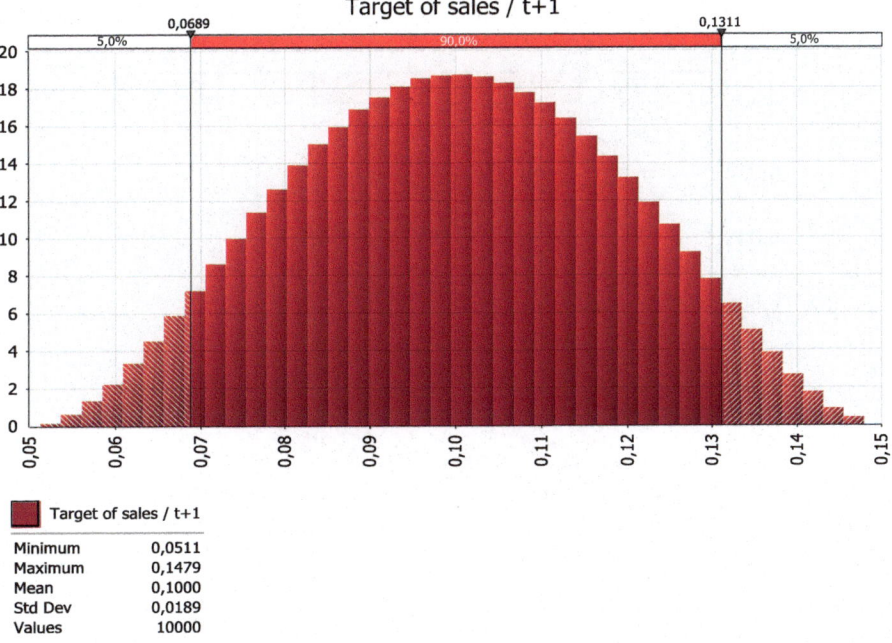

Fig. 2 PERT distribution for revenues/sales growth. Source: own calculations, based on volatility assumptions

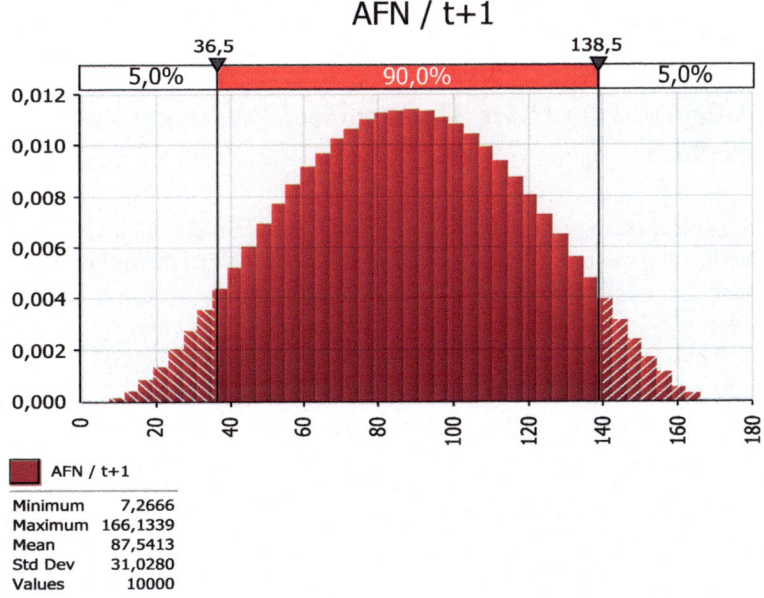

Fig. 3 PERT distribution for additional fund needed in programming period. Source: own calculations, based on volatility assumptions

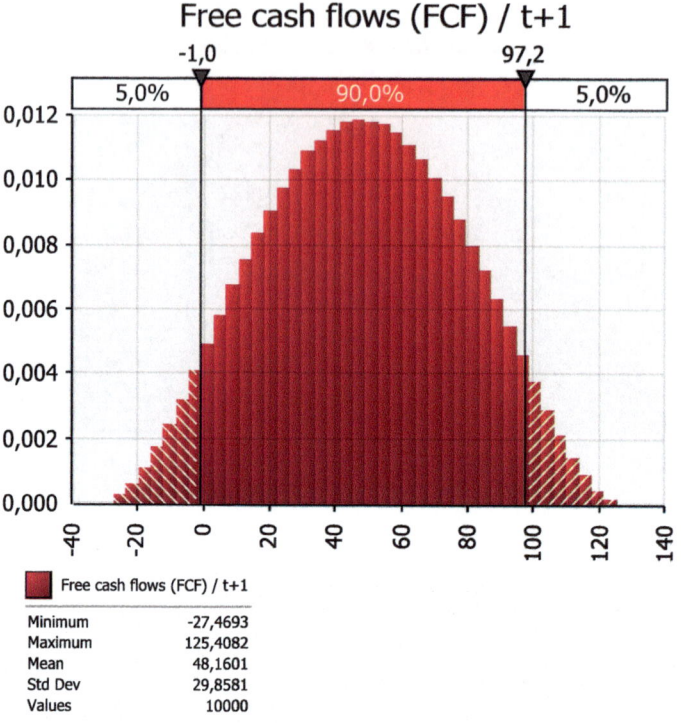

Fig. 4 PERT distribution for free cash flows in programming period. Source: own calculations, based on volatility assumptions

5.3 Policy-Making Using Mathematical Programming Methods

A useful application of our model is determining the optimal policies for businesses. The scientific approach to decision-making usually involves the use of one or more mathematical models (Winston 2004). For this paper's research purposes, we devised a policy problem to be solved by means of mathematical programming methods. Thus, we supposed that for the forecasted period there is no free credit limits or any decision to increase them (Eq. 24).

$$\textit{Objective function} \quad \text{AFN}_{t+1} = 0 \tag{24}$$

The adjustable variables under restriction are presented in Eqs. (25)–(29):

$$8\% \leq \text{Target of sales S } (t+1) \text{ (D3)} \leq 12\% \tag{25}$$

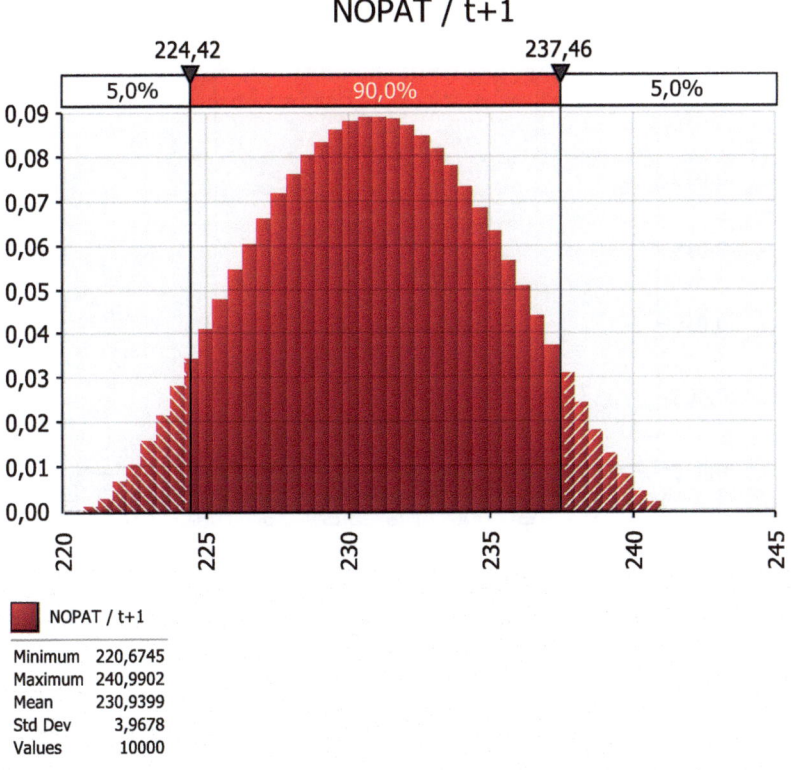

Fig. 5 PERT distribution for net operating profit after taxes in programming period. Source: own calculations, based on volatility assumptions

$$5\% \leq \text{Dividends per share growth rate (D6)} \leq 10\% \qquad (26)$$

$$86\% \leq \text{Costs of goods sold as percentage of sales (D7)} \leq 88\% \qquad (27)$$

$$12\% \leq \text{Accounts receivable as percentage of sales (AR) (D8)} \leq 13\% \qquad (28)$$

$$1.5\% \leq \text{Accounts payable as percentage of sales (APAY) (D12)} \leq 3\% \qquad (29)$$

Moreover, we set hard constraints as shown in Eqs. (30) and (31) in order to ensure an optimal policy:

$$\text{WACC (D78)} \leq \text{ROIC (D77)} \qquad (30)$$

$$\text{Dividends to common (D30)} \leq \text{FCF (D62)} \qquad (31)$$

A decision-making process with a multiple-criteria model has been addressed to solve capital budgeting problems (Kwak et al. 1996). What is more, financial planning via AFN models as a policy tool, should involve not only the implications

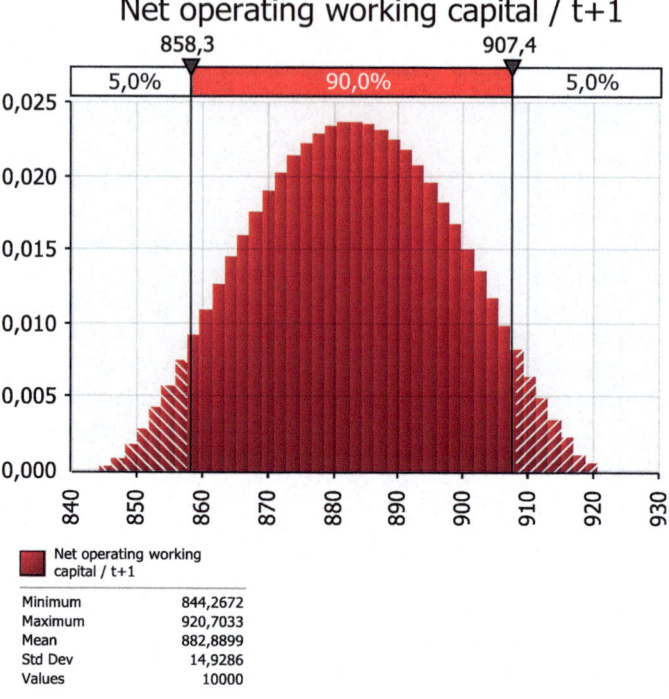

Fig. 6 PERT distribution for net operating working capital in programming period. Source: own calculations, based on volatility assumptions

to key financial ratios but also to the cost of capital, as well as the return on invested capital, and, therefore, the added value of the company. The cost of capital is calculated by the WACC method, and it is an important benchmark in many popular forms of performance analysis. These measures are important as they can be less sensitive to the distortions that can arise from traditional accounting measures (Knight 1997). The cost of capital or the weighted average cost of capital (WACC) is equal to:

$$WACC \text{ or } i_C = i_D(1 - \varphi)\frac{D}{D+S} + i_S\frac{S}{D+S} \tag{32}$$

where

i_D Average interest rate of debt capital
i_S Average interest rate of equity capital
D   Debt capital
S   Equity capital
φ Tax rate

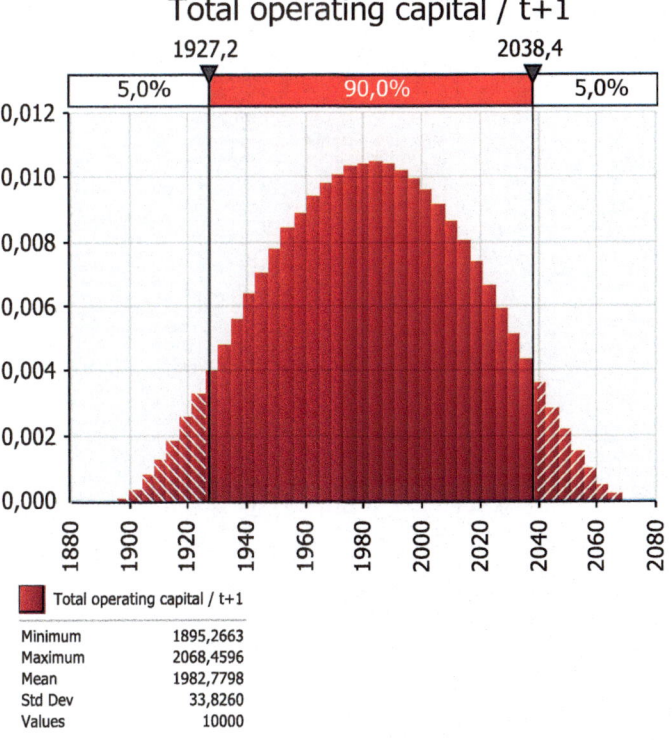

Fig. 7 PERT distribution in total operating capital in programming period. Source: own calculations, based on volatility assumptions

For our model, in order to calculate the average interest rate of equity capital, we used the dividend method or Gordon method (Gordon 1962) where the cost of equity capital is equal to:

$$[Cost\ of\ Equity] = i_S$$

$$= \left[\frac{EPS\ earnings\ per\ share}{P\ common\ stock\ Price} \right] + [Expected\ long\ term\ growth\ rate]$$

$$i_{Share\ Capital} = i_S = \left[\frac{EPS}{P} \right] + g \tag{33}$$

Recent studies (see Luoma et al. 2006; Luoma and Ruuhela 2001; Peters 1991; Thalassinos et al. 2006) based on this method continue to analyze the price to earnings (P/E) ratio, in order to calculate more accurate and relevant cost of equity.

P. M. Spanos et al.

Table 8 Descriptive statistics

Name	NOPAT (t + 1)	NOWC (t + 1)	TOC (t + 1)	FCF (t + 1)	AFN (t + 1)	Target of sales/t + 1
Minimum	221	844	1895	−27.47	7	5.11%
Maximum	241	921	2068	125.41	166	14.79%
Mean	231	883	1983	48.16	88	10.00%
Std deviation	4	15	34	29.86	31	1.89%
Variance	15.7436	222.8618	1144.196	891.5087	962.7363	0.000357184
Skewness	−9.3172E-05	−9.31725E-05	−9.31725E-05	9.31725E-05	−9.3173E-05	−9.31725E-05
Kurtosis	2.333653	2.333653	2.333653	2.333653	2.333653	2.333653

Source: Own calculations, based on volatility assumptions

For the purpose of this paper, it is assumed that the common stock price is equal to book value and the financial ratio; return on invested capital (ROIC) (Damodaran 2007) is calculated as:

$$\text{ROIC} = (1 - \text{tax rate}) \times \text{EBIT} \div (\text{Total liabilities and equity} - \text{cash}) \quad (34)$$

In order to secure that our policy will not affect the firm's value, we take as a restriction that the economic value-added spread or in our AFN model, the "AFN" economic spread will remain positive. So, under this framework, our problem has the best solution as shown in Fig. 8 and Table 9:

Our model concludes to the values as shown in Tables 10 and 11, thus, based on the described methodology, designing targeted policies and monitoring their implications.

Taking into account the best solutions in the progress steps, we consider only the simulations that meet our criteria and the optimizational range of each input variable as presented in Table 12.

The estimation of each range is very important to formulate the optimal policy. In our example, the data illustrates that if we want to support a growth of sales, without the necessity of additional funds (AFN = 0), the company can afford a range of multiple combined scenarios under the restrictions to formulate a dividend policy in a suitable FCF amount and a positive economic spread. Therefore, the decision-makers should implement the company's policy from current data (t) as presented in Eqs. (35)–(39):

$$8.24\% \leq \text{Target of sales S}\,(t+1)\,(\text{D3}) \leq 8.49\% \quad (35)$$

$$5.72\% \leq \text{Dividends per share growth rate}\,(\text{D6}) \leq 6.78\% \quad (36)$$

$$86.00\% \leq \text{Costs of goods sold as percentage of sales}\,(\text{D7}) \leq 86.51\% \quad (37)$$

$$12.24\% \leq \text{Accounts receivable as percentage of sales}\,(\text{AR})\,(\text{D8}) \leq 12.30\% \quad (38)$$

$$2.62\% \leq \text{Accounts payable as percentage of sales}\,(\text{APAY})\,(\text{D12}) \leq 2.96\% \quad (39)$$

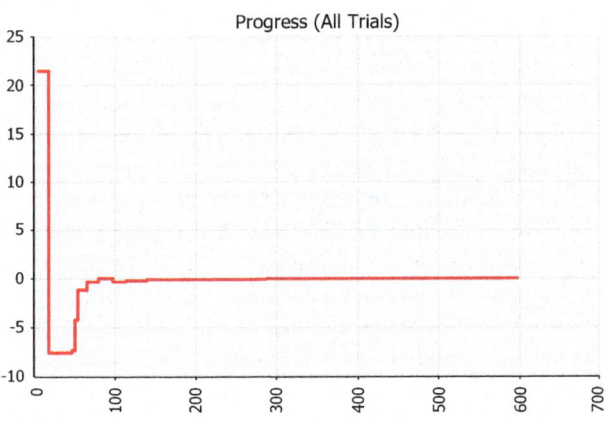

Fig. 8 Progress for all optimization trials. Source: own calculations, based on volatility assumptions

Table 9 Optimization output

Goal	
Cell to optimize	"MODEL!" D63
Statistic to optimize	Value
Type of goal	Target value
Target value	0
Results	
Valid trials	492
Total trials	604
Original value	N/A[a]
+ Soft constraint penalties	N/A
= Result	N/A
Best value found	0
+ Soft constraint penalties	0.00
= Result	0
Best trial number	528
Time to find best value	0:06:03
Reason optimization stopped	Stop button pressed
Time optimization started	27/3/2017 17:25
Time optimization finished	27/3/2017 17:32
Total optimization time	0:06:53
Precision	0
Evaluation time	Iteration
Satisfied for % of trials	82.78%
Simulation settings	
Number of iterations	5000
Sampling type	Latin hypercube
Random # generator	Mersenne Twister
Random # generator seed	475741056 (Chosen randomly)
Random seed changes	*FALSE*

Source: Own calculations, based on volatility assumptions
[a]AFN value is derived from the formula

6   Conclusions

In business, econometric models are not usually used as management concentrates on short-termed decision-making. The historical period could easily be composed with data of several years or several companies from the same industrial sector. Market conditions are changing tremendously fast, and sustainability in a business could be tested in a future research. Corporate financial modeling which employs AFN technique involves historicity which is transferred through stable indicators in the reference period. Such models are characterized by clarity and scientific competence while illustrating the effects not only in the production process but also the financial position of each company. The model in this paper is oriented toward demand, but it could easily be adjusted to different cost conditions through specific cost categories against revenue rates. It enforces controlling processes that can be

Table 10 Model input

Model input	Historical period (t)	Forecasted period (t + 1)
Target of sales		**8.45%**
Depreciation expense % ratio of net assets	10%	10.00%
Tax rate	26%	26.00%
Dividends per share growth rate		**5.89%**
Costs of goods sold as percentage of sales	87.21%	**86.07%**
Accounts receivable as percentage of sales	12.50%	**12.25%**
Inventory as percentage of sales	20.50%	20.50%
Interest rate loans	10.19%	10.19%
Cash Target		14.00
Accounts payable as percentage of sales	2.00%	**2.67%**
Accruals as percentage of sales	4.67%	4.67%
Net plant and equipment as percentage of sales	33.33%	33.33%

Source: Own calculations, based on volatility assumptions
Bold text indicates the important points for implementing the optimal policy scenario in this paper, Chap. 5.3

Table 11 Model output

Model output	Historical period (t)	Forecasted period (t + 1)
NOPAT	210	255
Net operating working capital	800	841
Total operating capital	1800	1925
Free cash flows (FCF)		130.04
AFN		**0**
Ratios	Historical period (t)	Forecasted period (t + 1)
Current ratio	3.23	3.09
Inventory turnover	4.88	4.88
Days sales outstanding	45.63	44.71
Total assets turnover	1.50	1.50
Debt ratio	48.00%	44.88%
Profit margin	4.70%	5.72%
Return on assets	7.04%	8.60%
Return on equity	15.05%	17.53%
Stock value	18.72	21.22
Cost of equity	12.40%	11.97%
Cost of debt	10.19%	10.19%
ROIC	10.55%	11.87%
WACC	9.81%	9.71%
AFN ECONOMIC SPREAD (ROIC-WACC)		2.15%

Source: Own calculations, based on volatility assumptions
Bold text indicates the important points for implementing the optimal policy scenario in this paper, Chap. 5.3

Table 12 Best solutions

Trial	Elapsed time	Iterations	Result	D3 (%)	Adjustable cells D7 (%)	D8 (%)	D12 (%)	D6 (%)
				8.00	86.00	12.00	1.50	5.00
14	0:00:38	5000	−8	8.18	86.18	12.35	2.96	6.70
45	0:00:59	5000	−7	8.16	86.13	12.32	2.88	6.61
46	0:00:59	5000	−7	8.18	86.21	12.37	3.00	6.97
47	0:00:59	5000	−4	8.23	86.24	12.40	3.00	7.58
52	0:01:02	5000	−1	8.24	86.46	12.30	2.96	6.90
64	0:01:10	5000	−0	8.41	86.16	12.27	2.75	6.27
77	0:01:22	5000	0	8.24	86.51	12.30	2.96	6.78
96	0:01:34	5000	−0	8.42	86.14	12.26	2.72	6.06
113	0:01:45	5000	−0	8.25	86.45	12.29	2.92	6.76
139	0:02:00	5000	0	8.42	86.14	12.26	2.72	6.09
166	0:02:17	5000	0	8.42	86.14	12.26	2.72	6.08
210	0:02:44	5000	−0	8.49	86.00	12.24	2.62	5.72
345	0:04:09	5000	0	8.45	86.08	12.25	2.68	5.91
356	0:04:15	5000	0	8.45	86.07	12.25	2.67	5.90
367	0:04:23	5000	0	8.45	86.07	12.25	2.67	5.90
378	0:04:30	5000	0	8.46	86.07	12.25	2.67	5.89
389	0:04:36	5000	0	8.46	86.06	12.25	2.67	5.88
392	0:04:38	5000	−0	8.45	86.07	12.25	2.67	5.89
395	0:04:40	5000	−0	8.45	86.07	12.25	2.67	5.90
429	0:05:01	5000	0	8.46	86.07	12.25	2.67	5.89
443	0:05:10	5000	0	8.46	86.07	12.25	2.67	5.89
454	0:05:17	5000	−0	8.45	86.07	12.25	2.67	5.89
480	0:05:33	5000	0	8.45	86.07	12.25	2.67	5.89
528	0:06:03	5000	0	8.45	86.07	12.25	2.67	5.89

Source: Own calculations, based on volatility assumptions

applied on alternative scenarios, working as a sensitivity analysis tool for each operational factor under conditions of either certainty or uncertainty. By posing uncertainty in our model, we examine the limits in the corporate financial structure, while simultaneously creating an envelope of results from diverse scenarios. On the other hand, by using mathematical programming methods, targeted policies could be designed and monitored for their implementation. This given research paper contributes with a model which is open to freely being extended, taking into consideration the complexity of each business in parallel with suitable techniques. Consequently, it is a useful tool not only for policy-making of entrepreneurs or financial directors but also a tool for investors or banks to be tested in stress conditions. Finally, corporate financial modeling becomes a beneficial application in a restructuring planning process for estimating base, adverse, and best business scenarios.

References

Bennett, J., & Ormerod, R. N. (1984). Simulation applied to construction projects. *Construction Management and Economics, 2*(3), 225–263.

Brigham, E. F., & Daves, P. R. (2007). *Intermediate financial management* (9th ed.). Mason, OH: Thomson.

Damodaran, A. (2007). *Return on capital (ROC), return on invested capital (ROIC) and return on equity (ROE): Measurement and implications.* https://doi.org/10.2139/ssrn.1105499

Gordon, M. J. (1962). *The investment, financing, and valuation of the corporation.* Homewood, IL: RD Irwin.

Hertz, D. B. (1964). Risk analysis in capital investment. *Harvard Business Review, 42*(1), 95–106 (Reprinted in Harvard Business Review, September/October 1979, pp. 169–182).

Knight, J. A. (1997). *Value based management: Developing a systematic approach to creating shareholder value.* New York: McGraw-Hill.

Kwak, W., Shi, Y., Lee, H., & Lee, C. F. (1996). Capital budgeting with multiple criteria and multiple decision makers. *Review of Quantitative Finance and Accounting, 7*(1), 97–112.

Loizou, P., & French, N. (2012). Risk and uncertainty in development: A critical evaluation of using the Monte Carlo simulation method as a decision tool in real estate development projects. *Journal of Property Investment & Finance, 30*(2), 198–210.

Lorance, R. B., & Wendling, R. V. (1999). Basic techniques for analyzing and presenting cost risk analysis. *AACE International Transactions,* K11.

Luoma, M., & Ruuhela, R. (2001). How to develop price per earnings ratio to fair valuation method of a stock? *Technical Analysis of Stock and Commodities, 19,* 34–38.

Luoma, M., Sahlström, P., & Ruuhela, R. (2006). An alternative estimation method of the equity risk premium using financial statements and market data. *Advances in Accounting, 22,* 229–238.

O'Byrne, S. F. (1999). EVA and its critics. *Journal of Applied Corporate Finance, 12*(2), 92–96.

Peters, D. J. (1991). Valuing a growth stock. *The Journal of Portfolio Management, 17*(3), 49–51.

Sizer, J. (1988). *An insight into management accounting.* Leicestershire: Penguin Business.

Thalassinos, E., Kyriazidis, T., & Thalassinos, E. (2006). The Greek capital market: Caught in between poor corporate governance and market inefficiency. *European Research Studies Journal, 9*(1–2), 3–24.

Vose, D. (1996). *Quantitative risk analysis: a guide to Monte Carlo simulation modelling.* Chichester: Wiley.

Winkler, D. (1994). Financing costs of additional funds needed: A modified equation approach. *Financial Practice and Education, 4*(1), 149–154.

Winston, W. L. (2004). *Operations research: Applications and algorithms* (4th ed.). Pacific Grove, CA: Cengage Learning Higher Education.

Wright, D. (1996). *Management accounting.* New York: Addison Wesley Longman.

Using Principal Component Analysis in Assessing Client's Creditworthiness

Anna Siekelová and Lucia Svabova

Abstract A company that provides trade credit must take into account the creditworthiness of its customers. The creditworthiness of customer is largely affected by its ability to repay trade credit properly and on time. The company usually follows the main financial indicators against which it receives a basic overview of the customer's creditworthiness. The basic indicators include indicators of activity, liquidity, indebtedness, and profitability. Within each group there are a number of indicators that can be monitored. Recommendations by authors who deal with this topic may also differ. There can be hidden relationships between the various. Monitoring two indicators among which exists a strong correlation is useless. The same amount of information can be obtained by monitoring only one of them. The aim of this paper is assessing the existence of hidden relationships between indicators that are most often recommended for the evaluation of the client's creditworthiness. There are many methods of analysis hidden relationships. Choice of the appropriate method depends on the type and number of variables. In our group the individual objects, i.e., businesses, are described by more than two quantitative variables, so we choose principal component analysis to describe hidden relationships. It is a statistical procedure that uses an orthogonal transformation to convert a set of observations of possibly correlated variables into a set of values of linearly uncorrelated variables called principal components.

Keywords Principal component analysis · Correlation matrix · Kaiser–Meyer–Olkin test for sampling adequacy · Trade credit · Creditworthiness

A. Siekelová (✉) · L. Svabova
Faculty of Operation and Economics of Transport and Communications, Department of Economics, University of Zilina, Zilina, Slovakia
e-mail: anna.siekelova@fpedas.uniza.sk; lucia.svabova@fpedas.uniza.sk

© Springer Nature Switzerland AG 2019 185
N. Sykianakis et al. (eds.), *Economic and Financial Challenges for Eastern Europe*,
Springer Proceedings in Business and Economics,
https://doi.org/10.1007/978-3-030-12169-3_12

1 Introduction

Nowadays, the provision of trade credit has become a normal part of business practice. However, surveys show that willingness to provide trade credit in Slovakia is much lower than in other advanced economies. Providing trade credit is associated with the risk of loss due to failure to pay properly and on time of the customer. This risk is inversely proportional to the payment discipline of the customer, whom was the trade credit provided. The question of granting or refusing trade credit is one of the core issues to be resolved within the claims management. The answer should be largely derived just from a correct assessment of the creditworthiness of a potential customer (Corejova and Al Kassiri 2016).

To assess the creditworthiness of the client, the professional literature recommends to monitor in general, solvency, the total debt, turnaround times, as well as selected indicators of profitability. When selecting specific indicators that will be taken into account when assessing the solvency of a potential client, we were inspired not only by foreign studies (Salek 2005) but also by domestic professional literature (Kadlecik and Markovic 2015; Svabova and Durica 2016; Petrach and Vochozka 2016).

Based on recommendations, we have chosen the following quantitative indicators which will be used for assessing the creditworthiness of a business partner within the paper:

- Quick ratio
- Total debt ratio
- Short-term debt ratio
- Credit indebtedness
- The absolute value of trade receivables
- The absolute value of trade payables
- Days sales outstanding
- Debt payable outstanding
- Commercial insolvency
- Return on assets
- Return on sales
- Indicator characterizing the imminent decline of the company

Subsequently Table 1 shows in detail the calculation used to calculate a selected indicator.

In our samples, we work with 9067 Slovak companies in which we calculate the chosen indicators.

1.1 Principal Component Analysis

In practice we often meet with a fact that a number of variables characterizing the object at the beginning is too high, which makes it very difficult to work with the set of these objects as well as to interpret the carried-out analyses. Therefore, it is

Table 1 Calculation of selected indicators

Selected financial indicator	Calculation
Quick ratio	$\dfrac{Financial\ Accounts + Short - term\ Receivables}{Short - term\ Foreign\ Resources + Short - term\ Accrued\ Liabilities}$
Total debt ratio	$\dfrac{Foreign\ Resources + Accrued\ Liabilities}{Total\ Assets}$
Short-term debt ratio	$\dfrac{Short - term\ Foreign\ Resources + Short - term\ Accrued\ Liabilities}{Total\ Assets}$
Credit indebtness	$\dfrac{Credits + Borrowings}{Total\ Assets}$
Days sales outstanding	$\dfrac{Trade\ Receivables}{Revenues\ from\ Sales\ of\ Goods, Products\ and\ Services}$
Days payable outstanding	$\dfrac{Trade\ Payable}{Total\ Cost}$
Trade receivables	The amount of the balance sheet
Trade liabilities	The amount of the balance sheet
Commercial insolvency	$\dfrac{Trade\ Liabilities}{Trade\ Receivables}$
Return on assets	$\dfrac{Earning\ After\ Taxes}{Total\ Assets}$
Return on sales	$\dfrac{Earning\ After\ Taxes}{Sales}$
Indicator characterizing the imminent decline of the company	$\dfrac{Equity}{Liabilities}$

necessary to identify hidden relationships between selected variables that are used to characterize the object (Kliestik and Majerova 2015).

In our case, we study the interrelationships between selected financial indicators describing the creditworthiness of the company, which is located within our data set. The aim is to replace a large number of primary variables with a smaller number so that we retain the greater part of the information provided by the original range of variables. Such examination shall use the methods of investigation of hidden relationships, which choice depends on the type and number of variables. Individual objects in our data set, i.e., businesses, are described by more than two quantitative variables (selected financial indicators). To analyze the relationship between these variables, we choose principal component analysis.

The author of the principal component analysis is an English mathematician Karl Pearson, who designed this method in 1901 to reduce multidimensional data. Later in 1933 it was generalized by American mathematician Harold Hotelling on random vectors, and he also suggested the use of this method for the analysis of covariance structure of variables (Stankovičová and Vojtková 2007). It is based on the fact that in the case where the variables are correlated with each other, you can get the same information by means of using a smaller number of variables, which can then be identified as the principal components. Principal component analysis is also known by the acronym PCA and is a mathematical–statistical method, which aims to convert the elements of the set of observations which can be correlated with each other, to the elements of such sets, among which there is no linear correlation using an orthogonal transformation (Stankovičová and Vojtková 2007). This is one of the oldest and also the most widely used methods of multidimensional analysis. Principal component analysis is conducted in order to find such a set of linear combinations of the original variables, which is characterized by not only preserving as much information about the original observations but also its dimension is as small as possible.

Using the procedure we achieve that a given set of businesses will be further analyzed in the subspace of smaller dimension, which is of great importance for the further analyses, which we will realize (Weissova and Durica 2016). Within the multivariate analysis, a statistical unit is characterized by several features, in this case by calculating financial indicators. These features can be imagined as points in p-dimensional space, where p is the right number of monitored variables. Each of these variables in the given set of objects has some variability measured by variance, which is the carrier of the information. The total volume of data in a multidimensional space is obtained by the sum variances of the individual information. In our case we have a 12-dimensional data, where each indicator calculated for the relevant year represents one dimension. Using principal component analysis, we examined the relationship between indicators in order to reduce the number of dimensions in an effort to preserve as much information about the observed objects, i.e., enterprises. It is therefore an ordinal method which allows reducing the number of dimensions in Euclidean character space so that there was a minimal loss of information.

2   Methodology and Results

For the implementation of principal component analysis, we used the software for statistical analysis in Excel XLSTAT.

One of the outcomes that we have chosen as required for analyzing the principal components was Bartlett's test. At the start we verify using Bartlett's test if some redundancy exists within our chosen variables, which is conditional on the variables being highly correlated, and thus using only one of these variables, we obtain the same amount of information about the examined object, in this case the company. This is a conformity test of more than two variances.

We test the null hypothesis against the alternative.

H₀ There is no correlation significantly differing from zero among the variables.

Hₐ At least between one of the pairs of variables, there is a correlation significantly differing from zero.

If k represents individual choices in size n_i variation S_i^2, then the testing statistic of Bartlett's test is:

$$\chi^2 = \frac{(N-k)\ln\left(S_p^2\right) - \sum_{i=1}^{k}(n_i - 1)\ln\left(S_i^2\right)}{1 + \frac{1}{3(k-1)}\sum_{i=1}^{k}\left(\frac{1}{n_i - 1}\right) - \frac{1}{N-k}}$$

where:

$$N = \sum_{i=1}^{k} n_i$$

We reject the null hypothesis H_0 of independence at the level of significance α, if the value of testing statistic χ^2 is greater than the critical value $\chi_\alpha^2(k-1)$ of the chi-square, which is used in the Bartlett's test.

Based on the results of the Bartlett's test, we can on the significance level $\alpha = 0.05$ reject H_0 and accept the alternative hypothesis H_a, which says that between at least one of the pairs of variables, there is a correlation significantly differing from zero, so we can assume there is a redundancy between variables.

Next, we must identify the pairs of variables with a significant correlation. This can be done based on the result of the selection correlation matrix R, which clearly shows the amount of correlation between variables. The general form of correlation matrix is as follows:

$$R = \begin{bmatrix} 1 & r_{x_1 x_2} & \cdots & r_{x_1 x_k} \\ r_{x_2 x_1} & 1 & \cdots & r_{x_2 x_k} \\ \vdots & \vdots & \vdots & \vdots \\ r_{x_k x_1} & r_{x_k x_2} & \cdots & 1 \end{bmatrix}$$

The correlation matrix for the selected variables used in the identification of the customer's credit score is shown in Table 2.

The arrangement of the variables within the correlation matrix is as follows:

1. Quick ratio
2. Total debt ratio
3. Short-term debt ratio
4. Credit indebtedness
5. The absolute value of trade receivables
6. The absolute value of trade payables
7. Days sales outstanding
8. Debt payable outstanding
9. Commercial insolvency
10. Return on assets
11. Return on sales
12. Indicator characterizing the imminent decline of the company

Table 2 The correlation matrix

Variables	1	2	3	4	5	6	7	8	9	10	11	12
1	1	-0.236	-0.248	-0.161	-0.073	-0.150	-0.012	-0.045	-0.029	0.146	0.019	0.629
2	-0.236	1	0.923	0.153	-0.057	0.006	0.027	0.060	0.042	-0.505	-0.050	-0.207
3	-0.248	0.923	1	0.122	-0.057	0.002	0.033	0.058	0.045	-0.534	-0.050	-0.200
4	-0.161	0.153	0.122	1	0.046	0.053	0.021	-0.021	-0.007	-0.178	-0.085	-0.128
5	-0.073	-0.057	-0.057	0.046	1	0.639	0.043	0.015	-0.037	0.047	0.016	-0.054
6	-0.150	0.006	0.002	0.053	0.639	1	0.010	0.099	0.032	0.008	0.012	-0.111
7	-0.012	0.027	0.033	0.021	0.043	0.010	1	0.152	0.051	-0.032	-0.328	-0.014
8	-0.045	0.060	0.058	-0.021	0.015	0.099	0.152	1	0.051	0.001	-0.018	-0.037
9	-0.029	0.042	0.045	-0.007	-0.037	0.032	-0.008	0.051	1	-0.026	-0.005	-0.017
10	0.146	-0.505	-0.534	-0.178	0.047	0.008	-0.032	0.001	-0.026	1	0.181	0.096
11	0.019	-0.050	-0.050	-0.085	0.016	0.012	-0.328	-0.018	-0.005	0.181	1	0.008
12	0.629	-0.207	-0.200	-0.128	-0.054	-0.111	-0.014	-0.037	-0.017	0.096	0.008	1

The prepared correlation matrix shows the degree of correlation for all of the pairs of the variables. The pair of indicators 5 and 6 reached a higher degree of correlation, i.e., trade receivables and trade payables, as well as a pair 1 and 12, quick ratio and an indicator of the imminent decline. The absolute value of the correlation coefficient above 0.5 is also observed between the indicators total debt ratio and return on assets and a pair of short-term debt ratio and return on assets. It is interesting to observe that in case the company uses external resources to finance its assets largely (total debt ratio increases), the amount of net profit, which is generated using one monetary unit of assets, decreases (return on assets declines). Significant correlation is mainly between the second and third indicator, i.e., indicator of the total and short-term indebtedness. The authors identify a significant multicollinearity, that is, the existence of the linear relationship between observed variables, in the case where the absolute value of the correlation coefficient of the two variables is equal to or greater than 0.8. On that basis, it was eligible to exclude one of these two variables: total debt ratio and short-term debt because the value of the correlation coefficient was at 0.923. We execute the selection based on the results of the measurement of the sample adequacy Kaiser–Meyer–Olkin Measure of Sampling Adequacy, which determines the adequacy of the sample data, while identifying factors that should be rejected, since they carry no information and the same amount of information can be obtained from the smaller number of factors. The KMO statistics is based on a comparison of correlation coefficients with partial correlation coefficients. Based on the test results of KMO, we came to the exclusion of the short-term debt ratio.

Next, we proceed to the actual analysis of the principal components. We follow eigenvalues, which are based on the correlation matrix eigenvalues and express the amount of variability that is captured by the respective component.

In terms of interpretation, the specific values are not important, but the expression of their share on the total variance is. Scree plot is a graphic representation of eigenvalues (variances) of all the factors in decreasing order. Thanks to them we determine the number of critical components by monitoring the cumulative expression of variability. They can be described as the principal components and based on the use of the results of PCA are thus possible to work with a smaller number of key components instead of the original 12 variables in further analysis.

The principal components have the following characteristics:

- Their number is significantly lower than the original number of variables.
- They describe almost the entire variation of the original characters.
- They are mutually uncorrelated.
- They represent linear combinations of the original variables (Kliestik et al. 2015).

As the main components represent a combination of the original variables, it is necessary to know the proportion of individual variables within the main components. Thus, here we ran into one of the major problems of the analysis of the principal components. It takes the resulting values of the indicators of financial analysis as numbers and does not reflect the logical relationships between them. So we decided to first organize the individual indicators into logical units and only then apply PCA.

So we conducted partial analyses of the key components for the following groups of indicators. The first group consists of debt indicators, i.e., the total debt ratio and credit indebtedness (the short-term debt ratio was excluded); another group is formed of indicators characterizing business transactions, hence the absolute amount of trade receivables and trade payables, days sales outstanding, days payable outstanding, as well as commercial insolvency; further group consisted of profitability indicators, namely, return on assets and return on sales; and finally the last group consisted of indicators of quick ratio and an indicator of imminent decline.

The results of partial principal component analysis are presented in the Tables 3, 4, 5, and 6.

In terms of interpretation, the specific values are not important but the expression of their share on the total variance. Using these we can determine the number of critical components by monitoring the cumulative expression of variability. For example, in this case, the principal component F1 with the percentage of cumulative

Table 3 Eigenvalues of the principal components for the debt indicators

	Principal component F1	Principal component F2
Eigenvalues	1.153	0.847
Variability (%)	57.659	42.341
Cumulative variability (%)	**57.659**	100.000

Table 4 Eigenvalues of the principal components for the variables describing business transactions

	Principal component F1	Principal component F2	Principal component F3	Principal component F4
Eigenvalues	1.654	1.139	0.854	0.353
Variability (%)	41.347	28.478	21.344	8.831
Cumulative variability (%)	41.347	**69.825**	91.169	100.00

Table 5 Eigenvalues of the principal components for the indicators of profitability

	Principal component F1	Principal component F2
Eigenvalues	1.181	0.819
Variability (%)	59.039	40.961
Cumulative variability (%)	**59.039**	100.000

Table 6 Eigenvalues of the principal components for current liquidity and an indicator of imminent decline

	Principal component F1	Principal component F2
Eigenvalues	1.629	0.371
Variability (%)	81.438	18.562
Cumulative variability (%)	**81.438**	100.000

variability is 57.659% that expresses the total variability in the data. Thus, in case that we decide not to use both indicators to describe indebtedness of the companies, but the created principal component F1, we capture up to nearly 60% of the variability in the data while reducing the amount of used indicators. Whereas the principal components are a combination of the original variables, it is necessary to know the ratio of representation of selected indicators of indebtedness in the principal component F1, and this representation is even 50% of the principal component that is formed by total debt ratio and 50% by credit indebtness.

As part of another group, we focused on indicators describing business transactions of a company. In the beginning, however, based the low value of KMO reached by the indicator of commercial insolvency, we came to its exclusion.

Based on the cumulative variability, it is possible to say that by selecting only the first principal component F1, we would describe only 41% of the variability of set, which is not sufficient. In this case, we have therefore chosen main components F1 and F2 whose cumulative variability is almost 70%, which is sufficient to describe the variability of the set. It can therefore be concluded that in contrast to the beginning, when business transactions were described by five financial indicators, based on the results of PCA for this group, we will continue to use only two created principal components in which is the following percentage of individual indicators. The principal component F1 is at 97% described by the absolute amount of trade receivables and trade payables, and principal component F2 is describe by turn-around times to a level of 98%.

As can be seen from the results of the Table 5, to describe almost 60% of the variability values, we need a principal component F1 in which is the representation of selected indicators of profitability even (50% return on assets 50% return on sales).

Within the last group of indicators, we focused on the remaining two, i.e., quick ratio and an indicator of imminent decline. Although they exhibit a higher degree of correlation, this is still not a significant multicollinearity, and therefore it is not required to proceed to reduction of their number. As in the previous case, the KMO value is sufficient. Results for the eigenvalues of the created principal components are in Table 6.

Based on the cumulative variability, we can conclude that using principal component F1, which is equally made up of current liquidity and an indicator of imminent decline, we cover up to 81.4% of the variability of the set.

3 Discussion

At the beginning, we decided to carry out an analysis of the principal components in all parameters at once. Based on the results, we came to the selection of six principal components. In addition to the creation of the principal components, our job was to ensure that we could consider the created components in further analyses and describe them relevantly based on the percentage of the original variables within the principal components. In some cases, however, we encountered a problem just at that point. Sometimes is the layout of the original indicators within the formed principal component quite similar and therefore is an interpretation of such formed component complex. That was possible to see, for example, within the principal component F3 when several indicators have higher percentage in this component, so that its interpretation was not as clear as in the case of the main component of F2, where trade receivables and trade payables clearly formed the basis for the component. Indicators of return on assets and return on sales together fall into the category of indicators of profitability and account for almost 34% of the principal component F3. A high percentage of representation was shown also by an indicator informing about the company's ability to repay liabilities (quick ratio) or indicator of imminent decline of the company. A principal component formed this way showed even more problems. Based on the correlation, it was possible to conclude that in the case where an indicator of quick ratio and an indicator of imminent decline increase, the principal component grows. The problem occurred in assessing the correlation between the principal component and indicators of return on assets and return on sales, when the correlation was negative, i.e., the growth of indicators of profitability caused a drop in principal component, and vice versa, which of course did not correspond with the results of the selection correlation matrix, where is clearly a positive correlation between the indicator quick ratio and return on assets. So here we ran into one of the major problems of the analysis of the principal components, which takes the resulting values of indicators of financial analysis as numbers and does not reflect the logical relationships between them.

So we decided to first organize the individual indicators into logical units and then to apply the PCA, as presented in the previous chapter. However, it should be noted that the components thus created do not pay, they are uncorrelated with each other, because they are the result of several PCA.

4 Conclusion

Based on the results of the analysis of the principal components within groups of indicators, we managed to reduce the number of dimensions in Euclidean character space from the original 12 financial indicators to 5 principal components so that there is minimal loss of information. Individual objects, in our case enterprises, will therefore also be characterized by five principal components. Based on which, we will greatly simplify the further work with a selected group of enterprises.

Acknowledgment This research was financially supported by the Slovak Research and Development Agency—Grant NO. APVV-14-0841: Comprehensive Prediction Model of the Financial Health of Slovak Companies.

References

Corejova, T., & Al Kassiri, M. (2016). Knowledge-intensive business services as important services for innovation and economic growth in Slovakia. In *CBU International Conference on Innovations in Science and Education (CBUIC)* (pp. 42–47). Prague.

Kadlecik, K., & Markovic, P. (2015). *Hodnotenie kreditného rizika odberateľa*. Bratislava: Wolters Kluwer.

Kliestik, T., & Majerova, J. (2015). Selected issues of selection of significant variables in the prediction models. In *Financial Management of Firms and Financial Institutions: 10th International Scientific Conference* (pp. 537–543). Ostrava.

Kliestik, T., Majerova, J., & Lyakin, A. N. (2015). Metamorphoses and semantics of corporate failures as a basal assumption of a well-founded prediction of a corporate financial health. In *Economics and Social Science: 3rd International Conference on Economics and Social Science (ICESS 2015)* (pp. 150–154). Paris.

Petrach, F., & Vochozka, M. (2016). Optimization of a company's capital structure: Global problem of the corporate finance and its possible solutions. In *16th International Scientific Conference on Globalization and its Socio-Economic Consequences* (pp. 1696–1703). Rajecké Teplice.

Salek, J. (2005). *Account receivable management*. Hoboken, NJ: Wiley.

Stankovičová, I., & Vojtková, M. (2007). *Viacrozmerné štatistické metódy s aplikáciami*. Bratislava: Iura Edition.

Svabova, L., & Durica, M. (2016). Korelačná analýza prediktorov použitých v bankrotných predikčných modeloch na Slovensku. *Ekonomicko manažerské spektrum, 10*(1), 2–11.

Weissova, I., & Durica, M. (2016). The possibility of using prediction models for monitoring the financial health of Slovak companies. In *8th International Scientific Conference Managing and Modelling of Financial Risks* (pp. 1062–1070). Ostrava.

The Way Out from the Public Sector's Labyrinth of Inefficiency? Alternative Governance Performance and Prospects in Greece

Sifis Plimakis

Abstract This chapter presents empirical research analyses and evaluates according to primary empirical data the viability and effectiveness of the alternative institutional arrangement for municipal services provision in the distinctive environment of Greek local government. The alternative provision appears to lead to cost reduction and quality improvement in most case studies analyzed, assuming, however, the appearance of a series of determinant factors of services performance, relating to the level of the competition and mainly the establishment of relationships of trust, mutual collaboration, engagement, and common culture among the partners and the stakeholders. Factors that transform the alternative provision from a simple cost rationalization tool into a promotion catalyst of a new governance model in Greek local government.

Keywords Local government reform · Alternative provision · Efficiency · Consultation · Competition · Social capital

1 Introduction: Efficiency in Greek Local Government—The Odyssey of a Forgotten Value

Efficiency in Greek local government, as a notion, comprises on its own a national paradox. Despite the fact that throughout the past 25 years, it has consisted of a basic rhetoric and a priority of all the reform programs and governmental commitments for the Greek government, it always ends up being incorporated into regulations of minor importance. In essence, a national void is observed in the estimation of the level of performance of Greek public services, in terms both of productivity and

S. Plimakis (✉)
Department of Political Science and International Relations, University of Peloponnese, Korinthos, Greece

© Springer Nature Switzerland AG 2019
N. Sykianakis et al. (eds.), *Economic and Financial Challenges for Eastern Europe*,
Springer Proceedings in Business and Economics,
https://doi.org/10.1007/978-3-030-12169-3_13

efficiency, such as in the presence of mechanisms and tools for efficiency improvement. Efficiency is again of particular interest both because of the strained financial crisis in Greece and the need that arises for cost constraints in the provision of municipal services and the simultaneous development of innovative models covering the growing needs of citizens.

Historically, Greek local government efficiency comprises a point of reflection and study, both pre-war and in post-war initiatives and projects for the reform of the public sector in Greece. Questioning the operation and efficiency of the mechanisms of central government and local government, although in most cases it is not an independent issue, but rather one in the context of promotion and decentralization of the Greek state and democratization of local government; however, it comprises an area where, over the years, the necessity for improvement and modernization have been highlighted (Makridimitris and Michalopoulos 2000; Konsolas 1997). The provision mechanisms of alternative service provision in Greece are evaluated as flawed and ineffective in all cases in respect of state reform, from Varvaresou's report on the Greek economy to the recent initiative of Kallikratis's project (Makridimitris and Michalopoulos 2000; Maistros 2009). The ascertainment of the need for improvement and modernization of the provision mechanisms of municipal services in Greek local government is timeless. An approach, however, which through the connection between the efficiency issue and the need to promote both decentralization of the central government and democratization of the local government resulted in the degradation of the acknowledgement of the role and contribution of the mechanisms improving and evaluating efficiency. The efficiency of the municipal services in Greece is analyzed and incorporated into the debate on the modernization of local government as an aspect of actions and initiatives, improving the operation of municipalities either in the context of the implementation of technical and development projects of national programming at a local level, or in the context of undertaking initiatives for the improvement of the financial management and administration of local government. A national framework of local government reform led to the downgrading of efficiency concept incorporation into the tools of government and the relevant regulation.

This view is confirmed by the analysis and coding of recent reform initiatives for the reorganization of local government, referring to the projects of Kapodistrias and Kallikratis, where efficiency is incorporated, institutionally and operationally, through activities such as the promotion of intermunicipal co-operation, the operational planning of municipalities, the implementation of municipal infrastructure development projects and the allocation of the municipal budget (Maistros 2009).[1] This confused view regarding the level and impact of municipal efficiency in Greece and the factors of containment and constraint affects its performance, both organizational and cultural, and bears the necessity for an evidence-based comparative evaluation of efficiency in Greek local government, a framework of analysis that comprised the incentive and the basis for conducting the present study.

---

[1]Qualitative and quantitative results of the empirical research of the present paper.

2 Literature Review: Theorizing Efficiency Under the Reform Pendulum of Local Government in Greece

Despite the significant lack of national empirical studies and evidence regarding Greek local government efficiency, the results of the available reports and research present a distinct view of limited efficiency, in terms of productivity and effectiveness of the municipalities (Dexia Bank 2004, 2011). This limited efficiency is reflected in the low standing that Greece holds, both on a European and an international level in areas such as the efficiency of municipal service provision, which is poorly rated in Europe, the operational costs of municipalities, and the association between the operational costs of the local government and the size of the workforce (Bouckaert and Halligan 2008; Dexia Bank 2004, 2011; Afonso 2010; Shah 2012; Van de Walle 2005). Low rates are respectively observed in the operation of Greek local government in a series of determining factors of efficiency, such as the cost of bureaucracy and red tape, the degree of deregulation of municipal services, the quality of local governance, the adoption of change management principles and tools, the degree of fiscal decentralization, the utilization of e-governance services, the incorporation of auditing in municipalities, and management by objectives. Barriers to efficiency and innovation in Greek local government also cause wider characteristics of the national social capital, such as public confidence in local government, inter-sectoral trust, corruption, network governance, and participation in deliberative institutions (Paraskevopoulos 2000; Karkatsoulis 2011; Featherstone 2008; Plimakis 2012; Dexia Bank 2011).

These factors are composed of a model of local governance, which appears to require, apart from the necessary institutional reforms, the immediate analysis of actions for the improvement of the municipal service provision mechanisms and the modernization of the existing model of municipal organization and regulation of local public goods (Tatsos 1999). In essence, both on a theoretical and empirical level, the problem of efficiency in Greece is predominantly a problem of governance (Yiannitsis 1994; Karkatsoulis 2011; Prime Minister Office - General Secretariat of Government 1992; Lavdas 1997; Kazakos 2001). These governance issues include the necessity for further assignment of authorities and resources from the central to the local state, the promotion of pragmatic multi-level governance, the modernization and simplification of local government audit and supervision, and the strengthening of its strategic planning and evaluation mechanisms (Yiannitsis 1994; Karkatsoulis 2004, 2011; Plimakis 2012). These problems of organization and operation of local governance in Greece are confirmed by recent reports of international organizations such as the European Union and the OECD, which emphasize the need to promote reforms that contribute toward the improvement of efficiency of municipalities and the promotion of a governance model, based on inter-sectoral and multi-level collaboration. Reform initiatives include the incorporation of strategic planning in municipalities, the evaluation of municipal service provision, the implementation of program budgeting, the reduction of administrative burdens, the promotion of inter-municipal and multi-level co-operation, and the development of co-operation with the private sector (OECD 2011; Dexia Bank 2011; Karkatsoulis 2011). Reforms focus on the improvement of municipal efficiency, through the modernization of the existing governance and management arrangements at local level and the promotion of a new philosophy of local government organization, adjusting to the pressures of fiscal austerity and the growing demand for quality services for citizens and enterprises.

These barriers to the efficiency of the Greek local government emerge from the existing model of local government organization and regulation, and from the wider resistance to change, that consist in a national characteristic (Maistros 2009; OECD 2011). The local government restructuring in Greece is considered to be incomplete, despite recent relatively successful reform initiatives for its modernization, most notably on a level of further democratization and decentralization of competences of the central government at prefectural and municipal levels. Maintaining centralization, especially in terms of funding, taxation, revenue, and fiscal autonomy of the local government, combined with the increased bureaucracy particularly at a level of costly central control and monitoring of the operation of municipalities and prefectures, cause a setback to efficiency improvement. Resistance to change, an after effect of the lack of co-operation, consultation and trust in the objectives and the reform inactions, in addition to the limited administrative capacity of municipalities to implement them, lead to the perpetuation of efficiency performance. A restriction to the success of the reforms, which, apart from policy design and implementation deficits, is caused by social capital limitations as the sustained low rates of trust, participation of citizens, adoption of innovation, governance regimes, and network performance (Maistros 2009; OECD 2011; Kazakos 2001; Pagoulatos 2005; Featherstone 2008).

The barriers of local government efficiency are further strained by the lack of effective consultation of central government with the local authorities for the design and specialization of national policies on a local scale and the restrictions imposed on the municipal entrepreneurship, an after effect of the often heightened and constant competition between central and local government. Counterpart restrictions on the efficiency of municipalities are caused by the limited integration and effectiveness of a series of recent initiatives, over the last decade, for the rationalization of municipalities' management and decision-making, municipal consultation and participatory planning, utilization of municipal property, and promotion of private sector participation (Cohen 2008; OECD 2011; Karkatsoulis 2011). The positive influence of the reform initiatives were particularly diminished at the implementation level, owing to the lack of multi-level co-ordination, essential strategic planning, consultation with stakeholders, and the appearance of increased bureaucracy and legislative complexity.

The efficiency crisis of Greek local government can be theoretically analyzed according to the theory of the new governance. Local government crisis is caused by the inability of the existing institutional and governance arrangements to support local development challenges and satisfy emerging citizen and social needs, the ineffectiveness of which diminishes municipal efficiency. Municipal efficiency challenges, whose improvement demands the restructuring of Greek local government, to a more participatory, decentralized and performance-oriented model of local government organization. Both the theoretical values and principles, in addition to the policy tools of the theory of the new governance, are based on the combination of two seemingly opposite, however fully auxiliary, principles of organization and change of the local state: the introduction of the model of local government competition, the deregulation promotion model, and the model of a local collaborative network. Seemingly opposite models of local government restructuring are put at the center of local governance reform, the development of partnerships with civil society and the private sector, for the provision of municipal services and the more effective fulfilment of citizens' needs, through the competition–collaboration nexus (Bouckaert and Pollitt 2010). According to the new governance theory, the traditional monopolistic role of the state in the provision of services and public goods is gradually replaced by a new model of organization, according to which the state's role is to regulate, steer, and assist the provision of services to citizens and enterprises from various social and economic stakeholders, to whom the state delegates authorities for efficiency, democratization, and proximity to the needs of citizens.

In this new emerging model of provision of public services and policies, the role of the state consists essentially in the regulation and control of public services, which are provided by the private sector and civil society, individually or in collaboration with the state (Stoker 2003, 2006; Peters 2004; Osborne and Gaebler 1992; Rhodes 1997; Denhart 2000). This assignment of authorities and the development of partnerships for the provision of public services contains several forms of governance, such as the collaboration and partnering of the state with private sector agencies and civil society organizations for the more effective provision of public services, the delegation of authorities from central state to lower levels of government, the contracting out of government services to the private sector, the development of policy networks with stakeholders, and the participation of public employees and citizens in the management of public services (Osborne 2008; Stoker 2006; Ostrom 1990). A changing model of local governance comprises the establishment of a new relationship among state, private sector, and civil society. In this new model of state organization, the role of citizens, stakeholders, and private sector is upgraded through the development of governance mechanisms and the institutionalization of their participation in the procedures of planning, provision, and evaluation of public services (Bouckaert and Pollitt 2010).

A new local governance paradigm, which, despite its national variations, appears to consist in the leading and increasingly diffused international model for public services reorganization, characterized by a new special place of the private sector in policy-making, especially in policy implementation (Hood 2006). Partnership with the private sector comprises the main political choice for the provision of efficient public services and the cost constraints of their operation. Moreover, the development of partnerships contributes toward the introduction of expertise and innovation to the public sector and the inflow of new private sources of funding for the provision of public services. The participation of the private sector is promoted through the development of partnerships, the inter-sectoral provision of services, and the provision of services by private contractors and in the context of policy networks (Agranoff 2004; Rhodes 1997; Warner & Hebdon 2001; Dollery 2007). New governance tools introduce and promote private initiative in local government, in the light of state regulation and the promotion of accountability, transparency, and consultation in their performance.

Correlating the scope of implementation and the principles of the new governance theory with the environment and the efficiency problems of Greek local government, its explanatory value is apparent. The crisis of efficiency in Greek local government can be explained through two basic levels of theoretical analysis. The incomplete nature of the delegation of authority from the central to the local state, particularly those of funding and taxation, limits the organizational capacity and flexibility of municipalities, impairing both the effective regulation of distinctive local needs and the performance of the municipalities. This institutional ineffectiveness is further enhanced by the substantial lack of networks and mechanisms of multi-level governance and co-ordination (Karkatsoulis 2004; Maistros 2009). In direct connection with this institutional inefficiency of Greek local government, lie the inadequate integration and implementation of modern tools and mechanisms of governance, on a level of provision of municipal services and implementation of public policies at local level (OECD 2011; Warner & Hebdon 2001; Warner & Hefetz 2002; Shah 2012). The incorporation of these alternative mechanisms for municipal services provision and the promotion of citizen and stakeholder participation in the management of the municipalities have proven to be troublous.

The limited adoption and performance of these new governance mechanisms in Greek local government are, according to the findings of this research, due to the limited administrative capacity of municipalities to incorporate them at an operational level and their limited responsiveness to local government needs, because of the inadequate participation of local government during their design and selection from central government. Furthermore, the introduction of new governance mechanisms and tools is limited by the lack of correlation with the implementation of strategic planning in local government agencies, the resistance of local government personnel to this new approach of municipal services provision, the limited political support, in addition to the essential lack of adopting a culture of participatory management in municipal decision-making and management (Maistros 2009). In this category of the inadequately functioning institutional mechanisms of new governance in Greek local government are included the partnerships between the public and private sector, concessions, social entrepreneurship, inter-sectoral co-operation, local development partnerships, and finally public consultation and participatory planning initiatives (Heinelt 2006). An implementation and diffusion deficit, which is largely based on the lack of a culture of consultation and co-operation in Greek local government and society in general, is a factor that is of great importance for the development of new governance at a local and a regional level.

2.1 Delimiting and Analyzing Alternative Provision in Greek Local Government: Methodological Framework

Based on the above-mentioned factors determining the efficiency of municipal services in Greece, current empirical research analyses efficiency issues in respect of the institutional choice of the selection of alternative models by municipalities. Before this performance analysis, it should be specified what constitutes alternative provision in Greek municipalities. In this selection labyrinth of the institutional form of private sector participation in Greek local government, the complexity caused by the preserve of the capability for alternative co-operation development with the private sector beyond formal public–private partnership (PPP) legislation and private contracts should be considered. A regulatory labyrinth that is promoted by the presence of 15 alternative legal acts for the implementation of alternative municipal services provision, with the participation of private partners, in areas such as waste management, utilization of municipal property, wastewater treatment, irrigation–water supply, in addition to the construction and maintenance of municipal infrastructure.[2] Owing to this institutional complexity, for the purposes of the research, these various forms of private sector participation in municipal services provision are classified into three distinctive categories: PPPs, hybrid local partnerships, and contracting out, which are analyzed in Table 1.

Participation and co-operation with the private sector, which is at the core of local governance reform at an international level and in line with the theory and practice of new governance. Institutionalization of private sector participation in municipal services provision, which, despite its perennial presence and formal legal recognition and regulation, is characterized by limited diffusion and only occasional successful implementation, a fact that prohibits it from being considered as a national coherent policy for the reform of local government and the promotion of private investments (Yetimis and Marava 2005; Lavdas 1997; Trova 2007). An alternative approach to analyzing the problem of local government reform in Greece, under the scope, principles, tools, and mechanisms of the new governance theory and the attempted theoretical and empirical reconciliation of contrasting principles of competition and co-operation in the provision of municipal services and widely in the modernization of the national model of local governance.

The empirical and evidence-based analysis of the efficiency of the alternative provision in Greek local government comprised a complex task. A complex and difficult task of efficiency assessment, owing to the inadequate record keeping of performance and management data by the Greek municipal authorities, the restricted publicity and accessibility of the data, and the lack of previous relevant empirical research. The extent of the research sample concerns 28 municipalities of the entire

---

[2]Indicative reference to the 3463/2006 Act on waste management and utilization of municipal property, the 59/2007 Presidential Decree on the deregulation of public and municipal services, the 3468/2006 Act on energy production, the 3581/2007 Act on utilization of municipal property, and the 2052/1992 Act on infrastructure protection for the environment.
A more detailed and comparative analysis of the regulatory labyrinth is presented in Table 1.

Table 1 The regulatory labyrinth of alternative governance in Greece

Model of alternative provision	Area of service provision (indicative)	Regulatory framework	Responsibility and mode of audit	Partnerships' management	Contract duration
Contracting out	Waste management Building maintenance Social services Property development Infrastructure development Administrative services IT support Vehicle maintenance	Code of local government procurement/ 7 different legal acts	Municipal authorities—outputs management	Legal contract execution	1 year with renewal possibility
Hybrid partnerships	Waste management Property development Energy production Social services	12 different legal acts	Municipal authorities—outputs management with (limited/differentiated per case) user participation	Hybrid partnership management committee—distinctive organization	2 to 5 years with renewal possibility
PPPs	Waste management Property development Infrastructure development Energy production	PPP legal framework	PPP Secretariat & Regional Authority & Municipal Authorities & SPV—outputs & outcomes management with (limited/differentiated per case) user participation	PPPs SPV	10 to 25 years

PPP public–private partnership, *SPV* special purpose vehicle
Source: Analysis from the author, based on the work of Savas (2000), Osborne (2004), Hodge (2010)

Greek territory (more than 50% of the municipalities have proceeded to the alternative provision in Greece) and a total of 89 services, which have been assigned to individuals during the period 2012–2014 and which originate from 11 different categories of municipal services. In terms of the institutional models examined, four particular forms of alternative provision are evaluated under the scope of the research, such as contracting out, concession contracts, public—private partnerships, and hybrid partnerships with private and public partners.

Overcoming the restrictions specified previously on finding empirical data, the comparative analysis between municipal and alternative private provision of municipal services, was based on the quantitative and qualitative analysis of a series of specialized independent and dependent variables assessing the alternative provision of municipal services. Variables emerged from an extensive analysis of the international literature and its harmonization with the particular environment of organization and operation of Greek local government (Boyne 1998; Fernandez 2009; Wollmann 2008; Hodge 2004; Greene 2002). The selected independent and dependent variables of the research analysis were based on both quantitative and qualitative data. The extraction of qualitative data on the municipal services and private contractor partners was carried out using official sources and documents of the municipal authorities responsible and the municipalities and private contractors. In terms of the comparative evaluation of the efficiency data between municipal and alternative provision, quantitative and operational data were further analyzed utilizing specialized and accredited methodologies and tools for measuring the efficiency of municipal services and the assessment of barriers and the actual cost of alternative provision (Brudney and Bozeman 2008; Warner & Hefetz 2002; Patton 2008).[3]

Apart from the quantitative data and official evidence, a qualitative research was conducted between 2012 and 2014 for the analysis of independent and dependent variables and factors affecting the performance of alternative provision in Greece. In the context of qualitative research, 86 semi-structured interviews and three focus groups were conducted, while 282 questionnaires were filled in by involved parties and recipients of services, with a response rate of 32%. The purpose of the qualitative research was the incorporation of views of the involved stakeholders and service recipients regarding the viability and effectiveness of alternative provision in Greek local government, and the acknowledgment of the effects of local social capital and national culture on the organizational design and efficiency of the services provided and the emergence of a new model of local governance in Greece.

2.2 The Decision on In-House or External Provision of Municipal Services—Incentives and Choice

In commencing the effort to empirically document the impact and performance of alternative municipal services provision in Greece, initially, the decision-making of the municipal authorities will be explored in an attempt to understand the incentives and expectations behind the private choice, whose impact is presented in Table 2.[4] The decision on selecting alternative models for municipal services provision involves both the municipalities and the private contractors in a complex process of evaluation and analysis of the incentives for participation.[5] It is also determined to

---

[3]In respect of the tools utilized, the following are indicatively referred to: red tape assessment tool, user participation assessment tool, quality of governance assessment methodology, for further analysis, see Bozeman (2011).

[4]Partner selection incentives are presented in Table 2.

[5]Incentive impact is presented in Table 2.

Table 2 Factors affecting the selection of alternative provision tools

Factors of alternative provision selection	Significance	PPPs	Hybrid partnerships	Contracting out
Limitation of the cost of provision	0.78	0.70	0.72	0.85
Fiscal constraints	0.68	0.79	0.71	0.58
Service quality improvement	0.42	0.48	0.61	0.21
Administrative reform promotion	0.22	0.37	0.22	0.12
Use of European Union funds	0.57	0.64	0.53	0.23
Promotion of collaboration with the private sector	0.19	0.43	0.27	0.07
Satisfying citizens' needs	0.38	0.41	0.57	0.22
Promotion of accountability and transparency	0.23	0.27	0.58	0.12

Source: Results based on the article's empirical qualitative research

a significant extent, beyond the fiscal and social factors of their promotion, by the level of transaction costs and administrative burdens in which their introduction results (Brudney et al. 2005; Fernandez 2009). According to the research, limiting the cost of services provision, both in the level of delivery and burdening of the available budget of the municipality comprises the primary factor for selecting private provision. Cost reduction is directly associated with fiscal constraints within municipalities, where the former do not allow the latter to continue funding the increased cost of services. Consequently, municipalities choose private provision in an attempt to provide the same quantity of services; however, with a perceptibly lower provision cost.

Another significant factor for the selection of alternative service provision by the municipalities, of less importance than the limitation of the cost of provision, comprises the utilization of innovative and modern financial tools for Greek local government. Modern financial tools, such as outsourcing, concessions, and PPPs, which provide municipalities with the opportunity to take advantage of their assets, in addition to providing their residents with services, which otherwise would not be capable of being provided monopolistically by municipal services owing to constraints in funding. The alternative service provision and the utilization of modern financial tools, however, limited from the increased bureaucracy, the complexity of the regulatory framework, and the delays regarding the development and licensing of the projects.

The selection of private participation in areas where the local government does not have the adequate expertise, technology, and experience, such as waste recycling, alternative energy production from renewable sources, integrated wastewater and water treatment, and management of complex technical projects, also consists in a factor promoting individual participation. Parallel to compliance with the agreed timeframe and the budget of projects and provided services, areas where their conventional implementation by the municipal authorities responsible is characterized by excesses, failures or frequent project cancellations, also consist in the significant factor of private initiative.

In contrast, in respect of the selection factors of the alternative services provision, the participation of factors relating to the promotion of administrative reform within municipalities, the improvement of quality and the promotion of transparency and accountability of the services provided are presented as limited.[6] The limited influence of these factors is reflected in the substantial absence of interconnection between the alternative service provision and the modernization of municipalities, in addition to the low priority given to accountability issues, transparency and citizens' participation, confirming the primary interconnection between the participation of private sector in local government with the increasing fiscal constraints and secondarily with the effective provision of complex services.

As to the selection of areas of interest of the municipalities regarding the development of the alternative provision of municipal services, the results of the empirical research are equally clear and distinct. The municipalities select the alternative provision of services with private sector participation in areas where they face serious operational issues, primarily in waste management and recycling, utilization of municipal property, cleanliness of streets, municipal building and infrastructure maintenance, development and operation of municipal infrastructure, and car parking. The construction and operation of complex technical projects are placed at the next level of interest, mainly in the areas of alternative energy production from renewable sources, replacement of municipal lighting with modern efficient and environmentally friendly technologies, and maintenance of municipal vehicles and machinery.

Complex and socially sensitive services, such as social protection services, public health and administrative services are areas that are not a priority for the municipalities present a low rate of interest and selection (Brudney et al. 2005). It should be noted that from the empirical research, and despite the degradation of the outcome at a level of statistical presentation, the need and demand of municipalities to develop partnerships with the private sector (PPPs) have been reflected, in addition to the increased sectoral selection in areas of services with immense local interest, such as are indicatively referred to, wastewater treatment and water supply to municipalities based on islands, energy-saving in urban and semi-urban municipalities, and the production of energy in rural and island municipalities.

Of particular interest, in accordance with the results of the quantitative and mainly qualitative empirical research, are the selection factors of the institutional form of individual participation in Greek local government as a tool of promotion of the efficiency of municipal services, as they are comparatively analyzed in Table 2 (Wollmann 2008). In this area, the effects of the quality of the institutional framework are presented as substantial and essential, as they shape the selection of the institutional form among traditional private contracts, PPPs, concessions, and hybrid partnerships. The selection of the traditional annual contracts is presented to be wide

---

[6]Qualitative and quantitative results of the empirical research of the present paper.

(over 80%), propelled by two main factors, the limitation of the impairment and the lack of confidence of the municipal authorities for the long-term and multi-year partnership with the private sector in addition to the impairments of the institutional framework and the increased bureaucracy for the development of PPPs.

Despite the temporal governmental rhetoric to promote PPPs in Greek local government and the positive expectations created by the enactment of the relevant legislation in 2005 followed by massive funding by the Ministry of Interior during the period 2006–2010 for the preparation and development of PPP projects in municipalities, the implementation of the institutional framework was inhibited at an important level of application, owing to the negative consequences of red tape, centralization, and lack of coordination, which led to multi-year delays and often suspension of the municipalities' initiatives.[7] Increased bureaucratic costs multiplied on a time and cost basis for municipalities in relation to the development of PPPs and concessions compared with the annual award contracts to private contractors.[8] Regulatory complexity, which supports the appearance and escalation of red tape and also determines the decision on alternative governance model selection, since the appearance of increased red tape on the licensing and auditing procedures of PPPs and local hybrid partnerships, contributes to the promotion of a short-term contracting out model of municipal service provision.[9] The impact of red tape, highlights the necessity for simplification and codification of alternative regulatory provision in Greece, to promote institutionalized and long-term collaboration against the short-term and rent-seeking impact of contracting out (Karkatsoulis 2011).

2.3   Comparative Evaluation of the Effectiveness of Alternative Service Provision Models

Continuing the evaluation of the impact and effects caused by the introduction of the private sector into the provision of municipal services, a definite reduction of the cost of municipal service provision through alternative models emerges, which, however, requires further analysis in respect of the factors reducing the cost, factors that are analyzed comparatively below and in Table 3 (Boyne 1998; Ferris 1986; Fernandez 2009).[10] The cost of provision reduction varies between 10 and 24%, a strong sectoral differentiation, despite the presence of increased transaction costs and

---

[7]A comparative assessment of factors' impact is presented in Table 2.

[8]Qualitative and quantitative results of the empirical research of the present paper. See Table 2.

[9]Indicative reference to the 3463/2006 Act on waste management and utilization of municipal property, the 59/2007 Presidential Decree on the deregulation of public and municipal services, the 3468/2006 Act on energy production, the 3581/2007 Act on utilization of municipal property, and the 2052/1992 Act on infrastructure protection for the environment.

[10]Qualitative and quantitative results of the empirical research of the present paper.

Table 3 Performance and impact of alternative provision models (Source: Results based on the article's empirical (qualitative and quantitative) research)

Service	Number of case studies	Efficiency	Efficiency range	Quality	Accessibility	User satisfaction
Waste management and recycling	18	+22%	10–25%	Improvement	Improvement	Improvement
Cleaning services	12	+21%	14–26%	Improvement	Improvement	Improvement
Catering services	8	+19%	15–22%	Improvement	Downgrading	Downgrading
Vehicle maintenance	8	+20%	18–28%		Improvement	Improvement
Water provision	2	+120%	90–150%	Improvement	Improvement	Downgrading
Social services	7	+10%	−10–18%	Downgrading	Downgrading	Downgrading
Administrative support/IT services	10	+15%	10–21&	Improvement	Unchanged	Improvement
Infrastructure management	9	+21%	10–25%	Improvement	Unchanged	Improvement
Street lighting	4	+50%	30–60%	Improvement	Improvement	Improvement
Energy production	6	+27%	20–33%	Improvement	Unchanged	Improvement
Parking facilities	5	+12%	5–20%	Improvement	Improvement	Improvement

bureaucratic barriers to private sector participation. It should also be noted that the fact that limitation of the provision costs of services, in most of the case studies and according to the results of the qualitative research, did not result in a simultaneous deterioration of the quality and the accessibility of the services provided, a common problem and accusation in cases of private provision of municipal services. In contrast, the quality of the services provided remained invariable, while in 60% of cases, the engaged stakeholders and users noticed improvement in the quality of services, compared with the previous provision by the municipal authorities responsible. Similarly, accessibility to the services provided remained at the same level of access to residents, without imposing restrictions on utilizing the services provided by individuals.

In areas of municipal services where constraint of the costs of provision occurred, the greatest benefits emerged through the treatment of water supply with substantia savings however, there were issues in respect of the quality of the service provided in one out of the three case studies, waste management and recycling, followed by maintenance of street lighting and small-scale energy production from renewable sources. The cost of maintenance of municipal infrastructure and premises also appear to be reduced, while the costs of management of previous municipal undertakings, such as municipal car parking and maintenance services of the municipal fleet vehicles, has also been reduced by around 20%.

Significant limitation of the provision cost of between 15 and 19% was also noted in administrative support services, such as accounting services, IT services, project management and training programs, services that are beyond the traditional categories of technical services and that municipalities most commonly assign to the private sector.[11] In the area of social services, the cost constraint was on a lower scale, a range between 5 and 10% with substantial variations; however, issues in respect of the quality and accessibility to the service provided, accessibility that was limited in some instances by 30% of the total beneficiaries.

Examining distinctively the crucial issue of quality and accessibility to the services provided by individuals, statistically and in most of the case studies, the assignment of services provision to individuals does not appear to have led to the deterioration of the quality and accessibility of services (Edwards et al. 2004; Hodge 2010). In contrast, in a substantial proportion of cases (around 60%), the quality was improved based on the views expressed by the beneficiaries and the engaged parties of the services, excluding the employees of the municipal authority previously responsible the service provision, the vast majority of whom (80%) consider that the quality of the service has deteriorated and therefore, responsibility should be restored to the municipality. Social services are a clear exception, as a clear view of quality deterioration of the provided services has been observed.[12]

Accessibility of the delegate services is of particular interest, because, except from the case of social services, where their provision by the private sector led to a

---

[11] Qualitative and quantitative results of the empirical research of the present paper.

[12] Column 5 of Table 3.

reduction of the beneficiaries of between 10 and 25%, in almost all the rest of the areas, accessibility by residents was enhanced. An increase in the citizens being served by recycling services, in roads being lightened, and the incorporation of new estates into the municipal drinking water network are indicatively referred to. Therefore, in respect of the efficiency of the alternative provision in Greek local government, a direct link between the degree of complexity of the service provided by individuals and the rate of constraint of the provision cost has been observed, always in association with issues of quality and accessibility to services, which are comparatively examined in the context of the particular research. The more complicated and socially sensitive a service is, the lower the degree of the provision cost constraint.

Another crucial determinant for performance of alternative governance, but one with very limited impact, according to research, is the promotion of choice among service users. With the exception of social services, and even there in a limited number of two cases, the introduction of alternative governance models has not been accompanied by the promotion of provider choice for service users. Alternative governance modes in Greek local government have failed, both in terms of accessibility and competition impact, because in almost all cases, the introduction of alternative governance merely replaces the previous municipal monopoly with a new private monopoly.

Of particular interest is the interconnection between the institutional form of co-operation with the private sector and the degree of cost reduction in the provision of services (Klijn 2004; Osborne 2004). A significant variation and range of efficiency improvements in service provision, determined from the actual performance of the selected institutional model, as presented in Table 3. In this area, the largest cost reduction percentage comprise the contracting out, followed by hybrid forms of co-operation with the private sector, and finally partnerships between PPPs, despite the temporal governmental rhetoric to promote PPPs in Greek local government and the provision of investment incentives from European Union programs, such as the Joint European Union Support for Sustainable Investment in City Areas program. This comparatively increased percentage reduction in the contracting out model, compared with PPPs, concession contracts, and hybrid partnerships, demonstrates the limitations of national culture in co-operation and collaboration between the public and the private sector, which extends to the temporally limited co-operation of 1 year.[13] Furthermore, significant questions are raised about the relationship of inter-sectoral partnership, trust, and efficiency in the environment of the Greek local government, which requires the implementation of a new, more long-term oriented, win–win, and mutually beneficial culture, which will replace the selfish profit of the partners.

Consistent with the degree of complexity and the constraint of a service provision cost, the factors regarding the size and the location of the municipality are placed, for which, however, a reversal of international experience is observed, namely, rural and

---

[13]Columns 3 and 4 of Table 3.

small municipalities illustrate a higher percentage of reduction of the provision costs for municipal services provided by individuals (Boyne 2000; Bouckaert and Halligan 2008; Savas 2000).[14] This fact, according to the illustrative results of the empirical research, is due to the increased cost of the previous municipal provision, which resulted from the lack of differentiation of the cost policy of the small and rural municipalities in comparison with the large and metropolitan municipalities, which resulted in an increased asymmetry between workload and provision cost, mainly salary costs, equipment usage, and fixed costs.

Based on the above, consistency between the metropolitan location of the municipality and the increased cost constraint of the private provision of services is not provided by the results of the empirical research, despite such a connection being documented in the international literature (Fernandez 2009). The national differentiation consists of two characteristics of the current organization of the municipal services among the metropolitan areas in Greece. First, from the comparatively higher degree of unionization of municipal employees in metropolitan areas, compared with rural and semi-urban areas, which acts as a barrier in respect of the participation of private contractors in the provision of municipal services. A second source of that national differentiation consists in the size and administrative capacity of the municipalities, which, because of their size, fulfil more adequately their residents' needs for services, compared with the problems of adequate budgeting and administrative capacity that smaller municipalities face.

The degree of fiscal pressure of municipalities appears to impair the provision costs, as from the empirical research it emerged that there is a correlation between the degree of constraint of the available funding of the service provided and the reduction of the provision costs. The impact of financial pressure is channeled to the selection of private contractors' solution, being imprinted within the service provision contracts, through the incorporation of references about meeting particular quantitative main provision standards, providing the service according to the limited available budget (Fernandez 2009; Bovis 2008; Bell 2008).[15] Correlation is also observed between the reduction of the cost of provision and the extent of private participation in a municipality. In municipalities with a larger percentage of delegation of services from the municipalities to the private sector, the cost savings appear to be higher, mainly because of the capacity of the municipality to effectively monitor the execution of the contracts and the trust-based relations being developed among the partners.[16] On a similar basis, repeated delegation of a particular service to private contractors, or the extension of existing contracts, also leads to cost reduction, estimated to be 5% higher compared with the individual assignments and the first assignment to private contractors, for reasons that are also related to the development of trust among partners, the progressively more effective

---

[14]Qualitative and quantitative results of the empirical research of the present paper.

[15]Qualitative and quantitative results of the empirical research of the present paper.

[16]For the sustainability of research and harmonization with Greek local government, this rate has been specified among municipalities with more than one service being assigned.

understanding of the real needs of the service provided, and the development of specialized skills for monitoring the provision contracts, by relevant staff and organizational units of the municipality.

Continuity in the leadership of the municipal authority and the re-election of the municipal authority that originally promoted private sector participation also contribute toward the increase in the efficiency of the alternative municipal service provision. Political leadership also appears to have two nondiscrete parameters influencing the efficiency of alternative service provision. The first parameter relates to Mayors working experience, which appears to operate in favor of efficiency, when associated with Mayors working experience in the private sector. Supplementary to the stability and continuity of the municipal authority, the degree of political consensus in the administration of the municipality is also beneficial, as in case studies where the decision for private provision of particular municipal services was made with an increased majority and with no objections made by the opposition, cost constraint appears to be greater, owing to the lack of protests and conflicts. Of particular interest are the elements that demonstrate the lack of effect in the selection and operation of the alternative provision by the political ideology of the municipal authority. An uncommon political neutrality regarding a politically strained model of local government reform, especially in an environment characterized from the politicization and the political competition.

In contrast, the degree of employees' opposition appears to be in contradistinction with the level of cost reduction of the alternative service provision. The management capacity of the municipal authorities also comprises a significant factor in favor of the efficiency of the assigned municipal services provided by private contractors (Bell 2008; Fernandez 2007). The empirical research presented data illustrating that the development and staffing of specialized units—offices for monitoring private contractors in the municipalities—assist the improvement of efficiency and the quality of the alternative provision. In addition to the management capacity of the municipalities, it also operates beneficially to integrate alternative provision into the operational planning of the municipalities and produce specific monitoring indicators, on the basis of the business plan and the implementation of the assigning contract. The support of the alternative service provision by maturation studies and planning of alternative provision beforehand maximizes further the level of efficiency and cost constraint of the provision, particularly in the areas of waste management, alternative energy production, maintenance of street lighting, and construction of car parking.[17]

In relation to the operational planning and preparation of the alternative provision within a municipality, a positive contribution is made through the assumption of initiatives for solving and undermining problems that derive from overlaps and failures of the regulatory framework. The greater the degree and actions on behalf of the municipality for resolving the restrictions of the regulatory framework and bureaucratic competition among the co-responsible public authorities in respect of

---

[17]Qualitative and quantitative results of the empirical research of the present paper.

the private sector participation, the higher the rate of improvement of efficiency is presented, owing to the support of the initiative by the municipal authority, the effective maturation, and the project preparation.

3 Discussion: Interpreting the Efficiency Gains— Degradation of Working Relations or a Rising Organizational Innovation?

Where does this apparent cost reduction from the alternative provision of municipal services, in the municipalities being examined, emerge from? Does the cost reduction consist simply of the outcome of the degradation of working relations and the working conditions of staff and the limitation of accessibility by citizens, as opponents and critics of the private provision in Greece and internationally claim, or does it comprise a more complex amalgam and indication of a necessary and at the same time viable rationalization of existing models and culture of municipal service provision in Greece? (Bell 2008; Dollery 2008; Fernandez et al. 2008; Hefetz and Warner 2004; Hodge 2010)[18]

Empirical data seem to confirm the second view of rationalization and restructuring of the existing models of municipal service provision in Greek local government, under the applied and constantly worsening pressure of fiscal limitations of municipalities and understaffing. In particular, the results generated tend to confirm the view that cost reduction of the services provided result primarily from efficiency improvement and, at a lower scale, associate this cost limitation with the downgrading of the quality service quality and working conditions of employees.

Limiting the provision costs to a rate of more than 65% is considered to emerge from the degree of efficiency improvement of the services provided, an after effect of the changes induced by private contractors in the organization and provision of services. Changes that concern the promotion of innovation in the organization and provision of services and the use of modern technological equipment, particularly in the cases of waste management, the maintenance of municipal infrastructure and equipment, and the production of renewable sources of energy, optimize the productivity of the infrastructure (Osborne 2004). Service provision redesign is based on the abolishment of the unnecessary and actions and regulations that have no administrative value, in addition to the rationalization of service provision channels according to the needs of service recipients, in terms of frequency, quantity, and quality of services. Service provision rationalization contributes considerably toward cost reduction through the optimal use of the available resources and infrastructures. Particularly prominent are the results of rationalization of the procedures being followed in areas such as waste management and recycling, maintenance of municipal infrastructure and equipment/machinery, and services of administrative support.

---

[18]Qualitative and quantitative results of the empirical research of the present paper.

At the same time, achieving economies of scale and scope, particularly in case studies of waste management, recycling, maintenance of municipal street lighting and infrastructure, catering, and alternative energy production, also contributes toward the cost constraint of provision. Economies of scale and scope, which are achieved through the policy of private contractors for the provision of services to neighboring municipalities, on an inter-municipal scale or in related activities such as cleaning of streets, waste management and recycling, and the preservation of urban greenery. In some of the case studies, economies of scale were achieved through the collection and disposal, on behalf of the municipal authority, of the total of the community infrastructure and resources related to the particular category of activities, as in cases of photovoltaic energy production systems and municipal lighting. Furthermore, private contractors often possess the required skills, expertise, and modern equipment for the more efficient provision of specialized services, such as waste recycling, treatment and supply of drinking water, and operation of alternative energy production infrastructure (Bell 2008).[19] The promotion of organizational innovation in contractor monitoring also contributed toward service cost reduction and efficiency optimization, in an increased volume of case studies evaluated.

In almost all case studies, specialized quality and expenditure indicators have been incorporated into the contracts for providing municipal services. The incorporation of such performance indicators is a priority in Greek local government and an area of reform with limited results. Almost all of these performance indicators do not relate to result-oriented and outcome indicators, but are instead indicators of service expenditure and quality characteristics, as in the case of waste management by indicating the required equipment, the frequency of itineraries, and the quality characteristics of treated drinking water and irrigation. However, the introduction of performance indicators contributes toward efficiency optimization and they secure the quality of the services provided by private partners. More evident is the positive effect of innovation in efficiency optimization of municipal services in the areas of waste recycling, treatment and supply of drinking water, energy production, and street lighting, where innovation lies with the technologies utilized, which limit the provision costs, while the introduction of modern technologies contributes toward the more effective control of the quality of the provided services and the immediate resolution of errors, as in cases of water treatment, alternative electric energy production, and energy-saving.

In a more limited volume of case studies, however, with particularly positive results, both at the level of efficiency optimization and quality improvement of the services provided, and at a level of promotion of social support and engagement, organization, and decision-making, innovation is recognized as the catalyst (Bouckaert and Halligan 2008). This organizational innovation highlights almost all the hybrid partnership projects of municipal authorities with the private sector, except for the treatment and management of drinking water, where a major quality failure occurred. Organizational innovation is also characterized in some case

---

[19]Qualitative and quantitative results of the empirical research of the present paper.

Table 4 Performance of trust and alternative municipal services models (Source: Results based on the article's empirical qualitative research)

Model of alternative provision	Trust in alternative provision (%)	Trust in other partner (%)	Trust in central government (%)	Trust in local government (%)	Trust in audit/ performance measurement of partnerships (%)
Contracting out	32	36	32	44	32
Hybrid partnerships	67	63	30	47	72
Public–private partnerships	68	69	47	35	75

studies, and by the participation of local community and citizens in project development and management in the areas of energy production from renewable sources, waste recycling, and the provision of social services. The engagement and accountability of selected alternative municipal service provision projects are institutionalized and supported by the participation of representatives of residents in decision-making and by integrating the needs and views of residents in project planning, management, and auditing. Citizen and stakeholder participation and engagement, which are formally recognized at a contractual level by the incorporation of mechanisms for the promotion of transparency and accountability, and finally, by the social return of service revenue in areas of advanced social significance for the local community, such as the financing of community health and social protection services and infrastructures (Bell 2008).

Trust in governance is another critical parameter for the success of alternative provision in Greece. A factor with increased importance in the case of Greek local government, is that national social, capital, and political institutions are characterized by very low levels of trust and the appearance of a long-term public–private dichotomy of the public sphere, which creates important cultural barriers (Pagoulatos 2005; Paraskevopoulos 2000). In this area of analysis, and despite the comparatively limited efficiency of PPPs regarding the other two forms of alternative governance, trust among PPP partners appear to have the higher score, with a positive impact on partnership organization and performance, according to the results of Table 4. Independent of variations in organizational models, alternative governance policy diffusion and performance determined from the limited trust in government are a result of the sustained red tape and administrative burdens on policy regulation.

Competition in the provision of municipal services comprises by far the most essential factor of cost reduction of the alternative provision (Wollmann 2008; Savas 2000).[20] In most of the case studies examined for the purposes of the present paper (65%), competition was satisfactory and capable of leading to cost reduction of the

---

[20]Qualitative and quantitative results of the empirical research of the present paper.

services provided. In many of the projects (70%), more than two private vendors participated in competitions, while in 50% of those, more than three participated, and as a result there was a real cost constraint of the provision by 10–15%, which occurred because of the reduced price offers made by the vendors. It should also be highlighted that the total provision cost of the services that were put into competition for the selection of the private contractor was considerably lower than the previous monopolistic private provision, as the project budgets were limited by 15 to 20% compared with the previous funding by the municipal budget. Consequently, the emerging empirical finding is that in a few selected cases out of a total of 12, the actual cost reduction of the provision can reach 30%, in terms of comparative accountability (Wollmann 2008).[21]

Competition has an effect on developing a maket for services that, however, is plagued and limited by the lack of a flexible and effective regulation and a national policy for the introduction of competition. Competition appears to operate regardless of the geographical location of municipalities. Cost reduction due to the competition of external contractors appears to depend upon the transparency of procedures for selecting contractors and the type of competitions, where the category of international open competitions involves more than four bids. Competition is rather constructive in case studies of services that are typical in their specificity and simplicity, such as waste management, recycling, catering services, cleaning and maintenance of municipal services, where economies of scale are achieved, and in cases of inter-municipal contractor selection. Moreover, as has already presented, the introduction of competition failed to promote service provider choice to citizens.

As for the interconnection between cost constraints of the operation of alternative municipal service provision and the degradation of working conditions and rights of employees, the following clarification should be made. Limitation of wage costs and alteration of the working relations of the employees engaged are reflected in the empirical research; however, these changes do not constitute more than 40% of the resulting reduction of the provision costs. Therefore, they consist of parameters of cost constraint of services, without concerning the total of such a constraint. The fact that wage costs in a few of the evaluated sectors, especially in waste management and secondarily in municipal transportation, are characterized as particularly increased, often surpassing 70% of the total service cost, should be noted. It is therefore a labor cost that is significantly increased compared with international practice, which varies between 40 and 50% and, within that scope, its limitation may be considered as an action of its rationalization (Wollmann 2008; Bell 2008).[22]

In terms of working relations, private provision changes the employment regime of employees from public to private law, which is characterized by a lower quality of insurance and wage benefits. As for the allegation of the limitation of personnel numbers, this particular factor seems to be confirmed on a significant level by the case studies examined, although results are weighted, as 55% led to the limitation of the number of personnel, inducing a dual explanation. The limitation of the number

---

[21]Qualitative and quantitative results of the empirical research of the present paper.

[22]Qualitative and quantitative results of the empirical research of the present paper.

of personnel on the one hand confirms the relevant allegations of the opponents standing against the assignment of municipal services to individuals; however, from a different angle, it produces the capability for improvement of the existing efficiency of municipal services, as in most of the case studies (75%), the reduction of the number of employed personnel did not result in a degradation of quality and accessibility to the provided service, instead maintaining or often improving it.

4 Conclusion: Beyond the Limits of Efficiency—Alternative Governance Arrangements and the Demand for the Emergence of a New Model of Local Governance

From the comparative analysis of case studies regarding the state of art of alternative provision in Greece emerges the definite cost reduction of service provision and the improvement of the efficiency level. However, this perspective requires further analysis on a case-study level by taking into account the non-economic factors, which are also found in the Greek case, to co-form the degree of efficiency improvement, through private participation and either the successful or the unsuccessful incorporation of alternative institutional arrangement from the municipalities (Peters 2004; Bouckaert 2011). These factors relate to the degree of trust and co-operation among the municipal and private partners involved, and the interconnection of the alternative provision with the emergence of a new model of local governance, based on inter-sectoral co-operation, the establishment of a local consensus, and the introduction of innovation into service planning and provision.

   In all good practices of selected case studies, and of cases achieving the highest rate of efficiency improvement, the level of confidence and trust were particularly high among the partners. The development of a high level of trust, which contradicts the low national average rate and the respective rates in local government, is based on a number of special characteristics. These special characteristics comprise the gradual transformation of individualistic and piecemeal co-operation with the private sector, in a long-term and repeated successful collaboration that contributes toward the development of mutual trust (Stoker 2006; Peters 2004). High level rates of trust between public and private partners are reflected in the analysis of project contracts that are less complex and have more room for flexibility in the provision of services. Alternative provision is evaluated in respect of the achievement of service-specific objectives and standards, in terms of service cost, quality characteristics, and outputs, and not according to the traditional and counterproductive evaluation of strict accounting and assessment of legal procedure compliance.

   The high rate of inter-sectoral trust among partners of alternative provision projects contradicts their low national average rate in the central government and the responsible agencies for the promotion of private participation in local government, such as the special secretariat for PPPs and the Ministry of the Interior, owing to the increased bureaucracy and the successive and costly control mechanisms. Lack of trust in the central government and an increased level of trust among partners, which led to the decision made by the parties involved, i.e., the municipalities, to select the alternative provision choice as a policy tool against the ineffectiveness and delays of the responsible central government authorities to support the expansion and performance of alternative provision, through the promotion of decentralization and the provision of adequate financial resources.[23] The influence of inter-sectoral trust is of equal importance, also in the context of selection made by municipalities of the alternative routes of the regulatory framework for the development of alternative provision, beyond the narrow limits of hardship of the PPP legislation.

Significant contribution toward the promotion of trust between the parties involved regarding the co-operation between the public and private sector is made through the institutionalized participation of municipal authorities in the management of projects, in addition to the provision of consultative and open procedures of disclosure and publication of their results. Deliberative and participatory processes and mechanisms improved the quality of municipal planning and the innovative provision of municipal services. The implementation of these initiatives to promote the engagement of partners and stakeholders and to strengthen public accountability operates positively in terms of the formation of the required alliances and the creation of a supportive environment for the introduction of alternative provision.[24] Participation and consultation are principles that contribute toward the ceasing of the common social contradiction and mistrust against municipal authorities in favor of alternative provision and the promotion of trust.

In addition to trust and engagement, local innovation also operates positively. Innovation in establishing incentives for co-operation between the partners and local community, perceiving different localization facets of alternative forms of municipal service provision and social redistribution of their revenue. More specifically, funding practices of social and medical services and municipal infrastructure for residents were recorded through the operation of alternative provision models, particularly in hybrid partnerships, while in four cases, communitization of the alternative provision concerned the participation of residents in the share capital, as part of the municipality participatory rate. This constantly increasing trend toward communitisation of alternative governance arrangements and their incorporation into the development programming of municipalities illustrates the gradual transformation of private participation from a simple mechanism of fulfilling local needs for municipal services into an influential catalyst of co-funding and supporting the implementation of local development planning at a local level (Bouckaert 2011).[25] The development planning will be based on partnership, consultation, and co-operation for the effective regulation of local problems and the promotion of real reform of the local state in Greece.

---

[23] Qualitative and quantitative results of the empirical research of the present paper.

[24] Qualitative and quantitative results of the empirical research of the present paper.

[25] Qualitative and quantitative results of the empirical research of the present paper.

An emerging model of local governance that exceeds the narrow limits of public–private spheres and places the spotlight on the effective regulation of the long-lasting local issues and the more efficient accomplishment of citizens' needs, based on the mutual utilization of public and private resources, financial or not, and the establishment of wider development alliances with the participation of central government agencies, local government institutions, private sector enterprises, and civil society. A new model of local governance, the viability and effectiveness of which, however, necessitates the implementation of a new framework of co-operation between the public and private sector at a local level, beyond centralization boundaries and the competition between central and local state and based on the development of a new culture of co-operation among public authorities, and among those of the private sector and civil society. Therefore, the challenge of alternative provision in Greek local government should not be considered to be simply the percentage reduction of the cost of provision of the municipal services, but more widely the development and diffusion of a new participatory and less bureaucratic model of local governance, where competition will be linked to consultation and efficiency improvement will be connected to the social effectiveness of the local state mechanisms.

References

Afonso, A. (Ed.) (2010). *Public sector efficiency: International comparisons*. EIB.

Agranoff, R. (2004). *Collaborative public management: New strategies for local government*. New York: Sunny Press.

Bell, G. (2008). Factors explaining local privatization: A meta-regression analysis. *Public Choice, 36*(2), 206–228.

Bouckaert, G. (2011). *Public management reform: A comparative analysis*. Oxford: Oxford University Press.

Bouckaert, G., & Halligan, J. (2008). *Managing performance international comparisons*. London: Routledge.

Bouckaert, G., & Pollitt, C. (2010). *Public management reform: A comparative analysis*. Oxford: Oxford University Press.

Bovis, M. (2008). *Public–private partnerships in European Union*. London: Macmillan Press.

Boyne, G. A. (1998). The determinants of variations in local service contracting: Garbage in, garbage out? *Urban Affairs Review, 34*(1), 149–162.

Boyne, G. (2000). *Public choice and local government reform*. London: Macmillan Press.

Bozeman, B. (2011). *Rules and red tape*. New York: Sharpe.

Brudney, J., & Bozeman, B. (2008). *Statistical analysis for public administration*. New York: Jossey Bass.

Brudney, J. L., Fernandez, S., Ryu, J. E., & Wright, D. S. (2005). Exploring and explaining contracting out: Patterns among the American states. *Journal of Public Administration Research and Theory, 15*(3), 367–391.

Cohen, S. (2008). Identifying the moderator factors of financial performance in Greek Municipalities. *Financial Accountability and Management, 24*(3), 265–294.

Denhart, T. (2000). *The new public service: Serving, not steering*. New York: Sharpe.

Dexia Bank. (2004–2011). *European public – Private partnerships market report*.

Dexia Bank. (2011). *Subnational governments in European Union*. Paris: Dexia Press.

Dollery, J. (2007). *Reform and leadership in public sector: A political economy approach*. Sydney: Oxford University Press.

Dollery, D. (2008). *The political economy of local government reform: A comparative analysis of advanced Anglo-American countries*. Oxford: Oxford University Press.

Edwards P., Shaoul J., Stafford A., & Arblaste L. (2004). *Evaluating the operation of PFI in roads and hospitals*. ACCA research report no. 88, London.

Featherstone, K. (2008). *The limits of Europeanization: Structural reform and public policy in Greece*. London: Macmillan Press.

Fernandez, S. (2007). What works best when contracting for services? An analysis of contracting performance at the local level. *Public Administration, 85*(1), 119–134.

Fernandez, S. (2009). Understanding contracting performance: An empirical analysis. *Administration and Society, 41*(1), 67–100.

Fernandez, S., Ryu, J. E., & Brudney, J. L. (2008). Exploring variations in contracting for services among American local governments: Do politics still matter? *American Review of Public Administration, 38*(2), 439–462.

Ferris, J. M. (1986). The decision to contract out: An empirical analysis. *Urban Affairs Review, 22*(2), 289–302.

Greene, J. D. (2002). *Cities and privatization: Prospects for the new century*. New York: Chatham House.

Hefetz, A., & Warner, M. (2004). Privatization and its reverse: Explaining the dynamics of the government contracting process. *Journal of Public Administration Research and Theory, 14*(1), 171–190.

Heinelt, H. (2006). *Legitimacy and urban governance: A cross-national comparative study*. London: Routledge.

Hodge, G. (2004). *Public–private partnerships: International comparisons*. London: Routledge.

Hodge, G. A. (2010). *International handbook of public – Private partnerships*. London: Macmillan Press.

Hood, C. (2006). *Transparency: The key to better governance*. Oxford: Oxford University Press.

Karkatsoulis, P. (2004). *State in transition*. Athens: Sideris.

Karkatsoulis, P. (2011). *Regulation, deregulation and reform of public policy*. Athens: Sideri.

Kazakos, P. (2001). *Between state and market*. Athens: Patakis.

Klijn, E. (2004). *Managing uncertainties in networks: Public–private controversies*. London: Edward Elgar.

Konsolas, N. (1997). *Modern regional economic policy*. Athens: Papazisis.

Lavdas, K. (1997). *The Europeanization of Greece*. London: Macmillan Press.

Maistros, P. (2009). *The three waves of public administration reform in Greece*. Athens: Papazisis.

Makridimitris, A., & Michalopoulos, N. (2000). *Expert reports on the Greek public administration*. Athens: Papazisis.

OECD. (2011). *Greece: Review of the central administration*.

Osborne, S. (Ed.). (2004). *Public-private partnerships. Theory and practice in international perspective*. London: Routledge.

Osborne, S. (2008). *New public governance*. Oxford: Oxford University Press.

Osborne, D., & Gaebler, T. (1992). *Reinventing government: How the entrepreneurial spirit is transforming the public sector*. Reading, MA: Addison-Wesley.

Ostrom, E. (1990). *Governing the commons*. Bloomington: University of Indiana Academic Press.

Pagoulatos, G. (2005). The politics of privatization: Redrawing the public-private boundary. *West European Politics, 28*(1), 111–131.

Paraskevopoulos, C. (2000). Social capital and public–private distinction in Greek Regions. *Journal of European Public Policy, 19*(2), 302–319.

Patton, J. (2008). *Realistic evaluation*. London: Prentice Hall.

Peters, G. (2004). *The future of governing*. Kansas: Kansas University Press.

Plimakis S. (2012). *Individual participation in the Greek local government: Regulation and accountability, under the constellation of bureaucracy*. Unpublished Doctorate Dissertation.

Prime Minister's Office – General Secretariat of Government. (1992). *Prospects and areas of private enterprise participation in local government*.

Rhodes, R. A. W. (1997). *Understanding governance: Policy networks, governance, reflexivity and accountability*. London: Open University Press.

Savas, E. S. (2000). *Privatization and public-private partnerships*. New York: Chatham House.

Shah, A. (2012). *Local governance in industrial countries*. Washington, DC: World Bank Publications.

Stoker, G. (2003). *Towards holistic governance*. Cambridge: Cambridge University Press.

Stoker, G. (2006). *Governance*. Oxford: Oxford University Press.

Tatsos, N. (1999). *Fiscal decentralisation: Theory and practice*. Athens: Tipothoto.

Trova, E. (2007). *Public–Private sector partnerships: European and national law*. Athens: Greek Lettering.

Van de Walle, S. (2005). *Measuring bureaucratic quality in governance indicators*. Leuven: Instituut voor de Overheid.

Warner, M., & Hebdon, R. (2001). Local government restructuring: Privatization and its alternatives. *Journal of Policy Analysis and Management, 20*(3), 315–336.

Warner, M. E., & Hefetz, A. (2002). Applying market solutions to public services: An assessment of efficiency, equity and voice. *Urban Affairs Review, 19*(1), 96–100.

Wollmann, H. (2008). *The provision of public services in Europe: Between state, local government and market*. London: Macmillan Press.

Yetimis P., & Marava, N. (2005). *New relations between private and public sector in the production and operation of high scale infrastructural projects in Greece. Trends and developments in the 1980 and 1990 decades*. Panteion University.

Yiannitsis, A. (1994). *Privatisation issues in Greece*. Athens: Livanis.

Competitiveness of the Greek Economy: Before and After the Crisis

George Galanos, Aggelos Kotios, and Manolis Koutoulakis

Abstract Greece in the last 7 years is experiencing an unprecedented economic crisis. The basis of the discussion is mainly in the fiscal deficit and public debt and consequently the implementation of those policies which will contribute to fiscal consolidation and resolving financial imbalances. However, as already shown by the implementation of the policies of the Stability and Reform Agreement, the Greek problem is much more complex (2013).

Today, Greece more than ever is facing the twin deficits problem: the fiscal deficit and the deficit of the current account reflect the deterioration of the competitiveness of Greek economy.

The main purpose of the article is to analyze the performance of the Greek economy on competitiveness and make a comparative analysis of its position before and during the crisis.

Article's specific objectives are to explore and analyze the causes of the reduced impact of policies to increase competitiveness of the country.

Keywords Structural weaknesses · Adjustment programs (VC) · International competitiveness · Political economy

1 Introduction

A multitude of determinants for competitiveness is recognized, with complex and often conflicting interactions. These determinants range from those referred in classical theories to those of more modern approaches that tend to involve parameters

G. Galanos (✉)
Department of Economics, Democritus University of Thrace, Panepistimioupoli Komotini, Greece
e-mail: ggalanos@econ.duth.gr

A. Kotios · M. Koutoulakis
Department of International and European Studies, University of Piraeus, Piraeus, Greece

© Springer Nature Switzerland AG 2019
N. Sykianakis et al. (eds.), *Economic and Financial Challenges for Eastern Europe*,
Springer Proceedings in Business and Economics,
https://doi.org/10.1007/978-3-030-12169-3_14

such as education, technological developments—either domestic or imported—macroeconomic stability, good governance, effective legislative framework, level of transparency, institutions' functionality, corporate and doing business culture, rules of demand, market size, etc. (Blanke et al. 2005).

In the international bibliography, a broad range of definitions has been provided for the "competitiveness" term, depending on researcher's or publishing entity's perspective, and the investigated range for it. A crucial parameter is the economical level at which we want to examine the concept of competitiveness. At microeconomic level, the term is rather well defined, as it is tightly linked to the capacity of each enterprise to face its competitors, to grow and demonstrate sustainable profitability. However, when we move toward studying the same concept at macroeconomic level, the whole picture becomes much more blared and exceptionally complex, since for each case definition depends on both viewer's perspective and also to the characteristics of each individual state (Annoni and Kozovska 2010). For example, we can examine the interpretation of a notable international organization, such as the World Economic Forum, which states that competitiveness is "the set of institutions, policies and factors that determine the level of productivity of a country"; it becomes evident from this definition that the two economic levels are interrelated, since according to this point of view, macroeconomic competitiveness provides the required fertile ground for the microeconomic level competitiveness to be achieved. State's wealth derives from its ability to exploit with the best possible way its factors of production and correspondingly increase its productivity. But productivity also depends to the microeconomic efficiency of the economy, which coincides with the business quality and efficiency (Porter et al. 2007).

Exactly for reasons as those outlined above, a broad range of definitions and interpretations have been articulated for the "competitiveness" term. Indeed, even the very same organizations or researchers are expressing differentiated formalizations in the course of time, the evolution of economic models, and the economic and trading developments and practices. The Organization for Economic Cooperation and Development in 1992 defined competitiveness as "the degree to which a nation can, under free trade and fair market conditions, produce goods and services which meet the test of international markets, while simultaneously maintaining and expanding the real income of its people over the long-term" (OECD 1992). In 1996, the same organization defines competitiveness as "...the ability of companies, industries, regions, nations or supranational regions to generate, while being and remaining exposed to international competition, relatively high factor income and factor employment levels on a sustainable basis" (OECD 1996).

World Economic Forum (WEF) is an organization that greatly reflects contemporary thinking regarding economy and global trading. Thus in 1996, WEF described competitiveness as "the ability of a national economy to achieve stained high rates of economic growth, as measured by the annual change in gross domestic product per person" (World Economic Forum 1996). In 2007, however, it gave a much more descriptive formulation for the same concept since it noted that "national competitiveness is the web of factors, policies and institutions that determine the level of productivity of a country. In turn, the level of productivity determines the sustainable level of prosperity that an economy can enjoy." In other words, most competitive national economies tend to be able to offer higher levels of income to their citizens. Productivity level also determines the return on investment ratio in a national economy. As yields are the key determinants for economic growth, a more competitive economy is the one that is more likely to grow faster in both midterm and long term (World Economic Forum 2007).

Since the beginning of the 1990s decade, European Union put significant effort in defining the competitiveness term but also these best methodologies for achieving its maximization in real economy and life. A key document for this process was the "Commission White Paper on Growth, Competitiveness and Employment" (European Commission 1993). In this document EU suggests that competitiveness is achieved by strengthening both economic activity and employability. The achievement of such goals is accomplished through the reinforcement of different parameters and factors, such as production capacities, skills, research, and education. Reflecting the special conditions for Greece, the National Council for Competitiveness and Development (NCCD) of the Hellenic Ministry of Development defines competitiveness as "the ability to sustain and improve the quality of life for country's citizens—upgrading business environment, boosting employment and actual cohesion, enhancing environment and its protection, constant productivity improvement—in a globalized environment." Competitiveness is therefore a multidimensional and dynamic concept that expands well beyond the narrow perception of economy's costing or exporting performance, incorporating parameters related to the long-term prospect of living standards, employment, social cohesion, regulatory framework, and most importantly the quality of life for state's citizens.

Of course, apart from the various global and regional organizations, a number of individual researchers have articulated numerous different definitions for competitiveness, without necessarily one interpretation contradicting with the other; we can rather state that all of them compose the complete competitiveness picture, reflecting indeed the complexity of modern economics and trading relations.

Scott and Lodge (1985) refer to competitiveness as the "country's ability to create, produce, distribute, and service products in international trade while earning profit." According to Fajnzylber (1988), competitiveness is defined as "a state's capacity to increase its international market share and simultaneously advance living standards for its citizens." Buckley et al. argued that the competitiveness concept contains both efficiency (achieving objectives at the lowest cost) and efficiency (aiming for the appropriate targets). Competitiveness includes both objectives and the means for achieving them (Buckley et al. 1988), while Tyson concluded that the term refers to our ability for offering goods and services that meet the international competition criteria, while citizens enjoy a sustainably growing living standard (Tyson 1992).

According to Fagerberg, state's competitiveness is reflected to its ability in achieving the set economic policy main objectives, primarily these of enhancing income and employment rates, without inducing arduousness in its payments balance (Fagerberg 1996). Similarly, Aiginger argues that a country is considered to be competitive if it manages to sell enough products and services, succeeding income levels compatible with country's current and future aspirations, under conditions (macroeconomic and social) that are considered satisfactory from its citizens (Aiginger 1996). In 2006 the same researcher adds to his view that national or regional competitiveness is the ability to establish prosperity (Aiginger 2006).

Based on these basic principles for competitiveness, and given that nowadays we are experiencing a strongly internationalized competitive environment, there is a number of key factors for defining if a state is competitive or not.

The most important of these are (Ezeala-Harrison 1999):

- Its capacity and ability to produce high-quality products and services
- Its competitive levels of production and distribution costs
- Its doing business ability

2   Competitiveness Measurement Systems

For assessing and measuring states' competitiveness properly, a large number of different models have been developed in these last decades by individual researchers and influential international organizations. A common approach for such systems is the use of indicators and parameters sets, which affect and to a certain extent determine state's productivity and overall population's prosperity, in a sustainable way.

Most models separate indicators into certain categories. Although each indicator's value calculation and their resulting groupings are done individually, it should however be noted that they are not independent from each other but usually somehow associated; the change in one of them induces alterations to the others. It is, of course, reasonable to assume that a change affects each indicator in a different way. We still have to pay attention in the fact that an identical set of criteria is not applied with exactly the same way in all countries; it is easy to understand the impact of the, for example, different size, structure, and characteristics of the Greek economy and this of the United States.

2.1   Global Competitiveness Report

This report aims in assessing each state's economy capacity in the globe in achieving sustainable growth. While in the past it was giving more weight to the macroeconomic environment, recently it altered providing additional focus to microeconomic level indicators, i.e., the level of enterprises. Through this approach, it is acknowledged that wealth of nations is actually constituted at microlevel, coming from the operating enterprises in each economy and the quality of doing business environment.

Table 1 WEF competitiveness pillars

Basic requirements	Efficiency enhancers	Innovation and sophistication factors
1. Institutions	5b. Human resources—higher education and training	11. Business sophistication
2. Infrastructure	6. Goods market efficiency	12. Innovation
3. Macroeconomic stability	7. Labor market efficiency	
4. Safety	8. Financial market sophistication	
5a. Human resources—primary education	9. Technological readiness	
	10. Extroversion and markets size	

World Economic Forum (2007), "The Global Competitiveness Report 2007–2008"

The model that WEF uses for performing its global rankings is extremely complex. In total it uses approximately 180 sub-indicators, which are grouped into 12 competitiveness pillars comprising 3 general axes (Table 1).

For determining the majority of sub-indicators' values, questionnaire-based surveys are conducted by the World Economic Forum among senior business executives. Due to the very nature of many questions, the provided answers (on a scale of 1–7) involve a sufficient degree of subjectivity. Subsequently these sub-indicators that are based on quantitative statistics are a minority.

2.2 World Competitiveness Yearbook

IMD foundation annually publishes its World Competitiveness Yearbook, which analyzes and compares the ability of nations to establish and sustain a supportive business environment, which in turn enhances their competitiveness. Its approach suggests that wealth is mainly generated at the business level; hence this very level of "business competitiveness" becomes critical. Howbeit since enterprises are operating in a national-level environment, which either strengthens or weakens their ability to compete, both domestically and internationally, "competitiveness of business environment" or "competitiveness of nations" gets a great importance too.

The competitiveness model, exploited by the Yearbook, partitions national environment into four main factors:

1. Economic performance
2. Government efficiency
3. Business efficiency
4. Infrastructure

These factors are further partitioned into 20 sub-factors and are rated based on more than 320 specifically selected criteria. It is noteworthy that with only slight changes in the overall index, the rankings can improve. In other words, there is a ranking "sensitivity" depending on the ranking neighborhood that a country can be positioned. So with just a slight improvement of 0.1% to the overall WCY score, a country could gain one position, while an improvement by a more respective 3.7% in other cases could provide just a poor gain of only five places. Such improvements can easily be achieved by improving the executives that complete the survey questionnaires or meliorate some of the objective indicators, wherever this is possible in the short term.

In order to get input for the needed indicators, IMD cooperates with other international bodies, getting access to statistical data for assessing quantitative criteria. In addition it conducts surveys for input regarding qualitative variables. Still, the weight factor for the objective elements is around the 2/3 of the global index, while subjective estimates are narrowed to the remaining 1/3. It is obvious that responses on qualitative estimations and perceptions enclose the element of subjectivity. The collection of qualitative data is based on questionnaires sent to senior executives (around 70 individuals per country). Overall, with respect to the WEF approach, in this IMD, the importance of subjective estimates is more limited. It should be noted however that WEF and IMD rankings demonstrate a high correlation factor (correlation coefficient = 0.9), but still their totals do not fully match.

2.3 World Bank Indicators

World Bank publishes a set of indicators regarding that examines establishment, operation, and termination of businesses. World Bank's indicators are considered extremely reliable since they are based on concrete exemplars. The methodology used for exporting the needed results includes the study of specific examples of a typical business entity, of the same characteristics for all acquired countries, and asks credible lawyers in each one of them, to assess the parameters for specific cases and procedures. These include:

- For accessing business establishment, it uses a typical limited liability company in the most densely populated city in the country.
- For accessing recruitment procedures, it examines the hiring of a nonexecutive employee for meeting the needs of a typical small- or medium-sized enterprise.
- For business closing, it also strictly defines a limited liability company, being in a specific bankruptcy state.

The reporting of such estimates for specific examples narrows the generality of the produced indicators, since despite leaving a number of parameters out of consideration, in the same time, it greatly enhances accuracy. In the parameters accounted, it does not include potential additional time or costs that can occur due to corruption phenomena.

Table 2 World Bank indicators	Indicators groups
	I. Starting a business indicators
	1. Start-up procedures to register (number)
	2. Time required to start a business (days)
	3. Cost of business start-up procedures
	4. Minimum required capital for business start-up
	II. Hiring personnel indicators
	1. Hiring barriers
	2. Working hours flexibility
	III. Enterprise termination indicators
	1. Time required to terminate a business
	2. Bankruptcy costs
	3. Claims recovery (after bankruptcy)
	https://data.worldbank.org/indicator

Such indicators demonstrate limited sensitivity. In other words, for achieving sufficient improvement, it is required that many parameters need to demonstrate an upturn, thus providing the needed boost in country's rankings (e.g., reduction of required procedures, lessen the required initial capital for establishing a company, improvements in the regulation for fixed-term employment contracts—Table 2).

2.4 European Union Indicators

In 2000 Lisbon European Council with the objective of moving toward a more competitive and dynamic Europe, EU decided to monitor a specific set of indicators. These 14 indicators cover specific competitiveness aspects (Table 3).

The European Union Index assesses both short-term and long-term prospects of European economies (Annoni and Kozovska 2010). It is based on the use of six indicator categories: GDP growth rate, public debt levels, surplus/deficit levels, rankings in Global Competitiveness Index, corruption index, and finally the cost of pensioning systems (or alternatively the rate of aging populations—future cost of aging). However we have to underline that the use of this model is limited only to EU countries, where specific conditions prevail and explicit policies are implemented.

2.5 Economic Freedom of the World Index

Economic Freedom of the World Index (EFW) is published by the Fraser Institute of the United States. This initiative was launched by M. Walker, member of the foundation, and the Nobel Prize awardee Milton Friedman in 1986. The index, the way it has evolved until today, measures "economic freedom's" basic dimensions,

Table 3 European Union indicators	Indicators
	1. Employment rate
	2. Elderly's employment rate
	3. Long-term unemployment
	4. Poverty threshold
	5. Regional unemployment distribution
	6. GDP per capita (in PPP)
	7. Comparative price level
	8. Productivity of employees
	9. Business investments
	10. Educational efficiency
	11. Research and development (% GDP)
	12. Greenhouse gases emissions
	13. Energy density
	14. Transportations volume

The EU Regional Competitiveness Index 2016

which relate with government's size, security of property rights, access to sound money, freedom to trade internationally, and regulation of credit, labor, and business.

Third-party data, in particular the WEF Global Competitiveness Report and the International Country Risk Guide, are being incorporated in the formulation of this index. In total it exploits 38 distinct criteria to synthesize the general index. Some of these third-party data come from surveys employing senior executives' personal opinion and thus introducing a certain amount of subjectivity. In general EFW demonstrates akin reliability levels to the aforementioned sources.

2.6   Entrepreneurship Indicators

Entrepreneurial Behavior and Attitudes Indicators are based on a survey performed by the Global Entrepreneurship Monitor (GEM). The survey is conducted individually in each country by a local team, in cooperation with the program coordinators "London Business School" and "Babson College" in Boston. It uses a common model for all countries, which defines the variables (both quantitative and qualitative), which are considered to affect entrepreneurship levels in a country. Each local team owes to collect and process the needed data.

Indicators estimates are based on data coming from three sources:

1. Field survey in each individual country, using a sample of 1000–2000 adults, aged between 18 and 64. In most cases the surveys are conducted by telephone, taking a random selection of houses equipped with a landline. Specifically for Greece, the survey was conducted by Metron Analysis by phone and included 2000 adults.

2. Standard ten-paged questionnaires, completed by interviewed specialists. These questionnaires are the source for several qualitative indicators. In Greece, the survey was carried out by IOBE (Foundation for Economic & Industrial Research), funded by the Ministry of Development and private Foundation's sponsors.
3. Statistical data from standardized international sources such as World Bank and IMF, United Nations, out of which basic characteristics regarding economic development, population distribution, educational efficiency, and infrastructure are extracted.
4. It is easy to spot however that data originating from interviews (cases 1 and 2) induce a level of subjectivity.

3   The Adaptation Policy in Greece: Objectives, Means, and Outcomes

From the initiation of the adjustment programs, the following short-term objectives were set:

- Restoring fiscal balance
- Ensuring financial stability and liquidity for the economy

  Respectively, the medium-term and long-term objectives were:

- Recovering of the Greek economy and securing debt serving capacity
- Improving Greek economy competitiveness
- Restoring external trading imbalances

  As the main economic policy instruments for achieving the aforementioned objectives, certain packages of measures were selected, partitioned in the following categories of interventions:

- Reduction of public expenditure, increase of tax revenues, and gradual development of primary surpluses.
- Enhancing internal devaluation through reductions in salaries, profits, and other incomes, setting as main goal to reduce domestic consumption, triggering prices reductions of internationally traded goods and services, and aiming to promote exports and substitute imports with local goods and services.
- Liberating goods, services, capital, and labor markets, combined with a wide range of changes and reforms in public sector, which were named as structural changes. Particular emphasis has been provided from the very begging, in deregulating labor market and limiting labor unions role.
- Implementation of an ambitious privatization program of state-owned enterprises and other public properties.

According to the adjustment programs' projections, the recessional effects of the restrictive fiscal policy would had be temporary, since the following dynamics were expected to gradually act countercyclically, i.e., in the direction of economic growth:

- The surfacing of the so-called non-Keynesian developmental impacts, through the increase of consumption demand due to the anticipated tax cuts. These cuts were thought to follow the budgetary adjustments and the enhancement of investments due to the anticipated reduction in government debt and hence in interest rates on consumer, housing, and business loans (confidence effect). At the same time, the reduction in total consumption would allow an increase in total savings and investments.
- The increase in external demand and exports, following the fall of exporting prices due to the domestic depreciation. In addition an increase in domestic demand was expected due to substitution of imports.
- Increased investments rates, particularly of the foreign direct investment, due to the improvement of business environment. These could be driven by privatization, liberalization, and deregulation of goods and services markets, as well as through the modernization of the public sector and the upgrade of its provided services.

But reality did not confirm these expectations.

4   Greek Economy Competitiveness

The reality is that the negative performance of the Greek economy during the economic crisis, in terms of competitiveness, has gotten worse as indicated by the country's economic efficiency and certainly the whole image did not reverse. Figures 1 and 2 illustrate the decline in country's competitiveness both compared with the relative consumer prices (CPI), overall weights, and with the relative unit

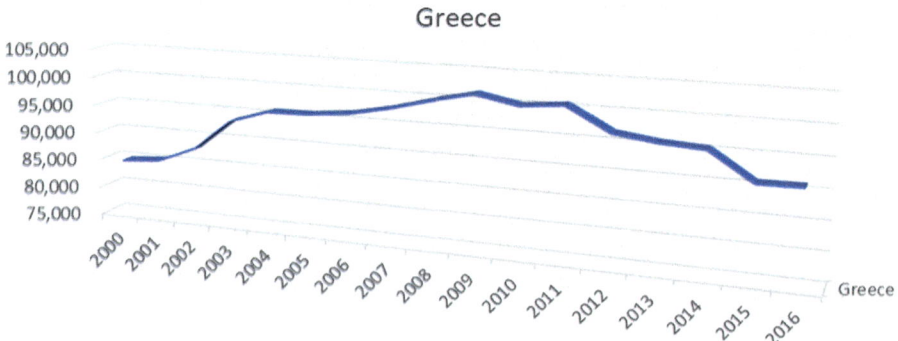

Fig. 1 Competitiveness indicator, relative consumer prices (CPI), overall weights. Source: Annual macroeconomic database (AMECO) 2017; Own calculations

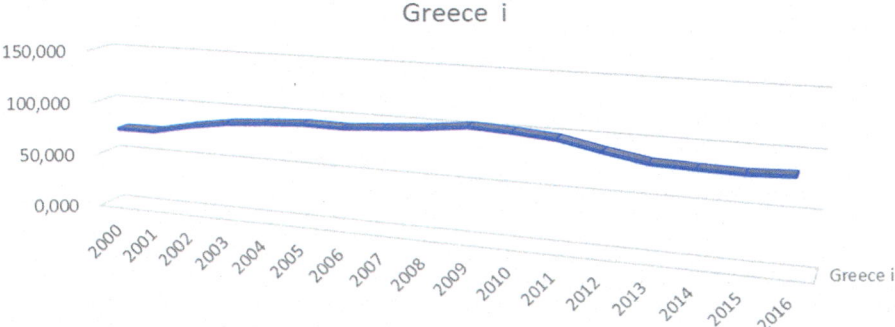

Fig. 2 Competitiveness indicator, relative unit labor costs, overall economy. Source: Annual macroeconomic database (AMECO) 2017; Own calculations

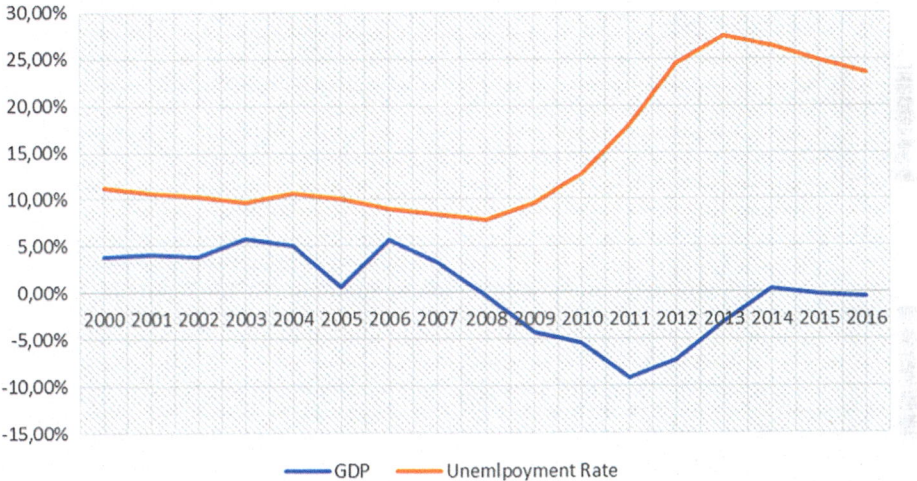

Fig. 3 GDP and unemployment rate in Greece (annual change in %). Source: Annual macroeconomic database (AMECO) 2017; Own calculations

labor costs, overall economy, which indicates the failure of the second midterm and long-term strategic target of boosting the competitiveness of the country. At the same time, the country experienced a stronger recession than expected, during which it cumulatively lost more than 25% of its GDP, which has led to a large increase in unemployment and the uprising of strong social problems. On top of these and despite significant fiscal consolidation efforts, debt ratio as a percentage of GDP increased rather than declining, while unemployment was rising (Fig. 3). At the same time, the failure of the implemented policies could clearly be mapped out in Figs. 4 and 5 where it is clearly demonstrated that the fall in wages cost had no positive effect on the unemployment rate, resulting in the failure of the first target as well.

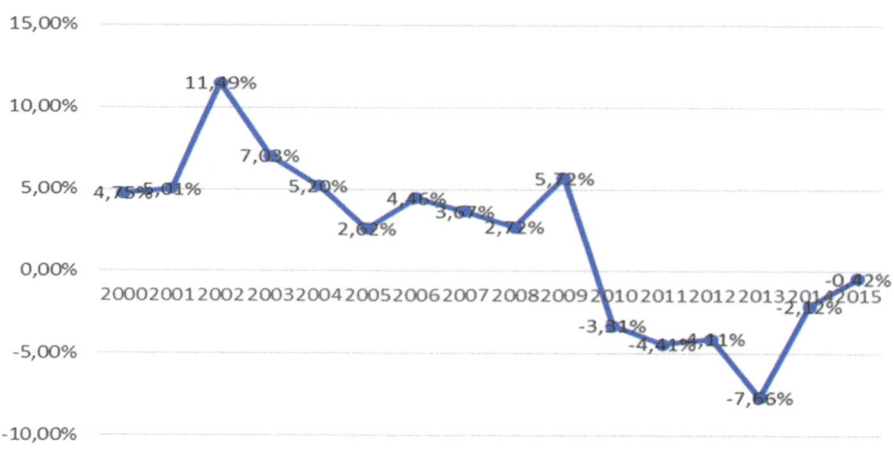

Fig. 4 Wages index (annual change in %). Source: Annual macroeconomic database (AMECO) 2017; Own calculations

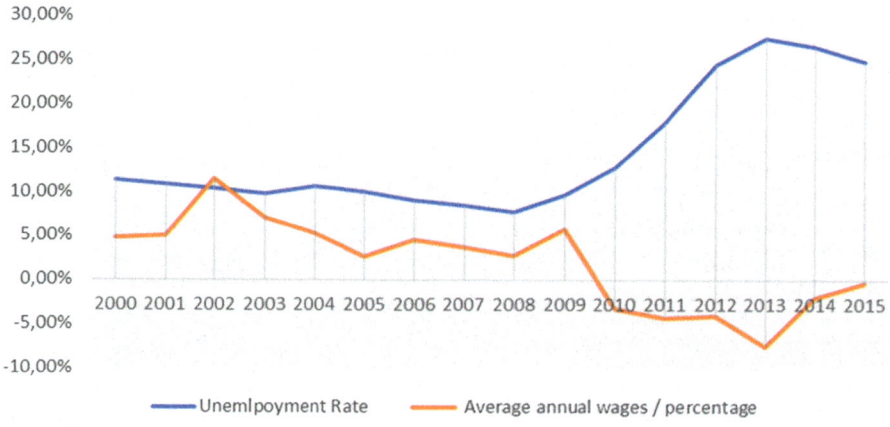

Fig. 5 Unemployment rate and average annual change of wages in %. Source: Annual macroeconomic database (AMECO) 2017; Own calculations

It is more than obvious that, following the imposition of the memorandums and fiscal adjustment measures, the unemployment rate was more than tripled (from 7.76% in 2008 to 27.47% in 2013), while the GDP index decreased significantly, at the first 3 years, while in recent years, it has "stuck" at particularly low levels. At the same time, during the last few years, the unemployment rate has not decreased more than 2.6% (2013–2015).

The wages index (Fig. 4) shows a significant constant decrease from 2009 onward. This decrease was relatively "stable" (3–4%) during the first 3 years (2010–2012) and got even worst (7.66%) on 2013, and even though it has stopped decreasing drastically, it has not been able to stop its downward trend in 2014 and

2015. As a result, Greece is experiencing the seventh consecutive year of wages reduction.

Regarding the third strategic objective of restoring the external equilibrium, it is observed (Figs. 6, 7, and 8) that after 2010 the large external deficits gradually disappeared. Indeed, in 2015, the country experienced a small surplus in the current account balance. In particular, country's low export performance in both products and services, although showing signs of improvement, is not to such an extent, in order to have a substantial positive impact on the current account deficit.

However, as the mentioned graphs indicate, this development is not a result of increased exports, neither through increased competitiveness or substitution of imports, but rather due to the large decline in imports, which is due solely to the fall in demand for imported goods due to internal devaluation and recession. In addition, the phenomenon of declining exports in certain years is particularly

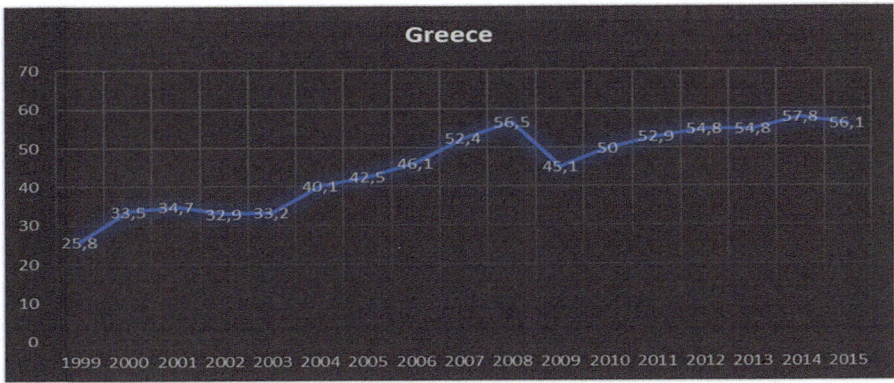

Fig. 6 Exports of goods and services at current prices (national accounts). Source: Annual macroeconomic database (AMECO) 2017; Own calculations

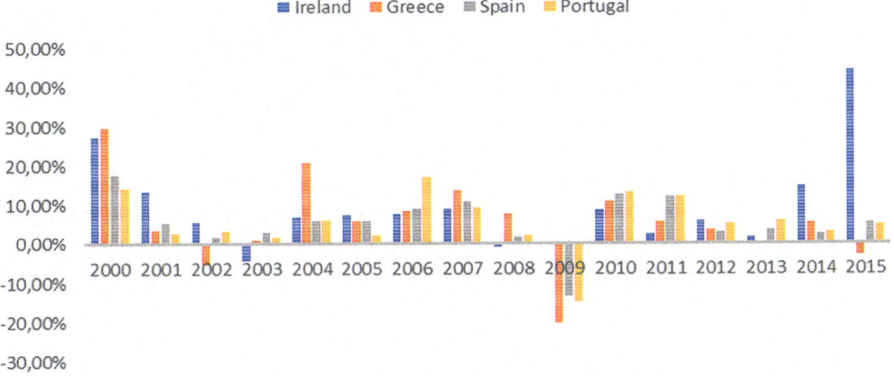

Fig. 7 Exports selected countries index (annual change in %). Source: Annual macroeconomic database (AMECO) 2017; Own calculations

Fig. 8 Export performance for total goods and services growth. Source: Annual macroeconomic database (AMECO) 2017; Own calculations

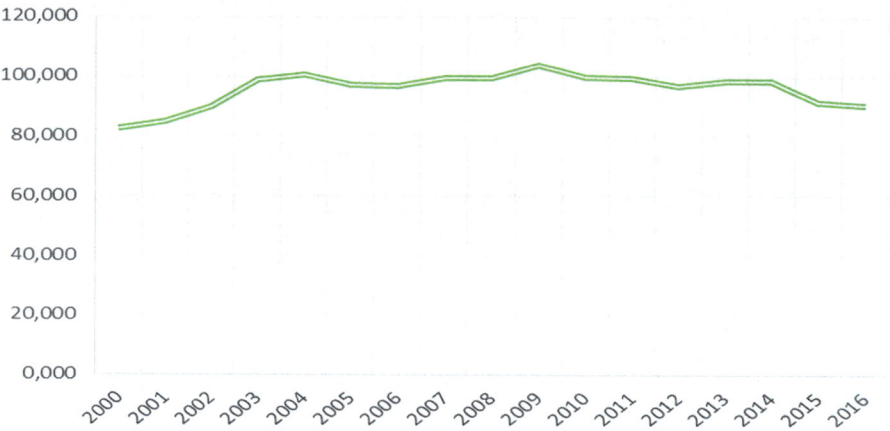

Fig. 9 Relative price of exported goods and services (Greece). Source: Annual macroeconomic database (AMECO) 2017; Own calculations

worrying, despite the relative recovery in international trade, and suggests the deterioration of the competitiveness of the Greek economy rather than its improvement.

One of the "positive" effects of fiscal adjustment should have been the improvement of the competitiveness of the country's exports by reducing the prices of the exporting products. Nonetheless, the "exports of goods and services at current prices (national accounts)" graph clearly shows an upward trend, surpassing (2014) the highest pre-crisis level (2008). The decrease of prices in 2009 can only be characterized as a temporary exception to the general rule (Fig. 9).

Similar policies do not affect all economies in the same way. Even though Ireland did more than well during the last 2 years (after a 4–5 year period of limited results) regarding its exports, Spain and especially Portugal and Greece witnessed an extremely narrow development of their exports during the last years of the crisis. This pattern doesn't seem to get any better in the near future for the three countries. In spite of the signing and implementation of more and more stringent memoranda and austerity measures in Greece than in the other countries, it is not possible to differentiate the "reaction" of the price level of the country's exporting products and services compared to those of Spain, Ireland, and Portugal. The lines are almost adjacent, and the derogations are considered negligible. Looking solely at the chart for Greece, a relative price stability is observed with a slight decrease during the last 2 years (Fig. 10).

Analyzing the imports and exports of goods and services as a percentage of the gross domestic product, one can emphasize on the fact that on both indexes there is an upward trend from 2009 to 2014 as they both decrease during the last year (Figs. 11 and 12). Another main characteristic of Figs. 11 and 12 is that imports and exports appear a significant conversion. It seems like the commercial balance has benefited from the increase of the exports and—at the same time—stability of the imports during the years of the economic crisis.

At the same time, as Figs. 13 and 14 show, consumption is still the key element in GDP formation, while the recession has increased the importance of declining imports. Calculating as base (100) the year 2010, the initiation year of the crisis and memorandums for Greece, it is more than obvious that during the first 3–4 years, despite the fact that the cost of wages had dropped significantly, the prices of exported products demonstrated a spectacular increase, reaching up to 35.90 points

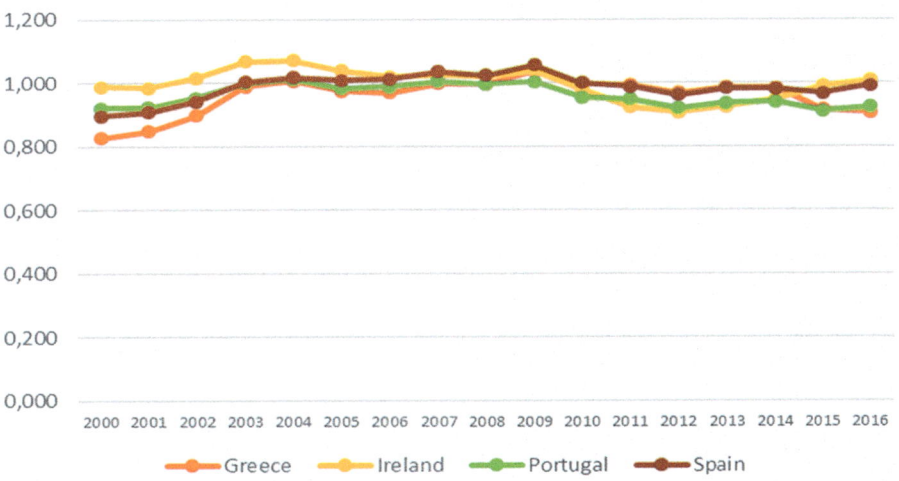

Fig. 10 Relative price of exported goods and services (selected countries). Source: Annual macroeconomic database (AMECO) 2017; Own calculations

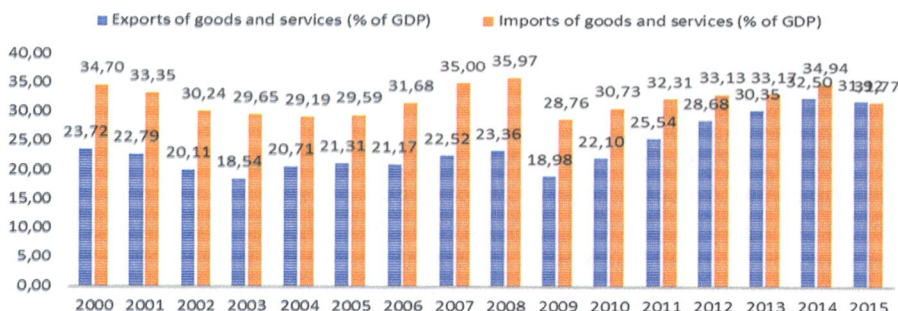

Fig. 11 Exports–imports (% GDP). Source: Annual macroeconomic database (AMECO) 2017; Own calculations

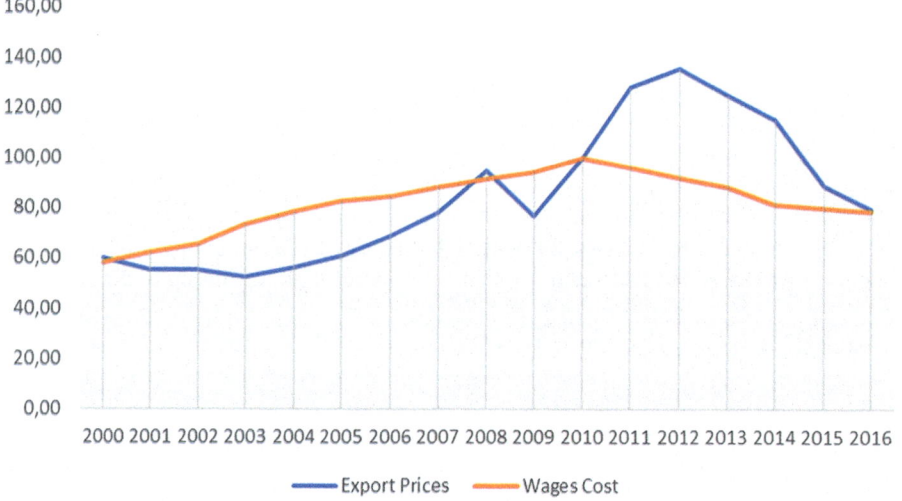

Fig. 12 Development of export prices and wage cost (2010 = 100). Source: Annual macroeconomic database (AMECO) 2017; Own calculations

over the base year. From 2014 onward, there is a clear trend toward reducing this phenomenon.

The indexes of the net national income, the total consumption, and the gross fixed capital formation (Figs. 13 and 14) all show the same trend: the drifting of the purchasing power and of households' income formation in Greece during the period of economic crisis and the imposition of memorandums. The inability to increase the formation of capital or higher consumption is not only a result of the reduction in net national income but also due to the imposition of significant additional taxes, as a result of the country's obligations that stem from the memorandums.

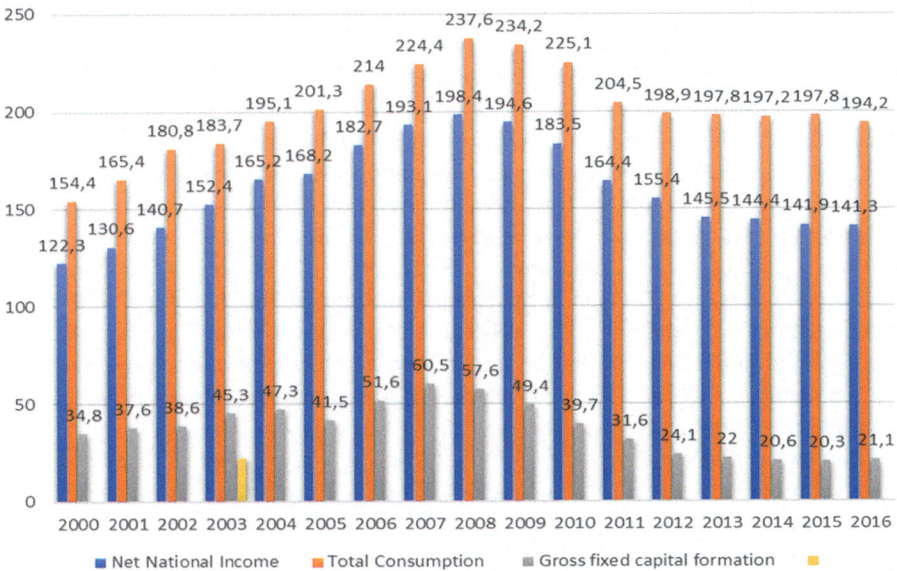

Fig. 13 Net national income—total consumption—gross fixed capital formation. Source: Annual macroeconomic database (AMECO) 2017; Own calculations

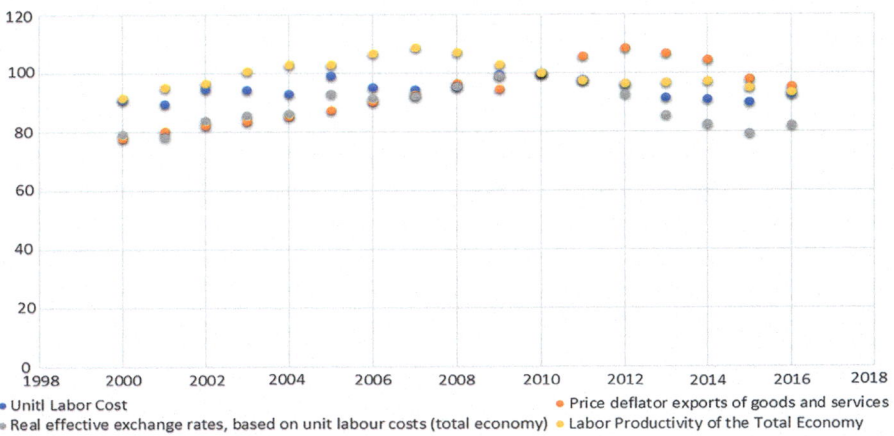

Fig. 14 Competitiveness factors (own calculations). Source: Annual macroeconomic database (AMECO) 2017; Own calculations

5 Conclusion

Despite the fact that over the past 7 years, three adjustment programs have been implemented to deal with the sovereign debt crisis, the Greek economy continues to experience a protracted recession and is plagued by competitiveness, political stability, and social cohesion. In addition, the fiscal adjustment policy does not solve the original sovereign debt problem. In particular, the adjustment policy reduced the overall consumption, but did not increase the rate of investments with respect to GDP, thus largely conserving the previous pattern of economic growth. The result of this inelastic policy is the gradual transformation of the Greek economy into one of the least extrovert countries—along with the corresponding index of extroversion for the Greek economy (sum of imports and exports to GDP), over the last 5 years. Continuing to illustrate the weaknesses of the Greek economy, we find that the erosion of competitiveness and thus the introversion of the Greek economy, in the last two decades, are reflected in the formation of the public deficit and thus in the public debt at the same time. This is because competitiveness and low extroversion are reflected in the financial figures and in key variables of the economy, as shown by the mentioned charts. The perpetuation of this situation has been accumulating and inflating Greece's public debt.

Similar are the conclusions for competitiveness with respect of labor costs; an indication of the extreme level of wages had reached just before crisis, without this being reflected to competitiveness performance at the same time. High level of taxation seem to have another side effect, that is, the rapid decrease of the gross fixed capital formation levels, an observation indicating that taxation absorbed a significant part of the produced added value of the economy, rather than this being invested. Unemployment rate is one worrying issue, that the country needs to find a way overcome. It is obvious that the outbreak of the crises resulted in a large shrinkage of GDP, which due to the introvert character of the Greek economy induced a rapid decrease of the offered job positions. Even the decrease of wages could not reverse this trend.

In addition the whole analysis indicates that the raised level of wages was not a main driver for the drop of Greek competitiveness. It is indicative that, despite the much deduced wages' levels, currently exports managed just to reach the before-crisis levels, instead of being skyrocketed. An explanation for this observation is the fact that export prices were intensively rising until 2012, and only after that point they dropped significantly, only to reach the same levels of 2008. It is important to mention at this point that Greek production was never really export oriented, and despite the fall of labor cost, still the country is not at the proper situation of taking advantage of it. From this we can rather directly assume that memoranda policies, that targeted in enhancing country's competitiveness, missed to achieve their goal, cause of the structural weaknesses of Greek economy. However an important and encouraging outcome is the neutral value of the payments balance that Greece succeeded in the last 2 years. This positive outcome resulted by the stronger increase of exports compared to the imports after the breakout of the crisis. It is crucial for this trend to continue in the future, based on the most extrovert parts of Greek economy, like tourism and agricultural production.

References

Aiginger, K. (1996). Creating a dynamically competitive economy: Defining the competitiveness of a nation and a case study. In P. Devine, Y. Katsoulacos, & R. Sugden (Eds.), *Competitiveness, subsidiarity and industrial policy*. Routledge.

Aiginger, K. (2006). Competitiveness: From a dangerous obsession to a welfare creating ability with positive externalities. *Journal of International Competition and Trade, 6*(2), 161–177.

AMECO database. (2017). http://ec.europa.eu/economy_finance/ameco/user/serie/SelectSerie.cfm

Annoni, P., & Kozovska, K. (2010). Defining regional competitiveness. *EU Regional Competitiveness Index, 2010*, 1–3.

Blanke, J., Paua, F., & Sala-I-Martin, X. (2005). *The growth competitiveness index: Analyzing key underpinnings of sustained economic growth* (pp. 3–28). Global Competitiveness Report 2004–2005. World Economic Forum.

Buckley, P. J., Pass, C., & Prescott, K. (1988). Measures of international competitiveness: A critical survey. *Journal of Marketing Management, 4*(2), 175–200.

European Commission. (1993). *White paper on growth – Competitiveness and employment – The challenges and ways forward into the 21st century*. COM (93) 700 final. Brussels.

Ezeala-Harrison, F. (1999). *Theory and policy of international competitiveness*. Westport, CT: Plaeger Publishers.

Fagerberg, J. (1996). Technology and competitiveness. *Oxford Review of Economic Policy, 12*(12), 39–51.

Fajnzylber, F. (1988). International competitiveness: Agreed goal, hard task. *CEPAL Review, 36*, 7–23.

OECD. (1992). *Technology and economy: The key relationships*. Paris: Organisation for Economic Co-operation and Development.

OECD. (1996). *Industrial competitiveness: Benchmarking business environments in the global economy*. Paris: Organisation for Economic Co-operation and Development.

Porter, M., Ketels, C., & Delgado, M. (2007). *The microeconomic foundations of prosperity: Findings from the business competitiveness index* (pp 51–82). The Global Competitiveness Report 2007–2008. World Economic Forum.

Scott, B. R., & Lodge, G. C. (1985). *U.S. competitiveness in the world economy*. Harvard Business School Press.

Tyson, D. A. (1992). *Who's bashing whom? Trade conflict in high-technology industries*. Washington Institute for International Economics.

World Economic Forum. (1996). *The Global Competitiveness Report 1996–1997*.

World Economic Forum. (2007). *The Global Competitiveness Report 2007–2008*.

Development of an Insurance Market in PIGS Countries After the Crisis

Adam Śliwiński, Tomasz Michalski, and Marietta Janowicz-Lomott

Abstract The insurance sector plays a crucial role in overall economic development. A studies published in the world literature have not finally confirmed the influence of the development of the insurance industry on economic growth; however, we may assume that the influence is positive. Countries in distress with regard to other activities such as fiscal or monetary policy should influence the overall development of the insurance sector. The paper is aimed at presenting the results of an assessment of the development of the insurance sector in chosen European countries such as Portugal, Italy, Greece, and Spain over the financial crisis, especially from the point of view of product innovation. We have chosen the countries stated owing to the economic situation against a background of the European Union. Those countries have faced budget deficits and were badly hit by the financial crisis of 2007. That is why it is interesting to study the progress of the financial sector, specifically insurance. The insurance market in a specific country is assessed by using taxonomy methods, in particular, two main measures: the distance measure and the similarity measure. The markets are described by a set of features divided into five groups: market structure, technical sphere, finance and investment, effectiveness, and product. The authors have calculated measures at two points in time: 1997 and 2013. The comparison between the level of taxonomic measures in those two years allowed the authors to draw the main conclusion that the financial crisis has stopped the speed of development of markets and has had a significant influence on other spheres as well. In countries such as Greece and Portugal, progress was even slower than that in post-Soviet countries such as Poland. External conditions have not imposed structural changes within chosen insurance markets. However, the general environment was conducive to supporting the expansion of the insurance markets only up to 2007. The influence of the crisis is very visible. The final conclusion is that the sectors were not innovative, mainly with regard to products. Product innovations give the insurer an opportunity to play an important role in contributing to sustainable development on a macroeconomic scale, or even more

A. Śliwiński (✉) · T. Michalski · M. Janowicz-Lomott
Warsaw School of Economics, Warsaw, Poland
e-mail: asliwin@sgh.waw.pl; majanow@sgh.waw.pl

© Springer Nature Switzerland AG 2019
N. Sykianakis et al. (eds.), *Economic and Financial Challenges for Eastern Europe*,
Springer Proceedings in Business and Economics,
https://doi.org/10.1007/978-3-030-12169-3_15

so—on a global scale. We are convinced that at the age of innovation, the insurance sector cannot remain insensitive to the need for innovation, not only in the area of insurance operation of companies, but also with regard to products. Innovations within the insurance sector become even more important in terms of building competitive strengths of an insurer. An innovative offer can maximize the insurer's revenue and profits.

Keywords Insurance · Taxonomy analysis · Financial crisis

1 Introduction

A few of observations motivated the authors to write this paper. First of all, a small amount of research focuses on innovation and development of an insurance sector and its influence on economic growth (Laeven et al. 2009; Tufano 2003; Allen and Gale 1994). The influence of the financial sector where insurance plays crucial role and its contribution to economic growth is not so clear. In history, there are a number of visible examples of the role of financiers in enhancing economic growth. For example, a special kind of investment bank and accounting system to enable screening and monitoring by distant investors were developed to finance the construction of railroads in the nineteenth and twentieth centuries (Laeven et al. 2009). A visible sample of the role of insurance in creating and supporting economic growth is the activity of Lloyd's of London, one of the largest world risk markets. Some historians state that the activity of the market contributed to helping England to become a global empire (Hodgson 1984). Studies published in the world literature have not finally confirmed the influence of the development of the insurance industry on economic growth; however, we may assume that the influence is positive. In the literature on the subject of the insurance sector, the impact on economic growth is not clear. At the same time, there is a lot of research to explain the impact of the banking sector on economic growth, with a relatively small amount of research devoted to the role of insurance. Some of the first studies on this topic were carried out by Outreville (1996). He proved the relationship between the development of the insurance industry and GDP growth. Another study was published in 2000 by Ward and Zurbruegg (2000). These studies have not clearly confirmed the impact of the insurance sector on the economy. As there were only a few articles with empirical findings concerning the relationship between the insurance sector and an increase in the real economy. For example, research conducted by Webb et al. (2005), Haiss and Sümegi (2008), Kugler and Ofoghi (2005), Adams et al. (2005), Wadlamannati (2008), and Zouhaier (2014) can be included. Studies about determining whether insurance promotes innovative actions are even less popular. This topic was taken into account, for example, by Ross Levine from the University of California, Berkeley (Laeven et al. 2009). The topic is also not alien to Polish commentators. However, there is little research in this area. As an example, we can state the works published by Michalski, Śliwiński and Karmanska (Śliwiński et al. 2013, 2014, 2017) and research published by Bednarczyk (2012). Therefore, it seems reasonable to conduct studies that answer the basic question: does the development of the insurance sector promotes economic growth and innovative actions? If so, to what extent? Insurance as a tool for risk transfer fully functions macroeconomically as well. In addition to the basic protective function, we can name for example, the redistribution of capital. Therefore, we put forward the following research hypothesis: the development of the sector has an impact on economic growth and promotion of innovative activities.

The second reason to investigate the subject is the situation after the financial crisis of 2007. The crisis was stated by many economists to be one of the most severe after the Great Depression in 1930. It hit a number of countries; however, from our point of view, it is interesting to see what has happened within the insurance sector from the perspectives of innovation and its influence on economic growth. In the paper, we take into the consideration selected European countries such as Portugal, Italy, Greece, and Spain, the so-called PIGS countries. The paper is aimed at introducing the results of an assessment of the development of insurance sector in PIGS countries during the financial crisis, especially the perspective of product innovation. The results obtained allow us to define the role of insurance in economic processes, planning, and innovative actions. The results are also of vital importance for both learning about finance, business practitioners, and people who are responsible for shaping economic policy, and the experience of Poland and the European Union.

2 The Economic Situation in PIGS Countries: Brief Characteristics

As mentioned above, the financial crisis of 2007–2008 (the global financial crisis) is considered by many economists to be the worst crisis since the Great Depression of the 1930s (Krugman 2009). It began in 2007 with a crisis in the subprime mortgage market in the USA, and developed into an international banking crisis. Disturbances in the financial system, together with the continual deterioration of the global economy, have caused a recession in the European Union (EU) countries (especially the Eurozone).

The crisis in the EU developed in two successive stages:

(A) Stage I—2007–2009. The negative "supply shock" in the Eurozone has been attributed to the systematic increase in the competitiveness of individual member states. This led to a deterioration of their competitive position in the pre-crisis period and a reduction in their share of global and European exports. As a result, there was a continuous acceleration of current account deficits in these countries. The GDP growth rate achieved by the Eurozone in 2009 was 4 percentage points lower than that achieved in 2007 (3%).

(B) Stage II—from 2010. The year 2010 brought a slight recovery in the European economy after a deep recession lasting almost 2 years. The growth of GDP in the European Union was 2.1% compared with a 4.3% decline in 2009 (mainly due to the improvement in world trade). The outbreak of the second phase of the Eurozone crisis triggered the negative reaction of global financial markets to deepening public debt. This affected five countries in particular: Greece, Portugal, Ireland, Spain, and Italy.

Owing to the global financial crisis, the name PIGS (P—Portugal, I—Ireland, G—Greece, and S—Spain) was created. These countries were characterized by a difficult budgetary situation and high public debt (Figs. 1 and 2). Later, Italy (I) was also included in this group and the name was modified to PIIGS. Ireland has been excluded from our study because of the relatively efficient anti-crisis policy and economic diversity.

A high level of public debt had already been recorded in 2002 (the year of joining the Eurozone). The PIGS countries (except Spain) did not meet the criteria of the

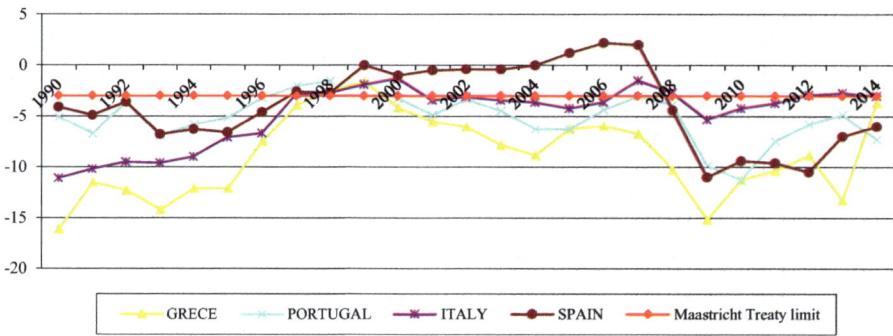

Fig. 1 Surplus (+), deficit (−) of the general government sector (in percentage of the gross domestic product [GDP]). Source: Own elaboration, Eurostat data

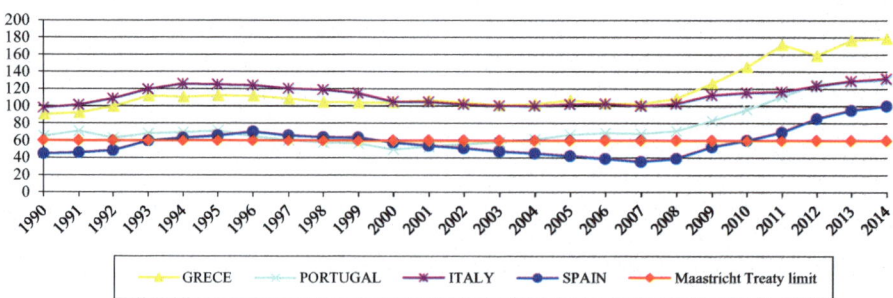

Fig. 2 Debt of the general government sector (in percentage of the GDP). Source: Own elaboration, Eurostat data

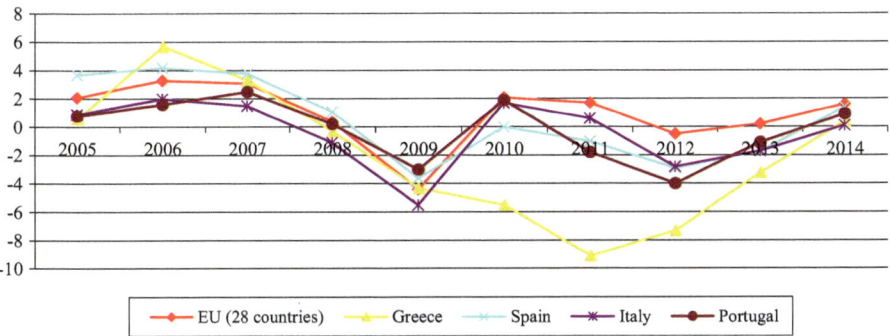

Fig. 3 GDP growth (%). Source: Own elaboration, Eurostat data

Maastricht Treaty, and some of them "applying restrictive policies" reduced debt and deficit. After the first period of crisis in the Eurozone only Greece had a unsustainable situation in public finance; the situation of other PIGS countries was critical (owing to Maastricht Treaty limits). In the second phase of the crisis, the situation of public finances (especially public debt) became worse. Recession in the PIGS countries was deeper than in other EU countries (Fig. 3).

The effects of the crisis on the economic situation have been studied frequently. In our article, we investigated the situation of the insurance market.

3   Insurance Market Development in PIGS Countries After the Financial Crisis of 2007

The insurance markets of the PIGS countries differ significantly with regard to the level of development. The penetration rate is most commonly used to determine the level of market expansion.

Among the PIGS countries, the Greek market is the least developed. Indicators of penetration for the Portuguese and Italian markets are close to the European average (Fig. 4).

The insurance markets of the PIGS countries were characterized by different developments in the collection of premiums and compensation paid after the crisis (Table 1). In Greece, there was a huge drop in contributions and at the same time a significant increase in compensation; a similar situation occurred in Portugal (although premiums decreased only 4%). Only on the Italian insurance market were a large increase in premiums and a decrease in compensation observed.

Also, the market structure of the PIGS countries differs (Table 2). In Portugal and Italy, over 70% of premiums were collected in life insurance. There was also a high share of motor insurance (especially in Greece and Italy).

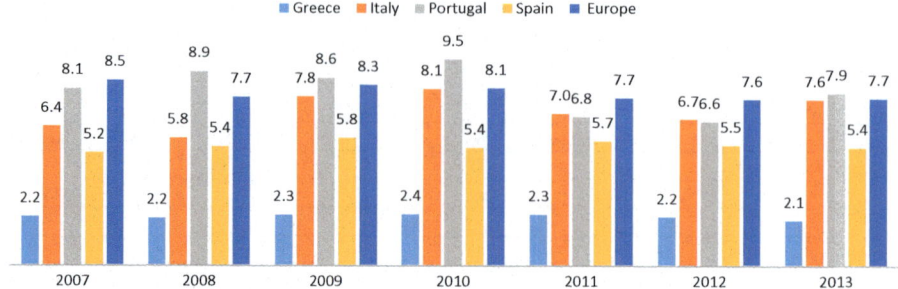

Fig. 4 Penetration ratio (premium to GDP; %). Source: Own elaboration, Insurance Europe data

4   Research Methodology: Description

We have conducted the research by means of multidimensional statistical analysis.
The comparative approach made use of taxonomic procedures. This study uses two
groups of measures: the distance measure and the similarity measure. Measure μ
describing the degree of similarity between dimension structures of the two objects is
defined by the following equation:

$$\mu_{i,p} = \frac{z_i{}^\circ z_p}{|z_i||z_p|}$$

where $z_i{}^\circ z_p$ denotes the scalar multiple of vectors z_i and z_p containing all dimensions
of the particular objects and $|z|$ the length of the vectors. This means that the value of
μ is between −1 and 1, as the scalar multiple is the cosine of the angle between the
vectors.

The measure of similarity of object dimensions $d*(i,p)$ is defined by the following
equation:

$$d * (i,p) = 1 - \frac{1}{2\sqrt{kn}} * d(i,p),$$

$$0 \le d * (i,p) \le 1$$

where k denotes the number of objects and n denotes the number of dimensions. This
is a normalized version of the differentiation of objects' dimensions $d(i,p)$.

$$d(i,p) = \sqrt{\sum_{i=1}^{k} \left(z_{i,i} - z_{i,p} \right)^2}$$

where d_{ip} denotes the distance between objects i and p and $z_{ij}z_{pj}$ the values of
dimension j of object i and p respectively.

Table 1 Premiums, claims, and benefits in the PIGS countries (Portugal, Italy, Greece, Spain)

		2007	2008	2009	2010	2011	2012	2013	Nominal growth 2013/2007
Greece	Premiums	5007	5085	5374	5237	4885	4320	3781	−24.48
	Claims	2320	2536	2883	2892	3036	3071	2642	13.88
Italy	Premiums	99,095	92,019	117,802	125, 720	110,228	105,128	118,787	19.87
	Claims	99,408	94,621	85,830	92,976	101,714	100,230	90,823	−8.64
Portugal	Premiums	13,751	15,326	14,516	16,340	11,669	10,911	13,105	−4.69
	Claims	9,589	3157	3193	14,304	18,132	13,595	12,533	30.70
Spain	Premiums	54,297	59,266	61,194	56,306	59,568	56,613	55,225	1.71
	Claims	40,133	48,401	48,409	46,905	44,230	48,529	44,608	11.15

Source: Own elaboration, Insurance Europe data

Table 2 Structure of premiums in insurance markets in PIGS countries

		2007	2008	2009	2010	2011	2012	2013
Greece	Life	50	49	47	44	44	45	44
	Nonlife	50	51	53	56	56	55	56
	Motor (in nonlife)	64	64	65	67	67	65	64
Italy	Life	62	59	69	72	67	66	72
	Nonlife	38	41	31	28	33	34	28
	Motor (in nonlife)	57	56	55	56	57	57	55
Portugal	Life	68	72	72	74	65	63	71
	Nonlife	32	28	28	26	35	37	29
	Motor (in nonlife)	44	42	40	40	40	39	38
Spain	Life	43	46	48	48	50	47	47
	Nonlife	57	54	52	52	50	53	53
	Motor (in nonlife)	40	38	36	37	35	34	33

Source: Own elaboration, Insurance Europe data

Fig. 5 Groups of features used in the study. Source: Authors' own material

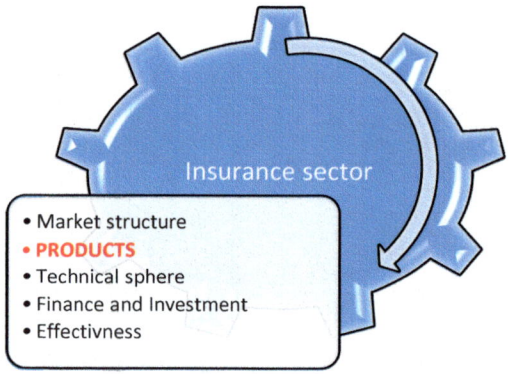

The analysis of the development of the insurance sector was conducted in relation to five groups of features: *market structure, technical sphere, finance and investment, effectiveness*, and *products* (Fig. 5). In each group there was a set of diagnostic features. We created the database including the implementation of selected diagnostic features in the years 1997 and 2010. Eventually, we decided on the number of features after the analysis of correlations between them, whereas the point of observation was determined on the basis of the implementation of features from all the groups.

The paper is aimed at demonstrating the lack of insurance product innovation. That is why we do not present a detailed description of all groups. The market structure group includes diagnostic features such as the number of insurance entities, the speed of changes within this number, the market share of the biggest insurers, the market concentration, the number of people employed by insurers or the presence of foreign insurers in the market. The technical sphere refers to the insurance operations. This group includes features such as the value of and changes in gross written

Table 3 Diagnostic features included in the products group

Symbol	Name of the feature
E1	Motor insurance gross written premium per capita
E2	Growth of motor insurance premium
E3	Share of motor insurance premium in total nonlife insurance premium
E4	Health insurance premium per capita
E5	Growth in health insurance premium
E6	Share of health insurance premium in total nonlife insurance premium
E7	Property insurance per capita
E8	Growth of property insurance
E9	Share of property insurance premium in total nonlife insurance premium
E10	Liability insurance premium per capita
E11	Growth in liability insurance premium
E12	Share of liability insurance premium in total nonlife insurance premium
E13	Marine, air, and cargo insurance premium per capita
E14	Growth in marine, air, and cargo insurance premium
E15	Share of marine, air, and cargo insurance premium in total nonlife insurance premium

Source: Authors' own material

premium, retention ratio, share of European countries in the total gross written premium, divided into nonlife and life insurance in addition to the reinsurance ratio. The finance and investment group is represented by features such as the value of total insurance investments in the European countries, the relation between investment and the gross written premium or changes in investment level between 1997 and 2010 (separately for nonlife and life insurers). The effectiveness group represents features that could be used to assess the development of the insurance sector from the macro perspective. In that group we have included features such as the share of the gross written premium in the GDP, the relation between insurers' investment and the GDP, and the gross written premium per capita separately for nonlife and life insurance. The most important feature from the perspective of the main aim of the paper is the group called products (group E in the graph below). It includes 15 features, which are listed in Table 3.

5 Results: Situation in PIGS Insurance Sectors

This part of the paper contain the results of our study. We have used the radar charts order to maintain the clarity of the presentation. The chart axes are the groups analyzed (in the case of sector analysis). Thus, A stands for market structure; B for technical sphere; C for finance and investment, D for effectiveness, and E for products. The results of the calculation for the measurement of differentiation of levels d∗ and structure similarity μ∗ are presented in the charts below respectively. The results for PIGS countries are presented in the graphs below. The values of the similarity measures are compared with each other within the separate groups at two points of time (1997 and 2010). This allows us to draw some conclusions about what has happened throughout the crisis. Therefore, we may see the influence of the crisis on the development of the insurance sector in the PIGS countries. On the other hand, objects (insurance sectors in each PIGS country) are compared with so-called reference objects. The reference object (benchmark) is set for comparison. In our case, the benchmark based on algorithms was set within the group of experts and presented by well-known statisticians (Z. Hellwig), separately for individual diagnostic features. In the case of *stimulants* (the higher the value of the feature, the better development of the insurance sector), the benchmark was calculated as a diagnostic feature of the maximum value in the period analyzed increased by a standard deviation for the whole time series. In the case of *destimulants* (negative relation to the development of the insurance sector) the benchmark value is 0 or a minimum value decreased by a standard deviation, depending on which of the two values is higher. The benchmark for *nominants* (the value of the features should be within a specific range or fixed) is set as an average value increased by a standard deviation or median depending on the character of the feature and the number of available observations. The value of the measures for the reference object after normalization is equal to 1. The measures of the object to be compared (in our case insurance sectors in chosen countries) varies from 0 to 1. A value of measure closer to 1 means that the study object is more similar to the reference object (in our case in terms of similarity of the structure and distance of chosen features). As has been stated earlier in the text, the calculation of the taxonomy measure at two different points in time allows us to associate changes throughout some chosen periods of time. In our case it is during the course of the financial crisis of 2007. The results are presented in Figs. 6 and 7 and Table 4.

The analysis shows that there are significant differences in terms of the PIGS countries (look at Table 4 and Figs. 6 and 7). The differences are particularly visible when we compare countries with a reference object. In general, the situation slightly improved after the crisis. For example when we look at Portugal, the improvement could be monitored in all groups except for group E (products). Portugal is the only country among those analyzed where there was no improvement in the group. Generally, the level of similarity of structure in terms of products is the lowest in all countries. In all countries, the value of similarity of the structure to the reference object for group E is below 50% (look at Fig. 6). Such a level should be assumed to be very low. The highest value of the measure occurred in terms of Italy followed by Greece and Spain. Similarity of the structure of features included in group B (the technical sphere) is the highest in terms of Italy. The technical sphere contains features connected to market development in terms of gross written premium such as changes in terms of gross written premium separately for life and nonlife insurance, penetration ration, reassurance ratio, and premium per insurance sector employee. Italy is one of the most developed countries among those analyzed and the insurance market there is established. That is probably why, in terms of market indicators, the value of similarity of the structure is approximately 80%. However, in terms of other groups, the value of the measure is below 50%, for example, that for group E is equal to 42%. When we look at the value for Poland (country after

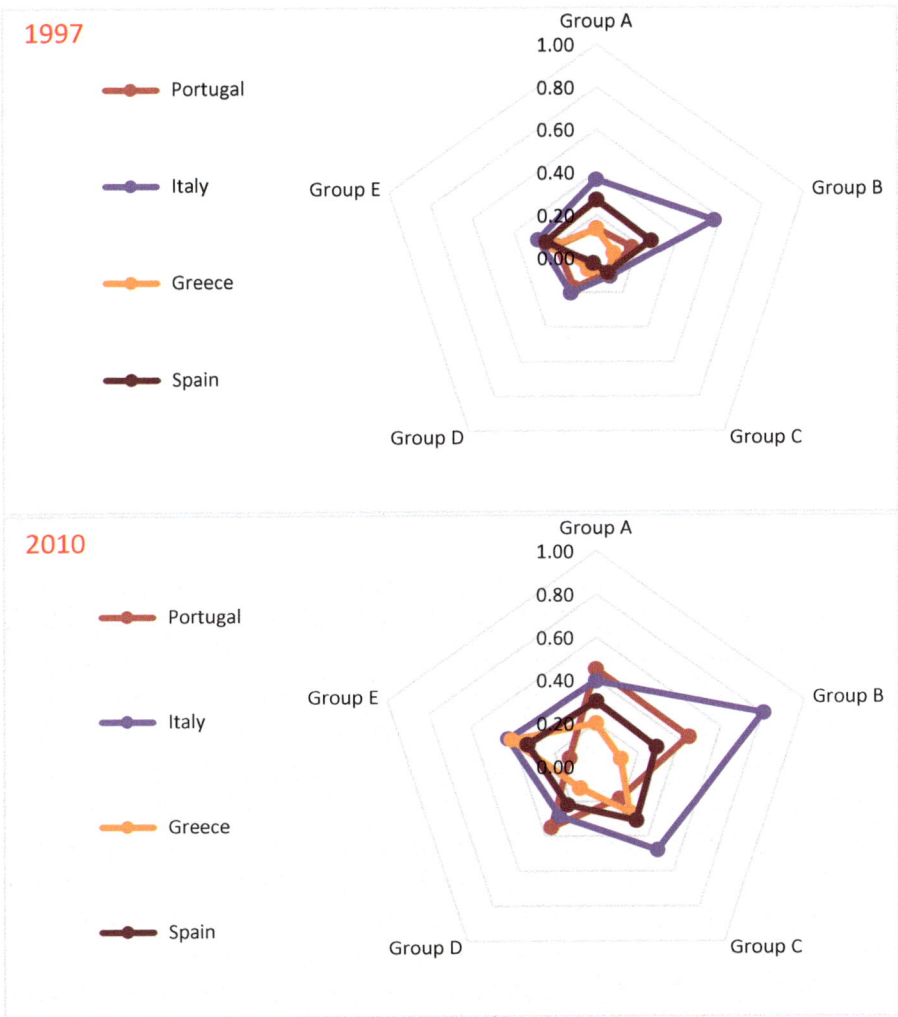

Fig. 6 Measure of structure similarity μ* for the PIGS countries in 1997 and 2010. Source: Authors' own calculation

transformation), it reached approximately 73% in relation to the similarity of structure to the reference object. We may conclude that the changes of development of group products in PIGS countries have been very slow. In our opinion, it is an effect of the crisis. After the crisis, insurers in the countries analyzed were very inactive in terms of developing innovative solutions linked to products. The lack of innovation has not changed the structure of the group, and the most significant source of premiums is still motor insurance.

The value of measure $d*$ (differentiation of levels) is very stable (look at Fig. 7), which confirms the earlier conclusion that the financial crisis has stopped the speed of development of insurance sectors in PIGS countries. The highest similarity in

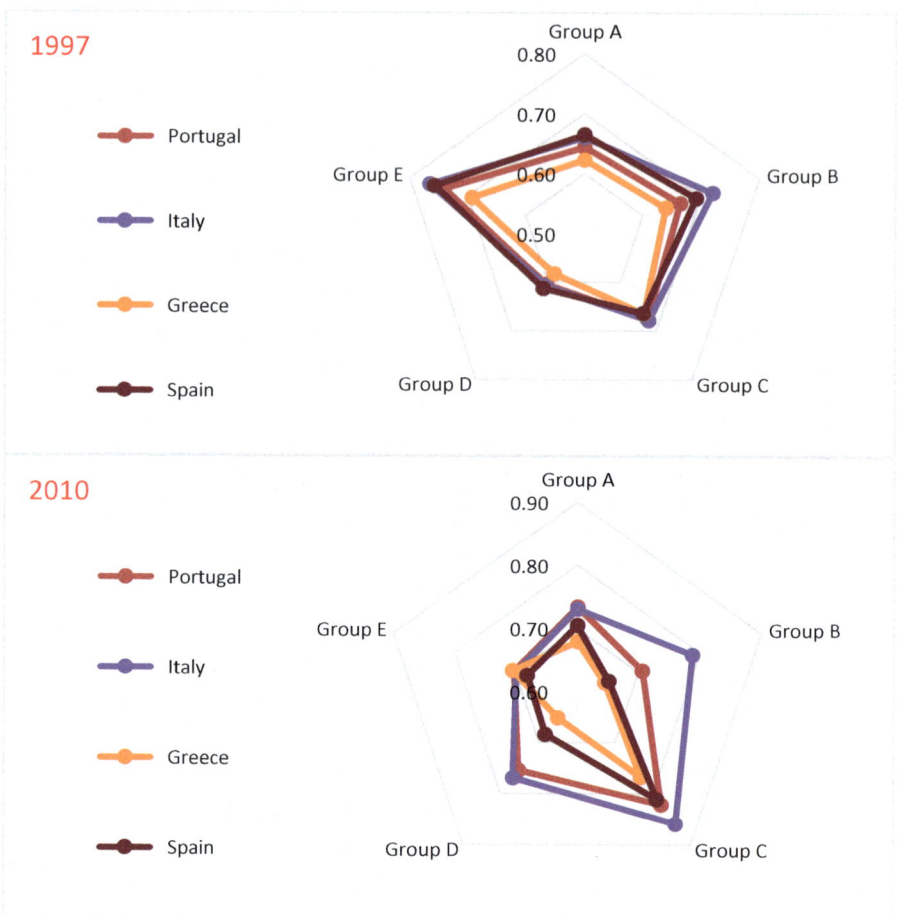

Fig. 7 Differentiation of levels $d*(i,p)$ for PIGS countries in 1997 and 2010. Source: Authors' own calculation

terms of the level of diagnostic features was observed for group C in 2010 in all countries. Group C contains features connected to finance and investments such as the value of investment of insurers calculated per capita, changes in level of investment, share of life insurers' investments in total insurance market investment, and the relation of investment to gross written premium in both life and nonlife insurers. It should be noticed that in group E the level of similarity was lower in 2010 in comparison with 1997, except for Greece. However, in terms of Greece, the change is very small. The measure $d*$ in 1997 was 0.69 and increased to 0.70 in 2010 (look at Table 5). The analysis of the results shown in Table 5 confirms the assumption that the development of insurance markets after the crisis was much slower, especially in positions of product innovation. The values of calculated measures of similarity of structures and differentiation of levels for countries analyzed at two points in time are presented in Table 6.

Table 4 Measure of structure similarity μ* for the PIGS countries in 1997 and 2010 (values)

	Group A	Group B	Group C	Group D	Group E
2010					
Portugal	0.4535	0.4470	0.1836	0.3499	0.1260
Italy	0.3971	0.8070	0.4802	0.2839	0.4201
Greece	0.2010	0.1175	0.2620	0.1233	0.4054
Spain	0.3018	0.2905	0.3117	0.2203	0.3304
1997					
Portugal	0.14009	0.17048	0.08672	0.17292	0.19208
Italy	0.36878	0.57359	0.10362	0.19924	0.28301
Greece	0.13821	0.08140	0.08808	0.06512	0.19959
Spain	0.27324	0.26484	0.08529	0.02967	0.24585
Benchmark	1	1	1	1	1

Source: Authors' own calculation

Table 5 Differentiation of levels d*(i,p) for PIGS in 1997 and 2010 (values)

	Group A	Group B	Group C	Group D	Group E
2010					
Portugal	0.7335	0.7060	0.8214	0.7546	0.7029
Italy	0.7302	0.7874	0.8595	0.7694	0.6992
Greece	0.6787	0.6443	0.7674	0.6519	0.7057
Spain	0.7043	0.6516	0.8109	0.6843	0.6816
1997					
Portugal	0.64353	0.66362	0.67603	0.60524	0.74135
Italy	0.65998	0.71919	0.67899	0.60728	0.76565
Greece	0.62231	0.63915	0.66537	0.58355	0.69307
Spain	0.66432	0.69111	0.66383	0.61336	0.75749
Benchmark	1	1	1	1	1

Source: Authors' own calculation

Table 6 Measure of structure similarity μ* for PIGS countries in 1997 and 2010 (values) within the product group

	Reference object			
	1997		2010	
	Structure similarity	Differentiation of levels	Structure similarity	Differentiation of levels
Country	$\mu*(p,i)$	$d*(p,i)$	$\mu*(p,i)$	$d*(p,i)$
1	2	3	4	5
Portugal	0.1920	0.7413	0.1260	0.7029
Italy	0.2830	0.7656	0.4201	0.6992
Greece	0.1995	0.6930	0.4054	0.7057
Spain	0.2458	0.7574	0.3304	0.6816
Reference object	1	1	1	1

Source: Authors' own calculation

6 Conclusions

The conclusions are as follows:

- The analysis of the aforementioned results shows the lack of significant changes in similarities of both structure and level differentiation. Structure similarity has changed more significantly, especially in Spain.
- The lack of significant changes in the structure and the sphere of products allows for the conclusion indicating the weak innovativeness of the insurance sector, especially in the sphere of products.
- In all countries analyzed, group C (finance and investment) gets closer to the reference object.

The main conclusion that may be drawn from the study is that the financial crisis stopped the speed of development of markets and had a significant influence on other spheres. In countries such as Greece and Portugal, progress was even slower than in post-Soviet countries such as Poland. External conditions have not imposed structural changes within chosen insurance markets. However, the general environment was conducive to supporting the expansion of insurance markets only up to 2007. The influence of the crisis is very visible.

Finally, the sectors were not that innovative, mainly in a Product sphere. Product innovations give the insurer an opportunity to play an important role in contributing to sustainable development on a macroeconomic scale, or even on a global scale. We are convinced that in the age of innovation, the insurance sphere cannot remain insensitive to the need for innovation, not only in the area of insurance operation of companies, but also in the area of products. Innovations within the insurance sector become even more important in terms of building a competitive strenghts of an insurer on the markets. An innovative offer can maximize the insurer's revenue and profits.

References

Adams, M., Andersson, J., Andersson, L. F., & Lindmark, M. (2005). *The historical relation between banking, insurance and economic growth in Sweden: 1830 to 1998*. Norges Handelshøyskole, Department of Economics Discussion Paper SAM, 26.

Allen, F., & Gale, D. (1994). *Financial innovation and risk sharing*. Cambridge, MA: Cambridge University Press.

Bednarczyk, T. (2012). *Wpływ działalności sektora ubezpieczeniowego na wzrost gospodarczy*, Wyd. Lublin: UMCS.

Haiss, P., & Sümegi, K. (2008). The relationship between insurance and economic growth in Europe: A theoretical and empirical analysis. *Empirica, 35*(4), 405–431.

Hodgson, G. (1984). *Lloyd's pf London, reputation at risk*. London: Allan Lane.

Krugman, P. (2009). *The return of depression economics and the crisis of 2008*. New York: W. W. Norton.

Kugler, M., & Ofoghi, R. (2005). *Does insurance promote economic growth? Evidence from the UK*. Working Paper, Division of Economics, University of Southampton. Retrieved 23 February 2009, from http://repec.org/mmfc05/paper8.pdf

Laeven, L., Levine, R., & Michalopoulos, S. (2009). *Financial innovation and endogenous growth*. NBER Working Paper No. 15356. Retrieved from http://www.nber.org/papers/w15356

Outreville, J. F. (1996). *Life insurance markets in developing countries. The Journal of Risk and Insurance, 63*(2)), 262–278.

Śliwiński, A., Karmańska, A., & Michalski, T. (2013). Innovations in risk management as exemplified by the Polish insurance market. *Journal of Reviews on Global Economics, 2*, 407–415.

Śliwiński, A., Karmańska, A., & Michalski, T. (2017). European insurance markets in face of financial crisis. Application of learning curve concept as a tool of insurance products innovation – Discussion. *Journal of Reviews on Global Economics, 6*, 404–419.

Śliwiński, A., Michalski, T., & Karmańska, A. (2014). *Innovations of insurers with respect to the use of management accounting – An example of insurance products*. Proceedings of Technology Innovation and Industrial Management, Seoul, South Korea.

Tufano, P. (2003). Financial innovation. In Constantinidis, G., Harris, M., & Stults, R. (Eds.), *Handbook of the economics of finance* (Vol. 1a: Corporate Finance, pp. 307–336). Elsevier North-Holland.

Wadlamannati, K. C. (2008). Do insurance sector growth and reforms affect economic development? Empirical evidence from India. *The Journal of Applied Economic Research, 2*(1), 43–86.

Ward, D., & Zurbruegg, R. (2000). Does insurance promote economic growth? Evidence from OECD countries. *The Journal of Risk and Insurance, 67*(4), 489–506.

Webb, I., Grace, M. F., & Skipper, H. (2005). The effect of banking and insurance on the growth of capital and output. *SBS Revista de Temas Financieros (Journal of Financial Issues), 2*(2), 1–32.

Zouhaier, H. (2014). Insurance and economic growth. *Journal of Economics and Sustainable Development, 5*(12), 102–112.

Usage Evaluation Through Data Analysis of the Greek Tax Information System

Stavros Valsamidis, Ioannis Petasakis, Sotirios Kontogiannis, and Fotini Perdiki

Abstract Every information system has to be positively accepted by its users in order to be successful in practice. Even though its usage is mandatory, the users have to use it without negative intention. Improving e-government services by using them more effectively is a major focus globally. It requires public administrations (PAs) to be transparent, accountable, and provide qualitative, trustworthy, controllable, and compatible services that improve users' confidence. The Greek taxation information system (Taxisnet) is now in the second decade of its operation and is characterized as a mature and expandable information system. The factors which affect its use by the tax office employees constitute an interesting field of study. The purpose of this study is to investigate the parameters affecting the positive or negative intentions of the office employees to use Taxisnet taking into consideration some critical parameters: Control, Complexity, Compatibility, Information Quality, System Quality and Trust. Data mining techniques and regression analysis are the main axes for the achievement of this goal. Although the research was conducted in the tax office employees of only four branches of the Region of Eastern Macedonia and Thrace (REMTh), the results can be generalized to the employees of other regions as well. This paper could also be a pilot for a general investigation of (1) the factors of acceptance of e-government systems by employees and (2) the factors that affect employees' intention to accept the e-government services.

Keywords Tax information system · Usage evaluation · Data mining techniques

S. Valsamidis (✉) · I. Petasakis · F. Perdiki
Department of Accounting and Finance, TEI of Eastern Macedonia and Thrace, Kavala, Greece
e-mail: svalsam@teikav.edu.gr; fperdiki@teikav.edu.gr

S. Kontogiannis
Department of Mathematics, University of Ioannina, Ioannina, Greece

© Springer Nature Switzerland AG 2019
N. Sykianakis et al. (eds.), *Economic and Financial Challenges for Eastern Europe*,
Springer Proceedings in Business and Economics,
https://doi.org/10.1007/978-3-030-12169-3_16

1 Introduction

Information communication technologies (ICTs) are literally changing the way that organizations are conducted, including government service. Government in emerging nations is relying on information technology as an important tool to improve the efficiency, cost, and quality of the government information and services provided to the citizens (Gupta et al. 2008). The rapid growth of investment to e-government has drawn attention to research on this area. Governments have a major opportunity to grant better and quicker services through the Internet. Internet-based technologies not only modify the habitual functions of public agencies but also introduce irreversible changes to the fundamental relations between government agencies and public (Golubeva et al. 2005). E-government is the use of information technology to enable and improve the efficiency with which government services are provided to citizens, employees, businesses, and agencies OECD (2008).

The e-government action programs are not always welcomed enthusiastically, despite the benefits they promise to bring. The use on large scale of information and communication technologies not only has advantages but also causes certain challenges (Davidaviciene 2008). The introduction of e-government services is not based on the assimilation of modern technology, but the degree of acceptance of the electronic services by the users, according to Anagnostopoulos (2006). Gaining full acceptance will require provision of information and adequate training (Floropoulos et al. 2010). The success of the informatization efforts depends, to a great extent, on how well the targeted users for such services, citizens in general, make use of them. Terzis and Economides (2007) as well Economides and Terzis (2008) highlighted critical factors that make a tax website successful. They developed an integrated evaluation framework across five quality dimensions. Then they used it to evaluate the tax websites of five countries. As governments develop e-government systems to deliver these services, there is a need for evaluation efforts that assess their effectiveness (Wang and Liao 2007). Such evaluation efforts can enable government agencies to determine if they are capable of doing the required task and delivering services as expected (Gupta and Jana 2003). The educational level of public employees and their continuing training are important factors for the successful implementation of information systems in the public sector (Lau and Halkyard 2003).

Taxisnet is an integrated computerized information system which operates as a platform for citizens, enterprises, and public sector organizations and allows various electronic tax transactions (Hahamis et al. 2005). It enables users to do electronic tax filing by using a computer or other electronic devices over public switched or dedicated telephone lines or via the Internet (Pant et al. 2004; Terzis and Economides 2007). This contributes to saving of productive working hours for both employees and tax payers. Taxisnet also provides full audit of economic activities and verification of declared elements for both natural and legal persons.

Data mining is an iterative process of creating predictive and descriptive models, by uncovering previously unknown trends and patterns in vast amounts of data, in order to extract useful information and support decision-making (Kantardzic 2003). Data mining methods are divided into three major categories (Witten and Frank 2005). The first category involves the classification methods, whereas the second the clustering ones and the third the association rule mining methods. Classification methods use a training dataset in order to estimate some parameters of a mathematical model that could in theory optimally assign each case from a new dataset into a specific class. In other words, the training set is used to train the classification technique how to perform its classification. Clustering refers to methods where a training set is not available. Thus, there is no previous knowledge about the data to assign them to specific groups. In this case, clustering techniques can be used to split a set of unknown cases into clusters. Association rule mining discovers relationships, sometimes hidden, among attributes (variables) in a dataset. In our research we apply methods from these three data mining major categories. Data mining techniques and knowledge management tools were used to Inland Revenue (Lau and Halkyard 2003). They also pointed out to that they have to pay attention on both adopting ICT and training the public employees.

The main purpose of this study is to investigate the use and evaluation of Taxisnet by the tax office employees, who are the link between the government and the citizen. It also tries to empirically investigate the perspective of the expert taxation agency employee by assessing the success of Taxisnet. Since employees work in a mandatory setting and do not have a choice, the adoption and use of Taxisnet are challenges that cannot be ignored. For the successful operation of a tax authority as well as of a government, the proper use of the public financial service information systems by the tax employees is essential (Beattie and Pratt 2003).

The paper is structured in five sections as follows: the second section overviews the baseline of our work, the third one describes the methodology, while the fourth section contains the results of the investigation. Finally, the fifth section highlights the findings of the results and draws useful conclusions.

2   Baseline

In this section we present a set of relative theories that constitute the baseline of our proposal. Empirical evidence relating to the impact of various factors on trust in e-government is sparse and rarely. Most of existing studies have included trust in broader adoption models, such as the technology acceptance model and the diffusion of innovation theory (Belanger and Carter 2008; Horst et al. 2007; Warkentin et al. 2002). In these models, the most analyzed determinants were trust in the Internet, trust in the government, perceived usefulness, and perceived quality of the e-government services.

Rogers' (1995) diffusion of innovation (DOI) theory is another popular model used in information system research to explain user adoption of new technologies. Rogers defines diffusion as "the process by which an innovation is communicated through certain channels over time among the members of a social society" (Rogers 1995). An innovation is an idea or object that is perceived to be new. According to DOI, the rate of diffusion is affected by an innovation's relative advantage, complexity, compatibility, trialability, and observability. Rogers (1995) defines relative advantage as "the degree to which an innovation is seen as being superior to its predecessor." Complexity, which is comparable to TAM's perceived ease of use construct (Davis et al. 1989), is "the degree to which an innovation is seen by the potential adopter as being relatively difficult to use and understand." Compatibility refers to "the degree to which an innovation is seen to be compatible with existing values, beliefs, experiences and needs of adopters." In compatibility, we examine the capability of the tax site to support various operating systems and various user devices, for example, if the tax site supports many browsers. Trialability is the "degree to which an idea can be experimented with on a limited basis." Finally, observability is the "degree to which the results of an innovation are visible" (Rogers 1995). After an extensive literature review, Tornatzky and Klein (1982) conclude that relative advantage, compatibility, and complexity are the most relevant constructs to adoption research. We do not include voluntariness and trialability. Voluntariness is the degree to which individuals feel they have the option to use an innovation or not. For the employees, the use of a web-based government service is a mandatory task and therefore inappropriate for our study. Trialability is the degree to which potential adopters feel that they can use the innovation before they actually adopt it. Again, it is doubtful that perceived trialability would display enough variance to offer explanatory power.

User's satisfaction regarding the quality of information he gets from a tax site is also an important factor. In quality, we examine at what extent the content is useful, relevant, simple, and clear. Moreover, it must be current and updated continuously (Terzis and Economides 2007). Do and Shih (2016) support that the quality of website or information system has a positive and significant impact on online users' intention. Related to willingness to use e-filing is whether websites with high information quality can be trusted or not. Sichtmann (2007) found that trust in high information quality from online websites positively affects using intentions. Wang and Emurian (2005) argued that the quality of information and service is one of the most important constructs in determining whether people will use an information system or not. "Reliability is the outward-facing feature of e-government - the part that constituents see, expect and depend on. When e-government infrastructures become hindered - unreliable and unavailable due to slowdowns or security breaches - the constituent experience and the rationale for undertaking the e-government initiative is threatened."

Trust in e-government is an abstract concept that underlies a complex array of relationships, so the method used to quantify trust in e-government should therefore account for this abstract nature. Grandison and Sloman (2000) report that the presence of various definitions of trust in the literature is based on two reasons:

(a) First, trust is an abstract concept, often used in place of related concepts, such as reliability, safety, and certainty. Therefore, clear definition of the term and the distinction between it and related concepts have proved a challenge for researchers. (b) Second, trust is a psychological concept with many facets, incorporating cognitive, emotional, and behavioral dimensions (Johnson and Grayson 2005). Perceptions of trustworthiness could also impact citizens' intention to use e-government services. Bélanger et al. (2002) define trustworthiness as "the perception of confidence in the electronic marketer's reliability and integrity." Privacy and security are reoccurring issues in e-government research (Hoffman et al. 1999; Chadwick 2001; Miyazaki and Fernandez 2001; Bélanger et al. 2002). Extending the work of previous researchers (Rotter 1980; Mayer et al. 1995; McKnight et al. 1998), McKnight et al. (2002) establish measures for a multidimensional model of trust in e-transactions, focusing on users' initial trust in a web service. Colesca (2009) identified what factors could affect the users' trust in e-government services. The findings indicated that users' higher perception of technological and organizational trustworthiness, the quality and usefulness of e-government services, the Internet experience, and propensity to trust directly enhanced the trust in e-government. Age and privacy concerns have a negative influence over trust. Initial trust refers to "trust in an unfamiliar trustee, a relationship in which the actors do not yet have credible, meaningful information about, or affective bonds with, each other" (McKnight et al. 2002). In initial relationships, "people use whatever information they have, such as perceptions of a web site, to make trust inferences" (McKnight et al. 2002).

Regarding the e-taxation services, Wang et al. (2005) argued that computer self-efficacy affects the users' behavioral intention to use a website. Ease of use, usefulness, and credibility are all important factors. Users in a tax site give very important information, so they must be secured in all their transactions. Tax site has to use security certifications and guarantees, and the possibility of encryption for the input or output data is also useful (Wang 2002).

3   Methodology

This research investigates the parameters that affect the employees' positive or negative intention of the use of information systems and the contribution of information systems to transactions. Six variables were defined as main parameters for data analysis: *Control, Complexity, Compatibility, Information Quality, System Quality*, and *Trust*. Finally, to measure the intention of employees to use the e-government, a seventh deterministic variable (intention to use) is used. In order to ascertain the views of employees on the usage evaluation of tax information systems in the prefectures of REMTh, the views of the users of tax information systems belonging to the public sector were recorded and processed.

3.1 Dataset

A self-administered questionnaire of 30 items was designed and delivered to be completed by respondents from the regions of Drama, Kavala, Serres, and Xanthi, in the first semester of 2015. It consisted of two components: (1) the first 21 items concern the attitudes of respondents, the factors that influence the employees to accept e-government systems and the results of the contribution of information systems in electronic transactions and (2) the last 9 items concern demographic data of the respondents (gender, age, education, residence, income, employment experience, etc.).

In the first part of the questionnaire, the 7-point Likert scale was used. For questions 1–18, 1 means "strongly disagree," and 7 means "strongly agree," while for questions 19–21, 1 means "not at all possible," and 7 means "possible." The recommended scales for use are either with 5 or with 7 points (Terpsiadou and Economides 2009; Raus et al. 2010). Specifically, Terpsiadou and Economides (2009) indicate that the greater the number of steps used in the scale, the greater the reliability of the scale. Hung et al. (2006) also use a 7-point scale to assess the online tax filling and return payments system OTFPS in Taiwan.

The deterministic variables are the questions of our questionnaire. After a thorough analysis, the questionnaire responses show us if the deterministic variables are suitable to measure the hidden variables and how they affect the formation of the employees' intention to use Taxisnet. The analysis of our model is focused on the six hidden variables (factors), each determined by some deterministic variables.

The dataset involves 150 tax employees from REMTh. The data are originally in ASCII format. The profile of each respondent is described by ten variables. The ten variables which are used in the analysis described in the methodology section are Gender, Age, Income, Education, Complexity, Compatibility, Quality_i, Quality_s, Trust, and Use. Table 1 describes each variable in detail.

Table 1 The variables used in our analysis

Variable name	Description	Type
Gender	The gender of the respondent (0, no, 1, yes)	Nominal
Age	The age of the respondent	Ordinal
Income	The income of the respondent	Ordinal
Education	The education level of the respondent	Ordinal
Complexity	The complexity of the Taxisnet	Numeric
Compatibility	The compatibility of the Taxisnet	Numeric
Quality_i	The quality of the information of the Taxisnet	Numeric
Quality_s	The quality of the system of the Taxisnet	Numeric
Trust	The trust of the system of the Taxisnet	Numeric
Use	The intention to use Taxisnet	Numeric

3.2 Data Mining Techniques

The WEKA (*Waikato Environment for Knowledge Analysis*) (Witten and Frank 2005) computer package was used in order to apply classification, clustering, and association rule mining methods to the dataset. WEKA is open-source software that provides a collection of machine learning and data mining algorithms. Figure 1 shows the basic graphical user interface (GUI) of WEKA. One of the main objectives of WEKA is to mine information from existing datasets (Cunningham and Holmes 1999), and this is the main reason why we chose it for analyzing our data.

There are various classification methods implemented in WEKA, like ZeroR, OneR, PART, etc. In the *classification* step, the algorithm *OneR* can parsimoniously discover and represent simple relationships between the real data (Cunningham and Holmes 1999). In our case the variable "Use" is used as a class and shows whether a tax employee uses Taxisnet or not.

The *clustering* step uses the k-means algorithm (MacQueen 1967; Kaufmann and Rousseeuw 1990), called *SimpleKMeans* in WEKA. K-means is an efficient partitioning algorithm that decomposes the dataset into a set of k disjoint clusters. It is a repetitive algorithm in which the items are moved among the various clusters until they reach the desired set of clusters. With this algorithm a great degree of similarity for the items of the same cluster and a large difference of items, which belong to different clusters, are achieved. The Euclidean distance is used to compute the differences concerning the intention to use. The variable "Use" is used in order to assess the accuracy of the clustering and investigate its impact on intention to use.

Association rule mining is one of the most well-studied data mining tasks. It discovers relationships among attributes (variables) in datasets, producing if-then statements concerning attribute values (Agrawal et al. 1996). An association rule $X \Rightarrow Y$ expresses that in those transactions in the database where X occurs, there is a high probability of having Y as well. In an association rule, X and Y are called, respectively, the antecedent and consequent of the rule. The strength of such a rule is measured by values of its support and confidence. The *confidence* of the rule is the percentage of transactions with antecedent X in the dataset that also contain the consequent Y. The *support* of the rule is the percentage of transactions in the dataset that contain both the antecedent and the consequent Y in all transactions in the dataset.

The WEKA system has several association rule-discovering algorithms available. The Apriori algorithm (Agrawal et al. 1996) is used for finding association rules over the discretized data of Table 1. Apriori (Agrawal and Srikant 1994) is the best-known algorithm to mine association rules. It uses a breadth-first search strategy to count the support of item sets and uses a candidate generation function, which exploits the downward closure property of support. Iteratively reduces the minimum support until it finds the required number of rules with the given minimum confidence.

There are different techniques of categorization for association rule mining. Most of the subjective approaches involve user participation in order to express, in

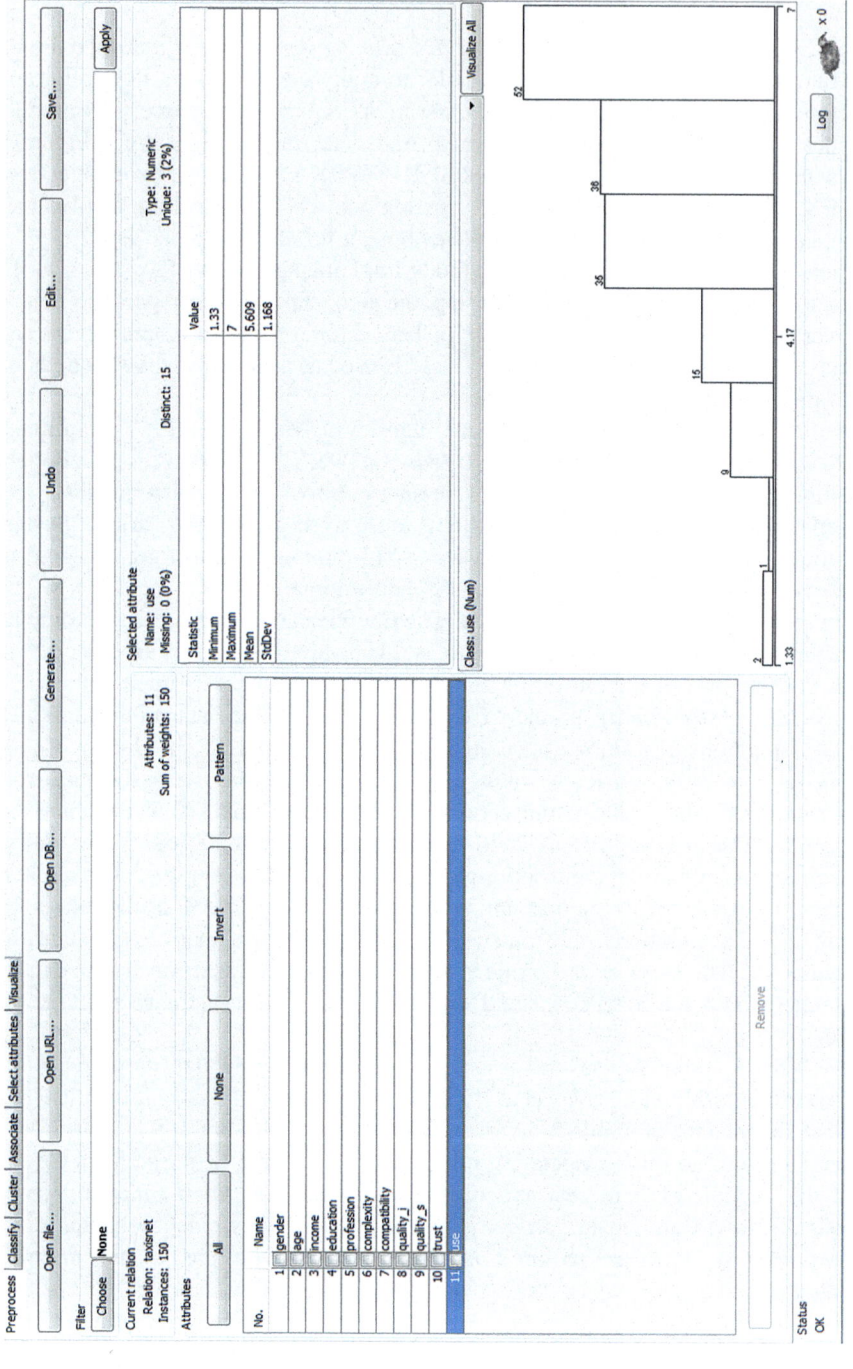

Fig. 1 WEKA environment

accordance with his/her previous knowledge, which rules are of interest. One technique is based on unexpectedness and actionability (Liu and Hsu 1996; Liu et al. 2000). *Unexpectedness* expresses which rules are interesting if they are unknown to the user or contradict the user's knowledge. *Actionability* expresses that rules are interesting if users can do something with them to their advantage. The number of rules can be decreased to unexpected and actionable rules only (García et al. 2007). Another technique proposes the division of the discovered rules into three categories (Minaei-Bidgoli et al. 2004). (1) *Expected and previously known*: This type of rule confirms user beliefs and can be used to validate our approach. Though perhaps already known, many of these rules are still useful for the user as a form of empirical verification of expectations. For agriculture, this approach provides opportunity for rigorous justification of many long-held beliefs. (2) *Unexpected*: This type of rule contradicts user beliefs. This group of unanticipated correlations can supply interesting rules, yet their interestingness and possible actionability still require further investigation. (3) *Unknown*: This type of rule does not clearly belong to any category and should be categorized by domain-specific experts.

4 Results

The first step before applying the data mining methods described in the previous section is the preprocessing of the data in order to prepare them for data analysis.

4.1 Preprocessing

Certain filters were applied to the data, such as the filter *NumericalToNominal* in order to convert numeric variables and their values to nominal. For example, number 1 and 2 in variable Gender are converted to nominal, where 1 signifies male and 2 signifies female. Furthermore, the filter *Discretize* was applied in order to discretize numeric variables and make them nominal. Figure 2 depicts all the variables used in our analysis.

4.2 Classification

In the classification step, the algorithm OneR is applied. The attribute "Use" is used as a class. Figure 3 presents the overall accuracy of the model computed from the training dataset and is equal to 90%. The worst performance based on the F-measure that combines precision and recall is for the class Use and equals 63.4%, whereas the best performance is for the class Not Use and equals 94.2%.

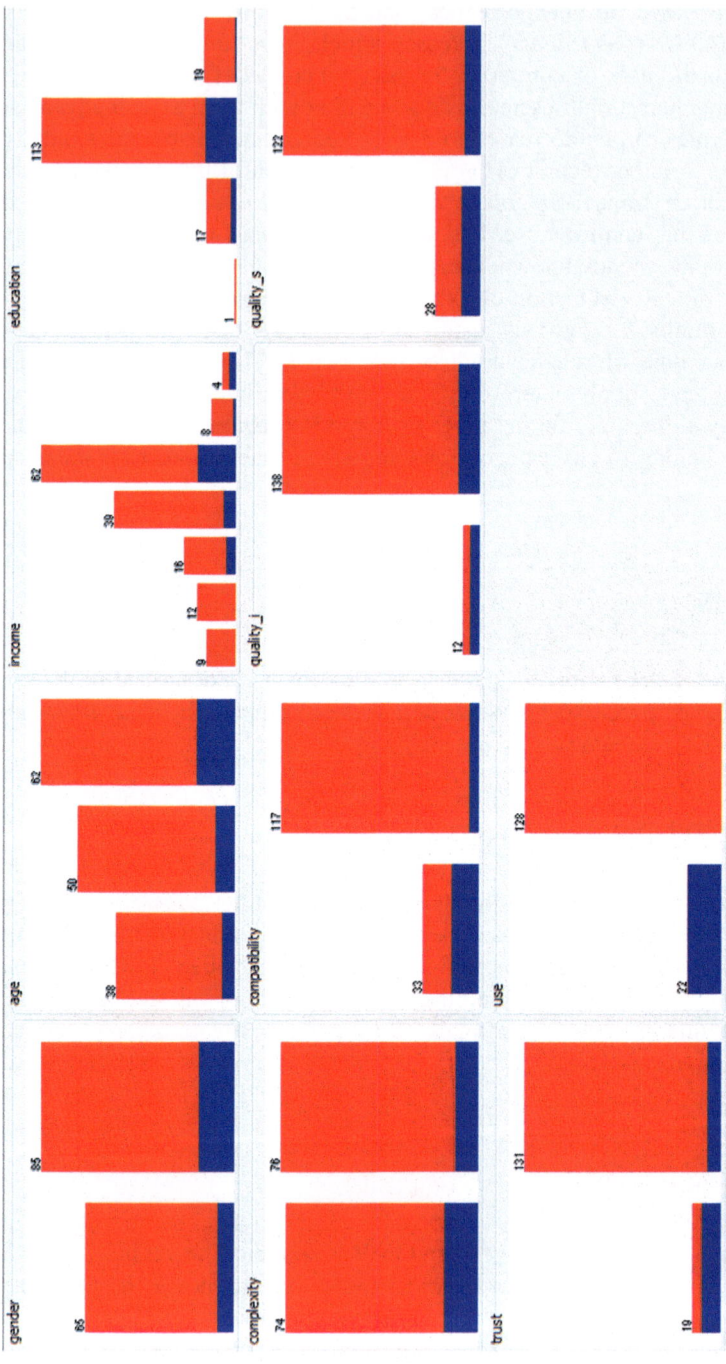

Fig. 2 Visualization of the attributes with class variable "Use"

```
=== Classifier model (full training set) ===

trust:
        '(-inf-4]'        -> '(-inf-4.165]'
        '(4-inf)'         -> '(4.165-inf)'
(135/150 instances correct)


Time taken to build model: 0 seconds

=== Stratified cross-validation ===
=== Summary ===

Correctly Classified Instances        135            90       %
Incorrectly Classified Instances       15            10       %
Kappa statistic                         0.5766
Mean absolute error                     0.1
Root mean squared error                 0.3162
Relative absolute error                39.3527 %
Root relative squared error            89.319  %
Coverage of cases (0.95 level)         90       %
Mean rel. region size (0.95 level)     50       %
Total Number of Instances             150

=== Detailed Accuracy By Class ===

             TP Rate  FP Rate  Precision  Recall  F-Measure  MCC    ROC Area  PRC Area  Class
             0,591    0,047    0,684      0,591   0,634      0,579  0,772     0,464     '(-inf-4.165]'
             0,953    0,409    0,931      0,953   0,942      0,579  0,772     0,928     '(4.165-inf)'
Weighted Avg. 0,900   0,356    0,895      0,900   0,897      0,579  0,772     0,860

=== Confusion Matrix ===

   a    b    <-- classified as
  13    9  |  a = '(-inf-4.165]'
   6  122  |  b = '(4.165-inf)'
```

Fig. 3 Classification results using variable "Use" as class

The results indicate that the attribute which describes the classification is variable Trust. This means that variable Use is more closely related to the variable Trust than the other variables, and therefore the use of Taxisnet depends on the trust of its users.

4.3 Clustering

The clustering step was performed using the k-means algorithm (*SimpleKmeans* in the context of WEKA). The number of clusters is set to 2, since the variable "Use" was used to compute the accuracy of the clustering and inspect the impact of the use of Taxisnet. Figure 4 shows the results of the clustering based on variable "Use." The clustered instances are 82 (55%) and 68 (45%), respectively. It is also evident from the cluster centroids that "Use" with higher values are in both clusters.

The differences in the two clusters are focused on demographic attributes: gender, age, income, and complexity.

```
kMeans
======

Number of iterations: 3
Within cluster sum of squared errors: 367.0

Initial starting points (random):

Cluster 0: 1,2,5,5,'\'(4.7-inf)\'','\'(-inf-4]\'','\'(4-inf)\'','\'(-inf-4.5]\'','\'(4-inf)\'','\'(4.165-inf)\''
Cluster 1: 2,3,6,3,'\'(-inf-4.7]\'','\'(4-inf)\'','\'(4-inf)\'','\'(4.5-inf)\'','\'(4-inf)\'','\'(4.165-inf)\''

Missing values globally replaced with mean/mode

Final cluster centroids:
                                            Cluster#
Attribute              Full Data               0              1
                        (150.0)             (82.0)         (68.0)
======================================================================
gender                      2                   1              2
age                         3                   2              3
income                      6                   5              6
education                   4                   4              4
complexity            '(4.7-inf)'         '(4.7-inf)'    '(-inf-4.7]'
compatibility          '(4-inf)'           '(4-inf)'      '(4-inf)'
quality_i              '(4-inf)'           '(4-inf)'      '(4-inf)'
quality_s             '(4.5-inf)'         '(4.5-inf)'    '(4.5-inf)'
trust                  '(4-inf)'           '(4-inf)'      '(4-inf)'
use                  '(4.165-inf)'       '(4.165-inf)'  '(4.165-inf)'



Time taken to build model (full training data) : 0.02 seconds

=== Model and evaluation on training set ===

Clustered Instances

0       82 ( 55%)
1       68 ( 45%)
```

Fig. 4 Clustering results. Variable "Use" is used for assessing the clustering

4.4 Association Rule Mining

The Apriori algorithm (Agrawal and Srikant 1994) was used for finding association rules for our dataset. The algorithm was executed using a minimum support of 0.1 and a minimum confidence of 0.9, as parameters. WEKA produced a list of 20 rules (Fig. 5) with the support of the antecedent and the consequent (total number of items) at 0.1 minimum and the confidence of the rule at 0.9 minimum (percentage of items in a 0 to 1 scale).

There are of course some uninteresting rules, like rules 9 and 11. There are some similar rules, rules with the same element in antecedent and consequent but interchanged, such as rules 12, 16 and 13, 20. There is also a similar triad of rules, rules with the same element in antecedent and consequent but interchanged, such as rules [5, 6 and 17], [1, 14 and 18], and [1, 7 and 10]. And there are also rules that show interesting relationships such as rules 13, 16, 19, and 20 which offer a lot of actionability in order to improve the intention to use Taxinet. Rules 4 and 15 can be useful since they prove that the quality of the system leads to both to quality of

```
Apriori
=======

Minimum support: 0.75 (112 instances)
Minimum metric <confidence>: 0.9
Number of cycles performed: 5

Generated sets of large itemsets:

Size of set of large itemsets L(1): 6

Size of set of large itemsets L(2): 8

Size of set of large itemsets L(3): 3

Best rules found:

 1. compatibility='(4-inf)' trust='(4-inf)' 112 ==> quality_i='(4-inf)' 112      <conf:(1)> lift:(1.09) lev:(0.06) [8] conv:(8.96)
 2. compatibility='(4-inf)' 117 ==> quality_i='(4-inf)' 116      <conf:(0.99)> lift:(1.08) lev:(0.06) [8] conv:(4.68)
 3. quality_s='(4.5-inf)' trust='(4-inf)' 115 ==> quality_i='(4-inf)' 113      <conf:(0.98)> lift:(1.07) lev:(0.05) [7] conv:(3.07)
 4. quality_s='(4.5-inf)' 122 ==> quality_i='(4-inf)' 119      <conf:(0.98)> lift:(1.06) lev:(0.05) [6] conv:(2.44)
 5. trust='(4-inf)' use='(4.165-inf)' 122 ==> quality_i='(4-inf)' 119      <conf:(0.98)> lift:(1.06) lev:(0.05) [6] conv:(2.44)
 6. quality_i='(4-inf)' use='(4.165-inf)' 123 ==> trust='(4-inf)' 119      <conf:(0.97)> lift:(1.11) lev:(0.08) [11] conv:(3.12)
 7. compatibility='(4-inf)' quality_i='(4-inf)' 116 ==> trust='(4-inf)' 112      <conf:(0.97)> lift:(1.11) lev:(0.07) [10] conv:(2.94)
 8. use='(4.165-inf)' 128 ==> quality_i='(4-inf)' 123      <conf:(0.96)> lift:(1.04) lev:(0.03) [5] conv:(1.71)
 9. compatibility='(4-inf)' 117 ==> trust='(4-inf)' 112      <conf:(0.96)> lift:(1.1) lev:(0.07) [9] conv:(2.47)
10. compatibility='(4-inf)' 117 ==> quality_i='(4-inf)' trust='(4-inf)' 112      <conf:(0.96)> lift:(1.15) lev:(0.1) [14] conv:(3.25)
11. trust='(4-inf)' 131 ==> quality_i='(4-inf)' 125      <conf:(0.95)> lift:(1.04) lev:(0.03) [4] conv:(1.5)
12. use='(4.165-inf)' 128 ==> trust='(4-inf)' 122      <conf:(0.95)> lift:(1.09) lev:(0.07) [10] conv:(2.32)
13. quality_i='(4-inf)' trust='(4-inf)' 125 ==> use='(4.165-inf)' 119      <conf:(0.95)> lift:(1.12) lev:(0.08) [12] conv:(2.62)
14. quality_i='(4-inf)' quality_s='(4.5-inf)' 119 ==> trust='(4-inf)' 113      <conf:(0.95)> lift:(1.12) lev:(0.09) [9] conv:(2.15)
15. quality_s='(4.5-inf)' 122 ==> trust='(4-inf)' 115      <conf:(0.94)> lift:(1.08) lev:(0.06) [8] conv:(1.93)
16. trust='(4-inf)' 131 ==> use='(4.165-inf)' 122      <conf:(0.93)> lift:(1.09) lev:(0.07) [10] conv:(1.92)
17. use='(4.165-inf)' 128 ==> quality_i='(4-inf)' trust='(4-inf)' 119      <conf:(0.93)> lift:(1.12) lev:(0.08) [12] conv:(2.13)
18. quality_s='(4.5-inf)' 122 ==> quality_i='(4-inf)' trust='(4-inf)' 113      <conf:(0.93)> lift:(1.11) lev:(0.08) [11] conv:(2.03)
19. quality_s='(4.5-inf)' 122 ==> use='(4.165-inf)' 112      <conf:(0.92)> lift:(1.08) lev:(0.05) [7] conv:(1.63)
20. trust='(4-inf)' 131 ==> quality_i='(4-inf)' use='(4.165-inf)' 119      <conf:(0.91)> lift:(1.11) lev:(0.08) [11] conv:(1.81)
```

Fig. 5 The association rule mining results based on the confidence metric

information and trust of the system. There are also rules which need further investigation such as 2 and 8, since they do not confirm user beliefs and they cannot be
used to validate our approach.

Summarizing the results from the classification, the clustering, and the association rule mining methods, we can conclude that:

1. The attribute which best describes the classification is the variable Trust. The
   attribute "Use" (intention to use) is used as a class.
2. Using "Use" as class attribute in clustering, the results show that employees who
   belong to the second cluster have better values in the parameters regarding the
   intention to use Taxinet.
3. In association rule mining, although there are some trivial rules, namely, expected
   and previously known like rule 15 that shows that the quality of the system leads
   to better quality of information, there are also rules like 13, 16, 19, and 20 which
   offer a lot of actionability. Quality of information, trust, and quality of system
   have great impact to the intention to use Taxinet.

Overall, low complexity, high compatibility, high quality of information, high
quality of system, and high trust lead to the intention to use Taxinet. It is surprising
that parameters such as gender, age, income, and education do not determine the
intention to use Taxinet.

5 Discussion and Conclusions

The application of three different data mining techniques in data about intentions to use Taxisnet by the office employees is presented in this paper. Some critical factors such as Control, Complexity, Compatibility, Information Quality, System Quality, and Trust and demographic characteristics such as Gender, Age, Income, and Education were taken into consideration. The dataset involves data of tax office employees of four branches in the Region of Eastern Macedonia and Thrace: Drama, Kavala, Serres, and Xanthi.

The results show some interesting outcomes. First of all, the classification method indicates that the trust is the most significant parameter for the use of Taxisnet. Furthermore, the clustering results show that there are no significant differences in the partitioned group of data. The last data mining method, the association rule mining, draws the conclusions that the quality of information, the trust, and the quality of system have great impact on the intention to use of Taxinet.

It is hardly possible to conduct a study that does not contain weaknesses or an element of bias. Therefore, there are some limitations in this study as well. The sample size is relatively small (150 employees) and may not be adequate to represent the whole population as the answers of the sample chosen may simply differ from the population. We selected only respondents of tax offices from four prefectures which may be addressed in future work so that the investigation can be extended to other prefectures of Greece and therefore to a larger sample of respondents. If the sample is selected from different parts of Greece, there will be an opportunity for researchers to broaden and deepen their survey and have more representative results that depict *different opinions* of tax officers using the Taxisnet. Being able to collect data from a diverse sample in terms of age, gender, and place of work increases the generalizability of the findings. Future studies should seek a broader set of tax officers to perform a more complex model testing and validate these results.

Furthermore, an increasing number of government operations take advantage of new technological advances (Kim et al. 2014; Tripathi and Parihar 2011) (e.g., Cloud and Big Data), improving e-government's performance. This direction could provide new challenges associated with compatibility, control, trust, and complexity of information. From a societal perspective, it is necessary to take into consideration citizens' attitudes in order to assess these services, and their perceptions on how public administrations (PAs) deal with their data along with the lack of transparency bottleneck the wide adoption of e-government (Eynon 2007). On the other hand, from a technical perspective, in e-government multiple organizations might require to process private data differently.

References

Agrawal, R., & Srikant, R. (1994). Fast algorithms for mining association rules. In *Proceedings of 20th international conference on very large data bases* (pp. 487–499).

Agrawal, R., Mannila, H., Srikant, R., Toivonen, H., & Verkamo, A. I. (1996). Fast discovery of association rules. *Advances in Knowledge Discovery and Data Mining, 12*(1), 307–328.

Anagnostopoulos, D. (2006). *Projects of the General Secretariat for Information systems*. In Speech in the context of the 1st EU Summit on observing IT society, Athens, Greece, pp. 27–29.

Beattie, V., & Pratt, K. (2003). Issues concerning web-based business reporting: An analysis of the views of interested parties. *The British Accounting Review, 35*(2), 155–187.

Belanger, A., & Carter, L. (2008). Trust and risk in e-government adoption. *Journal of Strategic Information Systems, 17*, 165–176.

Bélanger, F., Hiller, J., & Smith, W. (2002). Trustworthiness in electronic commerce: The role of privacy, security, and site attributes. *Journal of Strategic Information Systems, 11*, 245–270.

Chadwick, S. (2001). Communicating trust in e-commerce interactions. *Management Communication Quarterly, 14*, 653–658.

Colesca, S. E. (2009). Understanding trust in e-government. *The Engineering Economist, 33*, 7–15.

Cunningham, S. J., & Holmes, G. (1999). Developing innovative applications in agriculture using data mining. In *Proceedings of the Southeast Asia Regional Computer Confederation Conference*.

Davidaviciene, V. (2008). Change management decisions in the information Age. *Journal of Business Economics and Management, 9*(4), 299–307.

Davis, F. D., Bagozzi, R. P., & Warshaw, P. R. (1989). User acceptance of computer technology: A comparison of two theoretical model. *Management Science, 35*(8), 982–1003.

Do, T. H. N., & Shih, W. (2016). The Integration between the UTAUT with IS success model in case of online hotel booking user acceptance. *Research Journal of Commerce and Behavioural Science, 5*, 25–36.

Economides, A. A., & Terzis, V. (2008). Evaluating tax sites: An evaluation framework and its application. *Electronic Government, an International Journal, 5*(3), 321–344.

Eynon, R. (2007). *Breaking barriers to eGovernment: Overcoming obstacles to improving European public services* (p. 90). Brussels: DG Information Society and Media. European Commission

Floropoulos, J., Spathis, C., Halvatzis, D., & Tsipouridou, M. (2010, February). Measuring the success of the Greek taxation information system. *International Journal of Information Management: The Journal for Information Professionals, 30*(1), 47–56. https://doi.org/10.1016/j.ijinfomgt.2009.03.013.

García, E., Romero, C., Ventura, S., & Calders, T. (2007, September). Drawbacks and solutions of applying association rule mining in learning management systems. In *Proceedings of the International Workshop on Applying Data Mining in e-Learning (ADML 2007)* (pp. 13–22). Crete, Greece.

Golubeva, A., Merkuryeva, I., & Shulakov, N. (2005, Spring). Development of e-government in St.-Petersburg: Evaluation of Web sites performance and usability. *Occasional Papers in Public Administration and Public Policy, VI*(2), 15–30 (NISPAcee).

Grandison, T., & Sloman, M. (2000). A survey of trust in internet applications. *IEEE Communications Survey and Tutorials, 3*, 2–16.

Gupta, M. P., & Jana, D. (2003). E-government evaluation: A framework and case study. *Government Information Quarterly, 20*(4), 365–387.

Gupta, B., Dasgupta, S., & Gupta, A. (2008). Adoption of ICT in a government organization in a developing country: An empirical study. *The Journal of Strategic Information Systems, 17*, 140–154. https://doi.org/10.1016/j.jsis.2007.12.004.

Hahamis, P., Iles, J., & Healy, M. (2005). E-government in Greece: Bridging the gap between need and reality. *Electronic Journal of e-Government, 3*(4), 185–192.

Hoffman, D., Novak, T., & Peralta, M. (1999). Building consumer trust online. *Communications of the ACM, 42*, 80–85.

Horst, M., Kuttschreuter, M., & Gutteling, J. M. (2007). Perceived usefulness, personal experiences, risk perception and trust as determinants of adoption of e-government services in The Netherlands. *Computers in Human Behavior, 23*, 1838–1852.

Hung, S. Y., Chang, C. M., & Yn, T. J. (2006). Determinants of user acceptance of the e-Government services: The case of on line tax filing and payment system. *Government Information Quarterly, 23*, 97–122.

Johnson, D. S., & Grayson, K. (2005). Cognitive and affective trust in service relationships. *Journal of Business Research, 58*(4), 500–507.

Kantardzic, M. (2003). *Data mining: Concepts, models, methods, and algorithms.* New York: Wiley.

Kaufmann, L., & Rousseeuw, P. J. (1990). *Finding groups in data: An introduction to cluster analysis.* New York: Wiley.

Kim, G.-H., Trimi, S., & Chung, J.-H. (2014). Big-data applications in the government sector. *Communications of the ACM, 57*(3), 78–85.

Lau, C., & Halkyard, A. (2003). *From e-commerce to e-business taxation. Asia-Pacific tax bulletin* (pp. 1–12). Upper Saddle River: Prentice Hall PTR.

Liu, B., & Hsu, W. (1996). Post-analysis of learned rules. In *Proceedings of national conference on artificial intelligence* (pp. 828–834). Portland, OR.

Liu, B., Hsu, W., Chen, S., & Ma, Y. (2000). Analyzing the subjective interestingness of association rules. *IEEE Intelligent Systems, 15*(5), 47–55.

MacQueen, J. (1967). Some methods for classification and analysis of multivariate observations. In *Proceedings of the 5th Berkeley symposium on mathematical statistics and probability* (pp. 281–297). Berkeley, CA: University of California Press.

Mayer, R. C., Davis, J. H., & Schoorman, F. D. (1995). An integrative model of organizational trust. *Academy of Management Review, 20*(3), 709–734.

McKnight, D. H., Cummings, L. L., & Chervany, N. L. (1998). Initial trust formation in new organizational relationships. *Academy of Management Review, 23*(3), 473–490.

McKnight, H., Choudhury, V., & Kacmar, C. (2002). Developing and validating trust measures for e-commerce: an integrative typology. *Information Systems Research, 13*, 334–359.

Minaei-Bidgoli, B., Tan, P.-.N, & Punch, W.F. (2004). Mining interesting contrast rules for a web-based educational system. In *Proceedings of international conference on machine learning applications* (pp. 320–327). Louisville.

Miyazaki, A., & Fernandez, A. (2001). Consumer perceptions of privacy and security risks for online shopping. *Journal of Consumer Affairs, 35*, 27–44.

OECD. (2008). Annual report, public affairs division, public affairs and communications directorate.

Pant, V., Stiner, M. S., & Wagner, P. W. (2004). E-taxation: An introduction to the use of TaxXML for corporate tax reporting. *Journal of Electronic Commerce in Organizations, 2*(1), 29–41.

Raus, M., Lin, J., & Kipp, A. (2010). Evaluating IT innovations in a business- to government context: A framework and it's applications. *Government Information Quarterly, 27*, 122–133.

Rogers, E. M. (1995). *Diffusion of innovations* (4th ed.). New York: Free Press.

Rotter, J. B. (1980). Interpersonal trust, trustworthiness, and gullibility. *American Psychologist, 35*(1), 1–7.

Sichtmann, C. (2007). An analysis of antecedents and consequences of trust in a corporate brand. *European Journal of Marketing, 41*, 999–1015. https://doi.org/10.1108/03090560710773318.

Terpsiadou, M. H., & Economides, A. A. (2009). The use of information systems in the Greek Public financial services: The case of TAXIS. *Government Information Quarterly, 26*, 468–476.

Terzis, V., & Economides, A. A. (2007). Critical success factors for tax web sites. In J. Makolm, & G. Orthofer (Eds.), *E-taxation: State and perspectives: E-government in the field of taxation trauner verlag in its informatics series* (pp. 56–67).

Tornatzky, L., & Klein, K. (1982). Innovation characteristics and innovation adoption implementation: A metaanalysis of findings. *IEEE Transactions on Engineering Management, 29*, 28–45.

Tripathi, A., & Parihar, B. (2011). E-governance challenges and cloud benefits. In *Proceedings of IEEE international conference on Computer Science and Automation Engineering (CSAE)* (Vol. 1, pp. 351–354). Shanghai: IEEE.

Wang, Y. S. (2002). The adoption of electronic tax filing systems: An empirical study. *Government Information Quarterly, 20*, 333–352.

Wang, T. D., & Emurian, H. H. (2005). An overview of online trust: Concepts, elements, and implications. *Computers in Human Behavior, 21*, 105–125. https://doi.org/10.1016/j.chb.2003.11.008.

Wang, Y.-S., & Liao, Y.-W. (2007). Assessing eGovernment systems success: A validation of the DeLone and McLean model of information systems success. *Government Information Quarterly*. https://doi.org/10.1016/j.giq.2007.06.002.

Wang, L., Bretschneider, S., & Gant, J. (2005, January). Evaluating web-based e-government services with a citizen-centric approach. In *Proceedings of the 38th Annual Hawaii International Conference on System Sciences* (pp. 129b–129b). IEEE.

Warkentin, M., Gefan, D., Pavlou, P. A., & Rose, G. M. (2002). Encouraging citizen adoption of e-Government by building trust. *Electronic Markets, 12*(3), 157–162.

Witten, I., & Frank, E. (2005). *Data mining practical machine learning tools and techniques*. San Francisco: Morgan Kaufmann.

Urban Development

Alba Ramallari

Abstract Every government wants to achieve the necessary objectives timely and in defined manner.

The primary objective, however, remains realization of economic stability. When talking about stability, we take into account the relation with other influential factors with it for both positive and negative sides. The aim of this chapter is a significant manifestation that will be the link between economic stability and development of the country's urban infrastructure, water supply, sanitation, sewerage, better working conditions, etc., that is, keeping in mind the main objective: fair development among regions by utilizing all capacities and advantages.

Keywords Urban development · Infrastructure · Stability

1 Literature Review

Urbanization is the process of human migration from rural areas to towns and cities, thus rapid urbanization means that the rate at which the migration from rural to urban takes place is hurried that a country has no time to plan for their existence at the cities. According to a report compiled by the University of Michigan, the percentage of the human global population living in cities in 1950 was less than 30%, and by the year 2000, the figure stood at 47%. The study predicted that by 2025, the figure would be at 60% (World Watch 2011). George Murdock once said that a community is one of the two truly universal units of society organization, the other one being family (Schaefer, 461). We are all part of a community, and in many cases, we are a part of multiple ones. In chapter "Digital Practices of Greek Small Entrepreneurship: Social Media and Self-Employment" of our textbook, we are looking at communities and urbanization. It discusses urbanization and how communities originate. It also

A. Ramallari (✉)
Department of Economics Sciences, University "Aleksandër Moisiu", Durrës, Albania

© Springer Nature Switzerland AG 2019   277
N. Sykianakis et al. (eds.), *Economic and Financial Challenges for Eastern Europe*,
Springer Proceedings in Business and Economics,
https://doi.org/10.1007/978-3-030-12169-3_17

looks at the different types of communities. Communities are defined as "a spatial or political unit of social organization that gives people a sense of belonging" (Schaefer, 548). It can be based on a place of residence, such as a city, neighborhood, or a particular school district. It could also be based on common identity, such as gays, the homeless, or the deaf. The United Nations projects that developing countries will almost double their urban population by 2050, adding a further 2.4 billion urban dwellers. Urbanization in Albania has gone through three distinct phases since the fall of communism. The first phase was dominated by the informal sector. The second phase saw the consolidation of the informal sector and the emergence of a formal sector. The third phase, the current one in 2006, consists in the consolidation of the formal sector and the regularization of the informal sector (Alain Bertaud 2006). While the urbanization of the world's population has been accompanied by an "urbanization of global poverty" (Chen and Ravallion 2007), poverty continues to be overwhelmingly concentrated in rural areas. According to the World Development Indicators, almost two third of the poor globally are still rural. Thus understanding the implications of urban growth for rural poverty in developing countries is crucial for any global poverty reduction strategy. In a study created in India, Calì and Menon (2013) are examining the extent to which the growth in urban areas reduced poverty in surrounding rural areas. The focus on India is particularly relevant, as it is the country with the largest number of both rural and urban poor and with the largest expected absolute growth in urban population between now and 2050.

2 Introduction

Urbanization in Albania has gone through couple of phases starting with major changes in 1991 until currently, still in transition period. Looking at the world over 50% lives in urban areas. Over the years this figure has been rising and as such is projected. It is said that 80% of the GDP is generated in urban area. Urbanization could contribute in a stable development if every increased production is managed properly, allowing innovation and ideas to further develop.

However, the rapid growth and scale of urbanization introduce new changes, thus bringing increase in individual's demand, good interconnection of transport systems, other infrastructures, basic services, jobs, etc. It should be noted that at this stage work of individuals should be portioned out, who only work to improve their living standards (welfare).

To build cities that promise development and a better future, in particular promise safety and stability, requires intensive coordinated policies and solution to investments.

When cities are built its physical form and land can be used for generations. Important roles to act have the central and local government, to define the future and create other new aggregate possibilities.

The development of urban areas is still part of World Bank projects, and it is based on three main pillars:

(a) Tighter city/urban financing policies, planning, and a good management system
(b) Improvement in different dimensions of conditions, services in infrastructure, and living conditions in the neighborhood
(c) Support of urban changes and development through innovation in urban planning and land use, management, and implementation of integrated investments in infrastructure and offering services in order to improve urban environment and shape of the cities to make it more flexible, worth living, and productive

The three pillars of urban development in projects applied in World Bank have their six lines of actions:

(a) The city and economic development
(b) Poverty
(c) Infrastructure and services
(d) Land and comfort houses
(e) Urban management, leadership, and provisions
(f) Cities and urban environment

3   Urban Areas and Economic Development

When we refer to the cities development significant portion are developments that need to be taken to different programs, schools, and training, such as build new schools, update literatures, creating possibilities to learn and live better. All these are part of the urban development packages. In cases of economic growth remembrance, investing is what it needs. Nowadays most investments are private investments. In certain cases it may even develop public and private partnerships. In the case of private investments which require economic development of the country, there are different subsidies and interference with budget funds. Recently, such achievements are being seen in our country, such as building the "New Bazaar" and many other cases. Such changes occur throughout the world. It is worth mentioning that in order to have a development and economic growth in the cities, plans should be prepared and consolidated. Plans should be prepared for 4–5 year periods or even more. Despite the term, in context the plan must contain a coherent purpose, for instance, the realization of the quality of life for its inhabitants, to make it a cozy place to live and to visit.

If support is needed from private sector and subsidies are given, this would normally bring an economic growth.

We have received grants from the World Bank for urban development, despite a large portion of them has been used for countries that are part of UNESCO.

World Bank Board of Executive Directors has approved a financing grant of 71 million dollars for Urban Integrated Project Management and Tourism in Albania. This project will help create new job opportunities, increase in income, and support local economic development in selected districts in south Albania, known as main destination for tourism with big potential for economic growth. The project aims to improve urban infrastructure, increase the value tourism assets, as well as strengthen the institutional capacity to support tourism locally.

By linking up with other sectors, tourism contributes a fifth of economic activity and the creation of new jobs in the country, while in 2014 its direct share in the Gross Domestic Product was 5.9%. Tourism currently supports 50,000 jobs—a number expected to grow to 200,000 in 2025. However, inadequate urban infrastructure, lack of coordination of local and regional markets, and short seasonality of tourist activity pose serious challenges.

"This project will preserve the natural resources of Albania and its cultural richness making tourism more competitive." "This project will promote local economic growth by supporting urban regeneration and sustainable tourism" (Tahseen Sayed, the World Bank Office in Albania).

Often the plans drawn up in different places are taken and pursued as proper examples for other cities. But there are times when it does happen that way. In the best possible way, one city should have qualities and its living standards. A good example in the world gives the urban development plan of Dublin which stands on the principles of plans drawn up by the World Bank, but also urban development plans such as the Freiburg plan (Germany) which differs from the others preserve the origin of the city. Meanwhile, this is happening in our country.

It aims to provide an economic and social development, to be evenly distributed across the country, give priority to creating new jobs, foster support in the development of rural areas, ensure protection of the environment and natural resources, improve and develop transport, and support tourism development.

For the first time, it will be drafted and adopted the strategic document "National General Plan for Territorial Development," in investment and control of the territory.

All these will go in parallel with the implementation of territorial reform. Approval of the plan will be preceded by the adoption of Areas of National Importance, on the basis of which will be placed three important moratoriums on construction activity on the coast, forests, and surface water resources in all important areas for tourism.

However, the moment of creating a plan is not easy, affectionate. There are times when it does not go as foreseen, as in the case of New Zealand, which was not based on concrete facts but in predictive shade.

When we create a plan for urban development, we should visualize that three views of the planning process are distinguished, with their associated criteria of the quality of plans; planning as control of the future, implying that plans not implemented indicate failure; and planning as a process of decision-making under conditions of uncertainty, where implementation ceases to be a criterion of success, but where it becomes difficult.

Fig. 1 FDI stock by country. Source: AIDA (Albanian investment development agency) http:// aida.gov.al/fdi

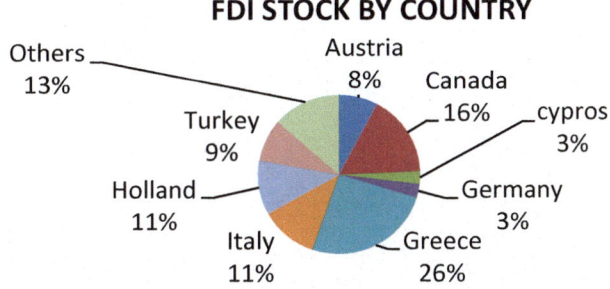

FDI STOCK BY COUNTRY

Table 1 FDI by country in million euro

Countries	2014 million euros
Austria	357
Canada	755
Cyprus	117
Germany	128
Greece	1169
Italy	526
Holland	505
Turkey	394
Others	614
Total	4565

Source: AIDA, (Albanian investment development agency aida. gov.al/fdi

4 Foreign Investments

Foreign Direct Investment Stock in Albania by Country of Origin (States)
Foreign direct investment stock (FDI) in the country at the end of 2014 amounted to 4565 million euros, increasing by more than 11% of the total FDI stock compared to 2013. The main share of the countries of origin of foreign investors in the stock of FDI invested in companies in Albania is from Greece, worth 1169 million euros or expressed in percentage 26% of the total stock. This state is followed by Canada in second place with 755 million euros or 16% of the total stock, and the third rank is Italy worth 526 million euros, or with a weight of approximately 11% of the total FDI stock. In the figures below is demonstrated FDI stock in Albania by country and by activities.

For being more understandable, the table below shows the value (related with the percentage of the Fig. 1) of foreign investments in Albania (Table 1).

Main economic activities that FDI stock is focused for 2014 are:

1. Extractive industry approx. 15% of the total
2. Processing industry approx. 9% of the total

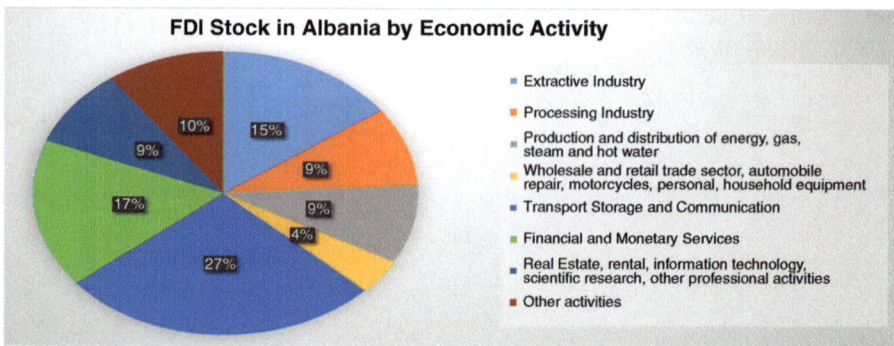

Fig. 2 FDI stock by economic activity. Source: AIDA (Albanian investment development agency aida.gov.al/fdi)

3. Production and distribution of energy, gas, steam, and hot water approx. 9% of the total
4. Wholesale and retail trade sector, automobile repair, motorcycles, and personal household equipment approx. 4% of the total
5. Transport, storage, and communication approx. 27% of the total
6. Financial and monetary services approx. 17% of the total
7. Real estate, rental, information technology, scientific research, and other professional activities approx. 9% of the total
8. Other activities approx. 10% of the total FDI stock

In Fig. 2 are shown the FDI by economic activity.

5 The Effects of Urbanization in Poverty

(a) Poverty fell by more than a half in middle and high income countries since 1981. However, the fight against poverty has been much slower in low-income countries, where poverty has only fallen by roughly a third since 1981.
(b) The speed with which the population is increasing in low-income countries makes it more difficult to pare poverty growth.
(c) The aggregate additional annual income needed to lift every individual out of extreme poverty in low-income countries rose by 33% between 1981 and 2010. This is due to an increase of 103 million in people living below the poverty line and "an average income among the poor that remained almost as low in 2010 as it was back in 1981" (World Bank 2013).
(d) In 2010, low-income countries were home to 29% of those in extreme poverty, second to India's 33%. The growth in this amount has been slowly decreasing since the turn of the century (World Bank 2013).

By the central government in our country, the urban poverty is related with migration. In recent years, a large part of the population is positioned in the capital, increasing it by territorial area, which adds even more focus on investments that need to be taken to the type of infrastructure, sanitation, roads, parking, gardens, schools, and everything else needed for a comfortable living with good conditions.

Rapid Uncontrolled and Unregulated Urbanization The post-communist period in Albania, beginning in 1990, has been characterized by massive population shifts from the countryside to large- and medium-sized urban centers such as Tirana, Durres, Vlore, Elbasan, and Saranda and to undeveloped coastal areas. Because the country lacks formal land and housing markets and a proper regulatory framework, this urbanization is occurring primarily through informal processes, particularly the development of *informal low-income settlements*.

All these changes create unemployment. INSTAT reported the unemployment rate in Albania to be 18.4% in 1999. In urban areas this figure is higher and even higher in periurban areas. High percentage of informal private businesses makes the employment very uncertain and keeps wages low.

Emerging of New "Pockets of Urban Poverty" Slum-like communities have formed around Tirana and other major cities, "lacking urban infrastructure and services."[1] The data of Living Standard Measurement Survey (LSMS) conducted in 1996 in Albania has indicated that poverty in Albania is a rural phenomenon with almost 90% of the poor residing in rural areas.[2] The emerging of "pockets of urban poverty" in the peri-urban areas is a pure response of the rural poverty to migration. People migrating from rural areas or other depressed regions of the country simply stake out and claim unused land on the outskirts of towns and build houses that are often quite substantial but don't have access to basic infrastructure.

Limited Access to Basic Infrastructure and Services During the last decade, after the demise of the communism the basic services deteriorated further. Current policies failed to respond quickly to the high demand from the growing population in the big inland urban or coastal urban areas. Investments in physical and social infrastructure have not kept pace with the rapid growth in settlements, and the percentage of the population without access to infrastructure has increased to around 50–60%. In addition, the existing infrastructure networks have not been maintained over the past decade due to lack of funding sources, and their deterioration has significantly decreased the quality of existing services.

---

[1] Albania-Interim Poverty Reduction Strategy Paper, Draft, pg. 2, April 8, 2000

[2] Ibid

6 Infrastructure

With regard to infrastructure, one of the largest projects was the completion of the highway Durrës-Kukës-Morinë, named "The Way of the Nation." The highway in question, with a length of 170 km, has had a positive impact on trade exchanges between Albania and Kosovo.

Albania has approximately 20,000 km of roads, and construction of roads is growing rapidly. Corridor VIII, which is under construction, will connect the Albanian Port of Durrës with Varna (Bulgaria) via Tirana, Qafë Thanë, Skopje, Deve Bair, Sofia, Plovdiv, and Burgas. This corridor will be the main east-west link through Albania and will become an important transport link between the Balkan and Mediterranean countries.

In 2008, special attention was paid to regional cooperation in the context of road transport with neighboring countries such as Macedonia, Kosovo, Montenegro, and Greece. During the year of 2011, 452 km of roads have been rebuilt across the country, of which 132 km have been completed and 320 are in the process of completion. Also, in 2011, has started the reconstruction of several major roads, including Tirana-Elbasan Highway, and two other segments, Librazhd-Neck Stud and Lin-Pogradec.

Also there are other projects being implemented which regulate and allow easy passage in certain areas of the country. These projects provide urban development, because there was no basis of regional preferences, but had all territorial expansion. Such is true for the tourism sector. But of course that development is not just about physical infrastructure, main services are priority; services that are provided by this physical infrastructure and of course challenges exist in this sector, such as reductions in tariffs. Similarly, in terms of services for passengers who travel and those who use interurban transport, conditions are improved, and new urban bus lines are available.

For the sector of tourism important is the infrastructure and water utility services, sewerage, and waste management. Albania has an international airport "Mother Teresa," which is located near the capital city, Rinas-Fushë Krujë (16 km from Tirana), which is the largest and most important investment implemented in this sector. The rail network in Albania consists of 441 km of main railways and 230 km of secondary railways. The main priority is the reactivation of the railway network through private equity instruments and financing available from international financial institutions and various donors. Maritime transport in Albania is carried out via four ports: Durrës, Vlora, Saranda, and Shëngjin. The largest and most important port is Port of Durrës, which realizes 81.8% of shipping across the country. If all this work continues in long-term period, a certain urban development will be realized.

7   Conclusions

Our country still has space available to carry out urban development. Renewal of the strategic plan is necessary in order to develop cities to have a more comfortable and productive life. The new territorial division brings improvements and opportunities in urban area development.

References

Papers

Bertaud, A. (2006, June 28). Urban development in Albania: The success story of the informal sector.
Calì, M., & Menon, C. (2013). Does urbanization affect rural poverty? Evidence from Indian Districts. *The World Bank Economic Review, 27*, 171–201.
Chen, Sh., & Ravallion, M. (2007, March). *Absolute poverty measures for the developing world, 1981–2004*, Shaohua Chen and Martin Ravallion*. Development Research Group, World Bank.
Murdock, G. (n.d.). *George Murdock's sociology theories on family and culture* (Chap. 3/Lesson 2).
Vivian, A. (2004, November 18). Personal interview: Treasure of a small town school.
World Bank. (2013). www.worldbank.org
World Watch. (2011). http://www.worldwatch.org

Annual Reports and Statistics

Aida. Retrieved from www.aida.gov.al/
Ministry of Urban Development, Albania. Retrieved from www.zhvillimiurban.gov.al/
Open Data Albania. Retrieved from www.open.data.al/

The Impact of Communication Quality, Partner Complementarity and Foreign Partner's Cultural Sensitivity on Inter-partner Trust in ISAs

Nikolaos Sklavounos, Konstantinos Rotsios, and Yannis A. Hajidimitriou

Abstract There has been an impressive growth in international strategic alliances (ISAs) numbers over the last decades since the formation of ISAs is considered one of the most important entry modes for firms to succeed in their internationalization efforts and to achieve optimal growth and competitiveness on a global basis. The role of trust on alliances' successful operation and performance has been highlighted in existing international business literature. In this paper, three propositions are developed in order to investigate the impact of (a) communication quality, (b) partner complementarity and (c) foreign partner's cultural sensitivity on the level of trust the foreign partner has towards the local ISA partner. The objective of this research is the attainment of an in-depth comprehension of the above factors. Furthermore, it provides the ground for future research to examine the importance of trust on ISAs in the South-East (SE) Europe region.

Keywords Trust · International strategic alliances · Communication quality · Partner complementarity · Foreign partner's cultural sensitivity

1 Introduction

During the past decades, globalization has motivated enterprises to participate in international strategic alliances (ISAs) in their effort to successfully enter into foreign markets. A strategic alliance is defined as an intentional relationship between two or more firms, which remain legally independent, involving exchange, sharing or co-development of resources, competences and capabilities (Gulati 1995). ISAs

N. Sklavounos (✉) · Y. A. Hajidimitriou
Department of Business Administration, University of Macedonia, Thessaloniki, Greece
e-mail: sklavou@uom.edu.gr

K. Rotsios
Perrotis College, American Farm School, Thessaloniki, Greece

© Springer Nature Switzerland AG 2019
N. Sykianakis et al. (eds.), *Economic and Financial Challenges for Eastern Europe*,
Springer Proceedings in Business and Economics,
https://doi.org/10.1007/978-3-030-12169-3_18

are very important for firms' survival as they provide access to vital resources for achieving and maintaining competitive advantages in today's uncertain international business environment (Cobeña et al. 2017). For firms, ISAs are a main instrument to ensure the knowledge improvement and the availability of complementary resources (Lubello et al. 2015). Nowadays, firms increasingly depend on external partners in order to reinforce their resources, increase their competitiveness and manage environmental hostility (Russo and Cesarani 2017). These ISA characteristics explain the fact that the rate and extent of ISAs has considerably increased recently despite the number of reports on their high failure rates (Kale and Singh 2009; Castro and Roldán 2015; Madhok et al. 2015; Linwei et al. 2017).

According to international literature, one of the key reasons for the failure of many ISAs is the lack of attention to the issue of relationship management among alliance partners (Brouthers and Bamossy 2006). Furthermore, Bell et al. (2006) note that there is a gap in literature, regarding a variety of aspects of partner cooperation in the context of ISAs. A significant determinant of the quality of relations among ISA partners is trust. Despite the fact that in recent years trust has become a central concept in international business literature, there is limited understanding of the antecedents that help partners build and maintain a trustworthy relationship. The aim of this paper is to propose a set of important antecedent factors for trust development among ISA partners. In this study three key factors related to trust building among ISA partners are identified. More specifically, the impact of communication quality, partner complementarity and foreign partner's cultural sensitivity on the level of trust the foreign partner has towards the local ISA partner is examined, and three propositions are presented to be tested empirically.

Prior research on the antecedents of trust has focused mainly on IJVs. This paper proposes the examination of these relationships in the context of ISAs. Additionally, previous research has focused mostly in several countries in North America, Asia and Western and Northern Europe. To the best of our knowledge, it is the first time that similar research will be conducted in the South-East (SE) Europe region. According to Triki and Mayrhofer (2016), the South and Eastern Mediterranean region has received little attention in the existing international business research as opposed to other regions such as Asia and Latin America. Moreover, this research focuses on a region and not just one country as most previous studies do (Nemeth and Nippa 2013). In addition, Park et al. (2015) note that the specific characteristics of each country do not allow the generalization of research results since specific local conditions and other parameters may vary among countries and time periods.

The remainder of this paper is organized in the following sections. First, a brief literature review of communication quality, partner complementarity and foreign partner's cultural sensitivity is presented. Next, three research propositions for the specific relationships among these antecedent factors and the level of trust the foreign partner has towards the local ISA partner are developed. The conclusions are drawn at the last section of the paper.

2 Development of Propositions

2.1 *Communication Quality*

Communication refers to the information exchanged among ISA partners and is defined as "the formal as well as the informal sharing of meaningful and timely information between firms" (Anderson and Narus 1990, p. 44). According to Nielsen (2004, p. 248), "communication can be described as the glue that holds together a channel of exchange". Social exchange theory (SET) proposes that communication is a key determinant of trust among ISA partners (Parkhe 1998a, b) because it aligns the partners' perceptions and expectations, lessens any misinterpretations and facilitates them to manage both the internal processes and external market conditions (Silva et al. 2012). According to Dyer and Chu (2000), the quality of communication provides crucial evidence for the interpretation of the partner's behaviour and motivations and, thus, is instrumental for trust development in the context of ISAs. Moreover, effective communication gives ISA partners the opportunity to learn more about synergistically combining resources and solving development challenges and issues (Ariño et al. 2001).

Hunoldt and Bausch (2009) note that trust influences the extent and the efficiency of information and resource exchange. Without the presence of trust among ISA partners, the perception of opportunistic behaviour may arise, and, consequently, information exchange may be low in terms of exactness, unity and actuality (Zand 1972). If knowledge transfer becomes more open and the circulation of knowledge is accelerated, the opportunities for organizational learning increase, and trust development among ISA partners is facilitated (Iles and Yolles 2002). Hennart and Zeng (2002) also state that an effective communication among ISA partners is critical to avoid misunderstandings and assists in trust development in the long run. According to Ellonen et al. (2008), institutional trust could be enhanced with the assistance of open and understandable communication, indicating that effective communication could result in mutual trust-based relationships, a view also shared by Ayoko and Pekerti (2008). De Jong and Woolthuis (2008) argue that in uncertain environments and when unexpected difficulties arise, accurate and timely communication is of great importance for trust maintenance among ISA partners. According to Thuy and Quang (2005, p. 394), trust in ISAs "cannot increase without exchange of information between partners".

The important role of communication quality as a key antecedent factor of trust has been shown in prior empirical research. For instance, Jennings et al. (2000) found that efficient communication facilitates not only the organization of the IJV activities but also assists in trust development among IJV partners. Dyer and Chu (2003) found a positive correlation between information sharing and trust, while Massey and Kyriazis (2007) showed that communication quality had an important effect on interpersonal trust between marketing and R&D managers during new product development projects. Huang et al.'s (2008) empirical findings showed that face-to-face communication has a broader impact in facilitating the interpersonal trust-building mechanisms. Moreover, Kwon (2008) found that communication between IJV partners was a crucial factor for trust development among them. Zeffane et al. (2011) showed that while a close link exists among trust, communication and commitment, the relationship between communication and trust is by far the strongest. Their findings reveal that trust is at the centre of the equation among these variables and that it depends highly on communication effectiveness. Communication quality prevents misperceptions which often lead to the development of feelings of mistrust, but when trust is established, actual feelings of loyalty and commitment are more likely to develop (Zeffane et al. 2011). Silva et al. (2012) also found that communication quality positively impacts trust among IJV partners. Furthermore, the empirical findings of Ali (2013) showed that communication has a positive effect on the development of trust among IJV partners. Thus, it is proposed that:

Proposition 1 Communication quality will positively impact the level of trust the foreign partner has towards the local ISA partner.

2.2 Partner Complementarity

Firms enter into strategic alliance agreements in order to "complement" their resources and, most importantly, to overcome their weaknesses (Kwon 2008). Among the four "Cs", firms should take into account when forming strategic alliances the "complementary of their skills" (Brouthers et al. 1995). As Ali and Larimo (2016) note, the combination of complementary resources of different firms is considered as a primary motivation for IJV establishment. Furthermore, ISAs are established when firms cannot acquire complementary resources in other ways (firm acquisitions or market transactions) as noted by Hennart (1988). Similarly, Park and Ungson (1997) note that the main motive for IJV establishment is for firms to jointly accomplish what they would not be able to accomplish on their own. Furthermore, firms seek partners with complementary resources to optimize benefits (Hamel et al. 1989). The combined efforts aim to better results than what firms would have on their own (Contractor and Lorange 1988).

As Madhok (1995) notes, the complementarity of partners' resources may have an important impact on trust. Similarly, when partners are not in competition and have mutual interests, the chances of opportunistic behaviour decrease (Hennart and Zeng 2005). It should also be noted that when the ISA performance depends on the combination of partner resources, the common objectives restrain opportunistic behaviour (Madhok 1995; Nielsen 2007). Furthermore, Kwon (2008) has shown that complementary of resources has a positive impact on trust. Ali and Larimo (2016) have also found that there is a negative relationship between resource complementarity and opportunistic behaviour among IJV partners. Similar are the findings of other researchers (Hennart and Zeng 2005; Zhang and Rajagopalan 2002). Khalid and Ali (2017) have empirically found that resource complementarity leads to trust among IJV partners. However they note that although previous research has shown that there is a positive relationship between resource complementarity and trust in IJVs, this evidence needs to be explored in different settings. Based on the above, it is proposed that partner complementarity will have a positive effect on the level of trust the foreign partner has towards the local ISA partner. Therefore, it is proposed that:

Proposition 2 Partner complementarity with the local partner will positively impact the level of trust the foreign partner has towards the local ISA partner.

2.3 Foreign Partner's Cultural Sensitivity

Nielsen (2001) notes that trust building among partners with different backgrounds can be very challenging bearing in mind that common expectations for the alliance might not be present. The success of ISAs has been linked to a firm's ability to adjust its approach regarding different cultures (Lorange and Roos 1993). This cultural adaptation is an indication of Johnson et al.'s (1996) definition of cultural sensitivity which includes the firm's sensitization and management of partners' cultural differences. Furthermore, Datta and Rasheed (1993) state that a lack of cultural sensitivity can lead to misunderstandings in cross-cultural interfirm relationships.

Cultural sensitivity is a crucial step for trust development in ISAs because it increases communication effectiveness. Communication is defined by Ali and Larimo (2016) as the exchange of information among ISA partners. Kwon (2008) argues that efficient communication adds to trust building and reduces the negative effects of conflicts and misunderstandings. Likewise, Voss et al. (2006) showed that cultural sensitivity reduces the negative impact of conflict and facilitates trust building among partners. Boersma et al.'s (2003) findings reveal that cultural sensitivity supports the decline of behavioural uncertainty and facilitates trust establishment in ISAs. Moreover, Johnson et al. (1996) showed that cultural sensitivity fosters the development of trust in ISAs. More specifically, when a firm makes the important investment of cultural adaptation, it signals commitment to the ISA implying that the firm cares about its partners. When the partner in an alliance feels valued, "it will come quickly to trust its counterpart" (Johnson et al. 1996, p. 986). In their recent empirical study, Khalid and Ali (2017) have also verified that cultural sensitivity has a positive impact on trust development among IJV partners. It is worth noting that a few prior empirical studies incorporate cultural sensitivity as an antecedent factor of trust development in ISAs. Thus, it is proposed that:

Proposition 3 Foreign partner's cultural sensitivity will positively impact the level of trust the foreign partner has towards the local ISA partner.

3 Conclusion: Implications for Further Research

In recent years large numbers of enterprises have formed ISAs in order to better handle the uncertainties and challenges of the international business environment and to achieve optimal growth and competitiveness on a global basis. However, the complexity of the relationships in ISAs and the environmental hostility have resulted to high failure rates; among the important reasons for the failure of many ISAs is the lack of attention to the issue of relationship management among alliance partners. Hence, further research is necessary in order to better understand the nature of these collaborative relationships.

This paper has focused on the construct of trust among ISA partners. Trust is considered as one of the most significant factors for ISA's successful performance, and in the often volatile social and economic environment in which most Greek ISAs operate, it becomes even more important. The first objective of this paper is to review and discuss some key parameters related to trust development. The recent findings in the international business literature regarding the impact of (a) communication quality, (b) partner complementarity and (c) foreign partner's cultural sensitivity on the level of trust the foreign partner has towards the local ISA partner are presented. The second objective is to develop three propositions based on the literature review to be tested at a later stage. It is proposed that communication quality, partner complementarity and foreign partner's cultural sensitivity will positively impact the level of trust the foreign partner has towards the local ISA partner. The contradictory findings on the relationship between communication quality and trust, the need of further examination in different settings on the relationship between partner complementarity and trust and the relatively small number of previous empirical research on the relationship among foreign partner's cultural sensitivity and trust underline the necessity for further research.

In general, there is a lack of empirical evidence for ISAs in the SE Europe region. As mentioned in a previous section, this region has received little attention in the existing international business research as opposed to other areas of the world. Moreover, this research focuses on a region and not just one country unlike most previous studies. This paper constitutes the basis for further research on the construct of trust in ISAs. The factors analysed in this paper will be investigated in the SE Europe region context, and any findings would be a useful contribution to existing literature since the specific region and country conditions do not allow for generalization of research findings (Park et al. 2015). A research questionnaire will be constructed and distributed to Greek firms that participate in ISAs abroad. The findings of the propositions developed will further build on the existing knowledge on trust among ISA partners. Additionally, a comprehensible understanding of the findings by managers and practitioners will make ISA management more efficient and will function as a valuable tool for overall ISA success.

References

Ali, T. (2013). *An integrative perspective of social exchange theory and transaction cost theory on the antecedents of trust and trust-performance relationship in international joint ventures: Evidence from Nordic multinational firms*, PhD dissertation, University of Vaasa, Acta Wasaensia 288, Business Administration 116.

Ali, T., & Larimo, J. (2016). Managing opportunism in international joint ventures: The role of structural and social mechanisms. *Scandinavian Journal of Management, 32*(2), 86–96.

Anderson, J. C., & Narus, J. A. (1990). A model of distributor firm and manufacturer firm working partnerships. *The Journal of Marketing*, 42–58.

Ariño, A., De la Torre, J., & Ring, P. S. (2001). Relational quality: Managing trust in corporate alliances. *California Management Review, 44*(1), 109–131.

Ayoko, O. B., & Pekerti, A. A. (2008). The mediating and moderating effects of conflict and communication openness on workplace trust. *International Journal of Conflict Management, 19* (4), 297–318.

Bell, J., et al. (2006). Dynamics of cooperation: At the brink of irrelevance. *Journal of Management Studies, 43*, 1607–1619.

Boersma, M. F., Buckley, P. J., & Ghauri, P. N. (2003). Trust in international joint venture relationships. *Journal of Business Research, 56*(12), 1031–1042.

Brouthers, K. D., & Bamossy, G. (2006). Post-formation processes in Eastern and Western European joint ventures. *Journal of Management Studies, 43*(2), 203–229.

Brouthers, K. D., Brouthers, L. E., & Wilkinson, T. J. (1995). Strategic alliances: Choose your partners. *Long Range Planning, 28*(3), 218–225.

Castro, I., & Roldán, J. L. (2015). Alliance portfolio management: Dimensions and performance. *European Management Review, 12*(2), 63–81.

Cobeña, M., Gallego, Á., & Casanueva, C. (2017). Heterogeneity, diversity and complementarity in alliance portfolios. *European Management Journal, 35*(4), 464–476. https://doi.org/10.1016/j.emj.2016.12.005.

Contractor, F. J., & Lorange, P. (1988). *Cooperative Strategies in International Business*. Lexington, MA: Lexington Books.

Datta, D. K., & Rasheed, M. A. A. (1993). Planning international joint ventures: The role of human resource management. In R. Culpan (Ed.), *Multinational strategic alliances* (pp. 251–272). New York: International Business Press.

De Jong, G., & Woolthuis, R. K. (2008). The institutional arrangements of innovation: Antecedents and performance effects of trust in high-tech alliances. *Industry and Innovation, 15*(1), 45–67.

Dyer, J. H., & Chu, W. (2000). The determinants of trust in supplier-automaker relationships in the US, Japan and Korea. *Journal of International Business Studies, 31*(2), 259–285.

Dyer, J. H., & Chu, W. (2003). The role of trustworthiness in reducing transaction costs and improving performance: Empirical evidence from the United States, Japan, and Korea. *Organization Science, 14*(1), 57–68.

Ellonen, R., Blomqvist, K., & Puumalainen, K. (2008). The role of trust in organisational innovativeness. *European Journal of Innovation Management, 11*(2), 160–181.

Gulati, R. (1995). Does familiarity breed trust? The implications of repeated ties for contractual choice in alliances. *Academy of Management Journal, 38*(1), 85–112.

Hamel, G., Doz, Y. L., & Prahalad, C. K. (1989). Collaborate with your competitors and win. *Harvard Business Review*, (January/February), 133–139.

Hennart, J. F. (1988). A transaction costs theory of equity joint ventures. *Strategic Management Journal, 9*(4), 361–374.

Hennart, J. F., & Zeng, M. (2002). Cross-cultural differences and joint venture longevity. *Journal of International Business Studies, 33*(4), 699–716.

Hennart, J. F., & Zeng, M. (2005). Structural determinants of joint venture performance. *European Management Review, 2*(2), 105–115.

Huang, X., Gattiker, T. F., & Schwarz, J. L. (2008). Interpersonal trust formation during the supplier selection process: The role of the communication channel. *Journal of Supply Chain Management, 44*(3), 53–75.

Hunoldt, M., & Bausch, A. (2009). *Factors influencing international equity joint venture performance: A meta-analytical review.* In Academy of international business annual conference, San Diego.

Iles, P., & Yolles, M. (2002). International joint ventures, HRM and viable knowledge migration. *International Journal of Human Resource Management, 13*(4), 624–641.

Jennings, D. F., Artz, K., Gillin, L. M., & Christodouloy, C. (2000). Determinants of trust in global strategic alliances: Amrad and the Australian biomedical industry. *Competitiveness Review, 10*(1), 25–44.

Johnson, J. L., Cullen, J. B., Sakano, T., & Takenouchi, H. (1996). Setting the stage for trust and strategic integration in Japanese-US cooperative alliances. *Journal of International Business Studies,* 981–1004.

Kale, P., & Singh, H. (2009, August). Managing strategic alliances: What do we know now, and where do we go from here? *Academy of Management Perspectives, 23,* 45–62.

Khalid, S., & Ali, T. (2017). An integrated perspective of social exchange theory and transaction cost approach on the antecedents of trust in international joint ventures. *International Business Review, 26*(3), 491–501.

Kwon, Y. C. (2008). Antecedents and consequences of international joint venture partnerships: A social exchange perspective. *International Business Review, 17*(5), 559–573.

Linwei, L., Feifei, J., Yunlong, P., & Nengqian, J. (2017). Entrepreneurial orientation and strategic alliance success: The contingency role of relational factors. *Journal of Business Research, 72,* 46–56.

Lorange, P., & Roos, J. (1993). *Strategic alliances. Formation, implementation and evolution.* Cambridge, MA: Blackwell.

Lubello, N., Albano, M., & Gordini, N. (2015). Il ruolo delle PMI nei processi di Open Innovation. In *4th Workshop—I Processi Innovativi nelle Piccole Imprese: Re-positioning of SMEs in the Global Value System* (Vol. 2), Urbino. doi: https://doi.org/10.13140/RG.2.1.3951.4645

Madhok, A. (1995). Revisiting multinational firms' tolerance for joint ventures: A trust based approach. *Journal of International Business Studies, 26*(1), 117–137.

Madhok, A., Keyhani, M., & Bossink, B. (2015). Understanding alliance: Adjustment costs and the economics of resource value. *Strategic Organization, 13*(2), 91–116.

Massey, G. R., & Kyriazis, E. (2007). Interpersonal trust between marketing and R&D during new product development projects. *European Journal of Marketing, 41*(9/10), 1146–1172.

Nemeth, A., & Nippa, M. (2013). Rigor and relevance of IJV exit research. *Management International Review, 53*(3), 449–475.

Nielsen, B. B. (2001). *Trust and learning in international strategic alliances.* Working Paper Series, Copenhagen Business School.

Nielsen, B. B. (2004). The role of trust in collaborative relationships: A multi-dimensional approach. *M@n@gement, 7*(3), 239–256.

Nielsen, B. B. (2007). Determining international strategic alliance performance. *International Business Review, 16*(3), 337–361.

Park, S. H., & Ungson, G. R. (1997). The effect of national culture, organizational complementarity, and economic motivation on joint venture dissolution. *Academy of Management Journal, 40*(2), 279–307.

Park, C., Vertinsky, I., & Becerra, M. (2015). Transfers of tacit vs. explicit knowledge and performance in international joint ventures: The role of age. *International Business Review, 24*(1), 89–101.

Parkhe, A. (1998a). Understanding trust in international alliances. *Journal of World Business, 33*(3), 219–240.

Parkhe, A. (1998b). Building trust in international alliances. *Journal of World Business, 33*(4), 417–437.

Russo, M., & Cesarani, M. (2017). Strategic alliance success factors: A literature review on alliance lifecycle. *International Journal of Business Administration, 8*(3), 1–9.

Silva, S. C., Bradley, F., & Sousa, C. M. P. (2012). Empirical test of the trust-performance link in an international alliances context. *International Business Review, 21*(2), 293–306.

Thuy, L. X., & Quang, T. (2005). Relational capital and performance of international joint ventures in Vietnam. *Asia Pacific Business Review, 11*(3), 389–410.

Triki, D., & Mayrhofer, U. (2016). Do initial characteristics influence IJV longevity? Evidence from the Mediterranean region. *International Business Review, 25*(4), 795–805.

Voss, K. E., Johnson, J. L., Cullen, J. B., Sakano, T., & Takenouchi, H. (2006). Relational exchange in US-Japanese marketing strategic alliances. *International Marketing Review, 23*(6), 610–635.

Zand, D. E. (1972). Trust and managerial problem solving. *Administrative Science Quarterly,* 229–239.

Zeffane, R., Tipu, S. A., & Ryan, J. C. (2011). Communication, commitment & trust: Exploring the triad. *International Journal of Business and Management, 6*(6), 77–87.

Zhang, Y., & Rajagopalan, N. (2002). Inter-partner credible threat in international joint ventures: An infinitely repeated prisoner's dilemma model. *Journal of International Business Studies, 33*(3), 457–478.

Digital Practices of Greek Small Entrepreneurship: Social Media and Self-Employment

Nancy Bouranta, Maria Tsampra, and Giannis Sklavos

Abstract The study explores the adoption of Information and Communication Technology and emerging digital marketing practices by microenterprises in Greece and, specifically, the perception of the self-employed and solo self-employed entrepreneurs for the social media as means/tools enhancing business resilience and performance in the current period of economic downturn. A sample of 418 usable questionnaires enabled exploratory and confirmatory factor analyses in order to validate the proposed constructs. The fit and predictive accuracy of the proposed model was estimated using AMOS software. Results on how Greek micro-entrepreneurs use digital marketing tools and, specifically, on whether they integrate social media into business practices illuminate important aspects of entrepreneurial motivation and perceptions and provide valuable information for both practitioners and policy makers. Interestingly, there is also a significant relation between social media usage, or lack thereof, and the industry/economic sector in which the self-employed engage.

Keywords Sales performance · Self-employment · Social media · Greece

1 Introduction

Self-employment has attracted particular attention in literature and research since the 1980s, due to its rising rates in all European economies. Since the outburst of the last crisis, self-employment has been further promoted by European Union (EU) economic policy as a way out of unemployment, and in fact, it has much

N. Bouranta (✉) · M. Tsampra
School of Business Administration, University of Patras, Patras, Greece
e-mail: nbouranta@upatras.gr; mtsampra@upatras.gr

G. Sklavos
School of Economics and Political Sciences, National and Kapodistrian University of Athens, Athens, Greece

© Springer Nature Switzerland AG 2019
N. Sykianakis et al. (eds.), *Economic and Financial Challenges for Eastern Europe*,
Springer Proceedings in Business and Economics,
https://doi.org/10.1007/978-3-030-12169-3_19

contributed to overall employment growth in certain countries amidst the crisis. In the economies of Southern Europe (notably Greece, Portugal, Spain, and Italy), self-employment with or without employees has traditionally been the backbone of the business sector—both in terms of employment and gross domestic product (GDP). Even in deep recession since 2009, in conditions of collapsed entrepreneurship and skyrocketing unemployment, self-employment in Greece appears to be resilient and even increased its rate to 31.9% (far above second-placed Italy, 23.4%, and Portugal, 21.1%) recording the highest score in the EU (Eurostat 2013).

Self-employed workers are often more focused on workmanship and much less on entrepreneurship. In other words, extended self-employment does not necessarily signify entrepreneurial initiatives of high aspirations and dynamic. Therefore, a thorough examination of the qualitative aspects of self-employed entrepreneurship is required for safe conclusions with regard to its contribution to job creation, economic resilience, and recovery. On this ground, the study of strategy and practices adopted by self-employed to enhance their business sales performance and competitiveness is essential. Recently emerging and broadly expanding digital tools for communication, networking, marketing, product/service customization, and development have formed new challenges and generated new opportunities for small enterprise and microenterprises (SmEs), such as the self-employed. The use of social media (SM) in particular, as the most user-friendly and popular Information and Communication Technology (ICT) means, has largely served SmEs' resilience in the postcrisis period of limited resources. It is considered challenge for businesses to measure the effectiveness of social media marketing (Palmer and Koenig-Lewis 2009). Jagongo and Kinyua (2013) proposed that further examination of the relationship between social media and business sales is needed. On this background, the aim of this study is to empirically explore the use of digital business tools by microenterprises in Greece, with particular focus on social media and their impact on sales performance. In addition, it is examined if self-employers' attitudes toward SM usage are significantly defined by the economic sector of their business.

The following part of the paper briefly refers to the concepts of social media and self-employment and presents the proposed theoretical model. Methodological analysis and results are described in the two subsequent parts, and then the final parts of the paper present the conclusions and practical implications of the present study.

2 Literature Review

Data for the use of social media and other digital technologies mainly concern the customer's side, i.e., the internet user. The Laboratory of E-Business Innovation, Strategy and Entrepreneurship (ELTRUN), Athens University of Economics, recently publicized the results of the 6th Annual Survey for Social Networking (2016). For the first time, data affirm an emerging trend of interaction between users and business—as recorded by Like in sites of commercial content and sites of specific companies and products. More illuminating information draws on the State of Digital Leadership 2014 survey (conducted by Valuecom in collaboration with ELTRUN). Greek SMEs are distinguished in three groups with regard to "how much digital is their marketing strategy and practice": 66% of SMEs are "traditional" firms of established presence in digital media; 18% are identified as "amateurs"; and just 16% of SMEs fit in the group of "pioneers" with a leading digital presence. As for the objectives to be served by digital media, 50% of Greek SMEs seek primarily the commitment of customers to the product and the brand; for 44% of SMEs, the main aim is to provide customer care; while for 33%, the priority is communication with customers, fans of the brand, and opinion leaders (SEPE 2015).

As observed, the efforts of companies to adapt to new digital market conditions vary in objectives as much as in results. Derham et al. (2011) proposed that even small enterprises can use social media for their daily transactions, as the cost is affordable compared with that of traditional media and requires a lower level of IT skills. The emergence of social media has created new opportunities, for micro-businesses in particular, to overcome "smallness," i.e., size-related liabilities by establishing direct and personal access to customers, sharing and collaborating, even interactively developing products/services, and raising brand awareness. Because of the low barriers against the use of SM, they present a free and efficient alternative for small business to promote goods and services directly to worldwide customers (Kadam and Ayarekar 2014; Sharma and Kalra 2011). It should also be noted, however, that data and related observations refer to large organizations and do not take microenterprises into account (Odoom et al. 2017). To fill in the gap, this research seeks to trace and conceptualize the mode of social media integration in the marketing practice of Greek micro-businesses, through questionnaires to self-employed and solo entrepreneurs.

RQ1 To what extent do Greek self-employed and solo entrepreneurs use social media?

There is evidence supporting the usage of major social media platforms, which varies by factors such as gender, age, educational attainment, etc. Some studies specifically showed that the reasons and frequencies of social media usage vary according to gender (Barker 2009; Mazman and Usluel 2011), supporting that females are more attracted to using SM than males (Misra et al. 2015). The age factor plays a significant role in the adoption of social networking sites, as the younger generation uses them more frequently (Chan-Olmsted et al. 2013). In addition, the level of a manager's education seems to play a significant role in whether or not to adopt a social media platform (Vlachvei and Notta 2014). Educated managers are more likely to use SM to promote their business or communicate with their customers (Damanpour and Schneider 2009; Vlachvei and Notta 2014). According to Sim and Pop (2014), the exposure on social media to a foreign language vocabulary can be beneficial to evolve it, and the participants were further encouraged to use it as a tool for that cause. Mahmud (2014), who conducted a similar study, distinguished three groups based on proficiency level and showed that social media as a medium can build confidence and promote language learning.

Also, as for the two groups, this encourages them to participate in online conversations. Business owners rarely possess all the skills and knowledge needed to expand their enterprise (Garrigos-Simon et al. 2012). It was found that information technology (IT)-based capabilities are particularly crucial in facilitating small- and medium-sized enterprise internationalization (Gabrielsson and Gabrielsson 2011; Zhang et al. 2013). Many self-employers are not technologically savvy and know little about social media. Thus, a major barrier for small businesses is the lack of knowledge that is necessary to start and maintain a web and social media presence.

RQ2 *Have the demographic characteristics (gender, age, educational level, language, and IT level of knowledge) of self-employed and solo entrepreneurs influenced the level of social media adoption?*

The use of social networking sites can be profitable for companies and their brands in terms of exposure, brand awareness, and actual sales; but it also can be detrimental if not managed correctly (Mihalcea and Savulescu 2013). In this line, Jagongo and Kinyua (2013) indicated that companies face social networks as valuable communication tools, which, if used properly, can help them to improve their web presence in order to effectively promote their brand. In addition, Kumar et al. (2013) showed that the social media community can strengthen customer-business relationships and lead to revenues. Empirical data also supported that the use of social networking has a positive and significant effect toward sales (Groza et al. 2012; Leung et al. 2015; Kwok and Yu 2013; Aladwani 2015). Idota et al. (2016) also reached the same conclusion, indicating that social media have a direct effect on Japanese companies' sales. The current research examines the relationship between SM usage and sales performance among self-employed and solo entrepreneurs.

RQ3 *Has the use of social media by self-employed and solo entrepreneurs a positive effect on business sales?*

Most of the aforementioned studies focus on a specific industry; thus, the current empirical research corroborates the relationship between social media and sales performance across various economic context. Odoom et al. (2017) proposed that further research should examine the possible disparities that exist between product-based SMEs and service-based SMEs. Dutot and Bergeron (2016) also recommended the comparison among different industries (e.g., technology, retail, communications) concerning the use of social media. Cross-sectional research may be valuable to explore how social media influences sales performance for specific types of companies and within particular industries. This prospective could allow managers to better understand what types of organizations are more likely to benefit from social media usage. However, little research has been done on the moderating effect of the business sector in the relationship between social media usage and business sales. Based on the above gap in the literature, the following research question can be formed:

RQ4 *Does the industry that the company operates have a moderating effect on the slope of the use of social networks sales of the enterprise?*

3 Methodology

3.1 Establishing the Constructs

Respondents were asked to identify the types of media used based on a given list (Kaplan and Haenlein 2010). The items concerning the reasons for using social media tools were based on previously developed measurements (Jagongo and Kinyua 2013; McCann and Barlow 2015). The 12 items were translated into the Greek language and took the form of a seven-point psychometric Likert scale (anchored on 1 = "strongly disagree" through 7 = "strongly agree"). The respondents were also asked about their perception of the impact of social media usage on firm performance. The measures based on managers' estimates were fixed versus the objective measures, which are based on independently observable facts. Ettlie et al. (1990, p. 68) proposed that it was necessary to rely on perceptual performance measures because of the virtual nonexistence of accurate, standard, and objective performance data and the practical difficulties associated with attempting to gather it. Other researchers have also supported perceptual measures as being useful and even necessary in the case of comparisons across units with different technologies and operation lines (Ketokivi and Schroeder 2004; Albacete-Sáez et al. 2011). Thus, sales performance is measured using the respondent's perception and based on three-item instrument. A sample item is: "The use of social media increase sales."

Finally, a series of questions were related to the demographic characteristics of the respondents (gender, age, education level, knowledge of a foreign language, computer literacy, marital status), as well as to their business (economic sector, size and type of the firm, etc.).

3.2 Sampling Process

Data were collected through field survey using a structured questionnaire administered exclusively to self-employed respondents. People out of employment (unemployed, looking for work), or in dependent employment (working for an employer) at the time of the survey, as well as atypical self-employed (students and pensioners) were excluded. Self-employed workers in Greece represent about 30.3%: 7.4% employing one or more employees and 22.9% with no employees. Family workers are also a significant component of employment, representing 3.9% of the employees (http://www.statistics.gr). Thus, the number of the target population was estimated to be 30.3% of the Greek population. The sample was formed by participants who fit the profile of the study and were therefore recruited with the snowball technique (Dragan and Isaic-Maniu 2013), as is usual in qualitative social research.

The questionnaires were filled out within 3 weeks, taking January 10, 2016, as a starting date for the data collection. The purpose of the study was explained to the sample participants, who were assured of total confidentiality and anonymity. A sample of 455 questionnaires was collected, 37 of which were not included in the following results as ineligible. Hence, the total usable sample for analysis consisted of 418 questionnaires. The demographic profile of the participants in this survey and the descriptive information of their firms are portrayed in Table 1. The sample consisted of 67% male and 33% female self-employers. The age groups were 18–24 years (8.4%), 25–34 years (18.9%), 35–44 years (29.2%), 45–54 years (31.5%), and over 55 years of age (12%). A total of 67.4% were married, while 32.6% were single.

4   Results

4.1   Exploring the Use of Social Media

The research findings indicated that 74.3% of respondents are aware of existing social media tools and use them in businesses, while 25.7% of them do not use social media tools at all. This question was important because it allowed the formation of two distinct groups (users and nonusers of social media) and the differentiation of results between them. The users were also asked to identify the types of social media used (Table 2): Facebook was by far the most commonly used (by 88.6%), followed by Twitter (21.3%), Blogs and Instagram (20%), YouTube (14%), and LinkedIn (7.6%). Interesting conclusions can be drawn for business by this question, as each type of social media serves different marketing strategies: Facebook is considered as consumer focused (and too social for B2B use), Twitter is interactive and serves business networking and innovation awareness, LinkedIn is more appropriate for staff recruitment, etc. The results also indicate that 35.8% of firms use only one type of social media, 19% use a combination of two, and only 6.7% use more than two types of social media.

Significant differences were found between male and female self-employers in social media usage (Chi squared 4.273; df. 1; sig. 0.039). According to results, female self-employed professionals use social media more (77%) compared to their male counterparts (66.8%). Age is also an important factor of differentiation: the higher rates of social media users are found among those younger than 54 years old (Chi squared 25.336; df. 4; sig. 0.000), ranging between 80.1% and 78.8% in the various subgroups. The usage of social media is limited to 50% of those older than 55 years of age. Chi-square analysis also indicated significant differences in the level of education between those who use SM and who do not (Chi squared 63.982; df. 4; sig. 0.000). Most of SM users of our sample have postgraduate qualifications (85.4%), many have completed tertiary (79.5%) or postsecondary technical/

Table 1 Demographic profile of the respondents and descriptive information for their firms ($N = 418$)

Type of classification	Category	Number of respondents	Percentage
Gender	Male	280	67
	Female	138	33
Age	18–24 years	35	8.4
	25–34 years	79	18.9
	35–44 years	122	29.2
	45–54 years	132	31.5
	55–64 years	50	12
Education	Received a postgraduate qualification	44	10.5
	Completed tertiary education	165	39.5
	Completed secondary education	118	28.2
	Completed postsecondary technical-vocational education	58	13.9
	Completed primary education	33	7.9
Knowledge of a foreign language	Excellent command	103	24.7
	Good command	176	42.3
	Basic skills	137	33
Knowledge of information technology (IT)	Excellent command	79	21.2
	Good command	155	41.6
	Basic skills	139	37.2
Marital status	Single	136	32.6
	Married	281	67.4
Sector	Tourism and catering	91	22.2
	Trade	89	21.8
	Non-service activities	118	28.7
	Professional services	112	27.3
Size in number of employees	None	198	47.4
	1–2 employees	105	25.1
	3–5 employees	69	16.5
	5 and more employees	46	11
Type of business	Home-based	198	65.3
	Non-home-based	105	34.7

vocational education (71.2%), while many have secondary education (67.8%). Those who have merely primary education are less likely (14.3%) to use social media. Apart from education, the knowledge of a foreign language as well as IT literacy significantly related to SMJ usage. The majority (51%) of those who do not use SM are not familiar with foreign languages (basic knowledge) and (53.1%) have limited knowledge of information technology. On the other hand, SM users who have a good (44%) or excellent (29.2%) command of a foreign language are comparatively more than nonusers of the same level of language knowledge

Table 2 Types of social media used

Types	Percentage
Facebook	88.6
Twitter	21.3
Social bookmarking	6.7
YouTube	14
Blogs	20
Wikis	1.3
Podcasting	1
Slideshare	1.9
LinkedIn	7.6
Instagram	20.3
Others	6.3

(good, 37.5%; excellent, 11.5%). The same applies for SM users and nonusers with regard to their level of IT literacy (Table 3).

4.2 Relating Business Motivation with the Use of Social Media

Respondents were also asked about the benefits of SM use that they identify for their business. Principal components analysis with varimax rotation was employed to the reasons for using social media tools. As displayed in Table 4, the factor analysis of the scale proved a good fit that revealed four factors that explain 66.2% of total variance. The Kaiser-Meyer-Olkin statistic was 0.872. The Bartlett test of sphericity also provided satisfactory results. In order to further examine the factors structure of the scale, a confirmatory factor analysis (CFA) was utilized. The four-factor structure shows an adequate model [$\chi^2 = 141.860$, $p = 0.00$, TLI $= 0.940$, CFI $= 0.958$ και RMSEA $= 0.71$]. The test for reliability instrument provided alpha (equal to 0.75) that exceeded the recommended level of 0.60 and rather strong item-to-total correlations. In addition, the Cronbach α values for the factors ranged from 0.77 to 0.91, suggesting that the constructs had high internal consistency. The measurement of the concept was based on previously developed instruments, so that content validity was assured. The analysis also verified that the factor loading of the concepts exceed the 0.5 threshold on its parent factor with low cross-loading, which supports that the measurement instrument reached convergent validity. Examining the discriminant validity of the instrument, it was found that the square root of AVE was greater than the coefficient, which demonstrated discriminant validity between the construct. The extracted factors are explained using the measured variable loadings and can be labeled/typecast as serving international perspective, customer communication, and business promotion.

Table 3 Use of SM and knowledge of a foreign language and IT

	Knowledge of a foreign language[a]				Knowledge of IT[b]			
	Basic skills	Good command	Excellent command	Total	Basic skills	Good command	Excellent command	Total
Users of SM	82 26.7%	136 44%	90 29.2%	308 100%	88 31.8%	118 42.6%	71 25.6%	277 100%
Nonusers	55 51%	41 37.5%	12 11.5%	108 100%	51 53.1%	37 38.5%	8 8.4%	96 100%
Total	137 33%	176 42.4%	103 24.7%	416 100%	139 37.2%	155 41.6%	79 21.2%	373 100%

[a]Chi squared 22.656; df. 2; sig. 0.000 (0 cell _ 0% _ have an expected count less than 5. The minimum expected count is 23.6)
[b]Chi squared 19.080; df. 2; sig. 0.000 (0 cell _ 0.0% _ have an expected count less than 5. The minimum expected count is 20.3)

Table 4 Factoring the reasons for using social media

Kaiser-Meyer-Olkin = 0.872	Factor loadings		
Items	International perspective	Customer communication	Business promotion
Expand business abroad	0.894		
Find suppliers internationally	0.863		
Immediate response to international customers	0.829		
Find international customers	0.808		
Better market research		0.783	
Reduced communication costs		0.720	
Better feedback from customers		0.715	
Gain more business contacts		0.653	
Showcase business offers			0.755
Establish relationship with customers			0.748
Immediate response to customer orders			0.672
Showcase business products and services			0.666
Eigenvalue	42.7	14.1	9.3
Cumulative variance %	26.6%	19.8%	19.8%
Cronbach α	0.91	0.78	0.77

As far as business performance concept, the factor analysis revealed a one-dimensional factor that explains 72% of total variance. Cronbach's alpha was 0.81. The results of both tests KMO and Bartlett were considered satisfactory.

4.3   Social Media and Sales Performance

Structural equation modeling was used to validate the cause-and-effect relation between social media usage and firms' sales. To estimate the parameters of the model, given that the data examination revealed no semantic normality violation, the maximum likelihood method and covariance matrix were used. The model indicates that χ^2 is 224.449 with 77 df ($p = 0.000$), supporting the assertion that the χ^2 relative value to degree of freedom (χ^2/df) does not exceed the proposed cutoff point of 3. The other indicators showed that the estimates for a set of recommended indices (IFI = 0.95, GFI = 0.94, CFI = 0.95, TLI = 0.94) were above or equal to the accepted threshold of 0.90. The RMSEA was equal to 0.07, which is considered adequate for the sample characteristics. The results indicated that all the social media reasons have a direct and positive effect on firms' sales at the p-value < 0.001 level (Table 5). Path estimates are identified as statistically significant in the predicted direction and with standardized residuals within the acceptable limits. Thus, the data

Table 5 Structural equation path coefficients

Relationships	Coefficient	CR (t-value)	p-value
Direct effect			
International perspective—sales performance	0.101	2.756	0.006
Customer communication—sales performance	0.714	6.227	0.000
Business promotion—sales performance	0.416	4.331	0.000

Note: t-values greater than 1.96 are significant ($p < 0.05$)

Table 6 Moderation tests

Model	χ^2	Df	GFI	CFI	RMSEA	$\Delta\chi^2$	Δdf	Sig.
Moderating variable: business sector								
Unconstrained	1027.215	385	0.96	0.97	0.035			
Constrained	1122.694	441	0.96	0.97	0.033	95.479	56	<0.05

analysis shows that the use of SM has a positive effect on sales as the p-value is less than 5%.

In order to test the moderating effects, a multiple group SEM analysis was selected, by using the unstandardized beta coefficients of the different groups. First the two models were tested unconstrained allowing all the parameters to vary freely across the subgroups. Next equality constraints were imposed on all the regression weights across the two subgroups. The moderator was the business sector. Each group has almost equal and adequate sample size (tourism and catering = 91; trade = 89; non-service activities = 118; professional services = 112). Both models (unconstrained and constrained) provided a good fit to the data (Table 6). The χ^2 difference was significant, providing evidence that the relationship between social media usage and sales performance are different among business sectors.

Next examined the path coefficients between four sector groups by using t-value over 1.96. The results, presented in Table 7, indicate that each sector perceives in a different way the social media dimensions' importance.

5   Discussion and Conclusions

In the globally expanding context of social media, consumers are no longer passive receivers but active participants in marketing and buying processes. Companies need to adjust to the new revolutionized market rules in order to gain a competitive advantage. According to the Social Media Marketing Industry Report (2015), most companies acknowledge the importance of these platforms: 93% declare they employ social media in their marketing strategy, with Facebook being rated as the top network (92%), closely followed by Twitter (84%) and LinkedIn (71%) (Stelzner 2011). Little is known, however, about whether small enterprise and microenterprises adopt social media and in what way they integrate them in doing business. Motivated by this lack of evidence, the paper investigates to what extent

Table 7 Structural equation path coefficients based on business sector

Paths	Tourism and catering			Trade			Non-service activities			Professional services		
	b	t	p-value	b	t	p-value	b	t	p-value	b	t	p-value
International perspective—sales performance	0.33	3.302	0.000	−0.083	−0.725	0.468	0.097	1.554	0.12	0.05	0.66	0.509
Customer communication—sales performance	0.774	3.096	0.002	0.396	1.203	0.229	0.992	3.914	0.000	0.529	2.335	0.02
Business promotion—sales performance	0.116	0.476	0.634	0.623	3.624	0.000	0.346	2.804	0.005	0.493	2.049	0.04

Note: t-values greater than 1.96 are significant

Greek self-employed and solo entrepreneurs use social media. Data analysis of this study supports that most of the small enterprise and microenterprises are aware of SM, and they use it for generating sales. The demographic characteristics of micro-entrepreneurs such as gender, age, educational level, language, and level of IT knowledge influence SM usage. The key deliverables that social media can provide are international perspective, customer communication, and business promotion, which play an important role in enhancing business sales.

According to recent research by Dosi and Tzortzaki (2016), many companies are unable to evaluate the broad potential of SM in doing business or to effectively manage the new ways of communication, access information, and interaction. The Greek business sector is the focus of research exploring SM integration in marketing processes (Dosi and Tzortzaki 2016). Findings indicate that Greek companies are aware of SM importance for marketing; those applying SM practices identify increased exposure and sales improvement as their main benefits. These results comply with the findings of the current study. The data analysis shows that, according to the respondents' perception, the use of social networking has a positive effect on their business sales. The study supported that most self-employed and solo entrepreneurs had not fully understood and internalized the potential of SM inter-national perspectives. Social media could enable small enterprise and microenterprises to acquire customers from all over the world (Cesaroni and Consoli 2015). However, the Greek micro-businesses in the majority seem not to reap the full benefits of this opportunity.

Some previous studies proposed to investigate the moderating effect of SM across different business sectors (Jagongo and Kinyua 2013; Odoom et al. 2017; Dutot and Bergeron 2016). Thus, the present research indicates that the perceived relationship between social media and sales varied among four industries (tourism and catering, trade, non-service activities, professional services). Small Greek businesses may be unable to reap the full benefits of the international perspective that SM provides except in tourism and catering. The industry seems to use SM simply to attract customers and increase sales. However, social media could enable small enterprise and microenterprises to acquire customers from outside their zone of operation (Cesaroni and Consoli 2015). On the other hand, business promotion appears to influence sales on the industries such as trade, non-service activities, and profes-sional services. Small businesses such as restaurants, cafes, and apartments may believe that SM cannot help them to increase their business' sales through promotion activities or they are unable to provide any kind of business offers because of low margins. Communication with customers seems to be important for all industries, except for trade, which believes it cannot help to improve sales. Through commu-nication, self-employers could improve their business image; customers appreciate the more personalize approached and typically leave comments about the products, thus providing valuable feedback (Rugova and Prenaj 2016). However, for the trade industry, the only deliverable that SM can provide is business promotion supporting its important role in enhancing business sales, thus negating the international perspective and communication with customers.

Finally, this study does have some limitations. Firstly, the context of the research should be tested in other countries to be able to make cross-cultural comparisons. The results of this research are influenced by the economic environment and the severe crisis in Greece. Caution should be taken regarding the impact of the economic crisis in each individual country and the diversity of cultures and social systems.

The present research examines the direct link between SM usage and business sales, assisting firms in predicting sales based on SM usage. Since SM usage explain only a part of the variance in sales, further research should investigate customer and contextual factors that may mediate the proposed relationship.

References

Aladwani, A. M. (2015). Facilitators, characteristics, and impacts of Twitter use: Theoretical analysis and empirical illustration. *International Journal of Information Management, 35*(1), 15–25.

Albacete-Sáez, C. A., Fuentes-Fuentes, M. M., & Bojica, A. M. (2011). Quality management, strategic priorities and performance: The role of quality leadership. *Industrial Management and Data Systems, 111*(8), 1173–1193.

Barker, V. (2009). Older adolescents' motivations for social network site use: The influence of gender, group identity, and collective self-esteem. *Cyberpsychology and Behavior, 12*(2), 219–213.

Cesaroni, F. M., & Consoli, D. (2015). Are small businesses really able to take advantage of social media? *The Electronic Journal of Knowledge Management, 13*(4), 257–268.

Chan-Olmested, S. M., et al. (2013). User perceptions of social media: A comparative study of perceived characteristics and user profiles by social media. *Online Journal of Communication and Media Technologies, 3*(4), 149–172.

Damanpour, F., & Schneider, M. (2009). Characteristics of innovation and innovation adoption in public organizations: Assessing the role of managers. *Journal of Public Administration Research and Theory, 19*(3), 495–522.

Derham, R., et al. (2011). Creating value: An SME and social media. In *PACIS 2011 proceedings. Brisbane, Australia* (pp. 1–9).

Dosi, C., & Tzortzaki, A. M. (2016). Managing social media as a marketing tool in the Greek business environment. *International Journal of Decision Sciences, Risk and Management, 7*(1–2), 48–69.

Dragan, I. M., & Isaic-Maniu, A. (2013). Snowball sampling completion. *Journal of Studies in Social Sciences, 5*(2), 160–177.

Dutot, V., & Bergeron, F. (2016). From strategic orientation to social media orientation: Improving SMEs' performance on social media. *Journal of Small Business and Enterprise Development, 23*(4), 1165–1190.

Ettlie, J., et al. (1990). *The research agenda for the next decade proceedings of the joint industry.* Ann Arbor, MI: University Conference on Manufacturing Strategy.

EUROSTAT. (2013). Retrieved from https://ec.europa.eu/eurostat/statistics.

Gabrielsson, M., & Gabrielsson, P. (2011). Internet-based sales channel strategies of born global firms. *International Business Review, 20*(1), 88–99.

Garrigos-Simon, F. J., et al. (2012). Social networks and web 3.0: Their impact on the management and marketing of organizations. *Management Decision, 50*(10), 1880–1890. https://doi.org/10.1108/00251741211279657.

Groza, M., et al. (2012). Social media and the sales force: The importance of intra-organizational cooperation and training on performance. *The Marketing Management Journal, 22*(2), 118–130.

Idota, H., et al. (2016). The effectiveness of social media use in Japanese firms. In *International Social Networks Conference on Social Informatics*. ACM, New York, NY.

Jagongo, A., & Kinyua, C. (2013). The social media and entrepreneurship growth: A new business communication paradigm among SMEs in Nairobi. *International Journal of Humanities and Social Science, 3*(10), 213–227.

Kadam, A., & Ayarekar, S. (2014). Impact of social media on entrepreneurship and entrepreneurial performance: Special reference to small and medium scale enterprises. *SIES Journal of Management, 10*(1), 3–11.

Kaplan, A. M., & Haenlein, M. (2010). Users of the world, unite! The challenges and opportunities of social media. *Business Horizons, 53*(1), 59–68.

Ketokivi, M., & Schroeder, R. (2004). Manufacturing practices, strategic fit and performance: A routine-based view. *International Journal of Operations and Production Management, 24*(2), 171–191.

Kumar, V., et al. (2013). Creating a measurable social media marketing strategy: Increasing the value and ROI of intangibles and tangibles for Hokey Pokey. *Marketing Science, 32*(2), 194–212.

Kwok, L., & Yu, B. (2013). Spreading social media messages on Facebook an analysis of restaurant business-to-consumer communications. *Cornell Hospitality Quarterly, 54*(1), 84–94.

Leung, X., et al. (2015). The marketing effectiveness of social Media in the Hotel Industry. *Journal of Hospitality and Tourism Research, 39*(2), 147–169.

Mahmud, M. M. (2014). Social Media: A Boon or A Bane? In *9th Global Conference: Cybercultures*. Exploring Critical Issues, Lisbon, Portugal. https://www.researchgate.net/publication/329706544_Social_Media_A_Boon_or_A_Bane.

Mazman, S., & Usluel, Y. (2011). Gender differences in using social networks. *Turkish Online Journal of Educational Technology, 10*(2), 133–139.

McCann, M., & Barlow, A. (2015). Use and measurement of social media for SMEs. *Journal of Small Business and Enterprise Development, 22*(2), 273–287.

Mihalcea, A. D., & Savulescu, R. M. (2013). Social networking sites: Guidelines for creating new business opportunities through Facebook, Twitter and LinkedIn. *Management Dynamics in the Knowledge Economy Journal, 1*(1), 39–53.

Misra, N., et al. (2015). Gender differences in usage of social networking sites and perceived online social support on psychological well being of youth. *The International Journal of Indian Psychology, 1*(2), 64–74.

Odoom, R., et al. (2017). Antecedents of social media usage and performance benefits in small and medium-sized enterprises (SMEs). *Journal of Enterprise Information Management, 30*(3), 383–399. https://doi.org/10.1108/JEIM-04-2016-0088.

Palmer, A., & Koenig-Lewis, N. (2009). An experiential, social network-based approach to direct marketing. *Direct Marketing: An International Journal, 3*(3), 162–176.

Rugova, B., & Prenaj, B. (2016). Social media as marketing tool for SMEs: Opportunities and challenges. *Academic Journal of Business, Administration, Law & Social Sciences, 2*(3), 85–97.

SEPE. (2015). http://www.sepe.gr.

Sharma, M., & Kalra, D. (2011). An empirical study of online social influence marketing with reference to Customer's product purchase decision and product recommendation. *Indian Journal of Marketing, 41*(8), 68–77.

Sim, M. A., & Pop, A. M. (2014). The impact of social media on vocabulary learning case study Facebook. *Annals of the University of Oradea, Economic Science Series, 23*(2), 120–130.

Stelzner, M. A. (2011). *Social media marketing industry report. How marketers are using social media to grow their businesses*. Retrieved from http://www.socialmediaexaminer.com/SocialMediaMarketingIndustryReport2012.pdf.

Vlachvei, A., & Notta, O. (2014). Social media adoption and managers' perceptions. *International Journal of Strategic Innovative Marketing, 1*(2), 61–73.

Zhang, M., et al. (2013). Drivers and export performance impacts of IT capability in 'born-global' firms: A cross-national study. *Information Systems Journal, 23*(5), 419–443.

The Conversion of Bank Deferred Tax Assets in 2016 to Bank Shares in 2017

Panagiotis Papadeas

Abstract This study correlates the provisions of CRD IV with the application of IFRS in banks operating in Greece. The accounting losses allow the creation of additional DTA which are transferred in claims against the state (tax credit). Thus, in 2017 conversion rights (warrants) may be issued which represent common shares of total market value equal to 100% of these tax credits. Then, equivalent special reserve is formed, and the equity capital of banks is increased, since the DTA are not deducted from the common equity tier 1 (CET 1) ratio.

Keywords Capital adequacy · Deferred tax · Loss provisions · Banks in Greece

1 Introduction

The existing laws and interpretations in different countries (members or not of the European Union) often cause deviations between accounting profits and taxable profits. These differences may be created in the following two manners:

1. Permanent differences are differences that never reverse. These are expense items that are included in bookkeeping, but are nondeductible, such as tax or insurance penalties, etc.
2. Temporary differences are differences between the tax basis of assets or liabilities, and they are reported amounts in the financial statements that will result in taxable or deductible amounts in future years, when the reported amounts of the assets or liabilities are recovered or settled, respectively. If such a temporary difference exists, an amount will be recorded and reported as either a deferred tax liability or a deferred tax asset depending upon the relationship between the reported net financial (book) value and the tax basis of the related asset or liability. When the temporary difference reverses, the recorded deferred tax

P. Papadeas (✉)
Department of Accounting and Finance, University of West Attica, Athens, Greece
e-mail: panapapa@uniwa.gr

© Springer Nature Switzerland AG 2019
N. Sykianakis et al. (eds.), *Economic and Financial Challenges for Eastern Europe*,
Springer Proceedings in Business and Economics,
https://doi.org/10.1007/978-3-030-12169-3_20

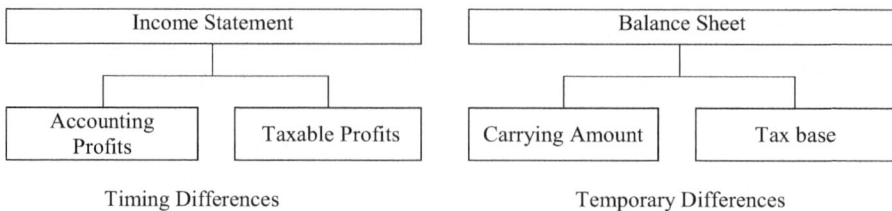

Timing Differences   Temporary Differences

Fig. 1 The liability method

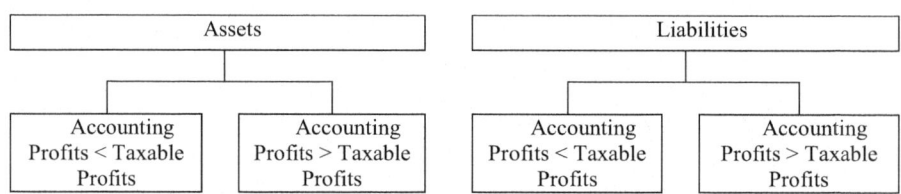

Fig. 2 Balance sheet–liability method

amount is removed from the balance sheet, and the amount removed results in an increase or decrease in income tax expense (see Fig. 1).

Under International Financial Reporting Standards, these differences should be accounted for using the principles of IAS 12: Income Taxes (see Fig. 2).

The revised IAS adopts only the liability method based on the balance sheet and temporary differences. For banks, the temporary differences arise from the valuation of financial assets (securities, derivatives) and assets, the credit risk provisions, and losses from the private sector involvement (PSI).

Deferred tax assets—the amounts of income taxes recoverable in future periods

Deferred tax liabilities—the amounts of income taxes payable in future periods in respect of taxable temporary differences (Merler 2015)

Finally, it should be clarified that according to IAS 12 if the company considers the possibility of setting off any losses against future profits, it is able to recognize deferred tax assets (Article 34). According to the Greek law 4172/2013, the use of losses can be offset against profits which will arise in the next five accounting periods (Article 27). If these profits are not enough to cover all the losses, this right is lost partially or totally (IASB 2012, IAS 12).

The main aim of this paper is to examine the revised Greek laws (4340/2015 and 4465/2017) along with the consequences of International (Accounting) Financial Reporting Standards/IFRS-IASB and deferred taxation for banks in Eurozone area. The analysis used data from annual reports of four systemic Greek banks, which control around 95% of the sector's assets and 90% of total deposits. The results suggest that increasing banks' losses may improve their capital adequacy. The paper is organized as follows: in the next section we briefly present interactions between IASB and BASEL aiming at preventing banking and accounting problems at international level during the last decades. This is followed by the comparative analysis of banking supervision accords and the presentation of International Accounting Standard 12: Income Taxes. The research methodology, the data sources used in the analysis, and research results are presented and discussed in Sect. 4. The last section summarizes the conclusions and presents further opportunities for research.

2 Legislative Developments: Bank Losses 2015 Similar to DTAS in 2016

Greek legislation has recently incorporated IASB regulations and Basel decisions, thus allowing deferred tax assets (DTAs) to be optionally converted to claims against the state, in case of accounting losses after taxes. In this way, statutory reserve funds are formed, which may subsequently be capitalized for the increase of share capital (L. 4302/2014, Article 23, Par. 1). Consequently, the DTAs of 2016 transform into TCs of 2017, i.e., these are not deducted from common equity tier 1 (CET 1) ratio but improve capital adequacy ratio (CAR) instead.

The actual value of TCs may be computed through the following ratio:

$$\frac{Deferred\ Tax\ Assets\ (DTAs) * Losses\ after\ Taxes\ (|L|)}{Equity\ (E) - Losses\ after\ Taxes\ (|L|)}$$

To gain a sense of the potential contribution of losses to the banks' capital adequacy, financial data of four systemic banks in Greece for the years 2011–2016 were used (Bank of Greece 2011–2017). We examine three variables: deferred tax assets from the balance sheet, provisions for loan losses and impairments, and profits/losses after taxes from the income statement.

Table 1 and Fig. 3 show the corresponding results for the National Bank of Greece. In 2011, the losses after taxes were highest because of the highest provisions for loan losses and impairments (13.9 billion euros). This amount includes the losses of PSI (10.6 billion euros). The year 2013 was profitable, while in the period 2015–2016 we notice that profits after taxes have an increasing trend (NBG 2017).

Table 1 National Bank accounting data (in '000 €)

Year	Deferred tax assets	Provisions for loan losses and impairments	Profits (losses) after taxes
2011	1,000,326	−13,962,983	−12,144,748
2012	1,085,038	−2,645,470	−2,935,625
2013	2,189,000	−1,026,000	618,000
2014	3,855,000	−2,370,000	−382,000
2015	4,906,000	−4,344,000	−4,540,000
2016	4,906,000	−819,000	9000

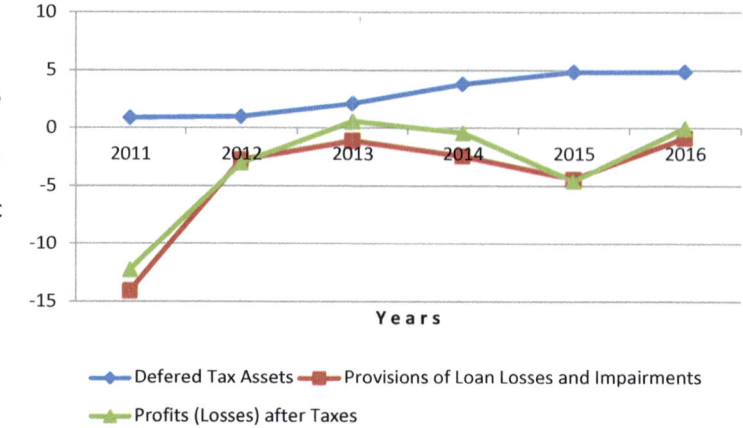

Fig. 3 National Bank of Greece. Source: Author's work

3 Legislative Developments: Bank Losses in 2015 Significantly Less than DTAS in 2016

Table 2 and Fig. 4 show also the corresponding results for the Piraeus Bank. In 2011, the losses after taxes were highest because of the highest provisions for loan losses and impairments (7578 billion euros). This amount includes the losses of PSI. The year 2013 was profitable, while in 2016 we can notice that profits after taxes are positive again (Piraeus Bank 2017).

Also, from the data of Eurobank (Table 3 and Fig. 5), we can observe that the largest losses after taxes and the highest provisions for loan losses and impairments occur in the years 2011 and 2015. The better financial results after taxes (loss reduction compared to the previous year) occur in 2013, while in 2016 they appear to have a positive sign (Eurobank 2017).

From the data of Alpha Bank (Table 4, Fig. 6), we observe that during the analyzed period, the losses after taxes were higher in 2011. In this year, the provisions for loan losses and impairments were 5.7 billion euros, which include losses of PSI (4.8 billion euros), while in 2016 they appear to have a positive sign (Alpha Bank 2017).

Table 2 Piraeus Bank accounting data (in '000 €)

Year	Deferred tax assets	Provisions for loan losses and impairments	Profits (losses) after taxes
2011	1,132,455	−7,578,403	−6,428,843
2012	1,754,746	−2,338,542	−804,665
2013	2,706,304	−2,298,793	2,506,328
2014	3,950,983	−4,038,759	−2,065,200
2015	5,012,800	−4,397,490	−2,389,397
2016	5,264,510		10,522

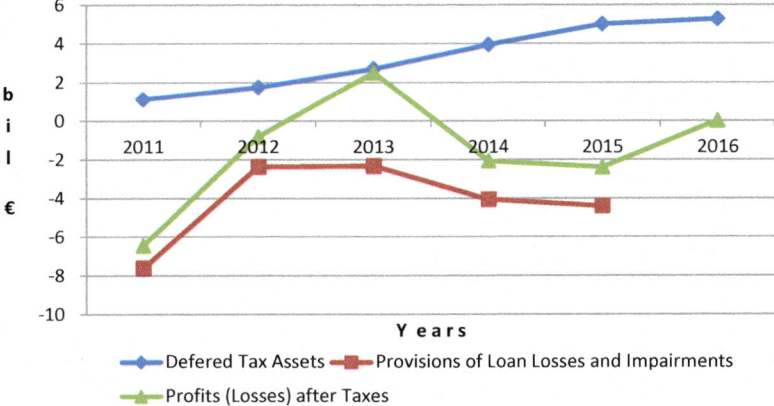

Fig. 4 Piraeus Bank. Source: Author's work

Table 3 Eurobank accounting data (in ′000 €)

Year	Deferred tax assets	Provisions for loan losses and impairments	Profits (losses) after taxes
2011	1,718,000	−1,086,000	−3,155,000
2012	2,037,000	−1,355,000	−1,368,000
2013	3,024,000	−1,587,000	−1,007,000
2014	3,871,000	−1,901,000	−1,383,000
2015	4,902,000	−2,503,000	−1,051,000
2016	4,918,000	−836,000	5000

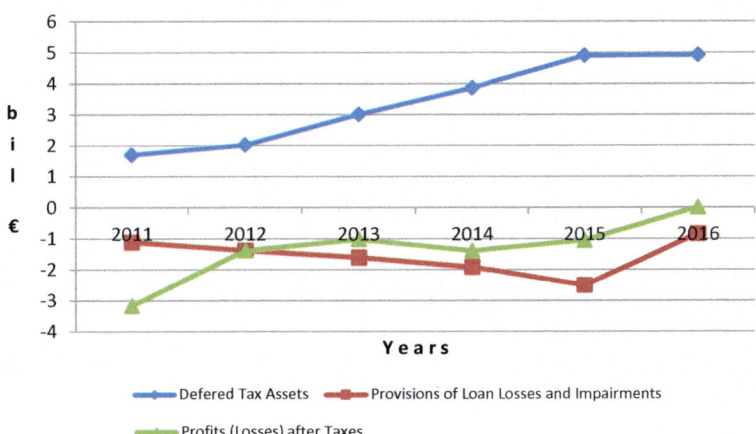

Fig. 5 Eurobank. Source: Author's work

Table 4 Alpha Bank accounting data (in '000 €)

Year	Deferred tax assets	Provisions for loan losses and impairments	Profits (losses) after taxes
2011	1,487,782	−5,685,460	−3,842,666
2012	1,786,612	−1,374,711	−1,732,934
2013	2,740,649	−1,609,775	2,857,021
2014	3,604,079	−1,386,598	−58,529
2015	4,372,486	−2,699,237	−1,032,276
2016	4,477,144	−1,170,200	260,618

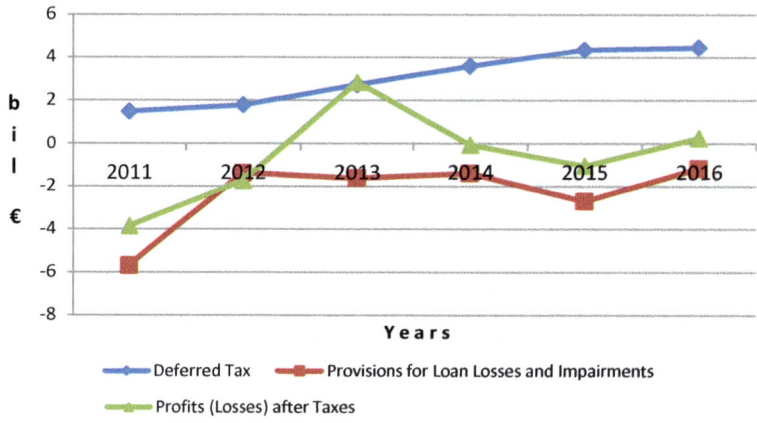

Fig. 6 Alpha Bank. Source: Author's work

4 Statistical Analysis

Recognizing the fact that ratio (Sect. 2) results from a combination of IASB and Basel Committee decisions, as adopted by the Greek legislation, we will henceforth refer to Sect. 2 as tax credits (TC).

Applying actual outturn data from all four Greek systemic banks for losses, DTAs, and equity for 2015, the corresponding TC indices for the next years, i.e., for 2017, are computed as follows based on the initial taxation (amounts in billion euros):

$$TC_{National\ Bank\ of\ Greece} = \frac{4.906 \times 4.540}{8.315 - 4.540} = \frac{22.273240}{3.775} = 5.90$$

$$TC_{Piraeus\ Bank} = \frac{5.013 \times 2.389}{9.608 - 2.389} = \frac{11.979958}{7.219} = 1.66$$

$$TC_{Eurobank} = \frac{4.902 \times 1.051}{6.131 - 1.051} = \frac{5.152002}{5.080} = 1.014$$

$$TC_{Alpha\ Bank} = \frac{4.372 \times 1.032}{8.418 - 1.032} = \frac{4.513612}{7.386} = 0.61$$

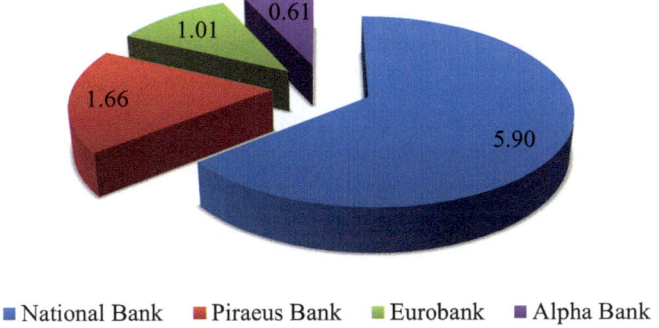

■ National Bank   ■ Piraeus Bank   ■ Eurobank   ■ Alpha Bank

Fig. 7 Tax credits for Greek systemic banks. Source: Author's work

Table 5 Tax credits (Laws 4340/01.11.2015 & 4465/04.04.2017)

NBG	5,770,000,000 € (instead of 5,900,000,000 €)
Piraeus Bank	1,357,000,000 € (instead of 1,660,000,000 €)
Eurobank	830,000,000 € (instead of 1,010,000,000 €)
Alpha Bank	470,000,000 € (instead of 610,000,000 €)

These values are shown in Fig. 7:

The relevant Greek legislation has recently changed (Law 4465/04-04-2017) and limits the amount of the deferred tax asset to the amount relating to the PSI's debit difference and to the credit risk provisions that have been calculated until June 30, 2015. As of December 31, 2016, the deferred tax assets, which is estimated to be part of the new legislation, amount to 4,800,000 million euros for NBG, 4,100,000 million euros for Piraeus Bank, 3,341,802 million euros for Alpha Bank, and 4,015,000 million euros for Eurobank. There is 2% reduction for NBG, 18% reduction for Piraeus Bank, 18% reduction for Eurobank, and 24% reduction for Alpha Bank. This will also have a similar effect on tax credits (Table 5).

Rearranging the terms appearing in Sect. 2, it becomes immediately apparent that TC is closely connected to the well-known and widely studied return on equity ratio (ROE)

$$\text{ROE} = \frac{Profits\ (or\ Losses)\ after\ Taxes}{Equity} = \frac{L}{E}\ \text{through the relation}$$

$$\text{TC} = \frac{DTAs}{|ROE|^{-1} - 1}$$

A straightforward computation shows

$$\frac{\partial TC}{\partial |ROE|} = \frac{DTAs}{(1 - |ROE|)2} > 0,\ \text{whereby the positive association of TC and } |ROE|$$

is readily revealed.

Our previous analysis may be illustrated through the use of financial data. The corresponding ratios TC and |ROE| of all four Greek systemic banks are gathered in Table 6:

Table 6 TC and |ROE| of all four systemic Greek banks

	Losses after taxes (billion euros)	Equity (billion euros)	|ROE|	TC
National Bank	4540	8315	0.546	5.90
Piraeus Bank	2389	9608	0.249	1.66
Eurobank	1051	6131	0.171	1.01
Alpha Bank	1032	8418	0.123	0.61

Source: Author's work

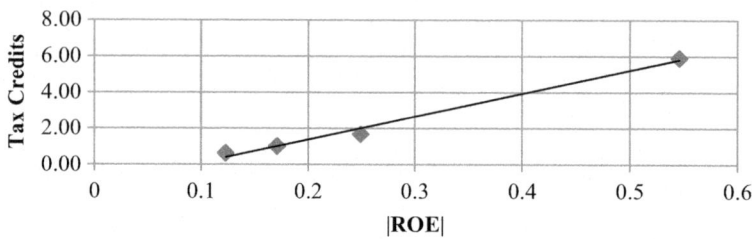

Fig. 8 Scatterplot. Source: Author's work

Table 7 Correlations

		|ROE|	TC
|ROE|	Pearson correlation	1	0.995[a]
	Sig. (two-tailed)		0.005
	N	4	4
TC	Pearson correlation	0.995[a]	1
	Sig. (two-tailed)	0.005	
	N	4	4

Source: Author's work
[a]Correlation is significant at the 0.01 level (two-tailed)

The DTAs of the banks for 2015 transferred to 2016 are certainly not identical. Nevertheless, their variance around their arithmetic mean (4,798,250 €) is small enough to allow the verification of the positive association of TC and |*ROE*| via the computations in Table 4.

An additional indication of the strong positive relation between TC and |ROE| is provided through Pearson's correlation coefficient. In fact, as attested by Fig. 8 and Table 7, correlation is statistically significant, identifying a 99% confidence level.

The Pearson correlation coefficient of 0.995 indicates, as expected, that there is a strong positive correlation between TC and |*ROE*|.

5 Conclusions

Credit risk in banks reflects a failure rate, for which the Basel Committee states:

Event of failure with respect to a borrower is observed when one or more of the following cases take place:

(a) when it is assumed that the borrower will not be able to meet his contractual obligations,
(b) when a credit is deleted or regulated,
(c) when the borrower has delayed debts more than 90 days,
(d) when borrower has submitted bankruptcy petition. (BCBS 1998)

The aforementioned cases have taken place in the Greek Banking System, to a big extent, between 2011 and 2016. In this study, the computed TC values confirm the contribution of losses to the banks' capital adequacy. In fact, recalling the definition of TC in Sect. 2, note that losses in 2015 are similar to DTAs 2016 result, leading to an increase of TC through two different routes: enlarging the nominator, as well as shrinking the denominator of ratio (Sect. 2). Hence, if the National Bank, which suffered the greatest losses (4540) in 2015 (when compared with either Piraeus Bank, Eurobank, or Alpha Bank—with respective losses in 2015 significantly less than DTAs in 2016/Sect. 3) were to transform its losses into DTCs, it becomes clear that it would enjoy the largest possible gain in capital adequacy ratio (CAR). This conclusion is supported by the fact that the TC Index for 2016 assumes its largest value for the National Bank (5.90), in comparison with Piraeus Bank (1.66), Eurobank (1.01), or Alpha Bank (0.61). Finally, it is not a simple matter of coincidence that the National Bank is the first one to have already decided the application of the new Law, converting its DTAs into DTCs, issuing warrants toward the Greek state and forming statutory reserves and bank shares in 2017.

The social cost of a bank failure exceeds the direct losses to the claim holders of the failing bank (Papadeas et al. 2016). Simultaneously the costs and externalities associated with a bank failure are likely to be much larger than those created by the failure of a commercial nonbank entity (Acharya et al. 2011; Kalfaoglou 2012). Consequently, it becomes obvious that the interest of banking supervisors (Basel Committee) is directed to the expansion of the capital adequacy of banks (Blundell-Wignall and Atkinson 2010; Gregoriou 2009) and to the wider disclosure of the respective comparable information through International (Accounting) Financial Reporting Standards/IFRS-IASB. One of the major accounting issues for banks (at the end of each year) is the deferred taxation. Then, the "right" for capitals' offsetting is guaranteed, without real capitals, but is measured and counted, subject to conditions, for the calculation of capital adequacy of banks (Hytis 2015). Furthermore, for some banks in the South of the Euro Area (i.e., Greece), legislative changes have been introduced that enable the biggest part of losses to contribute to the banks' capital adequacy in 2017.

References

Acharya, V., Mehran, H., Schuermann, T., & Thakor, A. (2011). *Robust capital regulation*. Federal Reserve Bank of New York, Staff Report No. 490.

Alpha Bank. (2017). *Financial information*, Athens.

Bank of Greece. (2011–2017). *The Governor's annual report*, Athens.

BCBS. (1998). *International convergence of capital measurement and capital standards.* Basel: Bank for International Settlements.

Blundell-Wignall, A., & Atkinson, P. (2010). Thinking beyond Basel III: Necessary solutions for capital and liquidity. *OECD Journal: Financial Market Trends, 2010*(1), 9–33.

Eurobank (2017). *Annual reports.* Athens.

Gregoriou, G. (2009). *Operational risk toward Basel III: Best practices and issues in modeling, management, and regulation.* Hardcover: Wiley.

Hytis, E. (2015). Why does the increase in taxation rates benefit the banks with losses? *EURO2day.* Athens (in Greek).

International Accounting Standards Board. (2012). *IAS 12 income taxes.* London.

Kalfaoglou, F. (2012, April). The framework of the banks' capital adequacy. *Economic Bulletin of Bank of Greece,* 36 (in Greek).

Merler, S. (2015). *Deferred tax credits may soon become deferred troubles for some European banks.* Retrieved from http://bruegel.org

National Bank of Greece. (2017). *Financial Report.* Athens.

Papadeas, P., Hyz, A., & Kossieri, E. (2016). IASBasel: The contribution of losses to the banks' capital adequacy. *International Conference on Business and Economic,* ICBU HOU, Athens.

Piraeus Bank. (2017). *Financial results.* Athens.

Quality Assurance in Education in the Light of the Effectiveness of Transformational School Leadership

Sofia Anastasiadou and Lazaros Anastasiadis

Abstract The main aim of the present paper is to endorse the effects of Transformational School Leadership on teachers and their teaching practices. Transformational School Leadership model, which comprises an essential element of quality assurance, is based on the constructs of Setting Directions, Developing People, Redesigning the Organizations, Reliability of Administrative Leadership. Measures of Teachers Capacities, Measures of Teachers' Motivation, Measures of Teachers' Work Setting, and Measures of Teachers' Classroom Practices. A survey has been conducted among secondary school teachers in Greece. In order to validate the measurement model and to test the hypothesized relationships, structural equation modeling was performed. The study provides useful insights on the era of quality assurance in education that lead to the improvement of teaching practices. The research findings reveal that Education Redesigning the Organization, Measures of Teachers' Classroom Practices, and Developing People are the most important factors among the seven dimensions on Transformational School Leadership. It was also found that Measures of Teachers' Motivation plays more important role than Measures of Teacher Capacities, Setting Directions, and Measures of Teachers' Work Settings.

Future research could apply this scale of transformational leadership on the secondary education system (in Greece) in order to compare the empirical results of this survey with the new results from secondary teachers across Greece.

Keywords Leadership · Transformational leadership · Quality assurance

S. Anastasiadou (✉)
University of Western Macedonia, Kozani, Greece
e-mail: sofan@uom.edu.gr

L. Anastasiadis
AUTH, Theesaloniki, Greece

© Springer Nature Switzerland AG 2019
N. Sykianakis et al. (eds.), *Economic and Financial Challenges for Eastern Europe*,
Springer Proceedings in Business and Economics,
https://doi.org/10.1007/978-3-030-12169-3_21

1 Theoretical Framework

Like any other organization, schools aim to attain their goals in an effective and efficient manner. Societies wish their citizens to have a high educational and intellectual level. The education, training, and culture of the youth are of the utmost importance for people, nations, economies, and cultures (Anastasiadou 2016).

Requirements posed by society on the quality in education and the pursuit of excellence are more than apparent. Quality in education includes a multitude of issues such as the role of leadership in the management of organizations, the strategy that each school unit develops on several academic issues that not only deals with the curriculum but also with the satisfaction of both the internal clients (students, faculty, and administration) as well as the external ones (parents, society). More specifically, Deming suggests that quality reflects the satisfaction of the customers and ought to focus on the satisfaction of immediate or future customers' needs (Steiakis and Kofidis 2010), while, according to Juran (1992), the dimensions of quality refer to the quality of a design and planning that rests on customer requirements for services/products (Stefanatos 2000; Steiakis and Kofidis 2010). Crosby (1979) claims that quality is conformance to requirements and specifications.

Adjusting the service, in the case at hand, education, to the customer's expectations and the non-conformance to customer requirements, the requirements posed by students, parents, educations and society, leads to the minimization of the quality of services (Goetch and Davis 2013). For Feigenbaum (1986), quality conforms with customer satisfaction at the lowest possible cost. Ishikawa emphasized and applied statistical techniques to improve quality (Atilgan and McCullen 2011). According to Ishikawa, 95% of the problems in an organization can be resolved using basic statistical tools (Steiakis and Kofidis 2010). He suggested in 1985 that a sufficient and necessary condition for the improvement of quality is to know customers' requirements and for the goal to be to satisfy them. Taguchi (1987) added that the right design and planning are a precondition for quality.

Moreover, human resource culture in education with respect to quality in schools changes and faculties strives to pose high academic goals. A significant role for the attainment of academic excellence and of the educational goals is performed by leadership who is charged with the development of the policy and strategy for the organization/school. It aims for the continuous improvement of the quality of the educational and academic work and of all the services the organization offers, the organization and continuous improvement (CI) of the evaluation system for all of its units and services, of the quality assurance system, and, finally, of the processes for its internal and external evaluation based on the framework for the Quality Assurance and Accreditation Agency in Higher Education (HQA) (Anastasiadou 2016).

Responsibility for quality in education belongs to its leadership. Deming considers that senior executives are responsible for 94% of potential improvements (Stefanatos 2000), thus ascribing the responsibility for problems and inexpediencies to the top of management (Steiakis and Kofidis 2010). Deming also focused his attention to management's responsibility and its commitment for continuous improvement (Lee et al. 1999). Furthermore, Juran supported the view that responsibility for low quality resides mainly with management (Stefanatos 2000) and that, more specifically, 85% of quality issues can be attributed to it (Wadsworth et al. 2002).

Leadership is a key factor that shares and establishes the procedures and practices applied in an educational organization. Leadership sets the goals and the vision and establishes the course and the future of the organization, while it attends to and promotes continuous improvement, the creation of a quality culture, and the attainment of business excellence. The implementation and application of the goals set by leadership presupposes the involvement of all interested parties and especially of human resources. Leadership is what inspires human resources on account of its organizational abilities and ethos. The implementation of activities that accentuate creativity and promote innovation is inspired and led by an effective leadership. A leader's or leaders' or the leadership's abilities, their actions and activities, and their morals, vision, culture, and training are strategic points in the course of an organization toward excellence (Martin-Castilla and Rodriguez-Ruiz 2008). Their impartiality, the way by which they manage human resources, and their focus not only on the satisfaction of the customer but also on satisfying all of the parties involved undoubtedly play a determining role not only for the viability but also for the development and continuous improvement of the organization (Martin-Castilla and Rodriguez-Ruiz 2008). The role of leaders for continuous improvement has been stressed by De Long and Fahey (2000). Mparoutas (2007) suggests that it is leadership that can become an inspiration to mobilize and maximize the performance of human resources, since by virtue of its insightfulness it can detect weaknesses, effect reforms, and, consequently, modernize the organization.

Detecting the weak and strong points, the disadvantages and advantages of an organization are key for the redesign of its organizing and continuous improvement (Day et al. 2004). Additionally, Morales-Lopez (2013) suggests that it is leadership that offers the motives and establishes both the framework as well as the rules for the conduct of the staff inside the organization. At this point, we must note that leadership and senior management in general are responsible for law quality, as Juran (1997), one of the "gurus" of quality, observes, while in addition to this, it is leadership that must initially commit to the improvement of quality (Crosby 1984).

Concomitantly, it is the requirement of students, parents, educators, the society, and the productive sector for there to be an effective and efficient management of education so that school units can fulfill their set goals effectively, just like any other organization (Kanugo 2001).

Leaders must possess those skills, abilities, capacities, behaviors, personality, knowledge of management techniques, vision, and charisma so as to be able to inspire the human resources they manage (Sağnak 2010) and to exercise effective management. The suitability of transformational leadership approaches and practices as the most appropriate and suitable management technique in education has been stressed by many researchers (Leithwood et al. 1996, 1999; Yukl 1999). According to Bass and Steidlmeier (1999), transformational leadership has its roots on the virtues and moral character, as pointed out by Socratic and Confucian typologies.

According to Yukl (1999), transformational leadership approaches and practices emphasize emotions and values while presupposing high levels of personal commitment to organizational goals for the entire managed human resources involved. Burns (1978) defined transformational leadership as moral leadership. Yukl and Van Fleet (1992) argued that leaders, in order to communicate their vision, must allow colleagues and followers to become informed about the significance of their actions and activates in accomplishing organizational visions and targets. Leithwood et al. (2004) stress that approaches and practices with respect to this form of leadership, transformational leadership, regard and involve the entire organization and every individual of human resources. Bass (1985) determined the dimensions of transformational leadership as idealized persuade, also called charisma, encouraging motivation, rational simulation, and individualized consideration.

Burns (1978) defined the characteristics of transformational leaders in moral terms. In addition, transformational leaders, based on their moral values and integrity, can inspire followers' behavior and put emphasis on moral values, such as justice and trust, as well as standards in order to increase the effectiveness of the organization (Grojean et al. 2004) and the use of constant universal values with the view to create the ideal vision of the organization (Mendonca and Kanungo 2007).

Mendonca (2001) emphasizes the special weight carried by the principles and integrity of the leader who adopts the transformational approach to leadership, with respect to establishing the lawfulness, justice, and reliability for all of its actions in order to attain his vision. Additionally, the virtues that characterize such as leaders are, among others, kindness, humanity, benevolence, trustworthiness, honesty, reliability, competence, and openness (Bass and Steidlmeier 1999). According to Leithwood (1992, 1994), Leithwood and Jantzi (2000, 2006), and Marks and Printy (2003), transformational leadership is the most suitable leadership approach in primary and secondary education because its goal aims for the development of innovation and the support of teachers.

Leithwood and Jantzi (1999) examined the relation between transformational leadership and commitment. Yu (2002) examined the effects of transformational leadership on teachers' commitment to change. Griffith (2004) emphasized the relation between transformational leadership and satisfaction, and Akbaba-Altun (2003) examined the primary school principals' perception and performance in relation to transformational leadership. Moreover, Leithwood and Jantzi (1999) studied the effects of transformational leadership on organizational conditions and student engagement with school.

Leithwood (1992, 1994) defined transformational leadership as a form of principal leadership which makes followers be highly committed in achieving school goals by setting direction, developing people, redesigning the organizations, and managing the instructional program. The Leithwood model conceptualized transformational leadership into nine dimensions referring to vision creation, group goal development, the maintenance and modeling of high performance, the provision of individual support, the provision of intellectual stimuli, the establishment of a productive school culture and building structures for collaborations (Leithwood et al. 1994), and building good relations with parents (Leithwood and Jantzi 2000).

Leithwood et al. (2006) summarized these dimensions in the following categories: Setting Directions, Developing People, Redesigning the Organizations, and Managing the Instructional Program.

Setting Directions refers to the actions taken by transformational leaders in order to build an ideal school vision and set up specific school goals while simultaneously helping teachers perform their best (Leithwood al. 1999; Leithwood and Jantzi 2006).

Developing People takes account of providing individualized support, intellectual stimulation, and modeling important principles and practices. The leader activities cited above aim to establish a culture within the school that solidifies the teachers' capacity while maintaining common goals. Additionally, they furnish examples of best practices and approaches to motivate teachers (Leithwood al. 1999; Leithwood and Jantzi 2006).

Redesigning the Organization includes the dimensions for building and developing a collaborative and productive school culture, for creating, maintaining, and fostering participative decision-making, for creating productive community relationships, and for building good relationships with parents (Leithwood et al. 1999; Leithwood and Jantzi 2006). Managing the Instructional Program amounts to the clustering of managerial best practices, including those behaviors that will establish a stable and secure organizational structure. It includes actions and practices for leaders with respect to staffing the program and providing instructional carry to monitoring school activities and buffering the staff and colleagues from distraction to their work while seeking continuous improvement (Leithwood et al. 1999; Leithwood and Jantzi 2006). In the context of transformational leadership model (Leithwood and Jantzi 2006), this paper investigates the dimensions it assumes with respect to quality in Greek secondary education.

2 Aim of the Study

The main aim of the present paper is to illustrate the effects of Transformational School Leadership on teachers and their teaching practices. Transformational School Leadership is based on the following constructs: Setting Directions, Developing People, Redesigning the Organizations, Reliability of Administrative Leadership. Measures of Teachers Capacities, Measures of Teachers' Motivation, Measures of Teachers' Work Setting, and Measures of Teachers' Classroom Practices (Leithwood and Jantzi 2006). A survey has been conducted among secondary school teachers in Greece.

3   The Instrument

The instrument, which was employed to measure secondary school teachers' opinions toward Transformational School Leadership, is K. Leithwood and D. Jantzi's scale (Leithwood and Jantzi 2006), which consists of 57 items, referring to 7 different attitude subscales as follows:

1. Setting Directions (three items, e.g., helped clarify the reasons for implementing the strategy)
2. Developing People (three items, e.g., given you individual support to help you implement the strategy)
3. Redesigning the Organization (three items, e.g., encouraged collaborative work among staff)
4. Measures of Teacher Capacities (eight items, e.g., I have the knowledge and skill I need to implement the strategy)
5. Measures of Teachers' Motivation (18 items, e.g., the aims of the strategy are clear to me)
6. Measures of Teachers' Work Settings (12 items, e.g., my colleagues and I function as a team in implementing the strategy)
7. Measures of Teachers' Classroom Practices (ten items, e.g., I have changed my teaching of reading/mental mathematics as a result of the strategy)

Each item of the instrument used a 7-point Likert scale that ranged from 1, strongly disagree, to 7, strongly agree. The value of Cronbach's α coefficient for this instrument in the sample of this study was 0.892.

One further question was included, which measured the existence of Transformational School Leadership in secondary education.

4   Methodology

Structural equation modeling was performed, in order to validate the measurement model and test the hypothesized relationships. It provides useful insights on quality assurance in education that lead to the improvement of teaching practices.

5   Research Hypotheses

The present paper examines the following research hypotheses:

Ho1: Setting Directions has a positive effect on Transformational School Leadership.
Ho2: Developing People has a positive effect on Transformational School Leadership.

Ho3: Redesigning the Organization has a positive effect on Transformational School Leadership.

Ho4: Measures of Teacher Capacities has a positive effect on Transformational School Leadership.

Ho5: Measures of Teachers' Motivation has a positive effect on Transformational School Leadership.

Ho6: Measures of Teachers' Work Settings has a positive effect on Transformational School Leadership.

Ho7: Measures of Teachers' Classroom Practices has a positive effect on Transformational School Leadership.

6 Sample

The research was carried out in Central and Western Macedonia, Greece. The sample consists of 127 secondary school teachers.

7 Results

The following tables present factor loadings and reliability estimates for each construct. The composite reliability scores range from 0.852 to 0.969, AVEs range from 0.570 to 0.716, and Cronbach's α estimates range from 0.776 to 0.921, indicating the reasonable reliability of all conceptual constructs. All these indices composite reliability and AVEs και Cronbach's α indicate the adequate reliability of the measurements or conceptual constructs (Fornell and Larcker 1981; Nunnally 1978).

Furthermore, all of the factors' loadings are large and significant, indicating convergent validity. The validities of the measurements were evaluated by comparing the average variance-extracted estimates with the squared correlations between constructs. For all construct pairs, the average variance-extracted estimates are greater than the estimated squared correlations of the factors, thereby proving evidence for discriminant validity (Fornell and Larcker 1981).

Setting Directions The reliability of the factor Setting Directions according to Cronbach's alpha coefficient is $\alpha = 0.776$ (Table 1). The composite reliability $CR = 0.911$ is observed to be larger than 0.7 ($CR > 0.7$), indicating internal consistency (Fornell and Larcker 1981). AVE assumes the price 0.659 and also supports the scale's reliability (Table 1) (Fornell and Larcker 1981).

In addition the eigenvalue for the conceptual construct Setting Directions is 2.142, and it furnishes evidence that all of the items across all structures load on one factor with an eigenvalue over 1, fact that verifies convergent validity (Kim et al. 2008) (Table 1).

Table 1 Setting Directions—factor loadings, eigenvalues, and reliability estimates

Construct	Items	Loadings	Cronbach's α	CR	AVE	Eigenvalues
Directions	Set1. Helped clarify the reasons for implementing the strategy	0.895	0.776	0.852	0.659	2.142
	Set2. Provided useful assistance to you in setting short-term goals for 1/n teaching and learning	0.823				
	Demonstrated high expectations for your work with pupils in 1/n	0.706				

More specifically, the conceptual construct Setting Directions με eigenvalue 2.349 collects or is constructed from items Set1, Set2, and Set3 and indeed with very high loads, 0.895, 0.823, and 0.706, respectively. From the eigenvalue or characteristic root criterion (eigen value ≥ 1), it is verified that the three items, Set1, Set2, and Set3, represent the same conceptual construct (Table 1).

The only extracted factor had an eigenvalue which met the criterion of being larger than 1 and the values of the loadings of the items of which the conceptual construct comprises support the acceptability of the convergent validity. More specifically, the three items, Set1, Set2, and Set3, which construct the factor Setting Directions verify that the measurements/items lead to the same results and render convergent validity acceptable (Spector 1992; Churchill 1979). All structures should load on one factor with eigenvalue over 1; thus convergent validity is acceptable. In addition the loadings of all the items Set1, Set2, και Set3 are over 0.50, and thus convergent validity is assessed (Wixom and Watson 2001).

Developing People The reliability of factor Developing People, according to the Cronbach's alpha coefficient, is 0.806 and is high. Values of Cronbach's alpha coefficient over 0.7 are considered as satisfactory (Spector 1992; Nunnally 1978). The composite reliability CR = 0.883 is shown to be larger than 0.7 (CR > 0.7), indicating internal consistency (Fornell and Larcker 1981). AVE takes a value of 0.716 and supports the reliability of the Developing People scale (Table 2) because values of the average variance extracted with the cutoff of 0.5 are considered as satisfactory (Fornell and Larcker 1981). Furthermore the eigenvalue for the conceptual construct Developing People is 1.894 and thus is evidenced that all the items of all the structures load on one factor with eigenvalue over one fact which verifies convergent validity (Kim et al. 2008) (Table 2).

More specifically, the conceptual construct Developing People with an eigenvalue of 1.894 collects or is constructed from items Dev1, Dev2, and Dev3 and, indeed, with very high loads, 0.885, 0.849, and 0.803, respectively. From the

Table 2 Developing People—factor loadings, eigenvalues, and reliability estimates

Construct	Items	Loadings	Cronbach's α	CR	AVE	Eigenvalues
Developing People	Dev1. Given you individual support to help you implement the strategy	0.885	0.806	0.883	0.716	1.894
	Dev2. Encouraged you to consider new ideas for your teaching of 1/n	0.849				
	Dev3. Modeled a high level of professional practice in relation to the strategy	0.803				

eigenvalue or characteristic root criterion (eigenvalue ≥1), it is verified that the three items Dev1, Dev2, and Dev3, represent the same conceptual structure.

The only extracted factor had an eigenvalue satisfying the criterion of being larger than 1, and the loadings of the items comprising the conceptual construct attest that convergent validity is acceptable. More specifically, the three items Dev1, Dev2, and Dev3, make up factor Developing People and verify that the measurements/items lead to the same results and render convergent validity acceptable (Spector 1992; Churchill 1979). All structures load on one factor with eigenvalue over 1, fact that suggests that convergent validity is acceptable (Kim et al. 2008). In addition the loadings of all the items Dev1, Dev2, and Dev3 are over 0.50, and thus convergent validity is assessed (Wixom and Watson 2001) (Table 2).

Redesigning the Organization The reliability of factor Redesigning the Organization, according to Cronbach's alpha coefficient, is 0.817 and is high. Values of the Cronbach's alpha coefficient over 0.7 are considered as satisfactory (Spector 1992; Nunnally 1978). The composite reliability CR = 0.853 is shown to be larger than 0.7 (CR > 0.7), indicating internal consistency (Fornell and Larcker 1981). AVE takes a value of 0.659 and supports the reliability of the Developing People scale (Table 3) because values of the average variance extracted with the cutoff of 0.5 are considered as satisfactory (Fornell and Larcker 1981).

Furthermore, the eigenvalue for the conceptual construct Redesigning the Organization is 2.713 and thus is evidenced that all the items of all the structures load on one factor with eigenvalue over 1 fact which verifies convergent validity (Kim et al. 2008) (Table 3).

From principal component analysis, only one factor was extracted, Redesigning the Organization. More specifically, the conceptual construct Redesigning the Organization with an eigenvalue of 2.713 collects the item's future intention to Red1, Red2, and Red3 and, indeed, with very high loads, 0.826, 0.814, and 0.795, respectively, and it is thus verified that the three items Red1, Red2, and Red3 represent the same conceptual construct. From the criterion (eigenvalue ≥1) and

Table 3 Redesigning the organization—factor loadings, eigenvalues, and reliability estimates

Construct	Items	Loadings	Cronbach's α	CR	AVE	Eigenvalues
Redesigning the Organization	Red1. Encouraged collaborative work among staff	0.826	0.817	0.853	0.659	2.713
	Red2. Created conditions in the school which allow for wide participation in decisions about the strategy	0.814				
	Red2. Helped develop good relationships with parents as part of the school's efforts to respond productively to the strategy	0.795				

the values of the loadings of all items Red1, Red2, and Red3 which are over 0.50, it is clear that convergent validity is assessed (Wixom and Watson 2001).

The only extracted factor had an eigenvalue satisfying the criterion of being larger than 1 and the loadings of the items comprising the conceptual construct attest that convergent validity is acceptable (Spector 1992; Churchill 1979). More specifically, the three items Red1, Red2 and Red3 make up factor Redesigning the Organization and verify that the measurements/items lead to the same results and render convergent validity acceptable (Spector 1992; Churchill 1979). All structures load on one factor with eigenvalue over 1 fact that suggests that convergent validity is acceptable. In addition the loadings of all the items Red1, Red2 and Red3 are over 0.50, and thus convergent validity is assessed (Wixom and Watson 2001) (Table 3).

Measures of Teacher Capacities The reliability of factor Measures of Teacher Capacities, according to the Cronbach's alpha coefficient is 0.896 and is high. Values of Cronbach's alpha coefficient over 0.7 are considered as satisfactory (Spector 1992; Nunnally 1978). The composite reliability CR = 0.934 is shown to be larger than 0.7 (CR > 0.7), indicating internal consistency (Fornell and Larcker 1981). AVE takes a value of 0.640 and supports the reliability of the Measures of Teacher Capacities scale (Table 4) because values of the average variance extracted with the cutoff of 0.5 are considered as satisfactory (Fornell and Larcker 1981).

Furthermore the eigenvalue for the conceptual construct Measures of Teacher Capacities is 1.952 and thus is evidenced that all the items of all the structures load on one factor with eigenvalue over 1 fact which verifies convergent validity (Kim et al. 2008) (Table 4).

More specifically, the conceptual construct Measures of Teacher Capacities with an eigenvalue equal to 1.952 collects items Mtc1, Mtc2, Mtc3, Mtc4, 1 Mtc5, Mtc6, Mtc7 and Mtc8, and, indeed, with very high loadings 0.841, 0.824, 0.803, 0.819,

Table 4 Measures of teacher capacities—factor loadings, eigenvalues, and reliability estimates

Construct	Items	Loadings	Cronbach's α	CR	AVE	Eigenvalues
Measures of Teacher Capacities	Mtc1. I have the knowledge and skill I need to implement the strategy	0.841	0.896	0.934	0.640	1.952
	Mtc2. I am having success implementing the strategy	0.824				
	Mtc3. I have many opportunities to think and talk about how practices recommended by the strategy relate to my own classroom practices	0.803				
	Mtc4. Had opportunities to practice and refine new teaching skills required for implementing the strategy	0.819				
	Mtc5. Strategy. My teaching of reading/mental mathematics has become more effective as a result of the strategy	0.783				
	Mtc6. My teaching of writing/mathematical concepts has become more effective as a result of the strategy	0.805				
	Mtc7. My pupils have benefited from the reading/mental mathematics component of the strategy	0.792				
	Mtc8. My pupils have benefited from the writing/mathematical concepts component of the strategy	0.728				

0.783, 0.805, 0.792 and 0.728, respectively. From criterion (eigenvalue ≥ 1), it is verified that these 18 items represent the same conceptual construct.

For only factor extracted, the value of its eigenvalue which meets the criterion of being larger than 1 and the loadings of the items comprising the conceptual structure support that the convergent validity is acceptable. More specifically, these eight items Mtc1, Mtc2, Mtc3, Mtc4, 1 Mtc5, Mtc6, Mtc7 and Mtc8 construct the factor

Measures of Teacher Capacities and verify that measurements/items lead to the same results and render convergent validity acceptable (Spector 1992; Churchill 1979). All structures should load on one factor with eigenvalue over 1, fact that verifies that convergent validity to be acceptable (Kim et al. 2008). In addition the loadings of all the items Mtc1, Mtc1, Mtc3, Mtc4, Mtc5, Mtc6, Mtc7 and Mtc8 are over 0.50, and thus convergent validity is assessed (Wixom and Watson 2001).

Measures of Teachers' Motivation The reliability of factor Measures of Teachers' Motivation, according to Cronbach's alpha coefficient, is 0.904 and is deemed high. Values of Cronbach's alpha coefficient over 0.7 are considered as satisfactory (Spector 1992; Nunnally 1978). The composite reliability $CR = 0.969$ is shown larger than 0.7 ($CR > 0.7$), indicating internal consistency (Fornell and Larcker 1981). AVE takes the value 0.638 and thus supports the reliability of the Measures of Teachers' Motivation scale (Table 5) because values of the average variance extracted with the cutoff of 0.5 are considered as satisfactory (Fornell and Larcker 1981) (Table 5).

Furthermore the eigenvalue for conceptual construct Measures of Teachers' Motivation is 2.739, and it, thus, serves as evidence that all the items of all the structures should load on one factor with eigenvalue over 1, fact that verifies convergent validity (Kim et al. 2008) (Table 5).

More specifically, the conceptual construct Measures of Teacher Capacities with an eigenvalue equal to 2.739 collects items Mtm1, Mtm2, Mtm3, Mtm4, Mtm5, Mtm6, Mtm7, Mtm8, Mtm9, Mtm10, Mtm11, Mtm12, Mtm13, Mtm14, Mtm15, Mtm16, Mtm17, and και Mtc18 and, indeed, with very high loadings 0.863, 0.794, 0.832, 0.798, 0.805, 0.811, 0.842, 0.831, 0.792, 0.763, 0.817, 0.763, 0.792. 0.765, 0.803, 0.826, 0.709 and 0.756, respectively. From criterion (eigenvalue ≥ 1), it is verified that these 18 items Mtm1, Mtm2, Mtm3, Mtm4, Mtm5, Mtm6, Mtm7, Mtm8, Mtm9, Mtm10, Mtm11, Mtm12, Mtm13, Mtm14, Mtm15, Mtm16, Mtm17, and Mtc18 represent the same conceptual construct.

For only factor extracted, the value of its eigenvalue which meets the criterion of being larger than 1 and the loadings of the items comprising the conceptual structure support that the convergent validity is acceptable. More specifically, these 18 items, Mtm1, Mtm2, Mtm3, Mtm4, Mtm5, Mtm6, Mtm7, Mtm8, Mtm9, Mtm10, Mtm11, Mtm12, Mtm13, Mtm14, Mtm15, Mtm16, Mtm17, and και Mtc18, construct the factor Measures of Teacher Capacities and verify that that measurements/items lead to the same results and render convergent validity acceptable (Spector 1992; Churchill 1979).

All structures should load on one factor with eigenvalue over 1, fact that verifies that convergent validity to be (Kim et al. 2008). In addition the loadings of all the items Mtm1, Mtm2, Mtm3, Mtm4, Mtm5, Mtm6, Mtm7, Mtm8, Mtm9, Mtm10, Mtm11, Mtm12, Mtm13, Mtm14, Mtm15, Mtm16, Mtm17, and Mtc18 are over 0.50, and thus convergent validity is assessed (Wixom and Watson 2001).

Measures of Teachers' Work Settings The reliability of factor Measures of Teachers' Work Settings, according to Cronbach's alpha coefficient, is 0.918 and is deemed high. Values of Cronbach's alpha coefficient over 0.7 are considered as

Table 5 Measures of Teachers' Motivation—factors loadings, eigenvalues, and reliability estimates

Construct	Items	Loadings	Cronbach's α	CR	AVE	Eigenvalues
Measures of Teachers' Motivation	Mtm1. The aims of the strategy are clear to me	0.863	0.904	0.969	0.638	2.739
	Mtm2. The aims of the strategy are consistent with my own aims about teaching 1/n in my classroom	0.794				
	Mtm3. I have been involved in setting key stage 2 targets in this school	0.832				
	Mtm4. I have been involved in setting curriculum targets for pupils in my class	0.798				
	Mtm5. I use the school's curriculum targets in my planning	0.805				
	Mtm6. If a pupil did not understand what I was teaching in a lesson, I would know what to do next to increase his/her understanding	0.811				
	Mtm7. If a pupil in my class becomes disruptive and noisy during 1/n lessons, I feel confident that I know some techniques to redirect him/her quickly	0.842				
	Mtm8. If one of my pupils could not do the work in 1/n. I would be able to assess whether the task was at the correct level of difficulty	0.831				
	Mtm9. If I really try hard, I can teach 1/n to even the most difficult or unmotivated pupils	0.792				

(continued)

Table 5 (continued)

Construct	Items	Loadings	Cronbach's α	CR	AVE	Eigenvalues
	Mtm10. The strategy training in which I participated was very useful	0.763				
	Mtm11. The climate in my school is consistent with efforts to implement the strategy	0.817				
	Mtm12. I have the flexibility that I need to implement the strategy in a manner that I believe is effective for my pupils	0.763				
	Mtm13. I have all the information that I need about the expectations associated with the strategy	0.792				
	Mtm14. I have access to the resources (e.g. people, materials) that I need to implement the strategy	0.765				
	Mtm15. I am able to find the teaching time needed to implement both the literacy and numeracy strategies	0.803				
	Mtm16. I am able to find the planning time needed to implement both the literacy and numeracy strategies	0.826				
	Mtm17. I receive useful feedback about my use of teaching practices related to the strategy (e.g. from the head teacher, coordinator, etc.)	0.709				
	Mtm18. The strategy has made my job more satisfying and engaging	0.756				

Table 6 Measures of Teachers' Work Settings—factors loadings, eigenvalues, and reliability estimates

Construct	Items	Loadings	Cronbach's α	CR	AVE	Eigenvalues
Measures of Teachers' Work Setting	Mtws1. My colleagues and I function as a team in implementing the strategy	0.746	0.918	0.944	0.585	2.542
	Mtws2. My colleagues and I build on one another's strengths in implementing the strategy	0.805				
	Mtws3. My colleagues and I assist one another, as needed, in implementing any new classroom practices required by the strategy	0.745				
	Mtws4. Structures (e.g., timetables, planning arrangements) in this school allow for opportunities to collaborate in teaching with colleagues	0.798				
	Mtws5. The physical layout of the school is school is conductive to discussion with colleagues about teaching and learning	0.702				
	Mtws6. Good teachers can teach 1/n to even the most difficult pupils	0.783				
	Mtws7. Teachers are very limited in what they can achieve in teaching 1/n because a pupil's home environment is a large influence on learning	0.643				
	Mtws8. When it comes right down to it, a teacher really can't influence 1/n much because most of a pupil's motivation and performance depends on his or her home environment	0.817				

(continued)

Table 6 (continued)

Construct	Items	Loadings	Cronbach's α	CR	AVE	Eigenvalues
	Mtws9. Colleagues in the second feel a sense of responsibility for the quality of teaching in their classrooms	0.814				
	Mtws10. Colleagues in the school feel a sense of responsibility for engaging in school-wide decisions that influence their teaching	0.769				
	Mtws11. Parents are supportive of this school's efforts in 1/n	0.782				
	Mtws12. Nonparent members of the community are supportive of the school's efforts in 1/n	0.753				

satisfactory (Spector 1992; Nunnally 1978). The composite reliability CR = 0.944 is shown larger than 0.7 (CR > 0.7), indicating internal consistency (Fornell and Larcker 1981). AVE takes the value 0.638 and thus supports the reliability of the Measures of Teachers' Work Settings scale (Table 6) because values of the average variance extracted with the cutoff of 0.5 are considered as satisfactory (Fornell and Larcker 1981) (Table 6).

Furthermore the eigenvalue for the conceptual construct Measures of Teachers' Work Settings is 2.542 and thus is evidenced that all the items of all the structures load on one factor with eigenvalue over 1 fact which verifies convergent validity (Kim et al. 2008) (Table 6).

More specifically, the conceptual construct Measures of Teachers' Work Settings, with an eigenvalue of 2.542 collects or is constructed from items Mtws1, Mtws2, Mtws3, Mtws4, Mtws5, Mtws6, Mtws7, Mtws8, Mtws9, Mtws10, Mtws11, and Mtws12 and, indeed, with very high loads, 0.746, 0.805, 0.745, 0.798, 0.702, 0.783, 0.643, 0.817, 0.814, 0.769, 0.782, and 0.753, respectively. From the eigenvalue or characteristic root criterion (eigenvalue ≥ 1), it is verified that the 12 items Mtws1, Mtws2, Mtws3, Mtws4, Mtws5, Mtws6, Mtws7, Mtws8, Mtws9, Mtws10, Mtws11, and Mtws12 represent the same conceptual structure.

The only extracted factor had an eigenvalue satisfying the criterion of being larger than 1 and the loadings of the items comprising the conceptual construct attest that convergent validity is acceptable. More specifically, the 12 items Mtws1, Mtws2, Mtws3, Mtws4, Mtws5, Mtws6, Mtws7, Mtws8, Mtws9, Mtws10, Mtws11, and Mtws12 make up factor Measures of Teachers' Work Settings and verify that the measurements/items lead to the same results and render convergent validity acceptable (Spector 1992; Churchill 1979).

All structures load on one factor with eigenvalue over 1 fact that suggests that convergent validity is acceptable (Kim et al. 2008).

In addition the loadings of all the items Mtws1, Mtws2, Mtws3, Mtws4, Mtws5, Mtws6, Mtws7, Mtws8, Mtws9, Mtws10, Mtws11, and Mtws12 are over 0.50, and thus convergent validity is assessed (Wixom and Watson 2001) (Table 6).

Measures of Teachers' Classroom Practices The reliability of Measures of Teachers' Classroom Practices, according to the Cronbach's alpha coefficient, is 0.921 and is high. Values of the Cronbach's alpha coefficient over 0.7 are considered as satisfactory (Spector 1992; Nunnally 1978). The composite reliability CR = 0.930 is shown to be larger than 0.7 (CR > 0.7), indicating internal consistency (Fornell and Larcker 1981). AVE takes a value of 0.570 and supports the reliability of the Measures of Teachers' Classroom Practices scale (Table 7) because values of the average variance extracted with the cutoff of 0.5 are considered as satisfactory (Fornell and Larcker 1981) (Table 7).

Furthermore the eigenvalue for the conceptual construct Measures of Teachers' Classroom Practices is 2.542 and thus is evidenced that all the items of all the structures load on one factor with eigenvalue over 1 fact which verifies convergent validity (Kim et al. 2008) (Table 7).

More specifically, the conceptual construct Ο παράγοντας Measures of Teachers' Classroom Practices with an eigenvalue of 1.761 collects or is constructed from items Mtcp1, Mtcp2, Mtcp3, Mtcp4, Mtcp5, Mtcp6, Mtcp7, Mtcp8, Mtcp9, and Mtcp10 and, indeed, with very high loads, 0.834, 0.827, 0.716, 0.752, 0.654, 0.763, 0.753, 0.803, 0.738, and 0.690, respectively. From the eigenvalue or characteristic root criterion (eigenvalue $\geq$ 1), it is verified that the ten items Mtcp1, Mtcp2, Mtcp3, Mtcp4, Mtcp5, Mtcp6, Mtcp7, Mtcp8, Mtcp9, and Mtcp10 represent the same conceptual structure.

The only extracted factor had an eigenvalue satisfying the criterion of being larger than 1, and the loadings of the items comprising the conceptual construct attest that convergent validity is acceptable. More specifically, the ten items Mtcp1, Mtcp2, Mtcp3, Mtcp4, Mtcp5, Mtcp6, Mtcp7, Mtcp8, Mtcp9, and Mtcp10 make up factor Measures of Teachers' Classroom Practices and verify that the measurements/items lead to the same results and render convergent validity acceptable (Spector 1992; Churchill 1979).

All structures load on one factor with eigenvalue over 1 fact that suggests that convergent validity is acceptable (Kim et al. 2008).

In addition the loadings of all the items Mtcp1, Mtcp2, Mtcp3, Mtcp4, Mtcp5, Mtcp6, Mtcp7, Mtcp8, Mtcp9, and Mtcp10 are over 0.50, and thus convergent validity is assessed (Wixom and Watson 2001) (Table 7).

The measurement model fits the observed data ($x^2 = 687.56$, $x^2/df = 1.78$, CFI = 0.95, GFI = 0.94, RMSEA = 0.03, AGFI = 0.90, IFI = 0.95) well.

The following table, Table 8, presents the descriptive statistics of and intercorrelations across the seven constructs used in this study. An assessment of the bivariate correlations indicates that all of the correlations are significant and are in the expected direction.

Table 7 Measures of Teachers' Classroom Practices—factor loadings, eigenvalues, and reliability estimates

Construct	Items	Loadings	Cronbach's α	CR	AVE	Eigenvalues
Measures of Teachers' Classroom Practices	Mtcp1. I have changed my teaching of reading/ mental mathematics as a result of strategy	0.834	0.921	0.930	0.570	1.761
	Mtcp2. I have changed my teaching of writing/ mathematical concepts as a result of the strategy	0.827				
	Mtcp3. I spend significantly more of my daily classroom time teaching reading/mental mathematics than I did before the strategy	0.716				
	Mtcp4. I spend significantly more of my daily classroom time teaching writing/mathematical concepts than I did before the strategy	0.752				
	Mtcp5. I spend significantly more time planning for 1/n teaching than I did before the strategy	0.654				
	Mtcp6. I spend significantly more time assessing pupils; work in 1/n than I did before the strategy	0.763				
	Mtcp7. My pupils spend significantly more of their time in school focusing on 1/n than they did before the strategy	0.753				
	Mtcp8. My pupils spend significantly more of their homework time on 1.n than they did before the strategy	0.803				
	Mtcp9. Parents spend significantly more time helping their children with 1/n now than they did before the strategy	0.738				

(continued)

Table 7 (continued)

Construct	Items	Loadings	Cronbach's α	CR	AVE	Eigenvalues
	Mtcp10. The literacy and numeracy strategies require me to use complementary forms of teaching	0.690				

Table 8 Descriptive statistics and correlation estimates

	Mean	SD	1	2	3	4	5	6	7
1. Setting Directions	4.07	0.13	1.00						
2. Developing People	4.23	0.12	0.46**	1.00					
3. Redesigning the Organization	4.16	0.23	0.37**	0.35**	1.00				
4. Measures of Teacher Capacities	4.03	0.15	0.24**	0.36**	0.28**	1.00			
5. Measures of Teachers' Motivation	3.98	0.51	0.41**	0.19**	0.22**	0.27**	1.00		
6. Measures of Teachers' Work Settings	3.84	0.42	0.34**	0.19**	0.23**	0.25**	0.31**	1.00	
7. Measures of Teachers' Classroom Practices	4.28	0.15	0.23**	0.27**	0.28**	0.19**	0.26**	0.29**	1.00

$**0.01$

In addition the seven hypothesized effects are supported (Table 9).

8 Conclusions

In general, this empirical study revealed the seven dimensions related to Transformational School Leadership on teachers and their teaching practices. Transformational School Leadership is based on the constructs Setting Directions, Developing People, Redesigning the Organizations, Reliability of Administrative Leadership, Measures of Teachers Capacities, Measures of Teachers' Motivation, Measures of Teachers' Work Setting, and Measures of Teachers' Classroom Practices.

Table 9 Hypotheses testing

Hypotheses	Standardized estimates	p-value	Results
Ho1: Setting Directions has a positive effect on Transformational School Leadership	0.34	<0.001	Supported
Ho2: Developing People has a positive effect on Transformational School Leadership	0.52	<0.001	Supported
Ho3: Redesigning the Organization has a positive effect on Transformational School Leadership	0.60	<0.001	Supported
Ho4: Measures of Teacher Capacities has a positive effect on Transformational School Leadership	0.36	<0.001	Supported
Ho5: Measures of Teachers' Motivation has a positive effect on Transformational School Leadership	0.39	<0.001	Supported
Ho6: Measures of Teachers' Work Settings has a positive effect on Transformational School Leadership	0.25	<0.001	Supported
Ho7: Measures of Teachers' Classroom Practices has a positive effect on Transformational School Leadership	0.56	<0.001	Supported

Transformational School Leadership is based on the constructs Setting Directions, Developing People, Redesigning the Organizations, Reliability of Administrative Leadership, Measures of Teachers Capacities, Measures of Teachers' Motivation, Measures of Teachers' Work Setting, and Measures of Teachers' Classroom Practices which have a strong direct effect on Transformational School Leadership.

In secondary education, Redesigning the Organization, Measures of Teachers' Classroom Practices, and Developing People are the most important factors among the seven dimensions on Transformational School Leadership.

In addition Measures of Teachers' Motivation plays more important role than Measures of Teacher Capacities, Setting Directions, and Measures of Teachers' Work Settings.

But future research may further investigate the role of these seven dimensions in relation to education assessment and quality assurance rewarding in primary, secondary, and tertiary education.

References

Akbaba-Altun, S. (2003). Eğitim yönetimi ve değerler. *Değerler Eğitimi Dergisi, 1*(1), 7–18.

Anastasiadou, S. (2016). *Evaluation of the implementation of TQM principles in tertiary education using the EFQM excellence model -research in educational departments of Greek universities.* Dissertation, Geek Open University.

Atilgan, C., & McCullen, P. (2011). Improving supply chain performance through auditing: A change management perspective. *Supply Chain Management: An International Journal, 16*(1), 11–19.

Bass, B. M. (1985). *Leadership and performance beyond expectations.* New York: The Free Press.

Bass, B. M., & Steidlmeier, P. (1999). Ethics, character and authentic transformational leadership behavior. *Leadership Quarterly, 10*(2), 181–217.

Burns, J. M. (1978). *Leadership.* New York: Harper & Row.

Churchill, G. A. (1979). A paradigm for developing better measures for marketing constructs. *Journal of Marketing Research, 16,* 64–73.

Crosby, P. B. (1979). *Quality if free: The art of making quality certain.* New York: McGraw-Hill.

Crosby, P. B. (1984). *Quality without tears.* New York: MacGraw-Hill.

Day, D. V., Gronn, P., & Sales, E. (2004). Leadership capacity in terms. *The Leadership Quarterly, 15,* 857–880.

De Long, W., & Fahey, L. (2000). Diagnosing cultural barriers to knowledge management. *Academy of Management Executive, 1*(4), 113–127.

Feigenbaum. (1986). *Total quality control* (3rd ed.). New York: McGraw-Hill.

Fornell, C., & Larcker, D. (1981). Evaluating structural equation models with unobservable variables and measurement error. *Journal of Marketing Research, 18,* 39–50.

Goetch, D. L., & Davis, S. B. (2013). In Tziola (Ed.), *Quality management and organizational excellence.* Thessaloniki.

Griffith, J. (2004). Relation of principal transformational leadership to school staff job satisfaction, staff turnover, and school performance. *Journal of Educational Administration, 42*(3), 333–356.

Grojean, M. W., Resock, C. J., Dickson, M. W., & Smith, D. B. (2004). Leaders, values and organizational climate: Examining leadership strategies for establishing an organizational climate regarding ethics. *Journal of Business Ethics, 33,* 223–241.

Juran, J. M. (1992). *Juran on quality by design: The new steps for planning quality into goods and services.* New York: The Free Press.

Juran, J. M. (1997). Early SPC: A historical supplement. *Quality Progress, 30,* 73–81.

Kanugo, R. N. (2001). Ethical values of transactional and transformational leaders. *Canadian Journal of Administrative Sciences, 18*(4), 257–265.

Kim, D. J., Ferrin, D. L., & Rao, H. R. (2008). A trust based consumer decision-making model in electronic commerce: The role of trust, perceived risk, and their antecedents. *Decision Support Systems, 44*(2), 544–564.

Lee, S. F., Roberts, P., Lau, W. S., & Leung, R. (1999). Survey on Deming's TQM philosophies implementation in Hong Kong. *Managerial Auditing Journal, 14*(3), 136–145.

Leithwood, K. (1992). The move toward transformational leadership. *Educational Leadership, 49*(5), 8–12.

Leithwood, K. (1994). Leadership for school restructuring. *Educational Administration Quarterly, 30*(4), 498–518.

Leithwood, K., Jantzi, D., & Fernandez, A. (1994). Transformational leadership and teachers' commitment to change. In J. Murphy & K. Louis (Eds.), *Reshaping the principal ship* (pp. 77–79). Thousand Oaks, CA: Corwin Press.

Leithwood, K., Tomlinson, D., & Genge, M. (1996). Transformational school leadership. In K. Leithwood, J. Chapman, D. Corson, P. Hallinger, & A. Hart (Eds.), *International handbook of educational leadership and administration* (pp. 785–840). Dordrecht: Kluwer Academic.

Leithwood, K., & Jantzi, D. (1999). Transformational school leadership effects: A replication school. *Effectiveness and School Improvement, 10*(4), 451–479.

Leithwood, K., Jantzi, D., & Steinbach, R. (1999). *Changing leadership for changing times.* Buckingham: Open University Press.

Leithwood, K., & Jantzi, D. (2000). The effects of transformational school leadership on organizational conditions and students engagement with school. *Journal of Educational Administration, 38*(2), 112–129.

Leithwood, K., Jantzi, D., Earl, L., Fullan, M., & Levin, B. (2004). Leadership for large scale reform. *School Leadership and Management, 24*(1), 57–80.

Leithwood, K., Day, C., Sammons, P., Hopkins, D., & Harris, A. (2006). *Successful school leadership: What is it how it influences pupil learning.* A report to the Department for Education and Skills.

Leithwood, K., & Jantzi, D. (2006). Transformational school leadership for large-scale reform: Effects on students, teachers, and their classroom practices. *School Effectiveness and School Improvement, 17*(2), 201–227.

Marks, H. M., & Printy, S. M. (2003). Principal leadership and school performance: An integration of transformation and instructional leadership. *Educational Administration Quarterly, 39*(3), 370–397.

Martin-Castilla, J., & Rodriguez-Ruiz, O. (2008). EFQM model: Knowledge governance and completive advantage. *Journal of Intellectual Capital, 9*(1), 133–156.

Mendonca, M. (2001). Preparing for ethical leadership in organizations. *Canadiam Journal of Administration Sciences, 18*(4), 266–276.

Mendonca, M., & Kanungo, R. N. (2007). *Ethical leadership*. New York: Open University Press.

Morales-Lopez, V. (2013). Leadership in organization knowledge to Mexico. *Procedia- Social and Behavioral Sciences, 6*(1), 19–44.

Mparoutas, S. (2007). In M. Paideia (Ed.), *Leadership today*. Thessaloniki.

Nunnally, C. J. (1978). *Psychometric theory*. New York: McGraw Hill.

Sağnak, M. (2010). The relationship between transformational school leadership and ethical climate. *Educational Sciences: Theory and Practice, 10*(2), 1135–1152.

Spector, P. E. (1992). *Summated rating scale construction: An introduction*. Sage University paper series on quantitative application in the social sciences, Newbury Park, CA.

Steiakis, E., & Kofidis, N. (2010). In Tziola (Ed.), *Management and quality control*. Thessaloniki.

Stefanatos, S. (2000). *Programming for quality* (Vol. B). Patra: Greek Open University (edus).

Taguchi, G. (1987). *System of experimental design*. Canberra: Unipub/Kraus, International Publication.

Wadsworth, H. M., Stephens, K. S., & Goldfrey, A. B. (2002). *Modern methods for quality control and improvement*. New York: Wiley.

Wixom, B. H., & Watson, H. J. (2001). An empirical investigation of the factors affecting data warehousing success. *MIS Quarterly, 25*(1), 17–41.

Yu, H. (2002). The effects of transformational leadership on teachers' commitment to change in Hong Kong. *Journal of Educational Administration, 40*(4), 368–389.

Yukl, G. (1999). An evaluation of conceptual weakness in transformational and charismatic leadership theories. *The Leadership Quarterly, 10*(2), 285–305.

Yukl, G., & Van Fleet, D. D. (1992). Theory and research on leadership in organizations. In D. Dunnete & I. M. Hough (Eds.), *Handbook of industrial and organizational psychology* (Vol. 3, 2nd ed., pp. 147–197). Palo Alto, CA: Consulting Psychologists Press.

The Impact of the Destination Image of Greece on Tourists' Behavioral Intentions

Amalia Triantafillidou, Prodromos Yannas, and Georgios Lappas

Abstract Greece's image has suffered from inconsistent advertising campaigns which positioned Greece as the ideal destination for summer holidays and heritage tourism. This fragmented image was further distorted as the result of the economic crisis. However, less is known about the current perceptions of foreign tourists regarding the image of Greece. The aim of the present study is twofold: firstly, to assess tourists' perceptions of the cognitive image of Greece and, secondly, to test the effects of the different cognitive image dimensions on tourists' revisit and recommendation intentions. Toward that end, a survey was conducted in the city of Athens using a self-administered questionnaire which was delivered to foreign visitors. Results indicate that Greece is perceived as a destination for heritage and leisure tourism. Moreover, the cognitive component of destination image is comprised of four factors, namely, natural/cultural resources, leisure/recreation, tourist infrastructure, and experience/value. Not all cognitive image factors exert influence on tourists' revisit intentions. More specifically, intentions to revisit Greece are primarily affected by the leisure/entertainment factor followed by experience/value and cultural/natural factors, while intentions to recommend are influenced mainly by the factors of experience/value and cultural/natural resources and to a lesser extent by the leisure/recreation factor. A number of managerial implications are discussed that would enable destination managers to better promote Greece and to entice tourists' loyalty.

Keywords Destination image · Cognitive component · Foreign tourists · Behavioral intentions

A. Triantafillidou (✉) · G. Lappas
Western Macedonia University of Applied Sciences, Kastoria, Greece
e-mail: a.triantafylidou@kastoria.teikoz.gr; amtriantafil@aueb.gr; lappas@kastoria.teikoz.gr

P. Yannas
Piraeus University of Applied Sciences, Aigaleo, Greece
e-mail: prodyannas@puas.gr

© Springer Nature Switzerland AG 2019
N. Sykianakis et al. (eds.), *Economic and Financial Challenges for Eastern Europe*,
Springer Proceedings in Business and Economics,
https://doi.org/10.1007/978-3-030-12169-3_22

1 Introduction

Tourism is an important industry for the Greek economy since it contributes to the country's GDP and employment. Greece is consistently investing in marketing and advertising programs in order to increase tourists' arrivals. Until 2009, Greece's promotional campaigns projected a fragmented image as a summer destination with an enormous cultural heritage (Kouris 2009). Economic crisis further deteriorated Greece's image and led the National Tourism Authorities in taking steps toward the re-branding of the image of Greece as a four-season destination offering different types of tourism (e.g., leisure tourism, heritage tourism, culinary tourism, adventure tourism, religious tourism, etc.).

Despite efforts made by Greece's authorities for repositioning the brand of Greece, less is known about the current perceptions of foreign tourists regarding the image of Greece as a destination. Research on the image of Greece has focused on measuring the image of specific Greek cities and islands (e.g., Athens, Thessaloniki, Mykonos, Pertouli, Corfu, Patra) (Kaplanidou 2009; Yannas and Simeli 2012; Zacharia and Spais 2017; Kokkali et al. 2011; Vitouladiti 2013; Papadimitriou et al. 2015). To fill this gap in relevant research the present study will examine how foreign tourists perceive the different attributes of the Greek tourism offering. Moreover, the study will shed light on the impact of tourists' perceptions on Greece as a destination as well as on their willingness to revisit the country within the next 3 years and recommend it through word of mouth to family, friends, and associates.

According to Martin and delBosque (San Martín and Del Bosque 2008), knowing tourists' perceptions about a destination can lead to (a) identification of the destination's strengths and weaknesses, (b) better and more efficient promotion of the destination, and (c) a competitive advantage. Moreover, understanding of the destination attributes that impact the behavioral intentions of tourists will improve promotional efforts of tourism managers (Chen and Tsai 2007) since they can carefully craft their communication strategy and messages, thus enhancing those aspects of the destination that were found to be determinants of tourists' loyalty (Chi and Qu 2008).

The present study is organized as follows. First, relevant literature on destination image components and the factors that affect image formation process are presented. Next, Greece's tourism promotional campaigns from 2000 and forth are analyzed followed by the presentation of the conceptual framework and research hypotheses. The methodology and results of the study are then described, and conclusions are discussed which focus on the theoretical and managerial implications of the study. Lastly, the main limitations of the study are outlined and future research suggestions are recommended.

2   Destination Image Components and Formation Process

Destination image is an important and intensively studied concept in tourism literature. Most destination image studies consider destination image as the "sum of beliefs, ideas, and impressions that people have of a place or destination" (Gertner and Kotler 2004) or "an individual's mental representation of knowledge (beliefs), feelings and overall perception of a particular destination" (Chen and Tsai 2007, p. 1116). Whereas the first definition emphasizes on the perceptual/cognitive component of destination image, the latter indicates that destination image is comprised not only by a cognitive component but also by an affective and an aggregate holistic impression of a destination (Martín-Santana et al. 2017). Specifically, the cognitive component refers to an individual's beliefs about the salient attributes of a destination, and the affective component is related to the feelings about the destination (Baloglu and McCleary 1999). According to Echtner and Ritchie (1993), the cognitive dimension of the destination image can be comprised of both functional/concrete characteristics of a place/destination such as climate, roads, and nightlife and psychological/abstract attributes like friendliness of people and perceived safety. On the other hand, the affective element of destination image captures an individual's feelings of pleasure, arousal (Beerli and Martin 2004), relaxation, and excitement (Baloglu and McCleary 1999). Gartner (1994) suggested that besides the cognitive and affective components, destination image is comprised of a conative element which reflects an individual's behavior or intention to revisit, engage in positive word of mouth, as well as recommend the destination to others (Agapito et al. 2013). These three elements—cognitive, affective, and conative—form the overall, global impression of an individual about a place/destination (Gartner 1994). Moreover, it should be noted that the cognitive component influences the affective (Baloglu and McCleary 1999) as well as the conative component (Agapito et al. 2013). Figure 1 better illustrates the different components of destination image and their interrelations. Thus, based on the above destination image is "an interactive system of thoughts, opinions, feelings, visualizations, and intentions toward a destination" (Tasci et al. 2007, p. 200).

Fig. 1 Components of destination image. Source: Tasci et al. (2007, p. 200)

It should be noted that individuals form images about destination even if they had not visited the place/destination in the past and had never been exposed to commercial messages about the destination (Echtner and Ritchie 1993). Moreover, destination image is not only related to individuals' perceptions about the characteristics of the place but is a complex construct intertwined with individuals' perceptions about the residents, retailers, other tourists, and employees of the destination (Gallarza et al. 2002). Destination image is also affected by elements that are not easily observable and controlled by destination managers (Gallarza et al. 2002).

Destination image is influenced by primary and secondary information sources as well as the personal characteristics of an individual (Beerli and Martin 2004). Primary sources are related to individuals' previous experience and familiarity with the destination. On the other hand, secondary sources can be classified in three broad categories: induced, autonomous, and organic (Gartner 1994). Induced information sources include advertisements on media by travel/tourism institutions, tour operators and wholesalers, as well as reports and articles about the destination and promotional activities involving celebrity endorsers. Autonomous sources are not promotional activities initiated by destination institutions and companies but are promoted by mass media in the form of broadcasting news, documentaries, films, and television programs for the destination. On the other hand, organic sources include information from friends and relatives and one's own knowledge and experience about the destination. However, one cannot ignore the Internet as another important secondary source of information about a tourist destination. According to Llodrà-Riera et al. (2015), these Internet information sources include search engines, web pages of official tourist information, forums and blogs specialized in tourism, social media, portals for hotel reservation (i.e., booking.com), websites with content generated from tourists (e.g., trip advisor), etc.

Personal characteristics like an individual's personal values (Baloglu and McCleary 1999) motivations, vacation experience, and other various sociodemographic factors could also influence the destination image formation process (Beerli and Martin 2004). For example, Baloglu (2000) revealed that motivations such as knowledge and escapism influenced significantly the various dimensions of destination image.

3   The Brand of Greece

Greece represents an interesting case for the study of destination image. Tourism in Greece has always been an important sector for the Greek economy that contributed to the GDP of Greece. Each year millions of tourists visit Greece (Table 1). In 2000, almost 13 million of tourists visited Greece. This figure, in 2008 was almost 16 million and in 2009 when the economic crisis hit Greece dropped to 14 million. From 2014 Greek tourism has largely recovered from the devastating effects of crisis and in 2016 broke all-time records with tourists' arrivals reaching almost 28 million tourists. Hence, in the midst of economic crisis, tourism revenues in Greece continued to increase, contributing to the recovery of the Greek economy (SETE 2016).

Table 1 Tourists arrivals in Greece (2000–2016)

Year	Tourists' arrivals
2000[a]	13,096,000
2001[a]	14,057,000
2002[a]	14,180,000
2003[a]	13,969,000
2004[a]	13,313,000
2005[a]	14,765,000
2006[a]	16,039,000
2007[a]	16,165,000
2008[a]	15,939,000
2009	14,915,000
2010[a]	15,007,000
2011[a]	16,427,000
2012[a]	15,518,000
2013[a]	17,920,000
2014[a]	22,033,000
2015[b]	23,600,000
2016[b]	27,500,000

[a]http://data.worldbank.org/indicator/ST.INT.ARVL?year_low_desc=true
[b]http://www.tradingeconomics.com/greece/tourist-arrivals

Greek National Tourism Organization (GNTO) under the supervision of the Ministry of Tourism is charged with the promotion and advertising of Greek tourism within Greece and abroad through the implementation of marketing programs, advertising campaigns (mass media and social networks), participation in tourism exhibitions, cooperation with tour operators, and dissemination of information in the GNTO webpage (visitgreece.com) (Annual Tourism Reporting Greece 2013). Up until 2009, most promotional activities of GNTO) had focused on creating a certain image for Greece as a summer holiday destination with great beaches and a rich cultural heritage (Acropolis, Olympia) (Kouris 2009). An evaluation of the communication strategies of GNTO revealed that from 2000 to 2009, GNTO changed its advertising campaigns and slogans eight times (*That's Life, Beyond Words, A New Point of View, Live Your Myth in Greece, The True Experience, Explore Your Senses, Greece 5000 Years Old: A Masterpiece You Can Afford, Kalimera*). As Table 2 shows, up to 2009, the key themes of the advertising campaigns were sea, sun, summer, culture/archeological attractions, nightlife, Greek local cuisine and traditional restaurants (taverns), and romance. Moreover, these campaigns generated stereotypical pictures and associations such as the image of Greek "Zorba" (locals who dance the Greek traditional dance of sirtaki). According to the GNTO's 2009 evaluation of the communication strategies used up until then, Greece promoted an old-fashioned, inconsistent national identity which was related to few types of tourism (summer holidays and heritage tourism) and was not differentiated from the images of competing destinations (e.g., Turkey, Spain, Egypt) that were more

Table 2 Promotional campaigns by Greek tourism national organization (2000–2015)

Campaign	Key themes
Greece: That's life	Summer, sea, beaches, sand islands, wine tourism
Greece: Beyond words	Summer, sea, sailing, local cuisine, byzantine heritage, culture/archeological attractions, theatre, water sports, group activities
Athens, Attica, Greece: A new point of view	Culture/archeological attractions, entertainment, Athens, Olympics, nightlife
Live your myth in Greece	Sea, beaches, sun, islands, acropolis, nightlife, "Zorba"
Greece: The true experience	Sea, sailing, culture/archeological attractions, countryside, wellness, luxury, meetings, city breaks
Explore your senses	Sand, beaches, sea, sailing, mountains (Meteora), nightlife, entertainment, romance
Greece 5000 years old: a masterpiece you can afford	Sun, summer, sand, locals, Olympic, romance, Syntagma, nightlife
Greece: Kalimera!	Sun, sea, local cuisine, romance, wine tourism, archeological attractions, new acropolis museum,
You in Greece	Sea, beaches, visitors' testimonials, summer, Greek restaurants (taverns), nightlife, luxury hotels, spa, golf tourism, diving, family-oriented, sea-sports, Mykonos, culture/archeological attractions
Gods, myths, heroes	Archeological attractions, sand, sea, beaches, sailing, wine tourism, locals, local cuisine, Greek restaurants (taverns), entertainment, nightlife, Greek traditions, winter tourism, wildlife, Olympics, churches, mountains, Greek dance (sirtaki)
Happening now, #greeksummer	Sea, beaches, sun, summer, sailing, local cuisine, Greek restaurants (taverns), churches, islands, entertainment

affordable (Communication Strategy of Greece 2013). This fragmented image of Greece was further damaged due to the economic crisis (Bisa 2013). The need for repositioning the brand of Greece was highlighted by Peter Economides (2011), a well-known brand strategist, who pinpointed that Greece needs to stop focusing only on beaches, heritage, and "Zorba." In 2008, Bozbay and Ozen (2008) conducted a survey of Turkish consumers regarding their perceptions of Greece as a tourism destination. Results suggested that Greece is perceived as a place with significant historical attractions, environmental beauty, and interesting local cuisine.

Acknowledging the need for re-branding the image of Greece, the GNTO initiated in 2010 a new campaign under the slogan "You in Greece" that was based on tourists' testimonials and aimed at positioning Greece as a "four-season destination" offering different types of tourism services. In the following years, GNTO continued to communicate the re-branded identity of Greece as a destination that can attract different types of tourists (winter tourists, recreation tourists, culinary tourists, wine tourists, sports tourists, religious tourists, adventure tourists). Moreover, endorsing new media's critical role in all stages of a traveler's experience (information search, choice of destination, evaluation, and post-visit behavior) (Hays et al. 2013), GNTO turned also to online platforms (Vazou 2014) in order to boost the "new image" of Greece. In 2015, GNTO launched the online campaign "Happening Now,

#greeksummer" aiming to attract online travelers and engage them by sharing their Greek summer experiences. The use of social media continued in 2016 when GNTO started the "Now is the Time" campaign that aimed to enhance online booking via the nowisthetime.gr webpage by urging online users to "book now" and redirecting them to the site of tripadvisor.com. Moreover, in order to increase awareness and engagement of users, a social media contest was initiated where users were nudged to share the photos from the nowisthetime.gr webpage in their Facebook accounts and win a 4-day trip (three nights) to Greece, for two persons.

It still remains to be seen whether the efforts of GNTO have altered tourists' perceptions of Greece as a destination. Toward this end the present study seeks to address the current perceptions and impressions of tourists for Greece.

4 Conceptual Framework

Destination image can affect perceptions and behaviors of tourists at any stage of the tourist experience (Agapito et al. 2013). According to Tasci and Gartner (2007), destination image can affect the pre-visit stage, the stage during the visit, as well as the post-visit stage of the experience. Specifically, destination could influence the information searching process, the visit intentions and destination choice, as well the tourists' feelings of anticipation prior to the visit. During the visit, destination image can affect tourists' evaluations (i.e., satisfaction) and emotions (i.e., enjoyment). Moreover, after the visit, destination image could affect tourists' revisit intentions, word-of-mouth behavior, and intentions to recommend the place to others. The present study will focus on the effects of destination image during the post-visit stage of the tourist experience and thus will draw a link between the cognitive and conative aspects of destination image.

A number of studies have explored the effect of destination image on tourists' behavioral intentions. For example, Chen and Tsai (2007) found that destination image is positively related to tourists' behavioral intentions (intentions to revisit and recommend the destination). In another study, Prayag (2009), examining visitors to the island of Mauritius, found that destination image had a significant effect on their future behavior. Zhang et al. (2014) in a meta-analysis of 66 destination image studies revealed that the cognitive image of a destination is a significant predictor of attitudinal (intention to recommend) and behavioral loyalty (intentions to revisit). Based on the above, the following two hypotheses were developed:

H1 The cognitive component of destination image will positively influence tourists' intentions to revisit Greece.

H2 The cognitive component of destination image will positively influence tourists' intentions to recommend Greece to others.

Figure 2 illustrates the conceptual model that will be tested by the present study.

Fig. 2 Conceptual model

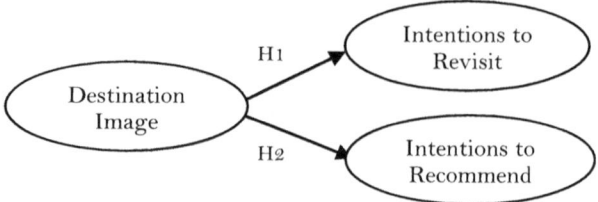

5 Methodology and Results

5.1 Measures

In order to measure tourists' cognitive destination image, the 18-item scale of Driscoll et al. (1994) was used. Specifically, respondents were asked to evaluate the 18 cognitive image attributes on five-point Likert scales ranging from (1) strongly disagree to (5) strongly agree. Behavioral intentions were measured using two items: intentions to revisit the destination and intentions to recommend the destination to others following Wang and Hsu (2010). These two items were rated on five-point scales with anchors (1) definitely would not and (5) definitely would. Finally, respondents indicated their demographic characteristics (gender, age, marital status, occupation, and nationality) as well as the number of their previous visits to the destination.

5.2 Data Collection and Profile of Respondents

A paper-and-pencil survey was conducted using a self-administered questionnaire that was delivered to foreign tourists who visited Athens during June and July 2015. Respondents were contacted on various touristic areas in Athens (outside the Acropolis museum, the Syntagma square, and Plaka). In total, 146 tourists answered the questionnaire. The sample characteristics are shown in Table 3.

Based on Table 3, most respondents were females (56.2%), single (54.8%), and aged between 18 and 35 years old (60.3%). Moreover, 47.3% of the respondents were private sector employees and 52.7% of them had visited Greece more the three times in the past. Regarding their nationality, most respondents came from the United States (20.5%), Australia (15.8%), and Italy (8.2%).

Table 4 presents the descriptive statistics (mean values and standard deviation) of the cognitive image items in a descending order.

Based on Table 4, it can be argued that, in general, tourists had a favorable impression for Greece as a destination. Specifically, attributes related to the cultural resources (M = 4.47, SD = 0.82), climate (M = 4.38, SD = 0.83), natural landscapes (M = 4.34, SD = 0.87), friendliness of locals (M = 4.30, SD = 0.85), and nightlife (M = 4.25, SD = 0.92) received the highest mean scores compared to

Table 3 Characteristics of the sample

Variable	Percentages	Variable	Percentages
Gender		Marital status	
Male	43.8	Single	54.8
Female	56.2	Married	41.1
		Divorced	4.1
Age		Occupation	
18–25 years	21.9	Freelancer	7.5
26–35 years	38.4	Unemployed	2.1
36–45 years	14.4	Private sector employee	47.3
46–55 years	15.8	Civil sector employee	16.4
Over 56 years	9.6	Student	17.8
		Other	8.9
Nationality		Number of previous visits	
United States	20.5	First time	19.9
Australia	15.8	2–3 previous visits	27.8
Italy	8.2	More than 3 previous visits	52.7
Germany	5.5		
Russia	4.8		
Romania	4.8		
Others[a]	40.4		

[a]Others include tourists from Belgium, the United Kingdom, Turkey, Sweden, Poland, Peru, Hungary, Ukraine, New Zealand, Malta, China, Spain, Ireland, Switzerland, Denmark, and France

Table 4 Descriptive statistics of cognitive image items

Items	Mean values	Standard deviations
Culturally interesting	4.47	0.823
Good climate	4.38	0.832
Natural landscape	4.34	0.874
Friendly people	4.30	0.850
Good nightlife/entertainment	4.25	0.921
Family-oriented destination	4.11	0.840
Safe for tourists	4.05	0.905
A different experience	4.03	0.838
An exotic place	3.99	0.939
Outdoor activities	3.96	0.846
Of religious interest	3.82	0.930
Modern facilities	3.76	0.857
Good value for money	3.75	0.931
A modern society	3.71	0.888
Easy access	3.71	0.903
Good shopping facilities	3.60	0.818
Organized activities	3.53	0.872
Clean environment	3.33	1.004

the other destination attributes. These findings are consistent with the earlier work of Baloglu and Mangaloglu (2001) who also found that Greece's cultural attractions, climate, and friendliness received high favorable ratings. On the contrary, the cleanliness of the environment, the satisfaction from organized activities, as well as Greece's shopping facilities received the lowest mean scores.

5.3   Data Analysis

First, an exploratory factor analysis was conducted to reveal the dimensionality and the internal structure of the cognitive image scale. The principal component analysis with varimax rotation technique was used to extract the cognitive image factors. Three items (i.e., exotic place, modern society, and religious interest) were dropped from further analysis as they exhibited factor loadings lower than 0.40. The remaining 15 items were factor analyzed again. Table 5 shows the results of the factor analysis as well as the descriptive statistics (mean and standard deviation) of the cognitive image items. Four factors with eigenvalues greater that 1.0 were retained. These factors explained the 77.22% of the total variance. Specifically, the first factor *natural and cultural resources* included items such as natural landscape, good climate, safety, and culturally interesting. The second factor was named

Table 5 Factor loadings of cognitive image items

	Factors			
Items	Natural and cultural resources	Tourist infrastructure	Leisure and recreation	Experience and value
Natural landscape	0.822			
Good climate	0.795			
Safe for tourists	0.766			
Culturally interesting	0.714			
Clean environment		0.770		
Modern facilities		0.757		
Organized activities		0.696		
Good shopping facilities		0.676		
Good nightlife/ entertainment			0.822	
Outdoor activities			0.725	
Friendly people			0.700	
Family-oriented destination			0.562	
Good value for money				0.865
Easy access				0.721
A different experience				0.549
Cumulative variance (%)	23.12	41.60	59.42	73.22
Cronbach's α	0.88	0.85	0.78	0.80

leisure/recreation and was composed of the following items: good nightlife/enter-tainment, plenty of outdoor activities, friendly people, and family-oriented destina-tion, while the third factor was *tourist infrastructure* and included items such as modern facilities, good shopping facilities, clean environment, and organized activ-ities. Lastly, the fourth factor was named *experience and value* and was comprised of three items, namely, a different experience, good value for money, and easy access. This factor is related to the psychological attributes of a destination's cognitive image (Echtner and Ritchie 1993). All items had factor loadings above 0.56 and exhibited adequate internal consistency as the Cronbach's alpha values ranged from 0.78 to 0.88 and exceeded the 0.70 criterion suggested by Nunnally and Bernstein (1994).

Next, four summative scales were developed for each factor by adding the items that comprise them. These summative scales were then used in order to test the two hypotheses. Correlation analyses using the Pearson's r correlation coefficient were conducted to test the study's hypotheses. Results are presented in Table 6.

There was a positive correlation between tourists' intentions to revisit the desti-nation and the cognitive image factors of cultural/natural resources ($r = 0.249$, $p = 0.002$), leisure/recreation ($r = 0.261$, $p = 0.001$), and experience/value ($r = 0.218$, $p = 0.008$). On the contrary, no correlation was found between the image factor of tourist infrastructure and revisit intentions ($r = 0.092$, $p = 0.272$). Thus, the attributes related to the cultural/natural resources, leisure/recreation ame-nities, and experience/value of a destination are positively related to tourists' revisit intentions. However, the above relationships were weak in strength.

Similar findings were observed in regard to the effect of the four cognitive image factors on intentions to recommend the destination. Specifically, a positive correla-tion was found between tourists' intentions to recommend the destination and the factors of cultural/natural resources ($r = 0.326$, $p = 0.000$), leisure/recreation ($r = 0.253$, $p = 0.002$), and experience/value ($r = 0.353$, $p = 0.00$). No correlation ($p > 0.01$) was found between the factor of tourist infrastructure and intentions to recommend the destination ($r = 0.168$, $p = 0.043$). Hence, WOM intentions of tourists are influenced in a moderate extent by tourists' perceptions about the cultural/natural resources, leisure/recreation amenities, and experience/value of a destination. Perceived experience/value of the destination proved to be the most influential factor on tourists' WOM intentions. It should be noted that the above three factors exerted stronger influence on intentions to recommend than intentions

Table 6 Results of correlation analyses

	Revisit intentions	Intentions to recommend
Factors	Pearson's r coefficient (*p*-value)	
Cultural and natural resources	0.249* (0.002)	0.326* (0.000)
Leisure and recreation	0.261* (0.001)	0.253* (0.002)
Tourist infrastructure	0.092 (0.272)	0.168 (0.043)
Experience and value	0.218* (0.008)	0.353* (0.000)

*Significant at the 0.01 level

to revisit based on the values of Pearson's r coefficient. Hypotheses 1 and 2 were partially supported for the three out of four cognitive image factors.

6   Conclusions

The present study examined the current tourists' perceptions of the Greece's cognitive image as a destination and tested the impact of the different cognitive image dimensions on tourists' behavioral intentions. Results indicated that despite the re-branding efforts of GNTO, Greece is still perceived as a destination for heritage and leisure tourism. This could be attributed to two main reasons (a) entrenched attitudes that are difficult to change and (b) failure of GNTO's promotional activities to project a differentiated image in the international tourism marketplace.

The study also shed light on the multidimensionality of the cognitive component of destination image. Consistent with other studies, the cognitive aspect of destination image is multidimensional in nature (Baloglu and McCleary 1999; Fakeye and Crompton 1991, Obenour et al. 2005; Hui and Wan 2003) comprising of four factors, namely, natural/cultural resources, leisure/recreation, tourist infrastructure, and experience/value. This four-factor solution exhibited high internal reliability and explained a large proportion of the data variance.

The present study also tested the impact of the different cognitive image factors on tourists' behavioral intentions as reflected in their intentions to revisit Greece and recommend the destination to others. Findings suggested that not all cognitive image factors exerted influence on tourists' revisit intentions. More specifically, the tourist infrastructure factor that was related to the tourist and shopping facilities did not influence behavioral intentions. Moreover, the effects of the remaining three factors were different for revisit intentions and intentions to recommend. For example, intentions to revisit Greece were primarily affected by the leisure/entertainment factor followed by experience/value and cultural/natural factors. On the other hand, intentions to recommend were influenced mainly by the experience/value and the cultural/natural resources and to a lesser extent by the leisure/recreation factor.

However, the effects of the three factors on behavioral intentions of tourists were found to be weak in strength. This poor "predictability" of the cognitive image factors was also found in the study of Stylos et al. (2016) and was attributed to the partial mediation of tourists' holistic image perceptions. Thus, it can be argued the holistic "overall" image of Greece as perceived by tourists—that was not measured in the present study—could be a mediating variable between the cognitive image factors and behavioral intentions.

This study has several managerial implications for managers of tourist destinations wishing to increase the loyalty of tourists to their destination. Destination managers should take into consideration the cognitive image factors that impact on tourists' behavioral intentions in designing their promotional messages. Specifically, two different promotional messages could be designed based on the desired outcome. For example, to entice repeat visits, messages should mainly position Greece as a destination for recreation and heritage tourism. This could be done by including content that shows the Greek nightlife and friendliness of locals combined with the outdoor and family activities in which tourists can engage when visiting Greece. In addition, these messages should simultaneously but to a lesser extent show images of the cultural heritage, the natural resources and the good climate of Greece. Greece should also be promoted as a "safe" destination for tourists in order to increase their behavioral loyalty. To enhance tourists' intentions to engage in WOM with others, a different blend of cognitive image attributes should be conveyed in the promotional messages. These messages should primarily promote Greece as a destination with good value for money where tourists can live an "authentic and alternative experience." Hence, promotional messages should place emphasis on the economic as well as the experiential value of a trip to Greece. In addition, messages should include snapshots of the Greece's culture and natural environment. This way, tourists will be more willing to share with others their experience in Greece.

7   Limitations and Future Research Suggestions

A main limitation of the study is related to the small sample size (n = 149) and the convenience sampling procedure that was used to collect responses. Therefore results should be interpreted with care as they are not representative of the study's population (foreign tourists to Greece). Another limitation stems from the measurement of the cognitive image. A limited number of attributes (18 items) was used to assess Greece's image. It is herein suggested that future researchers could use a more exhaustive list of attributes that capture in a more complete way the variety of the characteristics of Greece's tourism product.

This study focused only on the cognitive component of destination image. Future research could enrich the conceptual model by including all the components of destination image (cognitive, affective, conative, and overall) and their interrelations as well, thereby adopting a more holistic approach to examining the effects of destination image on tourists' behavioral intentions. In addition, adding the impact of social media as information sources on destination image, in the conceptual model, could also yield fruitful implications regarding the possible effect of social media in destination image formation process.

References

Agapito, D., Valle, P. O., & Mendes, J. C. (2013). The cognitive-affective-conative model of destination image: A confirmatory analysis. *Journal of Travel & Tourism Marketing, 30*(5), 471–481.

Annual Tourism Reporting Greece. (2013). Retrieved from http://ec.europa.eu/DocsRoom/docu ments/5957/attachments/1/translations/en/renditions/native

Baloglu, S. (2000). A path analytic model of visitation intention involving information sources, socio-psychological motivations, and destination image. *Journal of Travel & Tourism Marketing, 8*(3), 81–90.

Baloglu, S., & Mangaloglu, M. (2001). Tourism destination images of Turkey, Egypt, Greece, and Italy as perceived by US-based tour operators and travel agents. *Tourism Management, 22*(1), 1–9.

Baloglu, S., & McCleary, K. W. (1999). A model of destination image formation. *Annals of Tourism Research, 26*(4), 868–897.

Beerli, A., & Martin, J. D. (2004). Factors influencing destination image. *Annals of Tourism Research, 31*(3), 657–681.

Bisa, S. (2013). Rebranding Greece: Why nation branding matters. *Exchange: The Journal of Public Diplomacy, 4*(1), 61–67.

Bozbay, Z., & Ozen, H. (2008). The assessment of Greece's image as a tourism destination. *MIBES: Transactions, 2*(1), 14–27.

Chen, C., & Tsai, D. (2007). How destination image and evaluative factors affect behavioral intentions? *Tourism Management, 28*(4), 1115–1122.

Chi, C., & Qu, H. (2008). Examining the structural relationships of destination image, tourist satisfaction and destination loyalty: An integrated approach. *Tourism Management, 29*(4), 624–636.

Communication Strategy of Greece. (2013). Retrieved from http://www.eot.gr/sites/default/files/files_article/communication%20strategy_2010-2013_new_low.pdf

Driscoll, A., Lawson, R., & Niven, B. (1994). Measuring tourists' destination perceptions. *Annals of Tourism Research, 21*(3), 499–511.

Echtner, C. M., & Ritchie, J. B. (1993). The measurement of destination image: An empirical assessment. *Journal of Travel Research, 31*(4), 3–13.

Economides, P. (2011). Retrieved from http://brandinggreece.com/re-branding-greece-speech-by-peter-economides/

Fakeye, P. C., & Crompton, J. L. (1991). Image differences between prospective, first-time, and repeat visitors to the lower Rio Grande Valley. *Journal of Travel Research, 30*(2), 10–16.

Gallarza, M. G., Saura, I. G., & García, H. C. (2002). Destination image: Towards a conceptual framework. *Annals of Tourism Research, 29*(1), 56–78.

Gartner, W. C. (1994). Image formation process. *Journal of Travel & Tourism Marketing, 2*(2–3), 191–216.

Gertner, D., & Kotler, P. (2004). How can a place correct a negative image? *Place Branding and Public Diplomacy, 1*(1), 50–57.

Greece Tourist Arrivals. Retrieved from http://www.tradingeconomics.com/greece/tourist-arrivals

Hays, S., Page, S. J., & Buhalis, D. (2013). Social media as a destination marketing tool: Its use by National Tourism Organisations. *Current Issues in Tourism, 16*(3), 211–239.

Hui, T. K., & Wan, T. W. D. (2003). Singapore's image as a tourist destination. *International Journal of Tourism Research, 5*(4), 305–313.

International Tourism. *Number of arrivals*. Retrieved from http://data.worldbank.org/indicator/ST.INT.ARVL?year_low_desc=true

Kaplanidou, K. (2009). Relationships among behavioral intentions, cognitive event and destination images among different geographic regions of Olympic games spectators. *Journal of Sport & Tourism, 14*(4), 249–272.

Kokkali, P., Koutsouris, A., & Chrysochou, P. (2011). *Tourism destination image (TDI): The case of Pertouli*, Greece.

Kouris, A. (2009). Destination brand strategy: The case of Greece. In Cai et al. (Eds.), *Tourism branding: Communities in action (Bridging tourism theory and practice)* (Vol. 1, pp. 161–175). Bingley: Emerald Group.

Llodrà-Riera, I., Martínez-Ruiz, M. P., Jiménez-Zarco, A. I., & Izquierdo-Yusta, A. (2015). A multidimensional analysis of the information sources construct and its relevance for destination image formation. *Tourism Management, 48*, 319–328.

Martín-Santana, J. D., Beerli-Palacio, A., & Nazzareno, P. A. (2017). Antecedents and conse-quences of destination image gap. *Annals of Tourism Research, 62*, 13–25.

Nunnally, J., & Bernstein, I. (1994). *Psychometric theory* (3rd ed.). New York: McGraw-Hill.

Obenour, W., Lengfelder, J., & Groves, D. (2005). The development of a destination through the image assessment of six geographic markets. *Journal of Vacation Marketing, 11*(2), 107–119.

Papadimitriou, D., Kaplanidou, K., & Apostolopoulou, A. (2015). Destination personality, affective image, and behavioral intentions in domestic urban tourism. *Journal of Travel Research, 54*(3), 302–315.

Prayag, G. (2009). Tourists' evaluations of destination image, satisfaction, and future behavioral intentions—The case of Mauritius. *Journal of Travel & Tourism Marketing, 26*(8), 836–853.

San Martín, H., & Del Bosque, I. (2008). Exploring the cognitive–affective nature of destination image and the role of psychological factors in its formation. *Tourism Management, 29*(2), 263–277.

SETE. (2016). *Greek tourism: Developments-prospects*, Issue 1.

Stylos, N., Vassiliadis, C. A., Bellou, V., & Andronikidis, A. (2016). Destination images, holistic images and personal normative beliefs: Predictors of intention to revisit a destination. *Tourism Management, 53*, 40–60.

Tasci, A. D., & Gartner, W. C. (2007). Destination image and its functional relationships. *Journal of Travel Research, 45*(4), 413–425.

Tasci, A. D., Gartner, W. C., & Cavusgil, S. T. (2007). Conceptualization and operationalization of destination image. *Journal of Hospitality & Tourism Research, 31*(2), 194–223.

Vazou, E. (2014). From posters to posts: Greece moves beyond tourism campaigns to eDestination branding. *International Journal of Cultural and Digital Tourism, 1*(1), 38–52.

Vitouladiti, O. (2013). The comparison of secondary and primary tourism destination image: Serving as a bridge between expectation and experience and guiding effective marketing and management strategies. *Tourismos: An International Multidisciplinary Journal of Tourism, 8*(1), 53–91.

Wang, C. Y., & Hsu, M. K. (2010). The relationships of destination image, satisfaction, and behavioral intentions: An integrated model. *Journal of Travel & Tourism Marketing, 27*(8), 829–843.

Yannas, P., & Simeli, I. (2012). The destination image of Thessaloniki. In *Proceedings of International Conference on Contemporary Marketing Issues, Thessaloniki* (pp. 672–677).

Zacharia, A., & Spais, G. (2017). Holiday destination image and personality of a Greek Island during an economic recession period and the intermediate effect of the utilitarian and non-utilitarian needs. *Journal of Promotion Management, 23*, 1–22.

Zhang, H., Fu, X., Cai, L. A., & Lu, L. (2014). Destination image and tourist loyalty: A meta-analysis. *Tourism Management, 40*, 213–223.

A Differential Equations Analysis of Stock Prices

Georgios Katsouleas, Miltiadis Chalikias, Michalis Skordoulis, and Georgios Sidiropoulos

Abstract Stock price analysis is one of the most important issues concerning investments and financial decision-making. Thus, stock price analysis and estimation models can be very useful in the estimation of a firm's financial development. The aim of this paper is to propose a model of differential equations that will be able to be applied in the case of stock price analysis and estimation. The differential equations model will be based on Lanchester's combat model, a mathematical theory of war. In the field of business, such operations research models have been used in cases such as competition analysis and resources allocation optimization. The case to be examined in this paper refers to the healthcare services index stocks of the Athens Stock Exchange. A 7×7 differential equations model was developed to analyze the examined firms' stocks.

Keywords Stock price analysis · Stock price estimation · Differential equations · Athens Stock Exchange · Stock modeling

1 Introduction

A stock market is a public market to trade firms' stocks and derivatives at an approved stock price (Preethi and Santhi 2012). Moreover, it is affected by factors that are related to financial and political stability of each country and market expectation. These factors can influence stock price variation (Zhou et al. 2008a, b).

Stock price prediction is one of the main important subjects in investment and financial decision-making (Shi et al. 2012; Zhang et al. 2016). According to

G. Katsouleas · M. Chalikias · M. Skordoulis (✉) · G. Sidiropoulos
Department of Accounting and Finance, Piraeus University of Applied Sciences, Egaleo, Greece

© Springer Nature Switzerland AG 2019
N. Sykianakis et al. (eds.), *Economic and Financial Challenges for Eastern Europe*,
Springer Proceedings in Business and Economics,
https://doi.org/10.1007/978-3-030-12169-3_23

361

Diacogiannis (1996), stock price prediction models are very useful in order to investigate a possible corporate failure. Stock price prediction also involves the analysis of stock price series and the optimization of regression models (Kim and Kil 2013).

Spilioti (2016) indicated that key macroeconomic and psychological variables define the differences between predicted and realized stock prices.

Statistical results indicate that in the Athens Stock Exchange, investors are influenced by unpleasant and psychological factors as optimism and pessimism, and this fact can make stock prices to reflect the condition of the economy (Niarchos and Alexakis 2000).

Wenling Yang and Parwada (2012) in their research concluded that many variables such as the stocks net prices, the time between stock trades, the trade size, the trade imbalance, and the return on index are statistically significant almost for all stocks.

Glezakos et al. (2008) state that macroeconomic data, phases of the market, the maturity degree and the trade volume, the business profits, progress technology, globalization of markets, and the political situation of every country highly affect stock prices.

On the other hand, Kyriakides et al. (2016) concluded that in financial stock markets, the forecast of prices movements won't be attained because of the size of the market, the great liquidity, and the "dark pools."

Several empirical studies highlight the different methods that can estimate the stock prices. Mantegna's (1999) equation can calculate the daily logarithmic changes of every stock, for every day of the year as follows:

$$R_{i(t)} = lnP_{i(t)} - lnR_{i(t-1)} \tag{1}$$

On the other hand, Martikainen (1991) used the natural logarithm and concluded that stock returns and prices were connected to a firm's long-term profitability and capital structure on a cross-sectional level. The model is the following:

$$R_{i(t)} = log\, P_{i(t)} - log\, P_{i(t-1)} \tag{2}$$

Park and Shin (2013) developed a new method that didn't forecast stock prices based on the time series like other models, but it is possible to predict the stock price using a network by considering the economic indicator which changes the stock price and the range of other companies' stock prices.

Shi et al. (2012) combined autoregressive and moving average (ARMA), back-propagation neural network (BPNN), and Markov model, and they've created a new hybrid model, which is called ARMA-BPNN model, and it is considered to be a better method for stock price prediction.

Chih-Ming Hsu (2011) proposed a new hybrid model derived from a combination of self-organizing map (SOM) neural network and genetic programming (GP), which is named as SOMGP and considered that this model is effective and can be applied to stock price prediction.

Ballings et al. (2015) recommended random forest for stock price direction.

A different approach concerning the prediction of a market's data is based on warfare differential equations models. Warfare models based on differential equations have been used during WWI and WWII. By the end of the 1940s, such mathematical models were applied for first time in business cases.

The aim of this paper is to illustrate the healthcare services index stocks of the Athens Stock Exchange using a generalized differential equations model based on Lanchester's combat model.

Generalizations of this model have already been applied in business cases (Chalikias et al. 2016a, b). Chalikias and Skordoulis (2016) have used Lanchester's model in order to examine the supply chain in a duopoly. The differential equations model is the following:

$$\begin{bmatrix} \dfrac{dx}{dt} = -ay + f(t) \\ \dfrac{dy}{dt} = -bx + g(t) \end{bmatrix} \tag{3}$$

where $x(t)$ and $y(t)$ are the number of available product units for sale of firm A and firm B, respectively, $f(t)$ and $g(t)$ are the rates at which the available for sale product units are increasing and decreasing, and $ay(t)$, $ay(t)$, and $bx(t)$ are the rates of the available for sale product. Their research results indicate that model's fitting is very good to the examined case.

2   Differential Equations Model Formulation

Private health services in Greece include diagnostics centers and clinics, which are included, respectively, in primary and secondary healthcare. In the private health sector, the five largest groups account for 53% of all the market (ICAP 2016). This market consists of seven firms: Axon, Euromedica, Hygeia, Iaso, Iatriko Athinon, Lavipharm, and Medicon Hellas. Thus a 7×7 differential equations model will be developed.

Stock data used in this study were drawn from daily data files of the Athens Stock Exchange for the period from January 1 to December 1, 2015.

In order to construct the model describing the mentioned data, we use the variables T, U, V, W, X, Y, and Z which represent the stock prices of the seven companies examined. Furthermore we use a, b, c, d, e, f, and g to describe the firms' market quotas. So we have the following 7×7 differential equations model:

$$
\begin{cases}
\dfrac{dT}{dt} = \dfrac{b}{a}U + \dfrac{c}{a}V + \dfrac{d}{a}W + \dfrac{e}{a}X + \dfrac{f}{a}Y + \dfrac{g}{a}Z \\[2mm]
\dfrac{dU}{dt} = \dfrac{a}{b}T + \dfrac{c}{b}V + \dfrac{d}{b}W + \dfrac{e}{b}X + \dfrac{f}{b}Y + \dfrac{g}{b}Z \\[2mm]
\dfrac{dV}{dt} = \dfrac{a}{c}T + \dfrac{b}{c}U + \dfrac{d}{c}W + \dfrac{e}{c}X + \dfrac{f}{c}Y + \dfrac{g}{c}Z \\[2mm]
\dfrac{dW}{dt} = \dfrac{a}{d}T + \dfrac{b}{d}U + \dfrac{c}{d}V + \dfrac{e}{d}X + \dfrac{f}{d}Y + \dfrac{g}{d}Z \\[2mm]
\dfrac{dX}{dt} = \dfrac{a}{e}T + \dfrac{b}{e}U + \dfrac{c}{e}V + \dfrac{d}{e}W + \dfrac{f}{e}Y + \dfrac{g}{e}Z \\[2mm]
\dfrac{dY}{dt} = \dfrac{a}{f}T + \dfrac{b}{f}U + \dfrac{c}{f}V + \dfrac{d}{f}W + \dfrac{e}{f}X + \dfrac{g}{f}Z \\[2mm]
\dfrac{dZ}{dt} = \dfrac{a}{g}T + \dfrac{b}{g}U + \dfrac{c}{g}V + \dfrac{d}{g}W + \dfrac{e}{g}X + \dfrac{f}{g}Y
\end{cases}
\tag{4}
$$

The mathematical solution of the above model will lead to the understanding of how the examined market shares' prices evolve; thus, the stocks' prices forecast will become feasible as well.

3 Conclusions

Predicting stock prices is very important in investment and financial decision-making. Thus, many researches have used mathematical models to analyze and predict stocks' prices. The model proposed in this paper is a generalization of Lanchester's combat model which is based on differential equations. Such models have been successfully used in business cases by numerous authors. In order to examine the prediction ability of the proposed model, its results predictions have to be statistically analyzed and compared with the empirical observations.

References

Ballings, M., Van den Poel, D., Hespeels, N., & Gryp, R. (2015). Evaluating multiple classifiers for stock price direction prediction. *Expert Systems with Applications, 42*(20), 7046–7056.

Chalikias, M., & Skordoulis, M. (2016). Implementation of F.W. Lanchester's combat model in a supply chain in duopoly: The case of Coca-Cola and Pepsi in Greece. *Operational Research: An International Journal, 17*(3), 737–745. https://doi.org/10.1007/s12351-016-0226-0.

Chalikias, M., Lalou, P., & Skordoulis, M. (2016a). Modeling advertising expenditures using differential equations: The case of an oligopoly data set. *International Journal of Applied Mathematics and Statistics, 55*(2), 23–31.

Chalikias, M., Lalou, P., & Skordoulis, M. (2016b). Modeling a bank data set using differential equations: The case of the Greek banking sector. In *Proceedings of 5th International Symposium and 27th National Conference of HEL.O.R.S on Operation Research* (pp. 113–116). Piraeus, June 2016. Piraeus: Piraeus University of Applied Sciences.

Diacogiannis, G. (1996). The usefulness of share prices and inflation for corporate failure prediction. *SPOUDAI, 46*(3–4), 135–156.

Glezakos, M., Merika, A., & Georga, P. (2008). The measurement of share price volatility in the Athens Stock Exchange. *SPOUDAI, 58*(1–2), 11–30.

Hsu, C. M. (2011). A hybrid procedure for stock price prediction by integrating self-organizing map and genetic programming. *Expert Systems with Applications, 38*(11), 14026–14036.

ICAP Group. (2016). *Leading sectors of the Greek economy.* Athens: ICAP Group.

Kim, D. K., & Kil, R. M. (2013). Stock price prediction based on a network with Gaussian Kernel functions. In *International Conference on Neural Information Processing* (pp. 705–712). Berlin: Springer.

Kyriakides, G., Talattinis, K., Kyrmanidou, M., Ioulianou, M., & Stephanides, G. (2016). Assessing the predictive ability of a market's order book. A study on sports bet exchange. In *Proceedings of 5th International Symposium and 27th National Conference of HEL.O.R.S on Operation Research* (pp. 138–142). Piraeus, June 2016. Piraeus: Piraeus University of Applied Sciences.

Mantegna, R. N. (1999). Hierarchical structure in financial markets. *The European Physical Journal B-Condensed Matter and Complex Systems, 11*(1), 193–197.

Martikainen, T. (1991). Modelling stock price behaviour by financial ratios. *Studies in Financial Modelling, 12*(1), 119–138.

Niarchos, A., & Alexakis, C. (2000). The predictive power of macroeconomic variables on stock market returns. The case of the Athens stock exchange. *SPOUDAI, 50*(1–2), 75–86.

Park, K., & Shin, H. (2013). Stock price prediction based on a complex interrelation network of economic factors. *Engineering Applications of Artificial Intelligence, 26*(5), 1550–1561.

Preethi, G., & Santhi, B. (2012). Stock market forecasting techniques: A survey. *Journal of Theoretical & Applied Information Technology, 46*(1), 24–30.

Shi, S., Liu, W., & Jin, M. (2012, November). Stock price forecasting using a hybrid ARMA and BP neural network and Markov model. In *2012 IEEE 14th International Conference on Communication Technology (ICCT)* (pp. 981–985). IEEE.

Spilioti, S. N. (2016). Does the sentiment of investors explain differences between predicted and realized stock prices? *Studies in Economics and Finance, 33*(3), 403–416.

Yang, J. W., & Parwada, J. (2012). Predicting stock price movements: An ordered Probit analysis on the Australian Securities Exchange. *Quantitative Finance, 12*(5), 791–804.

Zhang, X. D., Li, A., & Pan, R. (2016). Stock trend prediction based on a new status box method and AdaBoost probabilistic support vector machine. *Applied Soft Computing, 49*, 385–398.

Zhou, J., Bai, T., Zhang, A., & Tian, J. (2008a). The integrated methodology of wavelet transform and GA based-SVM for forecasting share price. In *International Conference on Information and Automation, 2008* (pp. 729–733). ICIA 2008. IEEE.

Zhou, J., Bai, T., & Suo, C. (2008b). The SVM optimized by culture genetic algorithm and its application in forecasting share price. In *IEEE International Conference on Granular Computing, 2008* (pp. 838–843). GrC 2008. IEEE.

Cash Conversion Cycle and Firms' Performance: An Empirical Study for the Greek Listed Firms in the Athens Stock Exchange

Petros Kalantonis, Spyridon Goumas, and Maria Rodosthenous

Abstract It is commonly accepted that economic crisis has a negative effect on firms' liquidity. Therefore, liquidity management has become critical for firms, in order to be able to pay their short-term debts. Cash conversion cycle is used in order to measure the average collection period and days of sales in inventories less days of payables outstanding (Keown et al., Foundations of finance: The logic and practice of Financial management. Upper Saddle River, NJ: Prentice Hall, 2003). The main purpose of this study is to explore the relationship between cash conversion cycle and firms' financial performance in the era of financial crisis. For this purpose, we selected a sample of listed firms in the Athens Stock Exchange for the years 2012–2014, and using OLS regression, we investigated the impact of CCC on firms' size. Our findings differ from those of relevant studies which explored firms in the periods before the financial crisis or firms of countries which have not been significantly affected by the financial crisis.

Keywords Cash conversion cycle · Profitability · Firms' size · Liquidity

1 Introduction

It is commonly accepted that efficient liquidity management is a crucial factor in firms' viability. Furthermore, cash management, which is based on the development of a balance between current assets and current liabilities, is important for firms to obtain an efficient liquidity. Current liabilities include the short-term debt of firms. Analysts evaluate firms' ability to pay off their short-term liabilities examining the adequacy of current assets such as the inventories, the cash, the marketable

P. Kalantonis (✉)
Faculty of Tourism Management, University of West Attica, Egaleo, Greece
e-mail: pkalant@uniwa.gr

S. Goumas · M. Rodosthenous
Faculty of Accounting and Finance, University of West Attica, Egaleo, Greece

© Springer Nature Switzerland AG 2019
N. Sykianakis et al. (eds.), *Economic and Financial Challenges for Eastern Europe*,
Springer Proceedings in Business and Economics,
https://doi.org/10.1007/978-3-030-12169-3_24

Table 1 Managers who deal with short-term financial problems

Title of manager	Duties related to short-term financial management	Assets/liabilities influenced
Cash manager	Collection, concentration, disbursement, short-term investments, short-term borrowing banking relations	Cash, marketable securities, short-term loans
Credit manager	Monitoring and control of accounts receivable, credit policy decisions	Accounts receivable
Marketing manager	Credit policy decisions	Accounts receivable
Purchasing manager	Decisions on purchases, suppliers, may negotiate payment terms	Inventory, accounts payable
Production manager	Setting of production schedules and materials requirements	Inventory accounts payable
Payables manager	Decisions on payment policies and on whether to take discounts	Accounts payable
Controller	Accounting information on cash flows, reconciliation of accounts payable, application of payments to account receivable	Accounts receivable, accounts payable

Source: N. C. Hill and W. L. Sartoris, *Short-Term Financial Management*, 2d ed. (New York: Macmillan, 1992), p. 15

securities, and also the trade credit (accounts receivable) (Brealey et al. 2001). In other words, the relation, between current assets and short-term liabilities, is the key factor for the evaluation of the ability of firms to pay off their debt to the creditors.

Working capital is an indicator for the short-term financial health of firms and measures the difference between the current assets of firms and their current liabilities. Moreover, it is important accounting information for managers, who deal with short-term financial problems, as they have appeared in Table 1 which have been adopted by Ross et al. (2003).

Cash conversion cycle is an important metric financial tool which contributes to the improvement of working capital management and measures. Richards and Laughlin (1980) defined it as "the net time interval between actual cash expenditures on a firms purchase of productive resources and the ultimate recovery of cash receipts from product sales," and they also stated that using cash conversion cycle, we can evaluate the interrelated cash inflow-outflow pattern.

Ross et al. (2003) have presented graphically the short-term operating activities and the cash conversion cycle of manufacturing firms (Fig. 1). As they explain, additionally, "the time period, from inventory purchase until the receipt of cash, is the operating cycle which may not include the time from placement of the order until arrival of the stock," and "the cash cycle is the time period from when cash is paid out to when cash is received."

During the past three decades, many research studies explored the relationship between the liquidity and profitability. Cash conversion cycle (CCC) was used as an indicator for the liquidity measurement. In this research study, we explore the effect of cash conversion cycle on firms' value and profitability in the early years of financial crisis in Greece. Due to the fact that previous research has not focused on

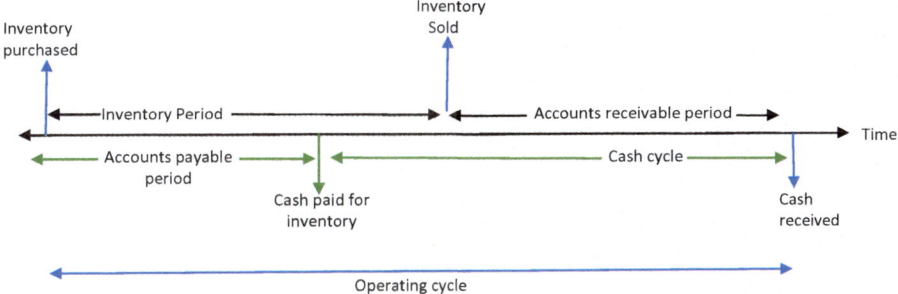

Fig. 1 Cash conversion cycle. Source: Ross et al. (2003): Fundamentals of Corporate Finance, Sixth Edition, Alternate Edition

economies which have been infected by the consequences of financial crisis, we will contribute in the research literature of cash conversion cycle studies examining if the cash management in the period of crisis affects firms' profitability and book value as it usually happens in non-emerging economies, according to the relevant research literature.

Our research study is structured as follows: in the next chapter, we will make a short literature review of relevant studies, and we will present definition approaches for cash conversion cycle. The research hypotheses and methodology are argued in Chapter "A Performance Measurement System for Staff of the Logistics Section: A Case Study for an Oil and Gas Company." We follow next with the analysis of our data and the discussion of our findings in chapter "Banks' Income Smoothing in the Basel Period: Evidence from European Union." The last chapter of this study includes the conclusion of the study.

2　Literature Review

The purpose of this study is to investigate the impact of cash conversion cycle on the profitability and firms' size. As we have already stated, cash conversion cycle has been defined as the length of time between cash inflow and outflow (Richards and Laughlin 1980). A similar approach to the cash conversion cycle definition describes CCC as the time difference between the firms' payment for their raw materials and the payments collection from their customers (Brealey et al. 2001). Since this approach concerns more on the manufacturing enterprises, the above authors stated also that "the longer the production process, the more the cash the firm must keep tied up in inventories." CCC has been expressed in the formula as follows:

$$Cash\ Conversion\ Cycle = (inventory\ period + receivable\ period)$$
$$- accounts\ payable\ period$$

Keown et al. (2003) and Uyar (2009) adopted a relevant formula in which three determinant variables of CCC are included:

$$Cash\ Conversion\ Cycle = Days\ of\ sales\ outstanding$$
$$+ Days\ of\ sales\ in\ inventory$$
$$- Days\ of\ payables\ outstanding$$

The determinant variables of the formula are explained as follows:

$$Cash\ Conversion\ Cycle = Days\ of\ sales\ outstanding$$
$$+ Days\ of\ sales\ in\ inventory$$
$$- Days\ of\ payables\ outstanding$$

$$Days\ of\ sales\ outstanding = \frac{Accounts\ receivable}{Sales/365}$$

$$Days\ of\ sales\ in\ inventory = \frac{Inventories}{Cost\ of\ goods\ sold/365}$$

$$Days\ of\ payables\ oustanding = \frac{Accounts\ payables}{Cost\ of\ goods\ sold/365}$$

The effect of cash conversion cycle on firms' performance has been explored in recent and past empirical studies. Specifically, Zakari and Sani (2016) searched for the effect of cash conversion cycle on corporate profitability of listed telecommunications firms in the Nigerian Stock Exchange for the period 2010–2014. Using Pearson correlation test, they found positive relationship between CCC and firms' profitability.

On the other side, Attari and Raza (2012), implementing the one-way ANOVA, have shown in the results of their study that CCC is correlated negatively with profitability and size of the manufacturing listed firms in Karachi Stock Exchange. In their research, they focused on automobile, cement, chemical, and food producers' firms for the period 2006–2010. An alternative approach for the determination of CCC effect on corporate profitability was adopted by Sabri (2012) who analyzed listed industrial firms in the Amman Stock Exchange for the period 2000–2007. More specifically, they applied the nonparametric test of Mann-Whitney and also the t-test to detect for significant difference between the profitability of firms with low CCC and of those with high CCC. They found evidence that CCC and profitability have an inverse relationship.

Also, Uyar (2009) has found evidence that CCC is correlated negatively with the size and profitability of listed merchandising and manufacturing firms of the Istanbul Stock Exchange for the year 2007. Moreover, Nobanee et al. (2011) examined the length of cash conversion cycle of Japanese firms from 1990 to 1994, and using the dynamic panel data regression, they investigated the relation between CCC and profitability of Japanese firms. They found a negative relation between the CCC and the return on investment (ROI) for the firms of all sectors except those of consumer goods and services.

Moreover, the return of invested capital, the asset turnover, the net balance position, and the invested capital have been used as dependent variables by Ebben and Johnson (2011) who investigated if the CCC and the liquidity level, the invested capital, and the financial performance of firms are related. Using a sample of small manufacturing US firms for the period 2002–2004, they stated that short cash conversion cycle maintenances lower levels of invested capital; it affects positively the financial performance of firms, and it is negatively related with liquidity.

The majority of the researchers argue that short length period of cash conversion cycle has positive effect on firms' financial performance. Their findings show on the one hand that the study of cash conversion cycle seems to improve the efficiency of cash management, and it also has a positive impact on firms' performance. However, these studies have not been focused on emerging economies. Besides, the test for the confirmation of the above studies' findings in Greek firms has been noticed in the aim of this study.

3 Methodological Aspects and Research Hypotheses

For the purpose of our study, we selected randomly a sample of 20 firms listed on the Athens Stock Exchange for the period 2012–2014. Banks and financial institutions have excluded of the firms' list of which we selected the sample of this study. We assumed that the year 2010 was the first year of financial crisis in Greece because the Greek economy has been under financial probation since the end of May 2010. However, the consequences of financial crisis appeared within the year 2011 in a period of political uncertainty, which stopped in the middle of 2012 after the national elections. In order to avoid the effect of political uncertainty on firms' performance, we selected a period with no significant political and governmental policy changes.

Following previous research studies of Uyar (2009), Attari and Raza (2012), Zakari and Sani (2016), Nobanee et al. (2011), and Ebben and Johnson (2011), in which the impact of CCC on firms' financial performance was investigated using profitability indices (Table 2) as dependent variables, we stated our first hypothesis:

H_o Greek firms' cash conversion cycle affects significantly on their return on assets and return on equity.

Ross et al. (2003) refer to the dictum "collect early and pay late," which could mean that financial managers must keep CCC in low levels in order to obtain adequate liquidity and therefore efficient working capital management. In those terms our research hypothesis could be also stated as follows:

Table 2 Variables of relevant research studies

Researchers	CCC formula	Dependent variables
Zakari and Sani (2016)	(Inventory turnover + average collection) − average payment	ROA
Attari and Raza (2012)	(Inventory turnover days + debtor turnover days − payables turnover days	ROA, ROE, total assets, total sales
Sabri (2012)	(Inventory period + accounts receivables period) − accounts payable period	ROA
Uyar (2009)	Days of sales outstanding + days of sales in inventory − days of payables outstanding	ROA, ROE, total assets, sales revenue
Nobanee et al. (2011)	Receivable collection period + inventory conversion period − payable deferral period	ROI
Ebben and Johnson (2011)	Days of receivables + days of inventories − days of payables	Invested capital, ROI, return on invested capital, asset turnover, net balance position

H_o CCC affects significantly on ROA and ROE, and there is negative relationship between CCC and these two indices.

As we have already argued, the aim of our study is also to explore if CCC affects firms' size. The size of firms is reflected in variables total assets and sales of firms in previous relevant studies (Table 2) which have been placed as dependent variables in models for the estimation of the association between CCC and firms' size. Therefore, the second hypothesis is as follows:

H_{o2} CCC affects significantly on total assets and sales of firms, and there is negative relationship between CCC and these two variables.

OLS regression equations will be developed in order to test our research hypotheses. OIS regression has been used from Muscettola (2014) who investigated the impact of cash conversion cycle on Italian manufacturing SMEs firms' profitability. Also, regression analysis has been applied by Ebben and Johnson (2011) to search for the relationship within cash conversion cycle, liquidity, invested capital, and firm performance. Cash conversion cycle has been stated as the independent variable. Separate regression equations have been developed for every one of the dependent variables. The dependent variables of our equations are total assets, sales, return on assets (ROA), and return on equity (ROE). Analytical determination of the variables is appearing in Table 3.

4   Discussion of the Results

The descriptive statistics of the financial variables include the measures of central tendency such as mean, median, minimum, and maximum and measures of variability such as standard deviation (Table 4). A decrease in sales per year of the examined period would be reasonably expected in an extended crisis period of the Greek

Table 3 Definition of the independent and dependent variables

Variables	Definition
Cash conversion cycle Uyar (2009)	Days of sales outstanding + days of sales in inventory − days of payables outstanding
	Days of sales outstanding = accounts receivable/(sales/365)
	Days of sales in inventory = inventories/(cost of goods sold/365)
	Days of payables outstanding = accounts payable/(cost of goods sold/365)
Return on assets	Net income/total assets
Return on equity	Net income/equity
Total assets	Logarithm of total assets
Sales	Annual sales

economy. However, the mean sales don't seem to be affected by the financial crisis. Due to the high variability of sales, we also examined the trend of sales using the median value of annual sales (Fig. 2), and we have found a negative effect of crisis on sales. No findings in the same direction have been observed for ROE and ROA. On the other hand, median total assets of firms become shorter year to year (Fig. 3). This finding could be expected as it could be associated with the negative ratios of growth for the Greek economy in the examined period.

An interesting finding in this study is the negative observed value of the mean and median length of cash conversion cycle. Further descriptive analysis showed that also the third quartile of CCC is a negative value, which means that at least 75% of the firms of the sample appear to have a negative cash conversion cycle length. According to these findings, we could argue that firms, during the crisis, don't pay their suppliers for the products they buy from them until after they sell the products and collect the relevant payment. Moreover, the high negative values of the cash conversion cycle reflect the low short-term paying off ability of firms. The fact, that the Greek banks almost stopped financing the business activity—after the beginning of crisis—and the uncertainty for the financial consequences of crisis in firms, could explain the high values of the days of payables.

To test our first hypothesis that CCC affects the profitability of firms, we implemented OLS regression for the whole period and also for every year separately (Table 5). In the total sample, according to the results of the regression analysis, and those of analysis of variance, ROE doesn't have any significant relationship with CCC (at a level of significance 5%). In contrast with this finding, we found evidence that on a significance level of 5%, the CCC has a significant impact on firms' profitability as it is measured by ROA. Nevertheless, no significant correlation between CCC and logarithm of total assets on the one hand, and between the CCC and the sales of firms on the other, was detected on a significance level of 10%, 5%, or 1%. In other words, there is no significant evidence that, in the early period of financial crisis in Greece, CCC has any impact on the firms' size. However, although a significant effect on ROA was detected, the variability of ROA which is explained by the regression equation is too low. No heteroscedasticity of the residuals of the above regression was observed.

Table 4 Descriptive statistics

Variable	Year	Mean	St. dev	Min	Median	Max
Cash	2012	−603	801	−2590	−318	123
Conversion	2013	−987	1884	−6944	−437	177
Cycle	2014	−753	1413	−5290	−209	87.7
Days of	2012	153.2	243.8	7.11	68.7	1067.5
Sales	2013	161.1	264.4	4.27	74.4	1160.3
Outstanding	2014	131.1	207.1	0.667	57.9	917.9
Days of	2012	342.3	338.5	17.9	250.5	1209.9
Sales in	2013	367	444	6.98	154	1561
Inventories	2014	251.8	300.1	18.8	127.8	1163.1
Days of	2012	2045	4382	141	739	20,043
Payables	2013	2404	4534	178	782	19,297
Outstanding	2014	3639	11,010	92.6	646	48,679
ROA	2012	0.0517	0.0941	−0.1223	0.0334	0.2053
	2013	0.0439	0.0786	−0.1426	0.0274	0.1482
	2014	0.0422	0.0724	−0.1020	0.0420	0.1704
ROE	2012	0.1675	0.2582	−0.4355	0.1251	0.6195
	2013	0.1772	0.2805	−0.2702	0.1658	0.9233
	2014	0.0660	0.3076	−1.1026	0.1042	0.3515
Sales	2012	997,338,826	2,368,906,885	8,911,000	91,174,353	8,739,275,000
	2013	1,020,738,474	2,547,344,946	9,513,000	83,784,403	9,681,883,000
	2014	1,015,406,217	2,501,579,055	5,346,000	79,167,368	9,282,339,000
Total assets	2012	688,667,027	1,642,295,441	25,123,831	139,396,000	7,210,700,000
	2013	689,893,215	1,650,315,802	23,108,222	132,306,000	7,235,100,000
	2014	689,392,307	1,643,129,564	21,560,689	127,869,773	7,250,100,000

Fig. 2 Median of annual sales

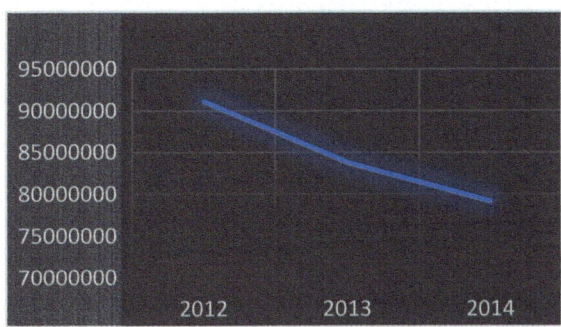

Fig. 3 Median of total assets per year

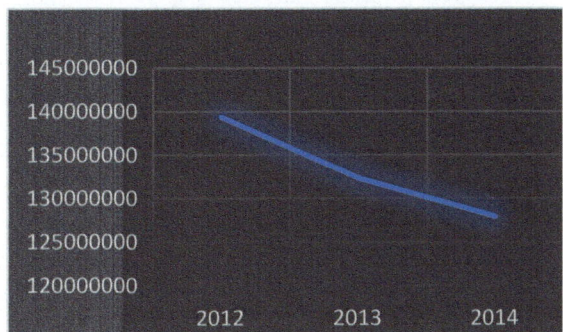

Testing the hypothesis, for every separate year, we noticed a significant effect of CCC on ROA, only for the year 2012. We could assume, from this finding, that as long as we remain in the status of financial crisis, CCC loses its impact on profitability of firms.

5   Conclusion

Cash conversion cycle is an important metric of cash management which is considered as a factor that could improve the profitability of firms (Muscettola 2014). Moreover, it is an indicator that shows how efficient a firm manages its working capital. The aim of this study was to detect if CCC affects the profitability and the size of firms during the early years of financial crisis. For this purpose, we analyzed listed firms in the Athens Stock Exchange from 2012 to 2014. Although it would be expected that effective cash management would be crucial for the profitability of firms, our findings are not relevant with those of previous research studies. Specifically, our findings for the negative relationship between profitability (measured by ROA) and cash conversion cycle are relevant with those of Uyar (2009) and Attari and Raza (2012). It must be noticed that none of the above research studies focused on emerging economies. No positive correlation between cash conversion cycle and

Table 5 Independent variable: cash conversion cycle

Dependent variables	Regression model statistics			Analysis of variance				
	Constant	Coef.	Sig	SSR	SSE	SST	F	Sig
Total period								
ROE	0.14664	0.00001	0.612	0.02195	4.553391	4.5787	0.26	0.612
ROA	0.07078	0.000230	0.007	0.08154	0.248282	0.286436	7.99	*0.007*
Sales	1,234,146,244	193,623	0.420	4.15371E+18	3.4351E+20	3.44505E+20	0.66	0.420
Log total assets	8.3087	0.0001	0.127	1.1202	25.2371	26.3572	2.40	0.127
Year 2012								
ROE	0.21231	0.00009217	0.240	0.09805	1.12480	1.22285	1.48	0.240
ROA	0.09479	0.00005730	0.023	0.037899	0.102373	0.140272	6.29	*0.023*
Sales	1,271,238,175	368,115	0.62	1.56398E+18	1.04030E+20	1.05594E+20	0.26	0.62
Log total assets	8.3519	0.0001734	0.389	0.3471	7.8636	8.2107	0.75	0.398
Year 2013								
ROE	0.16927	−0.00000425	0.910	0.00115	1.48821	1.48936	0.01	0.910
ROA	0.06643	0.00001827	0.158	0.008763	0.059569	0.068332	2.21	0.158
Sales	1,236,313,725	164,556	0.628	1.72975E+18	1.20486E+20	1.22215E+20	0.24	0.628
Log total assets	8.2795	0.00006728	0.462	0.2891	8.6940	8.9831	0.57	0.462
Year 2014								
ROE	0.09284	0.00002575	0.655	0.0225	1.7358	1.7583	0.21	0.655
ROA	0.06234	0.00001484	0.208	0.007482	0.069574	0.077056	1.72	0.208
Sales	1,277,319,467	198,766	0.672	1.34144E+18	1.15295E+20	1.16636E+20	0.19	0.672
Log total assets	8.3346	0.0001389	0.283	0.6551	8.4971	9.1522	1.23	0.283

Significance level: 0.05

profitability or firms' size was detected as it was argued in the study of Zakari and Sani (2016).

Furthermore, the negative values of cash conversion cycle which were not observed in previous relevant studies in the one hand and the significant low levels of firms' profitability consist of parameters that differ from those of firms in normal periods. We believe that an extended study for the total period of crisis in Greece and also a comparative analysis with the period before the financial crisis would offer more detailed view for the impact of CCC on profitability and on firms' size. However, the current research study showed that the cash conversion cycle and its impact on firms should be examined separately for emergent economies.

The small sample and the high volatility of the examined variables could be noticed as limitations of this study. This research could be extended in the future, searching a sample of more firms. This will allow analyzing firms' data per activity sector and may decrease the variability. In addition, more dependent variables could be tested such as liquidity of variable indicators.

References

Attari, M. A., & Raza, K. (2012). The optimal relationship of cash conversion cycle with firm size and profitability. *International Journal of Academic Research in Business and Social Sciences, 2*(4), 189.

Brealey, E. A., Myers, S. C., & Marcus, A. J. (2001). *Fundamentals of corporate finance* (3rd ed.). New York: McGraw-Hill Higher Education.

Ebben, J. J., & Johnson, A. C. (2011). Cash conversion cycle management in small firms relationships with liquidity, invested capital, and firm performance. *Journal of Small Business and Entrepreneurship, 24*(3), 381–396.

Hill, N. C., & Sartoris, W. L. (1992). *Short-term financial management* (2nd ed., p. 15). New York: Macmillan.

Keown, A. J., Martin, J. D., Petty, J. W., & Scott, D. F., Jr. (2003). *Foundations of finance: The logic and practice of financial management* (4th ed.). Upper Saddle River, NJ: Prentice Hall.

Muscettola, M. (2014). Cash conversion cycle and firm's profitability: An empirical analysis on a sample of 4226 manufacturing SMEs of Italy. *International Journal of Business and Management, 9*(5), 25.

Nobanee, H., Abdullatif, M., & Al Hajjar, M. (2011). Cash conversion cycle and firm's performance of Japanese firms. *Asian Review of Accounting, 19*(5), 147–156.

Richards, V. D., & Laughlin, E. J. (1980). A cash conversion cycle approach to liquidity analysis. *Financial Management, 9*(1), 32–38. (Published by Blackwell Publishing on behalf of the Financial Management Association International).

Ross, A., Stephen, A., Westerfield, W. R., & Jordan, D. B. (2003). *Fundamentals of corporate finance* (6th ed.). New York: McGrawHill-Irwin.

Sabri, T. A. (2012). Different working capital policies and the profitability of a firm. *International Journal of Business and Management, 7*(15), 50.

Uyar, A. (2009). The relationship of cash conversion cycle with firm size and profitability: An empirical investigation in Turkey. *International Research Journal of Finance and Economics, 24*, 186–193.

Zakari, M., & Sani, S. (2016). The impact of cash conversion cycle on firm profitability: Evidence from Nigerian listed telecommunication companies. *Journal of Finance and Accounting, 4*(6), 342–350.

Creativity Development and Educational Expenditures: An Exploratory Study

Fani A. Papoutsi

Abstract The creative idea's source lies in the Ancient Greece where Aristotle considered creativity as something that resulted "when one is bereft of his senses." Creativity entails generating and recognizing ideas; solving problems; viewing things from different perspectives and in different ways; changing or transforming an existing domain into a new one, in an innovative and unique way; and associating different fields of knowledge. Creativity development is an important consideration for many disciplines such as education, technology, engineering, cognitive science, business studies, and economics. The main goal of creativity is developing through exploration, decision-making, and expression. In an era defined by technological innovations and marked by financial crisis, developing the creative and innovative potential of students reflects the need of new educational methods. This necessity was recently reported to the European Commission's project entitled "Modernization on Education." The current research explores the different sources of funding (governmental or households), reports the spending per country on education, and, finally, emphasizes the importance OECD countries assign to education. This research aims at depicting the linkage between state budget spending on education and creativity development. It is purported that increases in expenditures on education may help foster economic growth, enhance productivity, contribute to people's personal and social development, and help reduce social inequalities. Educational expenditures include spending on universities, schools, and other private and public institutions.

Keywords Creativity in education · Creativity development · Educational expenditures · Modernization of education

F. A. Papoutsi (✉)
Kapodistrian University of Athens, Athens, Greece

© Springer Nature Switzerland AG 2019   379
N. Sykianakis et al. (eds.), *Economic and Financial Challenges for Eastern Europe*,
Springer Proceedings in Business and Economics,
https://doi.org/10.1007/978-3-030-12169-3_25

1 Introduction

For many decades, psychologists, philosophers, and educators have oscillated between the two aspects of creativity: innate or taught. The year 1950 heralds "the birth of the creativity movement" with Joy Paul Guilford's research on creativity which lasted for more than 20 years. Divergent thinking, method analysis, and the interaction between personality and creativity development are the main features that contribute to someone's creative ability. In 1953, Guilford's research supported that creativity is vitally important, everyone possesses creative potential, and the brainstorming technique is the best way to realize this potential. In 1974 Torrance's divergent thinking tests supported that creative ideas are unique and abundant and creativity can be measured (Davis and Rimm 1998). National governments must reorganize their educational systems in order to meet the challenges of the twenty-first century. Technological development, innovation, and creativity development are at the forefront of these changes. Recently, the aim of modernizing education[1] (especially higher education) in Europe—related to the quality of teaching and learning—figured at the top of commission's agenda for change.[2] Europe needs multiskilled and well-educated pupils capable of driving innovation, enhancing creativity, and increasing productivity and development in their daily lives. Investing on skills will lead to better socioeconomic outcomes. Investing on education means investing in society, its people, and its future. Education is affected by budget cuts, especially during the financial crisis. The impact of financial crisis and the social crisis as well have shifted the quality of education, the educational process, and the public spending on education.

2 Meaning of Creativity

Defining creativity is difficult due to the complexity of the phenomenon. According to some authors, creativity is the human ability to produce something new and to seek novel solutions to problems. Nowadays, it is mistakenly associated with artistic endeavors. Creativity, innovation, and invention are three different but also interrelated concepts. Creativity is the capability of conceiving something unusual or original. Innovation is the implementation of something new, while invention is the creation of something that has never been made before. Usually, creativity's process starts with the existence of a problem that needs to be solved. Generally, it is the ability to produce new solutions, without using conventional ways of thinking.

---

[1] http://ec.europa.eu/dgs/education_culture/repository/education/library/reports/modernisation_en.pdf

[2] http://eur-lex.europa.eu/legal-content/en/ALL/?uri=CELEX:52011DC05671

Taylor offers five levels of creativity[3] to answer the question how creative are we and people around us, while Hermann believes that everyone has a creative potential that can be expressed through creativity and can be taught through instruction (Stenberg and Lubart 2012). A creative person has the ability to look at situations from many perspectives, make connections and assumptions, and find problems and solutions as well as the ability to think outside the box. Creativity is the ability to illustrate what is outside the box from within the box (theory of conceptual blending).[4] Perkins[5] pointed out that creativity requires intelligence and talent. Wallas[6] mentioned a four-stage model for a complete creative process consisting of preparation, incubation, illumination, and verification. In order to support the creative individual, creativity development needs a "modern" educational environment, technologically equipped and full of materials, tools, and resources. According to a teachers' survey about creativity in schools in Europe (2009) launched by the European Commission,[7] more than 80% of 10,000 teachers believe that information technologies can be used to enhance creativity. Ninety percent of teachers support the idea, while less than 25% believe in the usefulness of ICT for creative learning. On average 4/10 teachers have received creativity training with large differences between countries. Thirty-six percent received training to use ICT in classroom, while 6/10 received training in innovative pedagogies or methods to improve creativity development and to modernize the traditional schooling methodology. An education indicator improves how healthy the educational system is. Moreover, the same indicator shows that the more highly educated people are, the more likely they will be employed in the future. Across OECD countries 93% of students reported using computers at home, and 72% reported using devices connected to the Internet at school. Enjoyment, fun, intrinsic motivation, tolerating ambiguity, experimenting, self-esteem, persistence, motivation, the willingness to take risks, and risk-taking are some serious indicators which play a large role in creativity and must be recognized by educators when it occurs.[8]

---

[3]The five distinctive levels of creativity by Taylor are expressive, productive, inventive, innovative, and emergent, where the last two can be attained by those with exceptional gifts. Born, not bred. A. Taylor, (1959) The nature of the creative process (In P. Smith, ed. Creativity), Mastering the 5 levels of creativity (Jeff DeGraff).

[4]Gilles Fauconnier and Mark Turner argue that all learning and all thinking consist of blends of metaphors based on simple bodily experiences. These blends are then themselves blended together into an increasingly rich structure that makes up our mental functioning in modern society. A child's entire development consists of learning and navigating these blends. *The Way We Think* shows how this blending operates; how it is affected by (and gives rise to) language, identity, and concept of category; and the rules by which we use blends to understand ideas that are new to us. The result is a bold, exciting, and accessible new view of how the mind works (The Way We Think: Conceptual Blending And The Mind's Hidden Complexities, Gilles Fauconnier, Mark Turner 2002).

[5]http://ei.yale.edu/wp-content/uploads/2014/02/pub61_MayerPerkins2001_EIandgiftedness.pdf

[6]Wallas' four-stage model: more than meets the eye? Eugene Sadler-Smith (Taylor and Francis)

[7]Eurodocs/European Commission/creativity in schools: a survey for teachers

[8]https://www.ajol.info/index.php/saje/article/viewFile/24914/20526

2.1 The Role of Modernization in Education

As a purposeful process, creativity occurs over time and it involves the unconscious mind. It entails risk-taking; it requires vision, space, time, innovative thinking, the appropriate environment, and the right skills and mechanisms in a place where innovative ideas are encouraged and failure is accepted. What is necessary is more than the ability to absorb information. Students need to be skillful and knowledgeable, and those skills must be applied in creative ways. School must teach them how to use this knowledge creatively to make an impact. Creativity is essential to survival in the twenty-first century (Hargreaves 1978). People need to be more creative in their daily lives, and this could be accomplished through collaborative pedagogies, where students are thinking, inventing, participating, learning, and developing their creative minds. But the main question is how to foster creativity in such a short teaching time, where the equipment and the teaching supplies and tools are inadequate. Educators must be able to reorganize and to answer some basic questions about creativity. What is it, why is it important, and how can they promote it? Public authorities and school leaders must develop comprehensive strategies and adopt new methods and models of teaching and learning. Modernization in education begins with technological equipment in classroom where the access to materials is plenty. Increasing teaching and learning quality requires investment and system reformation. The current situation of education is not unique. People tend to study online and blended learning is widely accepted. The multiplicity of the new modernized educational methods will offer online education, accessible to every student everywhere on earth 24/7. A variety of educational technologies is available in the field of online education and distance learning. Web pages, video tools, forums, course management systems, online discussions and opportunities for peer review, course reading on the Web, and teaching methods such as face-to-face online education, blended learning, and flipped learning are used to enhance student learning. As the world revolves around the Internet, these methods and those tools could benefit the educational system. With these opportunities at hand, students become more enthusiastic and can learn faster and better. The main aim is to modernize the way education is delivered to students and how they use this knowledge to become inspired toward lifelong learning. For the European Union, quality education is crucial to ensure continued social cohesion, competitiveness, and sustained growth. Investing in young people is the best investment a society can make. Equality in education is a prime concern as students with a vulnerable socioeconomic background abandon school. Also the recent refugee arrival requires an effective absorption strategy (e.g., social fairness, same opportunities for everyone, etc.).

The European Commission has put forth various initiatives to support modernization on education.

1. Building stronger links between educational institutes and businesses
2. Using the European Social Fund transnational networks
3. Helping students (equip them) with the best skills for the challenging society
4. Preparing students on problem-solving and analytical thinking

5. Promoting effective investment on education
6. Supporting E-Twinning (exchanging knowledge between educational institutions)
7. Supporting Member States ongoing efforts in keeping up with digital transformation in education
8. Enhancing creativity and innovation, including entrepreneurship, at all levels of education and training

Schools need to be modernized for a new era, and they need to be rethought for the digital, global, information economy. Reforming and replacing educational systems and preparing the youth to adopt the technologies (driven by the needs of the times and by the method of change) are the next steps for modernizing the existing educational systems. If all those reforms succeed, the results will benefit Europe as a whole.

2.2 Expenditure on Education and Educational Budget Cuts

Expenditures on education include direct public funding for educational institutions, transfers to households and enterprises, expenditures on ancillary services for students and families, and expenditure on schools, universities, and other public and private institutions delivering or supporting educational services. This indicator shows the priority given by governments to education relative to other areas of concern such as health care, social security, and defense. Education expenditures cover expenditure on schools, universities, and other public and private institutions delivering or supporting educational services. It is expressed as a percentage of each country's GDP, and in the last decade, there has been a downward trend for two thirds of OECD countries. In 2015, the general education expenditure in the EU-28 amounted to 4.9% of GDP.[9] As stated in the official publication of the EU, "at the level of the EU-28, government expenditure on 'education' as a ratio to GDP remained relatively stable over the 2002–2015 period, decreasing by 0.2 pp. from 5.1% of GDP in 2002 to 4.9% in 2015. However, since overall government expenditure as a ratio to GDP increased by 2.7 pp. (notably in the functions 'health' and 'social protection'), the share of expenditure on education in total expenditure decreased from 11.1% in 2002 to 10.3% in 2015" (Eurostat: Evolution of education expenditure 2002–2015).[10] Most education funding for 2013 (latest available data according to Eurostat) went to primary and lower secondary education. The highest amounts for primary non-tertiary education were recorded by Switzerland 10.8%, Iceland 10.1%, Denmark and Norway 8.7%, Sweden 7.5%, and Finland 7.0% of their GDP (Fig. 1).

---

[9]http://data.worldbank.org/indicator/SE.XPD.TOTL.GD.ZS

[10]http://ec.europa.eu/eurostat/statistics-explained/index.php/Government_expenditure_on_ education

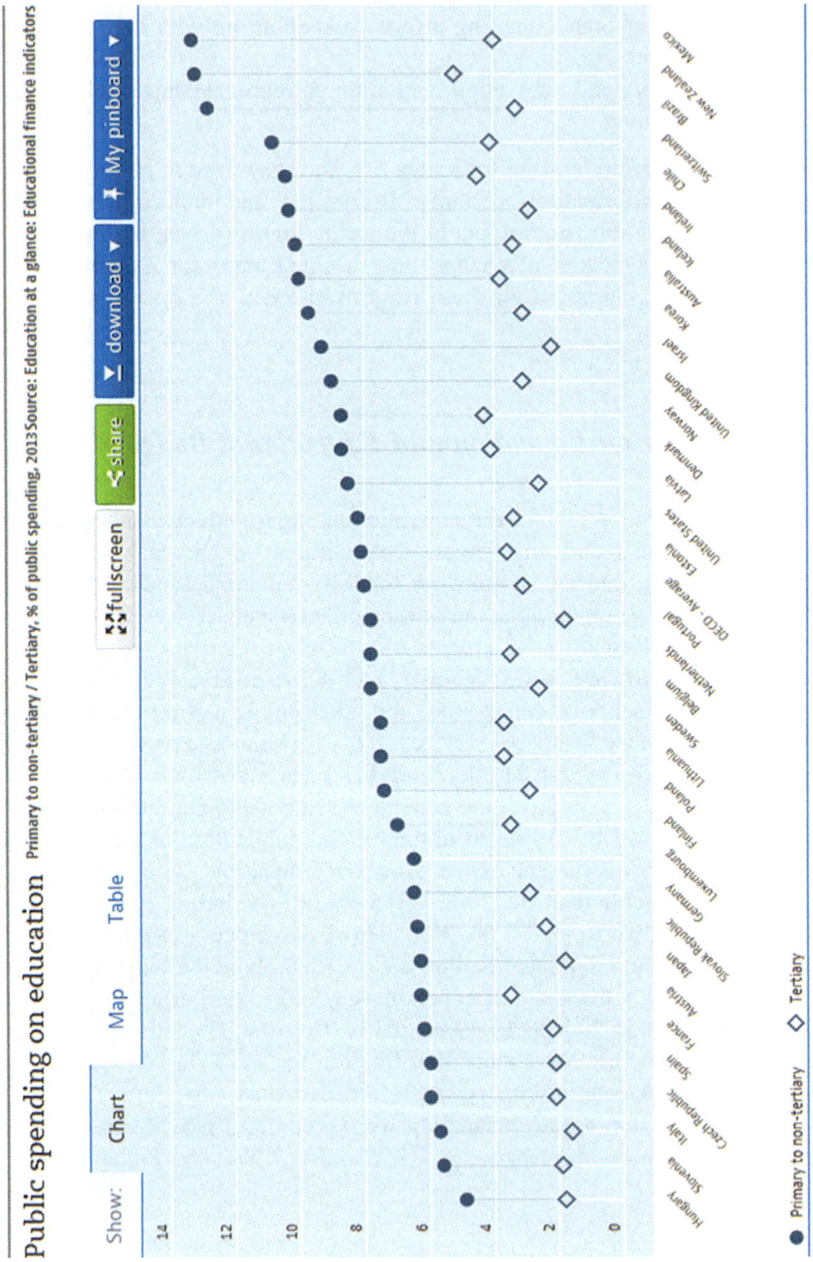

Fig. 1 OECD data. https://data.oecd.org/eduresource/public-spending-on-education.htm

Cut budget costs in education have had negative repercussions throughout the system, to mention just a few, increased costs to parents, loss of equal access to quality education (students with special needs and low-income families), overcrowding class-rooms as a result of consolidating schools, decreasing the number of teachers, larger student ratios per teacher, lower teaching quality ratios, and decrease in teacher–student attention.

2.3   EU Member States Debate

The debate between the EU Member States concerns the level of funding for education and whether the amount of funding impacts education quality. Financial crisis makes that challenge harder. More specifically, the debate concerns how to reform educational policies and systems and how to empower individuals with skills and increase the overall development levels for the future and for society. The financial crisis has adversely affected all state budget expenditures including educa-tional funding. Researches have concluded an increase in the educational budget per student has a significant positive impact on student achievement[11] (Lips, Watkins 2008). Furthermore, sustained improvements of funding can lead to improvements in the level and distribution of student outcomes (Bruce D. Baker 2012). In 1982 Eric Hanushek published a paper claiming that money doesn't matter when it comes to improving quality and student outcomes. On the contrary, 10 years later, Greenwald, Hedges, and Laine (1996) concluded that expenditures per student show strong and consistent achievements including teachers' quality. In 2011, Konstantopoulos and Bormang's re-analysis[12] of the Coleman report data[13] indi-cated that schooling quality has significant effects on student outcomes. Actually what matters *is not about how much money is spent but how money is spent*. At the same time, PISA findings[14] show that the success of a country's education system depends less on the volume of investment and more on how these resources are invested and how a school system's attitude impacts student performance. Differ-ences between PISA participants rely on their educational systems and their national wealth spending on education. For instance, PISA participating countries reward teachers with higher salaries and allocate more teachers in larger in size classes.[15] Also expecting high expectations for all of students is another positive indicator.

---

[11]Does spending more on education improve academic achievement?, Dan Lips, Shanea Watkins 2008. www.heritage.org.

[12]http://www.shankerinstitute.org/sites/shanker/files/doesmoneymatter_final%20April%20conver sation.pdf

[13]Coleman report data, http://files.eric.ed.gov/fulltext/ED012275.pdf and https://www.onemeck. org/wp-content/uploads/2016/03/BormanDowling_2010_Schools-and-inequality_TCR.pdf

[14]http://gpseducation.oecd.org/

[15]https://www.oecd.org/pisa/pisaproducts/pisainfocus/49685503.pdf

From one point of view, money alone can't lead to a better educational system, but on the other hand, what emerges from the available evidence is a combination of more accountability and more adequate funding for its use (Bruce Baker 2012). Furthermore, for systems that already provide the basic inputs (needed for educational quality improvement), efficient spending is more important than for those who spent less, and they should invest their budgets on basic resources and conditions in order to increase their quality education. Education systems should provide the same opportunities for every student to receive an equal, high-quality basic education (Berne and Stiefel 1984; Underwood 1995).[16]

2.4   "Educational Giants": Educational Success, Creativity Connection, and School Funding Affect

According to the "12 pillars of competitiveness ranking,[17] Finland, Estonia, and Switzerland are in the top 9 countries with the best educational systems worldwide." Based on the NCEE (National Center on Education and the Economy), in Finland, education is free except for fees regarding extracurricular activities in mornings and afternoons. The amount of federal money for education is determined by the number of students. In 2011, Finland spent $12,545 per pupil as compared to the OECD average $9377 in lower secondary education. Education in Finland is essential and is seen as a potential investment—not just an expenditure—in helping to develop innovation (Asplund and Maliranta 2006, p. 282). The principles that guide the Finnish education system are interrelated into a system that fosters equity as a basic value, flexible education system for LLL (lifelong learning), responsibility and local freedom, systems support, formative evaluation policy for promoting quality, and high-quality teachers and teacher education. Finnish schools are well equipped with computer-aided facilities and other kind of learning materials (Eurydice 2004, 2011), which are increasingly used in the learning process. Innovative pedagogies such as project and problem-based learning, as well as inquiry-based science education, are encouraged. During the computer-based discussions, comments, questions, problem solutions, and inventions in the discussion forum resulted from the collaborative work between students. This type of collaborative teaching and learning enhances group working and militates against cultural discrimination (as students work together, exchange opinions, and solve problems).[18] Many Finnish schools take advantage of the socio-digital revolution and produce novel and innovative approaches such as investing in technological tools and environments, becoming

---

[16]Berne, Robert, and Leanna Stiefel. 1984. The Measurement of Equity in School Finance: Conceptual, Methodological, and Empirical Dimensions. Baltimore: Johns Hopkins University Press

[17]http://www3.weforum.org/docs/WEF_GlobalCompetitivenessReport_2014-15.pdf

[18]Hurme, Merenluoto, and Järvelä (2009)

parts of pilot projects, and participating on teacher educational trainings.[19] Open online educational courses (MOOCs) and the use of WEB 2.0 technology tools[20] offer instant share of material representing a trend of "learning anytime–anywhere" and providing self-organized, creative approach to learning. Current practices have improved the Finnish PISA seemed efficient as have been resulted students' performance. According to data collected in 2015, Finnish students scored 511 in mathematics, 531 in science literary, and 526 in reading compared to mathematics, science literacy, and reading, scored with 511, 531, and 526 points compared to an average of 490, 493, and 493 in OECD countries (OECE 2015).[21] Classes in Finland are comparatively small (19 students), the average time per week spent is the shortest among PISA participants (24.2 h/week), and students spend almost 2 hours per day for studying after school. According to CCE[22] (Council for Creative Education), teachers are highly educated, they obtain a master's degree, many of them hold PhD degrees, and they have been trained on ICT in education. CCE is aimed to educate, invent, and promote creative education by providing support, innovation, and collaborative learning techniques (creativity features). Based on the Finnish National Curriculum framework,[23] teachers use "phenomenon-based teaching,"[24] students are involved in "helping to plan lessons," and there is emphasis on "student collaboration." This new approach upgrades the existing educational system (which ranks top quality) and facilitates the joy of learning where interaction, creative activity, and positive emotional experiences are blended together. The goal is to provide students the necessary skills for a more technological, global society.

Estonia's educational system is one of the strongest among OECD countries and is characterized as one of the best in the world. Basic education is the compulsory educational minimum which is provided by basic schools (grades 1–9). All young people receive at least 7–9 years of basic education. College is free and private schools are very few. In order to graduate from basic schools, students must present creative work and attain a high level in curricular subjects. In 1996, Estonia turned to Finland in order to learn, build, and follow a more effective education system. Many features of the Finnish curriculum directly inspired the Estonian system. In order to support weaker students and reduce inequalities, schools make a yearly development interview for students with unsatisfactory marks, they provide equal access to books, and learning materials have been provided for free. Compulsory education is free of charge, including learning materials and textbooks, the number of hours varies

---

[19]http://www.ubiko.eu

[20]Revolutionary new ways of creating, collaborating, editing, and sharing user-generated content online. It's also about ease of use. There's no need to download, and teachers and students can master many of these tools in minutes.

[21]Gpseducation.oecd.org

[22]http://www.ccefinland.org/

[23]http://www.oph.fi/download/151294_ops2016_curriculum_reform_in_finland.pdf

[24]http://innovatsioonikeskus.ee/sites/default/files/Konverents2015/17.04_Phenomenon_Based_Learning_KEKKONEN_LUOSTARINEN.pdf

according to the student's age, classes are particularly small (15–17 students), and students spend almost 2 hours per day after school in home studying. "Estonian Lifelong Learning Strategy 2020," adopted in 2014, is a national education plan. Lifelong learning opportunities for everyone through digital platforms and the Internet are at the core of this plan (Eesti elukestva õppe strateegia 2014). Efforts have been devoted to strengthen the use of technology in classes.[25] In Estonian education system, motivation is the absolute key to success, and teachers can use any kind of technology to mediate every learning practice, to provide creative learning experiences to all students. IT school usage is encouraged through some key educational initiatives such as Tiger Leap Foundation,[26] eKool[27] system, ProgeTiger,[28] and Tiger Leap plus.[29] The aim is to teach every young student. According to the Tiger Leap Program (1997),[30] all schools in Estonia are connected to the Internet. Estonia operates more than 100 different educational software programs, and 10,900 of 17,000 teachers have been trained in computer skills. According to the Creative and Innovative Good Practices in compulsory education in Europe,[31] Estonian teachers engage also outdoor teaching, in classes called open-air classrooms where they teach science, literature, languages, and geography. In such lessons, students must act creatively. They have to use their own measuring devices or technology, they usually work in teams or in pairs, and it is highly motivating for students and teachers as well. Moving from an indoor classroom to open-air classes increases student's curiosity, motivation, enthusiasm, creativity, imagination, and concentration. In PISA 2015, Estonian students performed high scores improving the effectiveness of their education system. Their scores were 534 to an average of 493 of OECD participants in science literacy, 520 in mathematics to an average of 490, and 519 in reading to an average of 490. In 2015, the index of schoolwork-related anxiety was one of the lowest among PISA-participating countries and economies.[32] Modern foreign languages, science, and social studies play the greatest role at lower secondary level.

In a multilingual and federalist country like Switzerland, education is under government's responsibility with the 26 cantons where their local municipalities finance the 90% of public educational budgets. Only 5% of the students attend private schools, and every student has the same opportunities. Public schools are free

---

[25]https://www.oecd.org/pisa/PISA-2015-estonia.pdf

[26]http://sange.fi/~ozone/Tigerleap.pdf

[27]http://tes.innove.ee/wp-content/uploads/sites/7/2016/04/TES-Guide-eKool-2016-update.pdf

[28]http://www.eun.org/c/document_library/get_file?uuid=f714002b-65ff-49cb-a6f1-74460eb108ce&groupId=43887

[29]http://ncee.org/2014/04/global-perspectives-e-stonia-how-estonias-investment-in-it-skills-impacted-improvements-in-the-economy/

[30]http://www.ut.ee/eLSEEConf/Kogumik/Magi.pdf

[31]http://ftp.jrc.es/EURdoc/JRC59689_TN.pdf

[32]http://www.oecd.org/education/skills-beyond-school/EDIF%202014%2D%2DN22%20(eng).pdf

of charge, the school duration is 11 years, and the school language depends on region's main language, German, French, Italian, or Romansh. Students also learn Swedish as second language and English as third. Ninety percent or more of the Swiss students graduate upper secondary education which automatically leads directly to the job market. It is reported that Switzerland is investing heavily in educational spending per student and teacher's salaries are the highest among the OECD countries. According to OECD data: "Switzerland spends US$16,090 per student, compared with the OECD average of US$9487 and the EU21 average of US $9531."[33] *In 2013 public expenditures, one education accounted for 14.9% of Switzerland's total public expenditure.*[34] Furthermore, as reported by SIS (Swiss International School), 47.7% of students obtain a bachelor's degree, students are 16–20 per class, and the state-of-the-art technology use enhances process and development. Besides, the Swiss educational methods promoting creativity, cognitive development, and the ability to "think outside the box."[35] Home schooling is uncommon. In Switzerland, all higher education institutions have implemented at least one LMS. Yet, based on numerous mutations (LLL) and reforms (Bologna), education systems moved away from teacher-centric methods, and the learner became responsible for his own knowledge and skill building. This trend gave birth to many new e-tools which provided autonomy to learners. The majority of the teachers are technologically literate (called innovative teachers), and for every field, there is an online platform, application, tool, or system which is used instead of a printed book and a technology—coordinator provides support when needed. The BYOD (bring your own device)[36] or BYOT (bring your own technology) is a source of information and advice which uses laptops, netbooks, tablets, and smartphones to support teaching indoors and outdoors, as all the devices are registered to monitor access and usage of content as required by Swiss law.[37] Devices have to be preregistered so that access can be monitored and filtered. By the use of such a system, there is plenty of freedom to create, both to the students and to the teachers, students benefit from using their own devices and through plenty of online information, and they learn in a safe environment focusing on technology and pedagogy with more enthusiasm and motivation. In 2015 Switzerland's student participants scored 506 points in science literacy, 521 in mathematics, and 492 in reading. The

---

[33]https://www.oecd.org/edu/Switzerland-EAG2014-Country-Note.pdf

[34]http://gpseducation.oecd.org/CountryProfile?plotter=h5&primaryCountry=CHE& treshold=10&topic=EO

[35]http://www.swissinternationalschool.ch/de-CH

[36]This initial guide, an online version of which will be regularly updated, has been developed by European Schoolnet as part of the work of Ministries of Education in its Interactive Classroom Working Group (ICWG)—http://fcl.eun.org/documents/10180/624810/BYOD+report_Oct2015_ final.pdf.

[37]The BYOD mobile devices, http://fcl.eun.org/documents/10180/624810/BYOD_Switzerland. pdf/b02f39c0-0c29-4550-b642-bc32ded77293

average time per week spent for learning is one of the shortest (25.1 h/week) among PISA participants; students spent a few hours after school for reading (1.5 h/day).[38]

3 Conclusion

Nowadays, digital literacy is important to school, and technology is the potential help to the "today's skills gap." In order to improve quality in teaching, so as in education, well-trained teachers and broad access to technology are some creative solutions to these challenges. As technology is only one tool in a mix of potential solutions, new pedagogies and learning methods and better teacher preparation are some further potential strategies for better quality of a school system. A higher level of skills, such as those useful for creating through new technologies, needs education system improvements like the training of teachers, the learning materials update, and the curriculum updating to make them appropriate to skill building, decision-making creativity development, and learning. The Directorate of OECD for Education and Skills developing and analyzing the quantitative, comparable indicators internationally (Education at a Glance 2014[39]) which could help governments to build more effective educational systems. As creativity development is a key indicator in educational development, a more detailed research on creativity and its relation with educational expenditures is crucial. Moreover, if education quality is related to the school budgets, spending for each European and non-European country, numerous indicators should be identified and analyzed. Teacher salaries, teaching hours, and age distribution are some indicators that affect the current expenditure which, in turn, affects educational quality and students' development. Educational expenditures are influenced by the teachers' salary cost, teaching time, and the class size. Student-teacher ratio is also an important indicator. Governments seek to provide better education and to ensure that education expenditures are spent efficiently. Reducing class size and increasing teacher's salaries are two main reforms of the OECD countries.[40] Modern schools in the twenty-first century include skills and abilities and teaching tools—materials and methods. What is necessary is to meet education's needs: communication skills and personal development. How and where education delivered are the main needs in modernizing. New technologies give the opportunity to learn from everywhere, in many different learning ways. Increased school funding may or may not guarantee better educational quality, but further investigation should be necessary. For the most successful education systems, their success begins with their teachers and their desire to see their pupils and the society as well improve and succeed later in life. Similar education systems, extracurricular

---

[38]http://gpseducation.oecd.org/CountryProfile?plotter=h5&primaryCountry=CHE& treshold=10&topic=PI

[39]https://www.oecd.org/edu/Education-at-a-Glance-2014.pdf

[40]http://www.oecd.org/edu/skills-beyond-school/EDIF%202012%2D%2DN9%20FINAL.pdf

choices and intrinsic motivation, rigor, and flexibility provide both educational and social services. Education is about creating a coherent and an effective teaching. Modernizing education reflects the changes occurring day after day in which we, as educators, need to adapt and to follow for a better socioeconomic future.

References

Books

Asplund, R., & Maliranta, M. (2006). Productivity growth: The role of human capital and technology in the road to prosperity. In A. Ojala, J. Eloranta, & J. Jalava (Eds.), *The road to prosperity: An economic history of Finland* (pp. 263–283). Helsinki: SKS.

Davis, G. A., & Rimm, S. B. (1998). *Education of the gifted and talented.* Needham Heights, MA: Allyn and Bacon.

Hakkarainen, K., Hietajärvi, L., Alho, K., Lonka, K., & Salmela-Aro, K. (2015). What engages digital natives. In J. Eccles & K. Salmela-Aro (Eds.), *International encyclopedia of the social & behavioral sciences.* Amsterdam: Elsevier.

Hurme, T.-R., Merenluoto, K., & Järvelä, S. (2009). Socially shared metacognition of pre-service primary teachers in a computer-supported mathematics course and their feelings of task difficulty: A case study. *Educational Research and Evaluation, 15*, 503–524.

Kampylis, P., Berki, E., & Saariluoma, P. (2009). In-service and prospective teachers' conceptions of creativity. *Thinking Skills and Creativity, 4*(1), 15–29.

Konstantopolous, S., & Borman, G. (2011). Family background and school effects on student achievement: A multilevel analysis of the Coleman data. *Teachers College Record, 113*(1), 97–132.

Leonard, P. A. (1910). *Open air school.* Whitefish, MT: Kessinger Publishing.

Journal

Alonso, J. D., & Sánchez, A. (2011). *Reforming education finance in transition countries: Six case studies in per capita financing system.* elibrary.worldbank.org

Anthony, G., & Walshaw, M. *Effective pedagogy in mathematics.*

Arundel, A. (2007). *Innovation survey indicators: Any progress since 1996?* European Commission, http://www.oecd.org/sti/inno/37436234.pdf

Boumová, V. *English language and literature, traditional vs. modern teaching methods: Advantages and disadvantages of each.*

Cachia, R., Ferrari, A., Ala-Mutka, K., & Punie, Y. *Creative learning and innovative teaching.* Final report on the study on creativity and innovation in education in the EU member states. http://www.eurosfaire.prd.fr/7pc/doc/1300702480_jrc62370_learning_teaching_2010.pdf

Creeemers, B. P. M. (2005). *Combining different ways of learning and teaching in a dynamic model of educational effectiveness.* Faculty of Behavioural and Social Sciences, University of Groningen, Lecture for the Lee Hysan Lecture Series, Hong Kong, https://www.rug.nl/staff/b.p.m. creemers/combining_different_ways_of_learning_and_teaching_in_a_dynamic_model_of_edu cational_effectiveness.pdf

Damodharan, V. S., & Rengarajan, V. *Innovative methods of teaching.* http://math.arizona.edu/ ~atp-mena/conference/proceedings/Damodharan_Innovative_Methods.pdf

Diem, A. (2015). *Studies on the Swiss education system.* Original document saved on the web server of the University Library of Bern, http://www.zb.unibe.ch/download/eldiss/15diem_a.pdf

Education at a Glance. (2007). *OECD indicators.* https://www.oecd.org/education/skills-beyond-school/40701218.pdf

Education at a Glance. (2014). *OECD indicators.* http://www.oecd.org/education/education-at-a-glance-2014-indicators-by-chapter.htm

Education at a Glance. (2016). *OECD indicators.* http://www.oecd.org/education/skills-beyond-school/education-at-a-glance-2016-indicators.htm

Education Expenditures by Country. (2017). *The condition of education.* https://nces.ed.gov/programs/coe/pdf/coe_cmd.pdf

Education Indicators in Focus. (2012a). *How does class size vary around the world?* http://www.oecd.org/edu/skills-beyond-school/EDIF%202012%2D%2DN9%20FINAL.pdf

Education Indicators in Focus. (2012b). *How well are countries educating young people to the level needed for a job and a living wage?* https://www.oecd.org/education/skills-beyond-school/Education%20Indicators%20in%20Focus%207.pdf

Education Indicators in Focus. (2012c). *What is the impact of the economic crisis on public education spending?* https://www.oecd.org/edu/skills-beyond-school/EDIF%202013%2D%2DN%C2%B018%20(eng).pdf

Education Indicators in Focus. (2017). *How innovative is the education sector?* http://www.oecd.org/education/skills-beyond-school/EDIF24-eng(2014)EN.pdf

Eesti elukestva õppe strateegia. (2014). https://eacea.ec.europa.eu/national-policies/eurydice/content/lifelong-learning-strategy-24_en

ELINET (European Literacy Policy Network). (2016). *Literacy in Switzerland.*

E-skills in Europe, Estonia – Country Report. (2013). http://eskills-monitor2013.eu/fileadmin/monitor2013/documents/country_reports/country_report_estonia.pdf

European Commission, Communication from the Commission to the European Parliament, the Council, the European Economic and Social Committee and the Committee of the Regions, Improving and Modernizing Education. (2016). http://eur-lex.europa.eu/legal-content/EN/TXT/?uri=COM:2016:941:FIN

European Schoolnet. (2015a). *BYOD bring your own device a guide for school leaders.* http://fcl.eun.org/documents/10180/624810/BYOD+report_Oct2015_final.pdf

European Schoolnet. (2015b). *A long-term approach is needed to achieve change with technology in Switzerland.*

Federley, M., Grenman, K., Kuula, T., Siltanen, S., VTT Palomäki, E., Stigzelius, E., Vartiainen, M., & Aalto/BIT. State of the art – *Overview of new applications, practices and concepts in utilizing technology in education, their use in work context, global/local aspects for multichannel online services.*

Frisch, J., & Kristahn, G. *Teaching intercultural communication competencies as an international student cooperation project – An innovative teaching approach.*

Glewwe, P., & Kremer, M. *Chapter 16 schools, teachers, and education outcomes in developing countries.* http://www.sciencedirect.com/science/article/pii/S1574069206020162

Grand-Duche De Luxemburg, Ambassade en Finlande, Finland – Education and Entrepreneurship.

Harris, D., & Plank, D. N. (2001). *Does class size reduction come at the expense of teacher quality?* Washington, DC: Economic Policy Institute, The Education Policy Center at Michigan State University. http://education.msu.edu/epc/forms/Policy-and-research-Reports/REPORT4.PDF

Hoeckel, K., Field, S., & Grubb, W. N. *Learning for jobs OECD reviews of vocational education and training*, Switzerland.

Hokanson, B. (2007). *By measure: Creativity in design.* http://hokanson.design.umn.edu/publications/2007Hokanson%20ByMeasureHokansonJIHE.pdf

http://ec.europa.eu/eurostat/statistics-explained/index.php/Europe_2020_headline_indicators

Innovative Schools; Teaching & Learning in the Digital Era. http://www.europarl.europa.eu/RegData/etudes/STUD/2015/563389/IPOL_STU(2015)563389_EN.pdf

Jackson, K. *The effects of school spending on educational and economic outcomes: Evidence from school finance reforms*. http://www.ipr.northwestern.edu/publications/docs/workingpapers/2015/IPR-WP-15-19.pdf

Kaagan, S., & Smith, M. S. http://ec.europa.eu/europeaid/how/evaluation/methodology/impact_indicators/wp_edu_en.pdf

Kampylis, P., & Berki, E. *Nurturing creative thinking*.

Keeble, G. Calculation of education educators, UNESCO Institute for Statistics.

Koh, K. H., Bennett, V., & Reppening, A. *Computing indicators of creativity*. http://citeseerx.ist.psu.edu/viewdoc/download?doi=10.1.1.303.2765&rep=rep1&type=pdf

Koitla, E. Information technology foundation for education, *Proge Tiger programme*.

Krzywacki, H., Pehkonen, L., & Laine, A. University of Helsinki, *Promoting mathematical thinking in Finnish mathematics education*.

Laanpere, M. *Implementing and evaluating the digital turn in Estonian schools: From spectacular to fundamental*.

Lafortune, J., Rothstein, J., & Schanzenbach, D. W. *School finance reform and the distribution of student achievement*. http://www.nber.org/papers/w22011

Lindenfeld, P., & Tang, Q. Switzerland (Bern), *Transforming education: The power of ICT policies*.

Magi, E. *Tiger leap program as a beginning of 21-st century education*.

Manuel Francisco Lobo, *Impact of the financial crisis on education sector, spending and government policy responses: Case note (Mozambique)*. http://unesdoc.unesco.org/images/0019/001913/191300e.pdf

Matilainen, M. *Finnish education model pedagogical approach*.

Mayer, J., Perkins, D., Caruso, D., & Salovey, P. *Emotional intelligence and giftedness*.

Moccozet, L., Benkacem, O., Ndiaye, B., Ahmeti, V., Roth, P., & Burgi, B., University of Geneva, Switzerland, *An exploratory study for the deployment of a techno-pedagogical staff learning environment*.

Niemi, H., Multisilta, J., Lipponen, L., & Vivitsou, M. (Eds.) *Finnish innovations and technologies in schools a guide towards new ecosystems of learning*.

OECD.org, *Public and private schools, how management and funding relate to their socio-economic profile*. http://www.oecd.org/pisa/50110750.pdf

Ottesta, G. *Innovative pedagogical practice with ICT in three Nordic countries – Differences and similarities*. http://onlinelibrary.wiley.com/doi/10.1111/j.1365-2729.2010.00376.x/full

Outcome and Impact Level Indicators Education Sector. http://ec.europa.eu/europeaid/how/evaluation/methodology/impact_indicators/wp_edu_en.pdf

PISA in focus 2015, OECD.

Sahlberg, P., & Lessons, F. *What can the world learn from educational change in Finland (second edition)*.

Sahlberg, P. *Education policies for raising student learning: The Finnish approach, Taylor & Francis online*. http://www.tandfonline.com/doi/abs/10.1080/02680930601158919

Sahlberg, P. *Lessons from Finland where the country's education system rose to the top in just a couple decades*.

School funding a review of existing models in European and OECD countries. https://www.nfer.ac.uk/publications/ESF01/ESF01.pdf

Sild, M. *ICT in education ICT in education e-school in Estonia administration of school systems*.

Snell, L. *School finance reform and student achievement*. https://www.hillsdale.edu/wp-content/uploads/2016/02/FMF-2013-School-Finance-Reform.pdf

Spyros, K. *Trends of school effects on student achievement: Evidence from NLS:72, HSB:82, and NELS:92*.

Swiss EQF-referencing report. https://ec.europa.eu/ploteus/en/referencing-reports-and-contacts

Tamme, T. *An overview of outdoor learning in Estonia*.

The Europe 2020 strategy, Europe 2020 headline indicators. http://ec.europa.eu/eurostat/statistics-explained/index.php/Europe_2020_headline_indicators

UNESCO Culture for Development Indicators. http://en.unesco.org/creativity/sites/creativity/files/cdis_methodology_manual.pdf

UNESCO Institute of Statistics, *Education indicators technical guidelines.*

UNICEF, *The investment case of education and equity.* https://www.unicef.org/media/50936/file/Investment_Case_for_Education_and_Equity-ENG.pdf

Vandeleur, S., Ankiewicz, P. J., de Swardt, A. E., & Gross, E. J., *Indicators of creativity in a technology class: A case study.* https://www.ajol.info/index.php/saje/article/viewFile/24914/20526

Vasileios, S., & Schwarz, J. F. *Phenomenon-Based teaching and learning through the pedagogical lenses of phenomenology: The recent curriculum reform in Finland.*

Vilalba, E. (2007). *The relationship between education and innovation.* http://publications.jrc.ec.europa.eu/repository/bitstream/111111111/5028/1/PUBSY%206992%20-%20EUR22797_EDandINN.pdf

Voogt, J., University of Twente, & Kasurinen, H. *Finnish National Board of Education, Finland: Emphasizing development instead of competition and comparison.*

World Economic Forum, *Education and skills 2.0: New targets and innovative approaches.*

Professors and Graduates at Greek Universities

Giannoula Florou

Abstract This work aims to trace and detect variations of both the number of professors (permanent staff) and graduates in Greek universities from 2011 until 2016. More specifically, a correlation between the number of professors and the number of graduates is assumed. Following this assumption, this work elaborates on statistical data concerning graduates taken from the Hellenic Statistical Authority and on data taken from the "Apella" system (website for formal registration election of faculty members). The study focuses on graduates' number; on professors' position, department, and gender; and on years of studies at universities. The inspiration behind this focus is that the number of professors has decreased dramatically in some departments, while the corresponding number of graduates has increased.

Keywords Greek professor · Graduate · Greek university

1 Introduction

In this work, we present data about the academic staff and graduates in Greece over the last years. We analyze the variation of the number of professors and graduates from 2011 until 2017, per gender, per years in tertiary institutes, and per university or technological institute.

We use Eurostat data and Hellenic Statistical Authority data about tertiary education. Due to the fact that there are missing data concerning the years 2014, 2015, 2016, and 2017, we have used data from the "Apella" system about professors and professors in 2017.

G. Florou (✉)
Department of Accountancy and Finance, Eastern Macedonia and Thrace Institute of
Technology, Kavala, Greece
e-mail: gflorou@teiemt.gr

© Springer Nature Switzerland AG 2019   395
N. Sykianakis et al. (eds.), *Economic and Financial Challenges for Eastern Europe*,
Springer Proceedings in Business and Economics,
https://doi.org/10.1007/978-3-030-12169-3_26

Despite the fact that a lot of research works have been done describing education data in Greece (Research about Greek University Education 2006; Livanos and Pouliakas 2011), almost none of these works have used the "Apella" system data.

2   Greek Tertiary Education

Greek tertiary education is divided into two sectors, universities and technological institutes. There are no private tertiary educational institutes. The Ministry of Education and Religious Affairs defines the number of students who are to enter each university or technological institute department per year.

Candidates participate in national-level exams (Panhellenic Examinations), and admission of new students to the abovementioned universities and institutes is correlated with their performance in these exams at the end of the third grade of upper secondary school (Lykeio).

2.1   Academic Staff

The academic staff has a triple role: teaching, research, and service or administrative responsibilities (Houston et al. 2006). A number of papers explore the organizational management literature and link it to the context in which universities operate (Kenny 2009; Kenny and Fluck 2017). In Greek universities, the academics take on administration role alongside their teaching or research work more often than in other countries, as there is not special administrative personnel.

In Table 1, we can see the number of professors in tertiary education per year in European and other countries (Eurostat). In Greece, until 2007, there were 28,998 people (academic staff both in universities and technological institutes). After 2008, there were not enough Eurostat data to be explored. In 2014, there were about 10,500 people (academic staff) in all Greek universities and about 4000 academics in all Greek technological institutes (Hellenic Statistical Authority), with a total number of 15,000 people in tertiary education. This number was about 30,000 in 2007. Unfortunately, the economic crisis had a very bad effect on the number of academics in Greece.

In Greece, in 2011 there were 22 universities with 11,508 people in the academic staff and 168,804 students at basic studies semesters. There were also 16 technological institutes with 6826 people as academic staff and 106,104 students. The corresponding ratio was 14.5 students per academic at universities and 15.5 students per academic at technological education institutes. The mean of European countries was 14.5 students per academic (Eurostat). The results of the economic crisis came up in Greek education system in 2011.

In 2013, the Greek government decided to abolish a number of tertiary education departments and some others to be merged under the "Athena" project. The objective

Table 1 Total number of tertiary academic staff per country per year

Geo/time	2003	2004	2005	2006	2007	2008	2009	2010	2011	2012
Belgium	25,364	25,602	25,774	26,067	26,298	26,619	27,418	28,957	28,579	28,859
French community in Belgium (including small German-speaking community)	11,681	11,791	11,872	12,011	11,961	11,994	12,147	12,074	11,815	–
Flemish community in Belgium	13,683	13,811	13,902	14,056	14,258	14,481	15,127	16,759	16,628	–
Bulgaria	19,104	20,944	21,102	22,306	21,447	21,380	20,848	20,855	20,648	22,955
Czech Republic	22,096	–	24,298	22,549	15,933	15,896	16,351	16,656	18,002	17,476
Denmark	–	–	–	–	–	–	–	–	–	–
Germany (until 1990 former territory of the FRG)	284,116	290,429	287,251	287,744	295,447	304,686	339,806	368,420	392,507	406,366
Estonia	6574	6630	–	–	–	–	–	–		–
Ireland	–	14,254	11,628	12,095	12,396	13,975	12,873	12,609	–	–
Greece	–	25,595	27,161	28,863	28,998	–	–	–		–
Spain	136,436	140,740	144,973	146,229	144,091	145,673	151,598	155,239	153,364	155,538
France	121,406	135,783	136,929	109,975	110,279	110,441	110,700	112,974	115,049	115,511
Croatia	8132	7917	8764	9486	13,075	13,866	14,995	15,721	16,319	–
Italy	87,215	91,978	94,371	99,595	104,421	103,283	110,314	106,119	103,468	–
Cyprus	1335	1460	1451	1723	1824	2339	2366	2553	2669	2710
Latvia	5360	5716	6268	6188	6867	7348	7731	6924	6340	6435
Lithuania	13,522	13,415	13,157	13,382	15,802	14,934	14,762	14,116	13,926	13,923
Luxembourg	–	–	–	–	–	–	–	1004	–	1619
Hungary	23,798	24,708	25,413	24,712	23,454	23,634	23,744	24,596	22,697	24,279
Malta	579	593	825	849	–	968	1271	1207	1386	–
Netherlands	44,092	44,768	44,656	44,414	44,632	47,389	50,029	51,675	51,675	59,431
Austria	28,698	–	–	40,186	29,367	32,686	34,800	46,651	43,807	50,431
Poland	87,158	–	95,144	98,223	99,014	100,500	101,390	102,595	102,621	101,407
Portugal	36,187	36,393	36,773	37,434	36,069	35,178	35,380	36,215	38,064	37,078

(continued)

Table 1 (continued)

Geo/time	2003	2004	2005	2006	2007	2008	2009	2010	2011	2012
Romania	29,619	30,137	30,857	31,543	30,583	31,964	31,973	31,103	29,746	28,365
Slovenia	3109	4143	4475	5246	5609	5939	6259	6947	7214	7348
Slovakia	12,601	12,635	12,709	13,101	13,606	12,284	12,573	13,333	13,080	12,887
Finland	17,988	18,520	18,605	14,370	13,535	14,225	14,545	15,414	16,480	16,164
Sweden	21,387	37,963	37,684	36,386	36,479	36,569	36,229	29,173	30,831	–
United Kingdom	101,040	111,830	122,305	125,585	129,930	134,170	137,950	140,354	139,758	139,785
Iceland	1979	1617	1782	1865	1961	2083	2178	2106	2123	–
Liechtenstein	–	0	0	0	0	–	–	–	109	–
Norway	15,181	15,806	–	18,169	19,182	20,268	21,011	21,807	22,600	23,627
Switzerland	20,417	26,234	34,076	32,545	31,725	33,797	37,235	39,842	41,480	46,193
Former Yugoslav Republic of Macedonia	2635	2627	2922	2857	2774	3506	3847	3464	3861	3662
Turkey	76,090	78,804	82,096	84,785	89,329	98,766	100,504	105,427	111,495	–
Albania	1699	–	–	–	–	–	–	–	–	–

Source: Eurostat (2017)

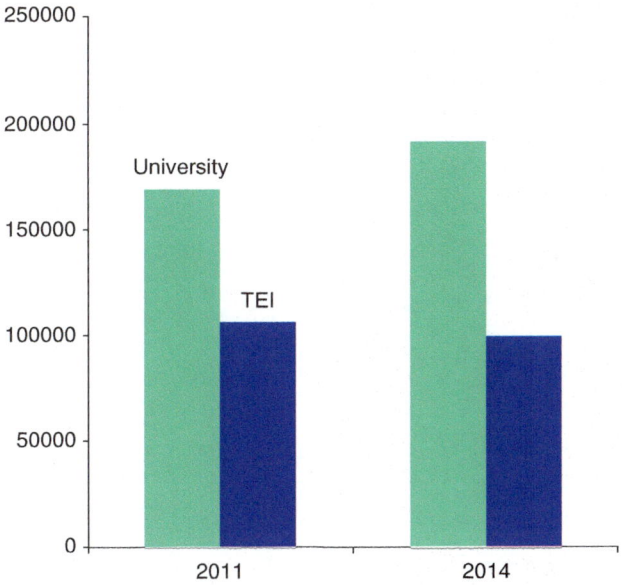

Fig. 1 Number of students 2011 and 2014

was a number of tertiary departments to be decreased for economic reasons. However, the government decided to increase the percentage of students who would enroll at university departments, while the academic staff was decreased as a great number of academics retired and new staff was not appointed. Therefore, since 2014 in Greece, there have been 20 universities with 7131 people in the academic staff and 190,835 students at basic studies semesters. There have also been 14 technological education institutes with 4140 academics and 99,391 students at basic studies semesters. The corresponding ratio has increased dramatically from 14.5 students per academic to 26.5 students at universities and from 15.5 students per academic to 24 at technological education institutes. The mean of European countries was stable at 14.5 students per academic (Eurostat 2017).

We observe that while the students' number increased, the academic staff number decreased, as we can see in Figs. 1 and 2.

The number of the academic staff at each university is presented in Table 2 and Fig. 2, using data from the Hellenic Statistical Authority tables.

The variation number of professors per university from 2011 and 2013 is presented in Table 3. The academic staff number has decreased from −6 to −39% in some universities. Only in two cases (universities), the academic staff number has increased (percentage 6.5% at Panteion University and 10% at the Agricultural University of Athens). The variation number of academic staff per technological education institute (from 2011 to 2013) is presented in the last column of Table 4. We observe that this number has decreased from −20 to −65% in some institutes.

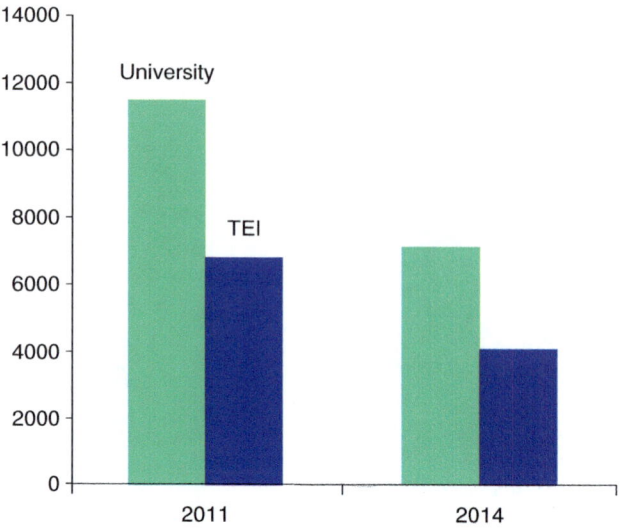

Fig. 2 Number of academic staff 2011 and 2014

Table 2 Academic staff per Greek university from 2011 until 2015

University	2011	2012	2013	2014	2015
National and Kapodistrian University of Athens	2139	2010	1997	2043	1992
University of the Aegean	420	405	343	383	366
University of Western Greece	74	67			
University of Western Macedonia	148	124	98	103	111
University of Thessaly	606	557	500	543	614
Aristotle University of Thessaloniki	2576	2405	2224	2342	2473
Democritus University of Thrace	778	764	630	668	641
University of Ioannina	604	594	542	585	586
University of Crete	603	588	526	528	555
University of Macedonia	284	275	277	266	296
University of Patras	848	790	802	833	819
University of Piraeus	196	192	186	196	196
University of Peloponnese	212	186	152	167	169
University of Central Greece	74	30			
Athens University of Fine Arts	74	69	70	51	47
Agricultural University of Athens	194	187	215	231	249
National Technical University of Athens (NTUA)	665	688	609	747	771
Ionian University	150	133	126	125	129
Athens University of Economics and Business	250	210	217	218	229
Panteion University of Social and Political Sciences	232	235	247	243	239
Technical University of Crete	291	213	177	201	213
Harokopio University	90	82	71	73	75

Table 3 University academic staff variation between 2011 and 2013

University	Variation 2011–2013 (%)
Aristotle University of Thessaloniki (2)	−13.7
National and Kapodistrian University of Athens (2)	−6.6
University of Patras	−5.4
Democritus University of Thrace	−19.0
National Technical University of Athens (NTUA)	−8.4
University of Thessaly	−17.5
University of Ioannina	−10.3
University of Crete	−12.8
University of the Aegean	−18.3
Technical University of Crete	−39.2
University of Macedonia	−2.5
Athens University of Economics and Business	−13.2
Panteion University of Social and Political Sciences	6.5
University of Peloponnese (3)	−28.3
University of Piraeus	−5.1
Agricultural University of Athens	10.8
Ionian University	−16.0
University of Western Macedonia (3)	−33.8

Table 4 Academic staff per Greek Technological Institute 2011 and 2013

	2011	2013	Variation 2011–2013 (%)
TEI of Athens	1286	999	−22.3
TEI of Thessaloniki	813	326	−59.9
TEI of Western Greece (Patra-Mesolongi)	721	362	−49.8
TEI of Crete	639	474	−25.8
TEI of Larissa (Thessaly)	581	205	−64.7
TEI of Piraeus	544	326	−40.1
TEI of Western Macedonia	436	311	−28.7
TEI of Stereas (Lamia Chalkida)	425	246	−42.1
TEI of Kavala (Eastern Macedonia)	347	137	−60.5
TEI of Epeiros	311	183	−41.2
TEI of Serres (Central Macedonia)	245	196	−20.0
TEI of Kalamata (Peloponisos)	176	165	−6.3
ASPAITE	152	108	−28.9
TEI of Ionian Islands	150	102	−32.0

2.2 Graduates

The total number of graduates in European countries (and other countries) is presented in Table 5.

Table 5 Graduates in European countries

	2003	2004	2005	2006	2007	2008	2009	2010	2011	2012
European Union (27 countries)	–	–	–	–	3,993,086	4,231,646	4,100,687	4,419,275	4,816,135	4,838,704
Geo/time	–	–	–	3,863,434	3,970,858	4,204,708	4,068,994	4,384,982	4,777,346	4,798,884
European Union (28 countries)	–	–	–	2,189,449	2,212,763	2,275,449	2,133,659	2,352,354	2,706,082	2,767,248
	–	–	–	2,163,035	2,186,011	2,251,279	2,107,652	2,325,809	2,681,229	2,745,776
Belgium	74,367	76,996	79,659	81,567	103,970	97,248	99,102	102,693	105,271	110,419
French community in Belgium (including small German-speaking community)	30,720	32,074	32,905	33,355	43,065	38,659	–	–	–	–
Flemish community in Belgium	43,647	44,939	46,754	48,212	60,905	58,589	–	–	–	–
Bulgaria	47,277	45,957	46,038	45,353	49,165	54,910	57,803	60,523	64,043	64,091
Czech Republic	47,178	54,341	59,256	69,312	77,580	88,975	96,207	101,188	107,118	107,773
Denmark	42,637	46,726	49,704	47,539	50,849	49,754	48,920	54,271	57,516	58,667
Germany (until 1990 former territory of the FRG)	304,773	319,791	343,874	358,706	376,898	398,537	466,196	493,249	527,108	554,215
Estonia	9877	10,235	11,793	–	12,612	11,345	11,489	11,450	11,828	11,497
Ireland	53,808	55,852	59,650	59,184	59,011	60,074	57,834	58,837	59,260	60,022
Greece	–	48,135	59,872	64,387	60,475	66,956	–	65,096	65,302	66,333
Spain	299,401	298,448	291,376	285,957	279,412	291,036	310,452	336,810	381,926	391,956
France	584,849	–	–	643,600	622,937	621,444	628,089	657,015	697,193	–
Croatia	16,891	18,508	19,548	20,687	22,228	26,938	31,693	34,293	38,789	39,820
Italy	292,015	350,125	386,186	400,860	401,469	398,194	226,012	214,965	388,837	383,332
Cyprus	3213	3547	3676	3858	4445	4228	4522	5053	5931	6173
Latvia	20,763	23,852	26,124	26,414	26,752	24,170	26,007	26,545	24,853	21,472

Lithuania	34,454	38,095	41,466	43,343	43,153	42,547	44,658	45,032	43,419	42,379
Luxembourg	–	–	–	–	–	–	–	–	1435	1289
Hungary	67,606	68,070	73,769	69,756	67,224	63,331	68,158	70,358	67,857	69,917
Malta	2145	–	2741	2676	2729	2792	2844	3032	3393	3463
Netherlands	89,341	96,890	106,684	117,392	96,004	92,545	93,746	96,101	138,772	152,049
Austria	29,176	30,664	32,925	34,825	36,429	43,644	52,157	57,538	63,754	69,385
Poland	477,785	486,313	501,393	504,051	532,827	558,023	574,972	624,799	648,045	638,957
Portugal	67,353	68,668	69,987	71,828	83,276	84,009	76,567	78,609	87,129	94,264
Romania	136,580	147,412	156,565	174,821	205,970	311,475	310,886	305,360	259,634	200,106
Slovenia	13,931	14,888	15,787	17,145	16,680	17,221	18,103	19,694	20,461	20,596
Slovakia	31,852	35,371	36,337	40,190	46,379	65,026	75,364	76,899	74,556	72,374
Finland	38,645	38,606	39,849	40,044	42,296	57,054	43,009	48,768	49,073	51,216
Sweden	49,345	53,848	57,611	60,762	60,243	60,434	59,320	61,217	69,322	69,140
United Kingdom	601,743	595,641	649,895	659,048	671,084	699,810	674,411	709,880	754,310	780,606
Iceland	2516	2841	2921	3404	3542	3627	3450	4105	4328	4096
Liechtenstein	61	73	132	132	146	176	211	200	258	211
Norway	30,127	32,043	31,929	33,529	35,410	35,214	35,272	37,844	40,379	40,346
Switzerland	57,524	61,395	52,000	56,320	63,687	67,334	68,829	73,159	74,149	79,148
Former Yugoslav Republic of Macedonia	4524	5187	5687	6501	8719	11,197	10,776	10,792	11,293	12,105
Albania	5202	–	–	7630	–	–	–	–	–	–
Turkey	311,235	258,858	271,841	373,375	416,329	444,758	488,803	573,159	534,055	607,981
United States	2,355,724	2,473,299	2,557,595	2,639,006	2,704,070	2,782,270	2,881,557	2,997,614	3,164,951	3,308,494
Japan	1,040,354	1,051,262	1,059,386	1,067,939	1,062,444	1,033,774	1,014,795	966,635	968,807	980,902

Source: Eurostat (2017)

Table 6 Graduates in European countries

Geo/time	2013	2014	2015
Belgium	46.7	47.4	–
Bulgaria	40.5	38.6	38.3
Czech Republic	42.5	41.7	–
Denmark	56.9	58.5	–
Germany	28.6	31.2	32.7
Estonia	39.8	37.7	38.6
Ireland	49.8	73.2	–
Greece	41.5	44.0	–
Spain	21.8	31.3	35.3
France	30.4	–	31.7
Croatia	36.3	34.4	36.9
Italy	31.8	32.4	–
Cyprus	23.1	25.6	25.8
Latvia	44.1	32.6	31.7
Lithuania	72.8	59.0	57.8
Luxembourg	8.7	8.2	–
Hungary	34.4	33.9	36.7
Malta	35.6	34.6	33.9
Netherlands	44.4	44.5	–
Austria	25.5	25.7	26.8
Poland	68.2	65.0	62.1
Portugal	43.7	41.4	42.4
Romania	37.3	32.0	30.3
Slovenia	36.7	38.7	42.5
Slovakia	40.3	38.5	35.6
Finland	49.4	50.4	54.3
Sweden	26.7	27.8	–
United Kingdom	46.5	51.1	–
Liechtenstein	47.4	38.3	41.4
Norway	42.0	43.6	43.5
Switzerland	52.0	53.9	54.6
Former Yugoslav Republic of Macedonia	28.3	29.5	–
Serbia	–	24.4	–

Source: Eurostat (2017)

The total number of graduates per 1000 inhabitants in European countries (and other countries) is presented in Table 6. For 2013 and 2014 in Greece, this number was 41.5 and 44, respectively, and it is among the highest percentages in European countries. Greek people consider education valuable and substantial for their children, and they believe that the impact of education on economic growth in Greece is very significant (Tsamadias and Prontzas 2012).

The number of graduates in each university is presented in Table 7 and Fig. 3, using data from the Hellenic Statistical Authority.

Table 7 Graduates per university

Educational institute	2001/ 2002	2003/ 2004	2005/ 2006	2007/ 2008	2009/ 2010	2011/ 2012	2013/ 2014
University of Western Greece	–	–	–	–	–	150	–
University of Central Greece	–	–	–	–	51	79	–
National and Kapodistrian University of Athens	6728	6950	9488	7455	6609	6757	6494
Aristotle University of Thessaloniki	7178	6810	6327	7948	6930	6902	5919
Democritus University of Thrace	1309	1650	2072	2034	2157	2286	2486
University of Macedonia	833	1044	1107	1006	1024	1033	2448
University of Ioannina	1142	1362	1392	1960	1636	1588	1897
University of Piraeus	1102	1337	1607	1428	1492	1204	1806
University of Crete	996	1334	1509	1447	1373	1341	1656
University of Patras	1448	1702	1782	2370	2659	2090	1529
Athens University of Economics and Business	998	1176	1518	1304	1114	1255	1461
Panteion University of Social and Political Sciences	972	1225	1354	1838	1480	1441	1371
University of Thessaly	396	696	879	908	998	1158	1314
National Technical University of Athens (NTUA)	1145	1295	1507	1383	1559	1456	1236
University of the Aegean	263	675	1086	1153	1008	974	1234
University of Western Macedonia	–	–	288	344	301	452	432
Agricultural University of Athens	268	292	264	241	273	321	413
University of Peloponnese	–	–	–	144	259	332	404
Technical University of Crete	111	158	152	217	233	215	294
Ionian University	172	184	230	208	223	214	290
Harokopio University	86	97	53	141	123	149	161
Athens University of Fine Arts	84	126	166	190	100	119	137

Source: Hellenic Statistical Authority

The number of graduates in each technological institute is presented in Table 8 and Fig. 4, using data from the Hellenic Statistical Authority.

2.3 Apella Data Base

"Apella" is a data base for formal registration of professors. In the Apella system, all professors and associate professors must be registered in order to participate in staff elections as evaluators.

The characteristics of Apella are voluntary registration for the selection of new academic staff and systematic registration of professors and associate professors, after 2013.

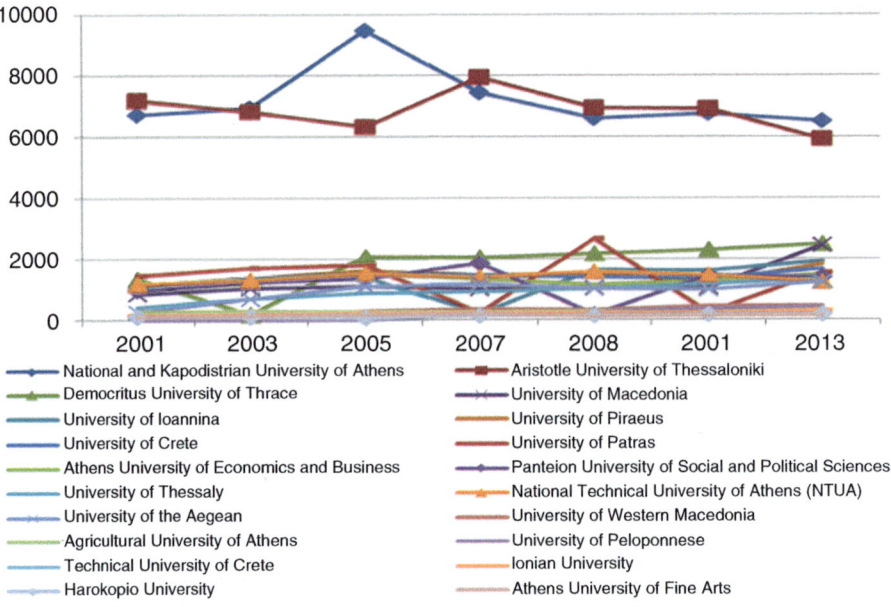

Fig. 3 Number of graduates per university

Table 8 Graduates per technological institute

Educational institute	2001/ 2002	2003/ 2004	2005/ 2006	2007/ 2008	2009/ 2010	2011/ 2012	2013/ 2014
TEI of Athens	2593	3392	3677	3567	3821	2907	2839
TEI of Western Greece (Patra-Mesolongi)	966	1389	2400	2138	2322	2343	2344
TEI of Thessaloniki	1622	2034	2209	2397	2377	2288	2152
TEI of Larissa (Thessaly)	913	1026	1603	1464	1622	1756	1729
TEI of Piraeus	946	1395	1313	1362	1508	1448	1450
TEI of Crete	649	852	775	1160	1515	1402	1435
TEI of Stereas (Lamia Chalkida)	785	1030	1317	974	1401	1588	1420
TEI of Western Macedonia	456	941	1166	1418	1395	1352	1117
TEI of Epiros	322	663	1045	1086	1000	1109	1086
TEI of Serres (Central Macedonia)	476	579	590	853	804	869	1015
TEI of Kavala (Eastern Macedonia)	385	517	802	932	902	907	865
TEI of Kalamata (Peloponnese)	236	323	407	429	574	635	619
ASPAITE	194	266	236	233	259	400	342
TEI of Ionian Islands	–	–	78	100	242	249	198

Source: Hellenic Statistical Authority

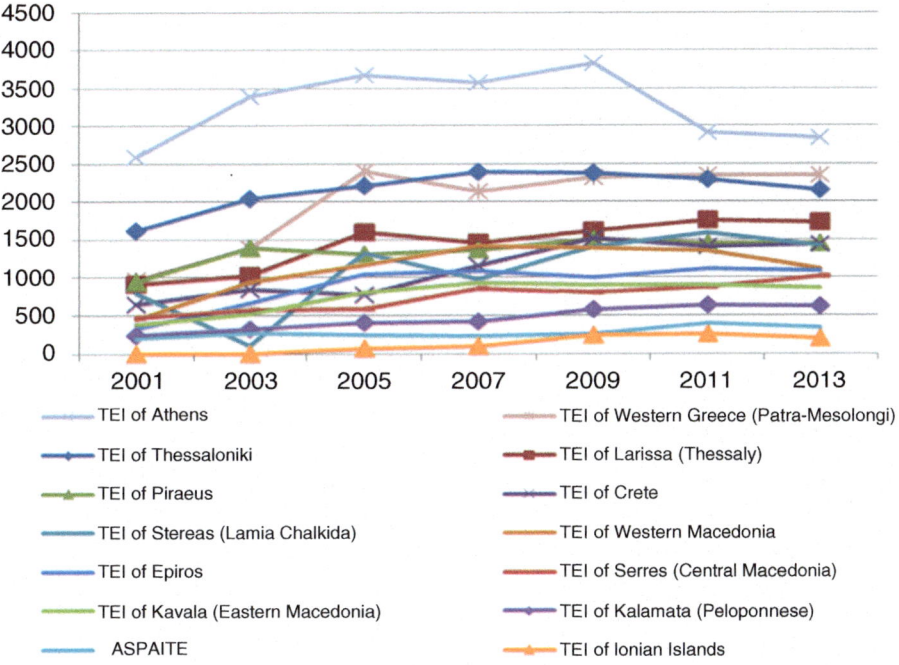

Legend:
- TEI of Athens
- TEI of Western Greece (Patra-Mesolongi)
- TEI of Thessaloniki
- TEI of Larissa (Thessaly)
- TEI of Piraeus
- TEI of Crete
- TEI of Stereas (Lamia Chalkida)
- TEI of Western Macedonia
- TEI of Epiros
- TEI of Serres (Central Macedonia)
- TEI of Kavala (Eastern Macedonia)
- TEI of Kalamata (Peloponnese)
- ASPAITE
- TEI of Ionian Islands

Fig. 4 Number of graduates per technological educational institute

Table 9 Professors per rank

	Frequency	Percent
Professor	1718	78.3
Associate professor	462	21.1
Assistant professor	10	0.5
Researcher	4	0.2
Total	2194	100

Since 2017, the registration of professors, associate professors, and assistant professors has been obligatory, but not all professors have registered yet.

We use data from the Apella system for academics registered until 15-3-2017. Mainly professors and associate professors are registered. The Greek professors registered in Apella on 15-3-2017 are presented in Table 9.

Mainly professors and associate professors are registered in the Apella data base. The percentage of Greek professors per institute in the Apella system is shown in Table 10. In the last column, we present the percentage of female professors which varies from 5 to 25% only.

The year that the last promotion (by appointment or election) took place for the academic staff in Apella is presented in Table 11. Forty-six percent of the professors have been evaluated after 2011 and 40% between 2001 and 2010.

Table 10 Professors per institute

Institute	Frequency	% Total	% Women
Aristotle Univ Thessaloniki	333	15.2	21.3
National and Kapodistrian Univ Athens	206	9.4	25.2
Patras Univ	170	7.7	8.8
National Metsobian Polytechnic	128	5.8	21.9
Democritus Univ Thrace	111	5.1	15.3
Ioannina Univ	107	4.9	11.2
Crete Univ	97	4.4	10.3
Economic Univ	92	4.2	13.0
Piraeus Univ	82	3.7	12.2
TEI Athens	74	3.4	20.3
Thessaly Univ	62	2.8	8.1
Agriculture Univ Athens	59	2.7	18.6
TEI Piraeus	58	2.6	17.2
Macedonia Univ	57	2.6	19.3
TEI Crete	56	2.6	8.9
TEI Thessaloniki	55	2.5	14.5
Crete Polytechnic	50	2.3	8.0
TEI Stereas	50	2.3	10.0
TEI East Macedonia Thrace	48	2.2	16.7
Aegean Univ	47	2.1	12.8
TEI West Macedonia	44	2.0	18.2
TEI Thessaly	43	2.0	4.7
TEI Central Macedonia	29	1.3	10.3
Panteion Univ	28	1.3	25.0
TEI West Greece	27	1.2	18.5
TEI Ipeiros	18	0.8	27.8
Peloponisos Univ	16	0.7	6.3
TEI Peloponisos	12	0.5	8.3
Harokopio Univ	11	0.5	36.4
ASPAITE	7	0.3	14.3
West Macedonia Univ	7	0.3	14.3
TEI Ionion	4	0.2	25.0

Table 11 Professors per election year

Year of last promotion or election	Frequency	Percent
Until < 1990	60	2.7
1991–2000	241	11.0
2001–2010	882	40.2
2011–2017	1011	46.1
Total	2194	100

3 Conclusions

In Greece, the number of graduates is stable between 2011 and 2014, while the number of academic staff has decreased up to 50%. Per 1000 inhabitants, 44 are tertiary education graduates. This number is among the highest proportions in European countries. One academic corresponds to 25 students nowadays, while in 2011 one academic corresponded to 15 students. The European mean is one academic per 14 students in tertiary education.

The graduates' number has no variation before and after the economic crisis. The female graduates' percentage is about 52%.

In the Apella system, all professors and associate professors must be registered in order to participate in staff elections (judges). 2194 academics from universities and technological institutes have been registered until 15-3-2017. Three percent of them started working in technological institutes before 1990 and 80% after 2000. Only 10–20% of the academic staff in the "Apella" system are women (min 6%–max 25%).

References

Eurostat. (2017). Retrieved March 15, 2017 from http://ec.europa.eu/eurostat/data/database

Houston, D., Meyer, L. H., & Paewai, S. (2006). Academic staff workloads and job satisfaction: Expectations and values in academe. *Journal of Higher Education Policy and Management, 28* (1), 17–30. https://doi.org/10.1080/13600800500283734.

Kenny, J. D. (2009). Managing a modern university: Is it time for a rethink? *Higher Education Research & Development, 28*(6), 629–642.

Kenny, J., & Fluck, A. E. (2017). Towards a methodology to determine standard time allocations for academic work. *Journal of Higher Education Policy and Management, 39*(5), 503–523.

Livanos, I., & Pouliakas, K. (2011). Wage returns to university disciplines in Greece: Are Greek higher education degrees Trojan Horses? *Education Economics, 19*(4), 441–445.

Research about Greek University Education. (2006). Retrieved March 15, 2017, from http://www.eliamep.gr/wp-content/uploads/2008/07/chapter1.pdf

Tsamadias, C., & Prontzas, P. (2012). The effect of education on economic growth in Greece over the 1960–2000 period. *Education Economics, 20*(5), 522–537. https://doi.org/10.1080/09645292.2011.557906.

The Three Paradigms of Social Organization

Theodore Papailias

Abstract The purpose of this paper, which is part of a more general research, is to investigate the determinant factors that often influence or control the changes in the organization of society.

The "paradigms" of social structure are three: nomadic life, city-state and state-empire. All of them co-existed and were dominant in the greatest part of world history. The development of social systems moves reciprocally between these three paradigms. In this framework, it is possible for the political regime, in each paradigm, to vary. However, the trend towards the "whole" (globalized society) seems to be something "natural".

The method employed is based on the analysis of historical development, while it attempts to estimate the trends.

Keywords Paradigm · Society structure · City-state · Nomads · Empire · Globalization

1 A General Review

The three *paradigms* of social organization were those of the nomadic life, the city-state and the empire.[1]

Up to the end of the Middle Ages all three seemed to co-exist, even though the first appeared to be the one that marked the social life of even today (gypsies, nomads in Africa, etc.). The second *paradigm* was dominant in antiquity and Greece (including Asia Minor). The third, even from the later Neolithic era (fourth to third

---

[1]Papailias (1999, 2002).

T. Papailias (✉)
University of West Attica, Aigaleo, Greece
e-mail: thpap@uniwa.gr

© Springer Nature Switzerland AG 2019   411
N. Sykianakis et al. (eds.), *Economic and Financial Challenges for Eastern Europe*,
Springer Proceedings in Business and Economics,
https://doi.org/10.1007/978-3-030-12169-3_27

millennium B.C.), as it was obvious, would become the dominant one. It is there that the roots of globalization[2] can be traced.

In the first *paradigm* the social structure was in a "juvenile" form. The various tribes, under the guidance of their leaders (chiefs), were segregated into lineages or (and) families.

The second, as well as the third, originated from the settlement of nomads in a certain location. This permanent settlement is what differentiates humans, transforming their perceptions, while it had the same significant consequences and gravity, one could claim, as the descent of humans from trees[3] (primates' evolution).

Organization became more complex, while at the same time, the individual, as well as the whole, was differentiated.

The cultivation of land, on the one hand, and the cities on the other are connected to this operational stage. The three *paradigms* were in constant conflict, since each differed on the basis of how it viewed the philosophy of history. Initially, the empire failed to subjugate the nomadic tribes of the North (i.e. Darius failed to defeat the Scythes in the Danube), as well as in the East (Cyrus was unsuccessful in enslaving the Turanian tribes) and in the West (all the efforts of Cambyses ended in failure to conquer the African nomads).

Initially, the empire failed to subjugate the nomadic tribes. And in the end, when the Macedonians enforced themselves on the city-states after Chaeronea (338) and on the Persian Empire in Arbela (331), a sort of balance will begin to emerge.

During that period, two major city-states, Rome and Carthage, compete against each other in the West, with the first eventually winning the battle. Nonetheless, its victory was accompanied by self-denial of its role as a city and its conversion into an empire. The transformation of the state's form (the institutions) was inevitable. The city's democratic regime gave its place to hegemonic rulership. Gradually, this differentiation became increasingly essential. The dwellers of Italy were the ones that first gained citizen rights and later on, in the third century, during the leadership of Karkalla, the whole dominion.

From Scotland to the Persian Gulf and from the Danube to Sahara, the "global village" that many embrace today had been formed, that is, the same law, two languages (Latin in the West and Greek in the East), one dominant currency, the Roman *dēnārius* (together with the local ones) and freedom in the market (laissez faire, laissez passer, etc.).

---

[2]This would efficiently result from the constant expansion in the area of Mesopotamia: Acadians, Sumerians, Babylonians, Assyrians, Medes, Persians and Macedonians. Each empire tended (or had the endogenous trend) to become greater than the former. In each stage, part of the heritage was destroyed. The vision, nonetheless, remained the same, i.e. the trend towards the whole. The administrative structures, despite the various regressions, still remained. In the times of Darius, organization reached its highest point. The empire was divided into satrapies, and the King himself as well as inspectors will centrally control this peripheral structure. Later on, Alexander tried to "inoculate" the Greek spirit with the Eastern practice. This interaction lasted for a long time (nearly one millennium), until the arrival of the Arabs.

[3]See in detail: Darwin (1871).

This world was destroyed by the first *paradigm*. It was the nomads that dismantled the system. In the chaos that dominated in the West, three were the major kingdoms that prevailed: the Ostrogoths, the Visigoths and the Franks. But the concept of rules and institutions had no sense and maintained an elementary authority, thanks to the accumulation of the past and the glory of heritage.

When everything was obliterated, the empire of Charlemagne was split into small fiefdoms. So, the *paradigm* of the city-state dominated again in another form, as an agrarian form. It seemed that the second paradigm was reborn, just as Phoenix did in mythology. So, Europe remained divided into numerous fiefdoms. This situation seems almost the same as that of many city-states of antiquity. Nonetheless, the invasion of new nomads, the constant pressure by the first *paradigm*, undermined the quasi function of the fiefdom. The Longobards were confronted by the Carolingian military machine. So were the Arabs—that is, before the dominance of the feudal regime.

The confrontation of Normans' or Magyars' incursions in the tenth century required a strong state. The weaknesses, inabilities and inadequacies of the second "solution" revival soon became very obvious.

That resulted in the establishment of a national state, since Charles V and Philip II failed to establish the new empire. In the East, the part of the old Roman Empire, Byzantium, was swept initially by the mishmash of feudal lords of the West (1204) and later by Turcoman hordes, in the fifteenth century.[4]

However, during these centuries the first *paradigm* had also been infected by the tendency towards the whole. In the thirteenth century, the Mongol hordes pursued expansion and created the largest empire that has ever existed. This change in thinking is reflected if one compares the social structure and the political conception of the Huns in the era of Attila, or of the Avars, to that of Genghis Khan or the Golden Horde of Tamerlane.

The main scope of the wars that broke out from the eve of the early modern period and up until World War II (or the Cold) was the creation or the obstruction of an empire. The collapse of the social "camp" after 1990 and the "invisible" accession of China in the ideology of the market triggered off the reinforcement of the trend towards globalization.

More specifically:

Nomad life was based on the least possible limitation of the individual. The nomad is under the loose supervision of the tribe and its leader. The limits of his freedom by the law (mainly the unwritten) were extremely constrained.

The defined rights of the citizen were usually written, but he had more constraints than the "apolis".[5] While in the first *paradigm* everything was owned by the tribe (or the leader as its representative), in the second there is private property (unlimited, one could perhaps argue with some degree of arbitrariness).

---

[4]For a more in-depth analysis, see the classical work of *Georgije Ostrogorski* (Ostrogorsky 1940).

[5]One who has no motherland.

The political rights of the citizen ranged from only a few (in the case of monarchy or tyranny) to fairly extended, as in the case of democracy. Generally, a kind of ambiguity and indeterminacy (or uncertainty) prevailed, since the regime oscillated between democracy and autarchy, with aristocracy, oligarchy and tyranny as middle points.

An empire may stem either directly from nomadic life, something that rarely appears (a situation that sometimes seems unnatural), or as the expansion of the city-state. The latter seemed to be the case during the ancient or medieval period. "Polis" in its process of expansion, almost inevitably, transformed into an empire. In ancient Greece, the Athenian hegemony was overthrown due to the coalition of the other cities. The same holds true for the Spartan or Theban hegemony. In contrast, in Mesopotamia, one of the first state amalgams in the Mediterranean (the other one was that of the Egyptians), the initial dominance of a city over the others and after that the absorption or the unification that followed led to the creation of the Sumerian empire. The Roman *paradigm* is the most characteristic one. "Polis" dominated over many cities and nations. The citizen rights were gradually passed over to all, while this administration process could not be realized under a democratic regime. So monarchy during the sovereign of Caesar became a dead-end and democracy seemed an anachronism.[6] An extended state could not be ruled by a group of citizens. The creation of bureaucratic mechanism was inevitable but this bureaucracy undermined the citizenship regime. For example, in the direct democracy of the cities, the existence of a complex administrative mechanism was limited. In a state or an empire, this was impossible.

2   Community-City-State: The Choice of Measure

The first establishment of the nomads was a primitive settlement, which in an immature form composed the community. The long stay broadened settlements and increased their number. In later stages, the unification of the settlements started in a more rapid momentum, resulting in the foundation of the city. Expanded cities came into conflict, retaining in this way some kind of a balance, as was the case in ancient Greece, or subjugating one another and forming up an empire. City-states are a characteristic example (Aristotle 1998). In Macedonia the unification of cities or, to state it more precisely, the lack of development of a spirit of autonomy led to the creation of the Macedonian dynasty and later on the Macedonian empire. In contrast, in the south of Olympus the spirit of locality and independence was so wide that it led to the establishment of the city-states. It seems that geography in this stage played a decisive role. In the Near East, nonetheless, the formation of an empire seemed to be unavoidable. The merge of communities in a unified authority (town) was what constituted the qualitative difference, the golden mean that led the nomads

---

[6]So Brutus and Cassius were never justified, just as Harmodius and Aristogeiton.

to detach permanently from the primary social organization. That is why in antiquity, the ones that acted in a similar manner were glorified and considered as founders and protectors of the city.[7] The quality difference was found in the gradual conversion of the existing regime. Monarchy in all cities was initially replaced by the aristocracy of blood and later of wealth. The leader of the tribe proved to be an anachronism, and so monarchy was incongruent with the new structure, whether anyone referred to the Phoenician regions or Great Greece or the Black Sea. The observation of the development of the Athenian regime provides a characteristic example. The "leader" king initially gave way to the quasi monarchy, where the top ruler was primus inter pares. The latter was gradually replaced by the aristocracy (the nobles). The evolution of exchanges (i.e. in commerce and manufacture) brought the class of artisans and traders into surface and the regime now approached timocracy. Tyranny and democracy constituted the developments that followed. The Athenian democracy quickly transformed after the Persian conflict into hegemony, so a coalition against it is created and finally after several processes the Macedonian empire prevails. In Rome, the expansion led to the abolition of democracy and the establishment of absolutism, which was the regime of the empire. Therefore, one can conclude that the growth of a city inevitably led to the third *paradigm*, that of imperial governing.

3   Commercial Capitalism

The existence of small autonomous cities led to the creation of commercial capitalism. The latter, in its current form, first appeared in Greece. More specifically, the division of the country into many small valleys and islands was what provided the potential for urban development. Despite the fact that there was some kind of loose bond between them, each city had its own protectors and currency.[8] Moreover, being a neighbour to the Eastern empires and their achievements was the factor that triggered the need for their own development. The cities of Minor Asia were pushed both linguistically (Greek borrowed the Phoenician alphabet and left Linear B) and in terms of science and belief to proceed to self-development. At the same time, the relevant distance between them and the empires gave the latter the ability to develop their own theory of the Cosmos (Weltanschauung). The Phoenician and the Greek cities of Asia Minor, initially, despite having taken precedence and having greater advantages, did not manage to create their own theory (worldview) since they were subjugated to the *paradigms* of the East (under the sovereignty of empire). In contrast, the cities of mainland Greece, Carthage and Rome, being far from absolutism, managed to stay independent and to develop. So the latter got the motive

---

[7]Theseus in Athens, who is the reason why the Panathenaea were celebrated as the most glorious celebration of the Athenians. Remus and Romulus in Rome, etc.

[8]Herodotus put emphasis on the three facts that united the Greeks: one blood, one language, one religion.

required for this economic and cultural "take-off" and at the same time, due to the abovementioned distance, survived up to the point that made them resilient to the pressure posed by the empire. However, the victory in the Marathon battle and the naval battle of Salamis seemed as something non-natural and was realized due to a number of favourable factors.[9] In the areas far from the East (and the state-empire), nonetheless, something additional developed, which was the spirit of atomism (the theory of individualism). That was one of the major characteristics of the Greek *paradigm* of the city-state. The king was considered the son of God since the early years (of the establishment of community), and his power was passed on to him by the latter (Pharaohs in Egypt, David in Israel, etc.). The power the leader of the nomads had was absolute (regardless of whether making reference to the Turanians, the Mongol Hans, the Turkish sultans, the Semitic rabbles, etc.). Thus Abraham had the right of life and death over his liegemen and, of course, his son. Similar examples can be found in the ancient Greek history as well. One of them is that of Agamemnon, who sacrificed his daughter to the Gods.

In the city-state, the overthrow of the king (a kind of *pieta* or *apokathilosis*) had penetrated into the whole ideology. In the first chapter of *Theogony*, as a belief, Greeks talked about Crones that ate his sons. Zeus, nonetheless, was the one that escaped and with the help of his brothers subverted his father. Thus, the son after his ascension to manhood threw off the paternal power and became autonomous, that is, a free citizen. Thus, while according to the nomad *paradigm* the patriarch, *fürer*, was the soul of the team, of the horde (something like that of animals), in the city-state its centre focused on the citizen. Each action originated from him.

4   The Empire: The Trend Towards the Whole

The empire *paradigm* was first imposed in Egypt and its more complete form in Mesopotamia. The attempt by Alexander was even more successful. He wanted to unite the two worlds, the Eastern and the Hellenic. His early death interrupted his work and the empire splintered. Caesar, led by the latter's vision, tried to affiliate the countries of the West and North to the "chariot" of the city-state Rome. The Roman Empire, which lasted for 500 years in the West and 1000 more in the East, took its position. The Roman state was a complete globalized economy. From Scotland to Africa and from Spain to Caucasus, the transactions and the economic activities were conducted under the same law. Capital, commodities and people circulated seamlessly.[10]

---

[9]Even the war technique was differentiated and supported the glory of the city-state. Empires, nonetheless, had a modern appreciation of war, resembling that of today.

[10]According to Max Weber, the three types of authority are the charismatic authority, the traditional (patriarchal) and the bureaucratic (Weber 1922).

5 Medieval Ages: The Partitioning and Disintegration of the Whole

At the beginning in the Middle Ages, various kingdoms were established in the West, which gradually got self-destructed and the fiefdom[11] dominated after the ninth century. This disintegration was the reverse direction of the former development (from the city-state to the empire). The reasons that led to this can be traced down to the defining factors of the establishment of a state. Each tribe created its own state (Vandals, Visigoths, Ostrogoths, etc.) over the ruins of the Roman world, but they did not have any bureaucratic apparatus. The passage from nomadic life to kingdom (without the middle stage, namely, the city) deprived them of those characteristics that would enable them to self-promote their further development. They made no contribution. They lived out of the lootings of the past.

The same disintegration was obvious in all aspects of life: education, technique, commerce etc. Therefore, Charlemagne's effort had a provisional character; he managed to unify the various kingdoms, but after his death, the empire collapsed. In contrast, the Ottoman Empire, which had been established on the ruins of the Byzantine and the long-lasting osmosis (one should not forget the fact that the sultans, up to their fall, used the Greeks or Muslims that had excelled in the Greek administration), managed to survive for a long time. However, its inability to be further developed and to establish itself for a long time led to its collapse.[12] Likewise, the imposition of the first *paradigm* failed to create a lasting state. The abovementioned can be rendered as eloquent, if the rapid degradation of the Mongol Empire is compared to the stability of the Chinese kingdom or the absorption of the Mongolian element in the Indian peninsula. The twilight of the medieval world was almost inevitable. Typically, the feudal society, through the partition it brought about, resembled that of the ancient city-state. However, there was still a very important difference. The economy had become rural and each fiefdom operated—to a great extent—as a closed economy.

The transition from the medieval economy to commercial capitalism and the national state came not as a result of the feudal transformation but of the development of the cities.

At first, they existed as quasi "parasites" in the feudal world.[13] The development of commerce, the accumulation of knowledge, originated from these commercial centres that gradually became autonomous. Due to the power they gained when the national state rose during the fifteenth to sixteenth century, they were also politically

---

[11]For some historians, the future of the Medieval West constituted the reflection of the developments in the East and more specifically, the descent of the Arabs (see Pirenne 1937).

[12]After the seventeenth and the eighteenth century it started declining (Ostrogorsky 1940).

[13]The noble, since he was only occupied with the art of war, aiming at the perseverance of his hegemony (or his ascension), had a disregard for the bourgeois professions (i.e. that of the lawyer, the doctor, the merchant etc.). Most of the cities, not belonging to a certain fiefdom, developed nearly independently (see Bloch 1940).

established as well. The states that remained agrarian declined and were marginal-ized. At the same time, in other places such as Italy, the powerful cities did not manage to survive, due to the competition with the West European states, and, as the case in antiquity was, the cities underwent an eclipse and submitted to them.

6 The Modern Period: National State

The unification of the fiefdoms and the dominance of the king over the toparches, which was often realized with the aid that was provided by the cities, and the emergence of the notion of national identity acted as a magnification example of the city-state. The reverberations of the Roman Empire, quite intense, especially in Germany (already from the eleventh century, the Holy Roman Empire) and the recollection of the Carolingian accomplishments in France reinforced competition among the emerging states. The Hundred Years' War would comprise, in essence, the last European feudal dynastic contradiction.[14] Nonetheless, in the whole Western and Central Europe a fierce competition prevailed.[15] More particularly, it was the common faith that held Europe united in its opposition to the East. The Latin language was the main language of science, at least for this first period. So the findings that took place in one area, soon expanded to even the far end of the continent easily, despite the fact that Protestantism constituted a rupture to this evolution. Nonetheless, it reinforced the transmission of knowledge, constituting in this way a shelter for the nonconformists.[16]

The prevailing antagonism in the Modern Period resembled that of the ancient times (conflicts between the cities in Italy, Rome and Carthage, Athens and Corinth or Megara, etc.). That fact resulted in the expanding knowledge in economic life and the accelerated development of the system.

In contrast, in the Ottoman Empire, in India or China, absolutism constituted a poisonous environment for the development of knowledge. It is not accidental that despite the initial dynamic that Spain showed, due to the discoveries, soon the regime (as a consequence of the political stillness it imposed) was pushed to stagnation. The same situation would be created in France during the reign of Louis XIV onwards, if the regime had not been overturned a little time later.

---

[14]"The war of the Roses" that followed in England was of a local interest.
[15]Le Goff (1964).
[16]The French Huguenots found shelter in Prussia, the Low Countries etc.

7 The Industrial Revolution: The Dynamics of the Economy

The industrial revolution was being prepared for many centuries (at least from 1400 onwards). It constituted the upshot of a long-lasting procedure that assimilated what was known to the world. In the middle and late medieval period, the knowledge of the Arabs and antiquity and the inventions of the East (China, etc.), such as paper, compass, gunpowder, etc., helped the take-off. And at the dawn of the modern era through the movements of Humanism and the Renaissance, the accomplishments and the spirit of the ancient world were rediscovered and revived. The intense competition among the various nations constituted the necessary condition for accumulation. The puritan ethic and the notion of non-consumption reinforced the trend towards capitalism that had already been invigorated with the New Man of the Renaissance.

Initially, it seemed that in the sixteenth century, Charles V would repeat the accomplishments of Charlemagne. An emperor that despite having dominions from the Baltic Sea to the Mediterranean and from the Atlantic Ocean to the Polish steppes failed, since all the major powers (France, England, the Pope, etc.) moved against him.

Although his army captured the king of France Francis I at Pavia, looted Rome and humiliated the Pope, Charles failed due to resistance from the home front. The German sovereigns, the remnants of the feudal structures, allied against the emperor and attained with the treaty of Augsburg (1555) the right to choose their preferred religion for themselves and for their subjects. His successor, Philip II, failed to crush England and the Low Countries.[17] From now on, a balance will prevail beyond any ideology and faith, and initially its apex will be recorded in Westphalia (1648) and will be completed in Yalta (1945). In those years the industrial revolution that had been prepared through knowledge acquisition and urbanization (and by the enclosures in England) will start exploding in the middle of the eighteenth century. At the same time, with the technical achievements accomplished, the ethical part had been altered. The up to the seventeenth-century condemned notion of the interest rate now became acceptable. The royal power was limited to England slowly but steadily (Cromwell, the glorious revolution, etc.). The weak kings will give precedence to the parliament (an amalgam from the class of the landowners and the bourgeois). The individual became the centre of society and liberalism the ensign of the era. Laissez faire, laissez passer will be justified with Smith. Personal benefits led to the general good. Anything supporting the profit and power of the kingdom constituted a principle.

So an unbridled capitalism broke out and Utilitarianism would warrant it. This ethic would easily prevail in the whole Western and Central Europe, since their history was parallel due to the osmosis. At the end of the nineteenth century, the national states, due to the fierce competition among them, turned to the exploitation of the rest of the world. The collisions between them led to the First World War and

---

[17]More analytically see Braudel (1949).

later on to the Second. During that period the system expanded to even more countries and eventually the whole world accepted the economic model. The revolution of the Bolsheviks, the triumph of the Red Army in 1945 and the dominance of the Chinese Revolution (1949) showed that there also existed another course of development.

The bloodless collision (cold war) led to the defeat of the socialist world and eventually its collapse. Presumably, today China politically stands for the communist regime. However, its collapse is just a matter of time. Capitalism is reinforced by the autarchies. But the system becomes more effective if there is a political struggle, even of a parliamentary type.

8 Globalization: The Squaring of the Circle

Therefore, after the collapse of the socialist countries, the undisguised truth came up. One language is the most dominant in the whole world, and that is English. One economic regime, that of the free market (laissez faire, laissez passer), is present. The same law dominates: the Anglo-Saxon. The World Trade Organization (WTO) and International Monetary Fund (IMF) lead all the countries to the arena of liberalism, to the abolition of every institutional barrier and the dissolution of the social welfare state. Health, education and culture tend to become uniform. In this sense, what smouldered for centuries emerged: globalization. In the ancient times, change came as a result of the absorption of one kingdom by another. The Sumerians were absorbed by the Babylonians, who, in turn, were absorbed by the Assyrians and so on. No state got self-destructed by the long-lasting stagnation and the intense class differences. The Egyptian regime, for example, lasted until its subjugation to the Persians. The Greek cities, despite the acute social problem they faced, remained timocratic regimes. Finally, the conservatives in the Hellenistic period, in order not to lose their benefits, called for help the ones that were outside. That is the case with Agis and Cleomenes, after the descent of the Macedonians, and so is the case with the entrance of the Romans as liberators. In Rome, the struggle was quite intense. But, contrary to Greece, there existed no exogenous factor. Democracy, inevitably, gave its place to the empire, which in turn, in an effort to survive, declared all citizens Romans. Nonetheless, the "class regime" generated such contradictions, that many accepted the Barbarians as some kind of a solution. Later on, parallel to the economic inequality, the religious one was added as well. The main provinces of the East Empire (Byzantium), after the battle in Yarmouk (636) or *Hieromyax*, and the capture of Alexandria (641)[18] will abandon and accept the Arabs (Syria, Palestine, Mesopotamia, Egypt, etc.). The same thing will happen with the arrival of the Seljuks after the Manzikert battle (1071).[19] In the medieval period, the social and

---

[18]Anderson (1974).

[19]Vryonis (1971).

political regime was dictated by the bourgeoisies and not by the serfs. In today's times it seems that nothing beyond the system exists. For the loyal Marxists, the end will be signalled by the contradiction of the bourgeoisies and the proletarians. Emmanuel (1969)[20] considered redemption something that would come from the new "barbarians", that is, the Third World.

References

Anderson, P. (1974). *Passages from antiquity to feudalism*. London: New Left Books.
Aristotle. (1998). The politics. Translated by C.D.C. Reeve. Indianapolis: Hackett Publishing.
Bloch, M. (1940). *La Société féodale*, Paris.
Braudel, F. (1949). *La Méditerranée et le monde méditerranéen a l'époque de Philippe II*.
Darwin, C. (1871). *The descent of man and selection in relation to sex*.
Emmanuel, A. (1969). *L'échange inégal: essai sur les antagonismes dans les rapports économiques internationaux*. Paris: Maspero.
Le Goff, J. (1964). *La civilisation de l'occident Médiéval*. Artaud.
Ostrogorsky, G. (1940). *Geschichte des byzantinischen Staates*.
Papailias, T. (1999). The defining factors of globalization. In *Proceedings of the 2nd International Conference in Messologi*, Greece.
Papailias, T. (2002). The community in the framework of globalization. In *Proceedings of the 3rd International Conference in Messologi*, Greece.
Pirenne, H. (1937). *Mahomet et Charlemagne* (p. 224, 1re édn.). Paris: Les Presses universitaires de France, 1992. Collection Quadrige.
Vryonis, S. Jr. (1971). *The decline of medieval Hellenism in Asia minor and the process of Islamization from eleventh through the fifteen century*. Berkeley: University of California Press.
Weber, M. (1922). *Die drei reinen Typen der legitimen Herrschaft*. Gesammelte Aufsätze zur Wissenschaftslehre.

---

[20]See the conflict between Bettelheim and Emmanuel Arghiri in Monde (1969). The relevant literature is included in the book of the latter "L'échange inegal".

Prospective Employee Attitudes Toward Public and Private Sector Employment: A Comparison Study of a Belgian and Two Greek University Student Groups

Alexandros G. Sahinidis, Georgia Tsakni, and Dimitrios Kallivokas

Abstract The increasing scarcity of talent and the graying of the labor market in western societies pose a number of challenges for the human resource departments of public sector organizations. Traditionally, the public sector fails to attract high-caliber professionals, since it lacks the resources of private organizations, unable to match their salaries and benefits. The situation is getting even more difficult for managers in the public sector, with the drives of downsizing and leanness, forced on them by the governments. Public organizations thus need to focus on finding high-quality talent, driven more by public service motivation (PSM) and less by extrinsic rewards. The purpose of this study is to examine the relationship between PSM and student choice of employer. Three samples were used in our analysis, one from a Graduate School of Economics in Belgium, another one from a Graduate School of Public Administration in Greece, and a third one also from a Graduate School of Business in Greece. We used SPSS and conducted a factor analysis, to ensure that the questions correspond to the expected dimensions of PSM. We then examined the relationship between the dimensions of PSM and the employer choices using correlation analysis. The hypotheses concerning the employer choices and the PSM dimensions were tested with ANOVA. The results partially supported the hypotheses proposed in this paper, demonstrating that PSM is a good indicator of an individual's propensity to give preference to working for a public organization, in spite of the less attractive rewards expected by doing so. The implications of the findings in this study are particularly significant for public organizations, since they highlight the value of PSM, as a predictor of how devoted to public service a future employee will be before recruitment. Public organizations can avoid turnover and achieve high levels of job satisfaction and employee motivation, if they use PSM when they recruit their staff.

Keywords Public service motivation · PSM · Employer choice · Greece · Belgium

A. G. Sahinidis (✉) · G. Tsakni · D. Kallivokas
Department of Business Administration, TEI of Athens, Egaleo, Greece
e-mail: asachinidis@teiath.gr

© Springer Nature Switzerland AG 2019
N. Sykianakis et al. (eds.), *Economic and Financial Challenges for Eastern Europe*,
Springer Proceedings in Business and Economics,
https://doi.org/10.1007/978-3-030-12169-3_28

1 Introduction

For a very long time, organizational analysis failed to distinguish between the management of public and private organizations, until two decades ago when in the early 1990s, the gap in the literature started to receive the scholars' attention and the management journals increasingly provided space, for the exploration of the particularities of public organization management (Wright et al. 2017; Homberg et al. 2015). The differences between public and private organizations are not limited to ownership, funding, and structure ones but also in the people employed in these organizations, their needs and wants, and their personality makeup in general (Perry and Wise 1990). Perry and Wise (1990), in their seminal work, introduced the concept of public service motivation (PSM), which is the prevailing term among others with relevant meaning, focusing on the motivational differences between the employees of public vs. private organizations. Other researchers expanded their work, examining issues of PSM effects on organizational outcomes such as job satisfaction, performance, turnover intention, absenteeism, etc. (Homberg et al. 2015; Ritz et al. 2013; Leisink and Steijn 2008; Lee and Wilkins 2011). Twenty years after the Perry and Wise (1990) study, 125 studies have been published about PSM (Perry et al. 2010), while Ritz et al. (2013), in their literature review, found 182 papers published by 2012, based on the Perry and Wise study, which had been further refined by Perry (1996, 1997), in terms of the measurement of PSM dimensions' reliability and validity.

There is fairly strong evidence, as reported by many researchers, that people with low PSM levels tend to work in private organizations, while public sector employees are characterized by high PSM levels (Wright et al. 2017; Homberg et al. 2015; Piatak 2016; Lee and Wilkins 2011; Ritz et al. 2013; Clerkin and Coggburn 2012). This is indicative of the need of public organization recruitment officers, to attract people from a talent pool of high PSM level prospective employees. Such employees will require less time to adapt to the organization due to the presumed person-job fit (Neumann 2016) or organization-person fit (Christensen and Wright 2011; Bright 2007), and the socialization effort they will need is going to be minimal (Perry 1997; Kjeldsen et al. 2013).

The abundance of research on PSM naturally generated numerous definitions, leading to inconsistent findings reported in the published studies. Perry and Wise defined PSM as "an individual's predisposition to respond to motives grounded primarily or uniquely in public institutions and organizations" (Perry and Wise 1990, p. 368), while Brewer and Selden (1998) thought of it as a force that makes people offer "meaningful public service." In another definition yet, Gould-Williams et al. (2013, p. 2) propose "PSM is an attitude that motivates both public and private sector workers to display altruistic or prosocial behavior." Rainey and Steinbauer (1999, p. 23), emphasizing the altruism aspect, define PSM as "a general altruistic motivation to serve the interests of a community of people, a state, a nation, or humankind." In spite of the slight variations, the majority of the PSM definitions describe the individual's concern for the public good. In this study, the Perry and Wise (1990) definition will be used, due to its prevailing presence in the literature and its acceptance by the majority of researchers.

The purpose of this study is to compare three different samples of students, from different background each, and ascertain the differences or similarities of those, in terms of their public service motivation. Furthermore, comparisons will be conducted to study where each of the samples stands in the four dimensions of PSM. Finally, the gender issue will also be addressed, to explore potential differences also.

The contribution of this paper is twofold: First, it is expected to help academics observe the PSM instrument behavior in two different cultures (Greek and Belgian) testing thus its reliability, as well as testing the PSM measure in samples from different subcultures (graduate students of public administration and business admin- istration graduate students). Second, the hypothesis of attraction vs. socialization (Kjeldsen et al. 2013) will also be tested, examining the PSM levels of public administration students compared to those of business and economics ones.

2 Literature Review

Numerous studies have shown that public service motivation (PSM) has a positive relationship with public sector employment (Ritz et al. 2013; Clerkin and Coggburn 2012). The topic has been receiving interdisciplinary attention, since the early 1990s, bringing into the discussion perspectives from human resource management (Naff and Crum 1999; Stazyk 2012), management theory and organizational behavior, (person-organization fit, Christensen and Wright 2011) and the attraction-selection- attrition theory (Wright and Christensen, 2010), public administration, and even behavioral economics (Kamenica 2012). Although some studies such as those of Christensen and Wright (2011) and Kjeldsen et al. (2013) called into question part or all of its capacity in the prediction of prosocial behaviors (Lee and Choi 2013), the studies reporting a positive of PSM with public sector employment by far outnumber the former ones (Ritz et al. 2013).

The ultimate question that is being addressed in the PSM literature is what are the characteristics or traits of the person who would be attracted to working in a public organization. Both attraction-selection-attrition and person-organization fit theories propose that people whose values are congruent with the organization (not the sector) will tend to be attracted to the organization and have greater job satisfaction and lower intention to leave. Naff and Crum (1999, p. 12) report that:

> . . .the typical 40-something, white male, grade 12 federal employee who has no motivation toward the public service would have only a 46 percent probability of being satisfied with his job. If the same employee were to have the "average" level PSM . . . his chances of being satisfied with his job would increase to 74%. With a maximum level of PSM, he would have an 85% probability of being satisfied with his job.

In the same vain, Lewis and Frank (2002) found a linear relationship between the level of PSM and the desire to work in the public sector.

Two studies disconfirming the assertions by the scholars mentioned above are one by Lee and Choi (2013) and another by Kjeldsen et al. (2013). The first of the two was conducted in Korea and reported that there was no relationship between PSM and prosocial behaviors and public sector's choice among students. Only job security was found to be a main reason why college students wanted to work for the public sector in Korea. The study by Kjeldsen et al., after having studied physical therapy students before and after their first job, reported that:

> ... PSM is relevant for neither attraction to the public sector nor actual sector of employment. This indicates that within a group of professionals, PSM is probably more associated with the nature of the public service work than the sector itself. Conversely, PSM is found to be severely hampered after job entry, which is interpreted as a shock effect. This effect is also moderated by sector, that is, public organizational membership prevents PSM from declining as much as in the private sector. This suggests that if PSM is associated with sector employment, then it is primarily a consequence of the sector affiliation, but in a more complex way than previously assumed.

In an effort to better understand PSM, some researchers focused on its antecedents. Camilleri (2007) proposes five types of antecedents, based a review of the literature. The first type relates to personal attributes of an individual such as education, job tenure, etc. and individual characteristics such as age, gender, and salary and the second, the role states; third, how the employee perceives the organization; fourth, employee-leader relations; and fifth, job characteristics (Perry 2000). In the Naff and Crum (1999) study of 10,000 public employees, women were found to have greater PSM levels, and bachelor holders or greater degree also had a greater PSM score than those with less education. Finally, Houston (2000) concluded in his study that public sector employees value more meaningful work than higher wages. In general he proposed that public employees place greater importance on intrinsic rewards and the sense of accomplishment rather than higher salaries and shorter work hours. Also, he sites other authors reporting the failure of pay-for-performance systems in public organizations, because such systems are linked to extrinsic rewards. Similar suggestions are offered by behavioral economists proposing that offering rewards for prosocial behaviors will likely lead to the extinction of such behaviors (Kamenica 2012).

Perry (1997) studied parental socialization effects on PSM, religious socialization, professional identification, political ideology, and demographics. Four variables, parental modeling, education, age, and closeness to God, were found to be associated to PSM. Also found against his expectations a negative association of PSM to Church involvement, while income showed a negative association with civic duty (Sahinidis and Kolia 2014).

Many studies report a strong relationship of PSM to organizational outcomes, such as employee commitment (Sahinidis and Kolia 2014; Crewson 1997; Naff and Crum 1999) and job satisfaction which in PSM research is treated as a consequence of PSM (Vandenabeele 2008; Perry and Wise 1990; Naff and Crum 1999; Kim 2005; Park and Rainey 2007, 2008; Bright 2007; Steijn 2008). Also, a positive relationship of PSM to individual performance was reported by Crewson (1997) and by Naff and Crum with the latter stating that: "...a low PSM individual would have a

29% probability of receiving an outstanding performance rating compared to 42% probability for an individual of an average level PSM and a 52% probability for the high PSM employee" (1999, p. 13). Other studies found a PSM relationship with organizational citizenship (Kim 2005; Pandey et al. 2007), lower turnover intention (Giauque et al. 2012), and work effort which was another variable also correlated with PSM, in studies by Wright (2003) and by Frank and Lewis (2004).

Based on the findings of the earlier studies mentioned above, we can form the following hypotheses:

H1 There is no difference between the student groups, represented in the study.

H2 There is no difference between male and female student PSM levels.

3 Method

Three distinct groups of graduate students comprise the sample of this study. The first one is a Graduate School of Public Administration in Greece (GSPAG), consisting of people from different educational backgrounds but joined the Public Administration Graduate Program ($N = 71$). The second one ($N = 141$) also from Greece are graduate students from a large Business School (BSG). The third group ($N = 135$) includes students from a Graduate School of Business and Economics in Belgium (GSEB). The background differences between the groups will enable us to compare the PSM levels of each and the potential differences between gender PSM levels.

PSM was measured with a 17-item Likert-type scale, previously used by Kim et al. (2013) and in Sahinidis and Kolia (2014). The above authors first used the 24-item instrument in Perry's (1996) study, which they revised in order to meet the criteria of their research. The final measure was tested in a CFA with success and its overall Cronbach $a = 0.87$. The four PSM dimensions whereby *PSM1 refers to self-sacrifice, PSM2 refers to attraction to public policy, PSM3 captures the compassion items, and PSM4 describes the commitment to public values* ranged in a values from 0.63 to 0.79. Also, the results provided support for both discriminant and convergent validity. The decision to use the particular PSM measure was based on its relative parsimony, without losing much of the richness of the original measure used in the literature. Some comparable studies have used 5-item or 11-item measures, raising the question of how reliable and/or valid the measure is, in capturing all four PSM dimensions content.

SPSS, v. 20 was used in the statistical analysis below, testing for differences between the groups in their employer preferences. The procedure ANOVA was employed (Table 1), which indicates a significant difference between the three samples, Graduate School of Public Administration in Greece (GSPAG) (1), Business School Greece (BSG) (2), and Graduate School of Business and Economics in Belgium (GSEB) (3).

Table 1 ANOVA, between GSPAG, BSG, and GSEB

ANOVA

		Sum of squares	Df	Mean square	F	Sig.
1. To what extent would you like to work for a public organization?	Between groups	170,810	2	85,405	67,716	0.000
	Within groups	433,858	344	1261		
	Total	604,669	346			
2. To what extent would you like to work for a large private organization?	Between groups	52,121	2	26,061	24,024	0.000
	Within groups	373,158	344	1085		
	Total	425,280	346			

Graduate School of Public Administration in Greece (GSPAG) (1), Business School Greece (BSG) (2), Graduate School of Business and Economics in Belgium (GSEB) (3)

3.1 Tables

As expected from the literature review, the null hypothesis H1 is rejected, and indeed there is a statistically significant difference between the three groups, potentially attributable to cultural differences between the Greek and Belgian samples or between the public administration students and the business and economics ones or both. A further analysis (multiple comparisons) will shed more light to the issue (Table 2).

Testing our second hypothesis for differences between male and female PSM levels, across all three samples, the null hypothesis is accepted since no statistically significant difference appears to exist, as we conclude from the similar employment preferences of the two sexes (Table 3). We then used factor analysis, to examine

Table 2 Multiple comparisons

Tukey HSD

Dependent variable	(I) Category	(J) Category	Mean difference (I − J)	Std. error	Sig.	95% confidence interval Lower bound	Upper bound
1. To what extent would you like to work for a public organization?	GSPAG	BSG	1.679*	0.163	0.000	1.29	2.06
		GSEB	1.793*	0.165	0.000	1.41	2.18
	BSG	GSPAG	−1.679*	0.163	0.000	−2.06	−1.29
		GSEB	0.114	0.135	0.677	−0.20	0.43
	GSEB	GSPAG	−1.793*	0.165	0.000	−2.18	−1.41
		BSG	−0.114	0.135	0.677	−0.43	0.20
2. To what extent would you like to work for a large private organization?	GSPAG	BSG	−1.043*	0.152	0.000	−1.40	−0.69
		GSEB	−0.789*	0.153	0.000	−1.15	−0.43
	BSG	GSPAG	1.043*	0.152	0.000	0.69	1.40
		GSEB	0.254	0.125	0.107	−0.04	0.55
	GSEB	GSPAG	0.789*	0.153	0.000	0.43	1.15
		BSG	−0.254	0.125	0.107	−0.55	0.04

*$P = 0.005$

possible differences in the samples' attitudes, in terms of the various dimensions of PSM. Table 4 shows the factors and the loadings of each, which indicates that the items loaded as expected, in accordance to the previous studies (Kim et al. 2013; Sahinidis and Kolia 2014).

Table 3 A PSM level means comparison males versus females

Group statistics

	Gender	N	Mean	Std. deviation	Std. error mean
1. To what extent would you like to work for a public organization?	M	179	2.87	0.097	0.097
				0.104	
				1.303	
	F	168	2.93	1.345	0.104
2. To what extent would you like to work for a large private organization?	M	179	3.76	0.080	0.080
				0.089	
				1.067	
	F	168	3.85	1.153	0.089

Table 4 Rotated component matrix

	Component			
	1	2	3	4
A1. I am interested in helping to improve public service	0.255	**0.825**	−0.133	0.036
A2. I like to discuss with others topics regarding public programs and policies	−0.006	**0.725**	−0.089	0.186
A3. It is important to contribute to activities that tackle social problems	0.138	**0.650**	0.358	0.162
A4. Meaningful public service is very important to me	0.107	**0.798**	0.196	0.120
A5. It is important for me to contribute to the common good	0.345	**0.571**	0.315	0.189
A6. I think equal opportunities for citizens are very important	0.079	0.338	0.277	**0.573**
A7. It is important that citizens can rely on the continuous provision of public services	0.312	0.063	0.078	**0.598**
A8. It is fundamental that the interests of future generations are taken into account when developing public policies	−0.064	0.160	0.007	**0.824**
A10. It is difficult for me to contain my feelings when I see people in distress	0.073	−0.003	**0.816**	−0.033
A11. I feel sympathetic to the plight of the underprivileged	0.305	0.060	**0.750**	0.131
A12. I get very upset when I see other people being treated unfairly	0.137	0.135	**0.582**	0.494
A13. Considering the welfare of others is very important	0.310	0.284	**0.495**	0.306
A14. I am prepared to make sacrifices for the good of society	**0.806**	0.211	0.171	0.181
A15. I believe in putting civic duty before self	**0.788**	0.064	0.143	0.210
A16. I am willing to risk personal loss to help society	**0.844**	0.198	0.071	−0.090
A17. I would agree to a good plan to make a better life for the poor, even if it costs me money	**0.646**	0.077	0.195	0.048

Table 5 Group comparisons in terms of PSM1, PSM2, PSM3, and PSM4

		Sum of squares	Df	Mean square	F	Sig.
PSM2	Between groups	813,028	2	406,514	28,537	0.000
	Within groups	4,900,418	344	14,245		
	Total	5,713,447	346			
PSM4	Between groups	149,805	2	74,902	13,665	0.000
	Within groups	1,885,613	344	5481		
	Total	2,035,418	346			
PSM3	Between groups	51,544	2	25,772	3884	0.021
	Within groups	2,275,927	343	6635		
	Total	2,327,471	345			
PSM1	Between groups	333,280	2	166,640	15,383	0.000
	Within groups	3,726,363	344	10,832		
	Total	4,059,643	346			

Graduate School of Public Administration in Greece (GSPAG) (1), Business School Greece (BSG) (2), Graduate School of Business and Economics in Belgium (GSEB) (3)

Table 5 shows that the three groups differ, as far as all four PSM factors are concerned. Table 6 describes the differences more lucidly, highlighting the similarities between the Greek and Belgian business schools and the statistically significant differences of both groups to the public administration student group.

4 Discussion, Implications, and Conclusions

The effort in this paper focused on examining the validity of the argument proposed by scholars in earlier studies that PSM is a major trait separating those who want to serve the public and derive motivation from, vis-à-vis, those motivated by other forces, needs, or wants. The findings in our study, not surprisingly, support the assertions by Perry et al. (2010), in the studies mentioned above, as well as Vandenabeele (2008) and Ritz et al. (2013) that public servants are motivated by forces other than private sector employees or aspiring employees. The magnitude of the PSM level difference, between the students of the Graduate School of Public Administration, on the one hand and the students of the two Graduate Schools of Business on the other, indicates that indeed different people are attracted to the two types of schools.

What is probably more important is that the findings of the present study fail to support the argument that PSM is acquired, or developed, as a result of socialization rather than being a characteristic of the employee (Wright and Christensen 2010). Also, our findings fail to support those of Lee and Choi (2013) and by Kjeldsen et al. (2013). Lee and Choi argue that the only motive of the public servants is job security and PSM does not relate prosocial behavior, while by Kjeldsen et al. (2013) posit that PSM is irrelevant to attraction to the public sector or actual sector of

Table 6 Multiple comparisons

Tukey HSD

Dependent variable	(I) Category	(J) Category	Mean difference (I − J)	Std. error	Sig.	95% confidence interval	
						Lower bound	Upper bound
PSM2	GSPAG	BSG	3.547*	0.549	0.000	2.25	4.84
		GSEB	3.988*	0.553	0.000	2.69	5.29
	BSG	GSPAG	−3.547*	0.549	0.000	−4.84	−2.25
		GSEB	0.441	0.454	0.597	−0.63	1.51
	GSEB	GSPAG	−3.988*	0.553	0.000	−5.29	−2.69
		BSG	−0.441	0.454	0.597	−1.51	0.63
PSM4	GSPAG	BSG	1.271*	0.341	0.001	0.47	2.07
		GSEB	1.789*	0.343	0.000	0.98	2.60
	BSG	GSPAG	−1.271*	0.341	0.001	−2.07	−0.47
		GSEB	0.518	0.282	0.159	−0.15	1.18
	GSEB	GSPAG	−1.789*	0.343	0.000	−2.60	−0.98
		BSG	−0.518	0.282	0.159	−1.18	0.15
PSM3	GSPAG	BSG	0.507	0.377	0.370	−0.38	1.39
		GSEB	1.032*	0.379	0.019	0.14	1.92
	BSG	GSPAG	−0.507	0.377	0.370	−1.39	0.38
		GSEB	0.524	0.310	0.210	−0.21	1.25
	GSEB	GSPAG	−1.032*	0.379	0.019	−1.92	−0.14
		BSG	−0.524	0.310	0.210	−1.25	0.21
PSM1	GSPAG	BSG	1.840*	0.479	0.000	0.71	2.97
		GSEB	2.674*	0.483	0.000	1.54	3.81
	BSG	GSPAG	−1.840*	0.479	0.000	−2.97	−0.71
		GSEB	0.834	0.396	0.090	−0.10	1.77
	GSEB	GSPAG	−2.674*	0.483	0.000	−3.81	−1.54
		BSG	−0.834	0.396	0.090	−1.77	0.10

*The mean difference is significant at the 0.05 level

employment. The findings of both of the latter two studies may be partially correct, if one is to assume that the cultural differences may explain a large part of the variation. However, the findings in this study depict a large difference between the PSM levels of the two Greek groups, which refutes the argument by Lee and Choi, especially given that in Greece the security offered by the public sector is highly valued too. In addition to that, the remarkable similarity between the Greek and the Belgian Business School students, in their PSM levels, both of which are characterized by low PSM compared to the Public Administration students, attests to the diverging interests and motives of the groups. The Kjeldsen et al. (2013) study using a sample of physical therapists reported that no difference was found in the employees' PSM, whether in the public or in the private sector. This may be correct for the specific profession; however, it needs further testing in other types of professions or jobs before drawing conclusions with a high degree of certainty.

The implications of the study are important for the human resource managers of public organizations, given that it is becoming increasingly difficult to attract highly qualified employees, in times of an unprecedented resource scarcity and high levels of employee mobility (the "brain-drain in Greece during its economic crisis is notable"). According to Paarlberg et al. (2008), several tactics can help public HR managers in their recruitment selection and retention practices, including the use of PSM in the selection process. People with higher PSM levels will be more compatible with a public sector job, will have more congruent values, and will tend to stay longer; they can teach the organizational values to the new employees; they can promote and reinforce the main tenets of PSM; and finally, they exhort leadership to be role modeling public service values.

Implication for researchers include further studying of the role of socialization and trait approaches to PSM and the possible difference variables such as the profession may make. Furthermore, studies of multiple cultures may provide greater insight, in the role PSM plays in employee behavior.

References

Brewer, G., & Selden, S. (1998). Whistle blowers in the federal civil service: New evidence of the public service ethic. *Journal of Public Administration Research and Theory, 8*, 413–440.
Bright, L. (2007). Does person-organization fit mediate the relationship between public service motivation and the job performance of public employees? *Review of Public Personnel Administration, 27*(4), 361–379.
Camilleri, E. (2007). Antecedents affecting public service motivation. *Personnel Review, 36*(3), 356–377.
Christensen, R. K., & Wright, B. E. (2011). The effects of public service motivation on job choice decisions: Disentangling the contributions of person-organization fit and person-job fit. *Journal of Public Administration Research and Theory, 21*(4), 723–743.
Clerkin, R. M., & Coggburn, J. D. (2012). The dimensions of public service motivation and sector preferences. *Review of Public Personel Administration, 32*(3), 209–235.
Crewson, P. (1997). Public service motivation: Building empirical evidence of incidence and effect. *Journal of Public Administration Research and Theory, 7*(4), 499–518.

Frank, S. A., & Lewis, G. B. (2004). Government employees: Working hard or hardly working? *The American Review of Public Administration, 34*(1), 36–51.

Giauque, D., Ritz, A., Varone, F., & Anderfuhren-Biget, S. (2012). Resigned but satisfied: The negative impact of public service motivation and red tape on work satisfaction. *Public Administration, 90*(1), 175–193.

Gould-Williams, J. S., Bottomley, P., Redman, T., Snape, E., Bishop, D., Limpanitgul, T., & Mostafa, A. (2013). Civic duty and employee outcomes: Do high commitment human resource practices and work overload matter? *Public Administration, 92*, 1–17.

Homberg, F., McCarthy, D., & Tabvuma, V. (2015). A meta-analysis of the relationship between public service motivation and job satisfaction. *Public Administration Review, 75*, 711–722.

Houston, D. J. (2000). Public-service motivation: A multivariate test. *Journal of Public Administration Research and Theory, 10*(4), 713–727.

Kamenica, E. (2012). Behavioral economics and psychology of incentives. *The Annual Review of Economics, 4*, 13.1–13.26.

Kim, S. (2005). Individual-level factors and organizational performance in government organizations. *Journal of Public Administration Research and Theory, 15*, 245–262.

Kim, S., Vandenabeele, W., Wright, B. E., Andersen, L. B., Cerase, F. P., Christensen, R. K., et al. (2013). Investigating the meaning and structure of public service motivation across populations: Developing an international instrument and addressing issues of measurement invariance. *Journal of Public Administration Research and Theory, 23*(1), 79–102.

Kjeldsen, A., Jacobsen, C., & Christian, B. (2013). Public service motivation and employment sector: Attraction or socialization? *Journal of Public Administration Research & Theory, 23*(4), 899–926.

Lee, G., & Choi, D. L. (2013). Does public service motivation influence the college students' intention to work in the public sector? *Korea Article Information.*

Lee, Y., & Wilkins, V. M. (2011). More similarities or more differences? Comparing public and nonprofit managers' job motivations. *Public Administration Review, 71*, 45–56.

Leisink, P., & Steijn, B. (2008). Recruitment, attraction and selection. In J. L. Perry & A. Hondeghem (Eds.), *Motivation in public management. The call for public service* (pp. 118–135). New York: Oxford University Press.

Lewis, G. B., & Frank, S. A. (2002). Who wants to work for government? *Public Administration Review, 6*(4), 395–404.

Naff, K., & Crum, C. (1999). Working for America: Does public service motivation make a difference? *Review of Public Personnel Administration, 19*(4), 5–16.

Neumann, O. (2016). Does misfit loom larger than fit? Experimental evidence on motivational person-job fit, public service motivation, and prospect theory. *International Journal of Manpower, 37*(5), 822–839.

Paarlberg, L. E., Perry, J. L., & Hondeghem, A. (2008). From theory to practice: Strategies for applying public service motivation. In J. L. Perry & A. Hondeghem (Eds.), *Motivation in public management: The call of public service* (pp. 268–293). New York: Oxford University Press.

Pandey, S. K., Wright, B. E., & Moynahan, D. P. (2007). *Public service motivation and organizational citizenship behavior: Testing a preliminary model.* L. Follette School Working Paper, (2007–0017), Retrieved October 22, 2007, from http://www.lafollette.wisc.edu/publications/workingpapers/moynihan2007-017.pdf

Park, S. M., & Rainey, H. G. (2007). Antecedents, mediators, and consequences of affective, normative, and continuance commitment: Empirical tests of commitment effects in federal agencies. *Review of Public Personnel Administration, 27*(3), 197–226.

Park, S. M., & Rainey, H. G. (2008). Leadership and public service motivation in U.S. federal agencies. *International Public Management Journal, 11*(1), 109–142.

Perry, J. L. (1996). Measuring public service motivation: An assessment of construct reliability and validity. *Journal of Public Administration Research and Theory, 6*, 5–22.

Perry, J. L. (1997). Antecedents of public service motivation. *Journal of Public Administration Research and Theory, 7*(2), 181–197.

Perry, J. L. (2000). Bringing society in: Toward a theory of public service motivation. *Journal of Public Administration Research and Theory, 10*, 471–488.

Perry, J. L., & Wise, L. R. (1990). The motivational bases of public service. *Public Administration Review, 50*(3), 367–373.

Perry, J. L., Hondeghem, A., & Wise, L. R. (2010). Revisiting the motivational bases of public service: Twenty years of research and an agenda for the future. *Public Administration Review, 70*(5), 681–690.

Piatak, J. (2016). Public service motivation, prosocial behaviours, and career ambitions. *International Journal of Manpower, 37*(5), 804–821.

Rainey, H. G., & Steinbauer, P. (1999). Galloping elephants: Developing elements of a theory of effective government organizations. *Journal of Public Administration Research and Theory, 9*(1), 1–32.

Ritz, A., Brewer, G. A., & Neumann, O. (2013). *Public service motivation: A systematic literature review and outlook. Public management research association conference.* Madison, WI: University of Madison-Wisconsin.

Sahinidis, A., & Kolia, A. (2014). Private or public sector? An investigation of employer preferences of university students using Herzberg's two factors theory of motivation. *Archives of Economic History, 26*(2), 1.

Stazyk, E. C. (2012). Crowding out public service motivation? Comparing theoretical expectations with empirical findings on the influence of performance-related pay. *Review of Public Personnel Administration, 33*(3), 252–274.

Steijn, B. (2008). Person-environment fit and public service motivation. *International Public Management Journal, 11*(1), 13–27.

Vandenabeele, W. (2008). Government calling: Public service motivation as an element in selecting government as an employer of choice. *Public Administration, 86*(4), 1089–1105.

Wright, B. E. (2003). *Toward understanding task, mission and public service motivation: A conceptual and empirical synthesis of goal theory and public service motivation* (7th ed.). Washington, DC: National Public Management Research Conference, Georgetown University.

Wright, B. E., & Christensen, R. K. (2010). Public service motivation: A test of the job attraction-selection-attrition model. *International Public Management Journal, 13*(2), 155–176.

Wright, B. E., Hassan, S., & Christensen, R. K. (2017). Job choice and performance: Revisiting core assumptions about public service motivation. *International Public Management Journal, 20*, 108–131.

ASPiRiN Methodics of Business-Planning

Mykhailo Maksymov

Abstract Business plan development is the basic method to describe decisions made before starting up a certain business. The estimating of the planned business is realized, and the decision about investment or crediting of a certain business is made based on a business plan. Business plan is also applied to perform the planned development of an already existing enterprise.

There are many different methods and standards of business plan creation. However, they are directed mainly to the specialists in the field of economics and business with a certain experience, specific knowledge, and improved abilities to work with information. Small business representatives usually do not have these knowledge and abilities. Consequently, we have the majority of small enterprise functioning without a business plan.

The result of it is that the small business acts "up to the situation" and does not apply the existing economical science achievements in the field of decision-making. It often happens that small and micro-business owners consider scientific methods too complicated and difficult to understand and apply to develop their business.

The researches in this field use the principles of a rational approach and do not take into account the peculiarities of making decisions by those who would work with such business plans.

The purpose of our research is to create a methodic of the business planning, which would, from the one hand, be efficient and based on the latest scientific achievements, and, from the other hand, would have to be so easy and clear that it might be used by an ordinary small business representative; at the same time it might be applicable for the current estimation and planning, and it must also have the algorithm of business plan making based on all of the current international standards.

We can confidently affirm that both creating and applying of a business plan have a general feature—they are developed and used by people. Whereby it is the small business that is characterized by a low acquirement level of people and the impact of their acquirement level onto the business planning result.

M. Maksymov (✉)
Karazin Kharkiv National University, Kharkiv, Ukraine

© Springer Nature Switzerland AG 2019
N. Sykianakis et al. (eds.), *Economic and Financial Challenges for Eastern Europe*,
Springer Proceedings in Business and Economics,
https://doi.org/10.1007/978-3-030-12169-3_29

Having used the achievements of the modern science such as economics (The Bounded Rationality Theory by H. Simon) and psychology (The Magical Number Seven Plus or Minus Two by G. Miller) and also the term of cognitive load (J. Julien), we can answer the questions of differences and formulate the criteria following to which would allow to develop a general approach to the creation and implementation of business plans making it possible for the small business to work with this instrument efficiently.

The Bounded Rationality Theory tells us that though a person makes rational decisions, he does it within certain limits of intellect, attention, willpower, and self-interest. At that, the supposition that the smaller the organized business is, the more limits a person has seems to be quite fair.

H. Simon describes the limits, but tells nothing about how they work. G. Miller though defines the quantitative parameters and the functioning principles of human attention. J. Julien, in his turn, represents us the qualitative estimation difficulties of the human comprehension.

The next work algorithm is proposed:

1. Presentation of the business "nucleus"—the obligatory elements with the mnemonic abbreviation ASPiRiN

2. Express estimation of each element working-out level: (1) is not reasoned out, (2) is reasoned out, (3) is written down, and (4) is described according to the methodic.

3. Based on the express estimation, the further plan is created, depending on the entrepreneur's purposes: (a) level 2 is sufficient for the micro-business; level 3 is sufficient for the small business; and level 4 is sufficient to apply the documents to the investor or crediting organization.

In our research the basic existing methods are chosen, which composes the notional base for small and micro-business development at the level of the increase of the made decisions efficiency. The algorithm presented hereby might be applied both for individual work of the small business representatives and for the work of business consultants who use the scientific approach.

Keywords Business plan · Small business · Cognitive load · ASPiRiN

1   Introduction

The small business is an important component of the modern state economy. One of the important features of the small business is that it might be started with almost any citizen.

This forms its important peculiarities such as numerosity of small businesses and, also, averagely low training level of small business leaders in the field of management and economics.

These peculiarities explain why those principles and patterns which work with medium and large business work weakly or do not work at all with the small business: medium and large business subjects employ management specialists with the eligible level of training and experience, while the small business management is realized with an entrepreneur, who had taken all the risks and organized the business process himself.

It is a feature of medium or large business leader either not to work for operational management at all or to hire the eligible specialists in those fields, in which he is not professionally trained.

For the small business, as long as it has significantly less resources, than the medium and the large one, such situation is less possible, because the operational management is executed by the owner himself and he takes the decisions corresponding his training level.

On the assumption of the abovementioned, the medium and large business development strategy consists in choosing the necessary employees for gaining the goals the company foresees, while the main strategy of the small business is the enterprise owner personal improvement or creation of the circumstances under which he could take efficient decisions with the current development level.

Working out a business plan as a component of the investment project is a zero-option condition of a business start-up preparation. A big number of organizations have developed their own business planning standards: KPMG, UNCTAD, EBRD, ISO, US SBA, Eurocommission, etc.

But practically all the developed standards are directed to people who are significantly trained; that is why the majority of small entrepreneurship subjects, as a result, do not use these methodologies, considering them too complicated or not useful at all. It means that the significant part of small entrepreneurship subjects work without any business plans.

This situation witnesses that currently the issue of creation of the method of business plan development, which would be applied for the small business, is actual and not solved.

The issue of business planning method analysis and structuring is not new; it is lit up in the researches (Shkurko 2013; Strantsov 2014; Sahlman 1997).

At the same time the existing business planning standards are studied from the organizational form point of view.

As it was stated above, the small business is characterized with the significant impact of the human factor onto the decision-making. It means that applying instrumentals of the economic directions, concerned with psychology and its achievements in the field of studying the process of human thinking and an individual's decision-making, might bring good results.

These directions might be observed in the bounded rationality theory by H. Simon (1978), in which he tells that human choice is rational but, to a certain extent, described as "rationality limits." Simon marked two fields of "rationality limitation" such as attention and intellect, and consequently he added willpower and self-interest.

There are also important researches, results of which allow to create methodologies for business plan development, such as the article "The Magical Number Seven plus or Minus Two" by G. Miller (1956) (a human comprehends from five to nine terms simultaneously, and if there are more terms, they unite in groups) and also the cognitive load theory by J. Sweller (the cognitive load is the quantity of mental efforts, necessary for achieving the goal) (Sweller 1988), and almost all practical researches of J. Julien in the field is user interfaces projecting (they represent the qualitative estimations of cognitive load) (Julien 2012).

The author has already conducted researches in the given field. In the article (Maksymov 2017) he studied existing business planning standards, defined the basic elements and united them into certain categories, and formulated the mnemonic abbreviation ASPiRiN, which describes the business plan basic elements.

The main purpose of this research is to develop a methodology of business plan creation, which could be efficiently used by the small business leaders through the most possible decrease of cognitive load, necessary for a business plan development.

2 Body of Paper

2.1 Principles of Cognitive Load

Hereby we will fix the qualitative estimations of the cognitive load.

2.2 Visualization of ASPiRiN Methodic

Hereby we visualize the basic business plan elements.

To decrease the cognitive load of working with these elements, we marked the sequence of elements and connection between each of them (nos. 2 and 4 in Table 1) and also conducted the search of existing methodologies, suitable for developing of the certain unit (no. 1 in Table 1), as far as in case of using the method, a business plan author does not create his own form, but answers certain questions described in the method.

It is also important to mention that modern economical science already has a lot of achievements which are possible to be applied to the corresponding business planning elements (no. 1, Table 1), as far as in case of using the methodology, the data standardized by the chosen methodology beforehand should be stated.

For visualization of the methodology elements, we used intellect cards, performed using XMind Software (no. 3, Table 1, Fig. 1), and BPMN 2.0 method using the ARIS Express software (Fig. 2).

Table 1 Qualitative estimations of the cognitive load

No.	Qualitative estimation of the cognitive load
1	Choosing from several variants < formulating an own variant (Julien 2012)
2	Sequence of choice from several elements without a certain result < sequence if choice from one element without a certain result (Julien 2012)
3	Digestion of the information presented in schemes and text < digestion of the information from one (Simon 1978)
4	Known < unknown (Julien 2012)
5	The volume of memory available—from five to nine elements (Miller 1956)
6	If the quantity of elements is increased, they are memorized by groups (Miller 1956)

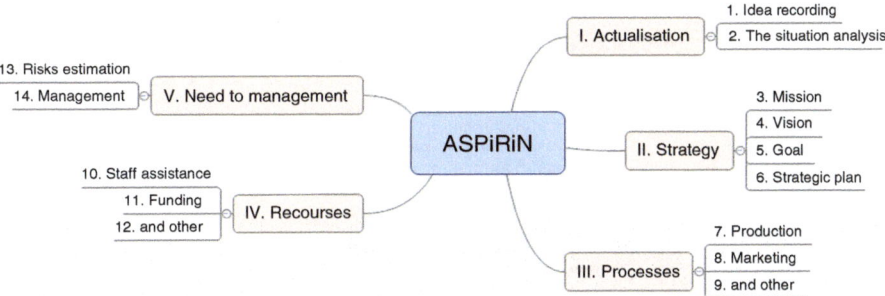

Fig. 1 The basic elements of a business plan based on the ASPiRiN methodology, performed using XMind software

All of the actions in the methodology are divided into blocks; the quantity of the actions in each block is not more than five (nos. 5 and 6, Table 1).

2.3 Critical Path Method for Business Plan Creating Project

But there is still a question that has no answer: how much time is needed to businss plan perform by methodology?

For the estimation the time for business plan development, we consider business plan development as a project and apply the method of critical way to it (Fig. 3). We accept as a supposition that a business plan is worked out by one person (the method of critical way allows calculating the time of business plan development if different blocks would be sent to other people to work them out).

The general time of performing the work for business plan creation might be described as follows:

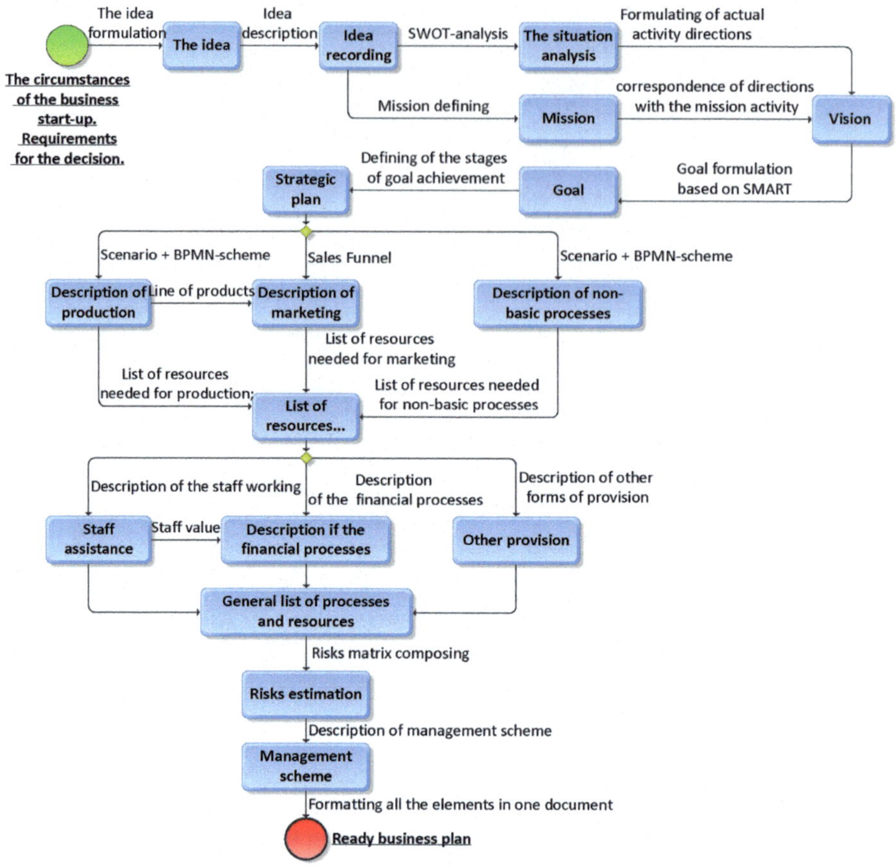

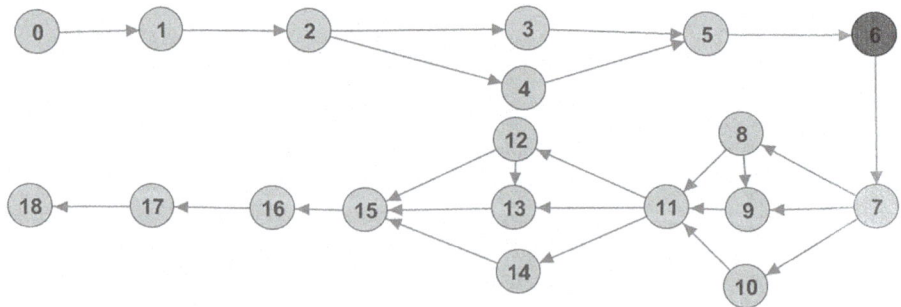

Fig. 2 Scheme of a business-plan creation, performed using BPMN 2.0 in ARIS Express software

Fig. 3 Graphic (network), based on the table of the critical way method

Table 2 Description of the project of a business plan creation based on the critical way method

#	Top	Action	Action description	# action	Carrier, methodology
0	The circumstances of the business start-up. Requirements for the decision				
1	The idea	0–1	The idea formulation	1	Mentally
2	Idea recording	1–2	Idea description	2	Recording on the material carrier
3	The situation analysis	2–3	SWOT analysis	3	SWOT analysis, PEST analysis
4	Mission	2–4	Mission defining	4	Recording on the material carrier
5	Vision	3–5	Formulating of actual activity directions	5	Recording on the material carrier
		4–5	Correspondence of directions with the mission activity	6	Recording on the material carrier
6	Goal	5–6	Goal formulation based on SMART	7	SMART
7	Strategic plan	6–7	Defining of the stages of goal achievement	8	Recording on the material carrier
8	Description of production	7–8	Scenario + BPMN scheme	9	BPMN
9	Description of marketing	7–9	Sales funnel	10	AIDA, sales funnel
		8–9	Product line	11	
10	Description of non-basic processes	7–10	Scenario + BPMN scheme	12	BPMN
11	List of resources needed	8–11	List of resources needed for production	13	Recording on the material carrier
		9–11	For marketing	14	Recording on the material carrier
		10–11	For non-basic processes	15	Recording on the material carrier
12	Staff assistance	11–12	Description of the staff working	16	Maslow's pyramid, EQ
13	Funding	11–13	Description of the financial processes	17	Financial coefficients
		12–13	Staff value	18	Average salary on the labor market
14	Other provision	11–14	Description of other forms of provision	19	Recording on the material carrier

(continued)

Table 2 (continued)

#	Top	Action	Action description	# action	Carrier, methodology
15	General list of processes and resources	12–15	Consolidation of all resources and processes	20	Recording on the material carrier
		13–15		21	Recording on the material carrier
		14–15		22	Recording on the material carrier
16	Risk estimation	15–16	Risk matrix composing	23	Risk matrix
17	Management scheme	16–17	Description of management scheme	24	Kanban/critical way method/scrum
18	Ready business plan	17–18	Formatting all the elements in one document	25	

$$T = \sum_{i=1}^{n} t_i$$

where t_{ij} is the time for doing the i-work and I is the number of the action in Table 2.

But it is worth mentioning that the variant described above is applicable on the condition that an entrepreneur has any preparations for business plan development. If such preparations exist, they have to be taken into account while defining the time necessary for performing a certain business plan stage.

It is also worth mentioning that for businesses of different size, the level of working out is also different. If for the level of self-employment the mental development might be enough, for the large business, a simple written description is sufficient; for the small business, the methodology application is needed; and for the medium business, the visualization of each element is also needed, for the core of the business-plan to be clear for all of the employees. At that it is efficient to develop a visualized business plan by iteration—from the reasoned out variant to the visualization.

In this case the project table will look like (Table 3):

$$T = \sum_{i=1}^{25} \sum_{j=1}^{4} t_{ij}$$

where t_{ij} is the time for doing the i-work of the j-type (1, reasoning out; 2, description; 3,description according to the methodologies; 4, visualization).

When choosing the final recipient of this research results, it is possible to define two categories: individuals, who make decisions, i.e. the small business leaders, and also business consultants, specialists in serving the small business.

The main targeted audience will be the business consultants, as far as they can apply these achievements in the process of their enterprises activity development.

Table 3 Description of the project of a business plan creation based on the critical way method for several variants of work

Activities	Number of activity	t_1	t_2	t_3	t_4
0–1	1	t_{11}	t_{12}	t_{13}	t_{14}
1–2	2	t_{21}	t_{22}	t_{23}	t_{24}
2–3	3	t_{31}	t_{32}	t_{33}	t_{34}
2–4	4	t_{41}	t_{42}	t_{43}	t_{44}
3–5	5	t_{51}	t_{52}	t_{53}	t_{54}
4–5	6	t_{61}	t_{62}	t_{63}	t_{64}
5–6	7	t_{71}	t_{72}	t_{73}	t_{74}
6–7	8	t_{81}	t_{82}	t_{83}	t_{84}
7–8	9	t_{91}	t_{92}	t_{93}	t_{94}
7–9	10	t_{101}	t_{102}	t_{103}	t_{104}
8–9	11	t_{111}	t_{112}	t_{113}	t_{114}
7–10	12	t_{121}	t_{122}	t_{123}	t_{124}
8–11	13	t_{131}	t_{132}	t_{133}	t_{134}
9–11	14	t_{141}	t_{142}	t_{143}	t_{144}
10–11	15	t_{151}	t_{152}	t_{153}	t_{154}
11–12	16	t_{161}	t_{162}	t_{163}	t_{164}
11–13	17	t_{171}	t_{172}	t_{173}	t_{174}
12–13	18	t_{181}	t_{182}	t_{183}	t_{184}
11–14	19	t_{191}	t_{192}	t_{193}	t_{194}
12–15	20	t_{201}	t_{202}	t_{203}	t_{204}
13–15	21	t_{211}	t_{212}	t_{213}	t_{214}
14–15	22	t_{221}	t_{222}	t_{223}	t_{224}
15–16	23	t_{231}	t_{232}	t_{233}	t_{234}
16–17	24	t_{241}	t_{242}	t_{243}	t_{244}
17–18	25	t_{251}	t_{252}	t_{253}	t_{254}

t_1—the time needed for reasoning out the work
t_2—the time needed for recording the work on condition that it is already reasoned out
t_3—the time needed to describe the work according to the methodology on condition that it is already described
t_4—the time needed to visualize the work on condition that it is described according to the methodology

3 Conclusion

1. The data about peculiarities of human conscience from the different theories and researches is gathered.
2. The research data allows to define all the necessary elements of a business plan for the planned business to be successful.
3. The proposed algorithm allows to develop each element of a business plan step by step, basing on the previous steps and using the modern methodologies.
4. The developed algorithm allows to unite the different existing methodologies into one noncontroversial whole, which includes the possibility to estimate a certain methodology working quality.

5. Applying the critical way method allows to estimate the time needed for the preparation of a business-plan for different levels of the material readiness and for business of various sizes.
6. As a direction of development for this research, we consider getting the average time needed to develop each element of a business plan and also creating a software which would help to develop a business plan efficiently.

Acknowledgment The given methodology is used for consulting the small business representatives, and it also is a ground for the school organized by the regional fund of entrepreneurship support that works at Kharkiv Regional State Administration.

References

Julien, J. (2012). What makes an interface intuitive? Understanding cognitive load and cognitive barriers to ease user experiences. *Uxmagazine*. Article no: 799. Retrieved from http://uxmag.com/articles/cognition-the-intrinsic-user-experience.

Maksymov, M. S. (2017). Reducing the cognitive load in the developing a business plan for small business. *Business Inform, 1*, 161–166.

Miller, G. A. (1956). The magical number seven, plus or minus two: Some limits on our capacity for processing information. *Psychological Review, 63*(2), 81–97.

Sahlman, W. A. (1997). How to write a great business plan. *Harvard Business Review, 75*, 98–109.

Shkurko, N. V. (2013). Metodicheskiy podkhod k razrabotke struktury biznes-plana v predprinimatelskikh strukturakh [Methodical approach to designing the structure of a business plan in business organizations]. *Sovremennyye problemy nauki i obrazovaniya, 1*, 299–310.

Simon, H. A. (1978). Rationality as process and as product of thought. Richard T. Ely Lecture. *American Economic Review, 68*(2), 1–16.

Strantsov, I. A. (2014). Metodicheskiy podkhod k formirovaniyu struktury i soderzhaniya biznes-plana investitsionnogo proekta [Methodical approach to formation of the structure and content of the business plan of the investment project]. *Vestnik AGAU, 118*(8), 159–163.

Sweller, J. (1988). Cognitive load during problem solving: Effects on learning. *Cognitive Science, 12*(2), 257–285.

Exploring Irrigation Water Issue Through Quantitative SWOT Analysis: The Case of Nestos River Basin

Dimitra Lazaridou, Anastasios Michailidis, Marios Trigkas, and Panagiotis Stefanidis

Abstract The irrigation sector in Greece has been recognized as the major consumer of water and, at the same time, a precondition of agricultural production. Impacts of agricultural practices on water quality and quantity are many and varied. This paper proposes a typology approach of irrigation water management problems in Nestos river basin, North Greece. A novel quantitative SWOT (strengths, weaknesses, opportunities, and threats) analysis is recommended for identifying the internal and external factors that influence the irrigation sector. Specifically, a double-round Delphi-type interactive survey method has been employed to rank and quantify environmental impacts of water use in agriculture sector, according to the literature, as well as a previous qualitative research conducted in the region. An independent group comprised of 20 experts engaged in irrigation water issues (academics, policy directors, business executives, and selected farmers) was invited to asses and rank all factors, identified by the SWOT. After experts' ranking, they were invited, in a second round, to propose potential policy implications for the major weaknesses and threats which emerged from the SWOT analysis. The results from this approach could be a tool for assisting the formulation of strategy in water management sector.

Keywords Irrigation water · SWOT analysis · Delphi method · Water resource management

D. Lazaridou · M. Trigkas
Faculty of Forestry and Natural Environment, Laboratory of Forest Economics, Aristotle University of Thessaloniki, Thessaloniki, Greece
e-mail: dimitral@for.auth.gr; mtrigkas@for.auth.gr

A. Michailidis (✉)
Faculty of Agriculture, Department of Agricultural Economics, Laboratory of Agricultural Extension and Rural Sociology, Aristotle University of Thessaloniki, Thessaloniki, Greece
e-mail: tassosm@auth.gr

P. Stefanidis
Faculty of Forestry and Natural Environment, Laboratory of Mountainous Water Management and Control, Aristotle University of Thessaloniki, Thessaloniki, Greece
e-mail: stefanid@for.auth.gr

© Springer Nature Switzerland AG 2019
N. Sykianakis et al. (eds.), *Economic and Financial Challenges for Eastern Europe*,
Springer Proceedings in Business and Economics,
https://doi.org/10.1007/978-3-030-12169-3_30

1   Introduction

Agricultural water management is an important component in achievement of efficient use of water resources and promotion of high agricultural yield. In the light of current economic and environmental conditions, it is of utmost importance to achieve a balanced relationship between the development of the agriculture sector and the water resources conservation (inland surface waters, transitional waters, coastal waters, and groundwaters).

In Greece, agriculture sector constitutes not only the foundation of national stability but also the precondition of economic and social development. At the same time, however, it has been recognized as the major consumer of water and a main source of diffusion pollution. According to Garrote et al. (2015), who studied water availability for irrigation in the Southern Mediterranean River Basins, the Iberian Peninsula and Greece are the areas where water resources will be most affected from the climate change as the water demand for irrigation purposes is very high.

So, the aim is to achieve a balanced relationship between the improvement of the agriculture sector and the water protection from quality and quantity degradation. Thus, it becomes very important to conduct researches in order to identify the strength and opportunities which will contribute to the further development of the irrigation sector, as well as to be recognized the weaknesses and threats which act as inhibitors for the irrigation sector and contribute to the irrational management of agriculture water.

In the last two decades had been addressed many surveys related to agricultural water management practices. In particularly, under the situation of increasing water demand and inadequacy of water resources, have been conducted many surveys oriented to agricultural water conservancy (Pereira et al. 2002; Gordon et al. 2010). Among them are restricted studies where it is applied the Delphi method to gather information from those who are immersed and imbedded in an under-investigated issue or a SWOT technique for a hierarchy analysis of the internal and external factors that linked to irrigation sector (Markou et al. 2014; Michailidis et al. 2015; Sun et al. 2017).

2   Study Area

Nestos, which is called Mesta in Bulgaria, is a transboundary river basin between Bulgaria and Greece. The total area of the catchment is around 5750 km², with about 60% lying in Bulgarian and the rest in the territory of Greece. Figure 1 depicts the geographical location of the watershed. The Nestos river source is located in the Rila mountain (southern Bulgaria), and it discharges into the Thracian Sea. Before Nestos flows into North Aegean Sea, it forms an extensive delta which regarded as one of

Fig. 1 Geographical location of the Nestos river catchment, Greek part (modified in ArcGIS 10.1)

the most significant wetlands in Greece. As a result of the variety of habitat types and flora and fauna species that are not found anywhere else in Europe, delta area is protected by the Ramsar Convention and is considered as a first priority site under EU Natura 2000 network (Dafis et al. 1997). The greater part of Nestos river basin is mountainous and semi-mountainous, while the delta of Nestos river is considered to be an extremely fertile and productive agricultural area.

This explains the fact that agriculture is the main economic activity in the Greek part of the basin, playing a decisive role in local financial development and having a significant positive impact on regional per capita GDP growth. It is estimated that approximately 40,000 ha of the catchment are irrigated from the Nestos river water (Anagnostopoulos and Petalas 2011), so the exploitation of the Nestos flow is inextricably linked with the development of the agriculture. Particularly, water in Nestos river basin is mainly used for hydroenergy production and irrigation purposes, and it is less exploited for urban and industrial use (Ganoulis et al. 2000).

The main products of the primary sector produced in the Nestos cultivated fields are corn, wheat, rice, vegetables, tree crops, asparagus, and kiwis. Some of the above products, mainly asparagus and kiwis, channeled into markets abroad. As far as the agriculture water distribution in the area is concerned, it is regulated by three local organizations for land reclamation: Chrysoupoli, Chrisochoriou, and Thalassia-Kremasti. Much of the cultivated land in the southeastern part of delta region is irrigated by numerous drillings that exist in the region, as well as from collective irrigation networks, but to a much smaller extent, which is supervised by a municipality. It is estimated that at least 2000 shallow drills exist in the area of delta (Myronidis and Emmanouloudis 2008). With regard to irrigation water pricing in the area, there are slight differences among the three TOEV although their common water resource. Particularly, fields being irrigated by the local organizations of Thalassia-Kremasti are priced at 90 €/ha while Chrysoupoli at 100 €/ha with the exception of rice cultivation which priced at 135 €/ha. TOEV Chrisochoriou prices the irrigation water at 95 €/ha for all crops and 125 €/ha for irrigated rice fields (the data gathered from TOEVs).

2.1 Water Quality and Quantity Status

Nestos is considered to be a water surplus basin. However, the continuously increasing water demands for agriculture purposes combined with climate change are projected to impact the water balance of the catchment, exacerbating the deterioration of water surplus (Myronidis and Emmanouloudis 2008; Doulgeris et al. 2015). The above described expanse agricultural activities exert an important influence on the water quality and quantity in the Nestos catchment. The extensive use of fertilizers, the overexploitation of groundwater, and the intensive use of drills have created water quantity and quality problems (Ganoulis et al. 2008). Specifically, in the southern part, the overuse of agricultural products (phosphoric fertilizers and pesticides) is responsible for a large amount of contaminated soils and groundwater (Papastergios et al. 2009; Pedreira et al. 2015). The nitrate concentration due to agricultural intensification leads to the deterioration of water quality, which exhibits a "moderate" status regarded to the European Water Framework Directive (WFD) (Skoulikidis 2009). The fact that the overall ecological status of delta Nestos catchments presented less than "good," as defined by the objectives of the WFD, is identified by Orfanidis et al. (2001) who evaluated the environmental state from "moderate" (in Agiasma) to "poor" (in Keramoti), as well as by Prieto Montes et al. (2009) who contend that Nestos main course appeared to have "moderate" ecological quality. The abovementioned leads to the adoption of supplementary measures to meet the environmental objectives of 2000/60 Directive. However, in the north part of the catchment, where exist a high percentage of forest ground cover and limited agricultural irrigated land, the ecological status exhibits "good" quality (according to the plan of the Greek Special Secretariat for Water, 2013).

Furthermore, the over-pumping of the coastal wells due to the agricultural development, mainly within the eastern delta of Nestos river, has led to lower the groundwater table and intrusion of seawater toward the mainland freshwater porous aquifer (Xeidakis and Delimani 2003; Pedreira et al. 2015; Gkiougkis et al. 2015). This saltwater intrusion into the aquifer system causes another type of water pollution, known as groundwater salinization. The water salinity problem is most acute on the coastal zone, where the seawater intrusion has been extended up to 5 km inland nowadays (Xeidakis et al. 2010), namely, in areas around the villages of New Erasmio, Maggana, Dasoxori, Agiasma, and Keramoti.

3 Material and Methods

This study employs a hybrid Delphi quantitative SWOT analysis method. The methodological framework proposed in this study is used to develop an expert-based decision-making tool for the sustainable irrigation water management in the Nestos river basin. In particular a Delphi-type double-round interactive survey method has been employed to rank the environmental impacts of water use in agriculture sector.

The Delphi method was developed at the Rand Corporation in the 1950s to obtain a method for achieving convergence of opinion from a group of knowledgeable individuals about certain topic areas (Dalkey and Helmer 1963). Despite its early inception, the most recognized description of the method was offered by Linstone and Turoff (1975). Its implementation is based on the creation of an expertise group of qualified people who have deep understanding of the subject under investigation. The Delphi technique is conducted in several rounds, and in each round the experts communicate their opinions through a questionnaire that is returned to the researcher. So, one important requirement that arises is the participation of qualified experts and another the selection and the precise wording of the survey subject. Choosing the appropriate subjects is the most critical step in the entire process because it directly relates to the quality of the results generated (Taylor and Judd 1989).

As far as the SWOT (strengths, weaknesses, opportunities, and threats) analysis is concerned, it is used for identifying the internal (strengths and weaknesses) and external (opportunities and threats) factors that influence the irrigation sector. Although dates back to the early 1950s, SWOT analysis has been used with outstanding popularity. According to Ghazinoory et al. (2011), 557 papers have been published up to the end of 2009, with percentage 5.7% of them related to environmental issues. Among the advantages of the technique are included its simplicity of design and its appliance, while the disadvantages refer to its subjective character.

The conventional SWOT analysis is based on the qualitative analysis and has no means of determining the priority of individual factors. Although in the present study it is conducted in a quantitative form where SWOT factors can be rated on a five-point Likert scale, in which 1 refers to least important and 5 refers to most important.

In this paper, the SWOT analysis is applied as a technique for the sustainable irrigation water management in order to protect water resources of the qualitative and quantitative deterioration. According to the methodology (European Commission 1999), it is necessary to identify the strengths and the weaknesses that influence the sustainable management of irrigation water, as well as to analyze the opportunities and the threats for the achievement of sustainable management of water resources in the catchment.

3.1 Research Questions and Strategy

The aim of this study is to investigate the environmental impacts of water use in agriculture sector. Through the literature, as well as a previous qualitative research conducted in the region in October 2016, there have been a number of factors identified which linked to the agriculture sector and have an effect on water quality and quantity in Nestos river basin.

In order to rank and quantify the abovementioned factors, we employ a research plan consisting of following step strategy. First of all, regarding the criteria used, individuals are considered eligible to be invited to participate in the study if they have somewhat related backgrounds and experiences concerning irrigation subjects in Nestos catchment and are capable of contributing helpful inputs (Pill 1971). Subsequently, it implemented a multiple-step procedure to categorize, identify, and select the group of experts, following the guidelines of Delbecq et al. (1975) and Markou et al. (2014). Figure 2 presents schematically the procedure for selecting experts.

The independent group comprised of 20 experts engaged in irrigation water issues. According to Ludwig (1997), the majority of Delphi studies have used between 15 and 20 respondents; for this reason expert panel is comprised of 5 academics, 5 policy directors, business executives, and selected farmers (presidents of agricultural cooperative and farmers' leaders).

Fig. 2 Procedure for selecting experts

3.2 Data Collection and Analysis

To address the research aim, the first version of the questionnaire asked for the expertise of Delphi panelists, through an e-mail survey, to rank the five most important SWOT factors linked to agriculture sector and the water resources. Considering that a double-round interactive survey is more time-intensive for the participants, we try to ensure that no one of the questionnaire would require more than 15 min to be completed. After the first e-mail, 20 fully completed questionnaires were returned with hierarchical classification of the most significant SWOT factors. The questionnaire from all experts analyzed together as various studies have found that, in group decision-making, heterogeneous groups are more creative than homogeneous ones (Okoli and Pawloski 2004).

From the results analysis emerged the most prevailing internal and external factors linked to the irrigation sector in Nestos watershed. These factors, weaknesses and threats, composed the second questionnaire of the survey. On the second round, the experts were called to propose water management measures for the crucial weaknesses and threats which arose. The response rate was found to be less on the second step, as 12 experts expressed policy proposals for confrontation of weaknesses and threats irrigation sector. Figure 3 depicts the described data collection process. The two phases of the survey were carried out from March to June 2017.

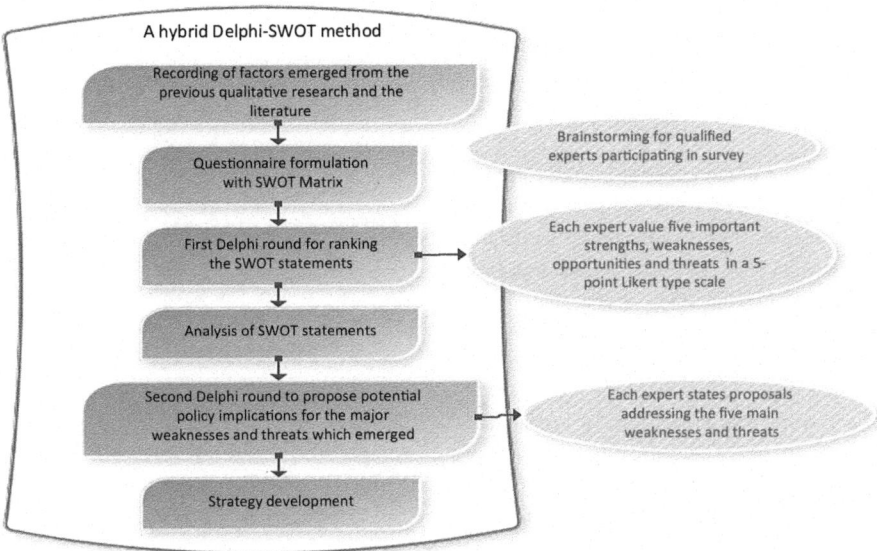

Fig. 3 Data collection process

4   Results

Tables 1, 2, 3 and 4 summarize the expert' rankings for internal and external factors of the agricultural water management in Nestos river basin. The evaluation resulted from the homogenization of the questionnaires and the extraction of overall results from the responses of participants composed the expert's panel.

As arose from the results shown in Table 1, the enlargement of the use of drip irrigation systems, as well as the fact that Nestos river basin, overall, is considered to be a water surplus catchment, is included among the strengths that have an effect on the irrigation sector. Moreover, the fertilization advisory provided by some agricultural cooperatives and the mitigation of the unreasonable use of agrochemicals are regarded as strengths. It is clarified that due to the reduction of their incomes and the high cost of agrochemicals, farmers use fewer quantities than they used in the past.

On the other side, as they are mentioned in Table 2, the low rate of adoption for water-saving technologies and the low level of advisory on rational irrigation practices are recognized as the most serious weaknesses. It is worth noting that this option has been declared from a significant number of farmers. The unreasonable management of water resources, which has been highlighted from academics, policy directors, and farmers, contributes to the weakening of integrated water management.

The prevailing opportunities that emerged from this research are about the human factor (engagement of young people with agriculture) but above all about the adoption of innovative irrigation systems and the creation of infrastructure projects in the region. The use of recycled water for irrigation purpose has been rated high, as

Table 1 Analysis of first rounds' results for strengths

Strengths	N	Min	Max	Sum
Enlargement of the use of drip irrigation systems	11	1	5	40
Adequacy of surface water	15	1	5	31
Mitigation the unreasonable use of fertilizers and pesticides	8	2	5	28
Fertilization advisory through agricultural cooperatives	5	4	5	24
Existence of regulatory irrigation dams	7	2	5	23
Production of high value agricultural products	9	1	5	21
Pesticide packaging recycling, in some local communities in the catchment	4	4	5	19
Low pricing of irrigation water from the three TOEV	5	2	4	16
Turn to less water intensive crops	6	2	5	16
Diminution of over-irrigation through drilling	4	1	5	16
Application of innovative cultivation methods	6	1	4	15
Recognition of the pollution caused by agriculture	5	1	5	14
Distribution of irrigation water from three TOEV	5	1	5	13
High percentage of forest cover in the mountainous part	4	2	3	10
Conversion of conventional crops into organic crops	4	1	4	8
Limited agriculture in the mountainous part of the catchment	2	2	4	6

Table 2 Analysis of first rounds' results for weaknesses

Weaknesses	N	Min	Max	Sum
Low rate of adoption for water-saving technologies	7	2	5	27
Low level of advisory on rational irrigation practices	11	1	5	26
Unreasonable management of water resources	8	1	5	22
Pollution of surface and groundwater due to the use of agrochemicals	5	3	5	21
Obsolete irrigation distribution networks	5	1	5	20
Some farmers' unwillingness to fulfill their financial obligations toward TOEV	5	2	5	19
Persistence in obsolete irrigation methods	6	1	5	19
No volumetric charging for irrigation water	5	2	5	17
Lack of environmental education	5	1	5	15
Existence of small fields with limited possibilities for modernization	5	2	4	15
Low educational level of farmers	6	1	4	14
High cost of innovation adoption in agriculture	4	1	5	12
Large number of drillings	4	2	3	10
Lack of sufficient knowledge of crops water requirements	4	2	4	10
Deficiency of land reclamation projects	3	1	5	10
Low level of advisory to the rational use of agrochemicals	2	4	5	9
Unauthorized drillings	3	2	4	8
Rural population aging	3	1	3	6
Consideration of over-irrigation as best practice for crops	2	1	5	6
Burning of crop residue	1	4	4	4
Soil erosion	1	4	4	4
Illegal import and use of unauthorized agrochemical products from neighboring countries	2	1	2	3
Specific mentality of farmers	2	1	1	2

it constitutes a mean of expand irrigated agriculture without depriving sufficient clean water of environmental purpose. Table 3 presents the corresponding results.

On the contrary, lack of modern irrigation infrastructure alongside the increased demand for irrigation water due to intensification of crops, as well as due to climate change, constitutes the future threats. Table 4 presents the ranking of main threats.

Further analysis suggests that greater convergence is indicated in statements of business executives and farmers, while worth mentioning convergence arises between academics and farmers too.

Figures 4, 5, 6, and 7 present graphically the quantification of the ten most significant SWOT internal and external factors that arose from the first round of the survey, using the average values of expert's ranking, and they are related to the agricultural water management in Nestos catchment.

Policy proposals, about the confrontation of water degradation problems in the research catchment, are summarized in Tables 5 and 6 in a ranking order. These measures are proposed as responses to major weaknesses and threats for the irrigation sector, and they have emerged from the second stage of the survey.

Table 3 Analysis of first rounds' results for opportunities

Opportunities	N	Min	Max	Sum
Subsidies to farmers for innovative irrigation systems	8	2	5	33
Developing new water-saving technologies	10	1	5	25
Creation of infrastructure projects	10	1	5	24
Engaging young people in agriculture sector	7	2	5	23
Use of recycled water for irrigation purpose	5	3	5	21
Agriculture sector is a pillar of the region's economy	10	1	4	20
Awareness that the future of the agriculture sector is intertwined with rational management	6	1	5	19
Pricing of irrigation water according to the full cost recovery/implementation of the polluter pays principle	7	1	4	18
Agro-environmental programs for nitro-pollution reduction	4	2	5	16
Pressure from market trends for environmentally friendly	4	1	5	16
Encouraging farmers to participate in water policy-making	4	2	5	14
Existence of advisory bodies for irrigation water-saving practices	6	1	4	13
Integrated water management at the river basin level	5	1	5	13
TOEV's network expansion	4	1	4	12
Strengthening environmental inspections and controls	3	3	5	12
Establish a contributory benefit for pesticide packaging recycling	2	1	4	5
Bilateral agreements between Greece and Bulgaria	2	2	2	4
Fair and rational irrigation water pricing	1	4	4	4
Construction of sprinkler washing facilities in remote locations away from streams and irrigation channels	1	4	4	4
Encouraging more environmentally friendly farming practices	1	4	4	4

Table 4 Analysis of first rounds' results for threats

Threats	N	Min	Max	Sum
Lack of modern irrigation infrastructure	12	3	5	48
Increased demand for irrigation water due to intensification of crops	8	1	5	28
Surface and groundwater nitro-pollution	9	2	5	27
Increased irrigation needs due to climate change	11	1	4	26
Absence of irrigation water-saving incentives	10	1	5	26
Salinization of aquifers (especially in the coastal zone)	8	1	5	24
Inadequate controls for the environmental conditions enforcement	6	1	5	24
Disturbance of the rainfall distribution	8	1	5	23
Further contraction in farm income	7	1	5	20
Transnationality of Nestos river/Greece is the downstream country	6	1	4	14
Sedimentation of underground aquifers due to over-pumping	5	1	4	13
High cost for reversing environmental degradation		2	4	8
Reduction of EU funds for the agriculture sector	2	2	4	7
Difficulties in authorization of land reclamation projects	1	1	5	5
Young farmers face problems in succession	1	1	4	4
Eutrophication in surface water recipients	2	1	2	3

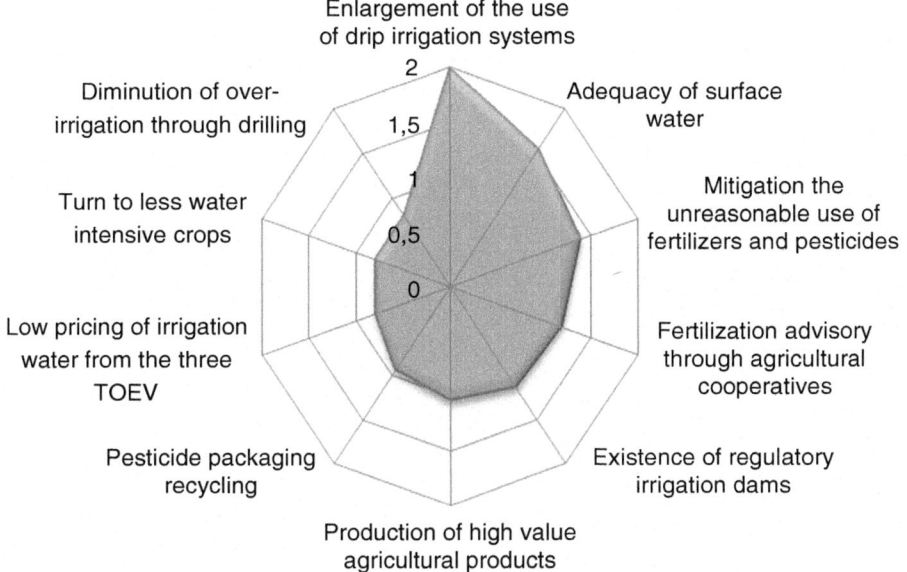

Fig. 4 Strengths of irrigation water management in the study area

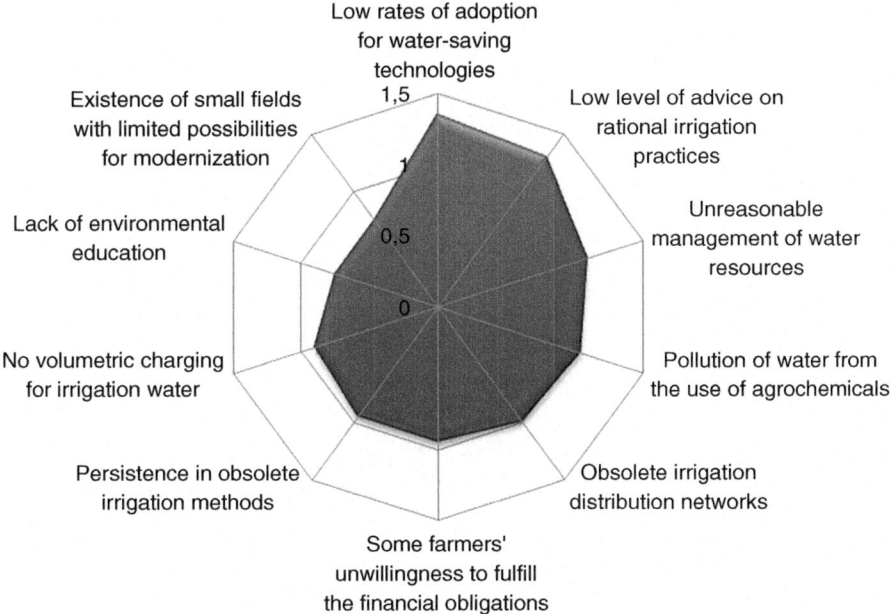

Fig. 5 Weaknesses of irrigation water management in the study area

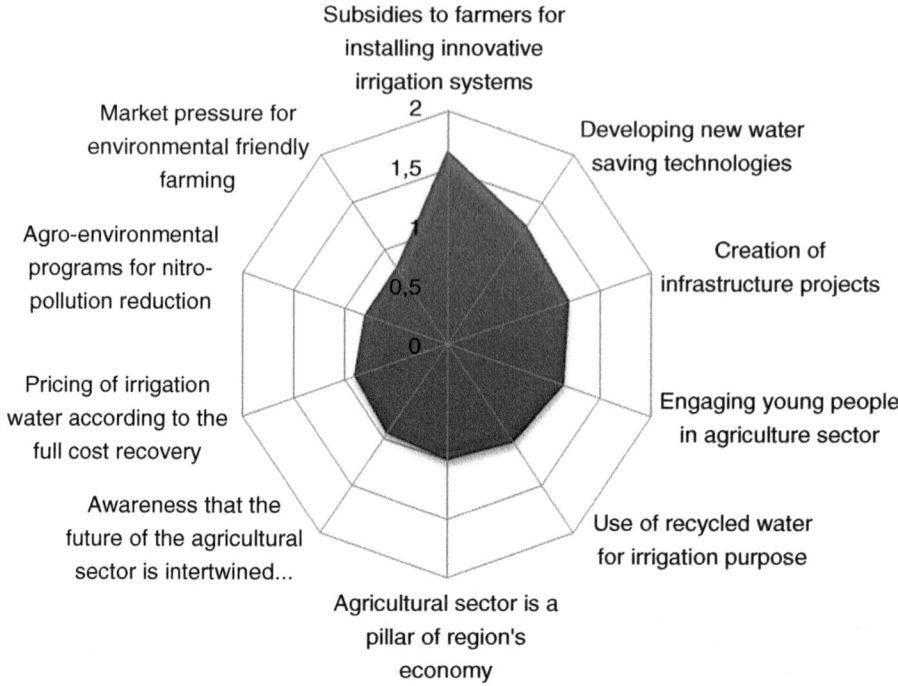

Fig. 6 Opportunities of irrigation water management in the study area

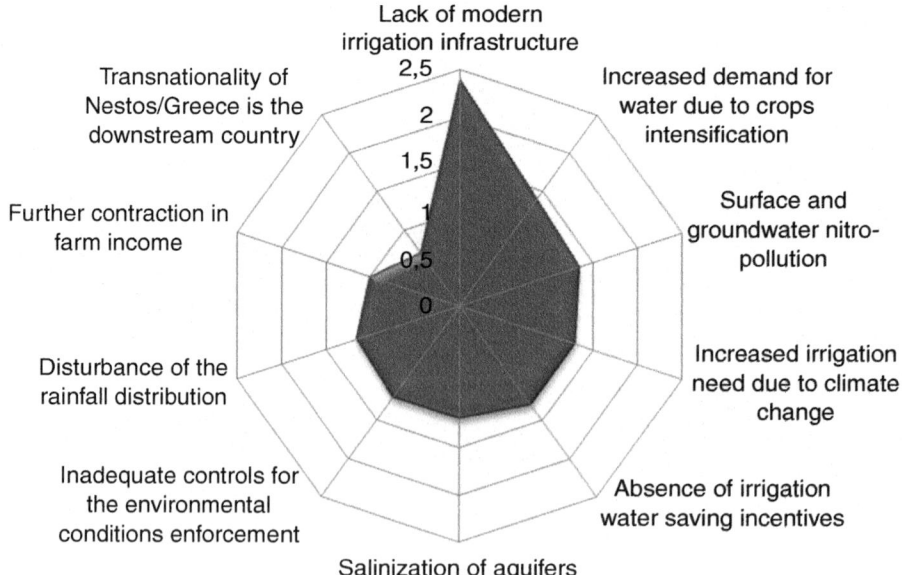

Fig. 7 Threats of irrigation water management in the study area

Table 5 Proposed measures of responses to major weaknesses

Weaknesses	Proposed measures	%
W_1: Low rate of adoption for water-saving technologies	• Informing/training of farmers for the adoption of new technologies	50.0
	• Harnessing national and European programs to fund innovative technologies	33.3
	• Further incentives for farmers to save water (volumetric pricing, programs for technology rehabilitation)	16.7
W_2: Low level of advice on rational irrigation practices	• Strengthening counseling programs (through TOEVs, agricultural cooperatives)	50.0
	• Organization of information seminars related to rational irrigation practices	25.0
	• Continuous and non-fragmentary counseling (interconnection with universities and research centers)	25.0
W_3: Unreasonable management of water resources	• Full cost recovery for irrigation water services/volumetric pricing	41.7
	• Farmers' training/information	33.3
	• Installation of smart irrigation systems	8.3
	• Environmental awareness of farmers	8.3
	• Implementation of strategies for farmers' behavior change	8.3
W_4: Pollution of surface water and groundwater due to the overuse of agrochemicals	• Pesticides prescription and empty packaging recycling	38.5
	• Stricter controls/imposition of fines	23.1
	• Adoption of organic farming methods	15.4
	• Implementation of the Code of Good Agricultural Practice (COGAP)	7.7
	• Information about good farming practices	7.7
	• Informing/sensitizing farmers about the effects of irrational use of water	7.7
W_5: Obsolete irrigation distribution networks	• Replacement of irrigation networks through National and European finances programs	41.7
	• Grounding/modernization of the irrigation networks	25.0
	• Replacement of irrigation networks (cost assumption by TOEV and farmers)	16.7
	• Counseling of local bodies for EU funds absorption	8.3
	• Upgrading irrigation networks through land consolidation programs	8.3

5 Conclusion

This study developed a hybrid model, combining SWOT analysis with the Delphi method to rank and quantify environmental impacts of water use in the agriculture sector. As it is indicated by the results, in the investigated area, there are opportunities and threats that come from external environment as well as strengths and weaknesses of the irrigation sector, which have an effect on water conservation in Nestos river basin.

Table 6 Proposed measures of responses to major threats

Threats	Proposed measures	%
T_1: Lack of modern irrigation infrastructure	• Grounding irrigation networks and maintenance water storage tanks	33.3
	• Harnessing national and European programs to fund innovative technologies	25.0
	• Installation electronic systems, instantaneous remote-sensing measurements, alarm systems	16.7
	• Upgrading irrigation networks through land consolidation programs	16.7
	• Counseling of local bodies for EU funds absorption	8.3
T_2: Increased demand for irrigation water due to intensification of crops	• Use of precision irrigation/drip irrigation	30.8
	• Control performing on the rational use of water/ establishment of a water ceiling per crop and per acre	23.1
	• Changes in kind of cultivation	15.4
	• Informing/training of farmers for its rational use	15.4
	• Water reuse and adaptation of relevant legislation	7.7
	• Change the pricing policy	7.7
T_3: Surface and groundwater nitro-pollution	• Inclusion in denitrification program the entire area of Nestos river basin	30.8
	• Implementation of dynamic policy, with correlation between subsidies and fertilizers consumption (imposition of financial penalties in the case of unreasonable use)	23.1
	• Lubrication only after soil analysis and foliar diagnosis	15.4
	• Informing/training of farmers for the rational use of agrochemicals	15.4
	• Promoting organic/chemical-free fertilizers	7.7
	• Establishment of integrated plant protection consultants/more rational use of crop inputs	7.7
T_4: Increased irrigation needs due to climate change	• Grounding of irrigation network to reduce evaporative water losses/prohibition of spray irrigation	33.3
	• Changes in kind of cultivation	25.0
	• Informing/training of farmers on rational use of irrigation water	16.7
	• Raising farmers' awareness on climate change issues	8.3
	• Long-term program on preventing climate change	8.3
	• Full cost recovery for irrigation water	8.3
T_5: Absence of irrigation water-saving incentives	• Full cost recovery for irrigation water	41.7
	• Volumetric pricing	33.3
	• Financial incentives for the replacement of old/ water-consuming irrigation systems	16.7
	• Correlation between agricultural subsidies and farmers' environmentally friendly behavior	8.3

Exploiting strengths, minimizing weaknesses, exploring opportunities, and facing the recognized threat could be components of a decision-making approach for the sustainable management of water resources in the region. The examination of the proposed acts, arose from this survey, for the confrontation of the problems which are over time detected, contributes to the formulation of an effective policy on water resource management.

References

Anagnostopoulos, K., & Petalas, C. (2011). A fuzzy multicriteria benefit-cost approach for irrigation projects evaluation. *Agricultural Water Management, 98*(9), 1409–1416.

Dafis, S., Papastergiadou, E., Georgiou, K., Babalonas, D., Georgiadis, T., Papageorgiou, M., et al. (1997). Directive 92/43/EEC: the project "Habitat" in Greece: Network natura 2000, life contract B4-3200/84/756, DG XI commission of the European communities. The Goulandris Museum of Natural History, Greek Biotope/Wetland Center, Thermi.

Dalkey, N. C., & Helmer, O. (1963). An experimental application of the Delphi method to the use of experts. *Management Science, 9*(3), 458–467.

Delbecq, A. L., Van de Ven, A. H., & Gustafson, D. H. (1975). *Group techniques for program planning*. Glenview, IL: Scott, Foresman.

Doulgeris, C., Georgiou, P., Papadimos, D., & Papamichail, D. (2015). Water allocation under deficit irrigation using MIKE BASIN model for the mitigation of climate change. *Irrigation Science, 33*(6), 469–482.

European Commission. (1999). *SWOT analysis. Evaluating socioeconomic programmes: Principal evaluation techniques and tools* (Vol. 3, pp. 41–45). Means collection, EC Structural funds, Luxembourg.

Ganoulis, J., Murphy, I. L., & Brilly, M. (Eds.). (2000). *Transboundary water resources in the Balkans: Initiating a sustainable co-operative network*. NATO ASI SERIES, Partnership sub-series 2: Environmental security (Vol. 47, 254 pp). Dodrecht: Kluwer Academic.

Ganoulis, J., Skoulikaris, H., & Monget, J. M. (2008). Involving stakeholders in transboundary water resources management: The Mesta/Nestos 'HELP' basin. *Water SA Journal, 34*(4), 461–467.

Garrote, L., Iglesias, A., Granados, A., Mediero, L., & Martin-Carrasco, F. (2015). Quantitative assessment of climate change vulnerability of irrigation demands in Mediterranean Europe. *Water Resource Management, 29*, 325–338.

Ghazinoory, S., Abdi, M., & Azadegan-Mehr, M. (2011). SWOT methodology: A state-of-the-art review for the past, a framework for the future. *Journal of Business Economics and Management, 12*(1), 24–48.

Gkiougkis, I., Kallioras, A., Pliakas, F., Pechtelidis, A., Diamantis, V., Diamantis, I., Ziogas, A., & Dafnis, I. (2015). Assessment of soil salinization at the eastern Nestos River Delta, N.E. Greece. *Catena, 128*, 238–251.

Gordon, L. J., Finlayson, C. M., & Falkenmark, M. (2010). Managing water in agriculture for food production and other ecosystem services. *Agriculture Water Management, 97*(4), 512–519.

Linstone, H. A., & Turoff, M. (1975). Introduction. In H. A. Linstone & M. Turoff (Eds.), *The Delphi method: Techniques and applications* (pp. 3–12). Reading, MA: Addison-Wesley.

Ludwig, B. (1997). Predicting the future: Have you considered using the Delphi methodology? *Journal of Extension, 35*(5), 1–4.

Markou, M., Michailidis, A., Loizou, E., & Mattas, L. (2014). Exploring climate changes issues related to eater resources and agriculture in Cyprus, employing a Delphi type method. In *Proceedings of ENVECON 2014 Conference "Economics of Natural Resources and Environment: Climate Change"* (pp. 184–195). Volos, March, Greece.

Michailidis, A., Papadaki-Klavdianou, A., Apostolidou, I., Lorite, I. J., Pereira, F. A., Mirko, H., Buhagiar, J., Shilev, S., Michaelidis, E., Loizou, E., Chatzitheodoridis, F., Restoy, R. C., & Lopez, A. L. (2015). Exploring treated wastewater issues related to agriculture in Europe, employing a quantitative SWOT analysis. *Procedia Economics and Finance, 33*, 367–375.

Myronidis, D., & Emmanouloudis, D. (2008). A water balance model of the Natura 2000 protected area "Nestos delta". *Journal of Engineering Science and Technology, 1*, 45–48.

Okoli, C., & Pawloski, S. (2004). The Delphi method as a research tool: An example, design considerations and applications. *Information and Management, 42*, 15–29.

Orfanidis, S., Panayotidis, P., & Stamatis, N. (2001). Ecological evaluation of transitional and coastal waters: a marine benthic macrophytes-based model. *Mediterranean Marine Research, 2*, 45–65.

Papastergios, G., Fernandez-Turiel, J. L., Georgakopoulos, A., & Gimeno, D. (2009). Natural and anthropogenic effects on the sediment geochemistry of Nestos River, northern Greece. *Environmental Geology, 58*, 1361–1370.

Pedreira, R., Kallioras, A., Pliakas, F., Gkiougkis, I., & Schuth, C. (2015). Groundwater vulnerability assessment of a coastal aquifer system at River Nestos eastern Delta, Greece. *Environmental Earth Sciences, 73*(10), 6387–6415.

Pereira, L. S., Oweis, T., & Zairi, A. (2002). Irrigation management under water scarcity. *Agricultural Water Management, 57*, 175–206.

Pill, J. (1971). The Delphi method: Substance, context, a critique and an annotated bibliography. *Socio-Economic Planning Science, 5*, 57–71.

Prieto Montes, M., Patsia, A., Angelakou, G., Kanli, L., Kasapi, K. A., Ntislidou, C., Kotzageorgis, G., Georgiadis, P., & Lazaridou, M. (2009). Ecological quality of river Nestos (Hellas) and its tributaries in September 2008. In *11th International Congress on the "Zoogeography and Ecology of Greece and Adjacent Regions"* (pp. 25–29). Irakleio, Greece.

Skoulikidis, N. (2009). The environmental state of rivers in the Balkans—A review within the DPSIR framework. *Science of the Total Environment, 407*(8), 2501–2516.

Sun, H., Wang, S., & Hao, X. (2017). An improved analytic hierarchy process method for the evaluation of agricultural water management in irrigation districts of north China. *Agricultural Water Management, 179*, 324–337.

Taylor, R. E., & Judd, L. L. (1989). Delphi method applied to tourism. In S. Witt & L. Moutinho (Eds.), *Tourism marketing and management handbook*. New York: Prentice Hall.

Xeidakis, G., & Delimani, P. (2003). Environmental problems of the coastal zone wet lands. The case of the Nestos Delta and Adjacent Areas, Northern Aegean Sea, Greece. In *2nd International Conference on "Ecological Protection of the Planet Earth"* (pp. 694–700). Sofia, Bulgaria.

Xeidakis, G., Georgoulas, A., Kotsovinos, N., Delimani, P., & Varaggouli, E. (2010). Environmental degradation of the coastal zone of the west part of Nestos River delta, N. Greece. In *12th International Conference of the "Geological Society of Greece (Bulletin of the Geological Society of Greece)"* (pp. 1074–1085). Patra, Greece.

How Do Mosquitoes Affect Tourism Enterprises in Greece?

Lambros Tsourgiannis, Giannoula Florou, Theodoros Markopoulos, Sofia Anastasiadou, and Christos Tsitsakis

Abstract During the period 2012–2014 a West Nile virus outbreak occurred in the Region of Eastern Macedonia and Thrace in Greece. This study is aimed at exploring the attitudes of tourism enterprises in this area toward the mosquito problem and at identifying the factors that have had an impact on those enterprises' losses due to mosquitoes. In particular, this paper is aimed at classifying tourism enterprises into groups according to their attitudes toward the mosquito problem; profiling each group identified group according to the type of enterprise, the regional district they operate, and their level of financial losses; identifying the opinion of each group of enterprises regarding the importance they give to vector control programs operating in the Region of Eastern Macedonia and Thrace; identifying the factors that affect those enterprises' losses due to mosquitoes. Multivariate statistical techniques, including principal component analysis, cluster analysis, discriminant analysis, logistic regression analysis, and nonparametric tests such as Chi-squared and Friedman tests, are used in this study.

Keywords Mosquitoes · Tourism enterprises · Public health

L. Tsourgiannis (✉)
Directorate of Public Health and Social Care of Regional District of Xanthi, Region of Eastern Macedonia and Thrace, Xanthi, Greece

G. Florou
Accounting and Finance Department, School of Business and Economics, Eastern Macedonia and Thrace Institute of Technology, Kavala, Greece

T. Markopoulos
Department of Agricultural Economy, Democritus University of Thrace, Orestiada, Greece

S. Anastasiadou
Early Childhood Education Department, University of Western Macedonia, Kozani, Greece

C. Tsitsakis
Department of Accounting and Finance, School of Business Administration, Technological Educational Institute of Central Greece, Psachna, Greece

© Springer Nature Switzerland AG 2019
N. Sykianakis et al. (eds.), *Economic and Financial Challenges for Eastern Europe*,
Springer Proceedings in Business and Economics,
https://doi.org/10.1007/978-3-030-12169-3_31

461

1 Introduction

Tourism and hospitality are key economic activities worldwide and therefore marketing plays an important role in the tourist industry (Morgan and Pritchard 2002; Tripathi and Siddiqui 2010; Williams 2006). Tourism activities cover a wide range of sectors, from agriculture to secondary industries, through many service suppliers (Proust et al. 2009). The tourism sector consists of a powerful developing force and it is a key sector in national economies (Proust et al. 2009). According to the Greek Tourism Confederation (2014), the tourism industry has played a significant role in the Greek economy by making a contribution to the GDP of 16.4%.

Knowing where consumers' preferences and their values reside, stakeholders can develop the necessary strategies to increase customer satisfaction, loyalty, and retention (Tripathi and Siddiqui 2010). Some crucial factors that affect the choice of tourists regarding their destination according to Hsu et al. (2009), Tripathi and Siddiqui (2010), Tsourgiannis et al. (2015) are: (a) psychological factors (escape and self-actualization); (b) physical factors such as rest and relaxation, medical treatment, health and fitness); (c) security including medical insurance, family safety; (d) value for money. On the other hand, the presence of mosquitoes seems to have negative impact on the tourism sector (Kumari 2016).

Mosquito vectors are solely responsible for transmitting malaria, dengue, West Nile virus (WNV), chikungunya, Japanese encephalitis, and lymphatic filariasis (Rozendaal 1997; Raghavendra et al. 2011; Pandit et al. 2010). In particular, the WNV not only poses a risk to health, but diseases in endemic areas place a burden on households, on health services, and on the economic growth of the local communities (Koenraadt et al. 2006; Tyagi et al. 2005). Therefore, protection of citizens and tourists against mosquito bites is very important for *public* health.

To face the problem, the Region of Eastern Macedonia and Thrace (REMTh) conducted a mosquito control program with aerial and earthly sprays. On the other hand, the WNV appeared in the REMTh and during the period 2012–2015 there were 154 infected people. Economic data regarding epidemics are of importance for estimating the costs and benefits of strengthening and maintaining prevention and control programs, improving existing surveillance systems, and introducing other proposed interventions (Zohrabian et al. 2004).

As tourism is an important pillar of the Greek economy—the safety of their family and health affect tourists' choice of holiday destination, and the presence of mosquitoes seems to have a negative impact on the tourism sector (Proust et al. 2009; Hsu et al. 2009; Tripathi and Siddiqui 2010; Greek Tourism Confederation 2014; Tsourgiannis et al. 2015; Kumari 2016)—in this study we tried to investigate how mosquitoes affect tourism enterprises in the REMTh in Greece.

In particular, this study is aimed at:

1. Classifying tourism enterprises into groups according to their attitudes toward the mosquito problem.
2. Profiling each group identified according to the type of enterprise, the regional district in which they operate, and their level of financial losses.

3. Identifying the opinion of each group of enterprises on the importance they give to vector control programs operating in the REMTh.
4. Identifying the factors that affect the losses of those enterprises due to mosquitoes.

2 Methodology

The null research hypotheses this study aimed to reject were:

- **Ho1:** Tourism enterprises cannot be classified into groups according to their attitudes toward the mosquito problem.
- **Ho2:** Tourism enterprises' attitudes toward the mosquito problem are not related to their opinion on the effectiveness of the vector control program.
- **Ho3:** Tourism enterprises' attitudes toward the mosquito problem are not related to their characteristics.
- **Ho4:** Tourism enterprises' financial losses due to the mosquito problem are not related to their characteristics.
- **Ho5:** Tourism enterprises' financial losses due to the mosquito problem are not related to their opinion on the effectiveness of the vector control program.

Figure 1 illustrates the conceptual model of the study.

An interview survey based on a structured questionnaire was conducted by the Directorate of Public Health and Social Welfare of Xanthi in September 2016 throughout the REMTh to gather the necessary information. A total productive sample of 162 tourism enterprises was used in this research. The sample is reasonably representative according to the methodology of Siardos (1997) ($z = 1.96$ and $d = 5\%$).

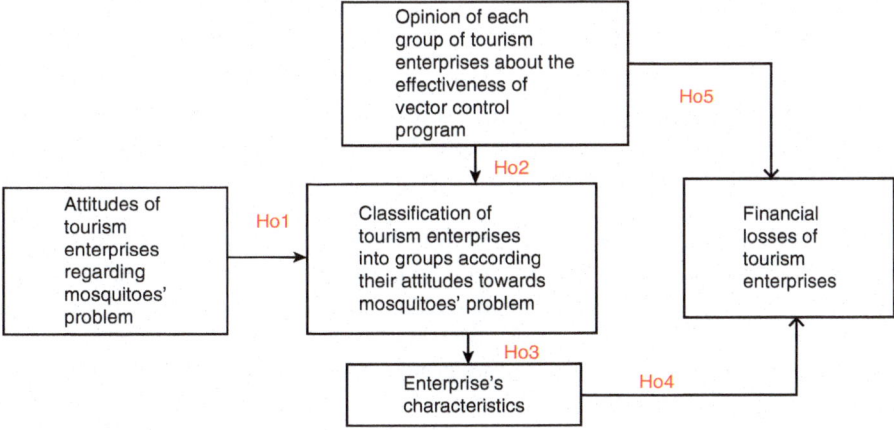

Fig. 1 Conceptual model

Multivariate analysis techniques were applied in three stages to the responses of the 162 tourism enterprises to reveal the key information that these contained. Principal component analysis (PCA) was used to identify the variables that accounted for the maximum amount of variance within the data in terms of the smallest number of uncorrelated variables (components). The anti-image correlation matrix, Bartlett's test of sphericity, and the measure of sampling adequacy (MSA) were used to check the appropriateness of the data for subsequent factor analysis. Variables with a high proportion of large absolute values of anti-image correlations and MSA less than 0.5 were removed before analysis. An orthogonal rotation (varimax method) was conducted and the standard criteria of eigenvalue $= 1$, scree test, and percentage of variance were used to determine the factors in the first rotation (Hair et al. 1998). Different trial rotations followed, where factor interpretability was used to compare the seven variables related to the main opinion of those enterprises on mosquitoes reduced through PCA to a smaller set of underlying factors. These PCA scores were then subjected to both hierarchical and k-means cluster analysis with group enterprises with similar patterns of scores into similar clusters regarding their attitudes toward mosquitoes (Hair et al. 1998). Quadratic discriminant analysis was performed to assess how accurately the key factors identified through factor analysis could predict and discriminate cluster membership. Furthermore, the Friedman one-way test was performed to identify what each group of enterprises believed about the effectiveness of the vector control performed in the REMTh. Chi-squared analysis was conducted to find out which factors/characteristics have an impact on the attitudes of tourism enterprises toward the mosquito problem. Logistic regression analysis and Chi-square analysis were used to identify which factors have an impact on the financial losses of tourism enterprises due to mosquitoes. Finally, the Friedman one-way test was performed to explore how the opinion of tourism enterprises regarding the effectiveness of vector control programs is affected by their financial losses.

3   Results and Discussion

The variables and the two main key factors affecting the attitudes of tourism enterprises toward the mosquito problem along with their eigenvalues, the scree plot test, and the percentage of variance results from PCA and factor analysis are portrayed in Tables 1 and 2.

Hierarchical and nonhierarchical clustering methods (Hair et al. 1998) were used to develop a typology of the tourism enterprises regarding their attitudes toward mosquitoes. Cluster analysis was conducted on all 162 observations, as there were no outliers.

Enterprises appeared to fall into two groups according to their attitudes toward mosquitoes (Table 3): (a) those who believe that mosquitoes are a major nuisance to people and (b) those who believe that people's fear about public health due to mosquitoes is a major problem.

Table 1 Variables affecting the key attitudes of tourism enterprises toward mosquitoes problem

Component	Eigenvalues	Percentage of variance	Cumulative percentage of variance
1	3.612	51.596	51.596
2	1.295	18.499	70.096
3	0.595	8.504	78.600
4	0.466	6.659	85.259
5	0.428	6.109	91.368
6	0.371	5.299	96.667
7	0.233	3.333	100.00

Table 2 What tourism enterprises think about the existence of mosquitoes in their area

Main factors	Factor loading
Mosquitoes are a nuisance to people	
How important a problem is the appearance of mosquitoes in your area in the evening?	0.887
How large a problem is the existence of mosquitoes in your area?	0.823
How important a problem is the appearance of mosquitoes in your area from a nuisance point of view?	0.809
How important a problem is the appearance of mosquitoes in your area early in the morning?	0.799
How important a factor do you consider the appearance of mosquitoes to be for the downgrading of quality of life?	0.736
Mosquitoes are a hazard to public health	
How important a hazard to public health do you consider the existence of mosquitoes to be?	0.900
How important a problem for public health do you consider the existence of mosquitoes to be in your area?	0.797

Kaiser–Meyer–Olkin measure of sampling accuracy $= 0.823$, Bartlett test of sphericity $= 479.169$, $P < 0.001$

Table 3 Classification of tourism enterprises regarding their attitudes toward mosquitoes

Key dimensions	Enterprises that consider that mosquitoes are a major nuisance to people	Enterprises that consider people's fear about public health due mosquitoes is a major problem	P
Mosquitoes are a nuisance to people	0.80343	−0.69261	**0.0001**
Mosquitoes are a hazard to public health	−0.46679	0.40413	**0.0001**
Number of consumers ($n = 162$)	75	87	

Values in bold are significant with $P < 0.001$ or $P < 0.05$

Enterprises that consider that mosquitoes are a major nuisance to people
comprise 46% of the sample. They mainly believe that mosquitoes are a large
problem in their area, mainly because of quality of life. They also think that the
appearance of mosquitoes in the evening and early in the morning disturb most of the
people in their area.

**Enterprises that consider people's fear about public health due to mosqui-
toes is a major problem** comprise 54% of the sample. They mainly think that
mosquitoes are a very important hazard to public health in general and in their area in
particular.

Discriminant analysis was performed to evaluate the prediction performance of
group membership with the predictors derived from the factor analysis. Initially, the
normality of the key strategic dimensions was checked. A summary of the cross-
validation classification derived through quadratic discriminant analysis is presented
in Table 4.

It is evident that the two attitude dimensions could accurately predict and
discriminate citizens' group membership.

Therefore, the hypothesis *Ho1: Tourism enterprises cannot be classified into
groups according to their attitudes toward the mosquito problem* can be rejected.

The Friedman nonparametric test was employed to investigate what tourism
enterprises believe about the effectiveness of the vector control program (Fig. 2).

As Fig. 2 indicates, most of the tourism enterprises believe that the vector control
program operated in the REMTh is very important, first of all, for the protection of
public health, and second, for facing the nuisance that mosquitoes are to tourists and
citizens. Furthermore, the enterprises of the second group (those who consider that
people's fear about public health due mosquitoes is a major problem) have the
opinion that vector control programs operated by the regional authorities are quite
important for touristic development. On the other hand, the enterprises of the first
group (those who consider that mosquitoes are a major nuisance to people) do not

Table 4 Summary of classification with cross-validation

	Predicted classification	
Actual classification	Enterprises that consider that mosquitoes are a major nuisance to people	Enterprises that consider people's fear about public health due to mosquitoes is a major problem
Enterprises that consider that mosquitoes are a major nuisance to people	72	4
Enterprises that consider that people's fear about public health due to mosquitoes is a major problem	3	83
Total number	75	87
Number correct	72	83
Proportion	96%	95.4%
$N = 162$	**Number correct = 155**	**Proportion correct = 95.6%**

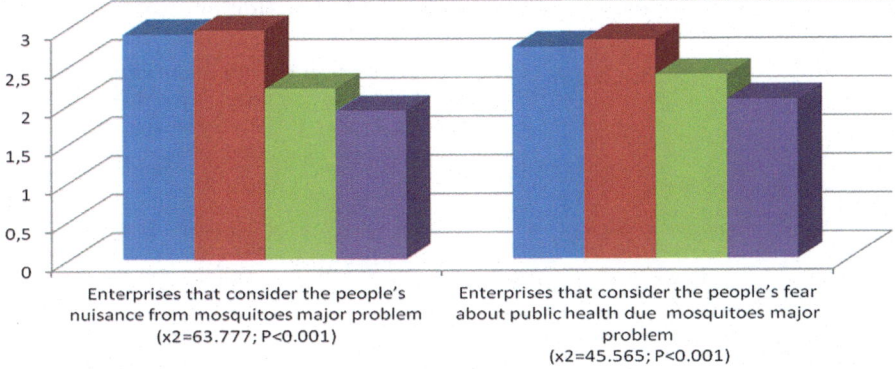

- How important factor do you consider the performance of vector control program in REMTh for facing the nuisense mosquiotes cause to citizens
- How important factor for the protection of public health do you consider the performance of vector control program in REMTh
- How important factor for the touristic development do you consider the performance of vector control program in REMTh
- How effective do you consider the performance of vector control program in REMTh

Fig. 2 What tourism enterprises believe about the effectiveness of the vector control program

consider vector control programs operated by the regional authorities to be important for touristic development.

Hence, the hypothesis, *Ho2:* Tourism enterprises' attitudes toward the mosquito problem are not related to their opinion on the effectiveness of the vector control program can be rejected.

Furthermore, Chi-squared analysis was conducted to identify the factors/characteristics that have a significant impact on the attitudes of tourism enterprises toward the mosquito problem (Table 5).

Therefore, most of the tourism enterprises that consider that mosquitoes are a major nuisance to people are based in Evros Regional District, they think that the problem is more intense in September, and most of these enterprises are cafe and beach bars. On the other hand, most of the tourism enterprises that consider that people's fear about public health due to mosquitoes is a major problem operate mainly in the Regional District of Xanthi, as in that area there were cases of WNV during the period 2011–2014. They think that the problem is more intense during July. Moreover, most of these enterprises are café and beach bars.

Hence, **Ho3:** Tourism enterprises' attitudes toward the mosquito problem are not related to their characteristics can be rejected.

Furthermore, logistic regression analysis (Table 6) indicates that the regional district in which tourism enterprises operate has an impact on the amount of their financial losses are due to mosquitoes.

The Chi-squared analysis also indicates (Table 7) that most of the tourism enterprises that have financial losses of less than 50 Euros per month operate in the Kavala Regional District and are mainly cafés/beach bars, whereas most of the

Table 5 Citizens whose factors/characteristics have an impact on the attitudes of tourism enterprises toward the mosquito problem?

Factors/characteristics		Enterprises that consider that mosquitoes are a major nuisance to people (%)	Enterprises that consider that people's fear about public health due mosquitoes is a major problem (%)
Regional district	Drama	11.6	17.1
$\chi^2 = 36.486$	Kavala	24.4	23.7
df = 4	Xanthi	18.6	**34.2**
P < 0.001	Rodopi	8.1	23.7
	Evros	**37.2**	1.3
Period of intensity	April	2.3	2.6
$\chi^2 = 12.869$	May	8.1	7.9
df = 5	June	12.8	28.9
P < 0.05	July	26.7	**35.5**
	August	15.1	6.6
	September	**34.9**	18.4
Type of enterprise	Café/beach bar	**48.8**	**46.1**
$\chi^2 = 16.258$	Tavern/restaurant	12.8	13.2
df = 4	Playground	1.2	2.6
P < 0.001	Hotel	30.2	11.8
	Other	7.0	26.3

Values in bold are significant with $P < 0.001$ or $P < 0.05$

Table 6 Which factors have an impact of the financial losses of tourism enterprises due to mosquitoes?

	Predictors	Coef	P	Odds ratio
51–100 € financial losses per month due to mosquitoes />=101 € financial losses per month due to mosquitoes	Constant	−1.69095	**0.484**	
	Regional District	−0.372559	**0.215**	0.69
	Period of intense	0.360535	**0.163**	1.43
	Type of enterprise	0.0124918	**0.932**	1.01
	Attitudes towards mosquitoes problem	1.33852	**0.101**	3.81
	Predictors	Coef	P	Odds ratio
<50 € financial losses per month due to mosquitoes />=101 € financial losses per month due to mosquitoes	Constant	2.61819	**0.204**	
	Regional District	−0.529180	**0.045**	0.59
	Period of intense	−0.104446	**0.615**	1.11
	Type of enterprise	0.170344	**0.168**	1.19
	Attitudes towards mosquitoes problem	0.240778	**0.732**	1.27

Values in bold are not significant ($P > 0.05$)

enterprises that suffer financial losses of between 51 and 100 Euros per month are based in Xanthi and are also mainly cafés/beach bars. In addition, the most of the tourism enterprises that have financial losses due to mosquitoes of more than 101 Euros exist in the Evros area and are also cafés and beach bars.

Table 7 The association between the characteristics of tourism enterprises and their financial losses due to mosquitoes

Enterprise's characteristics		<50 € financial losses per month due to mosquitoes (%)	51–100 € financial losses per month due to mosquitoes (%)	>101 € financial losses per month due to mosquitoes (%)
Regional district	Drama	16.8	7.4	0.0
$\chi^2 = 20.129$	Kavala	**24.4**	29.6	13.3
df = 8	Xanthi	22.7	**37.0**	33.3
P < 0.05	Rodopi	19.3	7.4	0.0
	Evros	16.8	18.5	**53.3**
Type of enterprise	Café/beach bar	**46.2**	**51.9**	**53.3**
$\chi^2 = 20.885$	Tavern/restaurant	8.4	25.9	26.7
df = 8	Playground	1.7	3.7	0.0
P < 0.05	Hotel	28.6	0.0	0.0
	Other	15.1	18.5	20.0

Values in bold are significant with $P < 0.001$ or $P < 0.05$

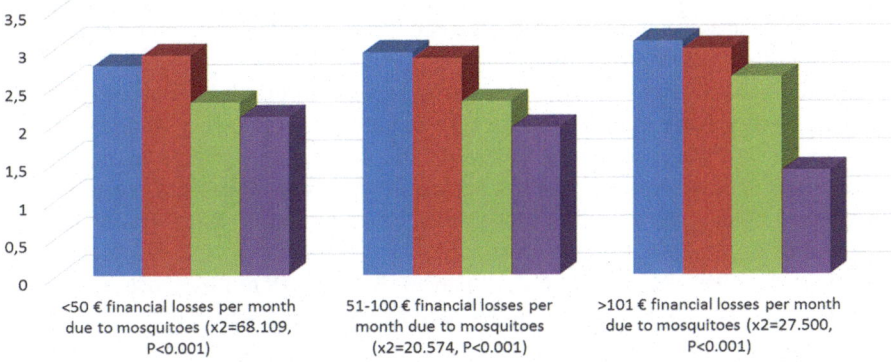

■ How important factor do you consider the performance of vector control program in REMTh for facing the nuisense mosquiotes cause to citizens

■ How important factor for the protection of public health do you consider the performance of vector control program in REMTh

■ How important factor for the touristic development do you consider the performance of vector control program in REMTh

■ How effective do you consider the performance of vector control program in REMTh

Fig. 3 How the opinion of tourism enterprises regarding the effectiveness of vector control programs affects their financial losses

Hence, **Ho4:** Tourism enterprises' financial losses due to the mosquito problem are not related to their characteristics can be rejected.

The Friedman nonparametric test was performed to explore how the opinion of tourism enterprises regarding the effectiveness of vector control programs affects their financial losses. According to the results of the test, as Fig. 3 illustrates, there is a significant association between the financial losses of tourism enterprises due to the mosquito problem and their opinion regarding the effectiveness of the vector control program operated by the regional authority. In particular, most of the tourism enterprises of the aforementioned three groups believe that the vector control programs operated by the regional authority are very important in facing the nuisance mosquitoes causes to citizens and in protecting public health.

Therefore, the hypothesis **Ho5**: *Tourism enterprises' financial losses due to the mosquito problem are not related to their opinion on the effectiveness of the vector control program* could be rejected.

4 Conclusions

According to the current study, the tourism enterprises that operate in the REMTh in Greece believe that the existence of mosquitoes in their area (a) are a nuisance to people and (b) constitutes a hazard to public health.

Hence, they can be classified according to their attitudes toward mosquitoes into two groups: (i) those who believe that people in their area are annoyed by the existence of mosquitoes, and (ii) those who believe that people in their area are aware of public health protection.

The regional district in which these enterprises operate, the period of the mosquito problem is more intense, and the type of enterprise all have an impact on their attitudes toward the mosquito problem. Furthermore, both groups of enterprises believe that vector control programs performed by local authorities are important for fighting against the nuisance mosquitoes cause to people and for public health protection.

This study also identified that the financial losses suffered by those enterprises due to mosquitoes are related to: (a) the regional district in which they operate, and (b) the type of enterprise.

Nevertheless, the current study is of value, because, to the knowledge of the authors, this is the first attempt to explore how mosquitoes affect tourism enterprises and in particular the attitudes of the tourism enterprises toward the mosquito problem, the factors that affect their attitudes, and their financial losses due to mosquitoes. On the other hand, even though those enterprises recognize that the vector control programs operated by regional authorities are effective and important in facing the problems mosquitoes cause to citizens, they should undertake their own actions (mostly preventive actions in their own private area), mainly during the period when the problem is more intense. Hence, a systematic information and awareness campaign by the relative stakeholders (regional authorities and municipalities) should be aimed at these target groups to learn what actions should be undertaken to avoid attracting and breeding mosquitoes in their private area. Furthermore, the operation of vector control programs by the regional and local authorities is very important for fighting the nuisance mosquitoes cause to people, for public health protection, and therefore for the development of the tourism sector.

References

Greek Tourism Confederation. (2014). *Greek tourism: Facts and figures* (2013 ed.). Athens.

Hair, J. F., Anderson, R. E., Tatham, R. L., & Black, W. C. (1998). *Multivariate data analysis.* New Jersey: Prentice Hall Inc.

Hsu, T. K., Tsai, Y. F., & Wu, H. H. (2009). The preference analysis for tourist choice of destination: A case study of Taiwan. *Tourism Management, 30,* 288–297.

Koenraadt, C., Tuiten, W., Sithiprasasna, R., Kijchalao, U., Jones, J., & Scott, T. (2006). Dengue knowledge and practices and their impact on *Aedes aegypti* populations in Kamphaeng Phet, Thailand. *The American Journal of Tropical Medicine and Hygiene, 74*(4), 692–700.

Kumari, S. (2016). *Mosquitoes drive Kochi's tourists away.* http://timesofindia.indiatimes.com/city/kochi/Mosquitoes-drive-Kochis-tourists-away/articleshow/53593003.cms

Morgan, N. J., & Pritchard, A. (2002). *Tourism, promotion & power: Creating images, creating identities.* Chichester: Wiley.

Pandit, N., Patel, Y., & Bhavsar, B. (2010). Awareness and practice about preventive method against mosquito bite in Gujarat. *Healthline, 1,* 16–20.

Proust, R., Angelakis, G., Drakos, P. (2009). *A study of tourist' attitudes and preferences for local products in Crete and changes endured by the current economic crisis.* In 133th, EAAE Seminar A resilient European food industry and food chain in a challenging world, Chania, Crete, Greece, 03–06 September 2009.

Raghavendra, K., Baril, T. K., Reddy, B. P. N., Sharma, P., & Dash, A. P. (2011). Malaria vector control: From past to future. *Parasitology Research, 108,* 757–779.

Rozendaal, J. A. (1997). *Vector control: Methods for use by individuals and communities.* Geneva: World Health Organization.

Siardos, G. (1997). *Methodology of agricultural sociological research.* Thessaloniki: Ziti Publications.

Tripathi, S., & Siddiqui, M. (2010). An empirical study of tourist preferences using conjoint analysis. *International Journal of Business Sciences and Applied Management, 5*(2), 2–16.

Tsourgiannis, L., Delias, P., Polychronidou, P., Karasavvoglou, A., Valsamidis, S. (2015). Profiling tourists who have holidays in the region of Eastern Macedonia and Thrace in Greece. Procedia Economics and Finance, 33, 450–460.

Tyagi, P., Roy, A., & Malhotra, M. S. (2005). Knowledge, awareness and practices towards malaria in communities of rural, semi-rural and bordering areas of East Delhi (India). *Journal of Vector Borne Diseases, 42,* 30–35.

Williams, A. (2006). Tourism and hospitality marketing: Fantasy, feeling and fun. *International Journal of Contemporary Hospitality Management, 18*(6), 482–495.

Zohrabian, A., Meltzer, M., Ratard, R., Billah, K., Molinari, N., Roy, K., Douglas Scott, R., II, & Petersen, L. (2004). West Nile virus economic impact, Louisiana, 2002. *Emerging Infectious Diseases, 10,* 1736–1744.

The Relationship Between Efficiency Measures and Environmental Pollution: An Empirical Study

Panagiotis Fotis

Abstract The aim of this paper is to empirically explore Environmental Kuznets Curve hypothesis within EU28 countries by utilizing dynamic panel data approach. The results show that economic growth positively affects environmental pollutants. Therefore, Environmental Kuznets Curve hypothesis does not exist within EU28 countries. The results also reveal that the use of energy efficiency measures negatively affects pollution, while energy intensity contributes to more air pollution.

Keywords Dynamic panel data · Environmental Kuznets Curve · Environmental pollutants · Energy efficiency measures

1 Introduction

The motivation of this paper stems from the environmental version of Kuznets Curve (Environmental Kuznets Curve, EKC) (Shafik and Bandyopandhyay 1992; Grossman and Krueger 1995; Holtz-Eakin and Selten 1995). EKC hypothesis basically states that pollution rises with income at low income levels (*degradation of environmental quality*), but at a higher income level, a turning point is reached and further income growth leads to lower pollution (Panayotou 1995). An opposite line of reasoning states that the relationship between pollution and economic growth is monotonically rising (Cole 1999).

This paper empirically explores whether or not an EKC actually exists and draws valuable policy implications regarding the effect of renewable energy use and pollution. For these purposes, we utilize yearly updated panel dataset of EU28 member states during the period from 2005 to 2013, and we employ dynamic

---

The views expressed herein are strictly and purely those of the author.

P. Fotis (✉)
Hellenic Competition Commission, Peristeri, Greece

© Springer Nature Switzerland AG 2019
N. Sykianakis et al. (eds.), *Economic and Financial Challenges for Eastern Europe*,
Springer Proceedings in Business and Economics,
https://doi.org/10.1007/978-3-030-12169-3_32

panel generalized method of moments approach to examine clustered patterns of EKC relationship.

This paper extents the literature by exploring the effect of various energy efficiency indicators on environmental pollutants within EU28 member states.[1] The energy efficiency indicators are the share of renewable energy in gross final energy consumption (RENWES), the electricity generated from renewable sources of gross electricity consumption (RENWEG) and energy saving from primary energy consumption (ES). The environmental pollutants are sulphur oxides (SO_2), nitrogen oxides (NO_X), non-methane volatile organic compounds (NMVOC) and greenhouse gas emissions (CO_2 equivalent, GGE). It also utilizes dynamic panel approach such as DIF-GMM methodology to examine clustered patterns of EKC relationship.[2]

The empirical results reveal that economic growth positively affects environmental pollutants. This implies that Environmental Kuznets Curve hypothesis does not exist within EU28 countries. The results also reveal that the use of renewable sources of energy negatively affects environmental pollutants. The more the renewable energy we use, the less the air pollution. Energy saving positively affects pollution, while energy intensity contributes to more air pollution.

The remainder of this paper is organized in the following way. Section 2 presents the notion of EKC hypothesis, and Sect. 3 reviews the literature. Section 4 presents the data and descriptive statistics of the employed variables, Sect. 5 presents the empirical model and the used methodology and Sect. 6 reports the empirical results. Lastly, Sect. 7 discusses the empirical results and provides some policy implications that emerge from them.

2 Environmental Kuznets Curve Hypothesis

Suppose the following empirical model where Y is a cubic function of X and Z represents control variables of the dependent variable Y: $\log Y_{i,t} = \alpha_i + \beta_1 \log X_{1,i,t} + \beta_2 \log X_{1,i,t}^2 + \beta_3 \log X_{1,i,t}^3 + \beta_4 \log Z_{i,t} + \varepsilon_{i,t}$. According to Dinda (2004), Richmond and Kaufmann (2006) and López-Menéndez et al. (2014) among others if:

(a) $\beta_1 > 0$, $\beta_2 < 0$ and $\beta_3 = 0$, then we observe an inverted U-shaped relationship between Y and X (existence of EKC hypothesis).
(b) $\beta_1 < 0$, $\beta_2 > 0$ and $\beta_3 = 0$, we observe a U-shaped relationship between Y and X.
(c) $\beta_1 > 0$, $\beta_2 < 0$ and $\beta_3 > 0$, then it must be so that it exists an N-shaped relationship between Y and X.

---

[1]See also Fotis and Pekka (2017) for an analysis within Eurozone.
[2]López-Menéndez et al. (2014) examines EKC hypothesis by including renewable energy sources as explanatory variables in the empirical models within a static environment (panel data models with fixed and random effects).

(d) $\beta_1 < 0, \beta_2 > 0$ and $\beta_3 < 0$, then it must be so that it exists an inverted N-shaped relationship between Y and X.
(e) $\beta_1 > 0, \beta_2 = 0$ and $\beta_3 = 0$, then it must be so that it exists a monotonically increasing relationship between Y and X.
(f) $\beta_1 < 0, \beta_2 = 0$ and $\beta_3 = 0$, then it must be so that it exists a monotonically decreasing relationship between Y and X. Obviously, if $\beta_1 = \beta_2 = \beta_3 = 0$, this indicates that there is no relationship between environmental indicators and income.

If we suppose the following quadratic empirical model where Y is a quadratic function of X, $\log Y_{i,t} = \alpha_i + \beta_1 \log X_{1,i,t} + \beta_2 \log X_{1,i,t}^2 + \beta_3 \log Z_{i,t} + \varepsilon_{i,t}$, and then if:

(g) $\beta_1 > 0\ (\beta_1 < 0)$ while $\beta_2 = 0\ (\beta_2 = 0)$, respectively, then there is a monotonically increasing (decreasing) relationship between X and Y.
(h) $\beta_1 < 0$ and $\beta_2 > 0$, then we observe a U-shaped relationship.
(i) $\beta_1 > 0$ and $\beta_2 < 0$, we observe an inverted U-shaped relationship between X and Y (existence of EKC hypothesis).

3   Literature Review

The EKC hypothesis has been studied for the EU countries and its subsequent members.[3] The empirical results show a considerable heterogeneity between environmental and economic growth variables. The main source of the divergence may be linked to the rate of productivity and member states' specific characteristics.

Particularly, Alvarez et al. (2005) analyse 15 European countries (all 15 members as of 2003, excepting Luxembourg plus 5 subsequent Eastern European members, Hungary, Poland, Czech Republic, Slovakia and Slovenia). The authors use each country's annual report between 1990 and 2000 on pollution (NO_x, SO_2 and CO_2), income (per capita GDP) and population. The empirical results revealed that air pollution, NO_2 and SO_2, decreased in the 1990s in most EU countries. The empirical results concerning CO_2 revealed different trends for middle-income countries (EU10; the EU14, except Greece, Ireland, Portugal and Spain). Even though for middle-income countries output growth is more intensely correlated with pollution growth, there is no evidence that income growth plays a critical role in pollution.

Richmond and Kaufmann (2006) analyse the effect of fuel mix, model specification and the level of development in 36 countries on the presence and size of a

---

[3]In this section we focus on the presentation of literature review concerning the validity of EKC hypothesis within the EU. For an application of EKC hypothesis in other countries except from European ones, see Wang et al. (2017), Yang et al. (2017), Wang (2013) and Zaim and Taskinm (2000). For a survey of the EKC hypothesis on an empirical and theoretical perspective, see Bernard et al. (2014). For relevant studies prior to 2010, see López-Menéndez et al. (2014), Markandya et al. (2006), Galeotti et al. (2009), Dinda (2004) and Stern (2004). Panayotou (2000) has also given a critical overview of the research done from 1992 to 2000.

turning point in the EKC relationship. The validity of EKC hypothesis depends on the employed variables in the empirical model (i.e. energy mix) and the sample mix. Income exhibits a positive relationship with carbon emissions, but there exists an inverted U-shaped relationship between income and carbon emissions if the effects of energy mix are included in the econometric model. Markandya et al. (2006) examine linkage between per capita GDP and SO_2 for 12 Western European countries (Austria, Belgium, Denmark, Finland, France, Germany, Italy, Netherlands, Norway, Sweden, Switzerland and the UK) over a period of more than 150 years (1850–2001). They find an inverted U-shaped relationship between the two variables. When they incorporated into their analysis environmental regulation (1972–2001) the empirical results show a lower EKC.

Coondoo and Dinda (2008) explore the relationship between the intercountry income inequality and CO_2 emissions and temporal shifts in such a relationship for a sample of 88 countries (22 EU member states) over the period 1960–1990. Based on a cross-country panel dataset and treating environmental damage as a private good, the authors argue that intercountry income inequality has a significant effect on the mean emission for all the sample countries. Also, evidences in favour of existence of EKC have been found for Europe for the period 1966 onwards.

Lee et al. (2009) explores the validity of EKC hypothesis for a sample of, inter alia, 19 EU countries, over the period 1960–2000. They find evidence of the EKC hypothesis for CO_2 emissions in a global dataset, middle-income American and European countries. Marrero (2010) examines the role of energy production on EKC. The author uses data on 24 EU member states (EU10 and Spain, Greece, Portugal and Ireland and East EU,[4] except Luxembourg, Malta and Cyprus) from 1990 to 2006 and concludes that the EKC hypothesis does not hold for the EU24 countries as well as for the most developed European countries (EU10 and Spain, Greece, Portugal and Ireland). Also, the empirical results show that there exists a convergence in terms of greenhouse gas emissions with no notable differences between the pre-Kyoto and the post-Kyoto periods.

Acaravci and Ozturk (2010) use autoregressive distributed lag (ARDL) bounds testing approach of cointegration for 19 European countries over the period from 1965 to 2005 to explore, *among others*, the validity of EKC hypothesis (CO_2 emissions and real per capita GDP). The empirical results reveal that the validity of EKC hypothesis holds only for Denmark and Italy. Jaunky (2011) uses the Blundell-Bond system generalized methods of moments (SYS GMM)[5] to test the EKC hypothesis for 36 high-income countries for the period 1980–2005 in a panel vector error correction model (VECM). The author supports the existence of the EKC hypothesis for Malta, Oman, Portugal and the UK.

Iwata et al. (2011) explore the validity of EKC taking into consideration the role of nuclear energy in the panel data analysis of 28 countries (17 EU countries) over

---

[4]Bulgaria, Czech Republic, Estonia, Latvia, Lithuania, Hungary, Poland, Romania, Slovenia and Slovakia.

[5]See, *among others*, Fotis and Pekka (2017).

the period 1960–2003. The empirical results show that CO_2 emissions increase monotonically in all countries under scrutiny, the effects of nuclear energy on CO_2 emissions are significantly negative and CO_2 emissions decrease and increase with income in OECD countries and non-OECD countries, respectively.

Donfouet et al. (2013) use data from 43 European countries over the period of 1961–2009 and present evidences regarding spatial EKC hypothesis.[6] The empirical results also confirm that the level of CO_2 emissions in Europe has been constantly increasing during the period under scrutiny and increased CO_2 emissions in a particular country affect CO_2 emission estimates in neighbouring states (spatial interdependence). The authors find evidence of an inverted U-shaped relationship between CO_2 emissions and per capita income after controlling for spatial interdependence. Danaeifar (2014) uses spatial panel data model to examine the spatial EKC hypothesis in 30 European countries over the period of 1992–2008. The results confirm the existence of an inverse U-shaped relationship between income, global CO_2 emissions and local aerosol pollutants.

Baycan (2013) examines the EKC relationship between the levels of environmental degradation [suspended particular matter (SPM), NO_2, SO_2 and CO_2] and real per capita income (PPS) in EU25 (EU15 and Cyprus, Czech Republic, Estonia, Hungary, Latvia, Lithuania, Malta, Poland, Slovakia and Slovenia) over the period from 1995 to 2005. The empirical results show a statistically significant U-shaped EKC relationship between each of the air pollutants employed and per capita income growth for EU15 and EU25 member countries. On the contrary, there is no statistically significant evidence for the existence of EKC hypothesis or a U-shaped relationship between air pollutants and per capita income growth for the remaining member states (10) of the study.

López-Menéndez et al. (2014) explore the EKC hypothesis for 27 European countries over the period from 1996 to 2010. Particularly, they use fixed and random effects panel models with additional explanatory variables related to the high renewable energy intensity (the proportion of electricity generated from renewable sources) in order to investigate the relationship between CO_2 emissions and GPD per capita. The empirical results show evidences of inverted N-shaped curve for the EU27 member states. However, the consideration of specific country effects in the empirical model leads to the conclusion that only 4 countries (Cyprus, Greece, Slovenia and Spain) exhibit an inverted U-shaped relationship, while 11 countries correspond to increasing patterns, 9 countries show a decreasing path and the remaining 3 countries lead to U-shaped curves.

Mazur et al. (2015) empirically explore the relation between CO_2 emissions and economic growth (GDP per capita) during the period 1992–2010, using panel data on EU28 countries (EU18 plus Czech Republic, Cyprus, Estonia, Hungary, Latvia, Lithuania, Malta, Poland, Slovakia and Slovenia). The authors employ both fixed and random effect econometric models, and they do not find strong evidences in

---

[6]The concept of the spatial EKC is similar to that of EKC, except that it considers spatial autocorrelation of environmental pollutants as one of the explanatory variables.

favour of EKC hypothesis. However, the graphical analysis demonstrates a justified turning point for CO_2 emissions as income per capita reaches the level of US $23,000. Also, when the empirical analysis is focused on the EU18 countries, the results confirm the existence of an inverted U-shaped relationship.

Ajmi et al. (2015) consider annual per capita data from 1960 to 2010 for energy consumption, GDP and CO_2 emissions for the G7 countries excluding Germany (Canada, France, Italy, Japan, the UK and the USA) in order to investigate, inter alia, the validity of EKC hypothesis. The authors support the non-existence of EKC hypothesis since they find evidences of cubic N-shaped (UK) and inverted N-shaped (Italy and Japan) relationships between CO_2 emissions and real GDP per capita.

Apergis (2016) explores the validity of EKC between per capita CO_2 emissions and real GDP by using panel- and time series-based methods of cointegration for a dataset of 13 European countries and Canada and the USA from 1960 to 2013. The empirical results are mixed both under panel or time-series techniques. However, when quantile cointegration is used, the results support the validity of EKC hypothesis for the majority of countries.

Rodriguez et al. (2016) examine the EKC hypothesis (CO_2 and GDP per capita) by using a balanced panel data of 13 European countries and Japan and the USA over the period 1979–2004. The authors provide evidences on the role of energy prices on EKC debate. They find a positive but marginal decreasing relationship between CO_2 emissions and GDP per capita and a relative decoupling between two variables. Fotis and Pekka (2017) analyse the relationship between pollution, income and energy efficiency indicators within Eurozone and conclude that there exists a dependence among the main components of energy policy mixture within Eurozone. Furthermore, they argue that perhaps not all Eurozone member states use energy efficiently at all stages of the energy chain from its production to its final consumption.

At the country level, Friedl and Getzner (2003) use panel data over the period 1960–1999 and show the existence of an N-shaped (cubic) relationship between environmental pollutants (CO_2) and income (GDP) for Austria. The authors also find evidences in favour of 'pollution haven hypothesis', that is, they support the hypothesis that higher imports lead to lower CO_2 emissions.[7] Also, they use value added produced in the service sector as a share of GDP in order to explain structural changes in the Austrian economy. The coefficient of value added in the service sector found to be significantly negative as a growing share of value added from the service sector reduces pollution-intensive industries and thus Austrian CO_2 emissions. Brannlund and Ghalwash (2008) found a positive (concave) relationship between income and environmental pollutants in Sweden from the years 1984, 1988 and 1996.

Soytas and Sari (2009) show that economic growth has no causal effect on the CO_2 emissions for Turkey over the period 1960–2000. The authors find no evidence

---

[7]The authors use imports as a ratio to GDP to account for the openness of the Austrian economy.

that CO_2 emissions Granger cause energy consumption and any long relationship between environmental pollutants and economic growth. Akbostanci et al. (2009) use panel data (1992–2001) and time-series analysis (1968–2003) and report evidences against EKC hypothesis for 58 provinces in Turkey. Especially, the estimated VAR model shows a positively monotonic relationship between CO_2 emissions and income (time-series analysis), while an N-shaped relationship between CO_2 emissions, particulate matter, PM_{10}, and income is reported by panel data analysis (the turning points of per capita income are calculated as \$1709 and \$5740).

Esteve and Tamarit (2012) examine the long-run relationship between per capita CO_2 and per capita income for the Spanish economy over the period 1857–2007. They use a two-regime threshold cointegration model (a nonlinear VECM of order $l + 1$) proposed by Hansen and Seo (2002) and confirm the nonlinearity relationship between the two variables and the existence of EKC hypothesis for Spain. The results yield a threshold at a per capita income of $\gamma = 8266$ euros.

Fosten et al. (2012) examine UK data on both CO_2 and SO_2 emissions over the long historic period from 1830 to 2003 (CO_2 model) and from 1850 to 2002 (SO_2 model). They found support for an inverted U-shaped relationship between GDP and emissions. The results reveal that the turning points for SO_2 and CO_2 occurred at GK \$8167 and GK\$7691 levels, respectively. The authors suggest that the asymmetry in the adjustment path towards the long-run equilibrium may be partially explained by technological change and energy prices.

Sephton and Mann (2013a, b) use the data employed by Esteve and Tamarit (2012) and show that economic growth and emissions are nonlinearly cointegrated, while the process to the long-run equilibrium involves asymmetric behaviour. By applying the Sephton and Mann (2013a, b) approach to the residuals from the nonlinear cointegrating MARS regression, they identify three thresholds in the equilibrating dynamics. Therefore, they generally support the existence of EKC hypothesis for Spain.

Shahbaz et al. (2013) apply unit root test and cointegration approach in the presence of structural breaks and econometric techniques to investigate the validity of EKC over the period of 1970–2010 for Turkish economy. The empirical results show that energy intensity and economic growth increase CO_2 emissions, while they validate the presence of EKC hypothesis. Sephton and Mann (2016) use the data by Fosten et al. (2012) to investigate the relationship between per capita emissions of SO_2 and CO_2 and per capita GDP in the UK. The empirical results support the EKC with estimated turning points in 1966 and 1967 for CO_2 and, SO_2 respectively.

4   Data and Statistics

4.1   Data

The econometric estimations are based on pooled time-series cross-section yearly (panel) data for EU28 member states (Table 1) covering the period from 2005 to

Table 1 Mean values of environmental pollutants, real GDP growth rate and control variables: EU28 (2005–2013)

	Environmental pollutants				Control variables				GDP growth rate
	SO$_2$	NO$_X$	NMVOC	GGE	ES	RENEWS (%)	RENEWG (%)	MI	I (%)
EU 28	189,489	349,238	282,610	157,230	40.24	16.52	22.73	232.42	1.38
Belgium	86,286	257,881	151,084	127,349	36.13	4.86	6.64	181.12	1.13
Bulgaria	534,513	157,257	102,675	52,414	9.52	12.69	12.21	717.86	2.55
Czech Rep.	174,175	233,732	176,453	134,982	25.02	8.74	7.38	378.79	2.12
Denmark	19,490	161,744	129,925	66,112	15.09	20.81	30.91	92.18	0.31
Germany	440,559	1,393,112	1,212,636	936,434	214.87	9.82	17.37	139.36	1.23
Estonia	65,748	39,156	26,675	14,329	2.92	21.57	7.09	490.42	2.64
Ireland	42,359	103,357	96,257	69,276	12.06	5.09	13.66	88.10	1.02
Greece	386,839	348,754	194,714	120,389	19.70	9.78	12.30	154.13	−2.12
Spain	673,427	1,112,679	705,394	355,167	90.40	11.97	27.10	142.20	0.56
France	330,818	1,159,437	881,986	467,390	153.02	11.49	15.10	149.51	0.91
Croatia	42,859	70,817	71,375	20,776	7.10	24.41	36.77	231.21	0.41
Italy	265,797	1,027,049	1,101,167	492,123	128.84	12.00	20.86	122.86	−0.47
Cyprus	23,528	20,179	10,405	8693	1.86	5.33	1.92	178.60	0.94
Latvia	6186	39,561	56,144	10,340	4.08	32.64	42.57	333.77	2.69
Lithuania	24,319	55,604	75,443	13,191	4.82	19.27	7.08	342.84	2.52
Luxembourg	1923	43,299	12,443	11,712	4.29	2.64	3.91	139.97	2.18
Hungary	34,236	143,662	129,545	63,775	16.38	7.42	5.62	286.22	0.63
Malta	9139	7804	3075	3121	0.46	1.18	0.36	172.08	2.33
Netherlands	45,292	313,578	163,941	211,285	52.92	3.82	8.36	150.89	1.05
Austria	20,288	190,265	122,169	78,389	27.46	28.90	65.40	129.38	1.40
Poland	1,042,823	841,407	631,323	361,238	62.80	8.76	6.18	332.08	3.84
Portugal	90,346	199,481	189,295	65,162	17.84	23.24	38.26	159.17	−0.38
Romania	431,437	273,608	365,980	114,090	23.44	20.86	30.73	411.49	2.63
Slovenia	15,647	49,754	40,387	12,307	4.94	18.48	30.70	232.74	1.10

Slovakia	70,252	92,539	122,120	40,253	11.06	8.64	17.96	384.18	3.91
Finland	65,948	174,014	112,777	41,804	25.42	31.94	27.88	215.10	0.81
Sweden	31,253	159,590	206,538	21,945	32.72	46.70	56.17	154.13	1.63
UK	500,382	1,280,183	946,262	616,985	142.92	3.21	7.37	111.39	1.05

Source: Author's elaboration of data from European Commission, Eurostat, European Environment Agency (EEA), (http://ec.europa.eu/eurostat/web/energy/data)

SO_2 sulphur oxides (total sectors of emissions for the national territory tonnes), NO_X nitrogen oxides (total sectors of emissions for the national territory—tonnes), $NMVOC$ non-methane volatile organic compounds (total sectors of emissions for the national territory—tonnes), GGE greenhouse gas emissions (CO_2 equivalent—all sectors and indirect CO_2—thousand tonnes), MI energy intensity (the ratio between the gross inland consumption of energy and the GDP—in kgoe per 1000 €), $RENEWG$ the ratio between the electricity produced from renewable energy sources and the gross national electricity consumption (% of gross electricity consumption), $RENEWS$ share of renewable energy in gross final energy consumption (%), ES energy saving from primary energy consumption (million tonnes of oil equivalent, TOE), I (real GDP growth rate) annual growth rate of GDP volume (percentage change on previous year)

2013 ($T = 9$, $N = 28$). The data source is Eurostat. The reason for using a panel dataset so as to investigate possible cointegrating vectors instead of time-series analysis is that residual-based cointegration tests are known to have low power and are subject to normalization problems. Since economic time series are typically short, it is desirable to exploit panel data in order to draw sharper inferences (Fotis et al. 2017; Christopoulos and Tsionas 2003; Polemis and Dagoumas 2013). Besides, cross-sectional data suffers from assuming that the same characteristics (i.e. structure of the markets, degree of regulation, etc.) apply to all national economies, while there are difficulties in obtaining reliable time-series data of sufficient length.

4.2 Descriptive Statistics

Table 1 presents the average values of environmental pollutants, real (per capita) GDP growth rate and control variables for all the cross-sections (member states) examined in this study. SO_2, NO_X and NMVOC present sulphur oxides, nitrogen oxides and non-methane volatile organic compounds correspondingly, while GGE presents greenhouse gas emissions (CO_2 equivalent).

The calculation of the real (per capita) GDP growth rate in terms of volumes is intended to allow comparisons of the dynamics of economic development both over time and between economies of different sizes. The GDP at current prices are valued in the prices of the previous year. Therefore, the computed volume changes are imposed on the level of a reference year, and they are not inflated by price movements (chain-linked series). MI denotes energy intensity, that is, the ratio between the gross inland consumption (the sum of primary production, recovered products, total imports, variations of stocks, total exports and bunkers) of energy and GDP. EI measures the energy consumption of an economy and its overall energy efficiency, and gross inland consumption of energy is calculated as the sum of coal, electricity, oil, natural gas and renewable energy sources (Shahbaz et al. 2013; Martínez-Zarzoso et al. 2007).

RENWES denotes the (%) share of renewable energy in gross final energy consumption, RENWEG denotes the electricity generated from renewable sources of gross electricity consumption in percentage terms and ES presents energy saving from primary energy consumption. ES consists of an indicator for monitoring progress towards energy efficiency targets of Europe 2020 strategy. All the environmental pollutants and control variables consist of emissions from all sectors of the country's territory under scrutiny.

Table 1 reveals that the mean value of real (per capita) GDP growth rate for EU28 countries under the period 2005–2013 is 1.38. Poland, Romania, Bulgaria, Czech Republic and Sweden exhibit high levels of growth rates, while Croatia and Hungary exhibit low levels of mean values of real per capita GDP growth rates for the period under scrutiny (0.41 and 0.63, respectively).

When we deal the relationship of environmental pollutants and real per capita GDP growth rate for each country of the sample separately, some important remarks emerge. Countries with the highest values of average real GDP growth rate (Bulgaria, Czech Republic, Estonia, Latvia, Lithuania, Malta, Poland, Romania and Slovakia) present both high and low levels of environmental pollutants. For instance, Bulgaria, Poland, Romania and Czech Republic exhibit high levels of pollution, but Estonia, Latvia, Lithuania and Slovakia exhibit low levels of pollution.

An explanation for this could be the high(low) ratio of energy intensity (MI) for the former(latter) group of countries. This may also imply a shift of structural changes in the economies of Estonia, Latvia, Lithuania and Slovakia towards environmental friendly energy use practices and technological developments at both demand and supply sides of energy, such as end-use appliances.

The countries with the highest levels of growth rate show low or at least modest values of environmentally friendly energy use (control variables). In support of our claim, Bulgaria, Czech Republic, Poland and Romania exhibit lower levels of the majority of control variables than their corresponding mean values. Exceptions that justify the rule are Poland and Romania, which exhibit one of the highest values of energy saving (ES) and high values of RENEWS and RENEWG within the EU28 countries, respectively.

Another characteristic of Table 1 is that countries with the highest levels of energy saving (ES) such as Germany, Spain, Italy, France, the UK and Poland show the highest levels of pollution among the EU28 countries under scrutiny. This evidence may be due to the fact that all these countries exhibit low levels of renewable energy use as a percentage share of gross final energy consumption and low levels of the contribution of renewable energy sources in gross final energy consumption (lower levels of RENEWS and RENEWG than the corresponding mean values).

Figure 1 shows mixed evidences concerning the relationship between environmental pollutants and real GDP growth rate for the EU28 countries during the period 2005–2013. Visual inspection of the figure supports a monotonic relationship between the variables under scrutiny. The majority of the sample countries[8] exhibits high and low levels of positive real GDP growth rate with low or at least modest levels of environmental pollutants. However, there exist some countries which exhibit a positive monotonic relationship between environmental pollutants with respect to real GDP growth rate. The group of these countries is divided into two samples: the first sample consists of countries associated with high levels of economic growth such as Poland, Bulgaria and Romania, and the second group consists of countries associated with low levels of economic growth such as Germany, Netherlands, France and Spain.

Lastly, there exist three countries (Greece, Portugal and Italy) which exhibit negative real GDP growth rates. Greece shows an almost double level of

---

[8]Belgium, Czech Republic, Denmark, Estonia, Ireland, Croatia, Cyprus, Latvia, Lithuania, Luxembourg, Hungary, Malta, Austria, Slovenia, Slovakia, Finland, Sweden, the UK and Norway.

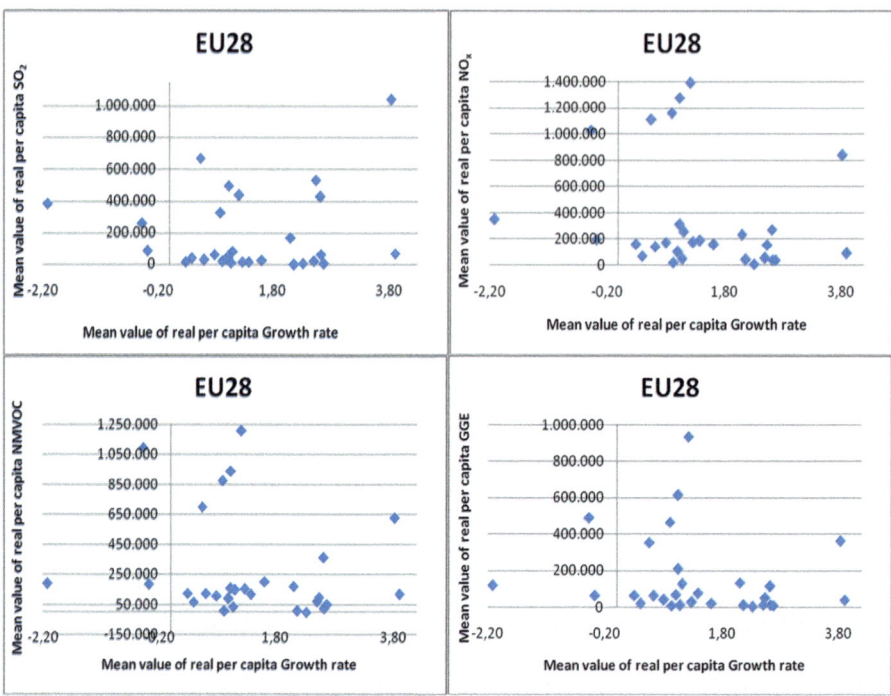

Fig. 1 The relationship between the environmental pollutants and the real gross domestic product growth rate for EU28 countries: 2005–2013. Notes: For all the graphs, the horizontal axis depicts the real GDP growth rate at 2005 constant prices, and the vertical axis depicts the average (2005–2013) environmental pollutant per capita at 2005 constant prices. The explanation of the variables is given in Table 1. Source: Fotis and Polemis (2018)

environmental pollutants with respect to the average level of EU28 countries, and Italy exhibits the same level of environmental pollutants with the corresponding average level. On the contrary, Portugal exhibits low level of environmental pollutants with respect to the corresponding average value, but its economic growth is much higher than the level of economic growth of Italy and Greece.

The aforementioned results of Table 1 and Fig. 1 reveal that for some sample countries pollution shows a stable path with respect to their economic development. In other words, pollution increases in the initial level of growth but remains at the same levels as growth continues to increase. For other countries pollution increases in the initial levels of growth and continues to increase as growth increases. Besides, we cannot find any point of return as EKC hypothesis.

Figure 2 presents the relationship between energy intensity (MI) and real per capita GDP growth rate. It is evident from the aforementioned figure that there exist a group of countries that exhibit a positive monotonic relationship between MI and economic growth but also there exist a group of countries which reveal stable levels of energy intensity as real per capita GDP growth rate changes.

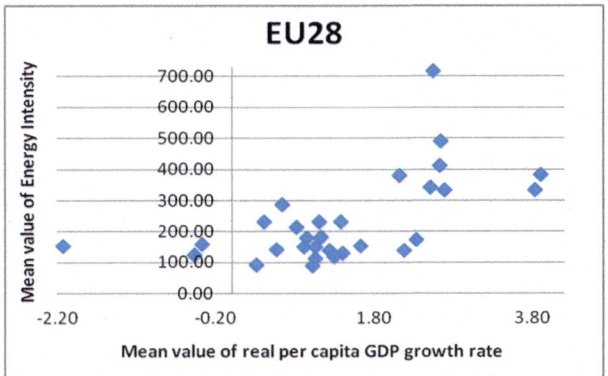

Fig. 2 The relationship between the energy intensity and the real per capita GDP growth rate for EU28 countries: 2005–2013. Notes: The horizontal axis depicts the real GDP growth rate at 2005 constant prices, and the vertical axis depicts the average (2005–2013) environmental pollutant per capita at 2005 constant prices. The explanation of the variables is given in Table 1. Source: Fotis and Polemis (2018) (only the EU28 figure)

The latter group of countries shows lower levels of economic growth than the former group of countries. Four countries with the highest levels of economic growth are not part of the Eurozone (Bulgaria, Czech Republic, Poland and Romania) and exhibit high levels of energy intensity. As a matter of fact, all of them show higher levels of MI than the corresponding mean level of EU28, and Bulgaria exhibits the highest level of energy intensity among all the countries under scrutiny.

5   Empirical Model and Method of Estimation

5.1   Empirical Model

Most of the researchers explore EKC hypothesis by estimating reduced-form models between per capita pollutant emissions, per capita real GDP and the squared-cubic values of per capita real GDP (Richmond and Kaufmann 2006; Stern 2004). An example of a cubic function is the semilogarithm Eq. (1) (Fotis and Pekka 2017):

$$\log E_{i,t} = \alpha_i + \beta \log E_{i,t-1} + \beta_1 \log I_{i,t} + \beta_2 I_{i,t}^2 + \beta_3 I_{i,t}^3 + \beta_4 X_{i,t} + \varepsilon_{i,t} \qquad (1)$$

Following standard notation, t stands for the period, and i stands for the countries under scrutiny. $LogE_{i,t} = \begin{bmatrix} \log SO_{2,t} \\ \log NO_{X,t} \\ \log NMVOC_t \\ \log GGE_t \end{bmatrix}$ denotes the vector of the environmental pollutants at period t, and $LogE_{i,t-1} = \begin{bmatrix} \log SO_{2,t-1} \\ \log NO_{X,t-1} \\ \log NMVOC_{t-1} \\ \log GGE_{t-1} \end{bmatrix}$ denotes the vector of the

environmental pollutants at period $t-1$. $Log\,SO_2$ is the natural logarithm of sulphur oxide emissions, $\log NO_X$ is the natural logarithm of nitrogen oxide emissions, $\log NMVOC$ is the natural logarithm of non-methane volatile organic compounds emissions and $\log GGE$ is the natural logarithm of total greenhouse gas emissions (CO_2 equivalent).

$I_{i,t}$ is the percentage ratio of real (per capita) GDP growth rate, and $\log X_{i,t}$

$= \begin{bmatrix} \log MI \\ \log RENEWS \\ \log RENEWG \\ \log ES \end{bmatrix}$ denotes the vector of control variables that influence environ-

mental degradation. Particularly, $\log MI$ denotes the natural logarithm of energy intensity, $\log RENEWS$ denotes the natural logarithm of the share of renewable energy in gross final energy consumption, $\log RENEWG$ denotes the natural logarithm of electricity generated from renewable sources (% of gross electricity consumption) and $\log ES$ denotes the natural logarithm of the indicator of energy saving for monitoring progress towards energy efficiency targets of Europe 2020 strategy. As usual $\varepsilon_{i,t}$ is the error term.[9]

The vector of the environmental pollutants $E_{i,t}$ constitutes the dependent variables of the empirical models. The share of renewable energy in gross final energy consumption ($RENEWS$) denotes an indicator which is calculated on the basis of data covered by Regulation (EC) No 1099/2008 (OJ L 304, 14.11.2008).[10] This indicator may be considered an estimate of the indicator described in Directive 2009/28/EC (OJ L 140, 5.6.2009, pp. 16–62).[11]

The indicator of electricity generated from renewable sources as a percentage of gross electricity consumption ($RENEWG$) is the ratio between the electricity produced from renewable energy sources (electricity generation from hydro plants, excluding pumping, wind, solar, geothermal and biomass/wastes) and the gross national electricity consumption (total gross national electricity generation from all fuels (including autoproduction), plus electricity imports, minus exports) for a given

---

[9]All the variables are measured in MWh at 2005 constant prices for all the countries under scrutiny and are deflated by the annual average rate of change of Harmonised Index of Consumer Prices (HICP).

[10]Regulation (EC) No 1099/2008 of the European Parliament and of the Council of 22 October 2008 on energy statistics.

[11]Directive 2009/28/EC of the European Parliament and of the Council of 23 April 2009 on the promotion of the use of energy from renewable sources and amending and subsequently repealing Directives 2001/77/EC and 2003/30/EC.

calendar year. It measures the contribution of electricity produced from renewable energy sources to the national electricity consumption.

The indicator of energy saving for monitoring progress towards energy efficiency targets of Europe 2020 strategy (log *ES*) is implemented by Directive 2012/27/EU on energy efficiency (OJ L 315, 14.11.2012, pp. 1–56).[12] The latter establishes a set of measures to help the EU reach its 20% energy efficiency target by 2020.[13] Under the Directive, all EU member states are required to use energy more efficiently at all stages of the energy chain from its production to its final consumption. The indicator of energy intensity is the ratio between the gross inland consumption of energy (the sum of the gross inland consumption of five energy types: coal, electricity, oil, natural gas and renewable energy sources) and the gross domestic product (GDP)[14] for a given calendar year. It is measured in kgoe per 1000 € and measures the energy consumption of an economy and its overall energy efficiency.

Real (per capita) GDP growth rate is the final result of the production activity of resident producer units. The squared real GDP growth rate is a measure that aims to capture the changes in environmental indicator trend across national economies. It captures changes in production and consumption patterns which affect the impact of potential real GDP growth rate on the environment and comprises a measure of the economic activity, defined as the value of all goods and services produced less the value of any goods or services used in their creation. We use the percentage ratio of real GDP growth rate rather than other measures of income utilized in previous literature (such as income in physical units) since it allows comparisons of the dynamics of economic development both over time and between economies of different sizes, and the computed volume changes are imposed on the level of a reference year, and therefore growth rate is not inflated by price movements.

Following Marrero (2010) the country specific terms α_i in Eq. (1) captures all fixed effects inherent in each member state national economy which are either not considered in the empirical model or not directly observed. The error term $\varepsilon_{i,t}$ encompasses random effects which are not considered in the empirical model. According to Arellano and Bond (1991), Arellano and Bover (1995) and Blundell and Bond (1998), α_i and $\varepsilon_{i,t}$ are independently distributed across i, $\varepsilon_{i,t}$ has zero mean and it is independent over t and i. Also, it is assumed that $E(E_{i,1}, \varepsilon_{i,t}) = 0$ for $i = 1 \ldots N$ and $t = 2 \ldots T$. The last assumption concerning the initial conditions of environmental indicators in conjunction with the assumptions regarding α_i and $\varepsilon_{i,t}$ suffices for a consistent estimation of Eq. (1) using DPGMM estimators for $T \geq 3$.

---

[12]Directive 2012/27/EU of the European Parliament and of the Council of 25 October 2012 on energy efficiency, amending Directives 2009/125/EC and 2010/30/EU and repealing Directives 2004/8/EC and 2006/32/EC.

[13]On 30 November 2016, the Commission proposed an update to the Energy Efficiency Directive including a new 30% energy efficiency target for 2030.

[14]The GDP figures are taken at chain-linked volumes with reference year 2005.

5.2   Method of Estimation

Ahn and Schmidt (1995) argue that the instrumental variables approach by Anderson and Hsiao (1982) fails to take all of the potential orthogonality conditions into account as well as the differenced structure on the residual disturbances (Baltagi 2005, p. 145). Therefore, the estimator by Anderson and Hsiao leads to consistent but not necessarily efficient estimates of the parameters in the model. Arellano (1989) also argues that for dynamic error component models, the estimator that uses differences rather than levels for instruments has a singularity point and very large variances over a significant range of parameter values (Baltagi 2005, p. 136).

In order to allow for the dynamic aspects in our empirical models, we investigate our main research questions by using dynamic panel data techniques such as PGMM estimators attributed to Arellano and Bond (1991).[15] The DPGMM estimator by Arellano and Bond (1991) is also known as a two-step difference GMM (DIF-GMM) where the lagged levels of the regressors are instruments for the equations in first differences. The DIF-GMM estimator is designed to deal with small T and large N panels, that is, few time periods and many individual units (cross sections). Recall that in this paper we deal with a short T dynamic panel data ($T = 9$ and $N = 28$).

6   Empirical Results

6.1   Stationarity and Cointegration of the Variables

Given the relatively short span of the cross-sectional element ($n = 9$), all the commonly used unit root tests separately to each country may have low power (Christopoulos and Tsionas 2003). Thus our results for the stationarity properties of the data could be seriously misguided. An increase in the power of individual unit root tests can be achieved by pooling individual time series and performing panel unit root tests (Banerjee 1999).

To test for the existence of a unit root in a panel datasetting, we have used various econometric tests, such as Breitung (2000) t-test, Im et al. (2003) W-test and Fisher-type tests (Maddala and Wu 1999; Choi 2001). In all the above tests, the null hypothesis is that of a unit root. The W-test is based on the application of the ADF test to panel data and allows for heterogeneity in both the constant and slope terms of the ADF regression. The Fisher-type tests (ADF and PP tests) under the null hypothesis are distributed as χ^2 with degrees of freedom twice the number of cross-sectional units. From the estimated results, we observe that the null hypothesis of a unit root cannot be rejected at 5% critical value for all of the relevant variables.

---

[15]See, inter alia, Polemis and Fotis (2013).

In other words they are integrated of order one including a deterministic component (intercept).[16]

The next step is to examine if there is a cointegrated relationship between the nonstationary variables of the models. The reason for using cointegration techniques is that nonstationary time series results to spurious regressions and hence does not allow statistical interpretation of the estimations. For this purpose we apply the Fisher-type test (Johansen 1992; Maddala and Wu 1999). This method allows us to examine whether there is a long-run co-movement of the variables. The maximum-likelihood eigenvalue statistics indicate that the null hypothesis (no cointegration) is rejected at 1% level for all the sample countries. The estimated results of the said tests and the estimated likelihood ratio tests depict that there is (at least) one cointegration vector for each model.[17]

6.2   Does the EKC Hypothesis Exist in the EU28 Member States?

Table 2 presents the DIF-GMM parameter estimates of Eq. (1). The said estimates are almost all highly statistically significant and robust given that Eq. (1) represents structural and not spurious long-run relation. GMM parameter estimates are shown for the one-step GMM estimator case with standard errors that are asymptotically robust to heteroscedasticity and have been found to be more reliable for finite sample inference than the GMM standard errors.

The estimation of β in Eq. (1) (E_{t-1}) is always highly statistical significant and smaller than 1 for all the dependent variables employed within the EU28 countries. This result reveals the importance of the inclusion of the lagged dependent variable in the right-hand side of Eq. (1).

Within EU28 countries the empirical results reveal a positive effect of economic growth on environmental pollutants. Even though there is a positive relationship between the two variables, the effect of real per capita GDP growth rate on all the environmental pollutants employed is quite close to zero. However, the nonstatistically significant parameter estimates of square and cube coefficients of income indicate that the EKC hypothesis does not exist in the EU28 countries for the time period in question. This result is consistent with the discussion made in Sect. 4.2.

In terms of the effect of control variables of Eq. (1) on environmental pollutants, it is evident that energy intensity (*MI*) positively affects all the environmental pollutants (the parameter estimates of coefficient *MI* under all empirical models employed

---

[16]The estimated results of the employed unit root tests are available upon request.

[17]The estimated results of the Johansen (1992) cointegration technique are available upon request.

Table 2 Estimation results from the EU28 countries: DIFF-GMM methodology[a] (2005–2013)

	EU28			
Independent variables (in logs)[b]	Dependent variables (in logs)			
	SO_2	NO_X	NMVOC	GGE
c^c	−0.13 (0.88)	1.54[*] (0.39)	1.40[*] (0.52)	0.81 (0.63)
E_{t-1}	0.52[*] (0.10)	0.48[*] (0.09)	0.59[*] (0.09)	0.32[*] (0.08)
I	0.01[*] (0.00)	0.01[**] (0.00)	0.00[***] (0.00)	0.02[**] (0.00)
I^2	0.00 (0.00)	−0.00 (0.00)	−0.00 (0.00)	−0.00 (0.00)
I^3	−0.00 (0.00)	−0.00 (0.00)	−0.00 (0.00)	−0.00 (0.00)
ES	0.62[**] (0.25)	0.63[*] (0.10)	0.36[*] (0.10)	0.72[*](0.22)
RENEWS	−0.23[**] (0.10)	−0.15[**] (0.06)	−0.04 (0.04)	0.04 (0.04)
RENEWG	−0.00 (0.00)	0.00 (0.00)	−0.00 (0.00)	0.00 (0.00)
MI	0.85[**] (0.40)	0.22[***] (0.13)	0.13[**] (0.06)	0.63[*] (0.20)
Wald chi^2	368.19[*] (0.00)	1495.52[*] (0.00)	513.90[*] (0.00)	411.82[*] (0.00)
No. of instruments	33	178	91	120
Max lags	5	5	5	5

The numbers in parentheses of the parameter estimations refer to the *robust standard errors* (*heteroscedasticity consistent asymptotic standard errors*). The italic numbers in parentheses of the Wald chi^2 estimations refer to the *p*-values of the individually significance tests
Source: Fotis and Polemis (2018)—(only the empirical results for EU28)
[*]1%, [**]5% and [***]10%, respectively
[a]One-step results
[b]*Except from real (per capita) GDP growth rate coefficients*
[c]*c* denotes the constant term

are statistically significant).[18] The empirical results also reveal that, mainly, energy intensity positively affects SO_2 emissions.

When we deal with the effect of energy saving on environmental pollutants, an interesting remark emerges. Under all models employed, the effect of energy saving on environmental pollutants is positive. This effect reveals an inefficient use of energy within EU. Different technological or regulatory aspects within EU member states may be critical factors affecting the way of use of energy saving towards monitoring EU's energy policy.

However, emissions from all the environmental pollutants are eliminated by the increase of the share of renewable energy in gross final energy consumption increases. This result reveals that the more the renewable energy we use the less the air pollution. The same could be said for the effect of electricity generated from renewable sources of gross electricity consumption (RENEWG) on environmental pollutants, at least in most of the models employed which the parameter estimate of RENEWG is statistically significant.

---

[18]A similar result regarding carbon dioxide (CO_2) emissions has been reported in the literature by Martínez-Zarzoso et al. (2007).

7 Discussion of the Empirical Results and Policy Implications

The estimated parameters of the empirical models employed in this paper suggest the non-existence of EKC hypothesis. The parameters of Kuznets Curve are found to be not statistically significant, and the obtained results suggest the existence of a monotonic pattern between environmental pollutants and real (per capita) GDP growth rate. These results are not surprising since they agree with the empirical investigations by Fotis and Pekka (2017), Mazur et al. (2015), Baycan (2013), Iwata et al. (2011), Marrero (2010), Martínez-Zarzoso et al. (2007) and Azomahou et al. (2006), which find increasing or non-inverted U patterns.

The use of the renewable energy intensity indicators (RENEWS and RENEWG) improves all the employed empirical models. The estimated coefficients of both energy efficiency indicators are found to be significantly negative. The share of electricity produced from renewable energy sources to the national electricity consumption (RENEWG) contributes to the elimination of emissions, but a more pronounced effect is revealed by the contribution of the share of renewable energy in gross final energy consumption (*RENEWS*). Therefore, Europe's energy policy within EU should be strengthened towards more installed renewable energy.

The empirical results derived from the indicator of energy saving indicator suggest that EU energy policy should be also strengthened towards a more efficient use of energy at all stages of the energy chain from its production to its final consumption. On the one hand, countries with the highest levels of energy saving indicator (Germany, Spain, Italy, France, the UK, Turkey and Poland) show the highest levels of emissions among the EU28 member states under scrutiny. This evidence may be due to the fact that all these countries exhibit low levels of RENEWG and RENEWS than the corresponding mean value of EU28 countries. On the other hand, most of the countries with low levels of energy saving exhibit high levels of RENEWS as well as high levels of RENEWG (Estonia, Croatia, Latvia, Lithuania and Slovenia). Therefore, a convergence of environmental policies towards more efficient energy use among EU countries should be in the merit of Europe's energy policy the next years.

The empirical results also reveal that, mainly, energy intensity positively affects SO_2 emissions. This is a very critical result for policy makers in order to prioritize their needs within future EU's energy agenda. Policy makers' energy strategy should be based on eliminating SO_2 emissions by using more efficient technology at all stages of the energy chain.

However, the statistical analysis of this paper reveals that countries with the highest values of average real GDP growth rate exhibit high ratio of energy intensity (MI) and high levels of pollution. This may also imply a shift of structural changes in the economies of Estonia, Latvia, Lithuania and Slovakia towards environmental friendly energy use practices and technological developments at both demand and supply sides of energy, such as end-use appliances.

The positive relationship between energy consumption and SO_2 emissions seems to be more important than the relationship between energy consumption and other pollutants. Even though energy intensity has reduced by 24% between 1995 and 2011 within EU28 member states, it seems that this endeavour must be reinforced in the future. As in the case of the renewable energy intensity indicators, the recent update by the EC of a new 30% energy efficiency target for 2030 will certainly improve more the elimination of emissions. However, energy intensity flows must be kept up more closely in nowadays.

Therefore, a further research on this topic should try to answer the question whether all member states use energy more efficiently, at all stages of the energy chain from its production to its final consumption, or European Commission has to reconsider its strategy for monitoring more efficiently progress towards European energy efficiency targets.

Further research opportunities on this topic are also essential for improving the estimated results. Do the expansion of EU affects the European energy policy and in which direction? Upon the empirical results, how can we improve the policy mixture underlying European Commission's 30% energy efficiency target for 2030?

References

Acaravci, A., & Ozturk, I. (2010). On the relationship between energy consumption, CO_2 emissions and economic growth in Europe. *Energy, 35*, 5412–5420.

Ahn, S. C., & Schmidt, P. (1995). Efficient estimation of models for dynamic panel data. *Journal of Econometrics, 68*, 5–27.

Ajmi, A. N., Hammoudeh, S., Nguyen, K. N., & Sato, J. R. (2015). A new look at the relationships between CO_2 emissions, energy consumption and income in G7 countries: The importance of time variations. *Energy Economics, 49*, 629–638.

Akbostanci, E., Turut-Asik, S., & Tunc, G. I. (2009). The relationship between income and environment in Turkey: Is there an environmental Kuznets curve? *Energy Policy, 37*, 861–867.

Alvarez, F., Marrero, G. A., & Puch L. A. (2005). *Air pollution and the macroeconomy across European countries* (Working papers 10 (FEDEA)).

Anderson, T. W., & Hsiao, H. (1982). Formulation and estimation of dynamic models using panel data. *Journal of Econometrics, 18*, 47–82.

Apergis, N. (2016). Environmental Kuznets curves: New evidence on both panel and country-level CO_2 emissions. *Energy Economics, 54*, 263–271.

Arellano, M. (1989). A note on the Anderson-Hsiao estimator for panel data. *Economic Letters, 31*, 337–341. https://doi.org/10.1016/0165-1765(89)90025-6.

Arellano, M., & Bond, S. (1991). Some tests of specification for panel data: Monte Carlo evidence and an application to employment equations. *Review of Economic Studies, 58*, 277–297.

Arellano, M., & Bover, O. (1995). Another look at the instrumental variable estimation of error component models. *Journal of Econometrics, 68*, 29–51.

Azomahou, T., Laisney, F., & Van Phu, N. (2006). Economic development and CO_2 emissions: A nonparametric panel approach. *Journal of Public Economics, 90*, 1347–1363.

Baltagi, H. B. (2005). *Econometric analysis of panel data* (3rd ed.). Hoboken, NJ: Wiley.

Banerjee, A. (1999). Panel unit root tests and cointegration: An overview. *Oxford Bulletin of Economics and Statistics, 61*, 607–629.

Baycan, O. I. (2013). Air pollution, economic growth, and the European union enlargement. *International Journal of Economics and Finance, 5*(12), 121–126.

Bernard, J.-T., Gavin, M., Khalaf, L., & Voia, M. (2014). Environmental Kuznets curve: Tipping points, uncertainty and weak identification. *Environmental and Resource Economics, 60*(2), 285–315.

Blundell, R., & Bond, S. (1998). Initial restrictions and moment restrictions in dynamic panel data models. *Journal of Econometrics, 87*, 115–143.

Brannlund, R., & Ghalwash, T. (2008). The income–pollution relationship and the role of income distribution: An analysis of Swedish household data. *Resource and Energy Economics, 30*, 369–387.

Breitung, J. (2000). The local power of some unit root tests for panel data. In B. Baltagi (Ed.), *Nonstationary panels, panel cointegration, and dynamic panels* (Advances in econometrics) (Vol. 15, pp. 161–178). Amsterdam: Emerald Group.

Choi, I. (2001). Unit root tests for panel data. *Journal of International Money and Finance, 20*(2), 249–272.

Christopoulos, D. K., & Tsionas, E. G. (2003). A reassessment of balance of payments constrained growth: Results from panel unit root and panel cointegration tests. *International Economic Journal, 17*, 39–54.

Cole, M. (1999). Limits to growth, sustainable development and environmental Kuznets curves: An examination of environmental impact of economic development. *Sustainable Development, 7*, 87–97.

Coondoo, D., & Dinda, S. (2008). Carbon dioxide emissions and income: A temporal analysis of cross-country distributional patterns. *Ecological Economics, 65*, 375–385.

Danaeifar, I. (2014). The estimation parameters of Kuznets spatial environmental curve in European countries (A case study of CO_2 and PM10 and incidence of tuberculosis and life expectancy at birth). *European Online Journal of Natural and Social Sciences, 3*(3), 439–448.

Dinda, S. (2004). Environmental Kuznets curve hypothesis: A survey. *Ecological Economics, 49*, 431–455.

Donfouet, H. P. P., Jeanty, P. W., & Malin, M. (2013). *A spatial dynamic panel analysis of the environmental Kuznets curve in European countries* (pp. 1–16). Center for Research in Economics and Management (CREM), Economics working paper archive, 2013–18.

Esteve, V., & Tamarit, C. (2012). Threshold cointegration and nonlinear adjustment between CO_2 and income: The environmental Kuznets curve in Spain, 1857–2007. *Energy Economics, 34*(6), 2148–2156.

Fosten, J., Morley, B., & Taylor, T. (2012). Dynamic misspecification in the environmental Kuznets curve: Evidence from CO_2 and SO_2 emissions in the United Kingdom. *Ecological Economics, 76*, 25–33.

Fotis, P., & Pekka, V. (2017). The effect of renewable energy use and economic growth on pollution in the EUROZONE. *Economic and Business Letters, 6*(4), 88–99.

Fotis, P., & Polemis, M. (2018). Sustainable development, environmental policy and renewable energy use: A dynamic panel data approach. *Sustainable Development, 26*(6), 726–740.

Fotis, P., Karkalakos, S., & Asteriou, D. (2017). The relationship between energy demand and real GDP growth rate: The role of price asymmetries and spatial externalities within 34 countries across the globe. *Energy Economics, 66*, 69–84.

Friedl, B., & Getzner, M. (2003). Determinants of CO_2 emissions in a small open economy. *Ecological Economics, 45*, 133–148.

Galeotti, M., Manera, M., & Lanza, A. (2009). On the robustness of robustness checks of the environmental Kuznets curve hypothesis. *Environmental and Resource Economics, 42*, 551–574.

Grossman, G. M., & Krueger, A. B. (1995). Economic growth and the environment. *Quarterly Journal of Economics, 110*, 353–377.

Hansen, B., & Seo, B. (2002). Testing for two-regime threshold cointegration in vector error correction models. *Journal of Econometrics, 110*, 293–318.

Holtz-Eakin, D., & Selten, T. M. (1995). Stoking the fires: CO_2 emissions and economic growth. *Journal of Public Economics, 57*, 85–101.

Im, K., Pesaran, M. H., & Shin, Y. (2003). Testing for unit roots in heterogeneous panels. *Journal of Econometrics, 115*, 53–74.

Iwata, H., Okada, K., & Samreth, S. (2011). A note on the environmental Kuznets curve for CO_2: A pooled mean group approach. *Applied Energy, 88*, 1986–1996.

Jaunky, C. V. (2011). The CO_2 emissions-income nexus: Evidence from rich countries. *Energy Policy, 39*(3), 1228–1240.

Johansen, S. (1992). Determination of co-integration rank in the presence of a linear trend. *Oxford Bulletin of Economics and Statistics, 54*, 383–397.

Lee, C.-C., Chiu, Y.-B., & Sun, C.-H. (2009). Does one size fit all? A reexamination of the environmental Kuznets curve using the dynamic panel data approach. *Review of Agricultural Economics, 31*(4), 751–778.

López-Menéndez, A., Pérez, R., & Moreno, B. (2014). Environmental costs and renewable energy: Re-visiting the environmental Kuznets curve. *Journal of Environmental Management, 145*, 368–373.

Maddala, G. S., & Wu, S. (1999). A comparative study of unit root tests with panel data and a new simple test. *Oxford Bulletin of Economics and Statistics, 61*, 631–652.

Markandya, A., Golub, A., & Pedroso-Galinato, S. (2006). Empirical analysis of national income and SO_2 emissions in selected European countries. *Environmental and Resource Economics, 35*, 221–257.

Marrero, A. G. (2010). Greenhouse gases emissions, growth and the energy mix in Europe. *Energy Economics, 32*, 1356–1363.

Martínez-Zarzoso, I., Bengochea-Morancho, A., & Morales-Lage, R. (2007). The impact of population on CO_2 emissions: Evidence from European countries. *Environmental and Resource Economics, 38*, 597–512.

Mazur, A., Phutkaradze, Z., & Phutkaradze, J. (2015). Economic growth and environmental quality in the European union countries – Is there evidence for the environmental Kuznets curve? *International Journal of Management and Economics, 45*, 108–126.

Panayotou, T. (1995). Environmental degradation at different stages of economic development. In A. Iftikhar & A. J. Doeleman (Eds.), *Beyond Rio: The environmental crisis and sustainable livelihoods in the third world, ILO study series* (pp. 13–36). New York: St. Martin's Press.

Panayotou, T. (2000). *Economic growth and the environment* (CID Working Paper no. 56). Cambridge, MA: Center for International Development at Harvard University.

Polemis, L. M., & Dagoumas, S. A. (2013). The electricity consumption and economic growth nexus: Evidence from Greece. *Energy Policy, 62*, 798–808.

Polemis, L. M., & Fotis, P. (2013). Do gasoline prices respond asymmetrically in the euro zone area? Evidence from cointegrated panel data analysis. *Energy Policy, 56*, 425–433.

Richmond, A., & Kaufmann, R. (2006). Is there a turning point in the relationship between income and energy use and/or carbon emissions? *Ecological Economics, 56*, 176–189.

Rodriguez, M., Pena-Boguete, Y., & Pardo-Fernardez, J. C. (2016). Revisiting environmental Kuznets curves through the energy price lens. *Energy Policy, 95*, 32–41.

Sephton, P., & Mann, J. (2013a). Threshold cointegration: Model selection with an application. *Journal of Economics and Econometrics, 56*(2), 54–77.

Sephton, P., & Mann, J. (2013b). Further evidence of the environmental Kuznets curve in Spain. *Energy Economics, 36*, 177–181.

Sephton, P., & Mann, J. (2016). Compelling evidence of an environmental Kuznets curve in the United Kingdom. *Environmental and Resource Economics, 64*(2), 301–315.

Shafik, N., Bandyopadhyay, S., 1992. *Economic growth and environmental quality: Time series and cross section evidence* (Working Papers for World Development Report 1992). Washington, DC: World Bank.

Shahbaz, M., Ozturk, I., Afza, T., & Ali, A. (2013). Revisiting the environmental Kuznets curve in a global economy. *Renewable and Sustainable Energy Reviews, 25*, 494–502.

Soytas, U., & Sari, R. (2009). Energy consumption, income, and carbon emissions: Challenges faced by an EU candidate member. *Ecological Economics, 68*, 1667–1675.

Stern, D. I. (2004). *The environmental Kuznets curve: A primer* (Centre for Climate Economic & Policy Working Paper, 1404). Crawford School of Public Policy, The Australian National University.

Wang, Y.-C. (2013). Functional sensitivity of testing the environmental Kuznets curve hypothesis. *Resource and Energy Economics, 35*, 451–466.

Wang, Y., Zhang, C., Lu, A., Li, L., He, Y., Tojo, J., et al. (2017). A disaggregated Analysis of the environmental Kuznets curve for industrial CO_2 emissions in China. *Applied Energy, 190*, 172–180.

Yang, X., Lou, F., Sun, M., Wang, R., & Wang, Y. (2017). Study of the relationship between greenhouse gas emissions and the economic growth of Russia based on the environmental Kuznets curve. *Applied Energy, 193*, 162–173.

Zaim, O., & Taskinm, F. (2000). A Kuznets curve in environmental efficiency: An application on OECD countries. *Environmental and Resource Economics, 17*, 21–36.

Exploring the Teaching Quality of Greek Accounting Studies

Sofia Asonitou, Athanasios Mandilas, Evangelos Chytis, and Dimitra Latsou

Abstract The present study aimed to explore the teaching quality of Greek accounting studies by examining the students' experience from their accounting studies at higher education institutions (HEIs) in relation to demographic characteristics. An exploratory factor analysis, from a sample of 268 students' questionnaires, identified four constructs, reflecting good teaching, generic skills, appropriate assessment and clear goals, and standards. The students' scores on all scales showed satisfactory levels of internal consistency. A reduced version of the CEQ in Greek is proposed as a measure of students' perceptions of the academic quality of programs in Greek higher education accounting studies, and its four dimensions are suggested as significant predictors of students' satisfaction.

Keywords Accounting · Teaching quality · CEQ · Greece

1 Introduction

Teaching quality and effectiveness have been extensively explored by academics (Entwistle and Ramsden 1983; Onwuegbuzie et al. 2007; De Jager and Gbadamosi 2013; Milton-Wildey et al. 2014). In most studies, teaching quality is investigated through the students' satisfaction rankings for a number of individual and environmental factors such as teacher's enthusiasm and passion, course interest, teacher's preparation and availability, concern for students, clear communication, assessment

S. Asonitou (✉) · D. Latsou
University of West Attica, Aigaleo, Greece
e-mail: sasonitou@uniwa.gr

A. Mandilas
Eastern Macedonia and Thrace Institute of Technology, Kavala, Greece

E. Chytis
Technological Educational Institute of Epirus, Preveza, Greece

© Springer Nature Switzerland AG 2019
N. Sykianakis et al. (eds.), *Economic and Financial Challenges for Eastern Europe*,
Springer Proceedings in Business and Economics,
https://doi.org/10.1007/978-3-030-12169-3_33

497

type, work load, fair grading, etc. (Okpala and Ellis 2005; Gerkin and Kierkus 2011; Alhija 2016).

The CEQ is a widely used tool for the assessment of teaching quality in Higher Education. The CEQ was developed by Ramsden (1991), while other researchers made significant extensions and amendments (Eley 2001; Griffin et al. 2003; Ginns et al. 2007; Wilson et al. 1997). The theoretical basis of Marton and Säljö (1976) and Entwistle and Ramsden (1983) on teaching and learning concepts has provided the framework for the development of CEQ, which is also used in conjunction to the students' approaches to learning tools (Trigwell and Prosser 1991; Lizzio et al. 2002).

Apart from Australia (Ramsden 1991), the CEQ has been used and checked for validation purposes in Western academic contexts, including the UK (Richardson 1994), the Netherlands (Jansen et al. 2013), Ireland (Byrne and Flood 2003), Italy (Barattucci and Zuffo 2012), and non-Western academic environments, such as Malaysia (Thien and Ong 2016), China (Law and Meyer 2011; Yin et al. 2014), Nigeria (Andrew 2010), and India (Chakrabarty et al. 2016) with mixed results.

The CEQ was validated in tourism industry studies held in Greece (Stergiou and Airey 2012), using the 31-item instrument of Möller (2002). Since various studies confirm that the CEQ' validity and reliability is equally related to the field of study and the culture and tradition of the academic setting (Richardson 2005; Thien and Ong 2016; Barattucci and Zuffo 2012), we investigated its use in Greek accounting studies.

The aim of this study has been to investigate the relationships between the teaching and learning environment (CEQ subscales) in relation to demographic and local educational system characteristics, such as students' first choice of study discipline and internship scheme.

The sections following the introduction will present the background to the study (Sect. 2); the methodology and the data collection methods of the study (Sect. 3); the data analyses (Sect. 4); the discussion of the results (Sect. 5); and, finally, the conclusions reached and suggestions for further research on the topic (Sect. 6).

2 Background to the Study

2.1 Literature Review

In the UK, Richardson (1994), using the 30-item CEQ, broadly identified the 5-factor scales reported by Ramsden (1991). Wilson et al. (1997), who investigated and validated both the 36- and the 23-item CEQ in their Australian survey, referred to items cross loading, indicating the potential for further improvement in subscales. Broomfield and Bligh (1998) reported satisfactory construct validity and reliability. Factor analysis yielded six factors (the good teaching was split into two factors), with alpha values ranging from 0.37 (clear goals and standards scale) to 0.78 (good teaching scale). Byrne and Flood (2003) surveyed an accounting group of students, using CEQ23, resulting in items loading in the intended factors and Cronbach alpha values ranging from 0.66 to 0.78. In the Netherlands, Jansen et al. (2013), using CEQ23, surveyed 956 students across 9 faculties and reported satisfactory alpha coefficients ranged from 0.75 to 0.87 and confirmed the original 5-factor structure of CEQ. In Italy, Barattucci and Zuffo (2012) used the 30-item SCEQ with a sample of 622 students belonging to different faculties. In the original version, the 30-item SCEQ did not provide satisfactory results; however, after the elimination of the Clear Goals and Standards Scale which presented unsatisfactory reliability (0.51), the 23-item SCEQ version showed that it was a reliable measure of the respective constructs. The authors decided that despite the clear differences of the Italian with the British and Australian contexts, and the need for further improvement, these instruments can be useful in the Italian academic environment. Stergiou and Airey (2012) used a 31-item CEQ, comprising 6 scales previously adapted by Möller (2002) for hospitality degree students in the UK. The adapted Greek version of CEQ had a 5-factor structure and satisfactory internal consistency.

Looking at non-European countries, the Nigerian SCEQ was validated with alpha coefficients ranging from 0.61 to 0.88 but with items' cross loading on scales other than intended (the good teaching scale), a pattern also seen in the study of Wilson et al. (1997). The authors concluded that the modified SCEQ is applicable for use with the Nigerian undergraduate students (Andrew 2010). In Japan (Fryer et al. 2011) and in China (Law and Meyer 2011), however, the surveys resulted in four scales and due to other findings also their authors proposed further development of the CEQ for its application in both countries. Price et al. (2011) in China, using the CEQ36, concluded in two-factor dimensions with regard to academic quality: students' perceptions of student support ($a = 0.92$) and students' perceptions of course demands ($a = 0.88$). Another study in China by Yin et al. (2014) reported acceptable construct validity, while Cronbach's alpha remained lower than 0.60 in three CEQ factors. The study of Yin et al. (2014) confirmed construct validity of the intended six factors for CEQ.

Ullah et al. (2011, 2016) used the CEQ36 to measure the students' perception of the teaching quality. The studies confirmed only four factors, while clear goals and the role of independence were not identified in the students responses, supporting the notion these ideas are not (yet) part of the discourse in non-Western countries. The CEQ36 was distributed to West Bengal students and identified four constructs (Chakrabarty et al. 2016). Finally, in Malaysia, Thien and Ong (2016) reported problems with reliability and construct validity raising questions for the applicability of CEQ23 to the Malaysian context.

In Greece there is no nationwide developed instrument to measure teaching quality as part of quality assurance framework. The Greek academic system is mainly teacher-centered, and, especially for accounting, studies are focused on information and technical regulation reproduction, with little effort to develop higher-order thinking skills and other employability skills (Kapardis et al. 2010; Asonitou 2015). Obviously there are concepts well settled in the Western environment (such as clear goals and standards, appropriate assessment, student independence, appropriate workload) but which are not yet developed in other countries; therefore, the CEQ instrument may not adequately reflect the local academic culture (Richardson 2005).

3   Methods

3.1   Participants

The sample of this study consisted of undergraduate students at the Departments of Accounting and Finance of the Technological Education Institutes of Piraeus, Epirus, and East Macedonia and Thrace. A higher percentage (56.6%) of students was enrolled in the seventh semester; 43.4% of study participants were attending an eight or higher semester. Data collection was conducted in the 2016–2017 academic year. Questionnaires were distributed by the researchers during class hours, following the assent of the class instructor. Before submission, students were given general instructions on the questionnaire. Students of TEI Epirus and East Macedonia and Thrace received an online questionnaire, sent by researchers to their email addresses. A follow-up letter was sent 2 weeks later to maximize the responses received.

3.2   Measures

Questionnaire CEQ23 was used in this study, and an agreement/disagreement 5-point scale from 1 (*strongly disagree*) to 5 (*strongly agree*) was used. Based on previous literature on the questionnaire, five scales were included: the Good Teaching Scale (GTS), consisting of six items measuring the lecturers' efforts to increase student interest and give feedback to students in order to motivate and guide them toward success; the Clear Goals and Standards Scale (CGSS), consisting of four items regarding the students' perceived degree of clarity in relation to graduation requirements; the Appropriate Assessment Scale (AAS), consisting of three items capturing the students' perceptions of the adequacy of assessment methods of the understanding of the materials versus rote memorization; the Appropriate Workload Scale (AWS), including four items assessing the perceptions of sustainability of the overall academic workload; and the Generic Skills Scale (GSS) comprising six items measuring the level of development of the students' analytic, problem-solving, and communication skills. The coding of the seven negatively worded items was reversed so that higher scores corresponded to more positive ratings. A pilot study with 40 students was conducted to test whether items were understandable. The pilot study used a test-pretest technique to measure the validity of the Greek version. The researchers reviewed the comments by members of the pilot sample and adapted the questionnaire accordingly.

4 Data Analysis

Descriptive statistics and bivariate analysis were performed. The results are presented as absolute (n) and relative (%) frequencies for the nominal and ordinal variables and as mean values for the quantitative variables. The focus of analysis was on the psychometric properties of its constituent scales as revealed by the standard application of item-correlation analyses and exploratory factor analysis. Kaiser-Meyer-Olkin (KMO) and Bartlett sphericity tests were used to test data compatibility for factor analysis. The value of the KMO test statistics was 0.858, which shows the very good suitability assessment. Also, the Bartlett's sphericity test was implemented and showed statistical significance ($x^2 = 1{,}410{,}443$; $p < 0.01$). The data follow the normal distribution.

Principal components analysis and oblique rotated component matrix were chosen as the factor analysis (Cattell 1978). Analysis showed that 23 items with the eigenvalue above value 1 have the same factor distribution as the original scale. A factor loading for a variable is a measure of how much the variable contributes to the factor; thus, high factor loading scores indicate that the dimensions of the factors are better accounted for by the variables. According to a rule of thumb, using an alpha level of 0.01 (two-tailed), a rotated factor loading would need to be at least 0.32 to be considered statistically meaningful (Tabachnick and Fidell 2007). A factor loading of 0.32 gives approximately 10% of the overlapping variance % overlapping variance = (factor loading)^2. The choice of cutoff may depend on the ease of interpretation including how complex variables are being handled.

Coefficient alpha of Cronbach was used in order to assess internal consistency. Multiple regression analyses using the backward method were conducted to investigate (a) the associations of CEQ scales (dependent variables) and characteristics of the sample (independent variables) and (b) the associations of overall satisfaction from accounting studies (dependent variables) and CEQ scales (independent variables). The SPSS 21.0 software was used for statistical analyses.

4.1 Results

4.1.1 Characteristics of the Sample

58.6% of the sample was female students. The mean age was 23.7 (S.D. 4.5). 35.4% of students had finished their internship. Accounting studies was the first choice for 54.5% of the sample.

4.1.2 Factor and Reliability Analyses

Values of sampling appropriateness (KMO $= 0.837$) and Bartlett test of sphericity ($x^2 = 1,602,993, p < 0.001$) showed sample adequacy. Six factors were extracted, explaining 55.8% of the variance. Items from the generic skills scale (items 2, 5, 9, 10, 11, 21) were loaded on Factor 1 (explained variance $= 25.2\%$). Factor 2 (explained variance $= 9.08\%$) showed salient loadings on three of the six items from the good teaching scale (items 7, 16, 15) and one item from the appropriate workload scale (item 20). The composition of the second factor suggested that the students associated the lecturers' teaching quality with the pressure of teaching staff in order to do well in courses. Factor 3 (explained variance $= 6.8\%$) showed salient loadings on one item from the appropriate workload scale (item 14), one item from the good teaching scale (item 3), and one item from the clear goals and standards scale (item 1). Review of these items suggested that the third factor involved students' perceptions as far as the motivation, the standard of work expected, and the time to understand things. Factor 4 (explained variance $= 5.2\%$) showed salient loadings on all three items from the assessment scale (items 18, 12, 8) and one item from good teaching (item 19). This factor reflects the interpretation factual knowledge associated with the interesting lesson of teaching staff. Factor 5 (explained variance $= 4.9\%$) showed salient loadings on one item from the appropriate workload scale (item 22) and one item from the clear goals and standards scale (item 13). The composition of the fifth factor suggested that students associated the understanding of accounting studies with the sheer volume and the teaching staff's expectations. The last factor (explained variance $= 4.5\%$) showed salient loadings on one item from the appropriate workload scale (item 4), two items from the clear goals and standards scale (items 6, 23), and one item from good teaching scale (item 17). The composition of the sixth factor suggested that the students associated the workload with the teaching staff's expectations and good teaching. From the above analysis, it is understood that many items did not load on the intended factors. However, the Cronbach's alpha of the overall questionnaire met the criterion of 0.781, which means adequate reliability; however, except from the good teaching (Cronbach's alpha $= 0.803$) and the generic skills scales (Cronbach's alpha $= 0.784$), the remaining scales were poor, with ranges from 0.418 to 0.124. Due to the issues highlighted by exploratory factor and reliability analyses, items of the appropriate workload scale were excluded from analyses.

A new factor analysis was performed. Table 1 shows factor loadings of the CEQ items. Four factors were obtained accounting for 52.18% of the variance. Factor loadings lower than 0.35 are not reported. Factor analysis showed that the 19 CEQ items represented the expected four-factor structure. The extracted factors were Factor 1, good teaching scale (explained variance $= 29.56\%$, five items); Factor 2, appropriate assessment scale (explained variance $= 9.39\%$, four items); Factor 3, generic skills scale (explained variance $= 7.61\%$, six items); and Factor 4, clear goals and standards scale (explained variance $= 5.62\%$, four items).

Table 1 Factor structure of CEQ item scores

		Components			
		GTS (first factor)	AAS (second factor)	GSS (third factor)	CGSS (fourth factor)
15	The staff made a real effort to understand difficulties I might be having with my work	0.762			
7	The staff put a lot of time into commenting on my work	0.749			
16	The teaching staff normally gave me helpful feedback on how I was going	0.698			
19	The teaching staff worked hard to make their subjects interesting	0.572			
3	The teaching staff of this course motivated me to do my best work	0.550			
12	The staff seemed more interested in testing what I had memorized than what I had understood		0.720		
13	It was often hard to discover what was expected of me in that course		0.670		
18	Too many staff asked me questions just about facts		0.628		
8	To do well in this course, all you really needed was a good memory		0.479		
21	My course helped me to develop the ability to plan my own work			−0.806	
2	The course developed my problem-solving skills			−0.787	
5	The course sharpened my analytical skills			−0.729	
11	The course improved my skills in written communication			−0.695	
9	The course helped me develop my ability to work as a team member			−0.582	
10	As a result of my course, I feel confident about tackling unfamiliar problems			−0.530	
6	I usually had a clear idea of where I was going and what was expected of me in this course				−0.815
1	It was always easy to know the standard of work expected				−0.674
23	The staff made it clear right from the start what they expected from students				−0.670
17	My lecturers were extremely good at explaining things				−0.561

CEQ Course Experience Questionnaire, *GTS* Good Teaching Scale, *AAS* Appropriate Assessment Scale, *GSS* Generic Skills Scale, *CGSS* Clear Goals and Standards Scale

Cronbach's alpha coefficient and the Pearson product moment correlation analysis are shown in Table 2. Based on instructions of Nunnally (1979) for the coefficient of internal reliability, values such as 0.5 and 0.6 are considered acceptable for the initial stages of a survey.

Table 2 Reliability and correlation analysis

	Cronbach alfa	Correlation analysis		
		ASS	GSS	CGSS
GTS	0.781	0.109*	0.563**	0.609**
AAS	0.535		0.145*	0.195**
GSS	0.784			0.487**
CGSS	0.688			

GTS Good Teaching Scale, *AAS* Appropriate Assessment Scale, *GSS* Generic Skills Scale, *CGSS* Clear Goals and Standards Scale
* Correlation is significant at the 0.05 level (2-tailed); ** Correlation is significant at the 0.01 level (2-tailed)

Table 3 Correlation analysis between CEQ scales and overall satisfaction of accounting studies

	Overall satisfaction from accounting studies
GTS	0.479**
AAS	0.252**
GSS	0.473**
CGSS	0.416**

CEQ Course Experience Questionnaire, *GTS* Good Teaching Scale, *AAS* Appropriate Assessment Scale, *GSS* Generic Skills Scale, *CGSS* Clear Goals and Standards Scale
** Correlation is significant at the 0.01 level (2-tailed)

4.2 Descriptive Statistics: Satisfaction and Background Characteristics of Students

Students have overall positive perception of their studies ($M = 3.3$, S.D. $= 0.5$); the mean score of good teaching was 3.05 (S.D. 0.77), the assessment scale was 3.33 (S.D. 0.67), generic skills scale was 3.43 (S.D. 0.69), and mean score of clear goals and standards scale was 3.55 (S.D. 0.65).

Further, statistically significant differences were found between the internship, good teaching, generic skills and clear goals, and standards scales. The mean score of the good teaching scale for students who have finished their internship was 3.20 versus 2.97 for those who had not (p value $= 0.024$). Similar results occurred for the generic skills scale and for the clear goals and standards scale, where students who had finished their internship, scored 3.66 and 3.69 versus 3.30 and 3.50 for those who had not, respectively (p value ≤ 0.001 and p value $= 0.022$). Respondents, who stated that accounting had been their first choice of study, were more likely to score higher in the clear goals and standards scale (3.67) and in the generic skills scale (3.62) versus students who negatively answered and scored lower in the above scales (3.45 and 3.24). These relationships were statistically significant (p value ≤ 0.001).

53.4% of students declared very/extremely satisfied from accounting studies. The correlation analysis conducted between CEQ scales and overall satisfaction of accounting studies showed that all scales correlate with the satisfaction criterion (Table 3).

Table 4 Model of linear regression analyses in CEQ scales and overall satisfaction

	Unstandardized coefficients		
	B	S. E.	Sig.
(Constant)	0.332	0.318	0.298
Good teaching scale	0.363	0.074	0.000
Assessment scale	0.248	0.071	0.001
Generic skills scale	0.370	0.083	0.000

B Beta, *S.E.* Standard error, *Sig* Significance

In order to determine the impact of CEQ scales in the overall satisfaction, multiple linear regression analyses were performed (Table 4).

5 Discussion

This study attempted to evaluate the accounting programs' teaching quality using the CEQ23 instrument. The results of this study reveal the accounting students' perceptions of the learning environment providing evidence about the psychometric qualities of the CEQ for its application in the Southwestern European countries, given that our results have similarities to the Italian results as well as the results from non-Western countries.

A four-factor structure was reached after eliminating the workload scale due its low reliability and the cross-loadings of factors. Low reliability ratings for certain scales and inability to reach the intended five-scale or six-scale structures (depending on the long or short form of CEQ) are met with the studies of Barattucci and Zuffo (2012) in Italy, Price et al. (2011) and Yin et al. (2014) in China, Ullah et al. (2011) and Ullah et al. (2016) in Pakistan, and the study of Chakrabarty et al. (2016) in West Bengal.

This study indicated that accounting students have not been able to identify the "appropriate workload" factor. This may be due either to the negative wording of three out four appropriate workload items or the high rate of absenteeism and the prolonged duration of studies noted in higher education (Katsikas and Panagiotidis 2011) or both. Students rated fairly higher their perceptions about clear goals and standards followed by the generic skills development and the proper assessment. These results may mirror the teacher-centered academic system, in which clear goals represent the "one book manual," the predetermined pages and exercises to study, and the information reproduction system which is most usually followed by accounting teachers. Internship influences positively the perceptions of students about good teaching, generic skills, and clear goals and standards, probably because students become more mature and realize the requirements of the profession and the importance of their studies. Further, the students who had clear intention to follow accounting studies (first choice) are positively influenced from clear goals and standards and generic skills, but their perception about good teaching is not impacted.

The evidence of the validity of the Greek CEQ is provided by examining the relationships between CEQ scores and external criteria like the overall course satisfaction (Ramsden 1991). All the Greek CEQ scales showed a significant positive correlation with overall satisfaction, strengthening the instrument's validity for use with Greek accounting students. Regression analysis revealed that the generic skills scale had the higher impact on students' satisfaction (0.370) perhaps due to the strong professional orientation of accounting courses followed by the good teaching (0.363) and the assessment scale (0.248).

6 Conclusions

The results from the present study apart from showing that the Greek CEQ could be used for evaluation purposes possibly reveal also a lag in the proper implementation of the EU requirements on modernization of higher education which subsequently may have implications for the teaching quality in HEIs. Quantitative results from CEQ should be supplemented with more qualitative data concerning students' rate of attendance and duration of studies that may seriously affect their learning process and their perceptions of the teaching and learning environment.

A limitation of this study was the convenience sample and the relatively small number of students (268). Given that the study did not include accounting students from Universities but only students from Technological Educational Institutions, the generalizability of the results needs to be examined in future work.

In response to the above empirical findings, we propose that more research is needed in order to confirm these results for Greek accounting students' experience and further validation of CEQ.

Acknowledgment This research is funded by the Special Account for Research Grants of the TEI of Athens, in the framework of the Internal Programme for the Support of the TEI of Athens Researchers, for 2015.

References

Alhija, F. (2016). Teaching in higher education: Good teaching through students' lens. *Studies in Educational Evaluation, 54*, 4–12.

Andrew, N. P. (2010). Applicability of the Student Course Experience Questionnaire (SCEQ) in an African context: The case of Nigerian universities. *Literacy Information and Computer Education Journal (LICEJ), 1*(3), 143–150.

Asonitou, S. (2015). Barriers to the teaching of skills in the Greek higher education accounting courses: Insight from accounting teachers. *International Journal of Strategic Innovative Marketing, 2*, 3.

Barattucci, M., & Zuffo, R. G. (2012). Measuring learning environment perceptions: Validation of the Italian version of the approaches to studying inventory and the student course experience questionnaire. *Testing, Psychometrics, Methodology in Applied Psychology, 19*(1), 15–33.

Broomfield, D., & Bligh, J. (1998). An evaluation of the "short form" course experience questionnaire with medical students. *Medical Education, 32*, 367–369. https://doi.org/10.1046/j.1365-2923.1998.00232.x.

Byrne, M., & Flood, B. (2003). Assessing the teaching quality of accounting programs: An evaluation of the course experience questionnaire. *Assessment & Evaluation in Higher Education, 28*(2), 135–145.

Cattell, R. B. (1978). *The scientific use of factor analysis in behavioural and life sciences.* New York: Plenum Press.

Chakrabarty, A. K., Richardson, J. T. E., & Sen, M. K. (2016). Validating the course experience questionnaire in West Bengal higher secondary education. *Studies in Educational Evaluation, 50*, 71–78.

De Jager, J., & Gbadamosi, G. (2013). Predicting students' satisfaction through service quality in higher education. *The International Journal of Management Education, 11*, 107–118.

Eley, M. (2001). The course experience questionnaire: Altering question format and phrasing could improve the CEQ's effectiveness. *Higher Education Research & Development, 20*(3), 293–312.

Entwistle, N. J., & Ramsden, P. (1983). *Understanding student learning.* London: Croom Helm.

Fryer, L. K., Ginns, P., Walker, R. A., & Nakao, K. (2011). The adaptation and validation of the CEQ and the R-SPQ-2F to the Japanese tertiary environment. *British Journal of Educational Psychology, 82*, 549–563.

Gerkin, M. P., & Kierkus, A. C. (2011). What makes a good criminal justice professor? A quantitative analysis of student evaluation forms. *The Journal of Effective Teaching, 11*(2), 18–39.

Ginns, P., Prosser, M., & Barrie, S. (2007). Students' perceptions of teaching quality in higher education: The perspective of currently enrolled students. *Studies in Higher Education, 32*(5), 603–615.

Griffin, P., Coates, H., McInnis, C., & James, R. (2003). The development of an extended course experience questionnaire. *Quality in Higher Education, 9*(3), 259–266.

Jansen, E., van der Meer, J., & Fokkens-Bruinsma, M. (2013). Validation and use of the CEQ in The Netherlands. *Quality Assurance in Education, 21*(4), 330–343. https://doi.org/10.1108/qae-11-2012-0041.

Kapardis, M. K., Montaño, J. L. A., González, J. M. G., Hassall, T., Joyce, J., Germanou, E., & Asonitou, S. (2010). The approaches to learning of European accounting students. *EuroMed Journal of Business, 5*(3), 345–362.

Katsikas, E., & Panagiotidis, T. (2011). Student status and academic performance: Accounting for the symptom of long duration of studies in Greece. *Studies in Educational Evaluation, 37*, 152–161.

Law, D. C. S., & Meyer, J. H. F. (2011). Relationships between Hong Kong students' perceptions of the learning environment and their learning patterns in post-secondary education. *Higher Education, 62*(1), 27–47.

Lizzio, A., Wilson, K., & Simons, R. (2002). University students' perceptions of the learning environment and academic outcomes: Implications for theory and practice. *Studies in Higher Education, 27*(1), 27–52.

Marton, F., & Säljö, R. (1976). On qualitative differences in learning: I-outcome and process. *British Journal of Educational Psychology, 46*, 4–11.

Milton-Wildey, K., Kenny, P., Parmenter, G., & Hall, J. (2014). Educational preparation for clinical nursing: The satisfaction of students and new graduates from two Australian universities. *Nurse Education Today, 34*, 648–654.

Möller, I. (2002). *The Ramsden course experience questionnaire: A pilot study of final-year students on hospitality, leisure, sport and tourism degree courses.* Retrieved February 10, 2010, from http://www.heacademy.ac.uk/assets/hlst/documents/projects/secq/ramsden.pdfS

Nunnally, J. C. (1979). Cited in: Churchill GA Jr. Paradigm for developing better measures of marketing constructs. *Journal of Marketing Research, XVI*, 64–73.

Okpala, C. O., & Ellis, R. (2005). The perceptions of college students on teacher quality: A focus on teacher qualifications. *Education, 126*(2), 374–378.

Onwuegbuzie, A. J., Witcher, A. E., Collins, K. M. T., Filer, J. D., Wiedmaier, C. D., & Moore, C. W. (2007). Students' perceptions of characteristics of effective college teachers: A validity study of a teaching evaluation form using a mixed-methods analysis. *American Educational Research Journal, 44*, 113–160. https://doi.org/10.3102/0002831206298169.

Price, L., Richardson, J. T. E., Robinson, B., Ding, X., Sun, X., & Han, C. (2011). Approaches to studying and perceptions of the academic environment among university students in China. *Asia Pacific Journal of Education, 31*(2), 159–175.

Ramsden, P. (1991). A performance indicator of teaching quality in higher education: The course experience questionnaire. *Studies in Higher Education, 16*(2), 129–150.

Richardson, J. T. E. (1994). A British evaluation of the course experience questionnaire. *Studies in Higher Education, 19*(1), 59–68.

Richardson, J. T. (2005). Instruments for obtaining student feedback: A review of the literature. *Assessment & Evaluation in Higher Education, 30*(4), 387–415.

Stergiou, D. P., & Airey, D. (2012). Using the course experience questionnaire for evaluating undergraduate tourism management courses in Greece. *Journal of Hospitality, Leisure, Sport & Tourism Education, 11*(1), 41–49.

Tabachnick, B. G., & Fidell, L. S. (2007). *Using multivariate statistics* (5th ed.). Boston, MA: Allyn & Bacon.

Thien, L. M., & Ong, Y. M. (2016). The applicability of course experience questionnaire for a Malaysian university context. *Quality Assurance in Education, 24*(1), 41–55.

Trigwell, K., & Prosser, M. (1991). Improving the quality of student learning: The influence of learning context and student approaches to learning on learning outcomes. *Higher Education, 22*, 251–266.

Ullah, R., Richardson, J. T. E., & Hafeez, M. (2011). Approaches to studying and perceptions of the academic environment among university students in Pakistan. *Compare: A Journal of Comparative and International Education, 41*(1), 113–127.

Ullah, R., Richardson, J. T. E., Malik, A. R., & Farooq, S. (2016). Perceptions of the learning environment, learning preferences, and approaches to studying among medical students in Pakistan. *Studies in Educational Evaluation, 50*, 62–70.

Wilson, K. L., Lizzio, A., & Ramsden, P. (1997). The development, validation and application of the course experience questionnaire. *Studies in Higher Education, 22*(1), 33–53.

Yin, H., Lu, G., & Wang, W. (2014). Unmasking the teaching quality of higher education: Students' course experience and approaches to learning in China. *Assessment and Evaluation in Higher Education, 39*(8), 949–970.

Corporate Governance: A Comparative Analysis of the Accounts of the Telephone Companies Cosmote, Vodafone, and Wind

Eleftherios Kleiousis, Angeliki Terzoglou, Dimitrios Valsamidis, and Lambros Tsourgiannis

Abstract The purpose of this paper is to present the structure governing corporate social responsibility in the mobile telecommunications sector in Greece. Because the sector is clearly oligopolistic and the competition in this type of the market is special, the corporate social responsibility plays a catalytic role in shaping the consumer perception of each company individually. Through this work the researchers hope to make clear the context of corporate social responsibility governing mobile companies in Greece.

Because these networks offer exclusively services and not products on the end consumers, the analysis will have a different manner than that is widespread in an ordinary industry. The comparative analysis of the three main players of this oligopolistic sector will hopefully yield useful findings, both at research level and at the level of quality improvement policies of certain services provided to all interested members of the mobile telecommunication sector in Greece. The comparative analysis is performed by the corporate social responsibility reports of the three companies for the years 2012, 2013, and 2014.

Keywords Corporate social responsibility · Mobile telephony · Oligopoly · Comparative analysis · Services · Accounts · Content analysis

E. Kleiousis (✉)
Department of Business Administration, TEI of Western Macedonia, Grevena, Greece
e-mail: e.kleiousis@kastoria.pdm.gov.gr

A. Terzoglou · D. Valsamidis · L. Tsourgiannis
Department of Accounting and Finance, TEI of East Macedonia and Thrace, Kavala, Greece

© Springer Nature Switzerland AG 2019
N. Sykianakis et al. (eds.), *Economic and Financial Challenges for Eastern Europe*,
Springer Proceedings in Business and Economics,
https://doi.org/10.1007/978-3-030-12169-3_34

1 Introduction

The corporate social responsibility (CSR) appears significantly in the mobile industry in Greece. This is due to the fact that the corporate social responsibility is a basic tool of suppliers of mobile telecommunications products and services both in Greece and in other European countries. Despite the fact that the real economy is interested in combining mobile telecommunication and corporate social responsibility, there are not many research references to the concrete combination as it is confirmed by Runhaar and Lafferty (2009). The telecommunication sector includes companies which provide voice and data services. There are a large number of bodies which focus on actions of suppliers for social issues, such as European Information Technology Observatory, European Telecommunications Network Operators' Association (ETNO), Global e-Sustainability Initiative, European Union, and World Health Organization. Forty-two companies are complete members which have committed themselves to the principles of ETNO at European level. In Greece the three main companies of the telecommunication sector seem to take due account of the corporate social responsibility.

Cosmote, Vodafone, and Wind are the basic members of the Greek Network for the CSR. The mission of the Greek Network is the promotion of the meaning of the CSR in the business community and the social environment. OTE-Cosmote is the only company of the three which is a complete member and has committed itself to the sustainable actions of ETNO. All of these telecommunication companies have an expert, separate CSR section which proves the great meaning of CSR for them. According to Douglas et al. (2004), the annual reports of CSR are optional in Greece, despite the fact that there is regulatory reference to the environmental dimension in some European countries. With regard to Greek telecommunication section, the Greek Ministry of Infrastructure, Transport and Networks and the National Regulatory Authorities determine the quality indicators. Moreover, they oblige all the telecommunication companies to publish their indicators on their official websites.

This paper is focused on traditional and innovative facts, figures, and information on the CSR that were found in sustainability reports and official websites of the companies. It is worth mentioning that the sustainability reports are posted mainly on official websites in Greece. This particular paper contributes to the bibliography in different ways. In other words, this study classifies, analyzes, and interprets the content of the CSR's information, so as to provide information to the readers. This information is related to whatever the CSR concerns, such as innovative approaches in the field of the sustainability reports, identifying similarities and differences among the three companies which have been studied in predefined categories and subcategories and have been concentrated on a specific section and a specific country, so as to being promoted information for the sustainability reports. In this paper, the word "sustainability" has the same meaning as the phrase "corporate social responsibility" (Marrewijk and Werre 2003; Marrewijk 2003; Dyllick and Hockerts 2002).

2 Baseline

There are plenty of studies from both individual authors and organizations which study the characteristics of the sustainability reports. CSR Europe (2000) noted that the companies adopt a variety of methods for the supply of CSR information. Idowu and Towler (2004) compared the content of the sustainability reports among 17 British companies of separate sectors. Birth and Illia (2008) refer the five most traditional channels of communication: internal communication, Internet, Social Report, code of conducts, and consultations with interested parties. A great survey relating to sustainability reports has been conducted by Giannarakis et al. (2011a, b), who present the characteristics of the reports, which describe providers of telecommunication services on the Greek market.

The main problem is that the basic characteristics of the sustainability reports are disregarded by related studies, such as characteristics of objective and comparative analysis. These characteristics are necessary elements for subjective assessments of interested parties. Moreover, they give an indication that they ensure a continuing improvement.

There are many determinants which are able to influence the corporate social responsibility, such as the size, sector, culture, and profitability of a company. According to Cowen et al. (1987), large enterprises which have many shareholders are likely to be moving in the direction toward social issues and programs. Watts and Zimmerman (1978) support that the large enterprises promote the corporate social responsibility so as to avoid the policy cost which is able to have a negative effect on the effective management. Adams and McNicholas (2007) concluded that the type of ownership could influence the sustainability reports. Sweeney and Coughlan (2008) had checked seven different sectors and found that the sustainability reports are influenced by the sector in which every company is operating.

The aim of a variety of assessments' approaches is to create a tool that will be suitable for comparing the sustainability reports with their completeness based on two main directions. The first direction is the quantitative one, which is referred to the number and percentage of words or sentences. The second direction is the qualitative, which includes the use of a scale for the assessment of the content (Giannarakis et al. 2011a, b). It is observed that in the bibliography, there is a comparison between companies which belong to a same sector or to different sectors. Additionally, there are surveys which try to evaluate the business efficiency in comparison with the economy of a country.

The tool of content analysis is used widely to the research sector of the corporate social responsibility in relation to analysis of noneconomic reports (Gray et al. 1995; Hackston 1996; Sweeney and Coughlan 2008; Milne and Adler 1999) and is used to gather and codify both quantitative and qualitative elements in predefined categories (Guthrie and Abeysekera 2006). The quantitative approach transforms from notes to quantitative statistical elements, while the qualitative summarizes, classifies elements or parts of references, and focuses on the feasibility and its impacts. Weber (1988) notes that the content of methodological analysis intends to codify and

512 E. Kleiousis et al.

summarize a text in different categories based on predefined criteria. Similarly, Krippendorff (1980) considers that the analysis of content is "a research technical construction and reproduction valid conclusions by data in accordance with their context." Moreover, Krippendorff gives particular importance relating to which content would be more appropriate for analysis. In contrast, Powell (1997) considers that the content analysis is "a systematic analysis of appearance of words, phrases, meanings . . . in books, movies and other types of materials." The analysis of content is a method for analyzing texts, images, illustrations, tables, photographs, cartoons, etc. (Kondracki et al. 2002). Content analysis is the most simplified type for the detection of existence or nonexistence of CSR information (Patten and Crampton 2004). Qualitative analysis of content is the subjective interpretation of CSR information. It takes place through systematic procedure of classification, coding, and detection of issues (Hsieh and Shannon 2005). The analysis of different units is used on the development of procedure of content analysis (Gray et al. 1995). Especially, the reports are controlled for the explicit or implicit interpretation of the corporate social responsibility. The elements are identified, codified, classified, and categorized in the report in accordance with analysis of the unit.

3 Approach

The lack of studies relating to surveys on a CSR model has extended an interest in creation of the concrete paper. This paper is restricted to analysis of sustainability reports in a particular sector and country. The study is based on a preliminary level of the sustainability reports and individual dimensions of the ones which are suggested by Sweeney and Coughlan (2008), Idowu and Towler (2004), and Ellerup Nielsen and Thomsen (2007). Sweeney and Coughlan (2008) adopted the content analysis and studied seven different companies' sectors in order to find the way with which the companies understand the sector of CSR. The stakeholders are classified in two categories, first and second level. Idowu and Towler (2004) analyzed the content of sustainability reports and presented information which is provided to readers by the sustainability reports. Ellerup Nielsen and Thomsen (2007) used a semantic thematic analysis, an analysis of a text and some rhetorical characteristics in order to identify strategies which are adopted by the companies. An important methodological restriction of these studies is the lack of information on identification procedure and description that are used. However, the proposed models have extended so as to include more categories and subcategories in order to further explore the characteristics of sustainability reports. Moreover, this extension increases the correlation between theory, bibliography, and sustainability reports.

In this paper, the content of sustainability reports will be analyzed using the official websites of the Greek mobile telecommunication companies. Their websites are the main channels of communication with the society and provide holistic information in the field of CSR. The sector of Greek mobile telecommunication consists of three main providers: Cosmote, Vodafone, and Wind. There are additional companies which provide mobile telecommunication services in Greece, but they do not have their own network. They are companies of telecommunication sector and resell it to final consumers. These companies are known as mobile virtual network operators. These companies are not going to be studied in this paper.

In the analysis of this paper, the comparative investigation of two out of three baselines of mobile telecommunication companies will be used: (a) their official website and (b) their annual sustainability reports. The time horizon of the research is 3 years, from 2012 to 2014.

Companies' websites, make an effort to reflect characteristics in tables, such as sustainable development, structure of operation of CSR sector, stakeholders, code of ethical behavior and CSR standards. The above information draws immediately some conclusions relating to the way every company understands the meaning of CSR.

As regards their annual sustainability, reports are more composite than their websites. It happens because these reports are published on an annual basis, and, as a result, there are small or big changes for every company. In this case, the annual representation per sector will give useful information for the development of every company relating to CSR during the period which is studied. In this paper, technical issues of the sustainability reports will be studied, such as certification, assessment, and size of the reports both regarding pages and the amount of data. The comparative analysis of these issues can give suitable, useful conclusion both to the company and to the other companies of the sector relating to the differences which appear to the period which is studied.

4   Results

4.1   Cosmote

In April 1998 Cosmote started its commercial activity in Greece as the third mobile telecommunication company in the country. Cosmote belongs to the OTE group and is active in Greece and other four countries increasing its penetration in the telecommunications services (Cosmote n.d.). The Cosmote's sustainability report has been the same with OTE—group' sustainability report since 2012 (Cosmote 2012). Moreover, there is a short presentation of the largest economic indicators of the group. The company presents its aims for different indicators not only for the previous years but also for the next year and compares their results among periods where there are suitable specific data (Cosmote 2005).

Cosmote considers that CSR creates value for the company, and as a consequence Cosmote incorporates the corporate social resource into its management and business processes. The company was certified with standard G.3.1 in the 2012, 2013, and 2014 year by the body GRI (Cosmote 2012, 2013, 2014). Cosmote has certified management systems by a variety of external entity, such as AssS 980ISO 22301:2012, BSI, BS 10500, ISO 27001, ISO 9001:2008, ISO ERM 31000,

OHSAS 18001, Tier III και FSC. Furthermore, its sustainability report follows guidelines of GRI. As regards the structure of the indicators per category, Cosmote has created four general categories by which Cosmote presents its activities in the field of CSR: (a) profile, (b) economy, (c) environment, and (d) society (Cosmote 2014).

Cosmote spends more and more money so as to increase the number of trainees and seminars every year. Moreover, health and safety of employees during the work are a very important aim of Cosmote, so its sustainability report refers to the indicator about accidents. Also, the company takes care of the existence of responsible communication with its customers relating to practices of responsible marketing. Cosmote has developed a paternal control service for parents to be able to follow the surfing the net of their children. In relation with the environmental dimension, Cosmote concentrates especially on the management of natural resources, material recycling, energy, and radiation. Cosmote supports social issues with a special emphasis on welfare of children, accessibility for people with special needs, equal access to education, and relief from disasters. The sustainability report is available to the public in the Greek and the English language (Cosmote 2014).

4.2   Vodafone

Greek Vodafone is owned 99.878% by Vodafone Group Plc. It provides a separate sustainability report from Vodafone Group Plc which is smaller regarding the number of its pages than the (one by) Cosmote. Particularly, Greek Vodafone's sustainability report was 91 pages and is separated to 13 units for the period from April 2011 to March 2012 (Vodafone n.d., 2003, 2012).

Vodafone is the only company on the telecommunication sector which has adopted a procedure CSR for its stakeholders since 2005 (Vodafone n.d.). Especially, there is a code of ethical behavior for its suppliers and an evaluation process with which the company takes notes of major issues such as working hours, child labor, and the environment (Vodafone 2003). The company encourages its suppliers to inform it for every possible problem in relation to the procurement process. As regards to its customers, Vodafone dumps practices to ensure and increase the trust of its customers. For example, Vodafone ensures activities for safer use of mobile phones from children and teenagers. The company emphasizes on CSR issues which are more important on the telecommunication sector, such as access to the telecommunication and health. Vodafone informs the general public about the functioning of new technologies, mobile telephone, supports information program in order to measure and control the electromagnetic radiation of radio frequencies, and publishes the results. As regards the environment, Vodafone is concerned about issues such as recycling, for the environmental damage to be reduced. As regards the digital divide, the company provides products and services to groups and people with special needs. In the section of social investment, Vodafone considers that children are a special social group and, as a result, supports those who adopt multidimensional programs. Investigations are conducted for employees of Vodafone in order for their needs to be detected. Some of the certificates of Vodafone's management system with various standards are the following: ISO 14001, OHSAS 18001: 2007, ISO 9001:2008, ELOTENISO/IEC 17025, ISO 27001: 2005, and ISO 22301:2012 (Vodafone 2014). Moreover, Vodafone's sustainability report is the only one of the three companies which provides a limited number of negative information, such as the problem of monitoring of safety in 2005 (Vodafone n.d.). The sustainability report of Vodafone is approved by GRI for the result to have standardization. The reports of the company are published from 2002 to 2003 (Vodafone 2003). Finally, its reports are translated in English (Vodafone 2012, 2013, 2014).

4.3 Wind

Wind Hellas belongs to Weather Group as Wind Telecomunicazioni which manages and provides the mobile and fixed telephony of Italy. Wind is concentrated on three main categories—business, environment, and society. With regard to the main category, the workplace is a basic subcategory, because the company supports that its employees are the most crucial factor for its reputation and success. This is the reason why Wind adopts a variety of practices, such as code of behavior, which gives priority on the health and safety of employees. A further subcategory is the market which gives information to both customers and suppliers. As regards the environmental category of CSR, Wind has an electromagnetic measuring of radiation with a view to the safe use of mobile telecommunications. The company adopted additional practices for the environmental category, such as waste management, energy sources, and environmental actions. In the third category, Wind supports directly or indirectly different groups of people and organizations. Wind is an important sponsor of social activities, for example, sport, theatre, and music. Its website involves information relating to coding and external certifications, such as TUV, OⓩSAS 18001, ISO9001:2008, CIA, CFE, and ISO14001:2004. Finally, there is a specific section which informs the customers for the infrastructure and network of the company. The sustainability reports are published in Greek and English language (Wind n.d., 2007, 2012, 2013, 2014).

The sustainability reports of 2012, as of the previous years, were not accessible by the official website of Wind when this paper was written (21 May 2016) (Wind 2012). The only reports accessible by the official website of this company were of years 2013 and 2014. For the purpose of this paper, it was necessary to research the Internet so as to find the sustainability report of the company for 2012 year. It was difficult for us to detect a report on the web. It generates objective problems to all stakeholders who want to have direct information for Wind's social activity before 2012.

The following indicators were presented on Table 1 of the annex by means of comparative analysis of the website of every company. What is found under the term CSR on the website? Does it refer to the meaning of the sustainable development? Is there any section of CSR? Which is its structure? Are there references to any matters of CSR, such as reference to stakeholders on the vision/mission or on the company's values? Is there mapping of the stakeholders and their engagement? Which/who are the main stakeholders of the company? Is there a code of ethical behavior? Do they adopt standards of CSR, such as AA 1000, EMAS, SA 8000, and GRI, and ten principles of global compact?

The compared sustainability reports are similar relating to their structure, content, and analysis. On Tables 2, 3, and 4, there is a presentation of characteristics of sustainability reports, where differences and similarities can be noted per year. Companies publish their sustainability reports on their websites as a means of communication. Furthermore, these three companies publish their reports in English. Moreover, they consider the meaning of CSR as a tool which is used for various issues and have similar stakeholders.

5 Discussion and Conclusions

The two out of the three companies which are discerned are Cosmote-OTE SA and Vodafone. According to indicators, Cosmote-OTE SA and Vodafone have degree "A+," while Wind has degree "B+." All of these companies publish the certificates of management systems and their awards so as to attract the social media and make their reports more attractive for readers. Cosmote-OTE SA and Vodafone publish information in their annual reports which provide information for more issues than a simple reader is interested. A similar conclusion was not found for Wind's reports although Wind is a recognized company.

The global business society has standardized all financial statements which are published on the media according to international accounting standards. With regard to sustainability reports, we believe that it is necessary to have a consultation in order for reports to be standardized. Up to now there are not widely acceptable standards so as to establish a uniform regulation.

In Greece, in particular on the mobile telecommunication section, the philosophy of CSR is in infancy. The companies of mobile telecommunication concentrate more on economic and competitive environment in accordance with the model of CSR.

On the overview of bibliography, there is a lack of publications for investigation of submission of sustainability reports on the mobile telecommunication section. The particular paper provides information relating to philosophy of the sustainability reports of providers of mobile telecommunication in Greece.

In this paper, we explore if these three Greek companies are social responsible relating to information which provide by their sustainability reports that is presented on their websites.

The proposed model can be used by both simple readers so as to be informed of the CSR of companies by the way that information of reports are presented, and managers of the telecommunication section who are interested in being informed of the CSR of their competitors based on their strategic reports.

Appendix

Table 1 A comparative analysis of websites of Greek mobile telecommunication companies (2016)

Characteristics of websites	Company		
	Cosmote	Vodafone	Wind
What is found under the term CSR on the website?	Strategy, marketplace, employees, society, environment, indicators	Management, environment, society, targets-indicators	Quality management, the market, employees, society, environment, targets-indicators
Does it refer to the meaning of the sustainable development?	Yes	Yes	Yes
Is there any section of CSR? Which is its structure?	Corporate responsibility	Sustainable development	Corporate responsibility
Reference to stakeholders on the vision/ mission?	Yes	Yes	Yes
Reference on the company values?	Yes	Yes	Yes
Mapping of the stakeholders and their engagement?	Yes	Yes	Yes
Is there code of ethical behavior?	1. Consumers and potential clients 2. The market 3. Science, research, education 4. NGOs and stakeholder groups 5. SMEs 6. State/governmental bodies 7. Employees, potential employees and their representatives 8. Suppliers 9. Shareholders, bond-holders, investors, analysts	1. NGOs 2. Government-local government-entities 3. Suppliers 4. Journalists 5. Academic community 6. Business community 7. Local communities 8. Owners of space for installation of base station 9. Parents-teachers 10. Employees 11. Customers	1. Shareholders 2. Employees 3. Commercial network 4. National regulatory authorities 5. SMEs 6. Local government 7. Suppliers 8. Collaborators 9. Customers 10. Central government 11. Academic community 12. NGOs
Is there code of ethical behavior?	Yes	Yes	Yes
Do they adopt standards of CSR?			

(continued)

Table 1 (continued)

Characteristics of websites	Company		
	Cosmote	Vodafone	Wind
• AA 1000	Yes	Yes	Yes
• EMAS	No	Yes	No
• SA 8000	No	No	No
• GRI	Yes	Yes	Yes
• 10 principles of global compact	Yes	No	Yes

Source: Cosmote (2012, 2013, 2014), Vodafone (2012, 2013, 2014), and Wind (2012, 2013, 2014)

Table 2 A comparative analysis of websites of sustainability reports of Greek mobile telecommunication companies (2012)

Characteristics of reports	Company		
	Cosmote	Vodafone	Wind
Name	Corporate responsibility report	Corporate responsibility report and sustainability	Corporate responsibility report
Size (pages)	127	91	144
Size (data MB)	33.1	3.8	14.3
In which by the three categories do indicators calculate?	GRI G3.1	GRI (2006)	GRI G3.1
Which and how many indicators are there in every category?	Strategy [2] Profile [10] Report [13] Governance [17] Economy [12] Environment [39] Work [21] Human Rights [13] Society [14] Product liability legislation [14]	Strategy [2] Profile [10] Report [13] Governance [17] Economy [7] Environment [17] Work [9] Human Rights [6] Society [6] Internal functions [8] Product liability legislation [4] Access [4]	Strategy [2] Profile [10] Parameters [13] Governance [17] Economy [3] Environment [9] Work [5] Human Rights [8] Society [4] Product liability legislation [5] Economic performance [6] Environmental performance [30] Social working performance [11] Social human right performance [10] Social product performance [6]

(continued)

Table 2 (continued)

Characteristics of reports	Company		
	Cosmote	Vodafone	Wind
Are there any changes in companies' reports over time? three (3) ages?	Yes	Yes	Yes
Are there differences between the three companies?	Yes	Yes	Yes
Are they certified?	Yes	Yes	Yes
• When?	2012	2012	2012
• By which organization?	ISO 14001:2004, CMS, OHSAS 18001-ELOT 1801	ISO 14001, EMAS, OHSAS 18001: 2007, ISO 9001:2008, ELO^{T}ENISO/IEC 17025, ISO 27001: 2005, BS25999-2:2007	ISO9001:2008, EN ISO14001:2004, TUV Hellas, MBCI
• Which was their degree?	GRI B+	GRI (2006) A+	GRI B+

Source: Cosmote (2012, 2013, 2014), Vodafone (2012, 2013, 2014), and Wind (2012, 2013, 2014)

Table 3 A comparative analysis of websites of sustainability reports of Greek mobile telecommunication companies (2013)

Characteristics of reports	Company		
	Cosmote	Vodafone	Wind
Name	Corporate responsibility report	Sustainability report	Corporate responsibility report
Size (pages)	242	92	145
Size (data MB)	6.8	2.6	5.4
In which by the three categories do indicators calculate?	G3.1	G3.1	G3.1
Which/who are the main stakeholders of the company?	Profile [42] Economy [12] Environment [39] Society [70]	Strategy [2] Profile [10] Report [13] Governance [17] Economy [7] Environment [17] Work [10] Human Rights [9] Society [7] Product liability legislation [4]	Strategy [2] Profile [10] Parameters [13] Governance [17] Economy [3] Environment [9] Work [5] Human Rights [8] Society [4] Product liability legislation [5] Economic performance

(continued)

Table 3 (continued)

Characteristics of reports	Company		
	Cosmote	Vodafone	Wind
		Internal functions [8] Access [4]	[5] Environmental performance [30] Social working performance [10] Social human right performance [10] Social product performance [6]
Are there any changes in companies' reports over time? three (3) ages?	Yes	Yes	Yes
• Are there differences between the three companies?	Yes	Yes	Yes
• Are they certified?	Yes	Yes	Yes
• When?	2013	2013	2013
• By which organization?	ISO ERM 31000, ISO 14001:2004, ISO 22301, OHSAS 18001, SOCAP, ISO 14001,	ISO 14001, OHSAS 18001: 2007, ISO 9001:2008, ELO^{T}ENISO/IEC 17025, ISO 27001: 2005, ISO 22301:2012	ISO9001:2008, ISO14001:2004, TUV Hellas, EΛO^T EN ISO/IEC 17025:2005, EΣ⊡Δ, CIA, CFE
• Which was their degree?	GRI 3.1 A+	GRI 3.1 A+	GRI 3.1 B+

Source: Cosmote (2012, 2013, 2014), Vodafone (2012, 2013, 2014), and Wind (2012, 2013, 2014)

Table 4 A comparative analysis of websites of sustainability reports of Greek mobile telecommunication companies (2014)

Characteristics of reports	Company		
	Cosmote	Vodafone	Wind
Name	Sustainability report	Sustainability report	Corporate responsibility report
Size (pages)	232	59	96
Size (data MB)	4.7	2.5	16.9
In which by the three categories do indicators calculate?	G 3.1	G 3.1	G.4
Which/who are the main stakeholders of the company?	Profile [42] Economy [12] Environment [39] Society [70]	Strategy [2] Profile [10] Report [13] Governance [17] Economy [7] Environment [17] Work [10] Human Rights [9] Society [7] Product liability legislation [4] Internal functions [8] Access [4]	Profile [14] Recognition of Limits [7] Participations [10] Governance [1] Ethical principle [1] Economy [2] Environment [11] Society [7]
Are there any changes in companies reports over time? three (3) ages?	Yes	Yes	Yes
• Are there differences between the three companies?	Yes	Yes	Yes
• Are they certified?	Yes	Yes	Yes
• When?	2014	2014	2015
• By which organization?	AssS 980ISO 22301:2012, BSI, BS 10500, ISO 27001, ISO 9001:2008, ISO ERM 31000, OHSAS 18001, Tier III, FSC	ISO 14001, OHSAS 18001: 2007, ISO 9001:2008, ELO^{T}ENISO/IEC 17025, ISO 27001: 2005, ISO 22301:2012	TUV, OℤSAS 18001, ISO9001:2008, CIA, CFE, ISO14001:2004
• Which was their degree?	GRI 3.1 A+	GRI 3.1 A+	GRI G4 (descriptive assessment)

Source: Cosmote (2012, 2013, 2014), Vodafone (2012, 2013, 2014), and Wind (2012, 2013, 2014)

References

Adams, C., & McNicholas, P. (2007). Making a difference. Sustainability reporting, accountability and organizational change. *Accounting, Auditing & Accountability Journal, 20*(3), 382–402.

Birth, G., & Illia, L. (2008). Communicating CSR: Practices among Switzerland's top 300 companies. *Corporate Communications: An International Journal, 13*, 182–196.

Cosmote. (n.d.). *Home page.* Retrieved May 21, 2016, from https://www.cosmote.gr/

Cosmote. (2005). *Corporate responsibility reports.* Retrieved May 21, 2016, from https://www.cosmote.gr/fixed/corporate/cr/reports

Cosmote. (2012). *Corporate responsibility report 2012.* Retrieved May 21, 2016, from https://www.cosmote.gr/fixed/documents/10280/788467/OTE-COSMOTE-CORPORATE-RESPON SIBILITY-REPORT-2012-gr.pdf/c914a303-163e-423a-8883-05a2ae526682

Cosmote. (2013). *Corporate responsibility report 2013.* Retrieved May 21, 2016, from https://www.cosmote.gr/fixed/documents/10280/788467/OTE-+COSMOTE+2013+CR+Report.pdf/ 623351d0-9f52-4b0e-ade4-3252563da0ea

Cosmote. (2014). *Corporate responsibility report 2014.* Retrieved May 21, 2016, from https://www.cosmote.gr/fixed/documents/10280/788467/ote_cosmotecr2014gr_final.pdf/1bf8cd1f-fb27-4cfd-816c-50a575ff810d

Cowen, S., Ferreri, L., & Parker, L. (1987). The impact of corporate characteristics on social responsibility disclosure: A typology and frequency-based analysis. *Accounting, Organisations and Society, 12*, 111–122.

CSR Europe. (2000). *Communicating corporate social responsibility.* Brussels: CSR Europe Publications.

Douglas, A., Doris, J., & Johnson, B. (2004). Corporate social reporting in Irish financial institutions. *The TQM Magazine, 16*(6), 387–395.

Dyllick, T., & Hockerts, K. (2002). Beyond the business case for corporate sustainability. *Business Strategy and the Environment, 11*, 130–141.

Ellerup Nielsen, A., & Thomsen, C. (2007). Reporting CSR – What and how to say it? *Corporate Communications: An International Journal, 12*(1), 25–40.

Giannarakis, G., Sariannidis, N., & Garefalakis, A. (2011a). The content of corporate social responsibility information: The case of Greek Telecommunication Sector. *International Business Research, 4*(3), 33–44.

Giannarakis, G., Sariannidis, N., & Litinas, N. (2011b). An analysis of corporate social responsibility in the Greek Telecommunications Sector. *Global Business and Organizational Excellence, 30*(4), 40–49.

Gray, R., Kouhy, R., & Lavers, S. (1995). Methodological themes: Constructing a research database of social and environmental reporting by UK companies. *Accounting, Auditing and Accountability Journal, 2*, 78–101.

Guthrie, J., & Abeysekera, I. (2006). Content analysis of social, environmental reporting: What is new? *Journal of Human Resource Costing & Accounting, 10*(2), 114–126.

Hackston, D. A. (1996). Some determinants of social and environmental disclosures in New Zealand companies. *Accounting, Auditing & Accountability Journal, 9*, 237–256.

Hsieh, H. F., & Shannon, S. E. (2005). Three approaches to qualitative content analysis. *Qualitative Health Research, 15*, 1277–1288.

Idowu, S., & Towler, B. (2004). A comparative study of the contents of corporate social responsibility reports of UK companies. *Management of Environmental Quality: An International Journal, 15*(4), 420–437.

Kondracki, N. L., Wellman, N. S., & Amundson, D. R. (2002). Content analysis: Review of methods and their applications in nutrition education. *Journal of Nutrition Education and Behavior, 34*, 224–230.

Krippendorff, K. (1980). *Content analysis: An introduction to its methodology.* New York: Sage.

Marrewijk, M. V. (2003). Concepts and definitions of CSR and corporate sustainability: Between agency and communion. *Journal of Business Ethics, 44*, 95–105.

Marrewijk, M. V., & Werre, M. (2003). Multiple levels of corporate sustainability. *Journal of Business Ethics, 2/3*, 107–119.

Milne, M., & Adler, R. (1999). Exploring the reliability of social and environmental disclosures content analysis. *Accounting. Auditing and Accountability Journal, 12*, 237–249.

Patten, D. M., & Crampton, W. (2004). Legitimacy and the internet: An examination of corporate web page environmental disclosures. *Advances in Environmental Accounting and Management, 2*, 31–57.

Powell, R. (1997). *Basic research methods for librarians*. London: Ablex Publishing Corporation.

Runhaar, H., & Lafferty, H. (2009). Governing corporate social responsibility: An assessment of the contribution of the UN Global Compact to CSR strategies in the telecommunications industry. *Journal of Business Ethics, 84*, 479–495.

Sweeney, L., & Coughlan, J. (2008). Do different industries report Corporate Social Responsibility differently? An investigation through the lens of stakeholder theory. *Journal of Marketing Communications, 14*(2), 113–124.

Vodafone. (n.d.) *Home page*. Retrieved May 21, 2016, from http://www.vodafone.gr/portal/client/cms/viewCmsPage.action?pageId=1032

Vodafone. (2003). *Corporate responsibility reports*. Retrieved May 21, 2016, from http://www.vodafone.gr/portal/client/cms/viewCmsPage.action?pageId=11293

Vodafone. (2012). *Corporate responsibility and sustainable development report*. Retrieved May 21, 2016, from http://www.vodafone.gr/portal/resources/media/Vodafone_Elladas/Etairikh_Ypeythinotita/Vodafone-annual_GR2012_LOW_lc.pdf

Vodafone. (2013). *Sustainable development report*. Retrieved May 21, 2016, from http://www.vodafone.gr/portal/resources/media/Vodafone_Elladas/Etairikh_Ypeythinotita/Vodafone-annual_GR2013_FINAL-low_lc.pdf

Vodafone. (2014). *Sustainable development report*. Retrieved May 21, 2016, from http://www.vodafone.gr/portal/resources/media/Vodafone_Elladas/Etairikh_Ypeythinotita/Vodafone%20annual_GR2014_final_low_lc.pdf

Watts, R., & Zimmerman, J. (1978). Towards a positive theory of the determination of accounting standards. *The Accounting Review, 53*, 112–134.

Weber, R. P. (1988). *Basic content analysis* (Sage University paper series on quantitative applications in the social sciences). Beverly Hills, CA: Sage.

Wind. (n.d.). *Home page*. Retrieved May 21, 2016, from https://www.wind.gr/

Wind. (2007). *Corporate responsibility reports*. Retrieved May 21, 2016, from https://www.wind.gr/gr/wind/gia-tin-etaireia/etairiki-koinoniki-euthuni/etairiki-upeuthunotita/apologismoi/?accept=1

Wind. (2012). *Corporate responsibility report 2012*. Retrieved May 21, 2016, from https://www.wind.gr/gr/wind/gia-tin-etaireia/etairiki-koinoniki-euthuni/etairiki-upeuthunotita/apologismoi/apologismos/?pdfID=126

Wind. (2013). *Corporate responsibility report 2013*. Retrieved May 21, 2016, from https://www.wind.gr/files/1/wind_v2/etaireia/PDF/Sustainability_report_2013_gr.PDF

Wind. (2014). *Corporate responsibility report 2014*. Retrieved May 21, 2016, from https://www.wind.gr/files/1/wind_v2/etaireia/PDF/Sustainability_report_2014.pdf

A Quantitative Analysis About Optimization of Number of Employees and Rebalancing Workload

Yılmaz Gökşen, Osman Pala, and Mustafa Ünlü

Abstract In an organization, the workload of the employees is very important in terms of efficiency and motivation toward work. Workloads must be at the same level as employees can achieve.

In the study, a large faculty of one of Turkey's leading universities was selected as a pilot. There are 25 different business units and 92 employees in the faculty. AHP and LP are preferred as models. With AHP, utility values of employees in each job type are calculated separately for 25 job types. The obtained utility values are assigned as the objective function coefficients of the decision variables of the LP model. Three different LP models were obtained and solved to obtain optimal workload values. According to the results of three different models, the manager will be able to complete the missing workloads of the employees from different units.

Keywords Workload of the employees · AHP and LP · MCDM

1 Introduction

According to the results of three different models, the manager will be able to complete the missing workloads of the employees from different units. A manager must be able to answer three questions in order to be able to evaluate their employees effectively. First, do they work in a job that suits their basic skills and training? Second, do they own the equipment they need to do their jobs? Third, are the physical and environmental conditions required by the job fulfilled? If all these questions are answered yes, the administrator can question his subordinates. It is extremely important that mathematical presentation of optimal distribution of workloads is made since managers will have different decision-making styles.

Y. Gökşen (✉) · O. Pala · M. Ünlü
Faculty of Business and Economics, Dokuz Eylül University, İzmir, Turkey
e-mail: yilmaz.goksen@deu.edu.tr; osman.pala@deu.edu.tr; mustafa.unlu@deu.edu.tr

© Springer Nature Switzerland AG 2019
N. Sykianakis et al. (eds.), *Economic and Financial Challenges for Eastern Europe*,
Springer Proceedings in Business and Economics,
https://doi.org/10.1007/978-3-030-12169-3_35

Making right decisions for encountered problems are always valuable for both individuals and organizations. In decision-making problems, the decision maker easily finds the best option when choosing between alternatives based on only one evaluation factor. However, in the case of decision making with multiple criteria, it is necessary to include the target aspects of the criteria, the weights, and the relationships between each criterion in the evaluation process. While attempting to decide the best among the options in the multi-criteria decision making (MCDM), the alternatives that constitute these options are evaluated on the criteria. Often the best alternative is not optimal for all of the selection criteria compared to other alternatives (Pala 2016).

2 Literature Review

Integration of MCDM approaches and LP are widely used approaches in decision making, some of such literature can be listed as follows: Ghodsypour and O'Brein (1998) indicated that managers should decide about two problems: which suppliers are the best and how much should be purchased from each selected supplier. They proposed an integration of AHP and LP in choosing the best suppliers and placing the optimum order quantities among them such that the total value of purchasing becomes optimum. Saaty et al. (2003) proposed a model which includes intangibles. They have shown that any current LP resource allocation model using ratio scale measurements for its coefficients can be transformed into an equivalent model whose coefficients belong to relative ratio scales. Chandran et al. (2005) present an approach based on linear programming that estimates the weights for a pairwise comparison matrix generated within the framework of the analytic hierarchy process and compare their results to other methods. Saaty et al. (2007) showed a way to apply the absolute measurement mode of the AHP together with LP to optimize human resource allocation problems. They indicate that the combined AHP and LP model is capable of solving hiring problems, such as when two people with different complementary skills work as a team. Gökşen et al. (2016) proposed a model for workforce assignment which is based on AHP and binary LP. They defined a utility function which is focused on both personnel and management views.

Workload in faculties and rebalancing workload to improve workforce productivity is well-known and widely studied subject in literature. Some of the most prominent studies in this field can be listed as follows: Diodato (1983) examined the activities of a faculty member and compared with other studies. Dairy questionnaire is used as method. He categorized activities as teaching, research, service, and others. Reid (1988) investigated mental workload which is divided into three subgroups: time load, mental effort, and psychological stress load in this study. The subjective workload assessment technique is proposed to explain mental workload. Burgess (1996) compared three different cases for planning workload of academic staff. Study concentrated on workload planning principles, computerized decision support, institutional contexts, the political dimension of workload planning, and the management of change. Seaberg (1998) compared workload of 40 selected faculties in the USA. Porter and Umbach (2001) examined 1104 faculties in the USA by the data of National Study of Postsecondary Faculty survey 1993. They compared classical regression models with a random coefficients model. Rhoades (2001) examined productivity in academic institutions. He discussed the definition of productivity and proposed different evaluation criteria. Also, some studies used LP as workload balancing tool: Jaumard et al. (1998) used generalized LP for nurse scheduling under constraints of satisfying demand of workload while minimizing salary costs and maximizing both nurse preferences and group balances. Aldowaisan and Gaafar (1999) combined business process reengineering approach with LP and redesigned activities of work types to balance workload of employees. Azmat et al. (2004) used mixed integer linear programming method to balance workloads of employees who work in a single shift workforce system under annualized hours.

3   Theoretical Background

There are numerous MCDM methods in the literature. Analytic hierarchy process (AHP), which is introduced by Saaty (1977) as an MCDM method, is the most popular among them. AHP is an analytical method, which can deal with both qualitative and quantitative criteria by using decision scale. AHP has become so widely popular in decision making due to its ease of comprehensibility by decision maker, applicability by researchers in various fields such as engineering and industry field when there is a need of decision making, and combinability with different methods like fuzzy, robust, and goal programming (Vaidya and Kumar 2006).

Hence, decision makers have to make pairwise comparisons for the same level criteria with using their knowledge and experience. Criteria must be independent between each other in AHP. In other words, there must be no interaction between criteria. AHP is composed of four basic stages: firstly, building structural hierarchy of the problem as seen in Fig. 1; secondly, making pairwise comparison between factors; thirdly, obtaining importance levels of factors, and lastly, evaluating consistency index (Ho 2008).

AHP ranks the alternatives with regard to their satisfaction levels for each criterion. In this process, importance levels are used for ranking criteria. AHP simply focuses on "which of them" question (Chen 2006). Implication steps of AHP are listed as follows (Aksaraylı et al. 2016):

- A square matrix is generated by using criteria, and the rank of criteria is same for both row rank and column rank of the matrix.
- Deciding a basis for comparison and making pairwise comparison with using 1–9 decision scale.
- Calculating eigenvector of matrix and assigning the weights of criteria and alternatives if the pairwise comparison matrix is consistent; otherwise turn one step back.

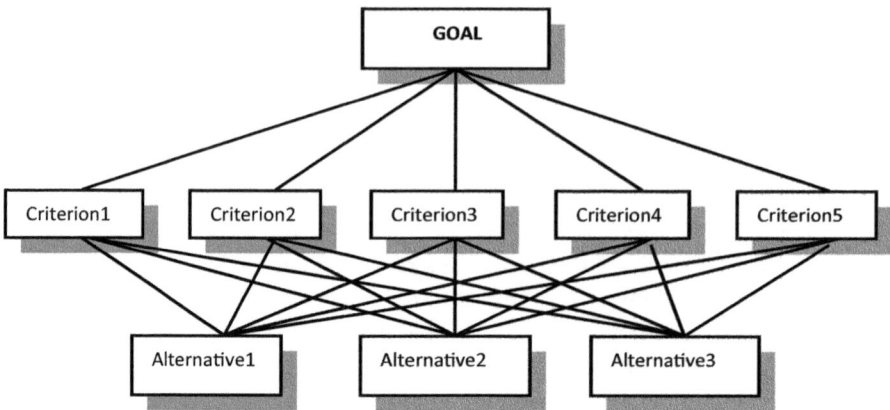

Fig. 1 Hierarchic Structure of AHP

- Multiplying each criteria weight with corresponding weight of alternative on criteria.
- Adding up weight of each alternative separately and using these sums for ranking alternatives.

LP is a tool for solving optimization problems where objective and constraint functions that are composed of decision variables and its parameters are both in linear shape. In 1947, George Dantzig developed an efficient method, the simplex algorithm, for solving linear programming problems. Since the development of the simplex algorithm, LP has been used to solve optimization problems in operational research field. In the method of linear programming, all variables take continuous values (Winston 1994).

Generally, LP model could be represented as follows (Öztürk 2002):

$$\max Z = \sum_{j=1}^{n} c_j x_j$$

Subject to:

$$\sum_{j=1}^{b} a_{ij} x_j \leq b_i \qquad (i = 1, 2, \ldots, m)$$

$$x_j \geq 0 \qquad (j = 1, 2, \ldots, n)$$

In this study, integrated AHP and LP models are used to solve the workload balancing problem in Dokuz Eylül University.

4 Methodology

Within *Dokuz Eylül University* Faculty of Economics and Administrative Sciences, there are 92 Administrative Staff who are appointed 25 different types of job. Administration of the faculty is studying about improving work productivity and satisfaction. Due to this reason, it is aimed to balance workloads of staff that are previously measured.

Workloads must be distributed to staff in a way that provides the most benefit to the job. For every kind of job, there are 3 features that staff needed as ability to perform better in the job:

C1: "Knowledge of legislation," knowing how work is done properly in the job type.
C2: "Learning ability," increasing with the number of different types of work that is done in the job type.
C3: "Technical competence," such as using computer and machine in the job type.

These 3 features are used as criteria C1, C2, and C3 in MCDM concept with AHP approach to evaluate who would be more appropriate for taking extra workload of specific job type. The weight of three criteria varies depending on the job, so we have to decide which criterion is more important for particular job and also we have to evaluate benefit that personnel provide for each work in the context of their original job to rebalance total workload of faculties. This approach allows us to distribute extra workload of a job to the personnel which he or she already employed with the nearest similar job. For this reason, we apply AHP to 25 types of job, and for every instance, we get weights of alternative jobs and paired them with staffs who are already appointed that kind of jobs. So we evaluate utility of staff for any kind of job over their original ones. For instance, when we make AHP judgments to determine which kind of job and its staff is a better candidate to take extra workload of job type 1, we include 24 different types of job except job type 1 in the analysis as alternatives.

Job types which are used in our study are listed in Table 1. For every job type, its name, total amount of workload, number of staff actually doing the job, and average workload of a staff are given. Last row includes total workload, staff, and average workload of a staff in faculty. So if we want to limit workload of a staff at the value of 1, we need (96.331–92) =4.3310 $\approx$ 5 new employee. We would use this information in LP models as new staff variable and would find where they needed most to be hired.

We compared 3 criteria to determine their importance level about 25 different types of job, and comparison matrix for X1, namely "administration manager," is given in Table 2. The answer of question that we seek for is "Which criterion is more important for doing job X1." So we make pairwise comparison and get result such as "C1 and C2 have equal importance for doing job X1," "C1 is 1.5 times more important than C3," and "C2 is 3.5 times more important than C3" with criteria weights, C1 = 0.3535, C2 = 0.4688, and C3 = 0.1777. Consistency rate of comparison matrix is 0.0819, which is under critical value of 0.1.

Table 1 Job types and its average workloads

No	Name of job	Total workload	Number of staff	Average workload of a staff
X1	Administration Manager	0.778	1	0.778
X2	Association Officer	0.685	1	0.685
X3	Executive assistant	0.553	1	0.553
X4	Planning Department	0.841	1	0.841
X5	IT Secretary	0.538	1	0.538
X6	Executive assistant of Dean	0.709	2	0.3545
X7	Executive assistant of Faculty Secretary	0.881	1	0.881
X8	Technical Services	3.154	4	0.7885
X9	Central	2.357	2	1.1785
X10	Postal Services	1.238	1	1.238
X11	Salary Services	1.801	4	0.45025
X12	Accounting	0.698	1	0.698
X13	Editorial Office	0.457	2	0.2285
X14	Material Office	2.62	4	0.655
X15	Personnel Office	0.556	4	0.139
X16	Bookstore	1.237	1	1.237
X17	Secretary of Economic Department	0.415	1	0.415
X18	Secretary of Public Administration Department	0.375	1	0.375
X19	Secretary of Business Administration Department	0.357	1	0.357
X20	Secretary of Public Finance and Econometrics Departments	0.714	1	0.714
X21	Culture, Art, and Sport Unit	1.326	1	1.326
X22	Student Affairs Unit	17.843	14	1.2745
X23	Auxiliary services	31.525	16	1.9703125
X24	Transportation services	1.816	2	0.908
X25	Security Guards	22.857	24	0.952375
TOTAL	All Jobs in the Faculty	96.331	92	1.047076087

Importance level of criteria, which is calculated within AHP structure for 25 different types of job, is given in Table 3. Ranks of criteria importance are not the same, but "technical competence" criterion is the least important criterion for all job types.

In Appendix 1, comparison matrix of alternatives for job type 1, X1: "administration manager," criterion C1: "knowledge of legislation" is given and variable names of job type are used which is previously mentioned in Table 1.

Importance levels of alternatives are given for every job in Appendix 2. We get job types in rows and corresponding importance levels of alternative job types that would take extra workload are listed in columns. For any job type, its own importance level is added as value of 1 to identify its superiority and also to use it in LP

Table 2 Comparison Matrix of Criteria for X1

X1	C1	C2	C3
C1	1	1	1.5
C2	1	1	3.5
C3	0.6667	0.2857	1

Table 3 Weight of criteria for each job type

	C1	C2	C3		C1	C2	C3
X1	0.3535	0.4688	0.1777	X14	0.5278	0.3325	0.1396
X2	0.3929	0.4779	0.1292	X15	0.5714	0.2857	0.1429
X3	0.5223	0.3464	0.1313	X16	0.4489	0.369	0.182
X4	0.4	0.4	0.2	X17	0.5978	0.2281	0.1741
X5	0.5135	0.3235	0.163	X18	0.5499	0.2402	0.2098
X6	0.5525	0.3329	0.1146	X19	0.5223	0.3464	0.1313
X7	0.6257	0.2426	0.1317	X20	0.5644	0.2883	0.1473
X8	0.6257	0.2426	0.1317	X21	0.5644	0.2883	0.1473
X9	0.5889	0.2664	0.1446	X22	0.4968	0.3792	0.124
X10	0.6396	0.2372	0.1232	X23	0.6466	0.245	0.1083
X11	0.5811	0.282	0.1369	X24	0.6169	0.2124	0.1706
X12	0.3313	0.3793	0.2894	X25	0.5336	0.3163	0.15
X13	0.5703	0.3096	0.1201				

model as coefficient. This approach makes LP models of the problem easier to establish and models become more flexible.

Administration of faculties has constraints of workload capacity for assigning both staff and job types, so we have to model the rebalancing workload problem as linear programming (LP) model in which we aim to maximize total utility for faculty. Our decision variables are quantity of the job's workload that a staff is assigned. Coefficient variables in objective function would be benefits that staff provides to the job type which are previously obtained by AHP.

Administration also proposed three different approaches and seeks to see differences between them and afterward select the most suitable one. So three different LP models of the problem with ensuring the utmost utility and their assumptions would be as follows:

Model 1 includes:

(A1) Each staff can be assigned to maximum value of 1 workload.
(A2) Workload of each job type must be satisfied with assigning sufficient staff.

Model 2 includes:

(A1) Each staff can be assigned to maximum value of 1 workload.
(A2) Workload of each job type must be satisfied with assigning sufficient staff.
(A3) All staff must be reassigned firstly their own job types.

Model 3 includes:

(A1) Each staff can be assigned to maximum value of 1 workload.
(A2) Workload of each job type must be satisfied with assigning sufficient staff.
(A3) All staff must be reassigned firstly their own job types.
(A4) Only particular group of staff can be assigned particular group of job types.

So with those assumptions as constraints we have LP models as follows:

$$i = \text{number of job type}, i = \{1, \dots, 25\}$$

$$j = \text{number of staff}, j = \{1, \dots, 93\}$$

$$X_{ij} = \text{quantity of workload assigned to staff } j \text{ for job type } i$$

$$C_{ij} = \text{quantity of benefit that provides staff } j \text{ to job type } i$$

$$J_i = \text{quantity of workload that has to be done in job type } i$$

$$O_{ij} = \text{quantity of workload of job type } i \text{ that is originally assigned to staff } j$$

$$Z_{\max} = \sum_{i=1}^{n} \sum_{j=1}^{k} C_{ij} X_{ij}$$

A1:

$$\sum_{i=1}^{n} X_{ij} \leq 1 \quad (j = 1 : 92), \quad \sum_{i=1}^{n} X_{ij} \leq 4.331 \quad (j = 93)$$

A2:

$$\sum_{j=1}^{k} X_{ij} = J_i \quad (i = 1 : 25)$$

A3:

$$X_{ij} \geq O_{ij} \quad (i = 1 : 25), (j = 1 : 92)$$

A4:

$$\sum_{j=1}^{50} X_{ij} + \sum_{j=93}^{93} X_{ij} = J_i \quad (i = 1 : 7), \quad \sum_{j=1}^{93} X_{ij} = J_i \quad (i = 8 : 22),$$

$$\sum_{j=9}^{93} X_{ij} = J_i \quad (i = 23 : 25)$$

$$X_{ij} \geq 0$$

All three models have the same objective function. Model 1 consists of constraints A1 and A2. Model 2 includes A1, A2, and A3 as constraints. Model 3 has A1, A2, A3, and A4 as constraints.

Coefficients of objective function C_{ij} for X_{ij}, which we got from AHP models, are utility values of staff "j" to corresponding job type "i." If there is more than one staff at a job, they have the same utility values for the jobs. Quantity of workload for each job type J_i must be fully occupied by staff. Calculation to assign staff for their original job type is simple and has one condition: if O_{ij} is less than one, it would remain same, and if it is greater than 1, then its value will be used as 1 to avoid loading workload greater than 1.

All calculations of AHP and LP models are evaluated in MATLAB. For instance, code of Model 3 is given in Appendix 3. Results of workload balancing with LP Model 1 and Model 2 are given in Appendix 4. Only decision variables with non-zero values are listed. All results are same for Model 1 and Model 2. The coefficients of staffs' utility are so high for their own job types that staffs are assigned firstly their own jobs in Model 1 without need of A3 constraints. Model 1 and Model 2 also share the same objective function value of 76.3837.

Model 3 with additional group constraint A4 is also solved and results are given in Appendix 5. Model 3 differs from Model 1 and Model 2 with objective function value of 76.3819. It can be seen that the increasing number of constraint tends to decrease the objective function value. Constraint type A4 is defined because of staff hierarchy. It is simply classified staff at three classes: class 1, which is from job type 1 to 7, can only do works from its own or class 2; class 2, which is from job type 8 to 22, can do every work; and class 3, which is from job type 23 to 25, can only do works from its own or class 2.

As results shown to Administration, they favor Model 3, due to ensuring all constraints they composed with slightly less utility value. Also "Where new employees needed most?" question has the same answer for all models as job type 23. In Model 3, workloads are balanced for every staff to value 1, with additional new staff to X23.

In the previous workload plan, Staff 1 has amount of 0.778 workload of job type X1; with Model 3, Staff number 1 has additional workload of job types X21 and X22 with the values 0.196 and 0.026, respectively. So with balancing workload, Staff number 1 has total workload of value 1. Also, Staff number 15 has amount of 1.238 workload of job type X10 in previous workload assignment. In Model 3, Staff number 15 has assigned workload value of 1 for X10, and the remainder of workload of X10 is shared by Staff numbers 9, 10, 11, and 12 with equal value of 0.0595. So with balancing workload, Staff number 15 has total workload of value 1.

5 Discussion

Decision problems with multi-criteria can be dealt with utility functions which can be obtained by MCDM approaches. AHP, which is one of the most popular and widely used MCDM techniques, can be used to determine utility values and importance level of alternatives due to its easy implementation and allowing decision makers to check their consistency on comparison matrix in all levels of its hierarchy. LP models are widely used in assignment problems. It gives flexibility with different types of constraints and provides optimum solutions easier than other optimization models. Integration of AHP and LP provides decision makers more solid results with systematically and analytically strong decision support.

Balancing workloads between staff have more than one benefit to organizations. Firstly, workforce productivity will increase due to taking extra workload from overloaded staff and passing it to less loaded staff. Secondly, satisfaction of job over staff will increase due to balancing workload with fair sharing. Last but not least, communication between staff will increase due to sharing same work more often.

Productivity of organizations is a major subject that must be dealt wisely to maintain competition with others. Workforce productivity is the most important type of productivity, especially in public services. Faculties which should be role model to society should also take the lead in this manner. The optimal values that arise as a result of the model support the management from the point of decision making. The manager can balance the missing workload of any employee by placing a job in a different business unit that best suits his or her wishes and abilities. The study provides optimal results by making quantitative model solutions.

In future works, workload balancing can be examined in a wider context. Different MCDM approaches such as TOPSIS, DEMATEL, and PROMETHEE can be integrated with multi-objective optimization to compare their performance in terms of determining utility values.

Appendix 1: Comparison Matrix of Alternatives for X1, C1

	x1	x2	x3	x4	x5	x6	x7	x8	x9	x10	x11	x12	x13	x14	x15	x16	x17	x18	x19	x20	x21	x22	x23	x24	x25
x1	1.0	1.0	1.5	2.5	1.5	2.0	2.5	2.0	3.0	2.0	1.0	3.0	1.5	2.5	1.5	2.0	2.0	1.5	1.0	2.5	1.0	1.0	2.0	3.0	2.0
x2	0.7	1.0	1.0	2.5	2.5	2.5	3.0	1.5	1.5	2.5	2.0	2.0	2.5	2.5	2.0	2.5	1.5	1.5	1.5	2.5	1.5	2.0	1.0	1.0	2.0
x3	0.4	0.7	1.0	1.0	1.5	1.0	2.0	3.0	3.0	2.5	1.5	1.0	1.5	1.0	2.5	2.5	2.0	2.5	1.0	3.0	1.0	1.5	1.5	3.0	2.0
x4	0.4	0.7	0.4	1.0	1.0	2.5	2.5	2.0	1.0	1.5	2.5	1.0	2.0	3.0	2.0	1.5	2.5	2.5	3.0	2.5	2.0	1.0	2.5	2.0	2.0
x5	0.7	0.7	0.4	0.7	1.0	1.0	2.0	1.5	2.5	2.0	2.0	1.0	1.5	2.5	1.0	1.0	2.5	1.0	1.0	3.0	1.5	2.0	2.0	2.5	2.5
x6	0.5	0.5	0.4	1.0	0.4	1.0	1.0	1.5	1.0	2.0	2.5	1.5	2.5	2.0	2.5	2.0	2.0	2.0	1.0	2.0	1.5	1.5	1.5	2.0	1.5
x7	0.4	0.4	0.3	0.5	0.4	0.5	1.0	1.0	2.0	1.5	2.5	2.0	1.5	2.0	1.5	2.0	2.5	1.5	1.5	1.0	2.5	2.0	2.0	1.5	2.5
x8	0.5	0.5	0.7	0.3	0.5	0.7	0.7	1.0	1.0	2.0	2.5	2.0	1.5	3.0	1.0	2.5	2.0	2.5	1.5	2.0	1.0	2.0	1.5	3.0	1.5
x9	0.3	0.3	0.7	0.3	1.0	0.4	1.0	0.5	1.0	1.0	2.0	2.5	1.5	1.0	2.0	2.0	2.0	2.0	1.5	2.0	2.0	2.0	1.5	2.0	1.5
x10	0.5	0.5	0.4	0.4	0.7	0.5	0.5	0.7	0.5	1.0	1.0	2.5	1.0	2.0	3.0	3.0	2.0	2.5	1.5	2.0	2.0	2.5	2.5	3.0	1.5
x11	1.0	1.0	0.5	0.7	0.4	0.5	0.4	0.4	0.4	0.5	1.0	1.0	1.0	2.5	2.5	1.5	2.5	1.5	2.0	2.0	2.0	2.5	2.5	2.0	2.0
x12	0.3	0.3	0.5	1.0	1.0	1.0	0.7	0.5	0.5	0.4	0.4	1.0	1.0	2.5	2.0	2.5	2.0	1.5	3.0	2.0	2.0	1.0	2.5	3.0	2.0
x13	0.7	0.7	0.4	0.7	0.5	0.7	0.4	0.7	0.7	0.7	0.7	0.4	1.0	1.0	2.5	1.5	1.5	1.0	2.5	2.0	3.0	2.5	2.0	1.0	2.0
x14	0.4	0.4	0.4	1.0	0.3	0.4	0.5	0.5	0.3	1.0	0.5	0.4	0.4	1.0	1.0	2.0	2.0	2.5	1.5	2.5	2.5	2.0	2.5	2.0	2.0
x15	0.7	0.7	0.5	0.4	0.5	1.0	0.4	0.7	1.0	0.5	0.3	0.7	0.5	0.4	1.0	1.0	2.0	2.0	2.0	3.0	2.0	1.5	1.5	3.0	1.5
x16	0.5	0.5	0.4	0.4	0.7	1.0	0.5	0.5	0.4	0.5	0.3	0.4	0.4	0.7	0.5	1.0	1.0	1.5	2.0	2.5	3.0	2.0	2.0	1.5	2.0
x17	0.5	0.5	0.7	0.5	0.4	0.4	0.5	0.4	0.5	0.5	0.5	0.7	0.5	0.7	0.5	0.5	1.0	1.0	2.0	1.5	1.5	2.5	2.0	1.0	2.5
x18	0.7	0.7	0.7	0.4	0.4	1.0	0.5	0.7	0.4	0.5	0.4	0.5	0.7	1.0	0.4	0.5	0.7	1.0	2.0	2.5	1.5	2.0	2.0	2.0	1.5
x19	1.0	1.0	0.7	1.0	0.3	1.0	1.0	0.7	0.7	0.7	0.7	0.5	0.3	0.4	0.7	0.5	0.5	0.5	1.0	1.0	2.0	2.0	2.0	2.0	2.5
x20	0.4	0.4	0.4	0.3	0.4	0.3	0.5	1.0	0.5	0.5	0.5	0.5	0.5	0.5	0.4	0.3	0.4	0.7	0.4	1.0	2.0	3.0	2.0	2.0	2.0
x21	1.0	1.0	0.7	1.0	0.5	0.7	0.7	0.4	1.0	0.5	0.5	1.0	0.3	0.4	0.5	0.3	0.7	0.7	0.5	0.5	1.0	3.0	2.5	2.0	2.0
x22	1.0	1.0	0.5	0.7	1.0	0.5	0.7	0.5	0.5	0.4	0.4	0.4	0.4	0.5	0.7	0.5	0.4	0.5	0.5	0.3	0.3	1.0	1.0	2.0	2.0
x23	0.5	0.5	1.0	0.7	0.4	0.5	0.7	0.5	0.7	0.7	0.4	0.5	0.4	0.5	0.4	0.7	0.5	0.5	0.5	0.5	0.5	1.0	1.0	2.5	2.0
x24	0.3	0.3	1.0	0.3	0.5	0.4	0.5	0.7	0.3	0.5	0.3	0.5	0.3	1.0	0.5	0.3	0.7	1.0	0.5	0.5	0.5	0.5	0.4	1.0	3.0
x25	0.5	0.5	0.5	0.5	0.5	0.4	0.7	0.4	0.7	0.7	0.7	0.5	0.5	0.5	0.5	0.7	0.5	0.4	0.7	0.4	0.5	0.5	0.5	0.3	1.0

Appendix 2: Utility Matrix for Job Types

	x1	x2	x3	x4	x5	x6	x7	x8	x9	x10	x11	x12	x13	x14	x15	x16	x17	x18	x19	x20	x21	x22	x23	x24	x25
x1	1.00	0.07	0.07	0.07	0.06	0.06	0.06	0.05	0.05	0.05	0.05	0.04	0.04	0.04	0.04	0.03	0.03	0.03	0.03	0.03	0.03	0.02	0.02	0.02	0.02
x2	0.07	1.00	0.07	0.07	0.07	0.06	0.06	0.05	0.05	0.05	0.04	0.04	0.04	0.04	0.04	0.03	0.03	0.03	0.03	0.03	0.03	0.03	0.02	0.02	0.02
x3	0.07	0.06	1.00	0.06	0.06	0.06	0.06	0.06	0.05	0.05	0.05	0.04	0.04	0.04	0.04	0.03	0.03	0.03	0.03	0.03	0.03	0.02	0.02	0.02	0.02
x4	0.07	0.07	0.06	1.00	0.06	0.06	0.05	0.05	0.05	0.05	0.04	0.04	0.04	0.04	0.04	0.04	0.03	0.03	0.03	0.03	0.03	0.03	0.03	0.02	0.02
x5	0.07	0.07	0.06	0.06	1.00	0.06	0.05	0.05	0.05	0.05	0.05	0.04	0.04	0.04	0.04	0.04	0.04	0.03	0.03	0.03	0.03	0.02	0.02	0.02	0.02
x6	0.07	0.07	0.06	0.06	0.06	1.00	0.05	0.05	0.06	0.07	0.05	0.04	0.04	0.04	0.03	0.03	0.03	0.03	0.03	0.03	0.03	0.03	0.02	0.02	0.02
x7	0.07	0.07	0.07	0.06	0.06	0.06	1.00	0.05	0.05	0.04	0.04	0.04	0.04	0.04	0.03	0.03	0.03	0.03	0.03	0.03	0.03	0.02	0.02	0.02	0.02
x8	0.07	0.07	0.07	0.06	0.06	0.06	0.07	1.00	0.06	0.07	0.06	0.06	0.05	0.05	0.05	0.05	0.04	0.04	0.04	0.04	0.04	0.04	0.03	0.03	0.03
x9	0.03	0.03	0.02	0.02	0.06	0.06	0.07	0.06	1.00	0.06	0.06	0.06	0.06	0.05	0.06	0.05	0.04	0.04	0.04	0.04	0.04	0.03	0.03	0.03	0.03
x10	0.03	0.03	0.02	0.02	0.06	0.06	0.08	0.07	0.07	1.00	0.06	0.06	0.06	0.05	0.05	0.04	0.04	0.04	0.04	0.04	0.04	0.03	0.03	0.03	0.03
x11	0.03	0.02	0.02	0.02	0.02	0.02	0.08	0.07	0.06	0.06	1.00	0.06	0.06	0.05	0.05	0.05	0.04	0.04	0.04	0.04	0.04	0.03	0.03	0.03	0.03
x12	0.03	0.03	0.03	0.02	0.02	0.02	0.07	0.06	0.07	0.06	0.06	1.00	0.06	0.05	0.05	0.05	0.04	0.04	0.04	0.04	0.04	0.03	0.03	0.03	0.03
x13	0.03	0.03	0.03	0.02	0.02	0.02	0.07	0.06	0.07	0.06	0.06	0.06	1.00	0.05	0.05	0.05	0.04	0.04	0.04	0.04	0.04	0.03	0.03	0.03	0.03
x14	0.03	0.03	0.02	0.02	0.02	0.02	0.08	0.07	0.06	0.06	0.06	0.05	0.05	1.00	0.05	0.05	0.05	0.04	0.04	0.04	0.04	0.03	0.03	0.03	0.03
x15	0.03	0.03	0.02	0.02	0.02	0.02	0.08	0.07	0.07	0.06	0.06	0.06	0.05	0.05	1.00	0.05	0.05	0.05	0.04	0.04	0.04	0.03	0.03	0.03	0.03
x16	0.03	0.02	0.02	0.02	0.02	0.02	0.07	0.07	0.06	0.07	0.06	0.05	0.05	0.05	0.05	1.00	0.04	0.04	0.04	0.04	0.03	0.03	0.03	0.03	0.03
x17	0.03	0.03	0.02	0.02	0.02	0.02	0.07	0.07	0.06	0.06	0.06	0.05	0.06	0.05	0.05	0.04	1.00	0.04	0.04	0.04	0.03	0.03	0.03	0.03	0.03
x18	0.03	0.03	0.02	0.02	0.02	0.02	0.07	0.07	0.06	0.06	0.06	0.06	0.06	0.05	0.05	0.04	0.04	1.00	0.04	0.04	0.03	0.03	0.03	0.03	0.03
x19	0.03	0.03	0.02	0.03	0.02	0.02	0.07	0.07	0.07	0.06	0.06	0.06	0.05	0.05	0.05	0.04	0.04	0.04	1.00	0.04	0.04	0.03	0.03	0.03	0.03
x20	0.03	0.02	0.02	0.02	0.02	0.02	0.07	0.07	0.07	0.06	0.06	0.05	0.05	0.05	0.04	0.04	0.04	0.04	0.04	1.00	0.04	0.04	0.03	0.03	0.03
x21	0.03	0.03	0.02	0.02	0.02	0.02	0.07	0.06	0.07	0.07	0.06	0.05	0.05	0.05	0.05	0.04	0.04	0.04	0.04	0.04	1.00	0.04	0.03	0.03	0.03
x22	0.03	0.03	0.02	0.02	0.02	0.02	0.07	0.07	0.07	0.06	0.06	0.04	0.04	0.04	0.05	0.05	0.05	0.04	0.04	0.04	0.03	1.00	0.03	0.04	0.03
x23	0.02	0.03	0.02	0.02	0.03	0.03	0.03	0.03	0.03	0.03	0.04	0.04	0.04	0.04	0.05	0.05	0.05	0.06	0.06	0.06	0.06	0.06	1.00	0.07	0.07
x24	0.02	0.02	0.03	0.03	0.03	0.03	0.03	0.03	0.03	0.03	0.04	0.04	0.04	0.04	0.05	0.05	0.05	0.05	0.06	0.06	0.06	0.06	0.06	1.00	0.07
x25	0.02	0.02	0.02	0.02	0.03	0.03	0.03	0.03	0.03	0.03	0.04	0.04	0.04	0.04	0.04	0.05	0.05	0.05	0.06	0.06	0.06	0.07	0.07	0.07	1.00

Appendix 3: Matlab Code for Model 3

```
clc;clear;
[wk1,CR1]=ahpkriter;
n=25;
wkrit=wk1';
[wa3,w3,CR2]=ahphesaplama;
for i=1:n
wkriter=wkrit(:,i);
wa4=cell2mat(wa3(:,i));
wkert=wa4*wkriter;
wkerti=wkert';
whedef(i,:)=wkerti;
end
whedef1=zeros(25,25);
whedef1(1,:)=[1 whedef(1,:)];
whedef1(25,:)=[whedef(25,:) 1];
for i=2:24
    whedef1(i,:)=[whedef(i,1:i-1),1,whedef(i,i:end)];
end
 whedef2=whedef1;
 eleman=[1  2  3  4  5  6  6  7  8  8  8  8  9  9  10 11 11 11 11 12 13 13 14 14 14 14 15 15 15 15
 16 17 18 19 20 21 22 22 22 22 22 22 22 22 22 22 22 22 22 22 23 23 23 23 23 23 23 23 23 23
 23 23 23 23 23 23 24 24 25 25 25 25 25 25 25 25 25 25 25 25 25 25 25 25 25 25 25 25 25 25
 25 25];
eleman=eleman';
elemanlar92=[];
for i=1:92
  ara1=whedef2(eleman(i),:);
  elemanlar92(i,:)=ara1;
end
elemanlar93=[elemanlar92' zeros(25,1)];
e=elemanlar93';
f=e(:)';
k3=f;
f=f.*(-1);
g1k1=kron([eye(7),zeros(7,18)],[ones(1,50),zeros(1,42),ones(1)]);
g2k1=kron([zeros(15,7),eye(15),zeros(15,3)],ones(1,93));
g3k1=kron([zeros(3,22),eye(3)],[zeros(1,8),ones(1,85)]);
k1=[g1k1;g2k1;g3k1];
k2= kron(ones(1,25),eye(93));
b1=[0.778  0.685  0.553  0.841  0.538  0.709  0.881  3.154  2.357  1.238  1.801  0.698  0.457  2.62
0.556  1.237  0.415  0.375  0.357  0.714  1.326  17.843 31.525 1.816  22.857];
b3=b1;
b2=[ones(1,92) 4.33104];
k3=k3>0.2;
k3=double(k3);
k33=[k3;zeros(24,93*25)];
k=93;
for i=2:25
k33(:,k+1:i*93)=circshift(k33(:,k+1:i*93),i-1);
k=i*93;
end
k3=k33;
k3=k3.*(-1);
bb3=[1 1  1  1  1  2  1  4  2  1  4  1  2  4  4  1  1  1  1  1  1  1  14 16 2  24];
for i=1:25
  if bb3(i)<b3(i)
     b3(i)=bb3(i);
  end
end
```

```
b3=b3.*(-1);
Aeq=k1;
beq=b1';
A=[k2;k3];
b=[b2';b3'];
lb=zeros(25*93,1);
[x,fval] = linprog(f,A,b,Aeq,beq,lb,[]);
matris=vec2mat(x,93);
matris1=matris;
for i=1:25
    for j=1:93
        if matris1(i,j)<0.001
            matris1(i,j)=0;
        end
    end
end
function [wk1,CR1]=ahpkriter
tmp=load('karark1.mat','AK1');
AK1=tmp.('AK1');
kn=3;
nen=25;
for i=1:nen
    A=AK1{1,i};
B=A*A;
C=A;
eps=ones(kn,1);
while max(max(eps))>1e-5
C=B;
B=B*B;
[a,b]=eigs(C);
wC=a(:,1)./sum(a(:,1));
[a,b]=eigs(B);
wB=a(:,1)./sum(a(:,1));
eps=abs(wC-wB);
end
wt=wB';
w=wB;
    for j=1:kn
        C(:,j)=A(:,j).*wt(:,j);%
    end
sumC=sum(C');
sumCw=sumC'./w;
emax=mean(sumCw);
CI=(emax-kn)/(kn-1);
RI=[0   0   0.52   0.89   1.11   1.25   1.35   1.4 1.45   1.49];
RI1=[0 0 0.49 0.8 1.06 1.18 1.25 1.32 1.37 1.41 1.42 1.45 1.46 1.48 1.50 1.51 1.52 1.53 1.53 1.54 1.54 1.55 1.55
1.55 1.56];
RIn=RI1(kn);
CR=CI/RIn;
    wk1(i,:)=w;
    CR1(i)=CR;
end
end
```

Appendix 4: Results of Model 1 and Model 2

Job type i	Staff j	Workload	Job type i	Staff j	Workload	Job type i	Staff j	Workload	Job type i	Staff j	Workload
1	1	0.778	22	19	0.0198	22	40	1	22	74	0.0476
23	1	0.222	22	19	0.53	22	41	1	25	74	0.9524
2	2	0.685	22	20	0.698	22	42	1	22	75	0.0476
22	2	0.315	22	20	0.302	22	43	1	25	75	0.9524
3	3	0.553	22	21	0.2285	22	44	1	22	76	0.0476
22	3	0.447	22	21	0.1185	22	45	1	25	76	0.9524
4	4	0.841	22	21	0.653	22	46	1	22	77	0.0476
23	4	0.159	22	22	0.2285	22	47	1	25	77	0.9524
5	5	0.538	22	22	0.1185	22	48	1	22	78	0.0476
23	5	0.462	22	22	0.653	22	49	1	25	78	0.9524
6	6	0.3545	23	23	0.655	23	50	1	22	79	0.0476
22	6	0.6455	23	23	0.345	23	51	1	25	79	0.9524
6	7	0.3545	23	24	0.655	23	52	1	22	80	0.0476
22	7	0.6455	23	24	0.345	23	53	1	25	80	0.9524
7	8	0.881	23	25	0.655	23	54	1	22	81	0.0476
23	8	0.119	23	25	0.345	23	55	1	25	81	0.9524
8	9	0.7885	23	26	0.655	23	56	1	22	82	0.0476
10	9	0.0595	23	26	0.345	23	57	1	25	82	0.9524
22	9	0.152	23	27	0.139	23	58	1	22	83	0.0476
8	10	0.7885	23	27	0.861	23	59	1	25	83	0.9524
10	10	0.0595	23	28	0.139	23	60	1	22	84	0.0476
22	10	0.152	23	28	0.861	23	61	1	25	84	0.9524
8	11	0.7885	23	29	0.139	23	62	1	22	85	0.0476
10	11	0.0595	23	29	0.861	23	63	1	25	85	0.9524

(continued)

Job type i	Staff j	Workload	Job type i	Staff j	Workload	Job type i	Staff j	Workload	Job type i	Staff j	Workload
22	11	0.152	15	30	0.139	23	64	1	22	86	0.0476
8	12	0.7885	23	30	0.861	23	65	1	25	86	0.9524
10	12	0.0595	16	31	1	23	66	1	22	87	0.0476
22	12	0.152	17	32	0.415	23	67	0.092	25	87	0.9524
9	13	1	23	32	0.585	24	67	0.908	22	88	0.0476
9	14	1	18	33	0.375	23	68	0.092	25	88	0.9524
10	15	1	23	33	0.625	24	68	0.908	22	89	0.0476
11	16	0.4502	9	34	0.357	22	69	0.0476	25	89	0.9524
21	16	0.0198	19	34	0.357	25	69	0.9524	22	90	0.0476
23	16	0.53	23	34	0.286	22	70	0.0476	25	90	0.9524
11	17	0.4502	20	35	0.714	25	70	0.9524	22	91	0.0476
21	17	0.0198	21	35	0.247	22	71	0.0476	25	91	0.9524
23	17	0.53	22	35	0.039	25	71	0.9524	22	92	0.0476
11	18	0.4502	21	36	1	22	72	0.0476	25	92	0.9524
21	18	0.0198	22	37	1	25	72	0.9524	23	93	4.331
23	18	0.53	22	38	1	22	73	0.0476			
11	19	0.4502	22	39	1	25	73	0.9524			

Appendix 5: Results of Model 3

Job type i	Staff j	Workload	Job type i	Staff j	Workload	Job type i	Staff j	Workload	Job type i	Staff j	Workload
1	1	0.778	12	20	0.698	22	41	1	22	74	0.0476
21	1	0.196	23	20	0.302	22	42	1	25	74	0.9524
22	1	0.026	13	21	0.2285	22	43	1	22	75	0.0476
2	2	0.685	16	21	0.1185	22	44	1	25	75	0.9524
22	2	0.315	23	21	0.653	22	45	1	22	76	0.0476
3	3	0.553	13	22	0.2285	22	46	1	25	76	0.9524
22	3	0.447	16	22	0.1185	22	47	1	22	77	0.0476
4	4	0.841	23	22	0.653	22	48	1	25	77	0.9524
22	4	0.159	14	23	0.655	22	49	1	22	78	0.0476
5	5	0.538	23	23	0.345	22	50	1	25	78	0.9524
22	5	0.462	14	24	0.655	22	51	1	22	79	0.0476
6	6	0.3545	23	24	0.345	23	52	1	25	79	0.9524
22	6	0.6455	14	25	0.655	23	53	1	22	80	0.0476
6	7	0.3545	23	25	0.345	23	54	1	25	80	0.9524
22	7	0.6455	14	26	0.655	23	55	1	22	81	0.0476
7	8	0.881	23	26	0.345	23	56	1	25	81	0.9524
21	8	0.119	15	27	0.139	23	57	1	22	82	0.0476
8	9	0.7885	23	27	0.861	23	58	1	25	82	0.9524
10	9	0.0595	15	28	0.139	23	59	1	22	83	0.0476
23	9	0.152	23	28	0.861	23	60	1	25	83	0.9524
8	10	0.7885	15	29	0.139	23	61	1	22	84	0.0476
10	10	0.0595	23	29	0.861	23	62	1	25	84	0.9524
23	10	0.152	15	30	0.139	23	63	1	22	85	0.0476
8	11	0.7885	23	30	0.861	23	64	1	25	85	0.9524

(continued)

Job type i	Staff j	Workload	Job type i	Staff j	Workload	Job type i	Staff j	Workload	Job type i	Staff j	Workload
10	11	0.0595	16	31	1	23	65	1	22	86	0.0476
23	11	0.152	17	32	0.415	23	66	1	25	86	0.9524
8	12	0.7885	23	32	0.585	23	67	0.092	22	87	0.0476
10	12	0.0595	18	33	0.375	24	67	0.908	25	87	0.9524
23	12	0.152	23	33	0.625	23	68	0.092	22	88	0.0476
9	13	1	9	34	0.357	24	68	0.908	25	88	0.9524
9	14	1	19	34	0.357	22	69	0.0476	22	89	0.0476
10	15	1	23	34	0.286	25	69	0.9524	25	89	0.9524
11	16	0.4503	20	35	0.714	22	70	0.0476	22	90	0.0476
23	16	0.5497	21	35	0.011	25	70	0.9524	25	90	0.9524
11	17	0.4502	23	35	0.275	22	71	0.0476	22	91	0.0476
23	17	0.5498	21	36	1	25	71	0.9524	25	91	0.9524
11	18	0.4503	22	37	1	22	72	0.0476	22	92	0.0476
23	18	0.5497	22	38	1	25	72	0.9524	25	92	0.9524
11	19	0.4502	22	39	1	22	73	0.0476	23	93	4.331
23	19	0.5498	22	40	1	25	73	0.9524			

References

Aksaraylı, M., Pala, O., Aksoy, M. A., & Turaba, L. (2016). A fuzzy mixed integer goal programming approach for academic performance modeling. *Akademik Sosyal Araştırmalar Dergisi, 4* (34), 14–32.

Aldowaisan, T. A., & Gaafar, L. K. (1999). Business process reengineering: An approach for process mapping. *Omega, 27*(5), 515–524.

Azmat, C. S., Hürlimann, T., & Widmer, M. (2004). Mixed integer programming to schedule a single-shift workforce under annualized hours. *Annals of Operations Research, 128*(1), 199–215.

Burgess, T. F. (1996). Planning the Academic's workload: Different approaches to allocating work to university academics. *Higher Education, 32*(1), 63–75.

Chandran, B., Golden, B., & Wasil, E. (2005). Linear programming models for estimating weights in the analytic hierarchy process. *Computers & Operations Research, 32*, 2235–2254.

Chen, C. F. (2006). Applying the analytical hierarchy process (AHP) approach to convention site selection. *Journal of Travel Research, 45*(2), 167–174.

Diodato, V. (1983). Faculty workload: A case study. *Journal of Education for Librarianship, 23*(4), 286–295.

Ghodsypour, S. H., & O'Brien, C. (1998). A decision support system for supplier selection using an integrated analytic hierarchy process and linear programming. *International Journal of Production Economics, 56–57*, 199–212.

Gökşen, Y., Aşan, H., Doğan, O., Ünlü, M., & Pala, O. (2016). The proposal model of rational workforce assignment in Dokuz Eylul University by analytic hierarchy process based 0-1 integer programming. *Scientific Bulletin – Economic Sciences, 15*(2), 54–66.

Ho, W. (2008). Integrated analytic hierarchy process and its applications: A literature review. *European Journal of Operational Research, 186*, 211–228.

Jaumard, B., Semet, F., & Vovor, T. (1998). A generalized linear programming model for nurse scheduling. *European Journal of Operational Research, 107*(1), 1–18.

Öztürk, A. (2002). *Yöneylem Araştırması*, 8. Baskı, Ekin Kitabevi Yayınları, The Bur, p. 167.

Pala, O. (2016). Bulanik Analitik Hiyerarşi Prosesi ve Meslek Seçiminde Uygulanmasi. *Dokuz Eylül Üniversitesi Sosyal Bilimler Enstitüsü Dergisi, 18*(3), 427–445.

Porter, S. R., & Umbach, P. D. (2001). Analyzing faculty workload data using multilevel modeling. *Research in Higher Education, 42*(2), 171–196.

Reid, G. R. (1988). The subjective workload assessment technique: A scaling procedure for measuring mental workload. *Advances in Psychology, 52*, 185–218.

Rhoades, G. (2001). AIR research and practice: Managing productivity in an academic institution: Rethinking the whom, which, what, and whose of productivity. *Research in Higher Education, 42*(5), 619–632.

Saaty, T. L. (1977). A scaling method for priorities in hierarchical structures. *Journal of Mathematical Psychology, 15*(3), 234–281.

Saaty, T. L., Vargas, L. G., & Dellmann, K. (2003). The allocation of intangible resources: The analytic hierarchy process and linear programming. *Socio-Economic Planning Sciences, 37*, 169–184.

Saaty, T. L., Peniwati, K., & Shang, J. S. (2007). The analytic hierarchy process and human resource allocation: half the story. *Mathematical and Computer Modelling, 46*, 1041–1053.

Seaberg, J. R. (1998). Faculty reports of workload: Results of a national survey. *Journal of Social Work Education, 34*(1), 7–19.

Vaidya, O. S., & Kumar, S. (2006). Analytic hierarchy process: An overview of applications. *European Journal of Operational Research, 169*, 1–29.

Winston, W. L. (1994). *Operations research: Applications and algorithms*. Belmont, CA: Duxbury Press.

The Effects of the Reformed CAP on the Local Economy in Rural Areas

Theodoros Markopoulos, Christos Karelakis, Konstantinos Galanopoulos, and Konstadinos Mattas

Abstract The impacts of the 2004 CAP reform on crop allocation, agricultural production, and the rural economy have been scarcely studied within a regional perspective. In this work, the impact of the CAP reform—and in particular the implementation of cross-compliance—on the region of Eastern Macedonia and Thrace (Greece) is studied with the use of factor analysis and structural equation modeling. Detailed qualitative and quantitative data were obtained through structured questionnaires and in-depth interviews of agronomists working in the local agricultural inputs sector. Results demonstrate that the CAP reform had primarily an adverse impact on both crop allocation and production, as well as on the local economy.

Keywords CAP · Local economy · Eastern Macedonia and Thrace · Factor analysis · Structural equation modeling

1 Introduction

Ever since the Treaty of Rome, the Common Agricultural Policy (CAP) has been reformed on many occasions and the impacts of each reform have been considered in terms of whether the goals, the perspectives, and the plans of the European Union (EU) have been realized. No doubt, the CAP is still one of the central elements for European integration and the most important EU common policy. During this

T. Markopoulos (✉) · C. Karelakis · K. Galanopoulos
Department of Agricultural Development, Democritus University of Thrace, Orestiada, Greece

K. Mattas
Department of Agricultural Economics, School of Agriculture, Aristotle University of Thessaloniki, Thessaloniki, Greece

© Springer Nature Switzerland AG 2019
N. Sykianakis et al. (eds.), *Economic and Financial Challenges for Eastern Europe*,
Springer Proceedings in Business and Economics,
https://doi.org/10.1007/978-3-030-12169-3_36

period, the initial aims of the EU policies changed from self-sufficiency, adequacy of agricultural products, and market stability to productivity increases and food safety and from there to the adoption of environmental parameters and animal welfare into agricultural production. The main tool for the implementation of all these reforms and changes was the method of calculation, the payment of subsidies, and a series of commitments that arose within this spectrum (Mousis 2008).

The reform known as "Fischler's reform" was launched in 2004 and was the most radical change among all CAP reforms. This reform changed the method of subsidies payment, while it introduced the concept of "rights" and the "decoupling" of subsidies from production. A key outcome of this reform has been that producers did not have to produce any quantities to be eligible for subsidized payments. Instead, subsidies were calculated based on historical data for areas, pastures, and animals for each farm. The subsidies calculation and payment system is known as the Single Farm Payments (SFP). All the conditions required in order for farmers to be eligible for subsidies, including environmental parameters and Codes of Good Agricultural Practices, including animal welfare, are known as "cross-compliance." It should be added that within this general framework each state had marginal options on a number of issues, which were set by the EU's decisions (Hüttel and Margarian 2009).

This CAP reform caused a number of important effects on most of the crops, the cultivation and production methods, and the use of production inputs. These effects furthermore extended to a wider range of subjects, such as transport and product trade and producers' investments. This chapter assesses the impact of the implementation of the CAP reform on the local economy of the agricultural areas of the Region of Eastern Macedonia and Thrace (also known as "Anatoliki Macedonia and Thraki"). In this region, agriculture is one of the main economic activities and accounts for a large share of regional GDP, employment, and income.

The remainder of the chapter is organized as follows: in the following section, the theoretical background is given, followed by the "research methodology section. Next, the study's results are presented, followed by discussion and concluding remarks.

2 Theoretical Background

Researchers in many scientific papers, even before the implementation of this reform, expressed concern that decoupling might cause a reduction in agricultural activity, reduce competitiveness, and then reduce the profitability of companies engaged in the transportation of agricultural products (Conforti et al. 2002). Other researchers expressed the view that there is an influence in farmers' behavior and in the choices and risks they are undertaking in the cultivation procedure (Bhaskar and Begin 2009). It is obvious that the impact of the revision in terms of culture and all the features regarding the productivity, intensification, and change in the size of farms ultimately affect farmers' income.

In a related scientific paper, the different characteristics of the agricultural households are highlighted for their ability to adapt to and adopt the changing agricultural policies brought about by the CAP reforms (Shucksmith and Herman 2002). This effect on farms is then transferred to the local market as well as in rural areas. Farmers are the main consumers who shape the conditions in the local market and furthermore in real estate, as in reconstruction and investments relating to the agricultural sector. Furthermore, the assessed CAP reform is estimated to affect employment. This is estimated to decrease family work input, as well as demand for personnel, mainly because of decoupling (Fasterding and Rixen 2005).

The impact of both Pillar I (direct payments) and Pillar II (rural development) in Austria was assessed by Schmid et al. (2006) and Schmid and Sinabell (2006), who found that market incomes rose by direct payments and agri-environment payments. Results of scientific studies showed that the impact of the weaknesses of the CAP reform expands in the agricultural employment sector, even extending over the nonagricultural workforce that may be involved in the rural labor market (Corsi and Salvioni 2012). Regarding Greece, Giannakis and Efstratoglou (2011) showed that the reform of the CAP and the payment of subsidies to the SFP system led to the transfer of land from intensive to extensive farming and also that the net production of the redistribution of land has been negative for the rural economy.

It should be noted that in this chapter, the term "local economy" includes the local market consumption, construction activity, the labor integration of agricultural crops, manufacturing facilities and warehouses, purchase of agricultural machinery, equipment and inputs from local suppliers, transportation, processing, and diversification of land value with respect to the purchase and renting of land.

3 Research Methodology

The research methodology includes a survey based on interviews with a questionnaire in the region of Eastern Macedonia and Thrace. The basic characteristics of the region are presented in Table 1.

The questionnaire included four sections. The items in the first section addressed the general CAP consequences on the population of the region, from the agronomists' point of view. The next section recorded the environmental issues of the CAP, and the third section addressed the financial consequences of the CAP. The last section investigated the CAP consequences on the local economy. The answers were given in the form of the five-point Likert scale, where 1 stands for "strongly agree" and 5 denotes "strongly disagree." The sample size was 212 participants who were agronomist scientists, store owners who sell pesticides and fertilizers, and other suppliers involved in input agricultural marketing in Eastern Macedonia and Thrace.

Table 1 Basic characteristics of the region of Eastern Macedonia and Thrace

Total area in km^2	Population (2011 census)	Agricultural area (m^2)	Agricultural area within CAP (m^2)
14,157	608,182	66,419,000	64,411,000

Resource: ELSTAT: National Statistic Authority

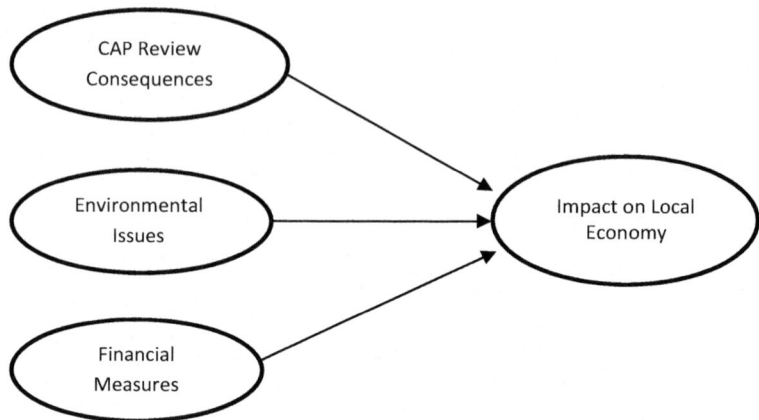

Fig. 1 The structural model under investigation

Agriculturalists were used for the correct completion of the questionnaires, who provided the necessary responses regarding the use of pesticides and fertilizers, which, play an important role in a local economy. The increasing age of farmers makes this problem even worse, since older people find it difficult to adapt to innovative ideas and changes, and so it is difficult in turn to follow the rules of the CAP reform. In most cases, the owners of these stores are Agriculturists themselves. Due to their direct cooperation with farmers, they can provide a broader view of the proper use of fertilizers and pesticides. Moreover, they are residents of the region, which means that they incur the financial consequences that the CAP may have, since they are not farmers but they are also part of the local economy.

Hence, it is important to investigate the role and the degree of CAP reform and of the environmental and financial issues in the local economy. Therefore, the following research hypotheses can be hypothesized:

H1 CAP review consequences have an effect on the local economy.

H2 Environmental issues have an effect on the local economy.

H3 Financial measures have an effect on the local economy.

The response rate of the survey was 65%, taking into consideration also the elimination of questionnaires which were poorly answered or included errors. The basic model under investigation is presented in Fig. 1.

4 Results

Initially, we summarize the basic descriptive statistics which correspond to the two parts of the demographic items of the questionnaire. The first part consists of the participants' demographics. The majority of the participants (41%) operate their store for more than 10 years continuously, mainly men aged between 36 and 45 years (47%). Moreover, most of the participants had graduated from Greek universities (60%). The second part consists of store demographics. The majority of stores (66.1%) were independent businesses, while the remaining 33.9% included stores as part of a broader business range. Regarding turnovers, the majority of the input stores declared between 200,000 and 400,000 € (26%), while 15% declared a number between 600,000 and 1,000,000 €. Finally, most of the stores (39.3%) are active in the wider region, which includes more than one municipality.

In order to determine the validity of the questionnaire structure, a factor analysis was conducted. The purpose of the analysis was the identification of the items that have the most significant impact on CAP reform, environmental issues, financial issues, and the local economy. Orthogonal rotation was used, since the factors are uncorrelated. Then, the observed variables were generated from the average of the respondents' answers to the corresponding variables. In this study, six factor analyses were conducted in order to extract the basic variables for the main analysis. For each one of the factors, reliability was examined with Cronbach's α criterion. A value of Cronbach's α greater than 0.6 indicates high reliability. The factors are presented in Table 2, where eigenvalues, total variance, and Cronbach's α are shown. The full table, including factor loadings, is presented in Appendix. More details on factors for the specific analysis can be found in Markopoulos et al. (2015).

Structural equation modeling (SEM) was then used in order to fit the investigated model described in Fig. 1 and to estimate its coefficients. This analysis is the appropriate method for processing in the case where the relationships lie between latent and observed variables, and between latent variables simultaneously, in order to validate or reject the assumptions made by the researcher (Schumacker and Lomax 2010). For this purpose, the statistical package AMOS 22 (IBM 2013) was used.

In this model, one variable from each group of observed variables that determine the latent variables had a factor loading fixed to the unit, or the variance of each latent variable must be fixed to one. The reason for imposing these constraints is the indeterminacy between the variance of a latent variable and the loadings of the observed variables on that latent variable. Utilizing either of these methods will eliminate the scale indeterminacy problem (Schumacker and Lomax 2010). Thus, the variables that are set to have loadings equal to the unit are "product production" (M1), "application accuracy" (M6), "marketing practices" (M13), and "areas in dependence on agriculture" (M45). The reason for this is that these variables identify to a great scale their respective factors, as is clear from the reliability analysis.

Table 2 Factor analysis results

N. of factor analysis	Factor code	Factor	Eigenvalue	Variance	Cronbach's α
1	M1	Product production	3.134	34.81%	0.801
	M2	Output reduction	1.434	15.93%	–[a]
2	M3	Differentiation	1.223	56.3%	0.609
3	M4	Human resources	3.243	29.98%	0.802
	M5	Farms	2.959	26.89%	0.795
4	M6	Application accuracy	2.676	29.73%	0.843
	M7	Financial consequences	1.915	21.27%	0.749
	M8	Impact	1.636	18.17%	0.589
5	M9	Farm Income from winter cereals	2.567	51.33%	0.893
	M10	Farm Income from summer cereals	1.662	33.23%	0.747
6	M12	Market bodies	2.131	16.39%	0.919
	M13	Marketing practices	1.955	15.03%	0.646
	M14	Marketing problems	1.468	11.29%	–[a]
	M15	Climate impact	1.201	9.23%	–[a]
7	M45	Areas in dependence on agriculture	4.258	32.75%	0.898
	M46	Boarder sectors	2.593	19.53%	0.827
	M47	Land value	2.106	16.19%	0.777

[a]This factor consists of only one item, so Cronbach's α cannot be extracted

The model shown in Fig. 2 can be expressed by the following equations:

$$(\text{CAP Review Consequences}) = \lambda_{11}(M1) + \lambda_{12}(M2) + \lambda_{13}(M3) + \lambda_{14}(M4) + \lambda_{15}(M5)$$
$$(\text{Environmental Issues}) = \lambda_{21}(M6) + \lambda_{22}(M7) + \lambda_{23}(M8) + \lambda_{24}(M9) + \lambda_{25}(M10)$$
$$(\text{Financial Measures}) = \lambda_{31}(M12) + \lambda_{32}(M13) + \lambda_{33}(M14) + \lambda_{34}(M15)$$
$$(\text{Impact on Local Economy}) = \lambda_{41}(M45) + \lambda_{42}(M46) + \lambda_{43}(M47)$$

and

$$(\text{Impact on Local Economy}) = \xi_1(\text{CAP Review Consequences}) + \xi_2(\text{Environmental Issues}) + \xi_3(\text{Financial Measures}),$$

where λ_{ij}, $i = 1, 2, 3, 4$, $j = 1, \ldots, 4$, and ξ_i, $i = 1, 2, 3$ are the coefficients to be estimated.

Based on the results of the factor analysis, the full model under investigation is illustrated in Fig. 2.

For the adjustment of the model, the unweighted least squares (ULS) procedure was used, because of the ordinal scale of the items. Therefore, they cannot be treated as quantitative, since their number is small, and consequently, it cannot be regarded that they follow the normal distribution (Schumacker and Lomax 2010). The overall fit of the model is very good, as indicated by the indices presented in Table 3.

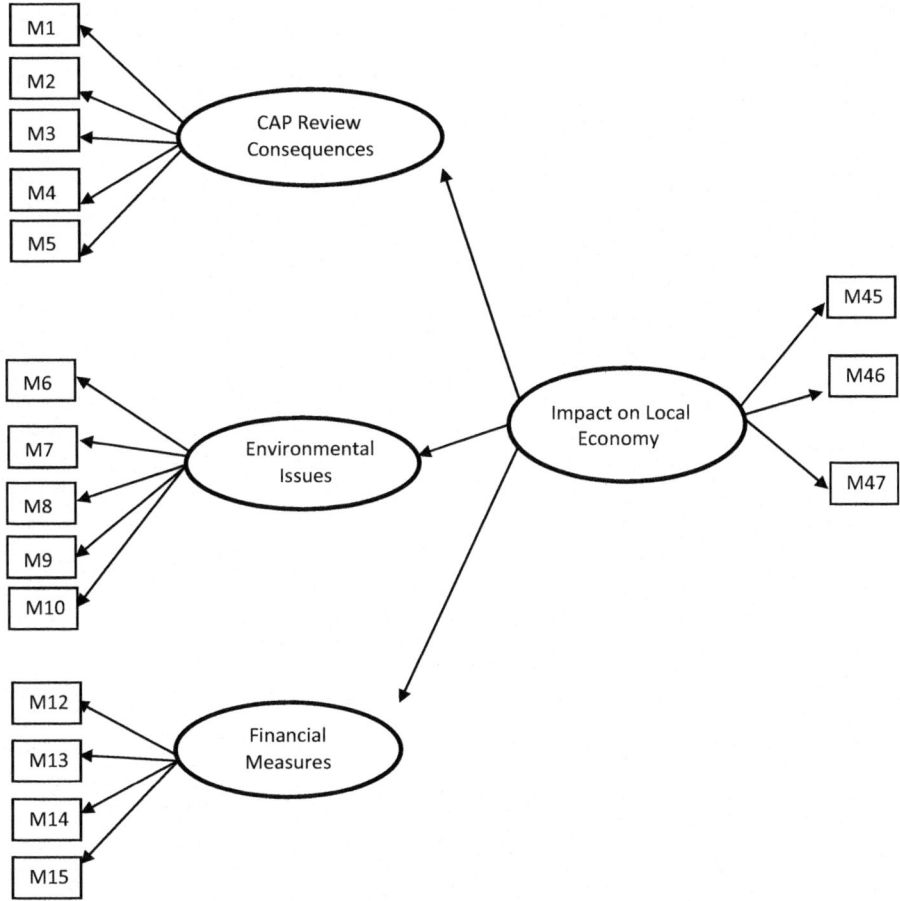

Fig. 2 Structural and measurement model of the research

Table 3 Goodness of model fit

Index	Values	Acceptable values
X^2	218.114	–
Degrees of freedom (df)	115	
X^2/df	1.896	<3
GFI	0.918	>0.9
RMSEA	0.056	0.05–0.08
AGFI	0.892	≥0.9

Table 4 shows the standardized factor loadings of the observed variables for each one of the latent variables of the model. All the coefficients have a significant effect on the corresponding variables at the 5% significance level.

Table 4 Standardized factor loadings

Coefficient	Estimate	Std error	p-value
λ_{11}	−0.920	0.233	<0.001
λ_{12}	−0.584	0.129	<0.001
λ_{13}	−0.553	0.311	<0.001
λ_{14}	−0.786	0.326	<0.001
λ_{15}	0.629	0.219	<0.001
λ_{21}	0.725	0.218	<0.001
λ_{22}	−0.240	0.172	0.012
λ_{23}	−0.518	0.122	<0.001
λ_{24}	−0.671	0.117	<0.001
λ_{25}	0.398	0.243	0.028
λ_{31}	0.312	0.017	<0.001
λ_{32}	−0.326	0.109	0.015
λ_{33}	−0.462	0.114	<0.001
λ_{34}	0.421	0.016	<0.001
λ_{41}	0.506	0.013	<0.001
λ_{42}	0.528	0.107	<0.001
λ_{43}	0.332	0.221	<0.001
ξ_1	−0.850	0.233	<0.001
ξ_2	−0.870	0.234	<0.001
ξ_3	0.704	0.208	<0.001

Hence, the equation using the estimated standardized coefficients becomes:

$$
\begin{aligned}
(\text{CAP Review Consequences}) &= -0.920(\text{M1}) - 0.584(\text{M2}) - 0.553(\text{M3}) - 0.786(\text{M4}) \\
&\quad + 0.629(\text{M5}) \\
(\text{Environmental Issues}) &= 0.725(\text{M6}) - 0.240(\text{M7}) - 0.518(\text{M8}) - 0.671(\text{M9}) \\
&\quad + 0.398(\text{M10}) \\
(\text{Financial Measures}) &= 0.312(\text{M12}) - 0.326(\text{M13}) - 0.462(\text{M14}) + 0.421(\text{M15}) \\
(\text{Impact on Local Economy}) &= 0.506(\text{M45}) + 0.528(\text{M46}) + 0.332(\text{M47}) \\
\text{and} & \\
(\text{Impact on Local Economy}) &= -0.850(\text{CAP Review Consequences}) \\
&\quad - 0.870(\text{Environmental Issues}) \\
&\quad + 0.704(\text{Financial Measures})
\end{aligned}
$$

$$\tag{1}$$

Equation (1) indicates whether or not the hypotheses of the research are verified. It is evident that there is a negative effect from the "CAP Reform Consequences" on the local economy. Moreover, "Environmental Issues" also seem to have a negative impact on the local economy, whereas "Financial Measures" have a positive effect on the local economy.

5   Discussion–Conclusion

The main purpose of the chapter was to investigate the impacts of CAP reform on the local economy of the rural areas of the region of Eastern Macedonia and Thrace. Moreover, some aspects of the CAP reform, such as environmental and financial issues, have also been considered to determine whether or not they affect the local economy of the region. The survey took into consideration the opinions of the agronomists who are responsible scientists at the stores for agricultural inputs, as they are more accurate in estimating the possible effects, due to their cooperation with hundreds of farmers each and their scientific background.

Results demonstrate the negative effect of the CAP reform on the local economy of the rural areas of the region. At this point, the meaning of CAP reform has to do with decoupling and, in general, the different way of calculating the subsidies for each farm. As for the environmental issues, there seems to be a negative effect on the local economy, and this is the result of the implementation of farmer cross-compliance. On the other hand, the factor related to financial measures has a positive effect on the local economy.

The equation created after the econometric processing confirms the existence of a clear influence between the changes in the CAP (the reform) and the local economy. The coefficients indicate that there is a clear effect on both Pillar I (decoupling and cross-compliance/preconditions for the payment of subsidies) and Pillar II (financial measures). According to this point, the three hypotheses described at the beginning of this chapter are accepted and positively confirmed.

Specifically, the effects brought about by the CAP formed three (3) latent variables. The first one represented "decoupling," different calculations, and payment of aid to beneficiaries, while the second represented "cross-compliance" which indicates the conditions for receiving community aid through the SFP system. The third latent represents the financial measures that accompanied the revision (Pillar II). Of the three latent variables, the first two had a negative effect while the third (financial measures) had a positive effect on the latent representing the local economy.

The negative impact of decoupling on the local economy is not easy to interpret, as the payment of the SFP subsidies creates better money liquidity conditions. However, the lower levels of agricultural production (Markopoulos et al. 2015; Markopoulos 2016) and the changes and conversion of the applied agriculture in a less intensive and more extensive way (Giannakis and Efstratoglou 2011) can be the basis of the explanation. A less intensive agriculture reduces the volume of produced products and therefore adversely affects some sectors of the local economy, such as transport. The same conclusion can be reached through the expected reduction of inputs used and less work, which will now be incorporated into a less intensive form of agriculture.

On the other hand, cross-compliance seems to negatively affect the local economy, which was considered a further commitment to the practice of farming. This may be due to the fact that the adoption of environmental measures did not bring the expected benefits to the agricultural environment or to the applied agricultural practice. Besides, all the factors which involve constraints provoke the reaction of those involved in the production process of agriculture.

Pillar II and particularly the financial measures it includes seem to be the only aspect of the reformed CAP which has a positive impact on the local economy. The financial measures (e.g., projects designed to improve the competitiveness of farms, action plans to improve the age composition by the installation of young farmers) require some consumption and purchase of equipment or the creation of new facilities that obviously impact positively on the local economy. At the same time, additionally, this positively affects production by modernizing farms and increasing their production capacity and competitiveness. This probably happened because financial measures contributed to the design, to the approval, and to the implementation of investments, which have a positive effect on the economy, especially the local economy. Moreover, it's worth mentioning that some of the financial measures help to increase the monetary liquidity of the economy and to create a positive climate for production and therefore for the local economy.

Here it should be noted that, as mentioned in the "Theoretical Background" section (Bhaskar and Beghin 2009), the reform and the CAP formulation affects the behavior of farmers with the two agents exerting a negative influence (decoupling and multiple compliance) and the third a positive one (financial measures).

Given the above conclusions, it is documented that the CAP as a whole, and in particular the changes, affects crop allocation, agricultural production, and the agricultural economy in general. Moreover, these effects are further extended over the local economy in rural areas. It can be accepted that the effects on purely agricultural issues are more direct and clearer and may be studied more easily, but beyond this, the CAP effects extend throughout the local economy on rural areas. Thereby the need for further study of the CAP effects in the local economy is confirmed via both subsidies and the monetary liquidity of farmers to develop, through the effects on crops, the inputs market, the changes in the value of land, as well as the impact on the psychology of farmers.

In conclusion, this study reveals significant impacts on the local economy of the region of Eastern Macedonia and Thrace and the implementation of the CAP reform that can be used as a guide to future reforms.

Appendix

Code	Factor	Items	Loadings
M1	Product production	Decoupling of aids changes crop synthesis in the region	0.599
		Decoupling of aids results in the increase of non-cultivated land in the region	0.551
		Decoupling of aids results in the decrease of product quality	0.580

(continued)

Code	Factor	Items	Loadings
		Decoupling of aids provides a significant negotiating advantage to farmers	0.751
		Decoupling of aids results in the adjustment of farms in the conditions of free market and competition	0.830
		Decoupling of aids has negative impacts on the marketing and processing of products	0.578
		Decoupling of aids has been accepted by local farmers	0.721
M2	Output reduction	Decoupling of aids results in production decrease	0.542
M4	Human resources	Grant of aids launches the non-agricultural use of money, taking resources from the productive process of the farm	0.661
		Grant of aids reduces production	0.680
		Grant of aids reduces intensive farming that requires high inputs	0.758
		Grant of aids reduces farmers' interest in risk taking	0.707
		Grant of aids is perceived as a non-farm social aid rather than as an agricultural community aid	0.650
		Grant of aids results in intense price fluctuations	0.645
M5	Farms	Grant of aids ensures conditions of stability and limited risk for farms	0.816
		Grant of aids results in better farm organization and programming	0.815
		Grant of aids results in better economic farm management	0.795
		Grant of aids results in attracting young farmers	0.636
		Grant of aids results in the increase of farm size	0.519
M6	Application accuracy	C–C was successfully applied to Greek farming	0.829
		C–C followed the necessary controls prior to implementation	0.888
		The relative bodies have been consistent regarding the announcement and implementation of C–C	0.863
		C–C appears to apply only to documents held concerning the CAP while they are not applied in practice	0.609
M7	Financial consequences	C–C has negative financial impacts in the short-term	0.887
		C–C has negative economic impacts on the farm	0.885
M8	Impact	C–C in the long-term has positive impacts on production and solving farm problems	0.838
		The implementation of C–C by some producers causes unfair competition and comparative disadvantage	0.600
		The non-implementation of C–C may result in the imposition of sanctions on our country by the EU	0.701
M9	Farm income from winter cereals	Durum wheat	0.942
		Soft wheat	0.867
		Barley	0.766

(continued)

Code	Factor	Items	Loadings
M10	Farm income from summer cereals	Corn	0.658
		Rice	0.964
M12	Cereals market bodies	Participation of NDP in collection and trade of cereals has fallen over the last eight years	0.934
		Participation of private traders in the collection and trading of cereals has increased over the last eight years	0.922
M13	Marketing practices	A significant number of farmers store the cereals they produce and market their own in times of higher demand	0.626
		Farmers in the region try to produce the quantities they need on their own farms	0.854
		There is evidence of 'concerted practices' among cereal merchants	0.608
M14	Marketing problems	The involvement of a large number of cereal traders in the region negatively affects "economies of scale"	0.503
M15	Climate impact	Climate change affects the production and quality of winter cereals	0.874
M45	Areas in dependence on agriculture	Diffusion of impacts of the CAP on other sectors of the local economy related to product processing	0.823
		Diffusion of impacts of the CAP on other sectors of the local economy concerned manufacturing	0.778
		Diffusion of impacts of the CAP on other sectors of the local economy related to product transfer	0.781
		Diffusion of impacts of the CAP on other sectors of the local economy concerned manufacture of packaging materials	0.892
		Diffusion of impacts of the CAP on other sectors of the local economy related to labour	0.801
		Diffusion of impacts of the CAP on other sectors of the local economy related to construction of storage infrastructure	0.668
M46	Broader sectors	Diffusion of impacts of the CAP on other sectors of the local economy covered the market of agricultural machinery, accessories etc.	0.553
		Diffusion of impacts of the CAP on other sectors of the local economy related to consumption	0.778
		Diffusion of impacts of the CAP on other sectors of the local economy covered standard of living	0.882
		Diffusion of impacts of the CAP on other sectors of the local economy related to construction activity in the area	0.742
M47	Land value	Diffusion of impacts of the CAP on other sectors of the local economy related to land purchase	0.772
		Diffusion of impacts of the CAP on other sectors of the local economy covered land rental	0.874

References

Bhaskar, A., & Beghin, J. C. (2009). How coupled are decoupled payments. *Journal of Agricultural and Resource Economics, 34*(1), 130–153.

Conforti, P., de Filippis, F., & Salvatici, L. (2002). *The mid-term review of the common agricultural policy: Assessing the effects of the commission proposals.* Working papers 14802, National Institute of Agricultural Economics, Italy INEA, Osservatorio Sulle Politiche Agricole dell'UE.

Corsi, A., & Salvioni, C. (2012). *Effects of the CAP reform on off-farm labour participation.* Selected Paper prepared for presentation at the International Association of Agricultural Economists (IAAE) Triennial Conference, Foz do Iguaçu, Brazil, 18–24 August.

Fasterding, F., & Rixen, D. (2005). *Analyse der Beschäftigung im Agrarsektor Deutschlands und Beschäftigungseffekte agrarpolitischer Maßnahmen.* Arbeitsberichte des Bereichs Agrarökonomie 05/2005, Institut für Ländliche Räume and Institut für Betriebswirtschaft, Bundesforschungsanstalt für Landwirtschaft; Braunschweig.

Giannakis, E., & Efstratoglou, S. (2011). An input-output approach in assessing the CAP reform impact of extensive versus intensive farming systems on rural development: the case of Greece. *Agricultural Economics Review, 12*(1), 81–90.

Hüttel, S., & Margarian, A. (2009). Structural change in the West German agricultural sector. *Agricultural Economics, 40*, 759–772.

IBM Corp. (2013). *IBM SPSS statistics for windows, version 22.0.* Armonk, NY: IBM Corp.

Markopoulos, T. (2016). *The reform of the common agricultural policy and its effects on agricultural production with particular emphasis on the cultivation of cereals.* PhD Thesis.

Markopoulos, T., Karelakis, C., Galanopoulos, K., & Mattas, K. (2015). Did the 2004 CAP Reform affect production practices of cereals? Insights from the agricultural input suppliers. *Scientific Bulletin Economic Sciences, 14*, 71–83.

Mousis, N. (2008). *European Union, loyal, economy, policy.* Athens: Papazisi.

Schmid, E., Hofreither, M. F., & Sinabell, F. (2006). *Impacts of CAP instruments on the distribution of farm incomes-results for Austria.* Diskussionspapier DP-13-2006, Institut für nachhaltige Wirtschaftsentwicklung, Universität für Bodenkultur Wien.

Schmid, Å., & Sinabell, F. (2006). On the choice of farm management practices after the reform of the Common Agricultural Policy in 2003. *Journal of Environmental Management, 82*, 332–340.

Schumacker, R., & Lomax, R. (2010). *A beginner's guide to structural equation modeling.* New York: Routledge.

Shucksmith, M., & Herman, V. (2002). Future changes in British agriculture: Projecting divergent farm household and behaviour. *Journal of Agricultural Economics, 53*(1), 37–50.